WINGS OF WAR

A Thousand Shall Fall is one of the most satisfying books ever written about air war: Once started, it is difficult to put down; when finished, it demands to be read again so that its complex layering of detail can be fully savored. With a compelling manner and a continually changing perspective, Murray Peden captures both the strategic and tactical aspects of air warfare. While painting in sharp, vivid strokes the horror of bitter combat at night, the author also poignantly conveys his deep sense of loss at the death of so many of his comrades. In counterpoint, he tells marvelous stories of his sometimes hilarious, sometimes moving, life as a combat crew member.

Peden's engaging writing style provides a perfect vehicle to relate the true history of the Royal Air Force Bomber Command's long campaign against Germany in World War II, a campaign that has in recent years been unfairly characterized by revisionist historians. More than forty years after the War, safe in the flakless groves of academe where no night fighters lurk, some writers now question the motives and actions of Bomber Command crewmen who fought at the sharp end of the stick, giving their lives by the thousands to defend the world from Nazism. *A Thousand Shall Fall* answers all their questions, showing clearly why Bomber Command conducted operations as it did—and how impossible it would have been to do otherwise given England's desperate situation and the technology at hand.

In many ways, the book is an autobiography not only of a young man who, upon reaching the age of eighteen in 1941, immediately joined the Royal Canadian Air Force, but also of a generation of young men who joined the RAF via the British Commonwealth Air Training Plan. Peden skillfully depicts both the vicissitudes and pleasures of learning to fly, interweaving the moments of fear and tragedy with the growing intoxication that comes with mastery of the aircraft. He shows how the difficult, demanding, and dangerous process molds young crewmen to endure the shock of sustained combat at night over Germany.

TIME-LIFE BOOKS INC., ALEXANDRIA, VIRGINIA 22314

An excellent, self-confident pilot, Peden flew the Short
Stirling, a huge aircraft that he came to love as the "Platonic
ideal" of a bomber despite performance limitations that meant it
must always be flown at the lowest (hence most dangerous)
altitude in the bomber stream. Peden's tour was more hazardous
than most, for it included clandestine resupply efforts with the
French Maquis resistance forces, and experimental work flying
American Boeing B-17s. His description of flying the corkscrew
evasive maneuver while being attacked by Messerschmitt night
fighters is heart-stopping. One can feel the G forces as he hurls
the huge Stirling through the night sky, unable to escape the
hammering of the German cannons: "I had instinctively thrust
the control column forward and twisted the ailerons to dive in a
violent corkscrew," he recalls. "The torrent of shells from the
Messerschmitt's cannons poured into us." With the control panel
shaking "as though the instruments were mounted on the sounding strings of some giant lyre," he rolled to begin his climb as
"frightening flames gushed out of the engine and were snatched
back across the cowling."

Peden survived the War and returned to Canada where he
became a distinguished jurist, serving as the Queen's counselor.
In the course of his career he became the friend of both Air Chief
Marshall Sir Arthur Harris and Harris's American friend and
counterpart, General Ira Eaker. Since his retirement from the
legal profession, he has devoted his attention to writing and to
his grandchildren.

Walter J. Boyne

*This volume, like every book in Wings of War, has been
reproduced photographically from an original edition. It thus
preserves the authenticity of the original, including typographical
errors and printing irregularities.*

A Thousand Shall Fall

by Murray Peden

A Pilot for 214

CANADA'S WINGS

The author, newly commissioned (1942).

DEDICATION

This book I dedicate to

Tommy Penkuri, Rod Dunphy, Freddie Taylor, Francis Plate

and to

THE VANISHED ARMY

the army of young aircrew who died in combat in the skies over Europe. Over 55,000 aircrew were killed serving in RAF Bomber Command, thousands of that number being fellow Canadians. The crews faced formidable odds, odds seldom appreciated outside the Command. At times in the great offensives of 1943 and 1944 the short-term statistics foretold that less than twenty-five out of each one hundred bomber crews graduating from Operational Training Unit would survive their first tour of thirty operations. On a single night Bomber Command lost more aircrew than Fighter Command lost during the Battle of Britain. Yet the crews buckled on their chutes and set out with unshakeable resolution night after night. They fell prey to the hazards of icing, lightning, storm and structural failure, and they perished amidst the bursting shells of the flak batteries. But by far the greater number died in desperately unequal combat under the overwhelming firepower of the tenacious German night fighter defenders. Night after night the battle was joined. In the morning the swelling roar of hundreds of Cyclones and Twin Wasps heralded the start of complementary operations of the Combined Bomber Offensive flown by Fortress and Liberator crews of our redoubtable partners, the US Eighth Army Air Force. Those daylight operations were carried out only at the price of a matching tax in blood levied against the American aircrew. I remember them all, with pride, respect and enduring affection.

v

First published in 1979 by

CANADA'S WINGS INC.
BOX 393, STITTSVILLE
CANADA KOA 3G0
Second edition August 1981

First   edition ISBN 0-920002-05-6
Second edition ISBN 0-920002-07-2

IWM   edition ISBN 0-901627-15-1

Dust Jacket design by George Mackie
Layout and Production by Rick Johnson
Printed by The Intelligencer, Belleville, Ontario

CONTENTS

FOREWORD

to

A THOUSAND SHALL FALL

by

Lt. Gen. Ira C. Eaker, USAF (Ret.)

One of the characteristic features of 1980 seems to be a revival of interest in the air battles of World War II. This was impressed on me since it has come to my attention recently that several books and motion pictures are in preparation for early release on phases of these aviation campaigns. New editions are also appearing of several recently released books on aviation subjects in response to this revived interest.

Among the best of these is Murray Peden's "A Thousand Shall Fall." This is an unusually entertaining and factual account of the air war which Britain and her principal ally, the U.S., waged against the vaunted German Luftwaffe. Eventually won decisively by the former, it made the sea and land victories possible.

Peden was an 18-year old Canadian who enlisted in the Royal Canadian Air Force in 1941, was sent to England the following year, and served the next three years with courage and distinction as a bomber pilot.

Two U.S. Air Force officers who participated in some of the air campaigns of this period read the book, "A Thousand Shall Fall," noted its unusual qualities and contacted the author: General Robert Dixon and Lt. General Ira C. Eaker. The former was a contemporary of Murray Peden in the RCAF, (a Spitfire pilot with the RAF) and prior to his retirement last year from the U.S. Air Force was commanding general for five years of Tactical Air Command.

I, as Peden knew, had commanded the U.S. Eighth Air Force from October 1942 to January 1944.

viii

We have each agreed, at Peden's request, to write a foreword to the new edition of this book, each discussing it from his own experience, I from the co-operative aspect of command and control and Dixon from the viewpoint of the courageous combat crews.

From my arrival at the Headquarters of the RAF Bomber Command, October 20, 1942, with a directive from General Arnold to understudy the bomber operations of the British, prepare the plans and launch our bombing forces when "I can get you some planes and crews," the RAF co-operated fully, in every possible way at all levels from Air Chief Marshal Portal, Chief of Staff, down the line and especially including Air Chief Marshal Harris and all his commanders and staff of Bomber Command.

Murray Peden mentions one of the retired Royal Air Force Seniors, Lord Trenchard, with deep affection and respect, as the father and founder of the RAF. All American leaders recognized Lord Trenchard, as did the RAF, as the author of the concept of strategic bombardment in World War I. He commanded the Independent Air Force in the late days of World War I, with a charter to conduct bombing operations beyond the battlefields of contending armies, against depots, rail networks and reserve forces, in order to affect decisively the land campaign.

It was Trenchard who influenced General William Mitchell and inspired his postwar campaign for a separate U.S. Air Force, which ultimately resulted in his court martial in 1925.

General Spaatz and I had contacted Lord Trenchard soon after arrival in England as observers in the Battle of Britain. He was always kindly and courteous in a fatherly fashion. The visits of this world-famous partriarch to our combat groups, during the early operations, proved a valuable morale factor.

The day prior to one of these visits, I read in the London Times that Lord Trenchard had just lost his last son as a casualty in the "Western Desert," the seventh son he and Lady Trenchard were to lose in World War II. I immediately called Trenchard saying I had seen that account, expressing my condolence and saying I would not call for him as planned, as we certainly did not expect him to leave Lady Trenchard in such a tragic time. He promptly stated that the visit to our groups should not be cancelled. His loss only confirmed his determination to carry on, doing whatever he could to destroy the Nazi menace. He did say that he would appreciate it if I could arrange that no mention of his late loss be made to him on the upcoming visit to our bases.

With the revival of interest in the air campaigns of World War II, much ill-conceived propaganda is being written, the general tenor of which is that RAF Bomber Command under the leadership of Sir

Arthur T. Harris, deliberately and without reason attacked civilians, including women and children.

No one can read Murray Peden's book without learning of the gallant effort bomber crews made to find and destroy their assigned military targets.

I can testify to the fallacy of this anti-humanitarian charge against British leadership, political and military.

I had many appointments with Prime Minister Churchill in order to show him photographs of the U.S. Eighth Air Force Bomber strikes or to discuss with him the great advantage of 'round the clock bombing — the British by night, the Americans by day.

Never at any time did he propose or encourage wanton attacks on civilians. No bomber strike was ever scheduled which was not aimed at an important element of the enemy's war-making capacity.

Sir Arthur Harris is now bearing the brunt of the charge of unnecessary "civilian brutality" by RAF Bomber Command. No one knows better than I that such charges and claims are entirely false and wholly unfair. For nearly two years I had daily conferences with him, concerning features of our joint bombing effort, targets, weather, results of the previous day's attacks, etc.

I can understand how present historians and pacifists with a pathological prejudice against warfare, even in defence of a nation and its people, can find some grounds which may be distorted to support such claims.

We were faced with constant Nazi propaganda designed to have the Allies call off their bomber campaigns as ineffective. To defeat this enemy effort, Air Marshal Harris devised a stereo box, showing his bombing attacks which showed workmen's homes without roofs in the Ruhr and elsewhere. They were surrounding vital targets, tank, airplane and gun factories. Such photographs were appreciated and approved by British subjects who saw the evidence of German attacks on Coventry and London.

Air Chief Marshal Harris believed, as I do, that the civilian who makes a weapon bears as much responsibility for warfare as the soldier who carries it into battle. When showing his stereo slides to members of Parliament and the news media, he often made the point that destruction of workmen's homes was a valuable contribution of the bombing effort: the reduction of the enemies' weapons capacity. This undoubtedly played a part in the Labor government's hostility to the Air Marshal and its failure to properly recognize the gallant combat crews as it did the veterans of other combat echelons.

No one who reads Peden's book can fail to recognize the unforgivable unfairness of this policy.

Another great satisfaction I derived from this book, was

confirmation of the fact that the young volunteers of Britain, the Commonwealth and the U.S. did not suffer irreparable damage from this demonstration of patriotism. The three or four years out of their normal education opportunities provided compensating advantages.

This is well illustrated by the life and career of the author as a distinguished member of the Canadian bar, in addition to providing us this historical and biographical masterpiece, "A Thousand Shall Fall."

Robert Dixon, who joins me in this foreword, is another outstanding example of this observation. He, like Peden, enlisted in the RCAF, but at age 21, after college, became a fighter pilot, and was sent to Britain before the U.S. entered the war.

Despite his loss of postgraduate education during his war service, this did not interfere with his education, through his own effort while in postwar military service. This is attested by the fact that he ultimately became a four-star general and commanded one of the U.S. Air Force's most prestigious organizations, the Tactical Air Command, for five years. After his military retirement, he became president of one of our leading aircraft manufacturing companies.

Finally, readers of Murray Peden's "A Thousand Shall Fall" will be rewarded by learning many of the reasons for our success in eliminating the Luftwaffe, leading to the destruction of Hitler and his Nazi tyranny.

Some of our present failures to deal properly with our present international crises will also become apparent.

Ira C. Eaker,
Lt. General USAF (Ret.)

FOREWORD

to

A THOUSAND SHALL FALL

by

Robert J. Dixon, General, USAF (Ret.)

Two great, good fortunes have been my lot — to learn to fly in the British Commonwealth Air Training Plan, and thus to make an operational contribution to World War II — and to relive that experience in the words of Murray Peden's superbly written classic "A Thousand Shall Fall."

I shall neither forget nor be able to repay the Royal Canadian Air Force for a second chance to fly — eventually to fly from age 21 to age 60 (since I am still at it), in three wars and during the intervening periods of uneasy peace.

In the summer of 1941, after graduation from Dartmouth College, at the age of 21 (barely), I joined the United States Army Air Corps as a pilot-trainee. Within months, while at Basic Training at Randolph Field, I was "washed out", declared unsuitable, by lack of inclination to discipline, to become a military pilot.

Within a year, I was a commissioned (Pilot Officer) graduate of the Commonwealth Air Training Plan, with a pilot's rating and a second navigator's "ticket". I had scrambled my way with liberal applications of help and practical discipline through the horrors of the Montreal Manning Depot in the cold of winter, Security Guard Duty at Brantford (Ontario) in even colder weather, Primary Training at Saint Catharines, final training at Aylmer, then Prince Edward Island (Navigation Training), to Dyce (Aberdeen, Scotland) for Spitfire OTU, and finally to 514 Squadron at Benson, Oxfordshire, England.

This progression was marked, then and now, in my mind and memory by the fundamental difference between the U.S. and the RCAF training methods. The former was pre-war, idealized, productive, and marked by focus on ground discipline in the cadet atmosphere — a peacetime, noble, and effective early effort to foresee the needs for and of dedicated aircrews in war. My youthful refusal to consider cadet "hazing" as practical military discipline resulted in failure to adapt successfully to U.S. Army Air Corps training. Others had the same experience. The same youthful attitude, moulded by a training system

xii

dedicated to the needs of a free commonwealth of nations *at war*, produced a trained and usable pilot — in my case and others.

The Tiger Moth, the AT-6, the Anson, the Miles Master at Wrexham, the Spitfire at Dyce, and later Benson, carried me through, with the aid of understanding instructors and superb ground school training. In those days, A.P. 1234, the world's best basic text for navigation, was never far from my hand. Years later, when my children were of age to fly, I managed to obtain a copy from the RCAF — and I still have it.

It was not a wholly joyous day when I transferred, with "my" PRU Spitfire Mark XI (and eleven more on reverse Lend-Lease), to the U.S. Army Air Corps at Mount Farm, near Benson. I left the RCAF (RAF), regretfully, to rejoin my fellow countrymen. My close association with Commonwealth aircrews — the British, Canadians and Australians I went through training with — gave me a window on a wider world of airmanship, fellowship, and esprit. The view of two training systems — and their differences, not all of which favored one system over the other — was most useful in later years in the U.S. Air Force. Experiences in training and in battle — in World War II with my ex-colleagues at Benson — in prison camp with a "mixed bag" of allied crewmen — in the Korean conflict with the United Kingdom unit at Kimpo — in the Vietnam war with the Australian ground forces — in peacetime with the Canadian-U.S. Regional Planning Group — and with Canadian and U.K. civil and military officials at the annual Survival Camp and Pine Tree meetings — at Winnipeg with the Wartime Pilots and Observers Association — all these experiences were of fundamental continuing value.

All those wonderful minutes, hours and days are brought back by the clear, bright recollections of Murray Peden — who, as his pictures attest, wore his military caps with a decidedly cheerful, independent, tilt, from his enlistment to his separation — and whose book, even in its tragic moments, attests to the free spirit that characterizes airmen the world over.

Robert J. Dixon,
General, USAF (Ret.)

CHAPTER 1

ENLISTMENT – THE RCAF

How dull it is to pause, to make an end,
To rust unburnished, not to shine in use!

Tennyson: Ulysses

I saw Air Marshal William Avery Bishop only once — at a recruiting rally in the Winnipeg Auditorium in the spring of 1941. I was seventeen, impatiently awaiting my eighteenth birthday so that I could join up. My classmate at Gordon Bell High, Rod Dunphy, sat beside me, both of us exhilarated by the pugnacious speech of the short, stocky flyer who, at that moment, was the greatest fighter pilot alive, with a score of seventy-two confirmed victories.

Eddie Rickenbacker, whose assessment in this field was based on solid credentials, once said that Billy Bishop was a man incapable of fear. Certainly the medal ribbons we could see on Bishop's chest afforded strong corroboration of Rickenbacker's assessment: Victoria Cross, Distinguished Service Order, Military Cross, Distinguished Flying Cross, to name only the ones we could identify. From the descriptions given by journalists and others I had come expecting to see a gamecock, and in that respect Bishop certainly lived up to his billing. But he was much more than that; he exuded as much dignity as daring, doubling the impact he made on an impressionable audience. Dunphy and I came away convinced that our original intent had been right, and that we should join the Royal Canadian Air Force as pilots as soon as we could qualify, namely, at age eighteen.

My eighteenth birthday fell on a Sunday in 1941, a sore disappointment to me since it prevented me from enlisting until the following day, Monday, October 20th. I was at the recruiting office in the old Lindsay Building when it opened Monday morning. I spent most of that day dressing and undressing in various offices and being subjected by impersonal doctors to highly personal indignities. The air-crew medical was devastatingly thorough.

Just before 6:00 PM I lined up with half a dozen other survivors, this time with my clothes back on, and was sworn in as a member of the RCAF. Our document folders were marked P/O, indicating that we would, if all went well, be trained as Pilots or Observers. (While the individual expressed his own preference, the Air Force made the binding decision, on the basis of performance at Initial Training School, as to whether he would be washed out altogether, or selected for training either as a Pilot or Observer.) I had entered the building in the morning as Mr. D. M. Peden. I left with a slightly swollen appellation: Aircraftsman Second Class (AC 2) PEDEN, DAVID MURRAY, R134578. I was also given an Air Force lapel pin to attest to my heroism, placed on leave without pay, and ordered to report back on November 6th, 1941, for the next draft to No. 3 Manning Depot, Edmonton.

On the appointed day, thirty of us assembled in the CN Railway Station, made our farewells, and, in the late afternoon, headed for Edmonton. After a casual inspection of our coach, I concluded that it had been amongst the rolling stock destroyed by General Sherman when he left Atlanta for his hike across Georgia, had been patched up after the termination of those hostilities and purchased by the Canadian Government for use in situations such as this, where it wished to transport the very cream of its manhood on important missions.

After three hours of drafty progress, I headed with some foreboding for the dining car, clutching a blue Air Force meal ticket in my hand, and assuming that if the meals harmonized with the accommodation I would shortly be struggling with serious gastric disorders. My fears proved groundless; the meal was excellent, and I returned in high fettle to the museum piece in which we were riding. That sensation was gradually eroded as the night wore on. Since our run of about eight hundred miles would be covered in one night, the Air Force policy was to allow its men to begin to develop character by spending the night sprawling in the upright seats of the ancient day coach, seats which I was sure were truncated church pews. It was a long night.

At 6:45 AM, November 7th, 1941, we rolled into Edmonton. The first fine careless rapture had evaporated. The weather in Winnipeg at the time of our departure had been quite pleasant for November, so most of us were lightly dressed. We lurched woodenly out of the coach vestibule and down onto the platform to find the Edmonton temperature some forty degrees colder. We stood for a few minutes with our teeth chattering until an Air Force Corporal gathered everyone together and

2

marched us a short distance to where, with a thoughtfulness which
we came in time to recognize as typical, the Air Force had provided
two open trucks to speed us to our new abode. On the ride over to the
old Exhibition grounds, now the site of No. 3 Manning Depot, with
the truck's speed contributing a 40 mile an hour windchill factor to the
frigid air, I realized that the doctors had wanted to be very sure about
our physical condition before letting us into the service so that the
number of trainees who died of exposure on the way to Manning Depot
could be kept within acceptable limits.

These Manning Depots of the RCAF were basically stations where
civilians were transformed into uniformed raw material suitable for
further training. We were issued dozens of items of standard kit,
everything from the various articles of our uniforms down to little
"housewives", or sewing kits for running repairs to uniforms. Despite
the age-old serviceman's complaint that there were only two sizes: too
big and too small, the stores clerks attempted, with moderate success,
to issue clothes that fitted. However, most of us spent five or ten dollars
of our own money and had the finishing touches in the way of final
minor alterations done by civilian tailors in town. In short order we
began to look like airmen.

As the lowest ranking humans on the station — we were the
service equivalent of vermin — we were subjected to further indignities
as a matter of routine, and were even preyed upon as fair game by
people who were almost as low-caste as ourselves.

The NCO in charge of our platoon, Flight Sergeant Tracy,
marched us one morning into the main arena inside the Exhibition
Building and left us standing in line, unsupervised, while he disappeared for a few minutes into one of the side offices. A Leading
Aircraftsman (LAC) — the Air Force equivalent of the lowly Lance-
Corporal — entered the arena and called us to attention in a
businesslike tone. He then told us to drop our trousers and shorts
around our ankles. "The MO's giving everyone another short-arm
inspection", he said, "I'll bring him in now".

He was referring to the standard test for hernia in males. We had
all had such a test upon enlistment, but by now saw nothing unusual in
a redundant repetition of any Air Force procedure. We all dropped
our slacks, underwear, and dignity, and stood in brutish splendour
awaiting the doctor resignedly. The LAC disappeared out another door,
undoubtedly choking with laughter as soon as he got out of sight.
Flight Sergeant Tracy came back on the scene a few minutes later. His
face was an interesting study in suppressed emotion when he beheld
his erstwhile immaculate platoon standing about like a gaggle of
practising homosexuals. When he could find his voice he asked the
obvious questions. We relayed the LAC's description and instructions,

3

and Tracy sprinted to the door in what proved to be a vain attempt to identify the humorist.

Our first "noc" parade took place a few days after the foregoing embarrassment. We had some inkling of what to expect, since the sadists who had already been through the ordeal were pleased to leak their horror stories amongst us. We paraded before Flight Sergeant Tracy one afternoon to learn that right now it was our turn for inoculations.

For those who dreaded needles, it was a memorable day. We rolled up our sleeves on both sides and walked between a bevy of white-gowned swabbers, doctors, and catchers. We got five needles in about a minute and a half, and I, who feared and loathed the things, was astonished to find that in our group about one in five simply keeled over and passed out when they got to the big TABT shot, which was third in the stabbing order. Mind you, there was a fearfully big cylinder on that needle. I suppressed a gasp with difficulty and forced myself to look away after I had allowed my gaze to linger on it for a little less than one microsecond; but in that brief appraisal I could see that it was the four cup size. I came through the assembly line quivering but vertical, and as I surveyed those who were horizontal and still showing only the whites of their eyes, my self-respect began to return.

After four weeks of Manning Depot we entrained for No. 7 SFTS (Service Flying Training School) at Macleod, Alberta, for a few weeks of what was officially styled "tarmac duty", a euphemism for a Joe jobs routine until an opening came up for our flight at an ITS (Initial Training School.) The train trip was uneventful until we got to Red Deer, where the conductor told us we had a 20 minute stop. Three or four of us promptly walked to a cafe about 200 yards away for a cup of coffee. There had been a slight breakdown in communication between the conductor and the engineer, who pulled out smartly and without warning after only ten minutes.

I almost caught up, pelting down the tracks only a few yards behind the train; then it pulled away. I had abandoned hope, although still running furiously, when someone pulled the emergency cord and the train stopped. The conductor was extremely angry, and thereafter no Air Force personnel were allowed out of the coach. I did my best to avoid the glances of my travelling companions.

I spent my first day at Macleod working in the kitchen. Even with its horrible odours and revolting messes it had its advantages, since it was bitterly cold outside, and Macleod was notorious for its continuous 30 mile per hour westerly wind funnelling in from the Crow's Nest Pass. (The whole time I was on the station, I saw them change the runway only once.) Some of our boys were stuck with guard duty, and even with the excellent parkas they drew, it was an uncomfortable and tedious way to put in the time. I was warm in the kitchen, and was not going to get militant about changing my job until I found something better. Fortunately I did not even have to look. Fate smiled on me the second day, and I gravitated into a sinecure.

Macleod had a station band, and a reasonably good one, under the baton of Corporal Norman Lehman. As soon as a new group of trainees hit the station, Corporal Lehman's extensively developed system of contacts screened them to find out whether any of them played military band instruments. I let it be known on the first day that I had played solo cornet for the Royal Winnipeg Rifles; and on the second day it turned out that what Macleod needed more than anything else in the world was a band librarian who could keep the music filed and organized, shine up the odd instrument, and play solo cornet.

It was an ideal arrangement. Corporal Lehman had been a barber in civilian life, and was not averse to making an extra few dollars by cutting his friends' hair at 25 cents a time. In return for my co-operation in helping him tidy up afterwards, and in keeping the whole operation more or less secret — for this moonlighting had to be done very judiciously — Lehman gave me the freest possible rein. Whenever I felt like it, I could go over to the flights and attempt to bum an aeroplane ride in an Anson, as long as there was an instructor along. More importantly, I could go to the Link Trainer instructor, Flying Officer Coghill, a World War I pilot who had flown with the redoubtable Raymond Collishaw, and try to find a free half hour in the Link.

This was extremely important to us potential air-crew, because we knew via the grapevine that when we got to ITS we were going to be tested in many ways to see whether we had the requisite co-ordination and reflexes to become pilots. One series of tests would be given in the Link Trainer, a very sensitive flight simulator; and we all wanted to sit in one and find out what it felt like so that we would not be completely unprepared when we got to ITS.

Strictly speaking, Coghill was not supposed to train us in the Link before we got to ITS, since the purpose of the ITS sessions was to test our aptitude and instinctive reactions, and see how readily we could get used to the hissing instability of the fidgety little trainer. Coghill knew this of course, and would never give any of us very much time in the Link, because too much would destroy the validity of the ITS tests. However, he was a warm-hearted and sympathetic soul, and he knew how desperately keen we were to make good. He reasoned that an hour or so in his Link would give us a little more confidence, take away some of the mystery and apprehension, and still not vitiate the ITS tests in any way. He was a flyer himself; he had the flyer's kinship with the new fledglings, and we could feel it.

He taught us in a nice way to conduct ourselves appropriately. Once when I carelessly transgressed the bounds of propriety by failing to salute when I entered his office — I was concentrating so much on what arguments I would use to try to get another 15 minutes in the Link that I completely forgot — he lectured me in a very fatherly way about remembering proper military courtesy, and then, with a twinkle in his eyes, said:

"Right. Now climb into the Link, put on the headphones and let's see what you can remember."

After 36 years, I think of him fondly still.

Our station band, complete with its accretion of three itinerant and very temporary air-crew members, numbered 27 players. We practised regularly three times a week, and for what was basically a pick-up group, the quality was not at all bad. My initial practice with the group produced a surprise for me that, for the first hour at least, threatened to destroy my usefulness. It came in the form of a burly French-Canadian mechanic with huge hands and knuckles, who would physically have been the best equipped member of the band to tote a big tuba on the march — or to carry an anvil under each arm if necessary. This burly bandsman played the piccolo, and when he got set to play, the tiny pipe would disappear within his huge hands.

Now, piccolo parts are the icing on the military band's cake, consisting largely of graceful and sweeping chromatic runs, embellishing echo phrases, and frequent, sustained trills. The parts are often demanding; hence our incongruously built musician made his share of errors. Following the more blatant and heinous auditory misdemeanours, Corporal Lehman would rap sharply with his baton in the time-honoured signal to stop and repeat the strain. The memory of the first time it happened in my presence remains etched on my brain.

A bird-like piccolo run, sweeping up and down over several bars to a high trill, was fractured beyond recognition. The bandmaster's baton rapped sharply against his music stand and the music ceased. In the momentary hush that followed, the piccolo player, his big hands poised ever so delicately before his pursed lips, brought his instrument slowly to his lap, squinted slightly under bushy black brows at the troublesome score, and began to speak. In comments representing the absolute nadir of foul profanity he raked the composer, publisher, distributor, and every other culprit sharing the slightest trace of responsibility for foisting this impossibly difficult passage upon unsuspecting piccolo artistes. What convulsed me was the fact that his extravagant French accent and wildly garbled mispronunciations somehow transformed the shockingly vulgar condemnations into something resembling an elegant critique.

The rest of the boys, being thoroughly inured to these ambivalent broadsides, merely chuckled, then lifted their instruments promptly at the bandmaster's signal. I was helpless for five minutes; after I did cork the laughing I lost control two or three times and unleashed triple forte blasts in the most inappropriate places as my thoughts strayed back to Frenchie's musical insights.

The band was scheduled to broadcast a concert at the radio station in Lethbridge three weeks from that date. One of the pieces on the program was a Gilbert and Sullivan medley containing several short solo passages which I was to share with the other solo cornet player. My recurring nightmare during the interval stemmed from my fear that my mind, through some horribly unavoidable process of thought association, would flit to one of Frenchie's outrageous expletives, and that I would forthwith blast out a sour note surpassing Gideon's in the middle of a solo.

Our musical responsibilities also included driving into Lethbridge every two weeks to play at the hockey arena for games between Macleod's team and teams from other Air Force stations. Our opening number at these functions was always Kenneth J. Alford's "The Voice of the Guns" — it was our loudest selection. Our team achieved an enviable record in these inter-station matches, since we had two top-notch former junior players on the roster: Max Mair, usually referred to by the sportswriters as "the bank clerk forward", who had played for Portage Terriers, and Red Hunter, formerly a star with the Winnipeg Monarchs.

Our band had a standing invitation to repair, after the games, to the banquet hall of a Lethbridge brewery, where a fine smorgasbord was always set out for us, together with unlimited quantities of the brewery's product. I was a teetotaler at the time, so the beer held no attraction for me, but as a trencherman I had no peer in the band, and perhaps none in the Allied Forces in North America. While the drinkers wasted some of their volumetric capacity on ale, I plugged myself with various kinds of sausage, pickled eggs, ham, cheese, sweet pickles, jelly, pie, cake and coffee. It is with considerable envy now that I recall that when I joined the Air Force I weighed 128 pounds, and that I was never able to put on a single ounce during my first three years.

The return trip to Macleod after one of the Lethbridge banquets was an experience that I did not look forward to. No one else had any qualms; they were all soporific from the beer. The road was a tricky one, twisting and turning every which way, and in some spots it bordered spine chilling vertical drops of several hundred feet. Our band travelled in two small vans. When I sensed that the party was about due to break up, it was my practice to address three or four seemingly nonchalant questions to each van driver, then, after guessing which one was the drunker of the two, make my way casually to the van of the other. When I emerged from the van at the far end of the run I usually, like Walter Scott's hero Fitz-James, "faltered thanks to heaven for life".

I gained other valuable experience as well. One afternoon, two of my new service friends, Gort Strecker and Billy Robertson, decided to venture into town that evening to attend the jitney dance, the cultural focus of the town's social whirl. They invited me to accompany them. I demurred, explaining that I could not dance. They absolutely refused to take no for an answer, scoffing at such a ridiculous reason for not going to a dance.

Strecker immediately set out to teach me how to dance, there and then, having first stationed Robbie in one of the adjacent top bunks with instructions to lean over the aisle and sing "Yes Sir, She's My Baby". He explained that it was to be sung very slowly, with heavy rhythmic emphasis, and hearty handclaps to go with Strecker's pulling and pushing and cries of "One, and Two, and One and Two". Perspiring copiously in his heavy underwear, Strecker did not convince me, even at arms' length, that dancing was a wonderful way to get to know girls; and I allowed myself to be persuaded, after ten minutes of concentrated practice on "Yes Sir", that if I became any more proficient I ran the risk of embarrassing the local belles by making them appear clumsy.

At the dance that night I did not embarrass any of the local girls with my newly acquired terpsichorean skill. About nine o'clock my instructors decided that they had had enough too, and decided to walk over to the nearby hotel for two or three beers before catching the bus back to the station. I went in with them, although I had no intention of taking a drink. However, Strecker ordered one for me, and once again I allowed my original intentions to be overborne and followed my mentors' example. This was the first glass of beer I had ever drunk. I did not enjoy it, but over the next hour or so I gagged my way through two more to prove that I was one of the boys.

It was when we got up to leave the table that I found I was not one of the boys. My co-ordination was definitely sub-standard and my faculties were all very much on the sluggish side. With minimal assistance from my friends I managed to board the bus, and we rode back to camp. During that quarter hour, my condition worsened somewhat, and because of my burning desire to have an exemplary conduct sheet, I chided myself for having been so stupid as to lower my guard and take a drink.

The bus pulled up opposite the guard-house, and we began to disembark under the eyes of the Service Police just inside. As I was stepping down from the front of the bus, striving earnestly to display the absolute ultimate in sang-froid, I missed the last step, lost my balance and fell ignominiously on my face in the drifted snow. Strecker and Robbie loudly made light of this, fishing me out and slapping some of the snow off me, and marched me through the guard-house like an unsteady penguin past the SP's who stared at me very suspiciously.

I was unable to contain myself. As soon as we were outside and clear of their scrutiny, I began to curse my traducers in a mumbled and maudlin harangue.

"You bastards, you've lost me my commission". I repeated it over and over, and each time their laughter grew louder.

It wasn't until I had slept it off that I saw any humour in the facts myself. The salient facts were, of course, that I was a lowly AC 2; that before I would ever be considered for a commission I would have to pass a whole series of physical and academic tests at ITS; I would have to pass an extensive ground school course at Elementary Flying Training School, together with a number of flying tests and Link Trainer tests; I would have to pass advanced ground school exams, Link Trainer Tests and flying tests at Service Flying Training School; and I would have to finish in the top third of the class both in ground school and in flying tests. It was with these requirements present in their minds that Strecker and Robbie found my accusation that they had lost me my commission so hysterically funny. They were right; it was a bit much.

Strecker, Robbie and I had quickly become fast friends, despite the fact that they were several years older than I was. Looking back, I think it was because we were opposites in so many ways. I was young, ingenuous, idealistic and highly impressionable. I took as unchallengeable gospel every edict the Air Force published. Strecker and Robbie were different; where the Air Force was concerned they were very strictly from Missouri. Their approach to a published order that held a potential for hampering them was to analyze it carefully for weaknesses and to determine whether and how it could be beaten.

On our first day at Macleod they too had been assigned to some obnoxious job. At the first possible opportunity they volunteered to fill two openings for electricians' helpers in the so called "Works and Bricks" department, and wound up as assistants to a middle aged civilian electrician named Mr. Whipple.

As their senior Mr. Whipple was entitled to make liberal use of their talents whenever there was a dirty or awkward job to be done. Somehow with Strecker and Robbie things never seemed to work out quite that way for Mr. Whipple.

The first time I ever came across the trio in action, a freezing gusty afternoon two days after Strecker and Robbie had launched their new careers in the electrical world, they were changing a street light at the top of a 20 foot pole. To my surprise, it was not one of the younger assistants I beheld balancing at the top of the rickety ladder, but the senior electrician, Mr. Whipple himself. I knew not what they were playing, or what they were dreaming of then, but a few moments after I passed I heard all three of them shouting.

I turned to see Mr. Whipple dangling by one arm from the outermost end of the horizontal lamp support and thrashing about very energetically. Instead of re-hoisting the ladder and rescuing their boss immediately, Strecker and Robbie scandalized me by indulging in shouted dialogue:

"Hey, look, Robbie! Look! It's a bird. It's a plane."

"No, no — it's WHIPPLE! YEA!"

Mid-way through this latter speech, Mr. Whipple uncorked a shout himself:

"Cut out the clowning you young buggers, and get that ladder up here!"

They did. They knew when to quit.

Ten days later it was announced that everyone on the station was going to receive five days leave. Half the station was to go two days before Christmas, the other half two days before New Year. Our group was in the first wave. We were to leave the station December 22nd; our passes would bear that date and were good until midnight on the 27th.

On the 17th Strecker approached me, shrouded in an air of mystery, and asked if I thought I could get permission to leave earlier, as early as the following day for example, if he could arrange to have our passes delivered to us that much ahead of schedule. My curiosity was aroused, but he parried my questions, telling me simply to ask the bandmaster and to tell him that Strecker and Robbie had secured their section head's consent.

Corporal Lehman was distinctly lukewarm about the idea, particularly when I was unable to explain how the passes would be forthcoming from the Adjutant's office so early, but he agreed to turn a blind eye to my absence with one reservation: if any officers came looking for me before the 22nd, he would plead ignorance of my whereabouts and guess that I had gone sick. I was mildly amused at his obvious suspicion that there might be some slight stench of fraud about the whole project, and left to pack, delighted.

The following day we went to the railway station and caught the train for Winnipeg. I had received from Strecker an official pass, made out in my name, bearing the Adjutant's stamp and signature. Aboard the train a short time later I received further evidence of the benefits which flowed from knowing the right people. From their haversacks

Strecker and Robbie produced a bountiful lunch of cold chicken sandwiches and big portions of pie. When we had gorged ourselves, I elicited the details relative to this minor miracle.

The materials for the feast had come from the officers' mess. Thinking ahead, Strecker had gone into the officers' mess on the 17th, ostensibly to replace some burned-out bulbs. This was his standard gambit. He invented trouble calls from any part of the station he wished to visit, then persuaded Mr. Whipple that there was no need for the section head to bother himself with something as mundane as replacing a few bulbs, and set off with Robbie to exploit whatever opportunities appeared. At the other end, of course, admission was secured by the brusque recital that Mr. Whipple had sent them to check out a trouble call.

On this occasion Strecker marched into the officers' mess kitchen, changed one or two bulbs that didn't need changing, then at an opportune moment, unscrewed the bulb inside the refrigerator and left. He returned an hour later in response to the cook's call, removed the undamaged bulb, shook it and announced that the filament was broken. He intimated to the cook that securing a replacement would be a lengthy if not impossible task for a man of normal talents, but that he would try.

Timing things nicely, Strecker showed up with a "replacement" the following day, half an hour before we were due to leave the station to catch our train. He explained to the cook that he'd had to make a special trip into town to get it. When the cook had been sufficiently impressed, Strecker made as if to leave and then, as an afterthought, asked if there was any chance of getting a couple of baloney sandwiches to take on the train since he and his companions didn't have any money for dining cars, and it was a 700 mile ride to Winnipeg. It was all he could do to keep the cook from coming with him and cooking for him on the train.

Next day as our train pulled into Brandon I got another insight into my friends' characters. I glanced at the platform just as we were shuddering to a stop and commented with no great interest that the DAPM (District Assistant Provost Marshal) and four SP's were going to board. To my surprise Strecker and Robbie leapt like panthers from their casual reclining positions and began pulling their kitbags off the overhead racks.

"What's the matter with you characters?" I asked. "We got passes."

Strecker paused just long enough to shove my gear into my hands and hiss: "Yeah, we got passes. You want to know who signed those passes? I did. Now come on into the vestibule. If they come through this coach climb out on the side opposite the platform and stay out of sight."

Later, when the DAPM had gone through and we were on our way again, Strecker explained that they had deliberately made a nuisance of themselves in the Adjutant's office a few days earlier, so much so that the Adjutant had taken himself off for a cup of coffee to avoid the clatter of their step ladder and the dust they showered onto him while cleaning the light fixture over his desk. No sooner had he gone out the door than Strecker came down the ladder, found the pad of pass forms, put the Adjutant's stamp on three or four of them, and tucked them into his tunic. Later, he had forged the signature creditably enough, after studying it on some posted orders and practising it, but he had wanted to avoid subjecting his handiwork to the acid test if at all possible. By the time we came back from leave we could wrinkle and crease our passes to disguise the shortcomings of the endorsement when presenting it to the SP's in our own guard-house; but it would look suspicious if we produced tattered, wrinkled passes at this stage of our leave.

I was again displeased with myself at having been led into a violation of Air Force regulations, and when Strecker phoned me the day before we were due to return to the station, I was in no mood for more shenanigans. This was exactly what he and Robbie were thinking of. We had left the station early; their thought was to go back late, returning with the second group, the ones who had received New Year's leave. I had no intention of tempting fate further and told him so. With a diligently creased pass, I entered the portals of Macleod unchallenged and on time.

On New Year's day the Air Force at Macleod put on a repeat performance of the feast it had presented on Christmas day. It was a turkey dinner that would have taxed most housewives to match. As they had on Christmas day, our officers honoured the old tradition and acted as the waiters in the airmen's mess. The tables were heavily laden with all the customary Christmas trimmings, including bowls of nuts and bottles of beer. The only perfectly routine feature of the meal was the appearance, part way through it, of the Orderly Officer, and his invariable shout: "Any complaints?" This day the ordained query brought a great cheer in response.

Three days later Strecker and Robbie showed up. Since their passes had long since expired I wondered how they were going to get past the SP's at the guard-house. Strecker was equal to the task. For three dollars he bribed the driver of the civilian laundry truck which came onto our station every day to let him and Robbie lie on the floor of the little panel truck. The driver then piled his parcels over the two delinquents and drove them onto the station undetected. When I saw how easy it had been I began to wonder if perhaps I wasn't a little too pure.

Shortly after their clandestine return, we had another Wings Parade, a station spectacle that always thrilled me. At these, the senior course — or, more accurately, those members of the senior course who had successfully weathered the battery of physical, academic, and flying tests thrown at them — received the symbol of their hard-won status as service pilots. It is difficult to convey to someone who has not been through wartime flight training the burning intensity of desire that most flight cadets lived with. We all knew it intimately. You recognized its concomitant when you saw a young man, who had just been washed out over at the flights, slumped on the edge of his bunk, eyes wet, misery and dejection written all over his face, oblivious to friends who tried awkwardly to console him.

The Wings Parades were the triumphs. I envied the lucky ones, and rejoiced with them. Our band always led the parade into the large hangar where the ceremony was to be performed. Accompanying the band, a few steps in front of it, marched Flying Officer Coghill, leading the station mascot, a huge Newfoundland dog with a head like a hassock. Every once in a while the dog would get bored with the straight-line progress and decide to scout around a bit on either flank. When the dog wandered, F/O Coghill's lot was not to reason why. He had to go where the dog led, and coax. He would disappear, sometimes abruptly, from my restricted field of view along the bell of my trumpet, then meander in again, unsteadily but smiling, with our friendly giant lumbering along beside him.

Inside the hangar the graduating class would be called up, one at a time, before a VIP, usually a visiting Air Commodore or Air Vice-Marshal who would acknowledge the cadet's salute, pin the coveted white pilot's wings on his chest, then shake his hand and give him a verbal pat on the back before the cadet marched off. I never tired of the drama implicit in the cadet's marching up in his plain, unadorned blue tunic, then turning about smartly and marching back toward the crowd of spectators with that clearly visible and impressive set of white-centered wings fairly glistening over his left tunic pocket. Parents and relatives of the graduates were welcome at these parades, and their obvious pride and enjoyment added to the exultant atmosphere radiating from the graduating platoon. I just could not visualize myself being good enough and lucky enough to reach a Wings Parade; at the same time I refused to contemplate the prospect of washing out as a pilot; that was the complete annihilation of the future as I saw it.

All through February rumours flew of impending moves to ITS for us. Each time the posting dates came and went and we remained in

Macleod. It began to look as though the Air Force had lost our documents and wasn't looking for them.

On February 26th Strecker and Robbie decided to check the Adjutant's office around coffee time again. After two or three minutes of their noise and dust the Adjutant left and the two electricians went over the correspondence on his desk. They struck pay dirt on the first pass. The posting order was there; we were posted to No. 4 ITS Edmonton as "G" Flight, Course No. 48, arriving March 1st, 1942.

Strecker and Robbie immediately headed for the barracks. Since the Air Force made a point of telling air-crew absolutely nothing about impending moves, they scented opportunity. First they told all the cooks that someone had seen our posting orders and that we were moving to the Saskatoon ITS on March 15th. After this rumour had gone through the camp from one end to the other, which it did at dinner time, one hour after they had lit the fuse, they confronted the dozen or so air-crew who by that time were claiming to have seen the posting order with their own eyes and bet them five dollars apiece that we would be out of Macleod at least a week or ten days before that date.

On March 1st we climbed into an Air Force bus and drove to No. 4 ITS Edmonton. Strecker and Robbie collected bets all the way, and most of the marks were so pleased to be starting real air-crew training that they didn't mind losing, fair and square.

CHAPTER 2

INITIAL TRAINING SCHOOL

Yesterday This Day's Madness did prepare;
Tomorrow's Silence, Triumph, or Despair;
Drink! for you know not whence you came, nor why:
Drink! for you know not why you go, nor where.

Rubaiyat of Omar Khayyam

We reached the end of our 300 mile bus ride that evening on the campus of the University of Alberta, in Edmonton, part of which had been taken over by the Air Force. We were quartered in fine old buildings that had formerly been the women's residence. The rooms were small, and it was two men to a room; but everything was spick and span. We soon learned how it was kept so spotless.

Next morning at 6:00 AM we were gently awakened by the fire alarm. I am not normally the fastest man in the west when it comes to rolling out of my warm bed, but I learned that morning that if you were going to do everything expected of you, your feet had to hit the floor the second the alarm began its clamour. The routine was as follows: reveille, 6:00 AM; wash up, shave, fold up blankets and sheets, polish boots and buttons, clean and dust your room *completely*, hustle to the adjoining building for breakfast, return and pick up books and march over to the gymnasium in time to go on parade at 7:15. A short time later, the officers appeared, and we received an inspection that would be described as pitiless even by the most charitable. We then marched, frequently in the howling March blizzards for which Edmonton is notorious, half a mile to the Normal School where we took classes from 8:00 AM until noon. We marched back at noon to the mess building, ate lunch at 12:15, and were back in the gym at 12:45 to march to the Normal School again for more lectures from 1:00 until 5:00 PM. We were given three hours homework each day on the off chance that we might otherwise find time hanging heavy on our hands.

After ten days of this hectic pace, someone coined a maxim that we thought summed up the ITS atmosphere fairly well: "If you stop for a leak — you'll fall a week behind".

Nevertheless, morale was sky-high, for many of the subjects on our curriculum were so clearly linked to the flying school training we would be moving to in six weeks — if we overcame all the ITS hurdles. Too, we were now clearly marked as flight cadets. At ITS all air-crew became entitled to wear, and were required to wear, a white flash in the front of their wedge caps. We were very proud of our white flashes. Subsequently some of us experienced a slight loss of self confidence when it came out that the ground crew, in a move designed to handicap potential competition, had circulated the canard amongst the young women of Edmonton that anyone suffering from VD was required by the Medical Officer to wear a white flash as long as the condition remained infectious.

The ITS course was essentially a six week ground school, during which the instructors, who were almost all former school teachers, tried to determine the aptitudes of the cadets. On the basis of their assessments they recommended the best cadets for further training, either as pilots or observers (navigators). Some cadets, who could not readily absorb the academic side of the course, were given a chance to try the wireless-operator/air-gunner's course, or the straight air-gunner's.

The toughest test of all at ITS was the M2, the second medical. This was a four hour ordeal, replete with careful colour vision and depth of vision checks, and odd items such as testing a man's ability to balance on one leg with his eyes shut. During the first two and a half weeks of the course, while the M2's were going on, people were frequently to be seen in their rooms teetering on one leg, eyes shut and arms outstretched, as they practised for this balance test. Since we were subsequently taught to disregard our unreliable senses completely and place our trust in instruments when visibility was cut off, I often suspected the Air Force of an inconsistency here — but I suppose one would have doubts about a person whose balance was so bad that he pitched onto his head the moment he closed his eyes, or who regularly soaked the linoleum with a coffee cup carried at a 45 degree angle.

My roommate at ITS was a former diamond driller from Oregon named Harry Peters. I had got to know him at Macleod. Harry was one of several Americans in our course, a fine, easy-going chap with a nice sense of humour. He and I got along famously for a couple of weeks, until he went over for his M2 one afternoon. When he came back he was very sombre, and told me he thought he'd flunked one part of the test for colour blindness. Next day his fears were confirmed and Harry was officially washed out. On the evening of March 17th, Strecker, Robbie and I went down to the station to see Harry off for Trenton, where all washed out air-crew were sent.

Robbie was next to go, but not for any shortcoming on his part. Robbie's wife had become afflicted with some rare glandular condition and required treatment with expensive drugs which he could not afford on an airman's pay. Reluctantly, he had to seek a compassionate discharge, which was granted. Once more we made the trip to the station. Randall, another American, left a day or two later. We were not of his retinue, so I did not attend the railway station leave-taking. I gathered from next morning's eye-witness reports that it was a typical, alcoholically maudlin ceremony, with much back slapping and "dog-gone-it" punching on the arms, until the conductor hollered "Board", at which time Randall was hoisted onto the lowest step of the vestibule, where he turned and faced his sorrowing, loyal buddies, and, as the train began to move, belched out his valedictory: "You're a bunch of runts, good-bye and pluck ya." Since his own alcoholic intake over the evening had been impressive, my informant had been suffering from a case of high frequency hiccups at that point, and when I questioned him was unable to attest with absolute certainty as to two of the words in the message.

Strecker and I carried on. With the exception of navigation, which was a completely new subject to me, I found the rest of the academic subjects on the course largely memory work, which came easy since I was fresh out of school. Strecker had been away from it for some years, and was rusty in mathematics. I had several sessions with him, reminding him of the rules and the short cuts. Lights out was at 11:00 PM; thereafter many apprehensive drudges carried their chairs to the large communal bathroom, where the lights still burned, and pored over the books and charts far on into the night.

Navigation was the heaviest subject, rightfully given a prominent place in the curriculum. Whether one became a pilot or a navigator, a working knowledge of aerial navigation was absolutely essential. In our six week stint at ITS we had 90 hours of navigation lectures, and perhaps 150 hours of navigation problems and plotting for homework. We learned the basic attributes of several cartographic projections and were taught the special advantages of the Mercator, the projection which we used for all our plotting thereafter. We learned the rhumb line — great circle route relationship, and a thousand other items of hitherto arcane knowledge.

In this scientific sphere we learned a new scale of values. To the aerial navigator, the *summum bonum* was the reliable fix. To have a fix was to know, or to be able to calculate from varying items of pertinent information, where one's aircraft was at a given moment in time. Fixes varied greatly in reliability depending upon the accuracy of the information on which they were based. A positive fix was a thing of beauty and a joy forever. It was the Holy Grail. It was the Platonic Idea of Truth. Even a good position line was something to be accepted by student navigators with deep gratitude, although, like Oliver, one was driven to ask for more.

With inky fingers and twirling dividers we checked innumerable references in latitude and longitude. With our Dalton computers we found the resultants of a million divergent vectors. We learned to average and apply temperature gradients, to sneer at IAS (indicated air speed) and convert it for the relevant altitude and temperature to TAS (true air speed). Likewise we converted magnetic bearings to true bearings, mumbling our rhyming guide like weak-minded children:

"Variation East, Magnetic least;
Variation West, Magnetic best."

Even then, we were not finished. We came to know that even an expensive aircraft compass such as our standard P4 did not speak the gospel from its lubber line, and that compass deviation, too, could lure you into a mountain. We mumbled more doggerel to reach the truth,

"Deviation West, Compass best;
Deviation East, Compass least."

We read that our aircraft altimeters were simply aneroid barometers, and that without the necessary pressure corrections in distant areas they could be dangerously misleading — this lesson I was to re-learn 18 months later in foggy blackness flying a few feet over the surface of the Kattegat. Soon we had the ability to trip lightly between confusing mixtures of statute and nautical miles, and we were taught to regard as a navigational impostor anyone who slipped and gave a speed as "200 knots per hour" instead of the correct "200 knots". We transposed position lines and grappled with the difficulties of six minute alterations of course. Ever and always we struggled for the good fix, that elusive jewel from whence one made a fresh start for the target, or for home, secure in the knowledge that at this moment one was right here on the chart.

While navigation was our heaviest course, it was only one subject among many on the curriculum. We also studied Theory of Flight and Airmanship. We studied Engines, in-line and radial, liquid cooled and air cooled. We applied ourselves to Aircraft Recognition and took lectures in "LDAO", Law, Discipline, Administration and Organization

18

of the RCAF. We took Signals, practising Morse on buzzers and on Aldis lamps as well. To qualify, we had to send and receive at a minimum rate of eight words per minute. We studied Armament, and War Gases, and we took an elementary course in Meteorology.

Our labours were not confined to the classroom. Every day we had PT, and every day we drilled on the parade square. It was when we first participated in these exercises that we came to know our disciplinary NCO, Flight-Sergeant Glaves.

Glaves had blond hair, and bright blue eyes which frequently held a spurious twinkle that could mislead one into thinking him a friendly soul. I found out differently one afternoon when I asked him for the pass which an air-crew cadet required to be off the station after 10:30 PM. My father was on his way to the west coast for a holiday, and was stopping off in Edmonton for the one day so that we could have a visit. Since I would be unable to get away to meet him until about 6:00 PM, I wanted to stay out two or three hours past our early curfew. Passes were given routinely by other NCOs for much less compelling reasons, but Glaves saw fit to refuse. I saw fit to go over his head, and got one without any trouble from Flying Officer MacDonald, an act which did not endear me to my twinkly-eyed friend.

I found Glaves an intensely interesting person. He stood about five feet nine, and I suspect that his mother would have described him as stocky. To me he looked like a cross between a Viking and a Sumo wrestler. His first appearance before our Flight, in his oversize PT sweatshirt, with its round crest framing his substantial paunch, earned him the nickname "The Great Circle" from Strecker. When he led us in our first warm-up sequence of feet astride jumping, and his hemispherical gut began its vertical yo-yo motion to the cadence of his jumping, I watched, fascinated, half expecting to see that mighty appendage tear loose and fall off like a thirty pound wheel cover.

Glaves frequently took us on route marches along the streets of Edmonton. It was on the first of these sorties that he demonstrated his rather distinctive command of the language. He was marching alongside the rear end of our platoon, ten or 15 yards behind me. March discipline seemed impeccable. We got lots of drill at ITS, and when the platoons were on parade, it showed. On this occasion, there were many people on both sides of the street standing and watching us march past. Out of a clear blue sky Glaves suddenly unleashed a raucous bellow that yellowed the plate glass windows for a block on either side of us:

"THERE'LL BE NO BASTARD TALKING!"

I mulled this pronouncement over for a hundred paces or so, but was unable to decide whether he meant bastard to be a noun or an adjective. While I was still considering the question, Glaves roared the admonition again, verbatim.

At regular intervals all the way back he repeated it, again and again, always in stentorian tones. The rhythmic cadence of the boots on the concrete caused my mind to flit to the two-line chorus of one of the Cavalier Tunes we had read in high school a year earlier, and I passed the rest of the march enjoyably enough reciting it to myself and trying to time it so that the Flight Sergeant's contribution came in at the appropriate moment. Once or twice I caught it perfectly and it went:

(Peden, *sotto voce*): "Marching along, fifty-score strong,
Great-hearted gentlemen, singing this song."
(Glaves, offstage): "THERE'LL BE NO BASTARD TALKING!"

I often wondered what the good burghers of Edmonton made of this performance. They probably pitied us. Actually, Glaves rose considerably in my estimation in later years because of the delivery of that somewhat profane stricture. What do *you* think — was it an adjectival use?

While the regimen at ITS was certainly arduous, it was not without its compensations. At Manning Depot we had slept in ordinary H-shaped barracks, and a routine we had found funny for the first few days consisted of flopping onto a bunk and dictating aloud a letter home beginning,

"Dear Mother, it's a bugger. Here we are,
sleeping 50 men by a room . . ."

At ITS we had small neat rooms, shared by only two men. Although the doors had been removed, there was little noise, and we were spared the earlier nightly chorus of 50 different levels of breathing and snoring, with the background accompaniment of grunts, groans, wheezes, whimpers and snorts generated by dreams and indigestion.

At Manning Depot a fatigue party had made toast every morning at 6:00 AM, as a special treat. When we walked in to eat at 8:00 AM, I would have defied anyone to state with assurance, after he had taken a few bites, whether he had eaten "toast" or a cold #2 cedar shingle rubbed lightly with Marfak. At ITS we ate excellent food, in a tastefully decorated mess that was presided over by a pleasant looking and smartly dressed woman — a switch from the sweaty and hirsute specimens in underwear shirts we had been favoured with hitherto.

As the ITS course wore on, we were summoned from time to time to the chamber where the Link Trainer instructors held sway. They put us through sessions in the stubby-winged little trainer from which I emerged sweating and trembly. The "feel" of the ITS machines was quite different from those at Macleod, and the knowledge that your future career in the Air Force depended upon your holding its nose in one position and keeping the fidgety machine from moving sideways while you rolled it over on its side, made the experience radically different from the enjoyable sessions we had had at Macleod with F/O Coghill.

If the Link Trainer sessions were a strain, I, for one, had a relaxing and distracting influence periodically available to me which offset them. Doug Cameron, another friend of mine from Gordon Bell High, had done his ITS in Edmonton, and had reached SFTS at Macleod while I was still there broadening my musical education. Since he was my friend, when he found out that we were posted to Edmonton ITS, he gave me the phone number of a girl he had met there, along with his earnest recommendation that I look her up.

I was very much the innocent in such matters, thoroughly inexperienced and naive; even so, I asked if he had a picture of her. Cameron produced a snap from his wallet, and identified her as a Miss Joyce Wright, a novice ballet dancer. Her father, he said, was semi-retired, a former member of the RCMP. I stared at the picture in frank admiration. The subject was undeniably a 24 carat charmer, so good that I double checked and verified the telephone number and address.

Most of the first week at ITS I was far too hurried, harried, and harassed to think of anything but service responsibilities; but the Air Force, after driving us until our tongues were lolling for five and a half days, dismissed us at 1:00 PM Saturday and let us have the afternoon off. Sunday was to be free too, once we had done our homework assignments.

Finding myself for the first time with an opportunity to draw a leisurely breath, I called the number Cameron had given me. A very pleasant young voice replied, and when I identified myself, and explained that common courtesy and a sense of obligation to my lifelong friend Cameron had compelled me to call and ask after her health, and for a date, she surprised me. She had made plans to do something else that evening, she said, but would be able to cancel them and entertain me at dinner with her parents instead. She gave me explicit directions for getting out there on the Bonnie Doon bus.

After I had hung up, I began to be assailed by grave doubts. Things had gone altogether too well. If this girl was so nice, how was it that Cameron was giving her up so freely — practically forcing her on me? Again, if she was such a catch, how was it that I could find her available on short notice — on a weekend — in a city overrun with airmen? Could it be that Cameron's questionable sense of humour had prompted him to line me up with some notorious beast, some fright, known to and shunned by everyone in ITS, and to show me a photograph of someone else to ensure ignition of the hormones?

21

I concluded that the die was now cast in any event, and that I should have to cross my fingers and face the moment of truth. I walked back to my billet in Pembina Hall slowly, inventing two or three plausible lies to feed Strecker to forestall any interrogation regarding my plans for the evening.

My trepidation vanished the moment Joyce Wright opened the door that night. Cameron's picture had certainly not been misleading, in fact it had not done her full justice. I took very careful physical inventory as I introduced myself and she took my coat. She was the answer to an airman's prayer: a petite brunette with sparkling eyes, intriguingly curvaceous.

Her parents were most hospitable. We dined royally, while they asked tactful questions about my success with the beginning of the ITS course, a subject on which they were understandably well informed. After dinner, when we had all pitched in and disposed of the dishes, they shooed us into a room by ourselves.

I discovered shortly that Joyce had made additional arrangements. I was going to be able to sit comfortably with her on the chesterfield until 11:40 PM — the normal cadet curfew of 10:30 was extended to midnight on Saturdays — at which time Mr. Wright was under orders to whisk me to the ITS portals in the family car. Leaving at 11:40 would get me in past the sentries with about three minutes in hand.

As I rode home that evening in the back seat of the family auto, snuggled up to a pretty girl, with a standing invitation to repeat the performance whenever I could get away, I thought ever so warmly of my dependable old friend Doug Cameron — surely goodness and mercy would follow him all the days of his life. If I had been a millionaire, I'd have altered my will that night and left him everything. The actual cash position being what it was, I settled for writing him a hurried letter next day saying thank you.

The following Saturday I took Joyce to the movies to see "Captains of the Clouds" starring James Cagney, ostensibly an epic about the RCAF. Much of the story was incredible claptrap, with Cagney and several accomplices at their unbelievable worst as a result; but the fearful dialogue was jettisoned from time to time to make way for some excellent flying scenes, and for five or ten minutes Billy Bishop played himself and gave one of his typical Wings Parade speeches to graduating pilots. That authentic sequence alone redeemed the picture as far as I was concerned, for Bishop came across on the screen or in person as just what he was, a gentleman with a lot of backbone, one of the type classified by Ovid as "the leader of leaders".

I managed to get out with Joyce most weekends during the first half of the course; but as we progressed to its final stages even

Saturdays and Sundays had to be used for cramming. Two straight weeks of this grind without a break indirectly led to my involvement in another clandestine venture with Strecker — with predictable consequences.

He and I worked on navigation one afternoon and evening until 9:45, with only 20 minutes off for supper, then decided we needed a breather before curfew. We picked up another companion and headed for the drug store a few blocks away at the end of the High Level Bridge. When we were half way there, a car with three girls aboard drove past, slowly.

"They'll be back," Strecker announced.

He spoke the truth. Moments later they pulled up beside us and invited us to join them. We piled in, no questions asked. We all introduced ourselves, and away we went for a drive. After 15 or 20 minutes, I brought up the topic of our 10:30 PM deadline, making pointed reference to the fact that it now lacked but ten minutes of the witching hour. Our hostesses fell silent. The other two musketeers, particularly Strecker, weighed in with several totally specious arguments as to why we should not worry about such peccadilloes. I allowed myself to be overborne by the force of their logic — I was thoroughly satiated with studying. On with the dance, I said, let joy be unconfined. We agreed that we would run half an hour or so over the curfew, and sneak in over the fence.

At 3:00 AM the girls dropped us a block away from our objective, and we began a stealthy trek towards the high wire fence. Our initial objective was a slightly sheltered spot where we could kneel in the hay and brambles and reconnoitre for a time without ourselves being observed.

We could see the sentry post covering the approach to Pembina Hall. The first fact we had to determine was whether there was actually a sentry on duty. In pooh-poohing my earlier pusillanimous suggestion of a timely and legal return to our quarters, Strecker had confidently predicted the presence of a sentry on that particular beat as an extremely unlikely contingency. As we huddled there, crouching, and surveyed the scene, it became apparent that in defiance of Strecker's astronomical odds, the unlikely contingency had in fact materialized, and there was a real live sentry in the sentry box, just 50 yards away from us. So much for Strecker's Assurance No. 1.

Every few seconds we saw a faint glow inside the sentry box. He was having an illegal smoke. I filed this scrap of information away as a possible bargaining point should the worst transpire.

When he had finished, the sentry came out of the box and began to patrol his beat. We noticed at once that he was not wearing a white flash in his cap — the flash would have guaranteed sympathetic assistance rather than hostile confrontation. So much for Assurance No. 2, quote: "Even if they have someone over in that sentry box, it's bound to be one of our gang; they've been sticking air-crew on sentry go all this week."

The closest the sentry came to us along the wire, we noted, was a point about 20 yards to our right. Then he reversed course and tramped about 100 yards the other way with his back to us. He carried a rifle garnished with a bayonet.

We held a whispered council of war and decided that we should climb the wire, one at a time, when the sentry was about 50 yards distant and heading away from us. Strecker was to go first and I was to bring up the rear.

Strecker clambered up the wire on schedule, seeming to have considerable difficulty surmounting the top two and a half feet of barbed wire which sloped outwards, towards us, at a 45 degree angle. Once on the other side, he slipped into the shadows and was gone well before the sentry turned to face us again.

My other accomplice was equally fortunate, and I prepared to follow in my turn. The sentry, however, decided to have another smoke, and disappeared into his shadowy lair again. But when he finished his smoke he did not come out, and I was loath to move in case he was gaping right at the bushes where I lay freezing.

After ten minutes of this, I decided that he must be dozing and that I must be off. I slipped forward silently and went up, out, and over the barbed wire like a cat. I was balanced at the most awkward point, turning to come down facing the inside of the wire, when the sentry came to life. I heard the ominous sound of a rifle butt being snatched across the sentry-box floor, and a startled shout: "WHO GOES THERE?"

I fell gracefully to earth like a sackful of anvils and shot across the campus like an Olympic sprinter, snatching off my wedge-cap lest I leave incriminating evidence behind. Another shout shattered the nocturnal tranquility, and I glanced back. My pursuer was running hard, rifle and bayonet properly in the "long point" position for mortal attack, obviously seizing upon this as a heaven-sent opportunity to win the Victoria Cross by impaling a dangerous air-crew cadet spy against the dormitory door.

I doubt whether this bloodthirsty sentinel could have got within clutching distance even if he had thrown his heavy rifle and bayonet away and saved his breath for running, because, under the sharp stimulus of fright, I was turning up take-off rpm; but lugging his trusty weapons, and bawling "STOP" and "HALT" every few yards, it was no contest, and he rapidly dropped astern.

I raced up the circular staircase in Pembina Hall to the third level, and paused to listen. He was just beginning to lumber up the first flight, banging his rifle butt repeatedly, so I flitted lightly down the hall to my own room, jammed a pillow under my blankets to make the bed look occupied in the darkness, and stretched out quietly on the floor beneath the lower bunk. In a few seconds he arrived on my floor, and came slowly down the wide corridor. He was trying to be quiet, but he was gasping for breath so strenuously that he couldn't have come up unheard behind a bull elephant trotting kneedeep through corn flakes.

I could hear him moving around for some time, then all was still, and I guessed that he'd gone into the only illuminated room on the whole floor, the large toilet-washroom. I quietly stripped, threw all my clothes on my chair, and ambled down the hall to confirm my suspicion. I entered the brightly lit washroom knuckling one eye and yawning, and simulated a sudden start at the sight of this perspiring warrior armed for strife. Despite my marvellous acting, I could sense that he was eyeing me suspiciously, and I prepared to allay those suspicions. Since I had been unable for six hours to do anything about a certain yearning except exert iron self-discipline, I proceeded to give a convincing demonstration of a genuine need to visit the facility, then left. The sentry never even looked to see which way I headed in the corridor. I was jubilant and thankful. Before dropping off to sleep, I re-dedicated myself to a monastic life of Air Force studies, and renounced again the pernicious trappings of existence outside the authorized service parameters.

In the morning we learned why Justice is depicted as a blind goddess. Our friends told us that shortly after curfew the night before, the Orderly Officer had conducted a surprise bunk check of the rooms on one side of the corridor — Strecker's side. Strecker's roommate, who had just been washed out, had come in tipsy just before the Orderly Officer's visit, and had crawled into Strecker's bunk instead of his own. He was snoring there when the Orderly Officer looked in a few minutes later. The Orderly Officer had promptly marked Strecker present and his roommate absent. Strecker accepted this additional windfall as nothing more than what was right and proper.

Having had only two hours sleep, I feared I might have some difficulty staying wide awake that day. As it turned out, I put in my most wide-awake day of the whole course.

Right after breakfast, Plate and I were ordered to visit the station dentist, who had worked his way through to the P's. When I sat on his plain steel folding chair, he rummaged roughly through my mouth and found eight cavities. In civilian life that would have meant three or four separate appointments to ration the agony into reasonably endurable sessions. Our dentist had an aversion to such complicated bookkeeping. You came to see him but once. If you had five cavities, you left with five new fillings. I writhed through two hours and 20 minutes of his entertaining monologue, while he plied needle and drill manfully, then tottered back to classes with my eight fillings, looking as though I were carrying a brace of golf balls in each cheek.

Next morning our whole Flight was paraded to a long shed-like building for what was billed on DRO's (Daily Routine Orders) as "A Test of the Service Gas Mask". I considered this either redundant or somewhat belated in April, 1942, but following hallowed tradition, no one asked me.

We donned our respirators and entered a room where visibility was virtually nil due to the dense concentration of tear gas. After ten minutes of wandering about comfortably in the mist, we were ordered to remove our masks, take a couple of breaths, and make for a door we would find at the far end. One at a time we choked and spluttered our way out of doors, where one of our officers explained gravely that we had been substantially asphyxiated thus "to give you complete confidence in your respirators".

As we sponged off the face-pieces of our masks I pondered this. I had been fully confident of the respirator before we started. Taking it off under orders and choking in the tear gas had not prompted me to alter my opinion of the reliability of the respirator, but it did leave me with a greatly enhanced respect for tear gas.

Examination time was now upon us, and every night after lights out the toilet was full of cadets studying. Some of the exams were very easy. I had whipped myself up to the point where I could send and receive Morse at 15 to 20 words per minute, so the test at eight was no strain. Aircraft recognition was another gift — for everybody. We sat in semi-darkness and wrote down the names of the 40 aircraft whose silhouettes were displayed in leisurely sequence on the screen before us. I had pored over the cards conscientiously and had them mastered. Strecker had done very little in this field of endeavour, but made amends by sitting next to me in the darkened projection room. He whispered "What?" so many times that even the tolerant sergeant administering the test began to grow testy and threaten to confiscate papers. Everybody within a radius of four feet of Strecker got 100 percent.

I worried about doing too well on the forthcoming Mathematics exam. The accepted dogma amongst the cadets was that if you did well in Maths and Navigation, the instructors would be strongly inclined to pick you as an observer (i.e. navigator), largely disregarding the remainder of your marks. On the Maths paper, therefore, I deliberately threw away seven marks — after I was sure I had racked up enough to pass — by failing to complete the answers.

A few days later I was called in for my personal interview. The interviewing officer was a small, spindly gentleman known to us as Pappy Yokum from his resemblance, in profile, to that worthy. The resemblance, I knew, was strictly superficial. Pappy was an excellent officer, a man who saw well below the surface. He referred to my documents in the file before him, and observed that I had earlier expressed the desire to be a fighter pilot. Now that I had had an opportunity to become a little more familiar with the various air-crew responsibilities, what was my preference? I told him with genuine enthusiasm that I wanted to be a fighter pilot, nothing else, a fighter pilot.

Abruptly Pappy changed the subject and asked bluntly why I had deliberately thrown away marks on the Maths paper. I started like a guilty thing, not having realized that my taking a dive would be so painfully obvious to an old school teacher. Pappy then proceeded to tell me that I had obtained a mark of 87 percent in Maths, and that he was perfectly aware that it should have been about 95 percent.

I came clean and admitted that I had been afraid of doing too well and being picked to go to Air Observer School. Pappy became quite nettled at that and said rather frostily that the Air Force would determine my aptitudes and decide what role I could best fulfill. I didn't want the interview to end on that note and reiterated my burning wish to be a fighter pilot. He seemed to thaw a little, and began asking me in a more sociable manner questions about my background and interests. I left after 15 minutes, highly upset at the thought that I might be denied a chance to go to a pilots school. I had absolutely no interest in becoming an observer. I had no delusions that navigation was easy; but I *knew* that I could ride in an aeroplane and navigate; it was no challenge. I would never know if I had the guts and skill to be a pilot if they packed me off to an AOS.

On April 19th, 1942, having completed the course and all our exams, we were each issued with two flying suits, one helmet and a pair of goggles. We still did not know our fate, but were told that in three or four days the evaluations would be completed, and we would get our promotions to Leading Aircraftsmen and our postings. The tension mounted noticeably.

On Thursday, April 23rd, the terrible moment drew near. In the afternoon we were marched to the classroom, issued with our new insignia of rank — a propeller badge to sew on our sleeves — and told to fall in to learn our classification and postings.

I lined up, hardly able to breathe. Flying Officer Milson began to shout out names, in alphabetical order. The first man's name was called: "LAC BAKER . . . OBSERVER . . . EDMONTON AOS". I almost choked. On he went, the next two picked as Pilots and sent to

Number 5 Elementary Flying Training School (EFTS) at High River. Then more Observers; back and forth. Suddenly he reached the P's and I stopped breathing:

"LAC PEDEN . . . PILOT . . . HIGH RIVER."

I was elated. I broke into a grin, then remembered guiltily that he hadn't reached the S's. In a moment it came:

"LAC STRECKER . . . OBSERVER . . . EDMONTON."

I walked over to him, ashamed at my own joy, and tried to think of something to say. His eyes were swimming.

"Ah, hell, I didn't want to be a Pilot anyway," he said brokenly.

Neither of us could say anything more for a while; the blow was too heavy.

But Strecker played it down, and soon we were talking about our forthcoming moves. The pilot trainees were to leave for High River on Sunday. We made ready, and we said our goodbyes.

At the same time, Rod Dunphy, who had accompanied me to the Winnipeg Auditorium to hear Billy Bishop a year earlier, was getting ready to leave Saskatoon for Air Observer School in Winnipeg. He had been too keen. He hadn't waited for me to reach my eighteenth birthday so that we could join up together, and had joined up himself a few weeks ahead of me.

CHAPTER 3

ELEMENTARY FLYING TRAINING SCHOOL

*"We cannot tell the precise moment when friendship is
formed. As in filling a vessel drop by drop, there is at last a
drop which makes it run over; so in a series of kindnesses
there is at last one which makes the heart run over."*

Boswell: The Life of Dr. Johnson

Sunday afternoon, brimming with enthusiasm, we struggled off
the train at High River, each lugging two duffel bags slung fore and
aft across one shoulder, in which we carried all our worldly possessions. Part of this burden was our bulky new flying clothing including
high-topped fur-lined boots, which henceforth accompanied us everywhere.

Standing near the platform to meet us was one Flying Officer
Hanbidge. Sporting short-cropped blond hair, and a certain steely look
in his blue eyes, he looked to me suspiciously like one of the Prussian
sadists so frequently portrayed by Erich von Stroheim. However,
nothwithstanding the unfailing reliability alleged to be the hallmark
of first impressions, subsequent experience revealed F/O Hanbidge as
a particularly considerate and intelligent officer.

It was a surprisingly warm afternoon for the end of April.
Through a purely routine oversight, the Air Force had neglected to
arrange for any transport, and we were a good deal warmer by the
time we had marched the three miles up the gravel road to the flying
field toting our kit bags.

Both the flying and ground school instructors at EFTS were
civilians. Their work was strictly supervised by a small cadre of RCAF

officers and NCO's, including of course, a Disciplinary NCO, Flight Sergeant Fines. Our instructors started us immediately on a new ground school curriculum, more advanced than the ITS course, but directly related to it. Here the great emphasis was on Navigation and Armament.

At the same time, our flying instructors introduced us to the aircraft we were going to attempt to fly, the DeHavilland 82C Tiger Moth. With a wing span of 29 feet four inches, she was a graceful, rather delicate looking biplane, with a perspex coupe top to cover the two tandem seats. She weighed only 1,115 pounds empty, and had a 145 horsepower, gravity fed, inverted Gipsy Major engine, which was extremely reliable. Being a Training Command aircraft, she was painted the standard (and beautiful) shade of yellow.

The preliminary familiarization exercises occupied us for only a few days. At the end of the fifth day we were told to report for morning flying class the following day. Upon receipt of this simultaneously welcome and worrying directive, we went into the flight room to hang flight gear in our newly assigned lockers. I couldn't help noticing the rather conservative motif of the room, sprinkled as it was with signs in heavy black script conveying this pointed message:

> ### "THERE ARE OLD PILOTS, AND BOLD PILOTS;
> ### THERE ARE NO OLD, BOLD PILOTS."

The organization of our morning flying class would have warmed the heart of Stonewall Jackson, whose written orders clearly showed his urge for starting the day's march "at early dawn". We were roused for morning flying class at 3:30 AM so that we could make ready and be sitting in our planes with the engines ticking over when the sun rose. The air was frequently rough over our field near the foothills of the Rockies, particularly during the middle of the day; so the instructors tried to get in as much time as possible early in the morning and during the last hours of daylight when the air was smooth. Every second morning we were allowed to sleep in until 6:00 AM. We would go to ground school until lunch time, and then take afternoon flying class, which went on until sunset.

We quickly got used to the routine on morning flying class. Each instructor had three or four new pupils, who would be awaiting his summons in the locker room. The instructor would shove his head through a small connecting window from the instructors' room and shout one name. That pupil would grab his seat-pack chute from the locker, fasten the shoulder straps, and waddle out to the flight line behind his instructor. The other instructors would follow suit in turn. Those of us who had not been called for the first flight would sit, wedged into our narrow lockers, and promptly fall fast asleep. An hour later the first lot of pupils would come back, parachutes slung over their shoulders bumping between the lockers, and the rest of us would rouse ourselves and wait to see whose names the instructors would call next.

Outside, everywhere one looked there were Tiger Moths. I never counted them, but I guessed there were about 60 all told on the station. At any one time one would see half a dozen being refueled, half a dozen taxiing out to the take-off point in the prescribed zig-zag pattern, one taking off, one or two climbing away after take-off, and two or three spotted about the circuit at various points preparing to land. It was a scene of immense industry, noisy and wind-blown; but blended into the over-all impression were prominent elements of soaring grace and frail beauty.

My instructor was Mr. Pearson, a pleasant man, only five or six years older than I. He had joined the RCAF, done well in his flying training, and been picked to train as an EFTS flying instructor, reverting during this period to the status of civilian instructor.

I had never even been up in an aeroplane when I joined the Air Force. I had my first aeroplane ride as a passenger at Macleod the day the Japanese decided to go for broke and attacked Pearl Harbor. On that occasion the instructor had scared me half to death mid-way through the trip by breaking off his pupil's instrument practice and taking control himself to give the pupil a rest. That was common practice, and so was what followed. Without warning he had pulled the Anson up vertically into a heart-stopping stall turn. I gripped the stanchion beside the navigator's table in a stranglehold and simultaneously suffered a traffic tie-up in the throat as my heart and stomach both lodged there for some minutes.

I had not forgotten that breath-taking stall, and the vertical dive that followed it, and had wondered apprehensively how my stomach was going to react to the generous dose of assorted aerobatics which I knew were on the EFTS curriculum.

Pearson initiated me gently into the wide range of new sensations which flying generated for the novice, explaining carefully, in advance, what he was going to do with the controls, and what response, in turn, we would get from our sensitive steed. After each demonstration, I tried — very gingerly at first — to duplicate his actions.

I gradually developed a modicum of confidence, although at first, when I was simply trying to keep the aircraft straight and level, it seemed to me that the moment I got the rudder centered and stopped the Tiger's yawing, two or three other problems appeared: the nose crept too high, or too low, causing the rate-of-climb indicator to rear up or sag accordingly, and the wings somehow tilted out of their parallel alignment with the horizon, causing the black ball in the turn and bank indicator to roll obstinately to the side of the dial and proclaim that we were side-slipping.

All the time, Pearson watched me intently in the round mirror mounted on the strut to the left of his head. I was very conscious of his appraising stare, and strove desperately to exude an air of nonchalance and serenity, even while my heartbeat fluttered around the 150 mark and my toes were scrunched up like the claws of a parrot on a perch.

I would clamber from the cockpit after an hour of this, with the sweat trickling liberally from under my helmet, wrench my face into a happy smile as I turned to face my instructor, then wobble my way back to the locker to settle down.

We knew from talking to the senior class that a sizeable number of people would probably be washed out fairly quickly, as the instructors concluded, from those pupils' attitudes and reflexes in the air, that they would be too slow in responding to the training. We also knew that about 90 percent of the remainder of our group would be expected to solo after receiving eight to ten hours of dual instruction. If you weren't ready to solo then, you were usually sent for a ride in the "washing machine" — i.e. a check ride with the Chief Flying Instructor, which in most cases was the final formality preceding the axe. In a very few cases, the Air Force would invest as much as 12 or 14 hours dual in a student in an attempt to get him solo.

We were all aware, too, that susceptibility to air sickness was likely to account for the early washing-out of a number of pupils. This doleful intelligence had been vouched for by the seniors. Thus, for most of us — for we were all nervous — each of these early flights was a dogged battle of mind over matter. It called for more than a touch of the stiff upper lip routine to have to finish an hour's dual with half a dozen power-on stalls and spins, and then climb out in front of one's instructor, conceal the fact that one was deathly ill, and say something hearty and keen like: "Gosh sir, that was fun; can we do some more later on?"

One of Pearson's other new pupils was an American lad named Francis Plate whom I had known slightly at ITS. He was only a few months older than I. Through having the same instructor we were now brought into constant contact, and quickly became fast friends. Plate came from a small town in Iowa called Bennett, but had somehow acquired the nickname "Tex". His mother was a widow and his older brother, Wilmer, had joined the American Army Air Force after Pearl Harbor. After a week or so of sleeping braced against each other's shoulders as we sat waiting for dawn on the locker room floor, we achieved that degree of mutual affection and intimacy which required the exchange of occasional insults and almost continuous ribbing.

Inside the Administration Building, in a prominent spot at the end of the main corridor, were handsomely mounted portraits of three famous Canadian Aces of the First War: Bishop, Barker and Collishaw. Duplicates hung in honoured spots in every RCAF station across the country, frequently in several places on the same station. Knowing that I had some slight regard for these three trusty warriors — about what a true Southerner would feel for Robert E. Lee, Stonewall Jackson, and Jeb Stuart — Plate started the ball rolling by feigning ignorance of their identity. Arranging to meet me he would say:

"Okay, Murray, I'll meet you in the Admin. Building — right under Rickenbacker's picture."

My response would be to clarify the situation:

"No, no, Tex, that's Bishop. You're getting confused because they both shot down 26 planes. But Bishop shot down 26 in one month and finished up with 72. Your man — what was his name Hickenlapper, no, Rickenbackett — he only got 26 in the whole War, and that was counting six French planes he shot down by mistake."

And so it went, with nothing sacred and no holds barred.

On May 11th we were all rushed into town as the High River began rising frighteningly — eight inches in one hour — toward the top of its banks. It felt to me that we carried a million sandbags apiece that day; but it was to no avail. By afternoon the town was flooded — in some streets the water was five feet deep. We were hauled out of our position on a horse-drawn wagon, and rode to the centre of town.

Opposite the St. George Hotel the driver pulled up as someone shouted to bring the Air Force in for a beer — why I don't know; the Queen Mary could have sailed through the area we had been dyking. Although the beer parlor floor was well above street level, the waiters inside were sloshing about serving beer in rubber boots at tables with water lapping half-way up their legs. No one seemed to think it odd; but if a band had struck up "Nearer My God To Thee" one could have visualized himself in the third class lounge of the Titanic at the moment of the grand finale.

Two weeks later the High River again demonstrated the aptness of its name, flooding the town for a second time to the same level. The railway tracks were awash, and there were no trains and no letters for a couple of days, then life went on as before.

Plate and I became increasingly edgy in the five days after the first flood. The odd member of our group began to go solo, and although these successful ones had an hour or two more dual than we had, we worried diligently because we could not see any indications that Pearson was approaching a frame of mind in which he would feel safe in turning us loose. Again the tension became oppressive, and we were fearful on each flight that it might be our last. We worked like dogs while we were in the air.

Then, on the morning of May 16th, Plate came into the locker room at 7:50 to shake me awake. He was ecstatic. He had just gone solo, and he was so excited he couldn't stand still. I clapped him on the back warmly, then grabbed my chute and ran as Pearson shouted for me.

It was a beautiful bright morning. At Pearson's direction I taxied out, zig-zagging carefully, turned out of wind and called off my cockpit check, turned into wind again, and took off. I made two reasonably good circuits and landings. As I made my third approach I was feeling more confident. Everything was going well. I levelled out smoothly, and prepared to ease the stick back as the Tiger floated and began to settle. Suddenly the stick jerked forward in my hands as Pearson deliberately bounced us high in the air. With adrenalin flowing by the gallon, I opened the throttle smartly, and was preparing to bring her in again when the stick was forced back in my grasp and we soared sharply upward. Again I had to give her full throttle and level out momentarily, then, since we were too far down the field, I had to climb away and do another circuit. I landed reasonably well, and Pearson sent me round again. I began to feel that he was in a sadistic mood, since he had chosen to spoil what was obviously going to be a good landing.

Again I made a normal approach and a reasonable landing. We taxied back to the control box in that mindless looking zig-zag, like an earthbound dragonfly run amok, and again I turned out of wind at Pearson's hand signal.

He hoisted himself out of the front seat, climbed back on the port wing step, and pulled off his helmet. My heart gave a great leap, for I now sensed what was coming, and simultaneously I realized that on the earlier circuit Pearson had simply tested my reactions in a perfectly justifiable manner. He had purposely bounced and nearly stalled the aircraft to satisfy himself that he had drilled me enough, and that if I had the bad luck to mess up a solo landing I wouldn't freeze and kill myself, but would go through the recovery procedure routinely.

I forgave him with my eyes.

"How'd you like to do it solo?" he called.

"I'd love it."

"Away you go then. And make it good; I'll be watching."

He tucked his chute up behind his back and walked away. I was all alone in the Tiger.

I lined her up carefully and fed her the throttle. The Tiger raced across the grass and soared into the air like a lark. My heart mounted up with her, thrilling to her response. She climbed away nimbly and beautifully, rising noticeably faster with only my own weight to lift. I made my climbing turn, after looking around with exaggerated caution, and soon I was at 1000 feet and turning onto my downwind leg, again like Tam o' Shanter: "glow'ring round wi' prudent cares".

Now I was heading downwind and the field lay spread out in the sun below me off the port wing. The dark brown fur on the arm of my flying suit rippled in the wind that whistled exhilaratingly past the open cockpit. My heart was bursting. Billy Bishop was never prouder. I revelled in the sensation. Here I flew, all alone. Down there was the field. I was going to bring this aeroplane round and land it right there, where I had taken off, myself.

I judged I was far enough downwind, and turned crosswind again, throttling back and gliding down to 500 feet as I estimated just where to begin my gliding turn into wind. Round I wheeled, reminding myself not to fall prey to the dangerous urge to hold off bank, but to keep the nose up with a gentle touch of top rudder.

Now I was sinking smoothly towards the field. I wiped my throttle hand dry on the furry knee of my suit and took hold again, opening the throttle a notch to make sure the engine was warm and responding. Now the critical moment was at hand. The grass began to stream past. I fixed my gaze resolutely on a point 70 yards ahead and to the left, as I had been taught, and began talking to myself, parroting Pearson, as I checked and began easing the stick back gently: "All right, check, steady, steady, back . . . back . . . right back . . ." She settled in with a tiny thump, and jounced along lightly for a moment before relaxing completely and trundling along with her full weight on the wheels. The stick was right back between my thighs. It was a good three-pointer, a heck of a good three-pointer, I told myself as I zig-zagged back for Pearson. He was smiling broadly as I pulled up.

"Nice going . . . that was a good one," he said.

I glowed with contentment. My log book would now show nine hours and 35 minutes dual, and *15 minutes solo.*

As soon as we finished ground school that afternoon, Plate and I headed for the store, where we each bought a polka dot white silk scarf. Hitherto I had worn a white towel draped around my neck inside my fur flying suit at the dawn flying class; but the accepted protocol at our EFTS was that a cadet acquired and wore a polka dot silk scarf as soon as he went solo. Plate and I were soon swanking about with our new scarves — despite the fact that the afternoon sun had brought the temperature up to 75° F. We now set our sights on the next badge of rank: every cadet on our station bought and sported a pair of Tone-Ray aviation-style sun glasses as soon as he passed his 20 hour check. These tokens of skill and superiority were not treated lightly in our society. When someone approached wearing a silk scarf and sun glasses you recognized that you were in the presence of a cosmopolitan AVIATOR, jaded with aerial adventure.

About a week later, recognizing the greatly elevated status which the surviving members of our course had achieved by soloing and buying silk scarves, the Air Force moved to preclude a possible marginal loss of prestige by giving us our first real all-in no-holds-barred anti-VD lecture.

Our medical evangelist came before us with an impressive array of impedimenta: graphs, charts, projector, screen and slides. He paced himself nicely, opening his lecture with a methodical recital of highly discouraging statistics, then moving on to a more lurid area, with harrowing details of the physical and mental consequences of syphilis.

He heightened the impact of this appealing subject matter by recourse to an extended series of slides. These featured unfortunate persons who, but for our lecturer's explanation, might have been taken for victims who had been lying asleep on the ground when several peckish divisions of army ants had used their faces as picnic grounds. With assorted parts of their visages either missing or in the process of falling off, none of these gentlemen would have been admitted to a self-respecting leper colony. By the time the projectionist turned the lights up, most of us were swallowing in some discomfort. But our performer was a showman. He had saved his best shot for the last.

He directed his assistant to set up a large chart on the easel, and continued with an arresting description of the requisite treatment for a complaint that he referred to as a highly contagious inflammatory disease of the genitourinary tract — and that the more worldly of our group called clap. He emphasized the narrowness of the passage in question by reference to the scandalously immodest gentleman on the chart, then flourished a lengthy instrument of arresting calibre which, he explained, had to be forced up the inadequate passage, while the unfortunate patient was biting through lead bullets like cashew nuts. He paused momentarily as he came to the *pièce de resistance,* placed the actual instrument in strategic position at the top of its stroke on our chart subject, then demonstrated that at this point the contrivance opened like an umbrella and was dragged out again, tearing and scraping the passage clean. He remarked, unnecessarily, that the treatment had to be repeated several times.

At this point most of us would have voluntarily submitted to amputation right there to preclude the possibility of having to submit to that fiendish umbrella treatment. The MO knew he had made his point and finished with one sweetly solemn thought:

"So just remember what you've seen here this afternoon men, and ask yourselves whether 15 minutes fun is worth all this, the pain, the suffering, and the ruin of your careers. Any questions?"

Plate stood up and spoke haltingly, simulating embarrassment and reluctance:

"Sir . . . ah . . . could you . . . ah . . . give us some tips on how to make it last for 15 minutes?"

Having taken the pressure off ourselves momentarily by soloing, Plate and I now indulged in the odd hour of relaxation, the first since we had set foot on the station. I spent half my pay those days putting nickels into the juke box in our canteen to play the current rage "Wait Till The Sun Shines, Nellie", sung by Bing Crosby and Mary Martin. One Saturday afternoon we decided to stroll into town on a little reconnaissance mission. We didn't spot any fillies of the type we had in mind, but we did see a lot of real horses, for we found ourselves on the outskirts of town watching a polo game. I hadn't seen a live polo game before, but that afternoon we saw what we thought was a pretty good one.

High River was in the heart of the Alberta ranching country; so I suppose we shouldn't have been as surprised as we were to see the polo players. By far the best known ranch in the area was the Duke of Windsor's, the "E P" Ranch, so styled when he had been Edward, Prince of Wales. It was only a few minutes from High River by Tigerschmitt (the name we now gave our aircraft) and held a special appeal for us. It was quite a show-place in those days, (compared with its rather tatty neighbours), with neatly painted buildings and corrals, easy to spot from the air.

A practice had grown up whereby the fortunate cadets who had successfully completed all their flying tests at Elementary would prove their prowess by low-flying over and around the Duke's ranch. Unauthorized low-flying was strictly forbidden, and anyone caught *flagrante delicto* could be washed out; but over the "E P" Ranch the feat had a certain snob appeal that seduced most of the graduates.

I had heard all about the custom from two Portage la Prairie boys who were in the senior class at High River, (with 21 hours each), when we arrived as juniors. Irvine Bradley and Bud Clarke had been well known to me when I lived in Portage a few years earlier. I liked them both, although I may have been slightly more gracious to Irvine Bradley because I had a soft spot for his attractive sister.

When Plate and I returned from the polo game, we walked over to their hut and looked up Bradley and Clarke for a short bull session before supper. A definite aura of furtiveness and worry clung to them on this occasion, in marked contrast to the bold and fearless air normally radiated by these silk-scarved Tone-Rayed warriors.

They fell prey to my subtle and penetrating questioning ("What's the matter?") and confessed that they had a suspicion that they were in the well known fertilizer up to their very eyeballs. When we heard the facts, their suspicion struck us as being well founded, to say the least. Both of them having been sent off solo to practise various exercises, they had made a clandestine rendezvous at 4000 feet just west of Caley, and engaged in a stimulating dog-fight. This was every bit as beneficial as the exercises they had been sent to do, and in fact included the full repertoire of prescribed aerobatics; but it did import the one disadvantage that it was vehemently forbidden by all instructors.

Tiring of the Roy Brown—Richtofen sequence at last, they had decided to do a little unauthorized low flying to relieve the tedium. They were weaving their way at 50 feet towards the "E P" Ranch, for a good close look at the natives, when a third Tiger came diving down from nowhere and overhauled them. Thinking that it was another hedonist, Bradley had made a steep turn at the aircraft as it came up, in a playful attempt to fly the interloper into the ground. It was not until he had forced the overtaking aircraft to manoeuvre sharply to avoid a collision that he got a good look under the coupe top and made the interesting discovery that there were two people in the aircraft, i.e. a nonentity like ourselves, and an instructor.

Brad and Clarke had immediately lost their appetite for checking the "E P", and headed smartly back to base, 1000 feet apart and climbing all the way. There was no doubt that the instructor had taken the letters of both their aircraft — he had pulled alongside for the express purpose and written them ostentatiously in a notebook. They had gleaned this last ominous detail out the corner of their eyes while pretending to concentrate their attention elsewhere.

Now they were waiting apprehensively for a summons to drop into the Admin. Building for a word with the Chief Flying Instructor. Their concern stemmed from a fear that the word might be "out". If Bradley's instructor had been available, the outlook might not have been so bleak, for Brad was a good pupil and his instructor had been very high on him. Undoubtedly he would have put a good word in for the pair in a pinch like this. But Brad's instructor had been killed three days earlier, while up dual with a student named Thomson, and his new instructor was a complete stranger. The forthcoming confrontation with the Establishment would therefore be about as evenly matched as an engagement between a battleship and a bumboat.

While we commiserated with the two malefactors, an airman came hotfoot looking for them, and they left, walking very close together for mutual support. It appeared to us unseemly that we should break bread until we discovered what Fate had in store for our friends, so we set off after them. We quickly noticed that their escort was taking them, not to the Admin. Building, but to a spot over by the rifle and machine gun butts. I wondered for a moment whether there was something in King's Regulations (Air) which authorized the Chief Administrative Officer to have them executed without a court martial.

They were out of our sight for a good 20 minutes, then they emerged again, homeward bound. Even from our vantage point 100 yards away the indications appeared favourable. They had their shoulders squared and were marching along briskly, and we saw teeth flash once or twice in nervous grins.

As we moved off together to rejoice over supper, Brad and Clarke took turns reproducing the conversation they'd had with the instructor who had caught them. We gathered it had been essentially a monologue after they had confirmed their identity. Fortunately the instructor was a good Joe who recognized that mercy droppeth as the gentle rain from heaven and so forth. What he dropped all over them for 20 minutes was not mercy, of course.

The instructor had gone up one side of them and down the other, chewing them out like a piranha. But the important fact was that he'd done it himself, without bringing the escapade to the attention of the CFI. After tearing a royal strip off both of them, he had reminded them that they could have been on their way to Trenton, and pointed out the risks they had been taking by engaging in such stunts with their limited flying experience. They had thanked him, with sincerity, for his forbearance, and left.

Three weeks later they were both graduated. Irvine Bradley won the second proficiency award for their course. On June 7th they left for SFTS at Macleod, where Doug Cameron was just finishing.

Flying training overshadowed all other subjects in importance at High River; but ground school was still an ever-present obligation. Our knowledge of Airmanship, Engines, and Theory of Flight continued to expand, and we spent many more hours on Navigation and Armament. We grew rather proud of our ability to strip a Browning .30 calibre machine gun, and to explain its principles of operation in a carefully memorized litany. In Armament class, we took turns simulating a mental block when it came to identifying a certain part known as the Trigger Motor Push Rod, so that our Instructor would have to give us the name. He was Scotch and burred every "r" like a roll on a snare drum. When *he* identified the Trrrrigerr Motorrrr Poosh Rrrrrod it stayed identified — for that class at least.

On May 20th the marks we had made on our mid-term tests were posted. I had done best in Navigation, with a mark of 96 percent; but I was happy with my over-all average of 84.3 percent. Plate accused me of sucking up to the instructors. His average was one point lower.

Once we had soloed, we did five hours solo practice on circuits and landings, with one check circuit accompanied by the instructor at the beginning of each of those five hours. Then, in more dual sessions, we began cautiously broadening our skills, progressing to steep turns, spins from turns with insufficient power, forced landing practice, and cross-wind landings and take-offs.

The first hurdle to be surmounted after one had soloed was the 20-hour check. This was administered by a testing officer, and covered all the basic skills imparted by the instructor up to that point.

On June 4th, when I had 25 hours and 30 minutes in my log book, I was called to take my 20-hour check with a testing officer named Stone. Stone was reputed to be a hot shot aerobatics pilot, and he was easy to identify. He never wore the standard bulky flying boots, preferring instead light running shoes, which gave him a more sensitive touch on the rudder pedals. He was friendly, but all business, as he sat in the front cockpit and got his check list and pad strapped above his knee.

I taxied out to the control box in the normal manner, turned out of wind and called off the six or eight items that made up the Tiger's take-off check. Amongst ourselves (and well out of the hearing of any instructor) we used to say that an adequate check for a Tiger Moth was: "Brake off, take-off"; but when riding with an instructor, and above all with a testing officer, one was careful to intone with appropriate solemnity the requisite checks of oil temperature, oil pressure, throttle nut tension, and the like.

As soon as I had taken off and we were nicely airborne and climbing, Stone cut the throttle completely (as I expected him to do) and called:

"Engine failure — what are you going to do?"

"Land straight ahead, sir" I replied, having already dropped the nose smartly the moment the power came off.

"Very well, open up again and continue your climb."

This was a standard and oft-repeated gambit, designed to make certain that novice pilots would ignore the dangerous temptation to turn back towards the field at low altitude if they had an early engine failure.

We carried on a few miles to an empty patch of sky, and Stone put me through my pedestrian paces: straight and level flying, medium turns, straight climbs and glides at constant speed, climbing turns, gliding turns, recovery from stalls, and recovery from spins.

All the time, I was conscious of a searching visual assessment — the eyes probed constantly from the mirror. (Orwell's 1984 surveillance would seem slipshod and disinterested to an EFTS graduate.)

"All right" Stone finally called, "take me home, join the circuit, and land."

I made for the station, at which point, in retrospect, my rejoining of the circuit could fairly be described as cavalier — or slipshod, or careless, or stupid, to employ a few of the adjectives my instructor applied to it subsequently. At that point I had not grasped the fact that the legs of the circuit pattern were supposed to be flown strictly as prescribed. I had a vague impression that, as long as one made the last two legs approximately at right angles and landed into wind, everything was ticketyboo. I made a good landing, and taxied back to the line.

As soon as I had switched off and we'd climbed out, I spoke to Stone:

"How did I make out, sir?"

He looked at me in a friendly fashion and grinned as he pulled his helmet off and we tucked our chutes up:

"Well, you didn't scare me very much, so I guess you're okay."

I was relieved at the verdict, since these checks were of crucial importance. Stone walked towards the instructors' room in the hangar, where he encountered Pearson, who was waiting to check the results. I hung about in the background in case I should be called upon. maintaining a very low profile, as current journalism would have it. and after a few minutes Pearson raised his voice and said testily:

"He can do a lot better than that — give him another check just on the circuit."

"No, no, there's no need. He's quite okay, it was just his circuit."

The conversation dropped back to an inaudible level, and after another two or three minutes they separated, Stone heading for his locker, and Pearson heading for me.

His normally pleasant countenance exhibited some traces of exasperation, and in a few terse sentences he gave me to understand that the only resemblance between my joining of the circuit and the one prescribed in our Flight Rules was that both terminated with a landing into wind. Beyond that, the Peden pattern embodied several features which contrasted sharply with the official version; features which I gathered I should scrap forthwith.

After he had delivered a few more volleys, I restored his customary good nature with my obsequious vows of reform, and he gave my sagging morale a needed boost by commenting favourably on the balance of my test performance.

Thereafter, when I rejoined the circuit after having been away from the station, I rejoined in copybook style — as I could just as easily have done on my 20-hour check if I'd understood that proper rejoining was *de rigueur*.

As our training proceeded I came to love the little Tigers more and more. Not only were they beautiful craft; but they were surprisingly rugged. In the early stages of our training we bounced them all over the aerodrome like rubber balls; but they kept coming back for more. The morning the mid-term results were posted, for example, we had nine minor accidents — most of them limited to heavy landings (which required a check of the aircraft) or ground loops in which a wing tip had dragged. A cadet named Dodwell had some tough luck — he ground looped and ran into another Tiger.

We had the odd engine failure — but surprisingly few for the number of hours we were putting on the machines. One morning I came close to witnessing one in the air. I had taxied out to the control box behind another Tiger, which proceeded to get its clearance and take-off as I was turning my nose out of the wind to do my check. I took my time so that his slipstream wouldn't be too rough if I hit it. When I did line up for take-off, I expected to see him climbing into the wind in front of me, but he was nowhere to be seen. I opened up and took off, climbing over the graveyard at the far side of our drome, and all at once I saw his plane in a field on the far side of the graveyard. He had obviously made his forced landing without any trouble, for as I skimmed down for a closer look he climbed out of his Tiger and waved at me to show that he was all right.

Another one of our boys, Goucher, had a more troublesome experience one morning while he was up solo. The perspex coupe top worked clear of its tracks, blew back suddenly in the slipstream and partially jammed his rudder and elevators. When he got over the shock, Goucher began experimenting cautiously, and found that he could get almost no response when trying to turn left or to climb.

He would have been fully justified in bailing out; in fact our instructions were to do just that if the aircraft was not responding in safe measure, and this one certainly fell within that description. Goucher decided to give it the old college try, however, and eventually manoeuvred himself into position for a run past the control tower. We had no radios in the Tigers, and Goucher wanted to draw his predicament to the attention of the control officer so that the crash tender would be in close proximity when he came in to land.

Flying past the control tower several times at 60 feet, Goucher did everything except hang from the wheels in an attempt to attract attention, but there was no activity in the bull pen to indicate that anyone was the least bit interested. He eventually decided that trying to land couldn't be any more dangerous than trying to stay in the air in this condition, and once more worked himself carefully into position down-wind of the field. As he began his approach the crash tender was sitting with a cold engine and everyone was studiously ignoring him in his hour of need.

Sweating copiously, he nursed the Tiger in, and landed precariously without injuring either of them. Then, for the first time, a dozen people noticed with horror that there was a Tiger with its cockpit cover jammed into the empennage, obviously in an unsafe condition. With the emergency over, red Very lights began soaring impressively from assorted locations on the field; someone woke the bloke on the crash tender, someone phoned the ambulance, and a horde of rescuers and vehicles churned out to Goucher's Tiger.

Goucher was hero for the day with those of us who had been witnesses to this genuine feat of airmanship; and after getting a full account of the exploit from the horse's mouth, we relayed the tale, suitably embellished to heighten the drama, to the half of the course who had been at ground school when it happened.

Those of us who had passed our 20-hour checks — a dozen of our course had left for Trenton by the last week in May — were now initiated to more demanding sequences, for the balance of the course included a minimum ten hours instrument flying (bolstered by 26 half-hour instrument sessions in the Link Trainer), about five to ten hours on forced landing and precautionary landing practice, five hours night flying (all dual), and some 20 or more hours of aerobatics. Our final test at Elementary was the 60-hour check, administered shortly after one had amassed that total; after which, if you passed, you were permitted to log up to 15 additional hours, depending upon how quickly your course's posting notice came through.

Pearson had actually given me my first taste of instrument flying a few days before my 20-hour check. I found it arduous work indeed once I pulled the hood over and my world shrank to the black-topped stick, the throttle, the rudder pedals, and the instrument panel in front of me. The Tiger was not equipped with an artificial horizon, so you determined whether you were climbing or diving by reference to the air speed indicator and the rate-of-climb indicator, both of which lagged somewhat before responding. The combination of human and mechanical imperfections resulted at first in the aircraft's tracing inexorably a ghastly roller-coaster path through the sky, weaving and skidding from side to side at the same time. The turning action of the aircraft —its "movement in the yawing plane" in officialese — was recorded by the turn and bank indicator, which by astute interpretation, could also be persuaded to reveal, indirectly, whether your wings were level or not.

For three-quarters of an hour I kept my eyes roving quickly from one instrument to another, and with foot, hand, and body English fought to stem the flood of evil tidings borne in upon me by the merciless gauges. Like most novices I over-corrected, and compounded my problems by concentrating all my attention on rectifying one undesirable aspect of our aerial posture, while two others went to hell on roller bearings. Like globules in the Chinese water torture Pearson's voice dripped through the ear tubes:

"Needle . . . ball . . . watch your airspeed . . . well, *do* something about it . . . needle . . . NEEDLE NEEDLE NEEDLE . . . now look at the ball . . . needle . . . ball . . . airspeed . . . needle . . . ball . . . airspeed . . ."

When I slowed the frequency of the pointed exhortations and got them back to a reasonably polite timbre so far as my straight and level efforts were concerned, Pearson added a few sadistic complications:

"Now try a rate one turn to the left through 90 degrees. Remember, in a rate one turn you'll be turning three degrees per second, so count 30 seconds to yourself, then level up. Here . . . I have control . . . I'll line her up due north and see how close you can come to due west. There . . . you have control."

"I have control" I echoed unenthusiastically, and initiated movements of the stick and rudder designed to produce a rate one turn to port. We lurched about erratically, and the "needle, ball, airspeed, oh hell" monologue flowed in again, *tempo prima*. After a dozen sorry substitutes for rate one turns, Pearson's compassion overcame his sense of duty.

"Right . . . that's enough for one day. I have control. Come on out and take a rest."

"You have control" I said, pulling back the hood and surfacing wearily for a breather. The time, I noted, was 7:35 AM.

It transpired that Pearson had not been simply wandering aimlessly through the skies in ordaining the various turns and straight legs I'd been struggling to execute, but had contrived to navigate us to the precincts of a farm. I could see the farmhouse like a tiny doll's house sitting just off the right wing tip, 3000 feet below us, smoke curling from the chimney. The whole scene was like a Currier & Ives print. As I was making careful mental note of the wind direction as revealed by the smoke — for it was drummed into us constantly to check the wind direction at every opportunity in case we should be faced with a forced landing — Pearson cut the throttle, and without so much as a by-your-leave dived straight for the back yard.

It was an exciting experience, for we plummeted at a rate which made the struts and flying wires whistle then shriek in a rising crescendo. As Pearson maintained the dive like a vengeful Stuka pilot, and the house swelled rapidly from dog kennel size to the full size real McCoy, I tried to gauge how much we would miss it by — if he levelled out, and if we missed it at all — and wondered for the first time if maybe the ratchet had slipped the whole way on Pearson.

I was practically shoving my boots through the floor of the Tiger, willing him to pull up, when he did so, and we swept across the back yard and flashed on toward the house at an altitude of about three feet.

We roared past the kitchen window at 120 miles per hour, but I got a clear look inside, and in a split second of time that somehow seemed protracted, I saw a housewife in an apron pouring coffee for a person seated at the near end of the table. I felt that I was close enough to reach out my hand and fill a cup from the streaming spout.

We rose steeply in a climbing turn and swung back, as I correctly presumed, for another pass. Now that I was satisfied that Pearson's flabbergasting performance was not attributable to suicidal tendencies I was thoroughly enjoying this exhilarating turn of events, for there can be few sensations as thrilling as precipitous dives and close quarters low flying in a light and delicately responsive aircraft like a Tiger. The risk attached to the performance simply gave an extra fillip to the experience, as did the knowledge that it was a gross violation of all flying rules, even for instructors. As we moved quickly into striking position again, I saw three people come hurrying out of the house, shading their eyes momentarily as they followed the Tiger past the sun, then waving in vigorous approval of the noisy assault. This time Pearson dove and levelled out well away from the house and we had a clear run at the little group, straight and level and about ten feet up, for about 200 yards.

Again we flashed across the backyard, sowing consternation and confusion in the chicken pen where birds fluttered about madly, colliding with one another in mid-air and flapping about in all directions at once. Two horses in the adjacent pasture galloped for the far side, and I could see that the dog was barking at the excitement, adding his little contribution to the general uproar. However, it wasn't the dog I wanted to check.

As we flew past the back steps I tried out my 20-20 vision on the girl in the middle of the threesome, the girl who had obviously motivated this pleasant but unorthodox visit. At 100 miles per hour I had to slide the mental calipers over her fairly nimbly, but even that brief inspection was ample to convince me that this boy Pearson was no mean judge of horseflesh.

We made one more spectacularly low pass, then climbed away, waggling our wings rhythmically to signal "finis." The moment he could do so with a modicum of safety, Pearson looked into the mirror and gave me a huge grin and a conspiratorial wink. I returned the smile and added a thumb and finger circle sign of ardent approval — this instrument flying was going to be less irksome than I'd feared with breaks like these. But on the flight back I recalled those first seconds of Pearson's manifestation of aerial schizophrenia and I guessed that I knew how those London girls must have felt when that nice 'andsome gent wot walked 'em 'ome turned out to be Jack the Ripper.

Two days after my 20 hour check Pearson introduced me to aerobatics, after warning me while we were starting up to be sure to pull my shoulder straps as tight as possible. It was an early evening flight and the air was beautifully smooth, but I awaited the experience with apprehension, knowing that a sizeable number of washouts flowed from an inability to withstand the bodily sensations produced by aerobatics without getting airsick.

We climbed to 4000 feet and Pearson demonstrated a loop, nosing down first to build our speed up, then coming back firmly on the stick and shoving the throttle wide open as he pulled up steeply to start into the loop. As the engine cowling rose high above the horizon and we climbed up past the vertical Pearson called:

"Put your head 'way back and watch for the ground to come back into view over your head . . . there you are, there it comes. Now we cut back on the throttle as we start descending on the other side . . ."

The earth appeared from the wrong side of my goggles; we swooped down gracefully, rounding out the loop, and hit our own slipstream with a churning thump — the sign that Pearson had kept the Tiger in a perfectly straight line all the way around. Now Pearson indicated that it was my turn, and as I tried to duplicate his actions he talked me round a second loop. I made it too tight, so much so that the G forces dragged my mouth open, but apart from that we got around all right, and Pearson once more took control to demonstrate a slow roll.

Again he dived to build up our speed, then, at 115 mph he raised the nose smoothly just above the horizon and applied full left aileron. Over we rolled until we were upside down, but this time there was no centrifugal force to hold us in our seats, we hung suspended in our harness like a couple of sacks of meal. Despite the fact that I had tightened my straps, I dangled down so far that I had difficulty keeping a grip on the stick, and my feet came off the floor like the dust which floated into my face. The roll continued smoothly and we came out the other side, Pearson explaining as we went round how the actions of the rudder and elevators were exchanged, then reversed, in the revolution.

Once more it was my turn to entertain. I had had so much trouble just trying to keep my hands and feet somewhere near the controls during Pearson's roll that I entered upon the performance with the zest of a condemned man crawling under the guillotine. I stiffened my legs to keep them from curling up under my chin like spaghetti again, took Lady Macbeth's advice re screwing one's courage to the sticking place, and stuck. Everything went reasonably well until we got upside down, at which point, between stifling the urge to scream and reminding myself that I now had to move the stick forward instead of backward to keep the nose up, I forgot to cut the throttle and experienced considerable difficulty maintaining enough leverage on the stick to keep the rate of roll constant. While we hung upside down again — me with all the cool poise of a man who has just tripped and fallen out a tenth storey window — the engine conked out because of its gravity feed, and Pearson gave me nine different suggestions for making my roll loosely resemble the manoeuvre he'd demonstrated. Ever mindful of those questioning eyes in the mirror — I noticed they bulged a little in my somewhat protracted upside down stance — I re-adjusted my now florid face, bared four top teeth in what I hoped was a convincing simulation of gaiety, and struggled to get us right-side up again. We surged and slipped back into an upright position, some 40 degrees off our original heading, and Pearson very charitably turned the conversation momentarily to the obvious need for more moisture on the back 40 of the farm we'd just tumbled over. I tried it again with a little more success and Pearson moved, gratefully I think, to a demonstration of a roll off the top. This manoeuvre started out as a loop, but when we were upside down at the top of it he cranked on full aileron and we half-rolled from the inverted position to resume level flight in the opposite direction. It needed a little more speed than the loop but was not as difficult as the roll to execute. My stab at it was acceptable enough as a first effort, and Pearson moved on to show me stall turns.

The stall turn was a lovely, graceful reversal of course movement, but it did shocking things to one's innards until you got used to it. The opening movement was simple: we built our speed up again so as to get a good high climb, then pulled back on the stick and soared into a vertical climb. In six or eight seconds the Tiger's speed fell off to the stalling mark and she began to shudder and prepare for a tail slide; at this point Pearson kicked on left rudder and she cartwheeled gracefully into a vertical dive, which imported a sensation like someone cutting an elevator's cable in a tall building. As we plunged down, leaving my stomach at the top of the stall 500 feet behind us, Pearson eased the stick back and we rounded out in a smooth arc back into straight and level flight. We did several of these, first on one side then the other. Each time, as we fell away from the stalling point I had the sensation that someone was pushing me off the high diving board, 500 feet up. Gradually I got a little more used to it; but I was glad when Pearson decided to call it a day and head out of the aerobatics area. I was beginning to feel clammy, and calculated that about two more stall turns and I would be trading my red inverted-flying face for a rich cucumber green visage. Over-all though, I felt a good deal more optimistic, having weathered an hour of new and vivid sensations coupled with new manoeuvres and unusual positions.

In actual fact it was this new confidence given to student pilots by aerobatics that was the chief value of the practice, and I gave the Air Force full marks for its flying curriculum on that score. In the solo practice sessions which immediately ensued we slow-rolled, looped, spun, stall-turned and whirled through rolls off the top until we were as much at home with the earth somewhere above the upper wing as we were with it in its rightful position. My confidence grew by leaps and bounds and on solo sessions at least I swaggered out to my Tigerschmitt in my silk scarf and Tone-Rays and went through my pre-flight check with a blasé air of knowledgeability and nonchalance appropriate to the man who had designed and built the aircraft.

We began doing a lot more flying now, about two-thirds of it solo. I racked up the course record for one day by getting in eight hours and five minutes. Plate and I frequently managed to get solo sessions at the same time. We would enliven these by arranging to meet over some town in the aerobatics area — usually Nanton — where we would proceed to take turns topping the other's performance. He liked to start the ball rolling by doing three or four loops in a row then flying alongside, taking his hands off the controls, and shaking them modestly over his head like the heavyweight champion of the world responding to the "And in this corner . . ." introduction. I would hold my nose in disgust, dive into a slow roll and follow it with a stall turn, after which he would waggle his wings to claim the spotlight again and launch into a new series of evolutions. After one of these sessions we would carefully separate before landing, approaching the field innocently from different directions, then sit and tell each other what red hot aerobatic specialists we were until we got the call for another flight.

But who knows what evil lurks in the hearts of men? Flight Sergeant Fines knew — Plate came in one afternoon, from a parade which I had resourcefully contrived to avoid, and announced with a lurid selection of profanity that our Discip. had given him three nights on Work Parade. With insufficient concentration and appreciation, I pointed out that there were a whole galaxy of punishments more onerous than Work Parade, which was essentially only two or three hours on light fatigues each night, and a long chalk from, say, three nights of pack drill, which Fines could have imposed if he'd been feeling his oats.

Plate responded to my Old Philosopher approach by asking me testily whose side I was on in this matter, and I hastened to ask him what he had done to merit the cruel retribution of Work Parade. He stated unequivocally that he had done nothing; but there was a certain fire lacking in his attestation which prompted me to probe the circumstances.

He explained that he had been standing erect and immaculate on parade, as was his wont, looking every inch the intrepid birdman of the RCAF recruiting posters, and listening intently and with appropriate military courtesy to one of Flight Sergeant Fines' familiar diatribes on observed departures from accepted Air Force protocol. At a highly unpropitious moment, when F/S Fines was referring to some of the drastic disciplinary measures he would reluctantly be forced to adopt to prevent the RCAF lapsing into total anarchy, an unidentified flying object of some type — a mosquito, or fly, or small bird of some description — had flown up one of Plate's nasal passages, causing him to snort explosively in an effort to repel boarders.

Flight Sergeant Fines had taken offence at the untimely interruption, and in an unaccountable display of cynicism had refused to accept Plate's explanation of the incident, cogent and compelling as it was. While I mentally conceded that Fines' scepticism had been 100 percent justified, I commiserated aloud, and compared Fines unfavourably with that air-crew paladin Flight Sergeant Glaves, who would undoubtedly have played down the incident and simply dismissed it by roaring: "There'll be no bastard snorting!"

The Work Parade sessions were not too onerous — in fact on two of the three nights all Plate had to do was wash a couple of the instructors' cars; but it had unfortunate consequences — (unfortunate in the sense that they ultimately involved me) — in that Flight Sergeant Fines made a mental note of LAC Plate, and filed away for future reference the fact that Plate was one of the ten or so Americans on the station. (All the Americans wore a "USA" lettering under their RCAF eagle shoulder patches.) This was a significant fact since there were approximately 250 air crew on the station at any given time, and 100 of these changed each month; so that the Discip. never really got to know more than a handful of people by name. Plate he knew by name.

A week after the degradation of Work Parade, Plate decided one evening, after a particularly revolting culinary failure in our mess, that we should trek into High River for a little exercise on the bowling alleys. I agreed that the objective was laudable but reminded him that our Flight was Duty Flight, and hence forbidden to leave the aerodrome. (I don't really know what function the Duty Flight was supposed to perform, but there was undoubtedly a logical Air Force reason behind it, e.g. if the Germans invaded North America and took the train to High River, the Duty Flight could go into town and buy rifles at the hardware store with which to defend the aerodrome. Something sound and sensible like that was behind it I'm sure.) I reminded him also that the SP's in the guard room knew which Flight was Duty Flight and that as soon as we picked up our bunk tags — you had to claim your bunk tag off the wall in the guard-house every time you left the station — they would arrest us.

Plate overcame these forensic difficulties by pointing out that there was a new crop of juniors on the station who would be too busy to think about going into town, and that we could easily borrow their bunk tags with no one being the wiser. I agreed that the risk was negligible and we wandered to an adjacent hut which was full of juniors and asked if we could borrow a couple of bunk tags. The juniors were properly accommodating, and we got the names of two of them and headed for the guard-house to sign out under their names.

With our mental equipment, deceiving the SP's was laughably easy, and we were soon on our way into town. At the alley we alternated our exercise between hurling the balls and patting ourselves on the back. Our self-satisfaction was further enhanced by the arrival of two girls who set up shop on the alley immediately to the left of ours. One of the girls could have climbed into mechanic's coveralls and gone the rest of her life unchallenged; but the other had been cunningly assembled and was obviously as approachable as a Venus flytrap.

Plate and I immediately began putting our powerful mental equipment to work to devise ways of attracting the girl's attention. In an unfortunate burst of inspiration Plate began bowling backwards, bending over with his head between his ankles and delivering the ball like a football centre on a place kick. This remarkable display of dexterity drew the attention, not only of the two girls, but of everyone in the building, including that of Flight Sergeant Fines who had oozed in unobserved. Our mental equipment had somehow overlooked the possibility of this contingency.

With Plate hanging upside down, Fines was not certain of his identification, so he moved closer. It was when Fines was about ten feet away, just on the far side of the sex symbol motivating us, that I first saw him. I immediately pulled out my handerchief and blew my nose 20 or 30 times, keeping nine-tenths of my face masked in the process. Simultaneously I began hissing warnings at Plate, who had warmed to his work and was performing feats of inverted bowling which I had never witnessed before, but it was in vain. Flight Sergeant Fines made sure of his man and then left to drive back to the station, obviously to do two things:

1. Verify that Plate's bunk tag was still hanging on the wall, and that Plate had committed two offences in leaving the station; and

2. Alert the SP's to check everyone wearing US shoulder patches coming in and make him produce his ID card, and to arrest LAC Plate and ascertain his alias when he came back.

As Fines left, I put my handkerchief away and advised Plate that unless we could beat the Discip. back to the station, we were in trouble. We abandoned our courting forthwith, and caught a bus ten minutes later for the station, hoping that Fines might not have homed directly to his objective.

Since it was doubtful that Fines had identified me, we assumed that if he had beaten us to the station he would tell the SPs to check the ID card of the person accompanying Plate. Plate spiked this plan by ignoring me and attaching himself to another cadet as we climbed off the bus and headed for the guard-house.

They checked Plate's companion closely, asking for his ID card; so it was obvious that the good Discip. had beaten us back. The best Plate could do was lie some more and say that the cadet whose name he had given had known nothing about the escapade and that he hadn't gone into town with anyone else but had gone alone.

I witnessed his interrogation from the far side of the guard-house, keeping eight or ten other cadets between us, hoping that the SP's would not be so insulting as to check all the rest of our bunk tags against our ID cards. In the bus I had re-read the name on the bunk tag I was carrying, to see who I was, and I affected a degree of nonchalance I was far from feeling as I signed in again as LAC Budd, and handed in his bunk tag. There were no questions asked, but I tactfully walked over to Budd's hut in case any SP's were watching.

This time Plate got four nights on Work Parade and, of course, Flight Sergeant Fines got to know him much better. Before we got to know Fines better we were exposed to a completely new experience: night flying.

No one who has not sat at the controls on a pitch black night can appreciate the enormous difference between day flying and night flying. The landing strip was marked by six small goose-neck kerosene flare pots set a hundred yards apart. As it happened, the first night flying Pearson gave me was on a very dark night. There was no discernible moon or starlight, and no visible horizon. When you took off, therefore, you went onto instruments immediately, and you were very careful to fly precisely and to watch the airspeed like a hawk until you got a few hundred feet of altitude under your belt. You were always cognizant of the fact that an engine failure at night meant, under most circumstances, a forced landing under forebodingly difficult conditions, or, if you were high enough, a blind parachute jump.

Although we were not sent solo at night at Elementary, we had five hours dual night flying during which we were expected to do the actual flying, with the instructor aboard to get us out of trouble if we blundered.

Single engine night flying, true night flying where you are dependent upon your instruments and your Maker, is a humbling experience. You realize so frequently how vulnerable you are if the slightest thing should go wrong. Another month was to go by before I fully realized the gulf that separated day flying and night flying; meanwhile I knew that it introduced a highly significant new factor into the general equation. Judging your position on the approach and during the landing flare-out solely by reference to those six flare pots was a whole new science. Since our necks could be at stake if we made a hash of it, we were diligent pupils. There wasn't much joking about single engine night flying.

The weather during this part of June had been most favourable for flying, and our course was accumulating flying time so well that the Senior Administrative Officer decided on Wednesday that we should be given a 48-hour pass the following weekend. At this point we had flown every Saturday and Sunday since we'd started, so the prospect of a weekend in Calgary or Edmonton stirred great expectations. We were to be released as soon as ground school was over on Friday afternoon.

Plate and I immediately began laying plans. We decided that if we could catch the bus for Edmonton on Friday night, we would go that far. It meant that I could have all day Saturday with Joyce, who had been writing to me faithfully, and Plate, who had played the field at ITS, was satisfied that with his contacts he'd have to let the Edmonton girls draw lots to see who would win his company. As it turned out, there was a bus we could catch, so we waited impatiently for Friday.

The great day finally arrived. Plate and I both got airborne before 5:00 AM and put in over three hours of aerobatics. Ground school seemed to drag that afternoon, although the last lecture had been cancelled so that those of us who chose to could catch the bus to Edmonton. As soon as it was over, Plate and I sprinted for the barracks, washed up with lightning speed, and set off in high fettle for the gate, assuring each other that God was indeed in His heaven and all was right with the world.

Our anticipation of our hard-earned pleasures to come was so keen, and we were so thoroughly wrapped up in discussing and extending our ambitious plans, that the raucous voice screaming from the orderly room behind us was repeating the shrill challenge before the fact was borne in on me that the shout:

"THOSE . . . TWO . . . MEN!"

was directed at us two men.

We froze, then turned in worried bewilderment to see the upper half of Flight Sergeant Fines projecting horizontally through a window which I then recalled having heard banged open. Fines imperiously made a scything gesture with his arm, then sprang back and slammed the window like a cuckoo popping back into its clock. He reappeared in a few seconds at the back entrance to the building.

"Ah, so it *is* you, Plate," he said, looking at the world's greatest inverted bowler as though he had just crawled before him out of a manhole, "I might have known. And where do you two think you're going?"

"We're going to Edmonton, Flight," I explained hopefully, holding my chest out so strenuously that my shoulder blades were in firm contact, "we've got passes."

"Not any more you haven't" Fines snapped. He seemed to have been dining on Ugly pills all afternoon. "You two men were talking in an Attention Area, and neither of you saluted the ensign. You're both confined to barracks for 48 hours. Maybe that will remind you of the fact that airmen march at attention in an Attention Area. They do not talk in an Attention Area."

"Quite right," I thought, "in fact one might go so far as to say that in an Attention Area there'll be no bastard talking."

"Furthermore," Fines went on, "when you pass the RCAF ensign you will do an eyes right or eyes left, as the case may be, and salute, at all times. Now, march down to the gate and back and let me see both of you conduct yourselves properly in the Attention Area."

We about-turned, and marched like wooden soldiers to the gate and back, snapping up salutes like propellers kicking over each time we came abreast of the flagpole. I had seen through the bluff, of course, and realized that Fines was just teaching us a lesson. I knew that when he saw our Coldstream Guards bearing, and the high-compression speed of our salutes, he would relent and reinstate our passes.

He taught us an even better lesson, as a matter of fact. When we marched up and halted before him again, he told us to march back to our barracks in the same fine style, and to march out just as briskly to attend Work Parade for the next two nights.

Looking back, and thinking of our shattered 48, I realize that Burns was prophetically correct in describing thus the transitory nature of our earthly joys:

"But pleasures are like poppies spread—
You seize the flow'r, its bloom is shed;
Or like the snow falls in the river—
A moment white, then melts for ever . . ."

I was too stunned to think of any retaliatory thoughts. I had to concede, too, that Fines had caught us dead to rights. But as we marched ever so smartly out of earshot, Plate indulged aloud in a medically improbable fantasy which envisaged his kicking Fines so forcibly in the jockey shorts that he could thenceforth pass for Quasimodo, the Hunchback of Notre Dame, and sing soprano in the church choir.

I attempted to soothe his ire by reminding him that the Discip.

was an honourable man, so were they all, all honourable men; and that, to give Fines his due, we had undeniably prejudiced the Allied war effort by our slovenly failure to display proper military courtesy in an area sacred to every right-thinking citizen, namely a High River Attention Area. Plate switched gears from anger to humour, then apologized for the unkind thoughts he'd had about our Discip. and pleaded with me not to write and let his mother know how he had tarnished the RCAF's tradition and honour in that afternoon's brief encounter. We progressed into a giggling fit, recalling how it must have looked to the numerous leave-bound onlookers when Fines threw up the window, shot into view like a gopher poking its head out of a hole, and began screaming at those two men. When we went to the mess hall for supper, I stopped Plate at the door and whispered warningly in his ear "If you see Quasimodo inside . . .," and got him giggling again.

We were only halfway through supper when F/S Fines entered the mess wearing the "OO" band identifying him as the Orderly Officer. (There were so few Air Force officers on the station that two or three of the senior NCO's took a turn at OO to spread the burden.)

As Fines intoned his rhetorical question: "Any complaints?" Plate rolled his eyes upward and murmured dreamily: "How do I love thee . . . let me count the ways . . ."

Between our sessions on Work Parade, Plate and I spent our lost weekend in an atmosphere of quietness, austerity, and meditation that would have made my Presbyterian ancestors glow with pride, if glowing with pride had not been sinful. When the madding crowd returned to our cool sequestered vale on Sunday evening with their envy-stirring tales of debauchery and licentiousness in Calgary and Edmonton, we suffered silently. My Christian charity wore paper thin as more and more fascinating stories filtered in, and I found myself hoping that when the roll was called up yonder, He would remember what a mean son of a bitch a certain spurious Orderly Officer had been.

When we resumed flying on Monday, we knew we were getting into the last lap and moving towards the final all-important test at Elementary, our 60-hour checks. A week or two before I had mine, I was subjected to an unplanned and very demanding test.

On June 18th I went up solo, mid-way through the morning, to practise more aerobatics. It took some time to climb the Tiger to 4,000 feet (we were under orders to recover from all aerobatic manoeuvres by 3,000 feet) since the elevation of the aerodrome itself was 3,400 feet, and in that relatively thin air our rate of climb was not too impressive. We tinkered around with our mixture control continually, leaning it out to get the best performance; but at best climbing was slow. I meandered 15 miles or so from the drome and began doing my slow rolls, climbing after each one to regain the bit of height I'd lost.

By the time I had put in my hour's cavorting, I was some 20 miles from the station, towards which I now turned.

When I looked in the general area of our field — the first time I'd taken a good look back that way since I left — I got a shock. The area was heavy with ominous black cloud. A local storm of considerable intensity had obviously moved in rapidly and unexpectedly, for we had heard no word of storms when we left.

The boundary of the storm area was quite clearly defined by the cloud and by the extremely rough air associated with it. I started into it twice, and broke off each time to fly back beyond it and skirt the edge to see whether I could find a less rambunctious approach route. We were all used to rough air flying — in fact High River was probably the best Elementary in Canada for getting that sort of experience — but what I was encountering was so vicious as to be dangerous. Even I recognized that.

I tried a third tack. It seemed marginally better at first, but soon the Tiger was bucking like a bronco and my mouth got as dry as popcorn. Updrafts would slam the little aircraft hard enough to snap my head unpleasantly. We would surge up giddily, then drop just as suddenly, rolling and twisting in boiling turbulence. To put the case in its best terms, I vibrated with apprehension. No longer did I feel like Billy Bishop — Chicken Licken would have been closer to it.

As I penetrated the storm further, the buffeting grew less but it began to rain heavily. Quickly the rain grew in intensity, to a point where the windscreen was streaming and visibility ahead, past the edge of the windscreen, was almost nil. I could still see the ground below my wing quite clearly, however, and it was by this means that I bucked my way homeward, hoping that there weren't many other blindfolded Tiger pilots cruising around in this storm.

Eventually I came to a town. In a minute or two I spotted the railway tracks, then flew along them and counted the grain elevators. There were five, indicating that I was back over High River. I set course for the field, and arrived over it in a few minutes. The rain slacked off to the point where I could see ahead, after a fashion, and I flew over the field twice to take a good look at it.

In most places it was like a lake; but on the high side, closest to the hangar, it looked merely puddly. On the low side, there was a barbed wire fence designed to keep animals from the adjoining farm from wandering into our path. A Tiger Moth with a torn wing was tilted up against that fence. Three or four people around the plane seemed to be working it clear of the fence and the liquid mud.

On my second pass, although my attention was primarily focused on the patch of mud and grass I was going to try to land on, I could see most of the cadets and instructors collecting expectantly at the edge of the hangar door to see how I would fare in my attempt to come safely back to earth. My own interest in the outcome required no whetting, particularly after noting that one Tiger had already come to grief. For the second time I carefully marked the best looking patch on the field, and hoped I could still see it when I finished my downwind leg.

With that object in mind, I cut the downwind leg quite short and sideslipped steeply, left and right, to kill off the excess height as I headed into wind, squinting into the rain as I lined up on my chosen landing site. Everything clicked as if for a good Hollywood finish, and with half the school lined up along the hangar watching me as I executed this spectacular fishtailing to within 20 feet of the ground, I prayed I would not publicly blot my copybook by hurling the aircraft ignominiously onto its back in the mire. I saw that I was going to touch down 50 yards too soon and cracked on an inch of throttle for a couple of seconds. She floated into place beautifully and as she settled I locked the stick right back in my belly so the tail would stay down when she dropped in.

My luck held. The Tiger kissed the sodden turf like a feather, briefly spraying high a sheet of water from each wheel, and rolled smoothly but heavily to a short stop. It was a real daisy-cutter of a landing, probably the best one I ever made in a Tiger.

In seconds a surplus of willing hands caught the grips on the wing tips to help guide me back to the line and make sure she didn't nose over in the heavy going on the way, and Plate braved the watery propwash to clap me on the back and shout encouraging insults over the blasts of the engine. I bumped and splashed forward happily, and then was doubly pleased to note that Pearson was in the forefront of the group waiting near the line.

When I cut the switches and hauled myself out Pearson was quick to congratulate me on a good performance. I sensed that he had been eating his fingernails watching me approach through the rain, and I was pleased that I'd done the job in a way that reflected credit on him. He told me, after he had inflated my ego, that a more experienced pilot would have stayed off the field and landed in a stubble field to wait out the storm. In fact, he said, two experienced instructors had done exactly that. Nevertheless he recognized that the proof of the pudding was in the eating, and commended me on the airmanship displayed in the precautionary survey and the slideslipping approach to the best spot on the field. I couldn't even feel the parachute on my back as I walked to the locker room, ten feet tall. Billy Bishop was back at the controls.

My 60-hour check on June 30th, again with Stone, was almost an anti-climax. Stone put me through my paces for an hour and 20

56

minutes, and if there was anything on the syllabus that he missed, I wasn't aware of it. He gave me to understand when we landed that I had passed my flying test okay and didn't have to sweat over it. I always remembered his thoughtfulness.

I stood sixth in our class of 120, and again registered my preference for fighters. On July 3rd we were told that there were postings open to No. 7 SFTS at Macleod or to No. 10 SFTS at Dauphin. We knew that the Cessna Cranes flown at No. 10 were not quite as stable and solid an aircraft as the Ansons at Macleod, and that electing for Dauphin might make our next course a little tougher on that account. Too, if we went back to Macleod, I could enjoy myself playing in the band in any spare time we had. But there was one factor that overrode all others. At SFTS the custom was to grant aircrew a 48-hour pass every fortnight or so. From Macleod all we could do on a 48 was travel to Lethbridge or possibly Calgary. From Dauphin I could get home on a 48, since it was under 200 miles to Winnipeg.

Plate knew my preference and never hesitated. He suggested we both choose Dauphin, and on July 5th we boarded the train for No. 10 to start Service Flying.

Oh, by the way, on July 3rd, Plate and I visited the Duke of Windsor's ranch and combed over the old "E P" extensively and at low level.

CHAPTER 4

SERVICE FLYING TRAINING SCHOOL

So Lycidas sunk low, but mounted high,
Through the dear might of Him that walked the waves . . .

John Milton: Lycidas

We wasted no time in getting acquainted with our new aircraft, the Cessna Crane. We arrived in Dauphin on July 6th and began flying on July 8th. After four hours and 25 minutes of dual instruction with the new instructor Plate and I had drawn, Pilot Officer Orr, I went solo.

The switch from Tiger Moths to Cessna Cranes was a big bite for us to digest at first. There were many differences to get used to. For a start, the Crane was a twin, powered by two Jacobs L4MB engines, and hence a much heavier and more powerful aircraft, with higher cruising and approach speeds and a greater range. Fitted with flaps and retractable undercarriage, and with most models sporting constant speed props, it was a more sophisticated aircraft all round, and the instrument panel reflected the change. Oil pressure gauges now came in pairs, so did oil temperature gauges, tachometers and cylinder head temperature gauges. In addition the instrument panel featured a directional gyro and an artificial horizon to go along with the other instruments we'd grown accustomed to in the Tigers.

Our take-off and other checks were now substantially longer and initially taxing, and we learned to chant magic alphabetical incantations on the crosswind leg to remind ourselves to check Trim, Mixture, Pitch, Fuel, Flaps, Gear and Gyros. The observer in the little control hut at the end of the runway was under orders to watch for any forgetful neophytes who might turn onto the final leg with their undercarriage

William Avery Bishop, VC.

The author, just before joining the RCAF.

Below: Tiger Moth 8965 is refuelled while its pilot waits. Note the voice tube just in front of the pilot's face.

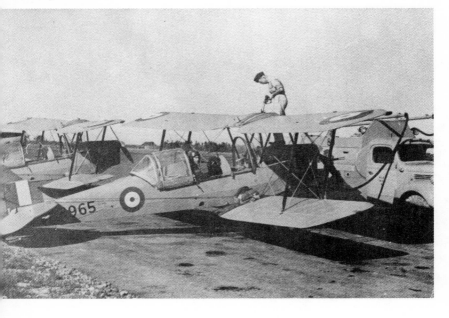

Above: The flood at High River, May 11th, 1942.

(RCAF

Below: Fledgling flight cadets at the relief field, High River, Alberta: the author in the dark flying suit. Tiger Moths at right are behind the white framed signals square.

Bud Clarke (standing) and Irvine Bradley get their wings at No. 7 SFTS, Macleod, September 1942.   (RCAF)

LAC Goucher (left), the author and friend.

Harvard II 2660. This particular aircraft survived with the RCAF from November 1940 until it was struck off strength in August 1955.

still up. If an aircraft did approach and come under 500 feet without sprouting wheels, he fired a red Very cartridge to warn the pilot, and subsequently reported the aircraft letters to the Chief Flying Instructor. The CFI in turn would invite the mortified culprit to drop in for a chat, bringing with him some documentary evidence of remorse and determination to improve, in the form of 1000 written assertions that "I must not approach to land with undercarriage retracted." Two or three unfortunates made this mistake — once. The penalty for a second lapse was a train ride to Trenton and a brand new career, and that prospect apparently kept everyone acutely conscious of the position of his undercart.

At SFTS the emphasis in the daylight flying program lay on cross-country navigational flights, instrument flying, and reconnaissance missions on which we were expected to make sketch maps of designated towns, outlining their road networks and the location of features such as bridges, railway yards, refineries and water towers which would have particular military significance. Our course also prescribed formation flying, various radio exercises in flight, and simulated bombing runs over a camera obscura. Night flying, we learned, was to be given much more prominence than at EFTS, and after we had gone solo and done a few sessions of circuits and bumps, we would be going on two or three night cross-country flights. The whole flying curriculum had a markedly more advanced and professional stamp to it, at least in our inexperienced eyes; and it was obvious that a good deal more responsibility and maturity would be expected of us in the air, where we would log approximately 150 hours — double the Elementary quota.

Plate and I, along with Charlie Payne, Claude Roy, and Freddie Taylor, found ourselves in "E" Flight. Our Flight Commander was Flight Lieutenant Jimmy Baird, a short, bustling individual who was all business. Prior to flying Cessna Cranes he had been on Harvards, single engined advanced trainers used on our station at Dauphin until a few months before our arrival. Baird was a hard but fair taskmaster who constantly strove to drum the basics of good airmanship into us. To illustrate his points he had a fund of authentic tales about former pupils. Perhaps because the opening scenes of the first tale had a familiar ring, it registered with indelible clarity. Let me relay it to you, only changing the name of the principal to LAC Strutter to protect the guilty.

Detailed to do solo exercises in Harvard 3022, Strutter made his way discreetly out of the area and headed for the farm where his current inamorata lived. Bear in mind that with its Pratt & Whitney Wasp engine and constant speed propeller, a Harvard in flight emitted a most distinctive and penetrating drone, highly satisfactory for signalling one's lady love. So loud was the engine that, to announce one's arrival to everyone in an area of ten square miles, all one had to do was ease back on the throttle momentarily then rev up again. The snarling, swelling roar that emanated while the prop was caught in the fully fine position would rattle window panes and china for miles around.

Strutter swirled ostentatiously onto the scene at a thousand feet, revving his engine dementedly, and shortly drew his audience into their back yard to watch admiringly while he passed in review. He executed two or three runs at roof top level in fine style, leaving the watchers breathless with delight and excitement, then climbed briefly so that he could build up a good head of steam for the *pièce de resistance* and grand finale.

Whistling in with 150 m.p.h. showing on the clock and absolute zero on the altimeter — this crude instrument was simply not up to Strutter's exacting flying standards, for later measurement proved conclusively that he was fully five feet ten inches clear of the ground — Strutter made a minor miscalculation, and with his right wingtip and an ear splitting crash tore the top off the family outhouse. Not to be outdone, the outhouse tore three feet off Strutter's wingtip, and the asymmetrical Harvard staggered leadenly away like a badly hit bird.

Never, I ween, was flyer in such an evil case. With his aircraft all but unmanageable after this shattering encounter, Strutter's first thought was somehow to escape the clutches of the toilet and to pull off one more good stunt — with his parachute.

By great good fortune the outhouse was not manned when Strutter de-roofed it, and the possible consequences, had a catalogue checker actually been in the blocks, might have given the local ranks of the medical profession pause. Such a victim, taking into account the physical impact (sanitary headquarters was shifted seven feet in the wink of an eye), the hellish burst of noise, and the blinding flash of the noonday sun as the roof left at 150 per, might well have had to concede the futility of ever hoping to achieve adequate peace of mind crouching indoors again, notwithstanding the undoubted propulsive powers of Exlax, Feenamint or Eno.

Finding that he could climb, albeit with difficulty, Strutter did lots of that, while he anxiously checked to ensure that the main parts of the aeroplane were with him and not threatening to separate from the big piece the toilet had left him with. Everything else appeared normal, and it began to appear encouragingly probable that he would survive to face the carload of charges that the Air Force would undoubtedly bring against him as soon as he put his two feet on the ground. Either of the two most serious charges meant being washed out and Trenton, if not jail, i.e. unauthorized low flying, and causing the loss of one of His Majesty's aircraft, to wit Harvard 3022, through gross negligence. The latter thought put Strutter to wondering if he could land the aircraft, save the Air Force 50,000 dollars, and thus reduce the staggering accumulation of prejudicial evidence to be adduced against him.

He patiently climbed still further and found by repeated experiments (with an apprehensive eye on the ragged wingtip) that the Harvard now stalled around 90 m.p.h. instead of around 60. That meant landing at over 100 to preserve a margin of safety, and wheeling her on in precariously unstable condition. Nothing daunted, Strutter decided to chance it, flew her back, and set her down safely at base, intact except for the three foot calling card beside his girl friend's open and airy outhouse.

Strutter's flagrant violation of the low flying prohibition could quite justifiably have been punished in the manner he had feared; but in an uncharacteristic display of common sense and magnanimity the Air Force took into account the coolness and sound airmanship he had displayed after the outhouse affair, and, instead of washing him out, they tossed him into the guardhouse and transferred him back to a later course. Eventually, despite the outhouse and the guardhouse, he won his wings.

Such tales went with F/L Baird and the heavier flying program.

The ground school course was also much heavier at SFTS. Navigation remained our most important subject, and the one which was allotted the greatest number of hours on the course. Fortunately for us, it was taught by a Jewish instructor named Flying Officer Solon who was admirably suited to the task of maintaining attention at a high level in a subject which could have been grindingly tedious in the hands of a less interested teacher. In a dozen different ways he embossed our endless series of hypothetical aerial journeys with the imprint of his gentle humour.

He would begin a lecture by explaining the salient features of the problem, which always stemmed from our wanting to go from A to B. *Why* we wanted to go to B in the first place was completely incomprehensible to him, he indicated: the place was devoid of interesting features; even the locals recognized its general unattractiveness and were emigrating in droves; and practically the whole way there and back we should undoubtedly be stormed at with shot and shell and subjected to fighter attack and other manifestations of disfavour. Nevertheless, the problem was predicated upon our implausible desire to fly from A to B, and in such a manner that our actual time of arrival would coincide with the Time over Target stipulated in an imaginary Operations Order.

Solon would then recite the series of meteorological mishaps which we would encounter en route, windy catastrophes which would make a shambles of our initial flight plan, based as it was upon winds predicted by met officers who must have been incompetent or treacherous. Each new problem embodied a new, complicating variant, in addition to the lengthening list of obstacles we had already learned to master. When he had outlined the new complication, Solon would move to the blackboard to diagram the problem.

Carefully he would place a dot on the board, circle it, and label it "A." A yard away he would place a second dot, which he meticulously rounded and marked "B." Next he would step back and eye the termini briefly, as though calculating the bearing of the imaginary metropolis at "B" relative to our aerodrome at "A." Then with a firm stroke of his chalk hand he would launch a freehand line from "A" which invariably missed "B" by two or three inches. With the blackboard eraser he would remove this effort, usually managing to damage the outline of "A" a trifle in the process, then lash out with another stabbing thrust at "B" which again passed wide of the mark. Then, with a straight face, he would clean the board completely with the eraser, draw a firm straight line freehand, mark one end "A" and the other "B", and face us with a smile of triumph to start the detailed exposition.

These were little things, admittedly; but on a July afternoon in a hot classroom, Solon's little touches sped the time along and kept our minds receptive. Just the fact that he was interested enough to expend a little extra energy to give us a laugh at his expense made him popular with the aircrew.

Our instructor in Armament was Warrant Officer Monk, a man we were to spend a lot of time with in the fifteen weeks of our course, since he not only served as a ground school instructor, but also discharged the less clearly defined duties of grand panjandrum, general factotum, and Discip. Armament was allotted many hours in the SFTS curriculum, as it had been at Elementary, and included a course of lectures on the various pyrotechnics in use as signalling devices. The first part of the Armament course promised to be tediously repetitious, since we had memorized the manual on the Browning machine gun at EFTS, and now had to repeat the performance. To complement this, the final part of the course was wasted on a detailed study of the composition and construction of a score of different pyrotechnics — as tedious and useless a body of knowledge as could possibly have been found. In fact, because of WO Monk, Armament turned out to be very easy to stomach.

Monk affected a terse, hard-bitten manner — and in truth he was tougher than a rhinosceros roast if he caught some cadet giving him short weight — but he was basically a no-nonsense, down-to-earth type, who knew he had to cover a large amount of work and who set about doing it in the most direct way. We recognized that we had a live one at the helm in the first minute of his first lecture.

Monk reminded us that we had studied the action of the Browning at Elementary, and gave us an individualistic review of the cyclical chain of events one initiated by pressing his thumb on the firing button. The King James version, which we had committed ineradicably to memory from our manual, began thus:

"When a round is fired, recoil action takes place, and gases are momentarily trapped in the muzzle attachment; these combined forces drive the recoiling portions to the rear . . ."

Monk jabbed his pointer at the cartridge shown in the cut-away diagram of the machine gun and spoke rapidly:

"Okay, a round is fired . . . the bullet f - - ks off down the barrel, and . . ."

He paused, feigning surprise at the burst of astonished laughter: "Whatsa matter — your manual not set up that way?"

The balance of the opening summary touched on vital actions of the goddam transporter arm, not to mention the bloody sear, and the remedial consequences of one hell of a reef on the cocking lever should this sonofabitchin' gun jam in a first position stoppage. An hour of the gospel according to Monk gave us revealing insights into the treacherous character of this firearm which we had hitherto accepted as just another inanimate and reasonably reliable automatic weapon. We left with a more optimistic outlook on the Armament course.

Monk gave us a further glimpse of his methods four days after we arrived. The practice at Dauphin was to give the aircrew a pass every second weekend, first a 36-hour pass, then a 48. As Monk explained the scheme to us on Friday, July 10th, the 36 we had coming to us at noon Saturday wouldn't really be much use to us. To get any time in Winnipeg, we would have to catch the Friday night train, which left Dauphin at midnight and arrived in Winnipeg at seven o'clock Saturday morning. The reason Monk needed us on the station Saturday morning (he explained) was so that he could get the ground school building and our barracks scrubbed out from top to bottom.

But, if we were minded, and I revert to his own crystal clear phraseology: ". . . to haul ass and scrub these buildings out to my satisfaction before 2100 hours *tonight,* I wouldn't be at all surprised if you could get out the gate then, which would leave you time to scoff a few beers in Dauphin before you catch the train."

We cheered mightily, had a fast supper, and then worked at top speed for two and a half hours getting everything shipshape. Monk walked through when we were finished, called for a few touch-ups, then opined, poker faced: "Hell of a mess. But I guess it's as good as you sonsabitches can do. Push off."

We savoured our 48 in Winnipeg; after all, it was the first pass we'd had since Christmas, thanks to our brief indulgence in the pleasures of stimulating conversation in the Attention Area. Plate came home with me and met the family, and we gave my mother a graphic demonstration of how much she had been saving on groceries through my being away in the service. Later on, Plate decided he would do a little solo reconnoitering and see for himself whether the Winnipeg girls measured up to the partisan endorsement I had given them. Neither of us had more than ten or 15 dollars; but I wasn't worried about Plate running short. Winnipeg was a good city for servicemen, and I knew that with his US shoulder patches he would fare even better than average.

He did even better than I'd bargained for. After passing the time of day with three or four girls who took his fancy, and making arrangements with the best endowed one to take her to the show that evening, he walked into a Salisbury House for a bite to eat and a cup of coffee. While he was eating, the gentleman who owned this local restaurant chain happened to come in. Seeing Plate, he came over and asked him what part of the States he was from, and they struck up a conversation. When Plate rose to go, the owner told him to put his wallet away and gave him a business card with a little signed message scribbled on the back entitling Plate and any friend he had with him to eat at any Salisbury House gratis whenever he was in the city. When Plate told me the story next day, I was a little sceptical until he showed me the card. Two weeks later, on our next 48, we had occasion to try it out together. When the waitress brought our order, Plate flashed the card, both of us half-wondering if it had somehow been revoked in the interval. Not a bit of it; it was as good as a line of credit with the Bank of England. As far as I know, that goodhearted gentleman is still around. I hope he lives to be a hundred.

After we had flown for four or five weeks and had become reasonably competent twin-engined pilots, with 45 or 50 hours on Cranes, our log books were stamped with this endorsement:

> Recommended as capable and
> Reliable to fly with other Pupils.
>> Jas. H. Baird F/L
>> For O.C. No. 2 Sqdn.

Once we had this endorsement we were clear to go on selected cross-country flights with other pupils. These flights we would do twice, once as pilot of the aircraft, the second time as navigator, keeping the log, map reading, and giving the pilot the various courses to steer.

On August 12th, I did a three-hour cross-country solo, and landed to find that Plate and I, along with other members of "E" Flight, were scheduled for our first twin-engined night flying. We checked the schedule and went off to supper together discussing it. Plate was on the first shift, but because of the time of year, even the first shift couldn't get started until about ten o'clock. I was on the second shift, and was supposed to report to the flight room at midnight. There was a movie being shown in the drill hall at nine o'clock that night, a movie which I thought held some promise. I tramped off to see it just before nine, telling Plate, who was lying on his bunk reading, that I would likely see him at the flights some time after midnight.

I left the drill hall before 11 and came back to my bunk to see if I could catch 40 winks before going night flying. I dropped off briefly and woke up about a quarter to 12 when someone came into the hut. It was Mullins; I caught a glimpse of his face as he passed under the small bulb in the vestibule and headed for my bunk. I swung my feet to the floor and rubbed the sleep out of my eyes as he came up to me. It was quite dark.

"Plate's dead, Murray," he said, speaking rather softly.

"That's a pretty poor kind of a joke" I responded; but as I looked at him I suddenly knew he wasn't joking and I stammered: "What do you mean . . . what happened?"

"He crashed on his first solo; I heard he just dove into the ground."

He stood there a few moments longer, saying nothing, and then moved down to his own bunk. For the next five minutes I sat staring vacantly at the next bunk trying to absorb the news. The shock began to make me shaky. I pulled on my tunic and walked in the darkness over to the flights, almost unconscious of what I was doing. The lights in the flight room were harsh and I screwed my face up and blinked as I entered.

"Hey, Peden, Pilot Officer Orr's looking for you," someone called.

I stuck my head into the instructors' room; Orr saw me and came over.

"We're in 7824," he said, "be ready in five minutes."

As we walked out to the aircraft he told me that Plate had taken off on his first night solo, climbed to 500 feet, begun his climbing turn to the left, and then somehow slipped into a spiral dive and failed to recover. He had gone in with full climbing power on, and must have been doing 200 miles an hour when he hit the ground. The impact threw his body through the upper and forward portions of the cabin, well clear of the wreckage, which burned.

We took off and flew right over the smouldering wreckage on three circuits. Then a rain squall moved in and the balance of the night flying program was cancelled. I walked back to the hut alone and lay awake until dawn.

The second evening after the crash we had a simple service, in the presence of Plate's classmates, in a little funeral chapel in Dauphin where his body had been taken. We were not aware at that time when and where the burial would take place, but the following morning I was ordered to report to Flight Lieutenant Baird's office.

"Do you want to take Plate's body back to the States, Peden — I understand you were his friend, that right?"

"Yes sir, I was his friend" I said, trying to think of the implications of the proposal. Before I could open my mouth Baird continued:

"We will be sending an escort with the body in any case; I thought it might be more appropriate if you went as the escort rather than an SP who didn't even know him."

"I'll go," I said. The last experience in the world that I wanted was to meet Plate's mother under these circumstances; but it was clearly my job. She would have dozens of questions, not just about the accident, but about everything her son had been doing and feeling for months. I was in a better position than anyone else to give her some answers, and since I knew Plate had mentioned me often in his letters home, I wouldn't be a complete stranger to her. The decision made, I asked Baird what this would do to me on the course.

"You'll be able to catch up," he said, "I've checked with your instructors. But you'll have to burn the midnight oil."

I left that night with the tickets, some documents for Mrs. Plate, and a route slip reminding me to check and see that the casket was transferred to the appropriate train at two or three different stops, including Minneapolis and Chicago. In Minneapolis it was cold, wet, and dark up on the platform, and as I came along to peer into the baggage car and make sure that the casket in its plain lumber outer covering was aboard, I noticed the curious glances at my unfamiliar Canadian uniform. After nearly two days I set out on the last lap from Chicago, through Rock Island and Davenport on the way to Plate's home town, Bennett, which was in Cedar County, Iowa. The sign in town said Bennett had 306 friendly inhabitants, and I wondered whether that included my dead friend.

A friend of the family had been sent to meet me at the station, and after we had spoken briefly with the local undertaker and seen the body placed in the hearse, he drove me to the Plate home. In Dauphin, Francis Plate had vowed several times that he would have me as his guest in Iowa to repay the hospitality my parents had shown him on our 48's. As we drove from the station I thought of the contrast between his conception and what was transpiring. I braced myself for the imminent meeting with Francis' mother.

I need not have worried about how Mrs. Plate would react at my appearance. She proved to be a warm, gracious lady with silver hair and an abundant strength of spirit. She shook hands with dignity, then pulled me to her gently, and hugged me in a tight embrace for several seconds as though I were her missing boy. Keeping one arm around me, she then introduced me to her other son, Wilmer, who was slightly older than Francis, and was now wearing the uniform of the US Army Air Force. Wilmer took me away to show me where I would be staying.

In a short time I rejoined the family who were gathered in the living room, obviously anxious to hear some explanation of what had happened, some details that might help make sense out of the blow. I told them everything I had been able to find out about the accident, and recalled for the first time that Francis had mentioned to me, in an offhand way, three or four days earlier that he had been having some minor trouble with his eyes. We speculated as to whether this had been a contributing factor, decided for various reasons that it probably had not been, and, in a short time, the hardest part of our dialogue was safely past for all of us.

After dinner, when we gathered for more conversation, Mrs. Plate seemed more relaxed, and I began, in a rather exploratory fashion, to tell her of some of the many experiences Francis and I had shared. She was able to smile and even laugh occasionally as I related a few of the scrapes we had gotten into.

"Oh, that sounds just like him," she said several times, smiling and dabbing at her eyes at the same time.

My heart went out to her, and I kept on with my recital, telling her every detail I thought she might be interested in of our few months together. I sensed that as long as I kept talking about Francis and about the recent experiences we had been involved in together, it half brought him back to her. We stayed there together until it was quite late.

In the morning a number of relatives and close friends came calling, and while Mrs. Plate was busy with them, Wilmer and I got out for a couple of hours together, walking to various places in town and discussing flying training in Canada and the United States. We returned to the house and then, just before two o'clock, we went to the funeral.

I had previously kept my emotions fairly well hidden, and my concern and sympathy for Lucy Plate had served to divert my attention from my own loss. Listening to the minister in the chapel I found it much harder to keep a firm grip on myself, particularly when he spoke of certain accomplishments which Francis had been too modest to mention to me himself.

The American Legion furnished an honour guard and a trumpeter for the service at the graveside. Here, standing hard by the grave, in view of all the other mourners, I particularly did not want to show my emotion openly, lest the Americans wonder whether the RCAF was composed of weeping weaklings; but as I took my leave of Francis Plate for the last time, saluting his flag-draped casket, I felt my own loss so keenly that the tears trickled down my cheeks despite my resolve.

F/L Baird had not fixed any definite return date for me, but I had vaguely assumed that once the funeral was over I would begin making arrangements to catch an early train back. The Plates would not hear of an immediate return. For another two days they drove me hither and yon about the country, showing me all Francis' favourite spots and re-introducing me to people whom I had met briefly at the funeral and to other friends who had been unable to get away from their jobs. Everyone was wonderfully friendly and obliging — it was as though they had reversed our roles and felt it their task to make me feel better.

Finally the time came when I could postpone my departure no longer. There were mutual sincere wishes of future good fortune, and promises on both sides to exchange letters. With a number of warm-hearted new American friends to see me off, I began my journey back to Dauphin. I felt as though I had been away for a month.

As soon as I arrived back I reported to F/L Baird and to his question I answered that I felt the family had appreciated the fact that the escort dispatched by the RCAF had not been a stranger. Baird thanked me briefly for undertaking the job, then began lining up a formidable list of work for me to start getting caught up on. It seemed that everyone in "E" Flight, except me, had already completed his 60-hour check. A few had failed and were no longer with us. Once more the butterflies started fluttering by the thousands in my stomach.

Two days later, Baird received a letter from Lucy Plate. He was so impressed and pleased by her message that he called me in to see him again and read the letter to me personally before he posted it up in our flight room for the whole class to read.

Mrs. Plate had expressed, in touching terms, her gratitude for the consideration the Air Force had shown in selecting a friend who had been so close to her son to bring him home to her. She had gone on to shower undeserved compliments on my conduct, and to stress the comfort she had been able to draw for several days from my presence. Her remarks were so generous as to be embarrassing, but it was nice to know that I had been able to help.

Baird lost no time putting me back to work, the first order of business being to get me solo at night. He gave me an hour and 15 minutes dual himself, then sent me on my way. As I lined up on the flare path I couldn't repress the recollection that 30 seconds after Plate had opened the throttles from the same position he had been killed. The green Aldis lamp flashed again and I got on my way.

The circuit was uneventful and my first solo landing at night a good one. Thereafter the tension gradually eased, although night flying in the vicinity of an aerodrome on a really dark night never became the routine or relaxed pastime day flying often was. With no moon or starlight the restricted visibility induced more than just normal alertness. In traffic, with aircraft winging in to join the circuit from various points of the compass, I fairly bristled with awareness.

Night cross countries were something else. Once away from the aerodrome traffic fell off to nothing, it was usually smooth, and in the denser cool night air the engines purred restfully. Darkness stretched ahead of us like black velvet, broken sporadically by the mass glitter of town lights and more frequently by the solitary, feeble little beams from lonely farmhouses. At infrequent intervals the instructor would bestir himself to ascertain whether you knew your position. If you appeared uncertain, as you often were, pending the hoped-for appearance of a prominent landmark, he would frequently drop a broad hint, corrective or confirmatory as the circumstances required, and the shared semi-reverie could be resumed.

As the work-crammed days flitted by I spent a lot of time in the air. On August 31st, seven days after my return from Iowa, I flew my 60-hour check under the supervision of our squadron commander, Squadron Leader Ball. I am pleased to record that Ball gave me a very fair test, with none of the miserable tricks or traps resorted to by one or two of the instructors who acted as examining officers. When he suddenly cut both throttles on me and called "Forced landing — where are you going to put her down?", I indicated a field within easy gliding distance, steered downwind, and kept doing "S" turns close to it until my altitude had dropped to the figure I wanted, then turned in and dumped the undercarriage. When Ball was certain that I would make it in without difficulty, he told me to open up, then said: "I think I would've picked that other field, to the north there. But, what the hell, this one is big enough; can't see any drainage ditches across it, and you were going to get into it okay — fair enough. Climb back to 3,000 and we'll do some steep turns."

In the third 70 degree steep turn he cut one engine on me and checked my single engine procedure. When I had run through it and got the aircraft stable and flying comfortably on one engine, he took the controls for a moment to check the trim I had applied, then told me to go back onto both engines and head for the barn.

As I approached the drome I was turning over in my mind the

question of whether to land in the orthodox and officially favoured three-point style or to wheel her in. I wasn't too worried about being able to deliver an acceptable three pointer, but they did have one disadvantage: unless absolutely perfect they always finished in a little bit of a bump. Like a true grandstander, I wanted to finish off in fine style. I had been practising wheel landings on most of my solo flights, so called because we came in on just the two main wheels, flying the aircraft right onto the runway with the tail wheel high. I was sure I could grease her on that way; so I decided to try a wheel landing and to say, if challenged, that it was the safer method in a cross-wind.

I wheeled in a beauty; the wheels kissed the concrete with a barely perceptible tremor and a moment or two later the tail sank, ever so gently, to provide the third point of contact.

Ball said "Passable", indicating that it was actually a thing of surpassing grace and elegance which satisfied him as much as me; then, to let me know that the orthodox theology was unchanged in the instruction manual, he cocked an eyebrow and said: "Why did you wheel it on instead of three-pointing it?"

"There was a bit of surface cross-wind just as I flared out sir" I replied, straight-faced; "I figured it was safer to wheel her in."

Ball grinned. "Quite so, quite so. I wondered whether you would spot it."

As we taxied briskly past the control tower, we both ignored the wind sock, which hung as limp as a balloon full of water.

Thanks to Squadron Leader Ball my 60-hour check was a decided success.

The Air Force now considered us competent enough to begin formation flying. We had all previously engaged in a few brief sessions, on the sly of course, for next to low flying there is nothing quite so hypnotically seductive — and dangerous — for novice pilots as the experience of formating on another aeroplane seemingly suspended 20 feet away from him in the air; but now we got formation officially, for an hour or two at a time, and we quickly learned how demanding and tiring tight formation flying could be. As a safety measure, when the instructor was not along with us, we always carried another pupil in the right hand seat to act as lookout. Actually, the leader of the formation was supposed to maintain the eagle-eyed vigil necessary to ensure that his formation kept out of harm's way, because the pilots formating on him had to keep all their attention riveted on his aircraft; but the Air Force recognized that with inexperienced pilots leading formations it was wise to splash extra lookouts around liberally. We all learned quickly the first cardinal rule of formation: don't move if one of your teammates disappears — you might move right into him.

Other rules, which required experienced judgment, were not so easy to apply.

On one of our early formation exercises I found myself flying as left wing man in a vic of three. I carried a student lookout. The lead aircraft was being flown by another student under the supervision of an instructor. I was finding out that judging accurately the distance between our aircraft was far from easy. Since we lacked radios on all but a few of our planes, we had to rely on hand signals. On this occasion I edged into position carefully and thought I was doing well until the instructor leaned over towards the window facing me and waved his hand in a vague gesture that didn't jibe with any of the precise and readily identifiable signals prescribed in the handbook. By a process of elimination I concluded that he must mean me to tuck my wing in closer or move it a little further away. Since he had beckoned only briefly and rather casually before turning his attention to the front again, I decided he wanted me in closer, reasoning that if I was too close he would be keeping a sharp eye on me until I had moved to a safer distance.

I pressed the left rudder pedal gently, to skid me two or three feet closer. Before the response was nicely started the instructor was framed in the window again. This time the signal was unmistakable — the palms of both hands were suddenly visible, pressed on the glass, on either side of a whitewashed face. I got the immediate impression that if I came an inch closer he would bolt right through the door and push me away.

Back on the ground he began talking to me as soon as I climbed out of my plane — while we were still a hundred yards apart. The only thing he didn't call me was chicken.

While I learned plenty from my own mistakes, I did pick up a few pointers from my classmates' bloopers. One of our boys, a day or two after I had put the formation instructor under medical care for shock, sat warming his engines on the tarmac as he prepared to take off on a three-hour cross-country navigational exercise with another pupil. It was fast approaching lunch time, and since flying took precedence over mundane pursuits such as eating, he had thoughtfully provided himself with an Oh Henry bar which he planned to gobble sometime before he took off. Noting that his engines were almost warm enough, he gulped down his bar and prepared to taxi. Responding instinctively to the Air Force's ingrained mania for tidiness, he opened his window and, without thinking, casually flipped out the light cardboard wrapper of his bar. It flew like a homing pigeon straight into his port propeller. To his surprise, the engine immediately rose to a new note, and simultaneously began vibrating so violently that he feared it would shake loose from its mountings. He switched off hurriedly and found, to his dismay, that when a steel propeller is turning at any significant speed, even something as light as a chocolate bar wrapper catching the tip of the blade can bend it out of alignment and generate sufficient vibration to wreck an engine. The rest of us were every bit as astonished as he was at the discovery, but not nearly as embarrassed — he got a blistering lecture on refuse disposal systems (and the inappropriateness of Jacobs engines for that purpose) from his instructor, with brief encores from the Flight Commander and the CFI.

We learned there were other flyers to watch out for. Just at dusk, another cadet, flying due east past the drome at 120 miles per hour, encountered a three-pound mallard drake cruising at 50 miles per hour due west. Paying no heed to Kipling, east and west did meet, and at the closing speed of 170, the duck nearly tore the Cessna's port wing off, burying himself dangerously deep in the main spar, and tearing a plate-sized hole in the fabric with his kamikaze attack. The tear began to spread quickly under the rush of air, and as the shape of the aerofoil grew more and more distorted, it lost lift, and the aircraft became dangerously unstable.

It was a greatly shaken pilot who crawled out in front of the flight office ten minutes later to verify what had happened and survey the surprising amount of damage. The dead mallard was still there, embedded firmly in the spar, and below him, to one side of the hole, the underside of the wing looked as though its fabric had been stretched over an enclosed tympani.

I got caught in my second bad storm a fortnight later, this time a freakish September snow storm which blew up from nowhere and engulfed me as I was winging home from a reconnaissance trip. The visibility, previously unlimited, shrank to about 200 yards in the blizzard of half-dollar-sized snowflakes, and it was obvious that if these conditions were widespread I was going to have my work all cut out for me finding dear old Dauphin.

I had always been impressed by the incredibly resourceful pilots of our Airmanship lectures who, when they encountered difficulties, invariably responded with prompt and positive countermeasures to nullify any troublesome situation arising — fire in the air, wing or prop falling off, tempest or typhoon — you name it, young Pilot Officer Paragon had a ready solution at his fingertips. After racking my brain for a few minutes, all I had on my mental exercise book was still the problem — "I cannot see; how do I find my way home?" — no answer.

Unconsciously broadening the parameters so as to accommodate illegal or unsporting solutions, I promptly thought of one. Less than five miles away was the railway line I'd left upon finishing my sketch plan of the town and making a bee line for base. By angling off my course, I could grope my way back to the railway — which ran into Dauphin after meandering through a few scattered whistle stops — position my aircraft over it like a Sperry car, and follow it to "E" Flight's back yard.

Officially, this primitive but ultimately effective navigational process — which we called "flying the iron beam" — was ferociously frowned upon. I was prepared to concede that it was not the neat and irreproachable solution Pilot Officer Paragon would have pulled out of his flight bag; but I took a liking to it, particularly to the fact that it was likely to get me and my aeroplane home intact. I altered course 45 degrees and began peering.

Even immersed in billions of snowflakes, finding the bright iron trail that wound its way to Dauphin took only a few minutes. Over the next few miles the visibility deteriorated further and I pulled in closer alongside the railway line to make sure I didn't lose sight of it. I had descended to 250 feet for the same reason, and by rights should have stayed there. But low flying is heady stuff, and here I was with a golden opportunity to do it legally. I assumed my Billy Bishop mien and slid down to 50 feet, enjoying myself hugely for a few minutes zinging along close to the tracks like a bat out of hell. The big snowflakes streaking by the millions past the cockpit heightened the exhilarating impression of blinding speed.

Suddenly a terrible thought crossed my mind. I pulled back the stick in panic and shot up to 200 feet, where I subsided momentarily, then began swearing.

"You stupid bastard," I said to Billy Bishop, speaking aloud and very distinctly to lend emphasis to the validity of the classification, for the thought that had suddenly invaded my smugly somnolent brain and galvanized me into such lively action had been the belated recollection of the quaint old North American custom of erecting 80 or 90 foot grain elevators at frequent intervals along railway lines. As it turned out, I did not pass one for a good five minutes after my panicky climb, but I did not erase that black mark against Bishop on that account. I knew all too well that I could easily have seeded 100,000 bushels of wheat spectacularly but posthumously if I had gone onto the iron beam a few miles further on than I actually did.

"Remember, Bishop," I said sternly, "there are old pilots and bold pilots; but there are no old, bold pilots, and don't you forget it. Stupid bastard."

Well clear of the drome I flew out of the storm and back into the soft bright September tranquility I'd been experiencing earlier. I checked the name on the next elevator — there were lots of them — to get my bearings, then climbed gracefully away, turning toward the sector from which our control tower would be expecting me to materialize. Simultaneously I checked the time and calculated that I had lost about nine minutes in crabbing up to the railroad and back. My innate modesty — and one or two other factors — forbade my claiming credit for the feat of airmanship I'd displayed in deciding to follow the trains to Dauphin, necessitating a few minor forgeries in my pilot's flight log to eliminate the wasted nine minutes.

Cooking flight logs so that they would show our earnest endeavours to best advantage was a science in which we were all past masters. Actually we felt it was only fair to our instructors, for the cooked efforts reflected much more credit upon their teaching prowess than the pitiable objects which a slavish adherence to the truth would have generated.

One application of my eraser, one modification of a figure, and lo! the time I had spent sketching the town's facilities was magically extended by nine minutes. In a few open spaces in the log — which we routinely left to accommodate just such eventualities — I inserted one or two observed pinpoints on the straight line track to base, points I would have observed if I had remained dead on my original course, and set down opposite them times which accorded with an appropriate ground speed.

With my documents fashionably falsified to record an impressively executed exercise, I flew serenely home to Dauphin, a wiser pilot.

The time for final tests was now upon us. On September 14th and September 18th, in sessions of 30 and 40 minutes respectively, F/L Baird gave me my instrument flying tests. On each of these flights we were accompanied by Freddie Taylor, another student. Freddie sat in the rear seat and acted as lookout on the left side while I was under the hood, then traded places with me and took his turn at instrument flying. While Freddie was taking his first session under the hood, Baird surreptitiously slipped his hand behind the left seat and turned off the gas cock controlling the fuel supply to the engine on that side. The second he turned away I surreptitiously kicked Freddie gently in the pants, through his seat, and as he glanced back, hidden from Baird by the hood, I waggled an accusing finger at the gas cock, which fully conveyed the message that his port engine would conk out in about 30 seconds. When it did, Freddie was ready, and swirled magnificently through his blind single engine drill. He would have done a respectable job in any case, for Freddie was a sound pilot; but at testing time we regarded ourselves as being locked in deadly combat with the testing officers, who could wash us out, and honour demanded that I give my fellow sufferer any advantage that lay in my power.

On September 28th Pilot Officer McAra rode with me for two and

Peden and Francis Plate (right) while on leave in Winnipeg.

Above: Cessna Crane 7892. This twin-engined trainer was widely used at SFTS stations.
(RCAF)

Below: Cessna Cranes from No. 10 SFTS (Dauphin, Manitoba) practise formation flying.

 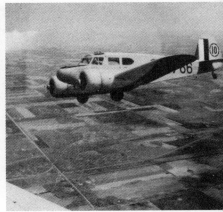

Lucy Plate and her son Wilmer (at right).

Above: After wings parade on October 23, 1942 a "Prairies" group display their newly pinned on wings. In the back row Barrie Dean, the author and Charlie Payne are 2nd, 3rd and 4th from the right, respectively. Claude Roy is 2nd from the left in the front row, and Walter "Watt" Wilton 2nd from the right.

(RCAF)

Right:
The author, newly commissioned.

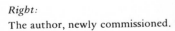

82

a half hours administering my Wings Navigation Test.

While these tests were very important — in fact each was a *sine qua non* — and kept us honed to a fine edge, the crucial one, marked on the syllabus forebodingly as "Wings Test" was still to come. We knew we would be called for it any day now, and its status as the make or break flight loomed larger and larger in our minds.

On October 4th I was despatched in Cessna 7929 to do some air to ground radio exercises. There had been considerable rain the previous week, with the result that our secondary practice or "relief" field, R1, had been unserviceable about 50 percent of the time. R1 had no runways, it was simply a good level grass field where pupils could practise forced landing or precautionary landing techniques away from the heavier traffic of our main drome. If we intended using it, we were required, before leaving the main field, to check its condition on the notice board in our flight office. I had not planned on doing any practice landings on this radio exercise, so I did not trouble to look at the board. I would have guessed R1 to be unserviceable in any event because of the amount of rain we'd had.

The radio was working with its customary efficiency, I found, which meant that the moment I got clear of the ground it delivered no intelligible sounds whatever. We had only four or five aircraft which carried radio, and the performance of these sets was uniformly atrocious. The whole time I was at SFTS I never heard a completely comprehensible sentence in plain English come in over an airborne receiver. Normally transmissions from the control tower sounded as though they were originated by an Abyssinian tobacco auctioneer with all his teeth pulled, standing at the machine gun butts during firing practice. In fifteen minutes, five under par, I progressed smoothly through the cycle of emotions inevitably associated with radio practice, i.e. irritation, anger, black rage and frustrated incoherence, and abandoned the exercise as totally futile. I decided to put the air time to good use by swinging over to R1 and practising all the preliminary drill on precautionary landings without actually letting the aircraft touch the ground.

Precautionary landings were always included in our flying tests. A precautionary entails flying low over the selected field, (usually a cow pasture), inspecting the proposed landing path to make sure it is suitably smooth, firm, and free of dangerous obstacles, then coming in slowly and dumping the aircraft in for a short landing run. A precautionary landing is made in the face of impending danger calling for a prompt and unscheduled landing — for example, when one discovers that his gas supply is down to 20 minutes and the nearest aerodrome is half an hour away.

As I flew in over R1, still thinking profane thoughts of Marconi and all his gremlin-ridden tribe, I spotted another Cessna on the far side of the field, and wondered idly if he too were practising approaches. I flew low over the grass field, just to one side of a portion which looked firm and dry, the area where I would touch down if I really intended to land, climbed around in a circuit, dumped my wheels and some flap while running cross-wind, and began turning into wind again to drag the aircraft in just over its stalling speed in the approved precautionary manner. To my surprise, the other aircraft was taxiing on the grass. He had landed on the lane I had picked out, and was taxiing back to the take-off end.

On the spur of the moment I decided to go all the way in and land. It was obvious that the field had been declared serviceable again; no one would dare take a chance on going into R1 while it was classified as unserviceable. The fact that the part I had just inspected was safe to land on had just been demonstrated to my satisfaction. I carried on with my approach, hovering just over the stall until I reached the portion of the field I had earlier picked out, then cut the throttles and sank quickly onto the turf.

In a few moments I turned clear of the landing path, at which point I was somewhat startled to see the other aircraft bearing down on me at three times the normal taxiing speed. When it was 40 feet away, its pilot twirled it about and stopped. I was now able to see that there were two occupants, and behind the sheen of the perspex I caught a vague flurry of hand waving which seemed to be aimed in my general direction. I came to a full stop and sat, interestedly awaiting developments.

A lanky figure sporting dazzling white coveralls and an officer's peaked cap emerged abruptly, jumped to the ground, and stalked truculently toward me. Under the officer's cap which marked him as an instructor, he wore a black look to set off his white getup, so I tactfully throttled my port engine right back to ensure that I didn't blow Flash Gordon off the wing and irk him further. He sprang up on the wing step, opened my door in a manner which made me wonder whether it would fasten again, crouched half-way into the cabin and glared at my questioning face for ten seconds before he spoke. When he did, his voice was hard and challenging:

"Don't you know that this field is unserviceable?"

"I thought it was, sir, until I saw your aircraft land," I replied. Apparently that was not the thing to say; his voice rose.

"I came over and inspected this field. Are you aware that there is only one part of it that is safe to use?"

" I landed on the same section you did, sir," I answered truthfully, staying in my defensive stance. This did not sit well either.

"What's your name — what flight are you in?"

84

"Peden sir; "E" Flight."

"Peden eh? All right, Peden, listen to me: taxi out behind my aircraft and take off on the same path I use. And next time check the serviceability of a field before you land on it."

"Yes sir."

He backed through the door, reminding me of Gary Cooper about to go for both six guns, uncoiled to his full six foot three, and strode back to his own plane.

I went back to practising precautionary approaches in the manner I had originally intended, but the practice was of little value for I was preoccupied, wondering whether this unknown instructor would report the incident to my flight commander and stir up some trouble. On meditation, I concluded that he probably would do nothing officially, since he could not push the matter very far without running up against the fact that a field flatly declared to be unserviceable was off limits to all pilots, not just those under six feet three inches. No mention was made of the incident when I landed, and I breathed a little easier — for a short time.

Bright and early the next day the members of "E" Flight began being called up for their Wings Tests. We hung about the flight room breathing shallowly and trying to think of pleasanter topics of conversation, but every time the testing aircraft taxied back in we waited with bated breath to see who was next. Early in the afternoon Freddie Taylor was called. He returned in 45 minutes, and my name was called. I hustled out, clipping in the leg straps of my chute in the gust from the port propeller as I reached the wing step. I entered the cabin, and my heart sank like a stone. The testing officer sat in the right hand seat writing up his final comments on Taylor's performance on the pad of test forms strapped around his thigh.

It was Flash Gordon, again in the white coveralls. From the notice board in our flight office which designated our testing officer, I now knew that his name was Flying Officer Sparling.

So far he hadn't even looked at me, concentrating fully on the test form, and I began to fan the hope that he might not remember me and the incident at R1. He flapped over a new page on his pad, still looking down, and spoke:

"Name?"

"Peden, sir."

"Ahhhh yes . . ." The sinister significance he managed to inject into those two words could not have been heightened if he had added the diabolical laugh of the Shadow. He remembered all right. I could see it was going to be a joyless flight.

My Wings Test lasted exactly 40 minutes, during which time Sparling put me systematically through the complete repertoire. It was a whole lot tougher test than my 60-hour check had been, but I could not truthfully say that it was unfair in any way. A friendlier atmosphere on the right side of the cockpit would have won a more confident performance from me; but even so, I felt that I had flown reasonably well. I was anxious to hear some reassuring comment from Sparling, but he maintained an impregnable silence as we taxied in.

When it was time for me to unfasten my seat belt and depart, I was unable to bear the suspense any longer. I turned toward him and forced myself to speak:

"How did I make out, sir?"

His eyes never moved. "We'll see . . .," he said heavily, the tone absolutely non-committal and devoid of the slightest spark of encouragement, "send Payne out next."

I sweated it out from that day, October 5th, to October 16th, the day I made my last flight at No. 10 SFTS. In that eleven-day interval I logged 23 additional flights, bringing my total flying time, at both schools, to 225 hours. All that time I agonized over that test, re-flying it mentally a dozen times a day and wondering if I couldn't have done better on some phases of it. Sparling's deliberate refusal to yield the slightest trace of encouragement made me worry that he intended to mark me down on my Wings Test as a result of what he might consider my temerity in joining him on the deck at R1 the day before the test.

Finally, on October 16th, when we had finished flying, my fears were dissipated by the cheering news that a wings party was being organized and that my name was amongst the officially sanctioned list of celebrants. I hardly dared accept this as a reliable guarantee, so shaken had I been by Sparling's attitude.

Equity compels the admission that my impression of John Sparling was completely wrong. In fact he was a flyer and a gentleman from top to toe. His preoccupation, and my own guilty state of mind, had combined to leave me with a totally unfair impression.

These wings parties were refined little soirees traditionally financed by the graduating class. The guest list invariably started with the social elite, the instructors, and it was common practice to invite deserving persons of our own lowly estate with whom we had a strong affinity: the line chiefs, and WAAF's from the parachute section and flight office. When the underwriting of the affair had been nailed down by the collection of ten dollars from each graduate, the proceeds were tastefully allocated on a basis which commanded broad public support, namely, 400 dollars for booze and 100 for salty food.

I was among the first of the graduates to arrive at the party, and paralleled that achievement by being the very first to leave. My early and horizontal departure was directly attributable to a discovery I made only a few minutes after I entered the gaily decorated hall. One of the instructors, in a display of amiability and good fellowship entirely appropriate to the occasion, called me over to the impressively stocked bar and asked me what I fancied. I knew the names of at least three alcoholic drinks, and, anxious to show a degree of *savoir faire* commensurate with my new status, I casually made it known that rye and coke was my customary libation.

From my sporadic studies of the drinking rituals portrayed in Western movies — which pretty well comprised the sum total of my experience with hard liquor — I vaguely expected to receive a searing potion which would burn like lye all the way down; thus I braced myself to keep the resulting gasps and grimaces within limits which would not betray the fact that this was my initiation. The moment I drank the first glass I made the discovery that my constitution was obviously quite different from that of most mortals, for they spoke of this stuff with great respect, whereas I was immediately aware that I could drink the concoction like lemonade. Nevertheless I did not throw caution to the winds there and then; I waited a good three minutes, then, noting that it had definitely failed of any effect, I marched up to the bar and requested another. I gave that one a fair six-minute trial too, but the second test only confirmed the tentative conclusions derived from the first data. I fell into line — there was now a short lineup at the bar — and obtained a third, and a short time later a fourth and a fifth.

At this point all guests were cordially invited, by repeated shouts and bellows, to sit down at the festive board. Five minutes later Flight Lieutenant Baird proposed the traditional toast to the King. I rose enthusiastically to participate, and that is the last detail of the evening which I can relate on the basis of firsthand knowledge. Credible witnesses have testified, however, that I was a new person to them, a life-of-the-party type rarely encountered in the bucolic surroundings of Dauphin, but that my overpowering ebullience lasted only 30 more minutes, at the end of which space I left the hall abruptly and shed the light of my countenance on the party no more.

Claude Roy found me lying in a heavy coma on the ground opposite a basement window of the hall a good half hour after that. He had gargled a few ryes himself by this time, but compared to me he was an old campaigner, meaning that he could still walk and talk. It was freezing outside. Claude wiped the frost off my face, and went back indoors, where the party was getting nicely underway, to organize a rescue squad. Three more benefactors, known only to the good Lord, came and helped him bear me on my shield to a taxi office a couple of blocks away.

I was sick for four days, and when I say sick, that word does not begin to convey the suffering I went through — it was really a lingering death that didn't quite come off. No party that I ever attended, before or since, remotely approached our Dauphin revel for vivid memorability. When I woke on the morning of the fourth day I felt ghastly, a state that represented a 90 percent improvement over my condition throughout the previous three days; and I set about making ready for our Wings Parade, scheduled for that afternoon. Such was the psychological lift immediately preceding and stemming from this long-sought ceremonial that by early afternoon the worst ravages of alcoholic poisoning were becoming only painful memories.

The excitement mounted until finally the great moment arrived for the members of Course 59. We marched into a hangar, where our parents and relatives had foregathered to share our moment of pride and pleasure, and after a brief wait were reviewed there by Air Commodore Shearer. He proceeded to make the customary congratulatory speech, which we were all prepared to accept as no more than our due, then began calling us before him individually to pin new wings on our carefully pressed blue serge. As he pinned on the wings and shook hands with each new pilot, there was a generous round of applause from the highly empathic spectators. When the Air Commodore pinned that coveted badge on my chest I distinctly heard a joyful Scottish hoot above the noise of the applause, certain evidence that my father had acted on my request that he attend and that he was sharing my own keen gratification.

One important question remained unanswered — which of us would be commissioned as officers. The customary practice was to award commissions to the top third of the class and promote the remainder to the rank of Sergeant Pilot. Those receiving commissions as Pilot Officers were generally notified at the same time as they received their wings; but in the case of Course 59 there had been an unexplained delay in the official communication from Ottawa, so that when we received our wings we all assumed the rank of Sergeant Pilot. We were ordered to hand in all our SFTS equipment, get our log books closed off and signed, and get cleared from all agencies on the station the following morning, Saturday, October 24th, 1942.

In the meantime there was the critical issue of postings to be settled. We were told that four of us would have to remain in Canada as instructors; also there were two or three postings to General Reconnaissance courses, which were frequently followed by Coastal Command work. The rest of us were to be posted overseas, and would report to No. 1 "Y" Depot, Halifax, Nova Scotia, in furtherance of those orders after two weeks embarkation leave. Most of us were eager to get overseas and wanted no part of instructing or GR courses; but there were a few, mainly men with wives to think about, who were content to settle for those assignments, so the arrangements were readily made to everyone's satisfaction. Several of us indicated, yet again, our strong preference for fighter pilot assignments; but for the moment we were more than satisfied to be wearing the badge of pilot and on our way towards the fighting.

We left the station *en masse* that night for one final fling in Dauphin before shaking its dust from our feet. We were excused all duties until eight o'clock the following morning, so many of us booked rooms in the Kings Hotel for the night — not that we were truly that anxious to stay off the station, but it gave us an excuse to sign the register as Sergeant Pilot Peden, or whatever, and let the world know that we had made the grade.

The rest of the boys wet their wings with gusto that night, but I played Stonewall Jackson and abstained from alcohol, not, as he did, because I had tried it once and discovered I liked it, but because I had tried it once and it nearly killed me.

We decamped the following day, and I came home to Winnipeg as a conquering hero to glory in a lazy regimen of sleeping in every morning, then idling away the day eating, visiting friends, and doing whatever I felt like.

Monday morning, the third day of my leave, I was still in bed and half asleep at a quarter to ten when my father came shuffling in with an oddly mischievous smile on his face and my freshly shined shoes in his left hand.

"Just your batman, sir," he warbled. Then, setting the shoes down he produced from behind his back a brown government envelope and held it so that I could see the address:

PILOT OFFICER D. M. PEDEN, J20216.

That put the icing on the cake.

I fully expected to be the butt of some robust ribbing from my father and his brother Jock over the remainder of my leave. Five Peden brothers had served in the Canadian infantry in the first World War; two were killed and Jock and my father were wounded. They had all served as privates, and my father and Jock, especially Jock, had come home highly unimpressed with officers generally, and their generals in particular. Jock was not a man to hide his sentiments, even where expression of them would violate the accepted social graces; in fact on a chance close-quarters encounter in a duck marsh with Sir Julian Byng, then Governor-General of Canada but remembered by Jock as the Commanding General of the Canadian Corps in 1916 and 1917, he had deliberately flipped his canoe to shower the Vice-Regal party with mud as an expression of his disapproval of Sir Julian in both capacities. But when I first put in an appearance in front of Jock in my new officer's uniform, he was sincerely complimentary and all his jokes were on himself.

All too soon the lovely lazy days of embarkation leave came to an end, for we were under orders to report to "Y" Depot on November 7th — a year and a day from our first appearance at Manning Depot — and we faced a three-day train journey getting to Halifax from Winnipeg. A sizeable segment of the clan, together with a sprinkling of other staunch friends, saw me off at the station. The leave-takings were full of synthetic cheerfulness, and I thought I reciprocated as well as could be expected in view of my awareness that the excellent turnout was partly attributable to a fear on the part of many of the wellwishers that they might well be enjoying their last look at a certain young Pilot Officer of whom I was very fond. Jock, who spent his working hours as a switchman leaping on and off freight cars, swung aboard my coach as the train began to roll and stood on the bottom step chaffing as she picked up speed; then, with an admonition to take care, and a final grin, he dropped off onto the end of the platform, ran a few steps and quickly dropped behind. I was on my way to Halifax.

CHAPTER 5

CONVOY

And I'm never, never sick at sea!
What, never?
No, never!
What, never?
Hardly ever!

W. S. Gilbert: H.M.S. Pinafore

Halifax we found squalid, dismally bleak, cold, wet, fog-drenched, and overcrowded — but otherwise very nice. As quickly as we assimilated that impression, the Air Force moved to forestall the onset of depression by calling a documents parade, having us make out our wills, and then complete a series of other forms each of which embodied a cheerfully innocent query as to the identity of our next-of-kin.

Halifax was a navy town. Its streets teemed with sailors, on liberty and on duty, and even our officers' mess harboured a sizeable number of naval officers engaged in duties connected with the transportation of airmen. We noticed that the Air Force was not the only service whose uniform was flaunted by the occasional four-flusher. Some of the saltiest naval specimens, tremendously extroverted matelots, were engaged full time on shore duties to which they clung tenaciously — meantime riding in the bow of the Dartmouth ferry twice a week to keep their cap badges impressively salt-stained. Usually it was one of the corvette boys, the genuine article in our navy, in for a drink in our mess with some overseas-bound airman friend, who tipped us off to these spurious sea dogs.

91

Our schedule at "Y" Depot was far from arduous, in fact we regarded it as pretty much of a rest cure; but we did have two or three additional tests to take during our sojourn. First of all, in groups of about ten, we took a series of "flights" in the decompression tank to see what limits if any would have to be imposed on our operating altitude. On the first test we stopped for ten minutes at 17,000 feet, without oxygen, to witness first hand the symptoms of incipient anoxia. Our respiration grew noticeably faster and deeper; even slight exertion brought on dizziness; and a distinct bluish tinge crept into our lips. Thereafter we put on oxygen masks and went to 25,000 feet, the limit on the first session. The medic who ran the section predicted that only about 46 percent of our draft would be able to get a clearance for 35,000 and above. I never did find out whether we ran true to form over-all, but when we had completed the remaining two decompression tests, Claude Roy and I were both cleared for 35,000 feet or over and had the inside cover of our log books stamped accordingly.

Next the Air Force re-inoculated us for all the old maladies we'd been jabbed for before, and broadened our experience by giving us another clutch of needles designed to immunize us against everything from poison ivy to cobra bites. While our arms, and certain other areas, were still throbbing and pulsating from this punishment, we underwent further tests for night visual acuity in a room in which any photographer could safely have developed his film.

Charlie Payne and I took these vision tests together, and performed fairly well after our eyes had adapted to the blackness of the test chamber. But for some reason, every time we brought our log books around to get this tester's endorsement, he was away, or tied up with other tests, or unable to find the proper batch of records. After four abortive attempts, Charlie and I decided we had had enough of trying to dance to his tune. We still had to have a night vision endorsement in our log books, but we felt that a scientific approach to that problem would yield quick results. We examined some of our associates' books to get the verbiage and format, noted that all we would require was a bottle of red ink, got it, then solemnly endorsed the fly leaf of each other's books "Night Visual Acuity = Average". Charlie and I subsequently had less trouble getting our log books cleared than many of our friends who had submitted to the eccentricities of the disorganized tester to secure the proper endorsement. That fact was not lost on us. Furthermore, as an incidental benefit, Charlie's red ink penmanship in my book later acquired the status of a conversation piece when Charlie flew the German generals to the surrender ceremony in May, 1945 — thoughtfully securing their autographs before they went back to face trial at Nuremberg.

Somewhat to my surprise, I discovered that the "Y" Depot had a

Link Trainer concealed within its precincts. My first session there began unimpressively as I found that having gone for three or four weeks without the benefit of any instrument practice had left me embarrassingly rusty. Towards the end of the exercise, though, what little skill I had formerly developed began to return, along with a trace of self-respect, and I felt better. Nevertheless I booked another period and, on the late afternoon of November 20th, had just completed it when some 90 members of our group were given an hour's notice to pack and parade, carrying with us all our worldly possessions, in front of a dozen trucks lined up on the square.

In the gathering dusk the drivers rushed us to the dock and we lined up briefly alongside the ship that we were to board. She was the S.S. *Cavina*, and although the grizzled old sergeant-major responsible for our draft said she was a Fyffes Line boat of 6800 tons, she didn't look to me to be big enough to send across Halifax harbour. I had been expecting to travel on the *Queen Elizabeth* (which did carry the remainder of our group from New York a few days later) and the old *Cavina*, by comparison, looked as though she could be hoisted up between the davits and carried as one of the *Q.E.'s* lifeboats.

As this thought crossed my mind, I heard the sergeant-major repeating his interpretation of the boarding drill, slowly and with emphasis, to an obtuse pilot with a larger than average mass of impedimenta sloped against his legs, "Now listen, you pick up all the gear you can lift and hang around your neck; you march up that gangplank once — and you don't come back." I didn't particularly appreciate the overtones of that last clause; but I dutifully clutched my trunk in one hand, my haversack and some odds and ends in the other, and filed up the gangplank.

In recognition of our new status as officers, we were favoured with something special in the way of accommodation — something specially small, that is, with four of us drawing a stateroom almost adequate for a pair of stunted Siamese twins. Presently the engines throbbed, and Charlie Payne and I squeezed clear of our bunkmates and came on deck to watch the *Cavina* back clear of her mooring, then move out into Bedford Basin to take position in the convoy waiting in the murk. A gust of the freshening wind tore Charlie's brand new peaked cap from his head, and in a moment it was bobbing on the light chop below us, the gorgeous red plush and gold silk embroidery of the badge sparkling wetly on the slate-coloured water as it slid quickly astern. As omens went, I couldn't say that I especially fancied the incident. The pitfalls of North Atlantic travel in wartime were not lost on airmen about to make the trip, particularly in November, 1942, one of the most successful periods of the whole war for the German U-boats. You didn't have to be an admiral to realize that our navy was overstretched and well on the way to losing the Battle of the Atlantic. I visualized the busiest man in the world as a German naval rating in running shoes keeping the U-boats' tonnage scoreboard current at Admiral Doenitz's headquarters.

When we woke up, we were riding to the firm but leisurely swell of the open sea. After we had bulled our way in, helter skelter, for breakfast, creating unnecessary problems for the staff, we were assembled in the main lounge where more orderly arrangements were laid on for all future meals. We were given table assignments and specific sittings. As a result of the Dauphin wings party I mustered little interest in the next topic of the speaker, which was the hours of bar service aboard the *Cavina*. (I never took a drink crossing the Atlantic — in fact during the whole trip I couldn't even stand close downwind of anyone who had.) While the official herald was still declaiming — now about the advisability of remaining constantly adorned with a lifebelt henceforth — an interesting rumour began to flit around, relegating the authorized orator's dissertation to the deep subconscious.

The scuttlebutt was that we had a famous movie star aboard. Freddie Taylor hoped aloud that it would prove to be Rita Hayworth, Betty Grable, or Linda Darnell, in that order. If we were to be fobbed off with an actor rather than an actress, he didn't really give a damn who it was — it might just as well be Mickey Rooney as Clark Gable. We got on deck shortly afterward for our first lifeboat drill, and took the opportunity to try and check over our convoy. I for one had more than a passing interest in what we had with us for escorts.

It was a large convoy. The *Cavina* seemed to have been positioned somewhere toward the centre, from what we could make out, although it was impossible to spot the extremities of the four widely spaced ranks of ships. From our vantage point we could see 20 or 30 ships, including two or three tankers, while close ahead plodded a pair of ten thousand-ton Liberty ships. Already they were rolling appreciably, despite the fact that the sea was still relatively untroubled. Their masts oscillated slowly and steadily, like tall black metronome rods.

Some of the crew were working forward, so we checked with them for more information. They told us that there were 50 ships in the convoy, and that its speed, set by the commodore to accommodate the slowest ship, was nine knots. Rather unsportingly I suggested that the *Cavina* herself was probably responsible for this cart-horse pace; but the crew loyally disabused me of that heresy, claiming that she was capable of absolutely hareing along, at 15 knots plus, should circumstances demand anything that radical.

The nine knot information caused a gloomy revision of our earlier estimates, which had optimistically paralleled the *Queen Elizabeth's* crossing time of five days, and we now reconciled ourselves to a longer holiday in the sea air. Our first drills over, we had a good walk around the ship to see what sort of armament she carried. Up near the bow she mounted a surprisingly large deck gun, much larger than anything I had expected to find her carrying. This piece was served by a Royal Navy gun crew who later demonstrated that they knew what they were doing. I guessed it to be a six-inch gun. Certainly it was bigger than a four; but with the cover on the muzzle we couldn't be sure. In various locations about the upper deck the *Cavina* carried Oerlikons, primarily for anti-aircraft protection. We concluded that she had been equipped to be an armed merchantman[1] capable of adding some useful punch to that of our light escorts should any surface action develop — like the "armed merchant cruiser" *Jervis Bay,* as Freddie Taylor commented sourly, sunk in the North Atlantic in a hopelessly one-sided fight with the *Admiral Scheer* in November two years earlier.

Barrie Dean strode up purposefully and delivered the latest communiqué on the mysterious celebrity. We definitely had an actress on board, and his was information we could rely on implicitly. Unlike the earlier untraceable rumour, he explained, this flash was practically straight from the horse's mouth, having originated with the helper of a steward who, in turn, was related by marriage to the purser. The patent authenticity of this bulletin bucked up Freddie Taylor no end; but, to even the score with him for the *Jervis Bay* reminder, I pointed out that the term "actress" left room for some pretty ferocious animals. Laurel and Hardy were *actors,* I said, leaving to his imagination the fearsome parallels one might draw on the female side.

During lunch further news drifted to our table: the actress was now reputed to be a British performer. Some wag threw out the name of Two Ton Tessie O'Shea to upset Freddie, who by now would stand still for nothing but a major league certified sexpot; but Barrie soothed him again by mentioning Margaret Lockwood as a possibility and describing her physical assets in sufficient detail to set Freddie's gastric juices flowing again. Another scrap of information which percolated through the cabbage fumes and cigarette smoke alerted us to the fact that every ship in the convoy would test its guns next morning in a scheduled firing practice.

At dinner there were a few vacant chairs in the dining saloon as the *Cavina's* remorseless rise and fall subverted the frailer constitutions. I noted with pleasure that my own cast iron constitution was remaining completely impervious to this hazard; I could sense that I was a natural sailor. Hard on the heels of our treacle tart sweet came

---

1. The *Cavina* was in Admiralty service. She was officially classed as an OBV (Ocean Boarding Vessel) and carried two six-inch guns.

the news that our movie actress was Anna Neagle, unquestionably a famous British actress, and one who was at the very height of her popularity following an inspired portrayal of Queen Victoria in a current movie. On learning of this feat, Freddie immediately expressed grave doubts that anyone who could convincingly play Queen Victoria in her eighty-second year could be a siren-type girl — never mind if she played her at 18 as well.

Nonetheless he willingly participated in the relay of deck patrols we organized immediately after breakfast next morning with the object of spotting Anna if she went on deck for a constitutional. Our tactics were successful very quickly. As soon as we got the message, we pulled on our greatcoats and hustled out on deck, walking against the sparse stream of traffic. In a minute she came towards us, on the arm of her director-husband, Herbert Wilcox, and even in the heavy clothing required for a tour on the deck it was apparent that Anna Neagle would emerge as a thing of beauty and a joy forever. Freddie himself — and he gave her the most searching scrutiny — acclaimed her as something very special; and although the novelty of seeing her soon wore off, she continued to get a lot of attention from us whenever she put in an appearance.

From a visual and aural standpoint the firing practice was spectacular. But the free and easy way the tracers were hosed about all over the convoy promptly put me on the side of the Iron Duke: I didn't know what effect they would have on the enemy, but they surely scared the hell out of me. I breathed a prayer that if any German planes fell upon us they would opt to stay at a respectable altitude, because a water level attack would clearly draw a lot of fratricidal flak between and into our own ships.

Before the practice had started, we had taken up a position commanding a close-up view of our own big deck gun. When the gong sounded, our navy gun crew came boiling out, and before you could say knife, the gun layer was spinning wheels and tracking briskly onto the imaginary target. They went through the motions of loading three or four times without actually firing. This was a bit of a letdown, and mentally I altered the reliability rating of our waiter, who had assured us at breakfast that they would actually fire the monster. Almost before I laid down the chalk, a loader produced a large bag of cordite, seemingly from his bell bottomed trousers, and in the twinkling of an eye the breech was snapped shut and the lanyard jerked. Came a flaming thunderclap, a shock wave like a slap in the face, and a cloud of dirty smoke blew back amongst us. My ears rang like the J. Arthur Rank gong, and the shock had been such that I felt it prudent to check and see whether the recoil had torn up the deck. The gunners grinned at each other. They knew they had caught us unawares — and they had ear plugs. We fell back ten yards and got ready to cover our ears if anyone else produced a powder bag. But that was it; the shoot was over.

As the *Cavina* snouted on, the weather deteriorated and the sea grew rougher with each passing day. Ahead, the masts of the Liberty ships traced a wider arc across the sky. Without those masts, or any other obvious indicators, a normal observer could have given an accurate description of the prevailing weather from one glance around the dining room at mealtime. The vacancies were eloquent. I checked their growing number with a faint touch of pride and blessed the heredity that had made me such a magnificent natural sailor.

The hurricane hit us a few hours later.

The afternoon of the fifth day, the wind began to rise above the 20 or 30 mile per hour strength we had grown used to. By dusk it was well over 50 and gave every indication of growing worse. We were no longer merely riding a heavy swell. Sitting braced in our chairs in the lounge, we could feel the enormous power of billows which lofted the *Cavina* upward for long, long seconds, rolling and twisting, then pitched her sickeningly down the other side, extracting a chorus of protesting creaks and cracks from her old beams. I decided I would forego the evening meal, purely in the interests of trimming my 128 pound figure, and ventured up to the deck entrance to see what was happening outside.

What was happening was dreadful. The gale had lashed the sea into a churning, heaving mountain range with peaks which capered madly under the blasts, then tore loose in driving sheets. Periodically waves pounded savagely along our starboard side.

Approaching us from the stern, a corvette zig-zagged its way past — the zigs and zags being in the vertical plane — its shuttered Aldis lamp flashing in rapid bursts against the gloom as it attempted vainly to keep its charges near their stations. I decided to watch for a few minutes to see whether it sank; but it slowly roller-coastered its way ahead to the first Liberty ship, just visible in the murk and spray, carrying my eye again to those waving masts. In this terrible sea they were heeling drunkenly from side to side, sweeping out tremendous arcs, with the ship seeming almost to capsize before fighting its way slowly upward again to repeat the hair-raising roll on the opposite side.

It was while I was staring fascinated at the terrible rhythm of those masts that the realization came upon me that environment, not heredity, was what really counted in a situation such as this and that even if my family tree had included all the Admirals from Horatio Nelson to John Jellicoe, I was still going to be desperately sick. I set course for the appropriate chamber below — it was like struggling over the tilted floors of the Crazy House — where I strained and choked through an interminable period, heaving as though trying to lift myself up with my shoelaces. When I was too weak to roar any more, I teetered back down the pitching corridor, one arm against the wall, the other towing my lifebelt along the floor.

The wind rose to hurricane strength and went beyond it to shriek for hours at 90 miles per hour, driving the sea to an ever greater fury. I clung to my bunk and wallowed in misery all night listening to the sledgehammer blows of the waves and not really caring any more whether we floated or sank.

By ten AM the following day the *Cavina* had come through the worst of it, and so had I. I cleaned up and headed for the deck again, by-passing the dining saloon. Outside I gazed around in bewilderment at the sight that met my bloodshot eyes. As the Ancient Mariner put it so clearly, we were "Alone, alone, all, all alone, alone on a wide wide sea." There was no trace of the convoy whatever — not a ship, not a wisp of smoke. The sea still raged, but it was a sane rage now, an ordinary storm, which I knew we could weather.

The *Cavina* had weathered a battle and bore scars attesting to its violence. The lifeboat directly in front of me had been pounded into kindling; a few feet further along the starboard side of the ship her plates had actually been breached by the force of the waves, necessitating some running repairs. Later, when the sea had subsided a little, the crew rigged a scaffold over the side and two men climbed out on this precarious perch and began to work. As I watched them moving coolly about on their narrow planks a few feet above the surging water, I experienced the gnawing tension that trapeze artists generate when performing without a net.

We had earlier been told that if anyone fell overboard, our ships would not be allowed to stop for any rescue attempt. However, we were no longer in convoy, and my first thought was that the rule against stopping might be waived if one of these men were to have an accident. Then I realized that it probably wouldn't make any difference whether the rule remained in force or not. With the sea running the way it was, it would be next to impossible to launch a small boat. My final thought on the matter was that the question was largely academic; the waters of the North Atlantic were now so frigid that a man bobbing in a life jacket would probably stay alive for only a few minutes anyway.

Seasickness was now practically universal among the *Cavina's* passengers. The dining room staff had few meals to serve, and below decks any tour along the corridors was made to an offstage obligato of strangled heaving from the uniformly green-gilled airmen behind the cabin doors. For two more days I curtailed the number of my visits to the dining room, and when I did force myself to eat, there was much

A convoy takes shape in Bedford Basin. (PAC)

The Ocean Boarding Vessel, HMS Cavina.   (IWM)

Anna Neagle won international acclaim with her performance as Queen Victoria in the movie "Sixty Glorious Years". In 1942 Billy Bishop, who had flown with her husband Herbert Wilcox in WW I, persuaded her to tour Canada with other stars on a bond drive. Here she is seen with the Air Commodore in command of the RCAF in Calgary.

(John Shipley, Shipley Photo Service, Calgary)

These two photographs show typical convoy scenes, and a couple of the methods
employed to protect them—a CAM-ship (Catapult Armed Merchantman) with a Hurricane
aboard and a Merchant Aircraft Carrier with two Swordfish.

Above: The Fw 200C Condor was a significant threat to Allied shipping because of its range. Apart from being able to bomb ships (this aircraft from KG 40 has two ship kills marked on its fin), they played an important role in vectoring U-Boats towards convoys.

(GG Hopp)

Below: An Fw 190 fighter-bomber of the type used on 'tip-and-run' raids against England. It was just such an aircraft that broadened the author's education shortly after his arrival in Bournemouth.

(USAF)

unessential fork work devoted to pushing aside the soggy overburden of potatoes and vegetables in search of a morsel or two with an appearance of edibility.

During this period every meal was a two-way experience. Progress of the upper alimentary canal toward normal operational efficiency was readily measurable by the slowly lengthening interval between the intake and exhaust strokes. The odors below deck played a significant part in retarding our recovery. The dining saloon was permeated with stale smells; a discriminating nose could readily identify the entrees of the last nine meals served, going back to Tuesday's breakfast kippers. This situation was not the crew's fault. All the portholes were dogged shut so that after dark no stray beam of light might escape to betray the convoy's position, and every vestibule opening onto the deck was swathed in stifling layers of black-out shielding. The result was that much of the time there was virtually no movement of air below decks and the atmosphere approached the solid state.

We learned that the navy brass shared the RCAF's basic operational premise: tell the vast majority of the people most directly affected by your plans and decisions absolutely nothing. This grand old service concept clearly had much to recommend it so far as the decision makers were concerned, since people who had been given no clue of the plan in the first place were hardly in an advantageous position to criticize it if it proved less than brilliant. The practice carried with it the incidental advantage that a totally specious but plausible-sounding argument could be made in its support — a one word argument delivered with impressive solemnity: Security.

The principle was applied rigorously now. The *Cavina*, sole survivor of the convoy for all we knew, began to steam at 15 knots instead of her earlier nine. The questions we had as to what had become of the convoy, where our escort had gone, why we had stepped up our speed, and whether we were going to join the convoy again, went unanswered.

We resumed what had become our chief form of recreation — playing bridge in the lounge. This was a bridge game, however, in which the talents of Ely Culbertson would have availed him nought, for after a few days we had tired of the orthodox rules of play and developed a code of our own. In our game, normal bidding technique was heavily supplemented by every hint and gesture capable of conveying information to one's partner. When the hand was being played the defenders relied heavily upon similar imaginative aids. To signal your partner to lead a diamond, for example, the Freddie Taylor convention called simply for a slow raising of the third finger, left hand. Whistling the opening phrase of Peg o' My Heart also avoided any strain, suspense, or surprise regarding the suit of the ensuing lead. A very apropos comment on the powers of deduction of Sam Spade had the desired result, as did a sudden steering of the conversation to the probable cost of membership in some outlandishly named club.

Reneging was considered excellent form, particularly if it went undetected, and it was routinely attempted whenever circumstances promised a better than even chance of success. Animated conversational flurries to distract declarer and reduce the likelihood of detection were frequent, and throughout the playing of a hand it was sound strategy on the part of the defenders to memorize the cards in dummy, for declarer was often moved to switch cards from dummy to his hand and vice versa, in the interests of maintaining a satisfactory degree of flexibility in situs of the lead.

Declarer's partner was expected to remain active in our game. Discharging this added responsibility entailed much "stretching of the legs" and visiting the toilet, and the maintaining of a high level of surveillance on the return journey to the table, following which meaningful looks were cast either to right or left at critical moments, the whole support manoeuvre resulting in the declarer's success rate in attempted finesses shattering all mathematical laws of probability. All in all we found "convoy bridge" a much more diverting and satisfying game than the denatured discipline espoused by Culbertson, Blackwood, et al, and we worked faithfully at devising new and more outrageous signals.

Next day our speed tapered off again as the great convoy reformed. How widely we had been scattered by the hurricane we never did find out, nor whether our escorts had somehow pulled all the ships together after the scattering — remembering that they could not break radio silence — or had flashed a rendezvous signal to each ship before the hurricane had cast us apart.

Three or four nights after the hurricane, as I sat chatting with Freddie Taylor in his cabin, he turned the conversation in an unexpected direction.

"Listen, Skeezix," he said, "there's a guy on the second sitting that owns a crown and anchor board — you know, not a regular board but one of those oilcloth kind you can roll up. I've spoken to him a couple of times and I think he would sell it. How would it be if I see how much he wants — you and I could buy it off him and go partners on the winnings. What say?"

I knew little about crown and anchor, having only a hazy recollection of the big circular boards that made their appearance once a year at the midway on the fair grounds. With identical frequency, I seemed to remember, howls would go up from the local sports, who swore that the wheels were gaffed — hence my general impression that crown and anchor as a recreational art stank slightly of fraud.

"No, not for me, thanks, Freddie", I replied. "I can think of better ways of losing money than gambling."

"Hell, crown and anchor isn't gambling", he laughed, "it's stealing. Just let me get hold of that board and I'll have every dime on the ship by the time we hit England."

How he financed its purchase, and on what terms, I do not know; but a day or two later he took me to his cabin to show me the new acquisition, simply a heavy black oilcloth ruled into columns with the various signs embossed in red and gold — complete with the dice. Freddie was now ready to provide tuition to all comers in the fine art of crown and anchor dice rolling.

It was at this stage of our crossing that the aircrew began to be called upon to take turns standing watch and manning the Oerlikons during the daylight hours. We deduced that we had now come within the operational radius of the Focke-Wulf Condors, the Germans' four engined maritime reconnaissance bomber whose primary mission was to search for convoys and report their positions for U-boat packs. The Condors were not yet restricted to searching, however, and during the months immediately preceding our crossing had inflicted heavy losses on lightly defended convoys with their bombs (they could carry loads varying between 3300 and 4600 pounds) and their cannon. From this point on we would remain within range of either the Biscay based or the Norwegian based Condor groups, and it behooved us to increase the numbers of our lookouts.

The aircrew stood only two-hour watches; but, if my experience was representative, after the first hour the additional safety factor stemming from our presence was too small to measure. The weather was frigid and the wind on deck cut like a knife. The sailors came to their posts bundled up like Arctic explorers, which was advisable if you wanted to be able to do anything after standing beside your gun for an hour. We were given no extra clothing whatever, and I showed up regularly in my parade ground greatcoat and dapper black unlined gloves. In half an hour I felt as though I were standing in a blizzard in a wet bathing suit. My eyes were so full of tears and freezing spray that if a Condor had collided with our mast I would only have been able to guess from the noise, and if anyone had sounded the alarm, my hands were so numb I'd still have been fumbling trying to untie the frozen gun shroud when the attackers were landing back at base. I came to have a great admiration for the sailors who stood four-hour watches regularly. With all the warm clothing you could pull on, standing out in that December wind and spray was no picnic.

The days dragged by slowly, and Freddie Taylor's foresight in acquiring the crown and anchor board was clearly demonstrated. The routine got to be bridge in the morning and afternoon, when the necessity of standing watches did not shatter our organization beyond repair, followed by crown and anchor in Freddie's cabin in the evening. Due to the very limited size of the casino, only four or five people on the very best of terms could be accommodated at one time. Although I was not a cash customer in the early rounds of the financial flogging that Freddie methodically administered, because of my special status as a very close friend I was allowed to hold a purely watching brief — I felt like the official witness at an execution.

After the first hour's play it was apparent that no one in his right mind would play crown and anchor in the expectation of leaving the game wealthier than he had entered. The odds were at least three to one in the operator's favour, and Freddie was surely the operator. Nevertheless, despite the patent inevitability of bankruptcy, every member of the group played at one time or another on the crossing. It was worth more than a few dollars, after all, to sit and pass the time pleasantly with friends, rolling the dice, making the odd side bet — the only kind that left you with a fighting chance — and pooh-poohing the gloomy reports we began to get at breakfast from our waiters when the dull thud of explosions had been felt during the preceding night.

When the handwriting on the wall unmistakably spelled mass insolvency, several strongly motivated entrepreneurs formed syndicates capable of mustering impressive blocks of capital — one as much as 50 dollars — and attempted to buy the board from Freddie. Freddie refused to sell at any price, knowing that he would harvest the 50 dollars in due course anyway — which he did, together with the other embryo capitalizations. It was our good fortune that Freddie was as generous as he was astute. He could have kept us in a state of thralldom until we got paid in England; instead all his friends and acquaintances, including me, got their money back in the form of interest free loans; but Freddie hung on to his oilcloth money machine, and his accounts receivable grew more imposing with every passing day.

A slow convoy journey was a far cry indeed from the pleasure-laden routine of a peacetime crossing; but our crew did everything they could to fend off the war and make the trip as much like a peacetime excursion for us as they could. Thus, disregarding the ever-present threat of torpedoes, the freezing weather, and a host of petty limitations and discomforts they could not avoid, they staged a traditional ship's concert for us on our fifteenth night at sea.

With Anna Neagle aboard everyone expected the star turn from her; and we were not disappointed. With next to nothing in the way of props or lighting she did a brief scene from her latest movie, and even we Philistines could appreciate her artistry. While no one else on the program came within hailing distance of her ability, there were two turns at the end of the program which made an impression.

The first of these featured as a singer the waiter who served our table in the dining saloon. He was a cheerful little character, even when swamped with work; here, in front of an appreciative audience, enjoying himself, he was effervescent, and he had a very pleasant voice.

A young man with a funny monologue followed. He pronounced the audience most receptive, in fact it was quite the most sensitive and responsive audience he had ever encountered, he said. He guessed that every single spectator in it must be far above average in responsiveness. Having reached that conclusion, he said, he would like to put his theory to the test with a couple of volunteers from the audience.

He gazed directly at one of the very few women in the audience and quickly persuaded her to volunteer. Blindfolding the woman, he silently recruited one of our pilots as his second assistant, while saying in a loud voice to the woman that he wished her to strain her imaginative faculties to the utmost for the next few minutes to induce a belief that everything he told her was true — much of it would be factually correct, he assured her, and if she entered unreservedly into the experiment he was certain she could demonstrate a state of empathy and responsiveness to suggestion far above average, thus preserving his reputation before this eager audience. He asked her again to strain her imagination to the utmost. She nodded.

"Very well", he said, "imagine yourself to be in Trafalgar Square. What lofty column can you sense towering immediately before you?"

"Nelson's monument" the young woman responded firmly.

"Absolutely right" said our tester, "and now I should like you to imagine that you are being transported to the very top of that great monument, 170 feet above the square. Standing directly in front of you now is Admiral Horatio Nelson."

He carried on: "Now take a moment and capture this impression thoroughly, because standing only a few inches before you is Lord Nelson himself; the great Admiral as he was when he stood on the deck of his flagship *Victory*. Have you captured that feeling? Can you sense that a living person, Horatio Nelson, is standing facing you just 12 inches in front of you?"

"Yes I can", said the woman, which was not surprising, for there was a living person standing a foot in front of her in the person of the other volunteer, the pilot. On whispered instructions he had taken his right arm out of its sleeve, and tucked the end of the empty sleeve in his tunic pocket.

"You may recall", said the tester, "that at Tenerife in 1797 Nelson lost his right arm. Let me have your left hand a moment —

there that's it — now reach out gently and feel the right sleeve of the Admiral's coat."

She started somewhat as she touched the sleeve and realized that something, or someone, was there. She checked a few inches of the empty sleeve between her thumb and finger, and one could sense the stirrings of pity and distaste at the dismemberment.

The tester was speaking again: "You may also remember that before this, in 1794, off Calvi in Corsica, Nelson lost his right eye, and that thereafter he always wore an eye patch? Here, take your right hand and touch the unwounded side of his face — see, you are touching his cheek bone. Now put your arm down for a moment and concentrate. Am I right in assuming that you can visualize with complete realism that the poor, blind, one-armed Admiral stands right here before you? Is it as vivid to your mind as I feel it to be?"

"Oh yes," breathed the woman, a trifle nervously, "it is very vivid."

As the tester had been speaking, he had quietly sliced an orange in half, and with the paring knife handed to him by one of the crew, cut a hollow the size of a quarter in the centre of the half he held, holding it towards us so that we could see it, meanwhile touching his lips to command silence as he beckoned the pilot away and stepped up beside the woman again.

"Now let's take your right hand again — just raise it and extend the index finger please, that's it — and you may touch the other side of the Admiral's face." (Here he gripped her raised hand with one of his and guided her outstretched finger slowly toward the hole in the orange.) "Oh, goodness, watch it, you're going right up under his eye patch" he called, and before she could withdraw jabbed her finger suddenly into the centre of the orange.

Her scream froze the blood in my veins. The fact that we had been braced for her reaction made us start all the more violently when it came.

Quick as a flash they whipped the blindfold from her eyes and showed her the "socket" which her well stimulated imagination had made so revoltingly realistic. She was a good sport, laughed at the violent distress she had exhibited, and got a great round of applause when she laid her hand on her bosom and heaved an exaggerated sigh of relief.

The morning after the concert, our sixteenth day aboard the *Cavina,* we spotted land on the horizon off to starboard, and at a very early hour we dropped anchor briefly in Belfast Lough before steaming on south through the Irish Sea. After we passed the Isle of Man, part of our convoy altered course to southeast, presumably making for Liverpool. I was as anxious as Columbus to set foot on terra firma again, but although we ploughed on steadily the whole day, dusk found us cruising once more at 15 knots, but still at sea. We did not know — and of course were not told — that we were approaching St. David's Head and would soon be swinging east into the Bristol Channel. When we climbed into our bunks the old ship was still hard at it. Sometime before dawn on the seventeenth day I sensed a great change having taken place and woke to find the engines off and the ship obviously snubbed up to a wharf. I went up on deck where I spied a solitary old gentleman in a battered yachting cap working away at some cases piled under a shielded light. At my shouted inquiry he told me we were docked in Avonmouth, a few miles down-river from Bristol. I went back to bed happy; after 17 days we had safely crossed the Atlantic and were now ready to begin our overseas careers. A few hours later we disembarked and took the train to Bournemouth, a city on the south coast about 80 miles southwest of London, site of No. 3 Personnel Receiving Centre, RCAF.

CHAPTER 6

BOURNEMOUTH – LEAVE –
ENGLISH MAP READING

Auld Ayr, wham ne'er a town surpasses
For honest men and bonnie lasses.

Robert Burns: *Tam O'Shanter*

Bournemouth was a lovely city in which to be introduced to the war-time way of life in England. In happier times it had been a restful south-coast haven, catering not so much to the younger, racy set, as to the middle-aged and older citizenry, who thronged there to enjoy its mild climate, beautiful beaches and headlands, its stately gardens and lush parks, and the handsome pavilion in which brass band and orchestra concerts, tea dances, and a variety of other pleasant affairs were presented. Over the years the city had accumulated a vast number of palatial hotels to handle the ever-increasing flow of resort traffic, but war had transformed the peaceful aspect of the city.

Now the beaches were heavily mined, all access to them barred by coils of rust-encrusted barbed wire. The elegant hotels had fallen on evil days, having been taken over by the Air Ministry and filled with transient Canadian airmen, most of whom must have struck their hosts as over-active thyroid cases compared with the sedate clientele of earlier years. Nevertheless, the city's beauty remained apparent despite the dense influx of boisterous servicemen. Our own small group, comprising 11 destitute ex-crown and anchor players, together with the opulent retired casino proprietor, found itself billeted in a tiny but immaculate hotel called Burley Court. A four-minute walk took us to the officers' mess, located almost on the sea front in the Royal Bath

Hotel. It was here in the swank Royal Bath that we were first exposed, on the first anniversary of Pearl Harbor, to the attractive appearance and appalling taste and texture of powdered eggs, which frequently masqueraded, marooned on a slice of parched toast with a small piece of grease-drenched Spam, as a hearty breakfast. With the powdered eggs we were sure we had experienced the culinary nadir, until our "chef" initiated us properly with his brussels sprouts.

The function of the Personnel Receiving Centre was to act as a holding unit and get us prepared for more flying training as soon as the Advanced Flying Units should make space available for new drafts. The first order of business was to issue us with battle dress and a generous allotment of clothing coupons which we would need for every article of clothing we bought thereafter. Next we had our photographs taken and were issued with our Form 1250 Identification Cards. On December 12th, six days after our arrival, we drew top quality new flying equipment: suits, silk and fleece-lined boots, chamois leather gloves, helmets and goggles. But although we now had the equipment, we were pretty sure from the crumbs of information we gleaned in a dozen different offices that we would not be going to any flying school until after Christmas.

Meantime we heard our first air raid sirens. In six days we experienced three alerts, all false alarms — at least we saw no sign of enemy aircraft. We flattered ourselves that we had adapted quickly to the eerie wail of the siren — it had sounded ominous the first time — and felt a trifle heroic marching disdainfully down the street ignoring the warnings. Our fine exhibition of *élan* was actually a manifestation of stupidity and a year or so later the RCAF in Bournemouth would pay dearly for treating the tip and run raiders so casually.

It wasn't too much later that I was out walking with Freddie Taylor on a headland overlooking the sea. It was a lovely day, and after half or three-quarters of an hour's brisk walking we sat down at the top of a narrow cut where we could dangle our legs, and lay back on our elbows enjoying the clear sweep out to sea and this wonderful example of Bournemouth's salubrious climate. There was a slight chop on the sea, causing continuously varying shades of light on a million waves to rise and fall in a mesmerizing cadence. I became vaguely aware that two small dark areas, unlike the others, were remaining unchanged, then realized that I was looking at two aircraft skimming towards us over the water.

"Here's a couple of our fighters coming back," I said to Freddie, taking four or five seconds to direct his gaze to them.

He murmured in assent and we watched to see what they would turn out to be, for they were still too far out to identify.

From our first day at Bournemouth we had frequently seen flights of Spitfires pass overhead, cleaving the air with the thrilling whispering whistle that was their trademark at speed, and we assumed that these two dots speeding at us were two of our fighters returning from patrol. They had grown a bit larger now and began to take shape.

"Christ, Freddie, they're Focke-Wulfs!" I blurted, sitting bolt upright as a I suddenly realized the significance of the radial engines racing at us six or seven hundred yards away.

As we both stared, fascinated, spouts of water leaped from the waves directly in front of the aircraft, and a second later we heard the rapid cough of a Bofors gun mounted down the coast. Simultaneously the two Fw 190's climbed abruptly and veered sharply to our right heading down the coast toward Poole as the air raid sirens began their banshee wail. Freddie and I exchanged vacuous stares. The Fw 190's should have been easy enough to identify, even head-on, had we first postulated the possibility of enemy aircraft intruding into our peaceful refuge. We left with a more realistic assessment of the possibilities, keenly aware that if our two German counterparts hadn't had bigger fish to fry, they could have terminated the war for us with one touch of the firing button. We headed for home, now keeping a hawk-like lookout to seaward until we got within sprinting distance of some air raid shelters.

We paraded twice a day, at 9:00 AM and again at 1:30 PM. There was so little work to be done that frequently we were dismissed immediately after roll call. This relaxation of the more onerous routine to which we were accustomed had an immediate effect: everyone became bone lazy and wanted to do even less. Many and varied were the facilities generously put at our disposal by the good burghers of Bournemouth, from archery ranges and cricket pitches to golf courses and sailing facilities. One day shortly after our arrival, we were marched to a theatre, where representatives of various clubs spoke to us outlining the facilities available and offering them for our use. A tennis enthusiast in our group queried one woman as to how early the courts would be open.

"Oh, we shall open up for you chaps any time at all, don't you know," chirped madam secretary; "if you find the clubhouse locked, you just go to the little house beside it and knock up the custodian."

She blinked in happy bewilderment as the hall rocked to laughter, applause, and roars of "Yes please!"

On several occasions we marched to a large indoor pool, known as Linden Hall Hydro, where we spent the afternoon swimming and practising crawling into rubber dinghies thrown onto the surface of the pool. These parades were a sore trial to the elderly English Squadron Leader who marched us down to the Hydro. When we first formed up, there would be much jockeying for position, the desirable location being as far as possible from the head end of the column. As soon as the roll had been called, the Squadron Leader would take his position at the front and move the parade off in column of route. Two hundred yards from the beginning of our march the road took a moderate curve to the left. From the moment he entered that first curve, the Squadron Leader began losing men faster than an Italian general in North Africa, as everyone safely out of his sight in the rear platoon ran for the sidewalk and immediately began walking in the opposite direction. English roads being what they were, the rate of attrition was fearful. Even where the road was straight, desertion was rampant; airmen would swing aboard slow moving buses, going either way, or step up on the sidewalk where a group of people offered concealment and walk into a shop. We would arrive at the Hydro with our original complement of 90 reduced by escapes to about 20, at which point the Squadron Leader would pull out his list and call off the 90 names. What bothered him was that every name he called was answered; in fact plans had had to be made so loosely and spontaneously for this contingency that embarrassing lapses occurred in which duets or even trios were heard in response to one name. There was a remedy for this sort of horseplay, of course, but the old Squadron Leader was too much of a gentleman to collect the ID cards of all those present and mark the rest absent.

Shooting crap on top of a tightly made bed in Burley Court was a common pastime for the period between lunch and the 1:30 parade. The stakes were necessarily miniscule, since we had not been paid since we left Canada — and in fact were not going to be paid in cash any more. As officers, we would now have £21 per month deposited to our account in a bank of our choice, and the balance of our pay sent home or held to our credit.

On one occasion when the lunch hour game broke up, I was on my way out the door with Freddie Taylor to attend the 1:30 parade when Barrie Dean called out and asked me to answer his name on parade, saying that he wanted to leave immediately to go downtown to a show. With some misgivings, I said I would. No sooner had we fallen in than the old Squadron Leader trumpeted:

"Pilot Officer Charles."

A voice shouted in reply: "Sir!"

"Pilot Officer Dean."

I had no time to think; I had to respond. I shouted "Sir!"

"Those two men fall out," said the Squadron Leader.

Pilot Officer Charles' feet began crunching on the gravel. I stood frozen for a moment, wondering what to do. The old Squadron Leader clearly had some special business to transact with these two, and I

113

could foresee serious trouble if I got myself trapped into signing documents or doing something else for Dean. I decided I'd better straighten this out in a hurry. The old boy was beginning to look questioningly in my general direction, since there was only one man approaching him and no sound of anyone else moving. Hastily pasting a doubtful look on my face, I walked out from the centre rank, past the front rank, and said:

"Did you say Peden, sir?"

The old gentleman looked at me, hard. I could practically hear him saying the names over to himself and concluding that there was a possibility — damned slight — of my having been mistaken.

"No, I did not. I want Pilot Officer Dean."

"Sorry sir" I said, edging my way discreetly back into anonymity.

"Pilot Officer Dean." Once more he shouted. There was no sound. He scribbled emphatically on his paper, glared in my general direction, then called the balance of the roll and dismissed us, sending the first officer, Charles, to the Paymaster to get some pay assignment tangle straightened out.

About 4:00 PM Dean came rolling home merrily, evidently having enjoyed himself all afternoon. I told him what had happened, and suggested that he cover his tracks by rushing over to the MO with a cock and bull story about a persistent, ghastly headache, procuring some aspirin to get his name in the MO's book, and telling our Squadron Leader, when taxed next morning with being absent, that he had been compelled to go to the MO for medication.

Dean left, on the fly, to fabricate an alibi with adequate corroborative detail, expressing his earnest gratitude for my co-operation as he ran out:

"Might have known you'd screw everything up, Peden," he said.

After dinner, with his tracks well and truly covered, he relaxed and prepared to bait Freddie Taylor. This was Dean's favourite sport, although he was careful not to get serious, for Freddie stood about six foot one, and was as lithe as a fencing foil.

"Going out tonight, eh Freddie?" he said, as Freddie slapped on some shaving lotion and picked out a fresh collar.

"Yes, boys, I am," Freddie smiled, "taking out the mayor's daughter again."

Barrie let that one pass, then tried another barb.

"Wilton tells me you were sucking up to that Limey Squadron Leader this afternoon trying to get an extra travel warrant."

Freddie gave himself a final fast check in the mirror, headed for the door as he pulled on his hat, then paused by Barrie's bed and clapped him paternally on the shoulder:

"You know, Barrie, I learned a long while ago that there are only two kinds of people in this world: suckholes, and assholes. I see you're still in the last group."

He swept out, leaving the rest of us chortling. But this was a running battle. Barrie made a few inquiries the following day, and somehow found out that the "mayor's daughter" was a nurse working at a nearby hospital. He spread the word. That night, as Freddie completed the preparatory grooming and headed once more for the door, Barrie spoke to him again, turning a page thoughtfully in his magazine, and expressing himself ever so casually:

"Stuck with the old pot-juggler again tonight, are you Freddie?"

Even Freddie collapsed in laughter at Barrie's choice of terminology.

With a lot of spare time on our hands, Freddie and I began to go to the gym every day for a workout. Our PT instructor was always there, a muscular English boy, a couple of years older than we were. He would work with us for an hour or so, going over the various tricks and holds that he had earlier demonstrated in the unarmed combat class, then leave us to practise by ourselves. I was just as fast as Freddie, but he was bigger, heavier, and stronger; and he used to remind me pointedly that a good big man could always beat a good little man.

Freddie was a friend in whom I had developed a special interest. After leaving school, he had worked as a lumberjack for a while in British Columbia. Because of his height and strength, he had later found a job in the mental institution at Essondale. After leaving that job, he had become involved in some sort of trouble — he was never specific — something that had caused a serious break between him and his father. Whatever it was, it had prompted his father to be contemptuously critical of Freddie, and the words he had used still festered in Freddie's mind. "I'll show him," was Freddie's constant thought, demonstrated by conduct every day, and expressed to me in so many words on one occasion when we were exchanging confidences, and he had reviewed with satisfaction his career in the Air Force thus far, and particularly his winning a commission as a Pilot Officer. But Freddie's determination was a positive feeling; he was going to prove his father's judgement wrong for the purpose of winning back his father's respect, not to flaunt success in his father's face as the basis for more recriminations. The sting of the reproach must have burned his soul like acid. His self-respect was tainted until the judgement was reversed. By the time we were at Bournemouth, Freddie and I had grown so close that I had unconsciously taken up his cause as my own, and waited hopefully for the day when some message from his home would signal a change of heart. Meanwhile Freddie's daily vow to himself was to prove his father wrong.

On December 22nd we were all given travel warrants and seven days leave. My father had come from Scotland as a boy, and still had relatives there, so there was only one place I wanted to go. The problem was money. We had received no pay for weeks — and were not going to receive any until our records caught up with us and the Air Force got untracked. I had filled in a form designating the London branch of the Bank of Montreal as the depository to which my pay should be sent; but the cupboard there was still bare. With only a handful of change and some big plans, I headed for Freddie Taylor. Several acquaintances had headed in the same direction at superior speed, and the best Freddie could do for me, leaving himself rather strapped, was three pounds. I foresaw seven days with many railway station lunches of a glass of water and a fly-bitten doughnut, but decided that a Scotch-Canadian could do it on three pounds if anyone could, and that I might be able to borrow another pound or two from some other Samaritan. I packed my big trunk in a touch under 30 seconds, and lugged it to the train.

I reached London about two that afternoon, and, recalling that it was Tuesday and still within banking hours, I squandered three shillings on a taxi and dismounted at 9 Waterloo Place, Pall Mall, the London office of the Bank of Montreal. From past experience I was not optimistic about the possibility of drawing money out of the bank before I had put any in, but deemed it worth a try.

In two minutes I was sitting in the manager's office explaining that I would lose a lot of weight on my Scottish tour if I couldn't get an advance of five pounds, mentioning also that I had designated his bank as the future holder of my funds. I was prepared to fall on my knees and shriek for mercy if that procedure seemed to hold promise; but before I had even finished the truthful portion of my story, the manager rang for the accountant and, without asking to see my identification card, instructed him to open an account in my name and bring in a five-pound advance. As I thanked him sincerely for his kindness he smiled and said:

"My boy is in the RAF. He has been training these last months in the States and Canada, and his letters are full of nice things people have done for him over there. I'm pleased to get the opportunity to treat a Canadian or an American the way they've been treating him. Are you sure now that five pounds will be enough?"

I assured him that eight pounds, which I now had, was more money than I had had in my pocket since I joined the Air Force, and left the good-hearted gentleman with a warm handshake and a warmer glow in my bosom.

I decided to ride over to the station from which my night train for Glasgow left, confirm the details of my warrant with the RTO

(Railway Transport Officer), check my cumbersome trunk, and then go and see some sights, starting with Buckingham Palace. I elected to travel on the underground, and went downstairs at the nearby station for my first look at tube travel.

The system was so well signed, and the maps so clear, that I had no difficulty getting to the railway station. On the subsequent tube journey to Buckingham Palace, I found myself sitting next to a window, and my eye was drawn to two signs, one authorized, the other somewhat anti-establishment, but definitely relevant. The transit authority sign had reference to the woven fibre material which covered the train windows completely, except for a small eliptical hole in the centre. Through this hole, if one craned one's neck sufficiently, the platform signs could be seen. The material had been installed as a safety measure to prevent shards of glass flying about in a blast, for the trains went to the surface (where they could be bombed) on some lines, and ran above ground for considerable distances. The authorized sign pictured, with strong reprobative overtones, a passenger scraping the fibre off the glass with his penkife. Below the picture appeared this prim chastisement:

"Pardon us for our correction
But this is here for your protection."

A heavily inked arrow led my gaze eight inches to the right, below an irregularly shaped porthole, recently hacked through the fibre by penknife or nail file, to the scrawled rebuttal of an unrepentant rebel:

*"That's OK Jack, but for your information
I want to see my f - - - ing station."*

There was something about the idiom that stamped it as Canadian composition beyond the shadow of a doubt.

I walked over to the Palace for my first look at the impressive old edifice. Two sentries stood, 40 yards apart, outside the lofty ornamental iron fence. As I strolled past the base of Queen Victoria's monument, taking everything in from a distance of at least 100 feet, both sentries suddenly snapped to attention, sloped arms with rigid precision, and delivered butt salutes with a slap like a beaver tail hitting the water. I realized vaguely that an officer of less than field rank must have passed by, and glanced back to see if someone had disappeared through the gate. No one was in sight, and I meandered another 50 feet before the realization suddenly came to me that these immaculately turned out robots had been saluting me. I resolved to correct the poor impression I had undoubtedly left by failing to acknowledge the salute. I carried on 100 yards beyond the second sentry, then turned back, this time at a parade ground pace, suitable to Buckingham Palace or a High River attention area, to do the job properly. Now I marched to the beat of a Guards' band playing "Imperial Echoes", audible only to me. At 25 yards, the first sentry, standing at ease, tapped his rifle butt sharply on the pavement twice, obviously the signal for his partner to begin counting. Seconds later they came smartly to attention, in perfect unison, and sloped arms. As I approached the nearer sentry, the butt salute flashed again. This time I snapped back a salute that fairly whistled. Flight Sergeant Fines, bless his rugged heart, would have led three rousing cheers and erased the work parade record completely.

I caught the train for Glasgow a few hours later, and in the morning, after a sleepless ride to that city, rattled on down to the tiny station at Dalrymple. It was a hilly mile from the station to Aunt Minnie's house on Garden Street, and after lugging my big trunk the first quarter of the distance, I resolved to travel a good deal lighter on my next journey.

I got a royal welcome, and for three days Min and her neighbours fussed over me, filled me with "halesome" food, including haggis, and made me feel at home. Min unearthed the swagger stick my father had left with her in Paisley during the first war, and every morning, after a good breakfast, I would take it and go for an early tramp along the banks of the Doon, which tumbled by in its rocky bed 100 yards from Min's door. The second day, I walked over to Maybole, my father's birthplace. He had walked it for fun, many a time as a boy, or so he had told me. I found that they had moved the town over a good bit since he'd been there — it was six long Scottish miles, and I concluded that the children of his day must either have been a little simple or else hard up for games. Since he had asked me to inquire after a boyhood friend of his named Tom McEwan, I set out to see if I could trace him. When last heard of, a few years before, Tom had lived on Dailly Road, so there I began my quest. It was late afternoon when I began, and 9:00 PM when I gave up. In the interval I had unearthed half a dozen McEwans, none of them related to the one I was looking for, and none in possession of any information except the address of another McEwan who might know where to find my father's friend. All told, I only walked about two or three miles during the five hours I hunted through Maybole; what took the time was the Scottish hospitality. None of these people even knew the man I sought; but when they heard the Canadian accent, they insisted that I come in while they got more particulars. Learning that my father and his parents had gone out to Canada from Maybole, every family I called on insisted on fixing me a cup of tea and a bite to eat, or pouring me "a wee nip" to ward off sunstroke, frostbite, or any other hazards I might be exposed to in carrying out my quest. I later found out that the Tom McEwan I was searching for had died some months before my arrival in Maybole; but in retrospect, I was glad I hadn't got the bad news at the first house.

On Christmas morning I went over to see Culzean Castle, ancestral

The following text appears on the inset inscription:

IN MEMORY
OF
ALEXANDER PEDEN,
(A NATIVE OF SORN)
THAT FAITHFUL MINISTER OF CHRIST, WHO
FOR HIS UNFLINCHING ADHERENCE TO THE
COVENANTED REFORMATION IN SCOTLAND, WAS
EXPELLED BY TYRANT RULERS FROM HIS PARISH
OF NEW LUCE, IMPRISONED FOR YEARS ON THE
BASS ROCK BY HIS PERSECUTORS, AND HUNTED
FOR HIS LIFE ON THE SURROUNDING MOUNTAINS
AND MOORS TILL HIS DEATH ON 26TH JANUARY 1686,
IN THE 60TH YEAR OF HIS AGE; AND HERE,
AT LAST, HIS DUST REPOSES IN PEACE AWAITING
THE RESURRECTION OF THE JUST.

SUCH WERE THE MEN THESE HILLS WHO TRODE,
STRONG IN THE LOVE AND FEAR OF GOD
DEFYING THROUGH A LONG DARK HOUR,
ALIKE THE CRAFT AND RAGE OF POWER

The monument to Alexander Peden, the doughty old Covenanter, at Old Cumnock, and *inset* the inscription on the monument.

(Rod Peden)

Tommy Penkuri during his early flying training.   (Jack Anderson)

Above: An RAF Tiger Moth R-4960, on loan to 402 Sqn. RCAF at High Post. The RAF Tigers differed from the Canadian DH 82C (below) in a number of respects — no canopy, wide wooden struts, no tail wheel and a different main undercarriage strut angle because of the lack of brakes.   (Above Don Whelmes via Norm Malayney. below PAC PMR 76-597)

Above: "Fearless" and "Stoneface" (right) at Sywell, their Tiger Moth in the background.

This Canadian Airspeed Oxford, seen at Trenton in December 1939, is similar to the type operated by the RAF.

home of the Marquis of Ailsa. (It was the top floor of this magnificent building that was given to Dwight Eisenhower by Scotland at the end of the war as a token of gratitude for great service rendered.) On the seaward side below the cliff on which it stood were the caves that my father and his friends played in as boys — and in which, legend has it, Robert the Bruce hid from his pursuers six centuries before. On my way back, I was amazed to see the Scottish farmers toiling in their fields on Christmas Day. I had known from experience that New Year's, Hogmanay, was of special importance to Scots, but had never realized how little attention they paid to Christmas.

In the afternoon I travelled over to Old Cumnock to see the graveside monument of an ancestor, Alexander Peden, recognized as the leader of the Ayrshire Covenanters in his day. I had heard many a tale of "Peden the Prophet" from my old grandmother, tales of the bloody days when those ministers who still stood firm behind the National Covenant or the Solemn League and Covenant, were hunted for their very lives. Aunt Min spoke of it all as though she and her family had personally witnessed the atrocities she described in such harrowing detail. Such was the height of her indignation at times, as she recounted the attempts on "auld Sandy's" life, that I almost began to think she had seen him, and that my rough idea of the dates involved must be 250 years out. At the graveside I checked the dates on Sandy's monument, and found I had been approximately correct. He had been born at Auchincloich, in Sorn, in 1626, and died in 1686 after living in the shadow of the gallows for years for his preaching. When the word got around that Peden had died, a squad of soldiers hunted out the grave, dug up his body and buried it by the gallows in Old Cumnock as a final insult. His last resting place came to be a place of honour, and others, when their time came, sought to have their bones laid by Sandy's. In the old graveyard I looked at the modest monument subsequently raised to his memory and experienced the touch of pride that comes with being linked, however tenuous the connection, with a good man. His best known prayer, uttered when it looked as though he and a handful of his followers were going to be run to ground and dangled by their necks "to glorify God", ran thus[1]:

Lord, it is Thy enemy's day and power. They may not be idle, but hast Thou no other work for them but to send them after *us?* Send them after those to whom Thou wilt give strength to flee, for our strength is gone. Twine them about the hill Lord, and cast the lap of Thy cloak over old Sandy with thir poor things, and save us this one time and we will keep it in remembrance and tell it to the commendation of Thy goodness, pity and compassion.

---

1. See page 55 *The Covenanters of Ayrshire* by Rev. R. Lawson, J. & R. Parlane, Paisley.

Following this practical plea, a dense mist descended, and old Sandy and his parishioners made good their escape.

I had to start back for Bournemouth Saturday afternoon, so on Saturday morning I caught the bus into Ayr. I had to slip over to Alloway, of course, to pay homage at the bard's birthplace, and to work in a fast visit to his monument and the auld brig o'Doon; but another object of the trip was to buy all the groceries I could get on the ration coupons they had issued me for my leave. The rationed goods did not make a very impressive pile, but I added so many unrationed items — in order to re-stock Min's larder properly — that I found myself in need of a shopping bag well before I had finished picking things up. I took one from a pile near the check-out counter, a fancy net article priced at two shillings. When I came up to the counter ten minutes later, I set out all the groceries, but forgot to say anything to the comely lass on the cash register about the shopping bag itself. I had walked half the distance to the bus station before I remembered. If the bag had been a five-cent paper one, I would not have bothered — custodian of the great Covenanter's name or not — but this bag was worth half a dollar. I trudged back lugging my cargo of groceries and came up to the girl at the counter. "Miss," I said, "I'm sorry, but I walked out of here without paying you for the shopping bag."

She smiled shyly. "I ken," she said, "I didnae like to say onything because I could see ye had forgotten."

On this touching note of sensitivity, I ended my first visit to Ayr, concurring whole-heartedly with Robbie Burns' description of it:

Auld Ayr wham ne'er a town surpasses
For honest men and bonnie lasses.

I detoured on my way back to Bournemouth, travelling down to the camp of my favourite infantry regiment after I reached London. Princess Patricia's Canadian Light Infantry were stationed just out of Eastbourne, and I was hoping I could pay a surprise visit to my cousin, Jim McKie. I hadn't seen him since he had gone overseas with First Division in 1939.

With considerable difficulty I found the regiment, then Jim's company, then Jim's platoon, then Jim's bunk — empty. He had gone to Scotland on leave the day before, I was told, passing my south-bound train to London on the north-bound train to Glasgow. That was as close as I got to Jim McKie until the war was over. As I headed disconsolately out of the barracks, now conscious once more of the weight of that cursed trunk, a soldier lying on a top bunk further down the room took a close look at me and jumped to the floor.

"Hey, Doc, where are you going?" he called, coming over to grab me by the arm.

It was Eugene ("Joe") McKay from Portage la Prairie, an old

classmate from Portage Collegiate who had served in the militia (the Manitoba Mounted Rifles) at the same time I had. I would have been glad to see any familiar face at that point, after wandering about for half an hour meeting little but challenging glances; but running into Joe was a real bonus. I parked the trunk and sat with Joe, happily swapping news until my train time approached. It was the last time I ever saw him. (Eight months later, with the Pats in Sicily, he lay on the ground outside Leonforte, badly wounded. Jim McKie lit a cigarette, placed it between Joe's lips, and tried to make him comfortable, propping a haversack under his neck; but in a few minutes Joe McKay was gone.)

I got back to Bournemouth on December 28th just in time for our group's first mail call since leaving Canada. So far as mail from home was concerned, it was usually a feast or famine situation. I made a hurried check and found 21 letters waiting for me, including one from Mrs. Plate advising that the ladies of her church in Bennett had just packed a huge food parcel for me — which arrived a few days later. For the next couple of weeks I was busy writing replies, showering carefully selected facts upon appropriate recipients. For example, I could tell my mother that we were about to embark on a short course of ship recognition, under naval auspices, and, a fortnight later, that we were engrossed in a program focused on aerodrome defence — in the course of which I handled a Sten gun for the first time, and was lucky enough to come away with all my fingers still attached. The first models of the Sten were ingeniously constructed so that if you held one with your left hand at the most natural point, your fingers would curl around the barrel and wind up on, and when fired, in, the breech mechanism. The Sten thus left a lot of its users with very stubby fingers until the efficient meat-slicer action of the breech mechanism was circumvented. What I did not pass along to my mother were items such as the fact that Morris, one of the four boys in our stateroom on the *Cavina*, had already gone to Advanced Flying Unit — he had 1700 hours in his log book compared to our 250 — and had been killed in a flying accident.

On January 22nd, Freddie Taylor and I were hurrying back to Burley Court from our morning workout at the gym, intent on listening to our newly acquired gramophone, when we heard a sound that brought us up short. It was the pipes. I recognized the march as "Blue Bonnets Over the Border" and hustled Freddie a block further over to check the source. We caught a sight that did our hearts good. Led by their pipers, a company of the Black Watch came swinging up the street in column of route, their bearing proud, their dressing excellent. Freddie and I eyed them critically, but they measured up well. After they passed and the lilt of the pipes faded hauntingly on the breeze, we popped into a record shop and picked up four more records to add to our embryo record collection. I picked up Crosby singing "Ain't Got A Dime To My Name" and the Ink Spots doing "Java Jive", while Freddie picked up Tommy Dorsey playing "Canadian Capers" and Glenn Miller's "Chattanooga Choo Choo".

Two nights later, Watt Wilton, another member of the five-man syndicate owning the gramophone, accompanied me to the Pavilion to sample some of the local beer, a responsibility I had not yet discharged. A number of the experts at Burley Court, brewmasters all, judging by the confidence of their assessments, had expressed the view that English beer was a pleasant but overly gentle beverage, with little in the way of alcoholic content, incapable of affecting the human system, except perhaps in the case of nuns or elderly divines. Fortified by this knowledge, Watt and I set about our cross-checking duties, bearing in mind that the weight to be attached to any observation we would subsequently make must necessarily be directly proportional to the scope and thoroughness of our test. Thus I played stag at eve and drank my fill; Watt displayed a little more caution and drank only five or six pints.

About ten o'clock I was forced to conclude that either the earlier research reports were grossly in error, or that I should be thinking of taking holy orders. I was not drunk, but I was better than half way there. In the warm glow of a friend-to-all-mankind mood, I set course with Watt for home. Along the way, we fell in with — would wonders never cease — four members of the Black Watch, jolly companions, outgoing and friendly to a fault. Fresh from my conquest of the homeland around Ayr, I was more than ready to meet them half way. One of them asked if we had ever heard of the Black Watch, and I proceeded to display my erudition by calling out, perhaps a bit louder than was necessary: "The Royal Highlanders — The Black Watch, originally Forty-second Regiment of Foot". This was well received, and we moved on slowly, with much back slapping and frequent exchanges of compliments until eventually we drew abreast of Burley Court and turned into the driveway, announcing to our jocund Scottish allies that this was where, alas, we must take our leave.

Here I must apologize for a slight hiatus in the story, for I was unconscious for the next two or three minutes. I awoke on my back, my face numb, tasting blood in my mouth. Thinking that a Focke-Wulf 190 must have flown into my face I rolled onto my arm to look for the wreckage, and saw Watt ten yards away absorbing heavy punishment from — what was this? — from two of our erstwhile bosom companions of The Black Watch. One of them had grabbed Watt's left arm and was struggling to press him tighter against the wall, while his sparring partner was using Watt's head for target practice. I noticed that Watt's head was commendably resilient for it bounced off the bricks several times without apparent damage. But Watt's assailants only had one arm pinned, and the general effect was of having a tom turkey by one wing — with his right arm Watt flailed away fiercely, keeping the unequal battle going. All this registered in a couple of seconds, for, as Scott said:

Thoughts from the tongue that slowly start
Glance quick as lightning through the heart.

I got to my knees and saw something that looked like two pairs of legs ten inches in front of me. As I digested this, the senior ruffian of the band drew his hand back approximately one yard and knocked me kicking again. Now I was getting angry — and smarter. This time I rolled clear in getting up, then staggered forward to get a shot in myself. One of the two in front of me began to retire. I fanned the air ineffectually a few times in the vicinity of the other's head, blocked a nicely aimed left with my mouth, and suddenly all the boys of the Gallant Forty-twa took to their heels as the door of Burley Court opened and Freddie Taylor came pelting out leading reinforcements, drawn by the noise of the carnage.

Watt and I tottered indoors looking for some surgical teams from the Mayo Clinic to make repairs. Freddie Taylor took on the medical chores, wiped our faces, waggled my loose teeth appraisingly and said they would tighten, and put cold towels on Watt's head to deal with the bell sounds and double vision he complained of.

The first question was "Why?" I was thinking a little more clearly than the others, and immediately concluded that it was a band of Scotch Catholics who had discovered my relationship with the great Covenanter. But when I searched for my wallet a moment later, I was relieved to find that it was not religious persecution at all, just ordinary robbery with violence. My money was gone, but that blow was as nothing compared with the loss of the irreplaceable clothing coupons we had been given. Freddie Taylor gave me a few of his, but it began to look like a long war, with a lot of darning. I decided, so far as the beer testing was concerned, that Freddie Taylor and Charlie Payne could take up the white man's burden and render the definitive verdict. I swore off strong drink in all its guises. The following morning, after asking myself what my reverend ancestor would do under this provocation, I turned both lumpy cheeks towards town and marched to a nearby shop where I purchased a knuckleduster of workmanlike design and fearful weight.

A few days later a number of us got short "fill-in" postings, designed to keep us busy for a fortnight or so. Obviously no postings to Advanced Flying Units were imminent. I was sent, on January 29th, 1943, for 12 days service with the 14th Canadian Tank Regiment, then stationed at Worthing. I found that they had taken over part of that south coast town and were living in what had been private houses. The officers' mess of my regiment — a Calgary regiment — was the front room of a well-weathered red brick house, and the bar, which I was directed to five minutes after my arrival, was a blanket-covered table in the bay window of that room. Beside the meagre supply of bottles was the tattered old scribbler in which one jotted his accounting for each drink he bought. I was not yet up to more testing duties, at least not for the time being, and in any event my vow was absolutely binding, so my entries over the 12-day sojourn were exclusively for mineral waters.

The first evening, we sat around chatting, and I acquired a little background on the Calgary boys. They were just nicely getting over the shock of the Dieppe raid. Five months earlier, while I had been attending Plate's funeral in Iowa, they had been sitting in their landing craft in Dieppe harbour, under heavy fire. Their efforts that day had been dogged from the outset by ill luck, and their gallantry had gone unrewarded by any tangible success. Their Colonel, and the rest of the crew in his tank, had perished in an attempt to lead some tanks ashore to help the infantry, driving off the ramp and plunging unsuspectingly into 14 feet of water. In the result, few, if any, of this squadron's tanks had got ashore. The bloody repulse sustained by the infantry in most sectors had yielded, as its only benefit, an object lesson of what to expect from muddled planning and woolly demarcation of authority and responsibility at the very top. With some helpful exceptions, notably some British Commandos and about 50 American Rangers of equal calibre, the entire landing force was from the Second Canadian Division. The Second Division commander, General John H. Roberts, had been placed in the almost impossible position of either accepting a plan about which he had grave reservations, or, by rejecting it, perhaps exposing to question the morale and readiness of his own troops — or indeed his own eagerness for combat. To a soldier there wasn't any real choice in that situation. Roberts took the plan and did his level best to make it work; but his fears as to its weakness, specifically in its lack of adequate naval and air bombardment, were tragically proved to be all too valid. The Calgary boys had clearly not forgotten Dieppe.

Next morning, struggling to preserve my poise in borrowed coveralls that would have left Fatty Arbuckle with a lot of slack, I climbed aboard a tank for my first ride. The regiment was equipped with Churchills, heavy "infantry" tanks, which carried a six-pounder as their main armament, together with two machine guns. A Churchill had a crew of five and was capable, with its 350 h.p. motor, of about 20 miles per hour at top speed. The tank commander had made arrangements for me to ride beside him in the second turret hatch so that I would get the best possible view of what was going on.

In describing the characteristics and capabilities of his vehicle, as we made ready for our ride, the tank commander repeatedly stressed its great weight. The phrase "43 tons" stuck in my mind — as he meant it to.

As we tested our radio, I noted that 90 percent of the sound it emitted was extraneous noise, principally shrill chirps and whistles accompanied by other exotic interference and a continuous backdrop of static resembling the amplified sound of pork chops sizzling over a torrid fire. I guessed that the tank sets were made by the same company that furnished ours.

Presently the tank commander ordered our driver to move out, and we clattered off, making a series of jerky turns with one track locked to get out of the tank park. Beyond, we picked up speed on a straight run and I thought the ponderous rush of an armoured vehicle was great fun until, as we were thundering toward a high bridge spanning a set of railway tracks, our driver came on intercom suddenly and announced in a panicky sounding voice that this bridge had a weight limit on it of 20 tons. While my pulse rate doubled, the tank commander wasted precious seconds checking a map and arguing that the driver was wrong. While I concocted a mental image of a top-heavy tank doing a falling half roll and landing on its turret — with us sticking two feet out of it — the commander ordered the driver to go over the bridge anyway, but to reduce speed and crawl over it very slowly. We rumbled across dead slow, while I cringed and the tank commander ran off a series of worried frowns; then we reached solid ground again, and I realized I'd been had when he slapped me on the back and the rest of the crew chortled delightedly at my manifest relief.

In fact there were several bridges in the area that would not support a Churchill, but the tank crews knew them all and avoided them. I got on the intercom after learning this and promised the boys that if I ever got a chance to get them up in an aeroplane with me, they would get a ride they would tell their grandchildren about. Later on, after a comprehensive demonstration of what a Churchill could do, they got back in my good graces when we stopped for a breather and a mug of coffee. Someone produced a loaf of bread — which I gazed at interestedly, since four hours had slipped by since breakfast — and I heard the tank commander telling him to "make the Air Force some tank bread". I was suspicious of a nauseous joke; but he cleaned off a hot spot around the engine manifold and produced the best toast I'd ever eaten.

Over the days that followed, the tank men engaged in a refresher course on all their weapons, and in odd hours that came available I gave them a series of lectures on aircraft recognition, using models, charts, and a blackboard the surface of which seemed to have caught a brief burst from a Sten gun. The tank crew's lack of knowledge in this field was exceeded only by my own ignorance of their specialty. However, after my intensive course of helpful tips and cinch clues for positive identification, there were a surprising number who were almost infallible in distinguishing a Focke-Wulf 190 (German, single engined fighter) from a Stirling (British, four engined bomber). Finer distinctions remained elusive however, and if I had been a Beaufighter pilot in their area, and if Junkers 88's had also been seen, I should not have come within range of any gunners of the 14th Canadian.

Moving from the academic to the practical, I learned that around Worthing in January, 1943, the smart thing to do if the air raid siren went — and it went fairly often — was to head for a shelter, giving your best impression of an Olympic sprinter while doing so. The German tip and run raiders — so called because they were fighters which shot in suddenly, dumped their one 500 pounder, and vanished back out over the sea — were far from being just a nuisance if you happened to be in the vicinity where the bomb landed.

I was in downtown Worthing one afternoon when the alert began to wail. I went from my casual window shopping pace to my Jesse-Owens-breaking-the-tape pelt in about two strides as I headed for cover; I had scarcely reached maximum cruising revs before a fierce blast roared and echoed from near the gasometer a couple of blocks away, and a moment later the siren went into its steady note signalling all clear as the lone raider hurtled back out over the sea. He left a number of dead and dying behind him, and one Canadian pilot with a much healthier respect for the damage bombs could do, even the penny packet loads of a fighter.

On the 10th of February I said goodbye to the 14th Canadian Tank Regiment, and boarded the train again for Bournemouth.

Freddie Taylor met me at Burley Court. I asked a few exploratory questions about the mail situation; but it was apparent that there had been no change on the home front. He was still in his father's black books. We took up where we had left off, going over to the gym each morning for a good workout, playing crap all through lunch hour, and going to movies and other affairs with the charming young ladies of Bournemouth in the evenings.

Apropos of the latter subject, I had enjoyed several evenings with a Bournemouth girl named Betty Collins before my posting to Worthing. The gravel in the sandwich so far as her society was concerned was the sharp-shinned hawk she had for a mother. When I first met the young lady, at the dry cleaners where she worked, and negotiated an evening with her at the movies, I had a premonition that the course of true love would not run smoothly and so forth when she told me that her mother insisted on her being home by 11. Nevertheless, knowing that the first show was over by nine, I remained confident that I could make great strides even within that limitation. When I called at her home to pick her up, though, mother took one look at me, another at the Canada shoulder patches, and moved closing time ahead one hour without blinking an eye. Over the next fortnight or two I weighed the question of whether she was a man hater or a mind reader. The blight of her maternal animus was a definite impediment, keeping me from hitting my best form, and I decided that despite Betty's undeniable charm a more flexible nocturnal timetable was mandatory.

Freddie Taylor had already transferred his allegiance from his first "mayor's daughter", having met a young lady whose development in the upper torso was verily historic and who, if Freddie's lurid accounts could be given credence, was virtually mad with desire for him. With this fine example before me, I decided when I got back from Worthing that I would not publicize in certain quarters the fact of my return. I took my uniform to a different dry cleaner, and began patrolling new precincts in the quest for pulchritude. I had another stroke of luck and got to know a charming young lady named Muriel Coleman. This relationship was kindling into a promising romance when the Air Force turned the fire extinguisher on it by posting me, on February 26th, to No. 6 EFTS, Sywell. Freddie and I were separated for several weeks at this point.

Sywell was half a dozen miles northeast of Northampton, or, to place it by reference to a better known city, 40 miles or thereabouts north northeast of Oxford. Sywell itself was a tiny hamlet, and our aerodrome was a barren grass and mud field just clear of the bush that lay south of the town. A satellite field which we visited occasionally was located at Denton, eight miles south southeast of Sywell. The Air Force's object in sending us to another Elementary Flying School was two-fold: to keep us from getting rusty so far as flying was concerned, and to get us used to map reading in England.

We were billeted in private homes in Northampton, and here the luck of the draw favoured us beyond anything we could reasonably have expected. Four of us, including Jim Watson, Barrie Dean and myself, were directed to the home of a Mr. and Mrs. Perkins. Freddie Taylor would have been right at home in their household since Mr. Perkins had recently been the mayor of the city, complete with robes and glittering chain of office, and he and his wife, (inevitably called Ma Perkins), had two very eligible and attractive daughters. Their contract with the Air Force required them to provide us with two bedrooms in which the four of us could sleep, nothing more. We ate our meals, such as they were, at the aerodrome; and all we were entitled to in Northampton was a place to sleep and wash up. With Ma Perkins that was not the way it worked at all. She regarded us as "her boys" and mothered us with genuine concern all the time we were with her. When we came back home from the aerodrome just after dinner, it was understood that as soon as we felt like it we were welcome to come down from our rooms and join the family in the living room.

After we had cleaned up and scribbled a letter or two, we invariably took advantage of our standing invitation and came down to join the family before the fireplace. One of the daughters was a Jean Sablon fan, and frequently played his records, and others, for us on the gramophone. She explained to me, in response to my blank look when she first mentioned Jean Sablon, that he was the French Bing Crosby. To demonstrate the great similarity, she played a disc and looked to me for confirmation of the resemblance. Since Jean Sablon's voice resembled Bing Crosby's about as much as mine resembled Caruso's, I had to tell her that in my opinion Jean would get the gong on Major Bowes' amateur hour. Despite my lack of appreciation of her favourite singer, our new friendship was unimpaired, and we went on to spend many pleasant evenings — unfortunately always with all my companions present — lying in front of the fire, on the rug, listening to records.

Being welcomed into the cosy living room every night was a gesture we particularly appreciated because of the noticeable difference in weather between Bournemouth and Northampton. While Northampton's winter was still a long chalk from the prairie winters I was accustomed to, it did produce the odd wisp of snow and a pretty steady diet of wet, raw weather. Ma Perkins didn't lower her high rating with us by her habit of rustling up a hot drink and a snack every night about ten.

In the mornings, at 7:15, we walked a couple of blocks down the road and an old bus that had been around the world several times picked us up and trundled us the six or seven miles over to the drome at Sywell. Our driver was a chap who was obviously cut out for better things — or faster things. We called him Mad George, because of his driving habits, particularly his penchant for flooring the throttle and roaring the ramshackle old bus around blind corners at its top speed of 25 miles per hour. Since the road we were using most of the way to the drome looked to be about five feet wide, the prospects if we met another adventurer coming full tilt the other way were frequently sombre. We used to tell Mad George that some day he would come hareing around one of these turns and meet a tank coming the other way. We were all quite impressed with tanks now, having just had our little training session with them, and that seemed like the ultimate threat to frighten some sense into our driver.

One morning on our way to work, that seemingly fanciful prediction actually came true; not on the worst corner, thank the good

Lord, but on a corner where the driver always retained about 50 feet of forward visibility even in the sharpest part of the turn. Mad George was in good form, obviously fancying himself in the Grand Prix or behind the handlebars in the Tourist Trophy, and slammed into the turn in grand style. Next moment there was a shuddering, shaking application of the brakes, and we were all pitched off our casual perches onto the floor as Mad George slid to a grinding stop five feet in front of an oncoming tank. The Canadian army was on a big scheme that morning, we discovered, and the roads were drenched in armour. Fortunately, the tank commander had been crawling slowly into the turn, fearful of posted anti-tank weapons, so we escaped a gory end. We addressed a few critical remarks to Mad George.

We wasted no time getting back in the air, starting with a review of some circuits and bumps and other basics the day after we got to Northampton. Again we were flying Tiger Moths. On February 27th I had an hour and 15 minutes with an instructor named Sergeant Macdonald; then I put in an hour and 20 minutes solo devoted to circuits and some general familiarization.

On March 2nd I went up for some local map reading. Just from what I had been able to see while doing circuits, I had twigged to the fact that from the air England looked much different than our prairies; but this flight forcibly brought home the realization that what we had called map reading at home had been child's play. At Dauphin we had grown accustomed to the helpful vista of mile after mile of uncluttered countryside tidily divided off by the section roads into neat squares lined up with the cardinal points of the compass. We were also accustomed to seeing one or possibly two railway lines running across a stretch of country, and one or two paved highways, along with a few side roads of gravel or dirt. Most importantly, we were in the habit, under normal circumstances, of looking ahead and around in unrestricted visibility, of being able to see 25 miles in every direction from 3,000 feet. Here at Sywell things were different. There was almost always low overcast, and flight rules recognized the fact that it was generally safer to limit your activities to 1,500 or 2,000 feet and stay under the stuff than to climb over it and hope you could find a hole when you had to come down. We learned to rate the visibility at Sywell A-1 if we could see about five miles at 2,000 feet. Frequently, between the industrial haze and the mist, we were lucky if we could see two miles.

But apart altogether from the greatly reduced visibility, map reading was rendered infinitely more difficult by the overpowering density of the detail on the ground. Railway lines ran to every point of the compass, like webs spun by industrious colonies of spiders, crisscrossing higgledly-piggledly in tangled skeins. The aerial panorama also took in a spaghetti-like tangle of roads, all of them paved, few of them straight for any worthwhile distance. Hamlets, villages, towns and cities had been sown with a profligate hand, in many instances merging into one another with no clear line of demarcation. Between them the farms and forests, large and small, had been strewn like an unending green jigsaw puzzle. Largely because of this bewildering super-abundance of detail, it was almost impossible to find an outstanding landmark capable of serving as a readily indentifiable and certain pinpoint — almost, but not quite.

Just a few miles from the drome lay a forest. It was of a size sufficient to attract the eye and to keep it from getting lost in the welter of nondescript detail scattered about it. Its shape was that of a rough trapezoid, but exactly in the centre was a perfectly circular clearing about 300 yards in diameter. From the air this round clearing was small but crystal clear. The forest was not extensive enough to rate an official name on our topographic map; but the aircrew of Sywell had disposed of that handicap without delay, recognizing a good thing when they saw it. They gave it a name which I thought should be commended to our official cartographer as possessing all the attributes that a good name should have: it was short; it was clear; it was graphically memorable once a pilot had seen the forest's central orifice; and it ran trippingly on the tongue. The mellifluous aircrew appellation in which the feature gloried was "Arsehole Forest."

Initially we stuck close to home when we went up on local map reading exercises, circling the fringes of Northampton until we got to know a few landmarks there, swinging down to the aptly named wooded area, over to the little town of Olney, and back to the field. (Olney, we learned, believed its name to be internationally renowned because of the famous pancake race its women held annually on Shrove Tuesday, the first day of Lent.) In a day or two we expanded our horizons, venturing north from Olney up to Wellingborough, on to Kettering, northwest to Market Harborough, southwest to the environs of Rugby, then southeast to Northampton and back to Sywell again. Gradually we began to acquire the facility of selecting an item we were looking for from the flood of detail on the ground, and our knowledge of the area increased more rapidly. Map reading did not suddenly become easy, but we found that with great concentration we could find our way from point A to point B and back again.

As we developed our map reading skill, our instructors checked our aerobatics as well. The English Tigers had no coupe tops on them, and when you went to do your first slow roll without one it required the hurdling of a minor mental block to bring yourself to hang upside down in your straps with nothing over your head — it was like hanging headfirst from a flying canoe.

One instructor checked me on stall turns, damned my efforts with faint praise, and said "That was okay, Peden. I know that's the Air Force's way — but you know, I think you get a lot more kick out of a stall turn if you pull her up steeper at the beginning. Here let me have her; this is how we used to do 'em on dive bombers."

He pulled the Tiger practically straight up, then went on to come slightly past the vertical. When he kicked on rudder as she stalled, we flicked over and began to fall like a bomb, still past the vertical. Gasoline sprayed out the top vent and we hurtled down with a far livelier sensation than I had ever experienced before in a stall turn. I knew that if I had not become reasonably inured to aerobatic sensations previously I should have been as sick as a dog. As it was, I quickly grew to like the breathtaking fall this new past-the-vertical approach produced, and I did my stall turns that way thereafter.

Each instructor had a favourite area to which he habitually resorted on our map reading exercises. Sgt. Macdonald used to like to fly over to Blenheim Palace and circle that magnificent edifice at a low level while reminding me that it had been the nation's present to the victorious Duke of Marlborough, and also the birthplace of Churchill. Blenheim was less than ten miles from Oxford, so it made a nice round trip of about 80 miles from Sywell.

Macdonald showed me an exercise not included in the syllabus, an exercise that I found particularly interesting. He would fly to an area where our map showed that a Roman road had once been built, perhaps 1600 years earlier. These roads that we searched for had now disappeared, and not a trace of them could be found at ground level without extensive excavation; but their boundaries could be faintly made out from the air due to an almost imperceptible difference in colour in the vegetation growing immediately over them. There were, of course, some Roman roads and walls scattered about the country which were completely visible, usually only vestigial remains; but I got a thrill out of searching for these buried ones, flying over a quiet farm at 1500 feet, peering intently, then, as the breeze waved the grass and the light hit it at just the right angle, suddenly spotting for a few fleeting seconds the ghostly highway of the Romans wending its way across the field, shrouded in the silence and mystery of forgotten centuries. For a moment I could hear in my imagination the measured tread of the vanished legions.

On March 9th our flight commander inserted another certificate in my log book: "Certified that P/O Peden is qualified to carry a Navigator or Air Bomber." In view of what was to happen on March 16th this verdict might have been considered questionable. What it meant in practice was that we now carried an Air Bomber or Navigator with us on most flights, since there were many of these trades with us at Sywell, and they too had to get in as much map reading as they possibly could.

While Macdonald leaned to the Blenheim Palace area, Sgt. Wright preferred to map read his way north about 100 miles and land at Brough, an aerodrome seven miles west of Hull on the north bank of the Humber. Usually this would take us an hour and a half or an hour and three-quarters each way, depending on the wind.

On March 10th, carrying a bombaimer by the name of P/O Coulson with me in the front cockpit, I set off on another trip to Brough. My pal Tommy Penkuri, also chauffering a bombaimer, teamed up with me on this venture. Formation flying was conspicuous by its absence in the list of duties we were to carry out on this flight; but in a hastily convened pre-flight conference in front of Penkuri's Tiger, he and I concluded, in lowered voices, that this was obviously an oversight on the part of the flight commander. We rectified it, flying tight formation the whole way once Sywell had disappeared from view in the haze.

The bombaimers found tight formation distracting, but overcame the handicap and map read us efficiently to the circuit at Brough. Here Penkuri and I found something to distract us. The Luftwaffe had paid a visit not long before by the look of the aerodrome; it was plentifully pock-marked with bomb holes, each marked with a red warning flag. Penkuri and I chose our approach with a great deal more than usual care, but once on the ground affected clouds of nonchalance, as though threading our way in through bomb holes was boringly routine where we came from.

By design, we had arrived just in time for lunch, since the offerings of Sywell's *chef de cuisine* were a touch on the loose — not to say swillish — side, and we all tucked in handsomely at the Brough officers' mess. When it came time to depart we found that there was no mechanic around to spin our props and get us started. Up to this point Penkuri and I felt that we had been reasonably successful in leaving with the bombaimers the desired impression that pilots as a class were omnipotent; hence we were unwilling to throw in the towel and shatter the image by saying that we would have to walk the 100 miles back to Sywell because we couldn't get an erk to spin the props. After another brief pre-flight conference, at the usual stand, and at the usual level of audibility, we resolved to preserve our Dawn Patrol image by pulling the props ourselves.

Since neither of us had actually spun a prop before, it was done very edgily, with noticeably eager snatching away of the business hand on each abortive kick, as though the propeller blade had suddenly turned white hot to the touch; but after half a dozen pulls — preceded by faultless verbal signals — we got both Tigers ticking over, so that we could swagger around to our respective rear cockpits basking in the admiring gaze of the bombaimers. We taxied out, goggles down, with many unnecessary but impressive hand signals to one another, picked our way through the craters again, and took off for an uneventful flight back to Sywell. Dinner that evening was another culinary catastrophe.

We practised aerobatics and other exercises for the next day or two. There was one unauthorized exercise, not recorded in my log book, which I attempted only once, unsuccessfully, and left unmastered. It was linked to the fact that our English Tiger Moths had no brakes, only tail skids, and to the complementary fact that 20 yards in front of our flight shack a large telephone pole lying on the ground barred the progress of all aircraft in case someone should taxi in too enthusiastically and chop up Squadron Leader Dalrymple, who sat just inside the first office.

On March 12th, P/O Jack demonstrated the challenging sport this telephone pole barrier could provide when the wind was in the appropriate quarter. He landed in a direct line towards Squadron Leader Dalrymple's office. We would land in this direction routinely in such a wind, but basic airmanship called for touchdown at least 350 yards away, with a final approach to the telephone pole at funereal speed, the plane being urged forward with gentle nudges of throttle.

P/O Jack kept us airborne until we were only 150 yards from Dalrymple's office. When we touched down he cut the switches and slewed the plane from side to side with rudder, dragging the tail skid for all he was worth. Initially I was sure that we were going to hurdle the pole and enter the Squadron Leader's office via the front windows. But Jack had obviously weighed with nice judgement all the factors involved. We decelerated rapidly in the last 40 yards, and fetched up gently and noiselessly against the pole. Perfect. I was captivated by the artistry of his judgement. This really was a challenge.

As he climbed out, P/O Jack waved an admonitory finger at me and grinned:

"Don't you try that, Peden. That takes a little more practice than you're going to get on this field."

I nodded dutifully, fully intending to give it a whirl the next time I got up solo.

As it happened, I was able to get the aircraft again that afternoon. When I came in to land I strove to approach on the identical glide path traced out by P/O Jack. But somewhere along the line, new and frightening aerodynamic and ballistic factors had been introduced, despite my best intentions, for at 100 yards, with throttle and switches off, the Tiger refused to stay on the ground. It kept leaping into the air and soaring forward like a charging panther. Dalrymple's thin-walled office approached at sobering speed. I slewed the Tiger's rear end back and forth like a hula dancer trying to sweep the floor, wishing fervently that the tail skid were a ploughshare, but results were slow to appear.

At 30 yards the Tiger was still trundling ahead about 20 miles per hour, swiftly and silently, the tail skid gouging "S" shaped furrows in the mud. I hit the telephone pole a horrid bump that rattled my teeth, rolled the pole over two or three turns, and stopped. Grateful that the undercarriage had not been sheared, and that there were no witnesses about, I hastened to roll the telephone pole from its incriminating position back into the shallow depression it had occupied before the sturdy stroke dealt it by my obviously incomplete calculations. With that step taken, I took ten seconds to throw my parachute in the flight office and sign in, then ambled nonchalantly back behind the Tiger and scuffed out some of the more desperate looking tail skid gouges leading to the machine. Then I slunk off, conceding that perhaps Pilot Officer Jack might have had a point, and deciding to defer additional telephone pole experiments until I had another few days' experience.

Each evening, in the comfort of Ma Perkins' living room, the conversation drifted, at one stage or another, to our flying duties of that day. The girls particularly seemed keen on discovering what new exploits we had recorded in our log books, and we required little in the way of urging. The law of averages obviously had no application to our training, because none of the flights recounted seemed to have been uneventful straightforward trips from A to B, as the Air Force meant them to be. On the contrary, the vast majority of the tales were action packed thrillers, high in entertainment content, but of dubious historical value. My own flair for hyperbole and selective recall — although rarely indulged, of course — was brought home to me one night when Ma Perkins was relaying an aerial saga to her husband (who had missed about three days' bulletins), and was three-quarters of the way through it before I recognized myself as the flyer who was acquitting himself so commendably.

Since a little timely embellishment of a flying story drew gratifying beams of admiration from the girls' sparkling eyes, I reasoned that an actual view of one of their aces in action was bound to make even more of an impression. Overcoming my natural tendency to self-effacement, I casually threw out the idea that it might be fun to bring a Tiger over the old homestead at Northampton and signal our presence to the family. This suggestion won the immediate approval of the girls — whose attitude contrasted sharply with Squadron Leader Dalrymple's where horseplay was concerned — so I undertook to fly such a mission at the earliest opportunity.

Opportunity knocked on March 15th and I set course for Perkins Manor full of enthusiasm despite a low ceiling and restricted visibility. Over Northampton I found my way with little difficulty to the long street of identical brick houses, checked for the dot of the pillar box on the corner and identified the house. I signalled my arrival with throttle and began circling in a steep turn. Thirty seconds went by, then Ma Perkins and one of the girls came hurrying into the backyard waving dishtowels vigorously. I dived the Tiger shallowly a few times, pulling up into a medium climbing turn before repeating the swoop on the opposite tack. The frequency of the dishtowel wig wags increased appreciably and I felt a sense of obligation to show my fans something a little more spectacular before departing for Sywell.

The problem was the 1,200-foot ceiling. To do aerobatics with any degree of safety required another 2,000 feet at least. I began to toy with the idea of a stall turn. That would be spectacular enough, but from 1,200 feet not really too bright a stunt to pull off, because, depending on how thoroughly the aircraft were stalled, it could drop for a few seconds — perhaps 400 to 800 feet — as though the wings had been removed. A quiet voice in the background began whispering something I couldn't quite make out, some pusillanimous sounding bit of doggerel about old pilots and bold pilots; common sense struggled manfully with vanity, but lost through crooked refereeing. I built up speed to go into a stall turn.

Following the recently recommended mode of initiating such a turn I soared up past the vertical and was just about sticking the Tiger's nose into the cloud when she stalled, totally, and, I quickly began to fear, irrevocably. Down we fell, plummeting towards Ma Perkins' backyard as though the fuselage had suddenly been poured full of lead.

The dishtowels froze into immobility as all three of us seemed to realize that there was an excellent chance of my riding the Tiger right down the chimney. At the point where I was noticing breathlessly that a number of the Perkins' roof tiles had hairline cracks in them, the speed hit 70 and I eased out of the dive, all the while expending enormous amounts of energy in up-turning body English. I left for Sywell without a backward glance.

The colour began creeping back into my cheeks just before Mad George dropped us back at the house that night, and I even managed to muster up some synthetic jauntiness when Ma and the girls rushed up to confirm that it was I who had given them such a thrill. I didn't tell them who had got the biggest thrill that day, carrying the whole thing off with a casual "Oh, that" gesture which was fairly convincing; but I had five plausible reasons for refusal ready should anyone ask for seconds.

The following day, the afternoon of March 16th, I met Pilot Officer Steele, not socially, but as the front seat occupant whom I was directed to chauffeur about the skies for an hour or so on a local familiarization and map reading flight. He was a pleasant young chap, a Canadian bombaimer, keen as mustard and terribly efficient looking. He was a relative newcomer to Sywell, and my first task was to fly him about within a rather limited radius and show him the local landmarks.

Before we took off, I showed him carefully on my own map what the landmarks were and where they were located. I mentioned first the vulgarly named forest. Steele was such a clean-cut innocent looking lad that I was tempted to inject an alias for the crude designation and call it Hole-in-the-Wall Forest, or Knothole Forest; but I knew that someone else would refer to it in its notorious form, thus generating confusion, so I gave it to him straight, i.e., anatomically. I went on to show him the famous Pancake Racecourse, the High Street of Olney, then showed him the relative positions of Wellingborough and Kettering, and where they in turn lay in relation to the much larger metropolis of North-ampton.

He took this all in, and then said:

"That looks like touring it shouldn't take more than 20 or 30 minutes. Would it be okay when we've finished if I get a little map reading practice for the balance of the exercise? Maybe I could try map reading us to three or four of these old windmills on the map? I'd like to see some of those."

He pointed to a few of the windmill symbols which dotted the map rather plentifully.

I was staggered by Don Quixote's display of industry, and allowed as how that would indeed be putting the time to good use. I had actually had something else in mind, but Steele didn't strike me now as the Roman road type.

In the air I quickly showed him the forest and the towns we had discussed on the ground, and then called to him and said: "Okay, where are these windmills you want to find?"

He shouted through the Gosport tubes — an extremely primitive form of intercom system with which we were cursed in all Tiger Moths — giving me a course to steer, and after I managed to get it straight, I swung off in that direction, keeping a sharp lookout myself for the object of our quest. In about ten minutes the windmill showed up just off our starboard wingtip. P/O Steele pointed down enthusiastically and, after checking his map, asked that I alter course some 50 degrees to port and head for another one.

He seemed to be doing fairly well with his map reading, so I was content to turn the navigating over to him and strike off in the new direction. Ten minutes later he called another course, again sub-stantially different from the one we had been on. I glanced around without too much interest, saw what could have been an old windmill a quarter of a mile off our port wing, did a steep turn, and headed off in yet another direction. Some 15 minutes went by before P/O Steele gave further signs of life. Then he asked for another substantial alteration of course, which we held for only six or seven minutes, following which he threw out a roughly southerly course which I once more dutifully steered.

Some ten minutes went by and I thought it behooved me to ascertain our position from the assiduous navigator and head back to Sywell. Squadron Leader Dalrymple did not mind us running ten or 15 minutes over the hour assigned for this type of flight, but beyond that he became somewhat uncharitable.

I called out to Steele: "Where are we?"

His answer was not reassuring: "I'm not sure."

"Well, where was your last pinpoint?" I shouted.

"That windmill I showed you" he shouted.

"You mean the second windmill?" I shouted.

"Did we find two?" he came back.

Conclusion after three additional queries: he had been lost for approximately 40 minutes — or more correctly, both of us had been lost for approximately 40 minutes, for I had assumed as we went along that he was finding all the pinpoints he was asking me to steer for. Inwardly I cursed him and his whole tribe, and then started on myself for not having kept track of his mindless wanderings.

I had not been keeping any air plot or pilot's log, such had been my confidence in the hard working windmill finder; and as I vainly strove to recall the various courses we had flown I realized that even a list of the headings themselves would not have helped since I had an even fainter recollection of the time spent on each leg. I did have a hazy notion, based on nothing but instinct, that the net result of our erratic meanderings had left us generally north and west of our base. (In actual fact, I discovered later, we were south and west of base, which accounted for the insuperable difficulty I had in trying to identify anything on the haze-covered ground.)

The prescribed method of map reading is from map to ground. But if one is not where he thinks he is, the prescribed method of map reading becomes a tantalizing exercise in wishful thinking. The triangularly-shaped lake shown on the map is compared, urgently and longingly, with the shoelace-shaped lake actually visible on the ground, and only with the utmost reluctance is this possible signpost to navigational salvation written off and a new map feature searched for. In short order the recommended method has to be sacrificed and its converse substituted, and the lost airman searches for some prominent landmark on the ground that shows promise of being identifiable on the map. There are usually a number of features that might serve the purpose if only the searcher could stop the relentless flow of detail and compare them carefully with the map; but the ground continues to slip by under the wing inexorably, the view is restricted by haze, smoke, shadows, or cloud, and the jigsaw puzzle stubbornly resists orientation.

I wasted a few minutes following the approved method, but my assumptions regarding our position did not pan out. I began searching for something on the ground that I could identify on my map, and in a few minutes — having turned southeast — saw a town ahead of me. Studying it with fierce concentration, I concluded that it might be Kenilworth. If it was, I should come to Leamington in five minutes. In five minutes I came to nothing. I gave it six minutes. Nothing. Eight minutes — nothing. I was still lost.

Presently I approached a grass drome, directly on my track; it had some Blenheims and Beaufighters scattered about its surface. I weighed the pros and cons of landing to find out where I was. It would be acutely embarrassing to have to walk up to the duty pilot like a person recovering consciousness and say "Where am I?" And recounting the salient facts of the performance later on in Squadron Leader Dalrymple's little confessional behind the telephone pole wasn't going to be jolly sport either. If I kept going for another few minutes I might get a fix and preserve my dignity.

On the other hand, there was only an hour's daylight left at most. I had already been flying for an hour and 25 minutes, and unless and until I ascertained my position I had no idea of how much longer it was going to take to get back to Sywell. Even if I got home in five minutes — which I was certainly not going to do — Dalrymple would have a word or two to say about my late return, and every extra minute I took would raise his word quota and his blood pressure. If he had to initiate a missing aircraft report — which he would soon have to consider — he would be really uncongenial. I decided to land.

I discovered that I had landed at Bicester, only ten miles from Oxford. If I had carried on for only a few more minutes I should have been back in familiar territory. I could have saved the 20 minutes I spent on the ground finding the duty pilot and avoided the humiliating conversation I had to have with him.

Smarting from the duty pilot's leaden witticisms, I returned to the aircraft on the run, my bitterness at Steele's perfidy temporarily revived. Again I cursed the maidenly modesty that had stopped him from telling me the moment he realized he was lost instead of keeping mum for half an hour. I told him curtly where we were, then started up and taxied hurriedly in the waning light to the take-off point. Just as I turned into wind, Steele looked at me in the mirror and called:

"Skipper, I think if you steer zero two eight with this wind I can take you right home."

I threw him a look that should have splintered the glass.

"Steele" I gritted, "belt up. You just sit there and watch *me* take *you* home."

I had already checked my map while I was at flying control and noted that about two miles out of Bicester I could get onto a railway line than ran within two or three miles of rectum wood at the other end. I flew the iron beam at low level to the forest and came in over the drome to find a line of flare pots for night flying already flickering.

I suspected that Squadron Leader Dalrymple would be nursing his wrath to keep it warm, and headed grimly to his office, alone, to report. Even with a little fiddling on the times, showing more time on the ground at Bicester than I had actually taken, I had had to log two full hours for a flight that was supposed to have been for one.

Dalrymple made rather heavy weather of it, delivering himself of some 15 short and fast pronouncements without troubling to take a breath. With the first two I could not quibble. One: Peden was pilot and captain of the aircraft. Two: Peden was a damned fool and had let an inexperienced Air Bomber get both of them thoroughly lost. The remaining barrage, directed at me, was more pungent, but I comforted myself with the promise that I would relay every significant feature of the monologue to Steele, with extra emphasis on the more defamatory parts.

Mad George had long since left with the bus, of course, and I feared that when the good Squadron Leader had shot his bolt I should be left like the ploughman to homeward plod my weary way. To my pleasant surprise Dalrymple, despite his fully justified ire, had been good enough to keep a vehicle about to run us into town.

I decided on the way home to stay in my room and write letters the whole evening. I was sure that Ma and the girls must be getting bored with all the flying stories.

One of our instructors was a precautionary landing specialist — or bug — depending on your point of view. Precautionary landing approaches were required to be made at slower than normal speed, the margin between safe flying speed and stalling speed usually being reduced to a point about ten miles per hour above the stall. With this instructor that margin was cut in half when the pupil was doing the flying, and when he himself had the controls, demonstrating the technique, he rejoiced in wallowing in just a mile or two over the stall, with the aircraft mushing in sluggishly, ready to fall the moment he cut the power off. Riding with him while he performed one of these approaches was far from boring; in fact it was as suspenseful as a murder scene in a Hitchcock movie.

He brought us in on a precautionary one afternoon, flopping us

143

into a small paddock bounded by a thick hedge. On the approach I was convinced for three or four seconds that we were going to blaze a prominent trail right through the hedge, but he nursed us over it by a whisker and set us down 60 feet inside the meadow. As we taxied back to the hedge and got ready to take off again, he directed my attention to the far side of the field where the line of the hedge was broken by a wide wooden gate which stood open.

"Remind me to tell you about that when we get home" he called.

When I raised the subject in the flight room at Sywell, he laughed and dropped into a chair beside me.

"I went into that same field on a precautionary a while ago," he said. "I was up by myself and I cut her a little too fine — I stalled into the hedge just about 20 feet to the left of that gate and the Tiger flipped over onto her back — damn near broke my fool neck."

By great good fortune she had not caught fire, but Mac had been slightly stunned in the crash. As he recovered his senses he found himself hanging upside down in the Sutton harness, his head swelling like a pumpkin and practically touching the ground. His maps and some other odds and ends from the cockpit had fallen out and were fluttering lightly in the breeze a foot away from him. He tried to collect his wits, realizing that he had to get out of the aircraft in case it did catch fire, but aware also that if he simply pulled the pin in his harness he could fall out and break his neck. However, there seemed nothing else to do, so he got one arm over his head, touching the ground, to try to cushion his fall, and pulled.

He fell heavily, and awkwardly, and was shaken up again.

"As I propped myself up on my elbow and pulled a map out of my face to see what was what," he said "a dear old lady out with her poodle walked by that gate and stopped to look at me. As I was thinking 'Thank goodness, she can flag down a car, or help me out of here and telephone the station', she called off her dog — which had already trotted over and sized up the broken propeller as a possible target — and she just paced quietly off and left my lying there in a puddle of gasoline. I could practically hear her saying 'Come along Hercules, don't bother the nice man while he's lying underneath his aeroplane map reading.' "

As it happened, both Mac and his aeroplane needed repairs, the aeroplane being in much the worse shape; but he always got a chuckle out of the old girl's imperturbable review of the crash.

Unknown to us, our sojourn at Northampton and Sywell was drawing to a close. It had been the closest thing to membership in a flying club for the idle rich that we had ever experienced. Those of us who had enjoyed the hospitality of the Perkins family in addition to the common privilege of having a fleet of Tiger Moths as our own playthings had had the best of all possible worlds. The fact that we had been blessed with a group of easy-to-get-along-with instructors, and had been subjected to no pressure in the form of tests, had been additional factors contributing to our contentment.

I flew twice with Sgt. Wright on Wednesday, March 17th; then on Thursday the weather lay on the ground and kept us there with it. Friday morning he and I got up again for 80 minutes' cross-country work. When we landed, I was planning a fast lunch — on the theory that the briefer the exposure to the daily dietetic miscarriage the less the damage to body and spirit — and then hopefully a spot of Roman road work, solo. It was not to be; my career as an aerial archaeologist was finished. The weather turned filthy and kept us on the ground again.

Next morning the weather was still dirty. About noon word came that we were to clear the station as quickly as possible, get back to Northampton to pack, and be at the railroad station to catch the train back to Bournemouth early that evening. The rumour was that there was an opening for 30 or 40 pilots at an AFU (Advanced Flying Unit). We scurried about getting our log books closed off and certified up to the end of the previous day — I had accumulated 42 hours and 15 minutes in our three-week refresher course — and rode with Mad George for the last time back into Northampton. Perhaps because we were subconsciously thankful for having escaped death at his hands, everyone chipped in at the end of the journey, and we left our driver thinking that Canadian pilots were all right — a little timid perhaps, but basically all right.

Farewells with Mr. and Mrs. Perkins and the girls were neither as casual nor as easy. They had made us members of the family for these few weeks. Several times Mr. Perkins had played his own records for us, including the Caruso records which he cherished. We were genuinely sorry to be losing their nightly companionship and the cordial atmosphere of the cosy living room.

At the railway station, in recognition of our status as holders of His Majesty's Commission, we were issued with travel warrants entitling us to First Class accommodation on the train. We learned that we were required to change trains in London on the way back. On the first train a few lucky fellows found seats in a Third Class carriage; the rest of us stood up in the corridor. According to the Air Force's travel schedule we would have a brief wait between trains. Actually we had fun standing around the platforms of Waterloo Station for a little over four hours while someone organized a train to Bournemouth.

When it eventually came along the situation improved. On this train they found space for all the officers — in a baggage car. This was not just any old baggage car, however, but one on which the sliding door would close only halfway, ensuring a fine view of the English countryside which was now being lashed with sleet and snow. The engineer made his contribution, jerking us along at 60 miles per hour, thus adding, to nature's endowment of invigorating air and snow, a worthwhile wind, together with generous consignments of coal dust, cinders and smoke. Some of us stood up and took it, some huddled together in the corners, some sat on suitcases, some sat on crates. Somewhere along the line, about two AM, we made a brief stop. Out of the snow a man loomed up on a wagon and chunked in 50 big bundles of wet newspapers. For the last hour everyone had a first class seat.

At three AM Sunday, looking like snow-bound sentinels from Stalingrad, we arrived in Bournemouth, an immobile, spectral force. After the power of movement returned we had a brief rest; then we trooped all over Bournemouth attempting to carry out the rather urgent orders we had been given and get various necessary clearances signed. Annoyingly, in view of the tenor of the orders, many of the offices we attended seeking clearances turned out to be closed on Sunday. I gathered from the inquiries I made that these places had been in the habit of closing every Sunday since about three weeks prior to the Battle of Hastings, and everyone in Bournemouth save only our Administrative Officer seemed to be well posted on that fact. However, after the Charlie Chaplin overtones of our train arrangements, this new evidence of the thoroughness and clockwork precision of Air Force planning was much less surprising.

My chief disappointment was that we missed Sunday Church Parade through our vain efforts to get cleared for the AFU draft. To the small minority to whom that might sound unconvincing I should explain that Church Parade in Bournemouth was an event that I greatly looked forward to, not, I regret to say, primarily for the spiritual uplift and the strengthening of moral fibre that were its main objectives, but for the pleasure of marching there behind our band and, later, listening to the band concert which the excellent RCAF band conducted by Flight Lieutenant Martin Boundy presented immediately afterwards.

Next day, we did get the balance of our clearances, and on Tuesday, March 23rd, 1943, 30 of our group left for No. 20 (Pilot) AFU at Kidlington.

CHAPTER 7

NO. 20 (PILOT)
ADVANCED FLYING UNIT

To teach vain Wits a science little known,
T'admire superior sense, and doubt their own.

Alexander Pope: Essay on Criticism

Kidlington, which none of us had ever heard of, turned out to be an aerodrome situated seven miles north of Oxford and only three miles east southeast of my old sightseeing headquarters, Blenheim Palace. Our quarters were very good by Air Force standards, although they naturally suffered by comparison with the Perkins' residence. But the huts were neat and clean, and we enjoyed the novelty of being wakened in the morning by WAAF batwomen who brought us steaming hot tea to get us off to a good start.

AFU training was designed to achieve three objectives: to improve our general flying skill and thus take us an additional step toward the standard required for flying on operations; to give us the experience to maintain that standard under worse weather conditions than we had previously been permitted to fly in; and to teach us the flying characteristics and "feel" of a heavier aircraft.

The plane we were to fly on this course was the Airspeed Oxford, a twin-engined advanced trainer powered by two 370 horsepower Cheetah X's. The "Ox-box", as she was often called, weighed 7,600 pounds loaded, and despite her 53 feet four inch wingspan she felt like an even heavier aircraft on the landing approach and touch-down. Flat out, she could be nursed to over 185 mph, but at cruising revs she purred along between 135 and 140. All in all, the Oxford could be described as a reasonably demanding but thoroughly reliable trainer.

I had been quite disappointed — as had a number of other pilots in our group — to learn that Kidlington was equipped with Oxfords. We had been hoping that our new steeds would turn out to be Miles Masters. The Master was a single-engined advanced trainer, and, had we been fortunate enough to catch it, we could pretty well have counted on getting onto operations on fighters. Even so, I did not entirely abandon hope, although I felt it politic to concede, on filling out my current "preference" sheet, that I would be happy to take even twin-engined fighters such as Mosquitos or Beaufighters.

But the handwriting was on the wall, or, more accurately, on the front pages of the daily newspapers. At the beginning of March, RAF Bomber Command had launched the first of the great aerial offensives for which its doughty commander, Sir Arthur Harris, had been struggling to prepare it. Now that the Pathfinder marking force could be led in by Mosquitos which themselves had been guided to the exact aiming point by the incredibly accurate navigational device called "Oboe", Harris had launched the Battle of the Ruhr, and every night the weather was halfway reasonable, an aerial armada fought its way through the defences of Germany to unload 1,500 tons or more of high explosives on the cities of the German industrial heartland.

Bomber Command had not yet attained the impressive size that it would achieve in only a few months, when the swelling tide of Lancasters, Halifaxes and Stirlings would permit the Air Officer Commanding-in-Chief to strike with 900 or 1,000 four-engined machines; but even now the Command could launch a mixed flotilla of over 500 twin-engined and four-engined heavies. Although the loss rate had been pared slightly below the previously prevailing 5.4 per cent, the Command was suffering a loss of 20 or 30 crews on each of these attacks. With losses of these dimensions — and the numbers were increasing each time out in proportion to the increase in the force — it was apparent that hundreds of new crews would have to be pumped into Bomber Command to fill up the holes in the squadrons and to build up the new formations planned for the bomber force.

Our ultimate destination was made more probable by the fact that Fighter Command's losses had fallen significantly once the Russian campaign had drawn the bulk of the German day fighters to that front. However, there was nothing to be gained by wringing our hands and bemoaning our fate. We settled down and began learning how to fly the "Ox-box". By a slight miscalculation on the part of the Air Force, our first familiarization flights took place 24 hours *before* April Fool's day.

On March 31st I had my first flight with the Flight Commander of "Y" Flight, Flight Lieutenant Waddington. He was a forceful character, and initially I found him quite brusque. As I got to know him better, I discovered that he was really quite a warm-hearted and considerate person. There was no doubt from the outset that he knew his job.

After I had flown with F/L Waddington on my initial 35 minute flight, I was assigned for general familiarization and solo preparation to Pilot Officer Leigh, and over the next three days I flew with him eight times. At AFU there was no rush to get people off solo. I spent a total of eight hours and 55 minutes with Leigh, so that I was thoroughly familiar with the Oxford's habits before he sent me solo on April 2nd; and before I took the Oxford up alone, F/L Waddington gave me one final 20 minute solo check himself in an attempt to ensure that I wouldn't bend the aeroplane.

We now realized that what we had been told and what we had read about the Oxford was true. It did not float after flare-out the way the lighter Cessna Crane had; and on the approach, particularly with flap down, the "settling" sensation was much more noticeable. To my surprise I found that flying it was much more exhilarating than I had imagined. I got to like the old "Ox-box", and soon began to experience a deeper satisfaction with my flying, the sensation that comes with stretching one's powers and mastering a more difficult task.

The AFU course was divided into three separate and distinct segments. The first portion, after the ground school, lasted three weeks, and was designed to make us thoroughly familiar with all the flying characteristics of the Oxford. Once we had accumulated a little solo experience, we embarked upon a series of 200 and 300 mile cross-countries to brush up our navigation. Interspersed between these flights were frequent sessions of instrument flying, some with our instructors, some with classmates acting as safety pilot. Jimmy Watson and I found ourselves paired up on a number of these instrument sessions.

No greater incentive could have been provided than to have one's performance under the hood monitored by a classmate. The judgement was always brutally frank, and, unlike the assessment of a regular instructor, was very apt to be broadcast to all and sundry within half an hour of landing.

We put in a lot of flying, considering that these aircraft were new to us and that first solo sessions are particularly wearing. On April 2nd I made five separate flights. On the 3rd I made five more, adding eight and a half hours flying time in those two days. Between April 4th and 6th I made 11 more flights. Unexpectedly, when flying was finished on the 6th, we were told that we could leave the station until morning roll call on the 8th.

Jimmy Watson and I decided to catch the train and have a night in London. When we got there we tried the Park Lane Hotel and were fortunate enough to get rooms. This was a pretty posh establishment for officers of our limited means, but in wartime London finding reasonably priced hotel rooms was hopeless. Frequently, finding a hotel room was hopeless.

Once safely based, Jimmy and I went out and blew ourselves to a good dinner, capped with Drambuie and cigars, the latter being formidable looking tubes of a distinctly cabbagey colour that we had spotted en route in a tobacconist's window. Cigars were hard to come by in England; in a short time I was wishing they were harder. I left about four and a half inches of my six-incher in the ash tray, but it had already done its work, and I began urging Jimmy not to linger longer as I felt in need of fresh air or a couple of cylinders of oxygen.

Half an hour's walking and deep breathing exercises in Green Park restored me to the point where my Scottish nature was no longer concerned over the possibility of losing my expensive dinner, so we struck off for Leicester Square and went to a movie. When we left the theatre a couple of hours later we thought that a few drinks wouldn't hurt us, so we took them. We washed them down with a few more, then, about midnight, made our way back to the Park Lane. We were in high spirits as we paid the taxi driver and came through the blackout screen into the spacious and elegant foyer that led back to the reception desk and to the elevator shaft beyond it in the corner.

We took off our raincoats and glanced around. The atmosphere struck me initially as perfectly sedate, precisely the atmosphere one expected for the rent levied, but a slight inclination of my gaze brought me up short, and I placed a restraining hand on Jimmy as I re-surveyed the scene.

Twenty feet in front of us two officers sat, quietly conversing over their drinks. Off to the left 30 feet further back another gentleman sat sipping brandy while he browsed through a newspaper. There was one other person sharing the relaxed scene with us, a gentleman in a tuxedo some 30 feet away from us, on the extreme right side. It was he who drew our gaze. He was standing on his hands, tilted toward the wall, his feet braced lightly against it; between his teeth he was clenching a stein of beer, working away successfully at drinking it upside down. The feature of the tableau that had me wondering whether I had slipped my cable was that no one in the room was paying him the slightest attention.

I looked at Jimmy and found him looking at me. We both looked back to the acrobat. His shoes were nicely shined, I noticed, and were set off to perfection by the immaculate wall against which they were planted; but the elegance of his pose was marred by the unbalanced display of more bare shank on one side than the other. He lowered his head and set the glass down carefully, his face resembling a large ripe tomato, burped, stretched his feet a bit higher on the wall, and got down to business again, ignoring the other occupants of the room as totally as they were ignoring him. I watched his Adam's apple make three or four very obvious round trips, and decided that he was either an extremely poised individual or . . .

I looked back to the first two officers, half expecting to discover that in the subdued light my first impression had been wrong and that they were institutional net men in white coats.

My first impression had been right; they were really in uniform. One was an American officer, a pilot; the other was a British colonel, complete with red collar tabs and a Colonel Blimp-ish cast to his features. The American officer looked distinctly younger than his companion, so much so that I took a second look at his shoulders to see what rank he carried.

"Great balls of fire Jimmy, he's a General" I said.

"Hoose General," said Jimmy, his gaze still riveted on the inverted extrovert who was sporadically giving off muffled metallic sounds as his pockets shed quantities of change and keys.

"That American pilot. He's a general."

"Okay," said Jimmy, squinting a bit to focus on the star, "if he's General let's get his autograph."

Before I could muster any arguments about propriety, he swished up to the General's table with the assurance of a waiter carrying up an overdue order of drinks, peered again at the shoulder badge, then, as the General looked up inquiringly, spoke:

"Could we have your autograph sir? We don't know any Generals."

This was spoken in a matter-of-fact tone, as though Jimmy were the General's tailor and was asking to double check his sleeve measurement.

Colonel Blimp didn't look at it so routinely. He worked a particularly glacial look onto his face conveying as clearly as a picket's placard the idea that he had but an indifferent opinion of this brashness on the part of junior officers.

The General looked at us, noticed our wings, and grinned.

"Sure thing, boys," he said, "have you got anything I can write on?"

As we fumbled for our inoculation cards, the colonel's temperature sank to absolute zero. He threw a look at us as we presented our noc cards that would have turned the water in the pitcher to ice cubes.

The General scribbled his name twice, and gave us a friendly smile again as we thanked him and moved off, heading for the elevator. As we stood there waiting for the attendant I checked the signature.

Our accommodating American officer was Brigadier General Frank A. Armstrong, Jr. Eight months earlier, on August 17th, 1942, he had led Mission No. 1, the first American attack by Flying Fortresses in western Europe. Twelve Fortresses of the 97th Bombardment Group bombed Rouen while the lead element of six Fortresses, headed by Armstrong, created a diversion to draw off the German fighters. On this attack, incidentally, General Ira Eaker had flown as an observer himself; and I remember reading in the American papers, while I was with Plate's mother, the warmly congratulatory message that Sir Arthur Harris had sent Ira Eaker on the successful completion of that historic mission.

This General Frank Armstrong was the man who later inspired the book "Twelve O'Clock High", the man upon whom Beirne Lay Jr. and Sy Bartlett based their memorable character General Frank Savage.

Jimmy and I could know nothing of this of course; and I had forgotten the name of the then Colonel who had led Mission No. 1; but what we did know was that we had seen a truly virtuoso beer drinker and had met a General, a friendly and obliging General, both items we could relay to the boys back at camp.

The ancient servitor in charge of the elevator scrutinized us covertly on the ascent, as the odour of Haig & Haig we were radiating reached him. He stopped the elevator three inches below our floor and left it there. Jimmy went to step out and promptly fell on his face. As I moved to pick him up, the elevator operator moved Jimmy's right foot clear of the door, with the same concern he would have shown in lifting a suitcase out, closed the door, and disappeared.

Jimmy started to giggle as I straddled him and tried to heave him erect, and when he got his knees under him, decided that that was good enough. I hadn't fully appreciated what a cargo he'd taken on until he moved off down the carpeted corridor on his hands and knees, giggling happily at each doorway, and looking up like an eager airedale to see if the number was his. The peak of his cap was impairing his visibility on these surveys, so he rotated it 90 degrees to starboard with one tug and carried on, looking from behind as though his neck had been broken. Next morning as I lay in bed giving the scene a mental replay, I wondered what Colonel Blimp would have thought of Jimmy's corridor patrol if he had happened to follow us to the same floor.

Back at Kidlington we were introduced to a new variant of instrument flying called Day Night training. This exercise was designed to complement the instrument flying we would get on the second part of our course, the beam training, and prepare us partially for the two-

week night-flying program with which we would finish our AFU training. In the DN sequences, as they were called, we wore on our heads a
device mid-way between a gambler's eyeshade and a welder's mask.
The dark eyeshade which this headgear held in position screened out
virtually all light except the tinted glow from the instruments and the
rays from the special runway lamps which provided the flarepath. The
total effect was reasonably realistic, or at least sufficiently so to keep
the instructors from growing bored. I did my first DN sequence with a
new instructor, P/O Thrower, and I could not help noticing that he kept
an exceptionally wary eye on every movement I made — as I would
have myself had I been in his place.

Our flying skills gradually expanded to accommodate the additional demands imposed by Oxford flying, and with the burgeoning
confidence that goes with youth we were soon looking for new fields to
conquer, confident that we should be able to pass the various tests
included in the AFU syllabus. Busy as we were, the days passed
quickly, and in no time we were into our third week and waiting
expectantly for the test we knew must be almost upon us.

On Thursday morning, April 15th, F/L Waddington came into the
flight room and told me to start up DF432 for a ride with him. I went
out and began warming her up. I was unconsciously tensing up by the
time Waddington climbed into the aircraft and settled himself in the
right hand seat; but he dissolved all the tension with his opening
remark:

"Figured I'd give you a little brush-up before your test. Head
down to Cirencester, then map-read over to Bristol, and we'll run
through a few sequences. Any that need a bit of polish you can work
on this afternoon, then I can set up a test for tomorrow."

With the pressure off, I relaxed and enjoyed myself. It was a
good day for flying, and for me it was one of those days when I
couldn't do anything wrong. In half an hour we were skirting the
environs of Bristol, having worked through single-engine drills, map
reading, timed rate one turns, and some climbs and descents both with
and without flap. I had the golden touch. When I did a rate one
climbing turn for 30 seconds I turned through exactly 90 degrees —
which a perfect rate one turn was supposed to produce. When I set the
power for a descent of 500 feet per minute, the needle on the rate of
descent indicator seemed to be stuck on that figure, and the altimeter
unwound with the smoothness of sand flowing out of an hourglass.

As we swung clear of Bristol and headed for home, Waddington
put me under the hood for ten minutes, caged the gyros, and put me
into some unusual positions to check my recoveries, then gave me a
workout on climbing and descending turns and steep turns, and finally
another single engine drill.

"All right, come on out" he said "you've earned a rest. I'll take her back to the circuit, then you can do a single-engine landing for me to finish off."

The landing went as satisfactorily as everything else, and I taxied in idly wondering what Waddington would tell me to concentrate on before the test.

After we had pulled our helmets off, he stood there jotting something in the notebook he'd been using from time to time in the course of our 55-minute flight, then said dryly: "Not much point in giving you another test; you couldn't do any better than you did today. Okay, that's it. You fellows will be going on your BAT course next Tuesday; meantime you can get in your No. 2 cross-country to St. Ives and Evesham — some nice country down in Cornwall."

I stammered my thanks and headed for the flight room, elated. I knew that I couldn't have flown a better test if I had practised for another fortnight. I also guessed, and later confirmed, that Waddington never did give any brush-up or warm-up flights. When you went with him at that stage of your course you were getting a test and that was that. But to avoid putting people under unnecessary pressure when they were called upon to demonstrate their command of the aircraft, he always resorted to this "practice session" device. He fully realized that a good performance would build confidence — and that shortly we were going to need a lot of self-confidence. I still rate him as one of the best instructors I ever had.

The night before our scheduled departure for Feltwell, Tommy Penkuri and I decided to catch the train into Oxford and socialize a little with the English citizenry. We had been warned that the trucks on which we would start our journey in the morning would be waiting for us at 6:00 AM, and that we should time our packing accordingly; further, that the last train back to camp left Oxford at midnight.

In due course we found ourselves in a pub in Oxford, and over a few pints wove ourselves into two or three of the numerous conversations being carried on by the locals. After an hour we elected to change our base, and after a slightly shorter interval in the second pub, decided that yet another change of publicans, barmaids, and philosophers would provide further stimulation.

We got slightly separated in the third pub, but this caused me no concern. I was catching glimpses of Penkuri through the crush, and knew that he would not leave without advising me.

He left without advising me, and it was probably an hour before that fact registered, my faculties being now less nimble. I immediately set off in hot pursuit, and had marched a mile or two with great vigour, thrusting inquiringly through every pub along the way like a fire inspector, before I called a halt briefly and faced up to certain pertinent facts: one, that I was walking about aimlessly in a totally unfamiliar city; two, that I had no idea of where I was myself, let alone where Penkuri was; three, that it behooved me to make tracks for the railway station ere long or, alternatively, gird myself for a seven-mile hike back to camp.

Realizing that the situation was serious enough to call for fresh, new, and innovative measures, I began taking them. I would walk briskly 100 yards or so, halt, and shout "Penky?" at piercing volume. In any period of time less than one full week, the odds against my achieving anything other than laryngitis with this fresh new approach were astronomical; but at the time it struck me as a sound and logical approach to the Penkuri problem. It was a dark night, and progress was halting in the blackout. Unanticipated variations in level jarred me frequently as I stepped off, or up onto, unseen curbs. As the spirit moved me — and I was chock-full of spirit — I made 90-degree course changes at intersections, always stopping to bellow "Penky?" at an early stage on the new heading.

A great deal of time passed; both my throat and my feet began to show the effects of wear and tear. For no good reason I made a right turn in an unlikely looking quarter — a residential district half a mile from the nearest pub or store — and in a few moments I paused to assess what I was heading into. I drew breath and bellowed another throat-rasping summons: " P E N K E E E E ?"

"Whaddya want?" came Penkuri's voice matter-of-factly, he ignoring the trifling three-hour hiatus in our conversation and appearing a shade unsteadily out of an alley ten feet away from me, his hands in the basic semaphore position as he buttoned up his fly. He frowned as he came up — I shouldn't be pestering him, I gathered — but his reproving glance lost considerable impact by being focused to one side of where I was actually standing.

We regrouped and set off for the railway station, repeatedly losing our bearings and having to seek assistance from the occasional figure that materialized out of the darkness. It took us almost an hour's zig-zag stalking to find it. With the exception of one old railway employee, whom we approached forthwith, the place was deserted.

"Where's the train for Kidlington?" we asked, Penkuri experiencing a little difficulty with the concluding syllables.

"The train's gone; it's gone two hours ago" said the railway's representative, leaning on his broom.

"Gone!" we echoed incredulously, unable to credit a British railway's deserting passengers simply for being two hours late.

We verified, about seven times, that no, there would be no more trains for Kidlington tonight, and that yes, the last one had indeed gone, leaving no trace. We then quizzed him on possible alternatives: No, there were no buses. No, there were no taxis; petrol was rationed and the drivers all packed it in early. Besides, he told us, they wouldn't drive all the way out to Kidlington anyway.

As we left the building and went back out onto the highway, we noticed a car sitting a few yards down the road. As we came up to it we could see a man inside at the wheel. The thought suddenly came to me that perhaps this gentleman was not sitting near the railway station, after hours, purely by chance. Possibly he ran a black market taxi; or possibly we had been lucky enough to find a good samaritan.

We introduced ourselves and explained our predicament in emotional terms, not forgetting to emphasize the consequences which would ensue if we actually missed our draft. Our listener bore up well under the harrowing tale. I thought about walking another seven or eight miles on top of what I had already done that night, and meditated less than a second before deciding that, reprehensible as black market taxi operators undoubtedly were, and ruthlessly as they and their passengers were dealt with by the law, one should face this sort of situation with an open mind and give private enterprise a fair chance. I mentioned the sum of three pounds, which was all I had in my pocket; Penky mentioned the 30 shillings he still had; the gentleman behind the wheel then mentioned that it was our good fortune that he just happened to be heading out Kidlington way to visit an old friend who lived opposite the drome.

We climbed in, paid off, and rolled. I sank back and experienced the greatest enjoyment of the whole evening just resting my throbbing feet. The car turned this way and that for about ten minutes, then began to clear the city and finally got onto what promised to be a highway to our drome. Fully relaxed, I checked the time — 25 to three — and was about to close my eyes and start freshening up for our impending 5:00 AM call when our driver blurted savagely:

"Just my bleddy luck . . . imagine, John Law on this road. Keep mum back there, Canada."

Ahead of us on the side of the road we could faintly discern the silhouette of a Bobby. He stood there waving our car down with his flashlight, and our driver stopped 20 feet short of him, to give himself time to run over the indignant denials he was about to make, I supposed. I knew it would be useless — we were caught with our hands in the cookie jar — and braced myself for a night in the cooler and for an even more unpleasant sequel. The helmeted symbol of British Justice stalked toward us deliberately. Three feet away he signalled briskly to our left with his flashlight and called out in a coldly polite tone:

"Pull right the way over on the verge, please."

As we did so we drew up even with him, and his flashlight probed suspiciously, first into the back seat to reveal Penky and I, frozen guiltily, bolt upright and wordless, then into the front seat and across our driver's face. The policeman's voice came to us a moment after his beam touched our driver's face:

"Ow, it's you Alf — you've chynged cars again."

His attitude changed on the instant. He clicked off the flashlight, opened the door to plant his foot on the sill, and bent down to our driver's level to chat. Accepting a cigarette from our driver, whose own attitude had changed remarkably, he delicately steered the conversation to the pleasant topic of the soccer disaster that had overtaken the Bolton Wanderers in their last contest. Penky and I began to unstiffen again.

Presently, in a warm glow of camaraderie, we left the impartial embodiment of Justice and a few minutes later disembarked circumspectly 200 yards from our guardhouse.

We got to bed at 3:30, and our heartless batwoman carried out orders and roused us an hour and a half later. At six, Penkuri and I moved onto parade looking like a couple of wounded holdovers of Napoleon's retreat from Moscow. 'Twas thus on April 20th we journeyed to Feltwell, about 90 miles northeast of Kidlington, to start what was called the BAT course (Beam Approach Training) at No. 1519 BAT Flight.

The beam could be described in simplified terms as an intersecting pair of audible aerial highways, crossing over the aerodrome and dividing the territory for 30 or 40 miles around into four quadrants. One highway, i.e. one leg of the beam, was lined up with the main runway, so that a homing aircraft coming towards the aerodrome within the confines of its "on-course" signal would be brought, in time, directly along the path of the runway. If it carried on, it would then move away from the station in the same line. At intervals an identifying signal in the form of a pair of Morse call letters was transmitted, so that a pilot could verify that he was in fact homing onto the correct radio range. A less certain check existed in the fact that the ranges transmitted their signals on varying frequencies, which were specified on the map.

For example, if the Feltwell beam were shown as 250 Kilocycles, you tuned your receiver to that frequency, then when the aircraft began to approach the aerodrome the signals would become audible, faintly at first, then in growing strength so long as the aircraft moved towards the aerodrome, the point of origin of the signals. But because of the vagaries of radio reception and the narrow separation of the bands, the frequency check on identification, while useful, was not foolproof — hence the addition of the periodic call signal, which was tantamount to a reassuring voice saying "You *are* listening to the Feltwell range station."

Where a pilot was uncertain of his position relative to the drome, he could, by following the prescribed beam procedure, bring himself directly over the centre of the radio range — where a sudden "cone of silence" conveyed that welcome information unmistakeably. The pilot's first step once he was close enough to receive the signal — perhaps 30 or 40 miles away from the drome — was to figure out which of the four quadrants he was in. In two of the quadrants the predominant signal would be a Morse "A", in the other two an "N". From the first reception of the signal, therefore, the pilot could eliminate two quadrants and narrow the problem to ascertaining which of the remaining two he was actually in. To do this he flew a course which would produce a clean intercept of the beam legs and listened to find out whether the signal was growing in volume or fading. If the signal was fading, the pilot immediately turned 180 degrees and flew the reciprocal, holding that course until he passed through the "twilight" zone, where "A's" and "N's" began to blend, and cut right across the steady note of the on-course signal, the central axis of the beam leg. (The Morse code for "A" produced the sound "dit-dah"; the "N" was the reverse sound, "dah-dit". The continuous blended note of the on-course signal resulted from the simultaneous reception of both the "A" and the "N", and that happened only on one of the four beam legs.) As soon as he crossed the beam, a 90-degree turn enabled the pilot, the moment he learned whether the resulting signal was an "A" or an "N" to eliminate a third quadrant and identify with certainty the quadrant he was actually in.

Once the homing pilot had thus positioned himself in a known spot on one of the beam's legs, ancillary signals enabled him, if he found it necessary, to make an approach and landing on the runway even when the visibility was greatly restricted by mist or fog, or when the cloud ceiling was far too low to permit a normal visual contact circuit.

These additional features of the radio range that permitted a pilot to fly blind in what would normally have been perilous proximity to the ground were two vertically transmitted beams, situated on the approach to the runway, known respectively as the outer and inner markers, the latter being located just short of the near end of the runway. The vertical signals produced distinctive notes in the pilot's headphones as the aircraft receiver passed directly over them. On our specially equipped Oxfords, the inner marker, which gave off the more rapid and urgent-sounding signal, also activated a bulb in our instrument panels and gave us a visible light signal synchronized with its rapid beeps.

Thus if an aircraft approaching the aerodrome lined up on the beam and passed over the outer marker at an altitude of 600 feet, then made its descent at the prescribed rate, it would reach the inner marker at 100 feet, a stone's throw from the runway. If the pilot had not made visual contact with the runway at that point, it would be dangerous to carry on and actually make the landing; but in desperate circumstances it might well be attempted, and with a fighting chance of success.

Most of our air time on the course was devoted to practice approaches and landings using the outer and inner markers. We did run through one or two homing problems, adding to the nine hours preparatory Link practice we had done on homing problems before leaving Kidlington. But in the air, the homing exercises were time-consuming if they originated at a point far enough from the drome to make them challenging and realistic; so as soon as the novice beam pilot demonstrated an adequate grasp of the technique involved, the instructor transferred him onto close-in approach work, with its heavy emphasis on precisely timed procedure turns and carefully controlled descents over the markers.

Except when Mother Nature gave us some solid morning mist — which she did two mornings out of the six we flew at Feltwell — we flew our exercises entirely on instrument under the hood. Our instructors, however, preferred the realism that came with dispensing with the hood. They were enthusiasts, skilled enthusiasts, and the dirtier the weather the better they liked it, especially if it was thick enough to permit them to leave the hood off. They were so familiar with their beam layout, and so skilled in its use in the Oxford, that we swore they could pick their teeth nonchalantly while doing a beam landing in fog as thick as porridge.

In decent weather — which we perversely got gobs of, now that we didn't want it — our instructors would frequently have us fly blind until we had come in past the inner marker's adrenalin generating warning, meanwhile watching us fight to keep the crosswind from squeezing us off the ever-narrowing beam, then, when we were only 15 feet in the air, assume control and tell us to lift the hood. It was always a thrill to snatch it up and find the aircraft speeding above the runway like some huge bird, particularly after having sweated for 15 minutes seeing and hearing nothing but the demanding, wavering instruments, and the monotonous theme of the untiring beam. As a variant of this, my instructor twice talked me down the last ten or 15 feet, so that I brought the aeroplane right onto the concrete, blind. The instructors had a reason for doing this, a reason going beyond the simple gratification of our vanity, for it bred confidence, confidence in the reliability of the beam, and confidence in our own ability to exploit its resources if that should prove necessary.

On Monday, April 26th, I made my final flight of the BAT course. For six days, both in the air and in the Link trainer, we had lived with

"The Beam," seeking its blended on-course signal from every point of the compass, listening intently to the unbalanced duet of "A's" and "N's", and transposing their cryptic messages, now fading, now swelling, into developing mental images of our aircraft's position relative to the cone of silence. For 16 laborious hours, 11 in the air and five in the Link, we had flown solely on instruments, confined by the blindfold of the black canvas hood to a darkened hemisphere 20 inches in diameter, and drawing from only the glowing instruments and the ubiquitous monotone of the radio range information enabling us to find the field, position ourselves on the axis of its main runway, and sink gently at 100 miles an hour to the vital concrete ribbon we sought. We were beam pilots now, and if the need arose could fall back with assurance on its lifesaving potential.

On Tuesday Penky and I rode with the rest of our draft to Croughton, a satellite drome of Kidlington's located 12 miles north and three miles east of Kidlington itself. Here, the following day, we started the two-week concentrated session of night flying that would complete our training at No. 20 Advanced Flying Unit.

On April 28th, following a brief afternoon air test with P/O Thrower and two or three solo daylight landings, I went up with him for my first hour of night dual in an Oxford. On May 1st he gave me another 35 minutes night dual and sent me off on my first night solo on the Ox-box. As soon as I had done one solo landing he gave me another hour's dual, this time devoted to what was called beacon flying or "pundit crawling". A pundit crawl was a night navigational exercise which consisted of flying to four or five aerodromes in a sequence designed to take about one hour and to cover about 120 miles. Every aerodrome in the country had a tiny red beacon (pundit) mounted on it or near it. At dusk each pundit would begin flashing low-powered signals — usually a combination of two letters in Morse Code — enabling pilots who had an up-to-date list of the various call signs to identify the aerodrome.

Thrower let me do the navigating as well as the flying, and I discovered that finding these aerodromes was more difficult than I had expected. Until you were very close to the pundit you could not see it at all, and although our forecast winds turned out to be surprisingly accurate, both as to speed and direction, we flew almost to the last minute of our ETA each time before I spotted the pundit just ahead of me.

Thrower and I returned to the Croughton circuit a little after midnight — our trip had taken 55 minutes — and I assumed that I was finished for the night, having already logged three flights. But Thrower had other plans for me, as I realized when he told me to take my fountain pen and write down seven or eight aerodromes and their pundit signals on the back of my left hand. This was the standard procedure, and it imported the advantage that you could not go up in the air and forgetfully leave your list on the ground. There were disadvantages too, of course — the writing surface available on the back of the left hand was limited, particularly for me, and penmanship suffered unbelievably in any encounter with veins and hair. Writing additional letters on the palm of the hand was of no use because your palm would sweat on the control column and render the letters indecipherable. Of the eight pundits I listed, four represented aerodromes that I was actually going to fly to after I worked out a course and ETA from the winds given us by the met section. The other four were the insurance provided in case you missed one or more of the aerodromes you were searching for, in which case, if you were in luck, you might find yourself near one of your "spares". On the other hand you might not — a thought which greatly heightened our alertness since, in typical Air Force fashion, having just been thoroughly drilled in the mechanics of availing ourselves of the lifesaving properties of the radio range, we had been sent back to do our night flying on aircraft which didn't even have radios, let alone a complete beam panel.

I went looking for someone to give me a hand starting up and spotted Penkuri slumped on an apple box in the flight shack trying unsuccessfully to sleep and keep from falling off the apple box at the same time. I stirred him up, friendship having a stronger claim than Morpheus, and we went to start my aircraft: I to wield the crank and do all the work, Penkuri to sit out of the wind in the cockpit and flip the switches in response to my urgent signals.

That scene, and a score of carbon copies, form one of my clearest and most enduring memories of AFU — going out after midnight, red-eyed and tired, on a black, damp, cold night, to start an aeroplane. To perform this feat one knelt in an attitude of supplication on the wing — which always felt like frost-bound granite on the knees — shoved the crank into a recess in the nacelle, and wound mightily on the starter mechanism. Despite the astronomic gear ratio, it was heavy work, and you had to keep it up until the rising whine of the starter reached a pitch that promised sufficient energy to turn the heavy engine over. At that point you took one hand off the crank just long enough to signal your assistant in the cockpit to engage. Typically the engine would kick over briefly, with a dry, lifeless cough, then freeze again with a jerk into Paleozoic immobility. You began winding again, occasionally gasping an ugly word into the crank orifice to signify that you were displeased and wanted no repetition of this obstinacy. People in top physical condition and with exceptionally strong Christian upbringings had been known to wait until the third unsuccessful attempt before beginning to swear, but I frequently gave the port engine a few words of encouragement when I stuffed the crank into it at the outset. On the average about four windings were required before the engine's stubbornness would be overborne and a staccato bark would be coaxed into the smooth steady roar that was the prerequisite of reliable work. Then the process would have to be repeated on the starboard engine — usually equally recalcitrant. One sometimes wondered, leaving the frigid slipstream of the port engine and heading around the rudder to start its mate, whether the better course might not be simply to screw the fuel cap off and drop a match in the tank.

This time it was not too bad, the engines still being reasonably warm, and in a few minutes we had both engines snarling away satisfactorily, belching lurid gouts of bluish flame from the exhausts. Penkuri climbed out and vanished into the darkness. I climbed unenthusiastically into the cockpit and began taxying cautiously to the far end of the drome. In a few minutes I was lined up on the row of flickering paraffin flares, got an answering green flash from the ACP's Aldis lamp in response to my signal on the recognition light, and took off.

To this day I remember that solo pundit crawl as the loneliest flight I ever made, perhaps because while I was afloat in that night's dark and stormy skies my loneliness was accentuated by fear. Leaving the friendly twinkling of our flarepath behind, I conned my noisy little galleon with trepidation into the trackless void ahead. For 20 minutes it was as though the aircraft had been draped from end to end in black velvet, with nothing visible outside the cockpit except the faint red and green glow at my port and starboard wingtips. Twenty minutes in engulfing darkness, tossed like chaff on the wind, unable to see anything anywhere offering a clue to your whereabouts, takes a long time to pass. I was down to the last minute of my estimated time on the first leg before I saw the weak glow of a pundit ahead, and during the two or three minutes immediately preceding the sighting I checked my watch at least five times.

The remaining legs were shorter; but the recurring anxiety during the final minutes did not diminish, and my relief, firstly on finding a pundit of any description, and then on verifying it to be the one I was searching for, was intense. I arrived back over our home beacon exactly one hour after takeoff, and was on the ground five minutes later. Wearily I signed in and climbed out of my gear; then, as I was about to leave, I was touched to notice that Penkuri had waited for me to get back, trying awkwardly to sleep on a hard narrow bench. I was more than pleased that I was going to have some company on the long walk back to our hut.

I woke him up and he grinned at me sleepily, "Fearless, my boy, you is back" he croaked.

Penky's sister sent him the Fort William paper every week, and he and I were faithful followers of L'il Abner. L'il Abner, in turn, was occupied with the adventures of his detective hero, Fearless Fosdick, who was grappling during this period with that implacable antagonist Stoneface. An evening or two before this solo pundit crawl, when I had confided to Penkuri that I had just scared myself livid on a bad night landing, he had immediately christened me Fearless, and thereafter we invariably addressed each other as Fearless and Stoneface. This prompted a few odd looks from senior officers in the mess when we greeted one another ringingly in their presence.

We got into the habit of waiting for each other at the flights each night, and then walking back to the hut together. The last man to land would find and rouse the other and we would start the chilly walk together, usually about two o'clock in the morning.

It transpired that Penkuri and I had things in common apart from our vocations and our enjoyment of Fearless Fosdick and the misadventures he endured for his salary of a cool 28 dollars a week. We shared similar wide-ranging tastes in music, deriving as much pleasure from our few classical records as from Crosby doing "Yodelin' Jive". We shared a cordial hatred for Frank Sinatra and, to our mutual surprise, a fondness for the French-Canadian dialect poetry of William Henry Drummond. On our nocturnal walks back to the hut, we often passed the time prompting each other through "Leetle Bateese," "Keep Out Of The Weeds," and "The Last Portage," three of our favourites. Freddie Taylor and our other friends of Dauphin, the SS *Cavina*, and Burley Court, had not been with us for some weeks, having been posted to different AFU's, and the loneliness flowing from the loss of their company was another factor that tightened the bond between Penkuri and me.

Our flying training went ahead steadily. We re-discovered the fact that flying aircraft at night was much more demanding than day flying. The Oxford was certainly not a vicious aeroplane, at least not if you treated her with respect. But if you were inattentive or careless, she could scare the liver out of you, or kill you, depending on what liberties you were foolish enough to take.

The weather on most nights during this period was marginal for flying, marginal even by our new and tougher standards. This added significantly to the strain of the pundit crawls, and the single-engine night landing practice, a strain that most of us would have found heavy enough under ideal conditions, and I found myself glad to see the end of the night training approaching.

Just before that happy event took place, I went into the mess one day and found my name — or rather a name obviously intended to be mine — listed in the DRO's (Daily Routine Orders) as being designated to serve as Orderly Officer for the following day. I had been expecting it, since Penkuri and a number of other pilots on course had already been stuck with that duty. Strictly speaking, we were not supposed to be saddled with this when we were on flying duties; but there weren't too many Admin types around Croughton to take turns at the job, and as we knew it would only happen once or twice during our course we did not elect to make an issue of it. It was not really an onerous duty anyway, just a series of time-consuming formalities that chopped a day into useless remainders: visits at meal time to the airmen's mess to inquire whether there were any complaints, inspection of fire pickets, visits to the sick quarters and the guardhouse, and finally, at Retreat, the ceremonial hauling down of the ensign, with the Orderly Officer, in the presence of the official party, whipping off his smartest salute as the flag came down the halyards. But I noticed with a glimmer of interest that my name had been misspelled — it appeared as Reden — and that no service number appeared after it, thus leaving me homefree to ignore the duty with impunity and play dumb when the Adjutant played hell.

I did, and he did, and I got away with it. But two days later he put my name on again, this time correctly spelled, and nailed down with the J20216 that eliminated everyone else on our side in a blue uniform. I made a splendid Orderly Officer, and even volunteered to enlarge the normal duties of the office and inspect the WAAF's quarters for good measure, an offer which the WAAF "G" officer declined with a frosty smile. I completed my performance with an elbow-cracking salute at Retreat, under the burning gaze of Penkuri and two WAAF officers whom he had coaxed to come to the window to witness Fearless in action — a show studiously ignored by every other soul on the station.

On May 11th, 1943, we completed the AFU course and had our time certified and our course assessments entered in our log books. To my great delight I was assessed "Above the Average", the only one on our course to get it so Waddington told me. Protocol precluded my hiring heraldic trumpeters and making a public announcement of the fact, but it did not stop me approaching every other pilot on the course, steering the conversation in the right direction with a word or two on the tests, asking what assessment he had received, and then letting nature take its course and allowing the delicious information to be extracted from my modestly reluctant lips.

We were given a week's leave and ordered to report on May 18th to No. 12 OTU (Operational Training Unit) at Chipping Warden for heavy bomber training on Wellington III's. Thus, despite my frequently expressed preferences, my pleas and my prayers, I was to be denied the chance to fly fighters. A number of others, including Penkuri, had expressed the same preference for single-engine fighters, and got the same blanket assignment to bombers.

I always believed with Omar Khayyam that once the Moving Finger had writ you might just as well swallow hard and move on to the next row of hurdles. I tried my best to do just that, swallowing my disappointment — and make no mistake about it, realizing that Billy Bishop and I were not going to pursue parallel careers after all was a bitter draught to put down— and reconciling myself to a basic change in the flying career I had hoped for.

Of course, to the world at large we did the only thing we could: we pushed the line that any damned fool could fly a single-engined fighter, but it took a pilot of top quality to qualify for multi-engined bombers.

CHAPTER 8

OPERATIONAL TRAINING UNIT (FIRST PHASE)

'Tis all a Chequer-board of Nights and Days
Where Destiny with Men for Pieces plays:
Hither and Thither moves, and mates, and slays,
And one by one back in the closet lays.

Rubaiyat of Omar Khayyam

Our very first glimpse of the Wellington III's, squatting heavily in the dispersals ringing the drome at Chipping Warden, made us sharply aware of the nearer presence of the God of War. For the Wellingtons looked very much like what they were, battle-tested operational heavy bombers, still in use by several units in Bomber Command, although declining in numbers and importance alongside the streams of four-engined Stirlings, Halifaxes and Lancasters now widely replacing them in squadron service. Further, the aircrew grapevine, which normally functioned incalculably faster and more reliably than official channels, had also disclosed to us that fatal accidents were commonplace at OTU and that our "graduation exercise" at the end of the course would be a flight over enemy-occupied France to drop bales of propaganda leaflets.

The instructors and Admin officers, who wasted no time getting hold of us, organized the group into classes and laid out our syllabus. They dropped the word that within about ten days we would be teamed up in crews of five, each consisting of a pilot, bombaimer, navigator, wireless operator and air gunner. Equal numbers of each of these trades had been brought together to form our course at Chipping Warden, and we were told that if any five could agree amongst themselves that they wanted to form a crew and fly together, the Air Force would oblige and crew them up officially. But at the end of the ten-day period all those who had not made their own arrangements would be crewed up arbitrarily by the staff; and probably, we guessed, by purely random selection.

Although offered to us *bona fide*, this opportunity to crew up on the basis of our mutual and personal choices was largely illusory in practice. The reason for anyone wishing to crew up and fly with certain other selected individuals was generally self-preservation pure and simple; you wanted to have crew members with you who were good at their jobs and who could perform them efficiently under the grinding stress of operational conditions.

Most of the pilots considered it a hopeless task to pick a crew member, say a gunner, on the basis of the scanty information available. How could we judge whether or not a man wearing a gunner's wing on his chest was good at his job when all we had to go on was a glimpse of him in class? We did not have a clue as to his scores at gunnery school, or as to his psychological make-up. This latter point was of importance in connection with all aircrew, and particularly so with a gunner. If he could respond and return well-aimed fire in the face of the terrifying hail of incandescent cannon shells that an attacking night fighter could launch at him, he just might be able to drive the fighter off or shoot him down, despite the one-sided odds favouring the night fighter in most of these point-blank combats. But if the gunner could not control his fear, and froze in the face of the fighter's onslaught, the bomber crew's only hope was that their pilot could corkscrew the bomber violently and skillfully enough to prevent the fighter's blowing them out of the air. Similar considerations applied with respect to most of the other aircrew trades.

Looking at the other side of the coin, the other crew members had just as hard a decision to make in trying to size up a pilot, and the consequences of a poor selection — whether made by them or made by the Air Force for them — were even more frightening. Choosing a pilot could be a much more critical decision than choosing a wife. A bird-brained wife might still make life worth living, and remain an object to cherish. A bird-brained pilot was likely to kill everyone who flew with him, soon.

And yet the indicia of competence were nowhere to be found with any degree of reliability until a crew had had an opportunity to fly with a pilot and judge his performance in the actual handling of an aircraft under a series of tests. They knew that if a pilot had been commissioned on graduation he had stood well in his class; but that was a rough and often unreliable guide, no matter which way you applied it. One of the finest pilots and aircraft captains I ever flew with was an NCO, a diminutive English Flight Sergeant named Sellar who was as cool as ice water in a crisis, and handled a 35-ton bomber as easily as though he were flying a Link Trainer in smooth air. Some pilots who had earned good training records up to this point had reached, or were approaching, their psychological limits, and would experience increasing difficulty coping with the OTU aircraft's greater demands on their nerve and reflexes. In short, people other than pilots had to go through an even more worrisome ordeal than the pilots themselves while waiting to be crewed up.

Despite the impracticability of attempting to pick other trades, I decided initially that there might be some merit in trying to size up the navigators from the way they handled themselves in the classroom discussion of navigational problems. One chap in particular impressed me as being articulate and skillful in his analysis of problems, so, feeling that I should be doing something about the composition of my own crew, I approached him after class one day and asked him if he would be interested in crewing up with me. He thanked me for the implied compliment, but said he had already agreed to fly with another pilot, a chap with whom, as it happened, I was on very friendly terms.

I decided there and then that I was damned if I was going to run about canvassing a classful of navigators, cap in hand, to come and fly with me. I knew there were enough members of each trade to make up a complete crew for every pilot, and I determined to sit tight and take what the Air Force gave me.

It was while I was still snorting to myself in this vigorous anti-social frame of mind that Penky happened along and brightened my day tremendously by telling me that he had just learned that Freddie Taylor was also at No. 12 OTU. In fact, Freddie had gone over to the satellite aerodrome at Edge Hill, where we got our initial flying training on Wellingtons, just a few days before our arrival. I was elated and could hardly wait until afternoon lectures were over to place a call to the officers mess at Edge Hill. The old crown and anchor king was not in the mess, but in 20 minutes he returned my call. The obvious pleasure in his voice did my heart good. In a few moments we had arranged to meet for dinner the following night in Banbury. It was the only town of any size in the immediate area, and lay about halfway between the two aeodromes.

Penkuri was unable to come, so Freddie and I met opposite Banbury Cross (of nursery rhyme fame) and made our way to a restaurant a short distance up the street. He insisted on ordering, and subsequently paying for, the most elaborate dinner our host could provide, and over our meal we exchanged snippets of news and gossip on everything that had happened since our days together in Bournemouth.

Freddie, too, had been cast adrift from the remainder of our old gang; Watt Wilton was gone, Charlie Payne, Barrie Dean, all our friends had been scattered to flying schools in different parts of the country. Freddie was clearly as delighted as I was to think that he and I and Penky would be together at Chipping Warden and Edge Hill for the next month or two. We began indulging the rather unlikely hope that all three of us would wind up on the same squadron.

Freddie appeared to be doing extremely well on the OTU course. He was happy with the crew he had drawn, and liked the challenge of flying Wimpies, but as we discussed them he interjected a warning comment on their badly worn condition. This was one of the principal factors contributing to the high accident rate at OTU; the other was simply the greatly increased weight, speed, and complexity of the aircraft themselves. Until a short time before, OTU Wellingtons had come from the squadrons actually using them on operations, and were pretty thoroughly used up before they were relegated to OTU service. Freddie warned me in advance that the engines on all our Wimpies were "de-rated", meaning that a pilot could not open the throttles fully and secure emergency boost, otherwise the engines might blow up. Strands of wire at the top end of the throttle quadrant precluded the pilot from forgetting this if an emergency did arise. However, despite the rather precarious condition of the aeroplanes, Freddie liked them and was keen as mustard about his crew's progress.

I steered the conversation around to the family situation to see whether his father's unrelenting attitude had softened now that Freddie was on the point of taking his crew on ops over Germany.

Freddie shook his head, his expression conveying a hint of wistfulness and more than a hint of stubbornness. His father had not mellowed noticeably, other than to indicate occasionally, through a third party, that he had received some word of his son's progress. Just one word of praise or recognition indicating that he understood what Freddie had accomplished since joining up would have been like giving a drink of cool water to a desert-parched wayfarer.

Our conversation turned back inevitably to the Wellingtons and what they were like to fly, and we spent two and a half hours over dinner trading the pleasantest kind of shop talk. After that there wasn't much to do except walk to the bus stop and get ready to head in opposite directions. Freddie's bus left last, so he saw me off, shouting a promise to get together with me in a few days when I got my crew and came over to Edge Hill.

On May 28th we learned that our course was to be crewed up the following day. During lunch hour on the 29th, I was sitting playing cards with Penky and two other pilots when a lanky bombaimer wearing Canada patches walked hesitantly toward us.

"Is there someone named Peden here?" he asked in a high-

169

pitched, gravelly voice.

I glanced at him with more interest as I replied:

"Yes. I'm Peden. What do you want?"

His eyes crinkled as he spoke again. He was as friendly as a puppy wagging its tail, and as compellingly likeable:

"My name is Waters . . . J. B. Waters . . . I'm assigned as your bombaimer."

"Well, you lucky son of a bitch," I said, simulating great heartiness, and shaking hands briefly before resuming play. I meant it to be a joke and thought that must be obvious, but I discovered later than when J. B. walked away he was doing a slow burn and thinking hard thoughts about what a conceited bastard he'd drawn as a pilot.

As soon as the hand was over, I hurried over to check the notice board. My newly-constituted crew was midway down the list:

CAPTAIN & PILOT:	P/O D.M. PEDEN
AIR BOMBER:	P/O J.B. WATERS
WIRELESS OPERATOR:	SGT. A. STANLEY
REAR GUNNER:	SGT. E. JARVIS
NAVIGATOR:	SGT. S. MATHER

Eddie Jarvis, our rear Gunner, was another Canadian, making three Canadians and two Englishmen in the crew. "Stan" Stanley, the Wireless Operator, and Sam Mather, the Navigator, both hailed from Manchester. I don't know what the others thought of their pilot, but my first impression of all of them was good; they seemed to have their heads screwed on right, and to be keen — I myself was so keen at this milestone in our careers that I practically needed chaining down, and I sensed similar enthusiasm in my new compatriots.

Keen they undoubtedly were, but initially they were certainly in no danger of being swept away with a new sense of collective responsibility.

Two days later, "Peden's crew", as we were henceforth described, was detailed to do a "Grope" along with five other crews. This was basically an exercise that simulated the navigational and other problems a crew could expect to encounter on an operation. It was carried out in a large, gymnasium-like building that was divided at the back into half a dozen twin-level studios, each housing one crew. The pilot and bombaimer were ensconced in an open area on the higher level, and the remainder of the crew in the ground-level portion of the "aircraft". While the exercise was going on, simulated engine noise necessitated the use of intercom between the different crew positions. The multitudinous problems we encountered on our simulated raid — on Bremen — were mainly of the variety we had encountered on earlier classroom plotting problems, but an additional complication was introduced by the fact that the large wall clock that governed all our actions travelled at one and one-half times normal speed. This kept everyone nipping about like road runners in an attempt to keep abreast of developments. To project a six-minute alteration of course, the navigator actually had to do the necessary calculations in four minutes, and new drift readings and other corrected information kept streaming in at a dizzy pace.

At noon everything ground to a halt as the clock was shut off, and six slightly dishevelled crews were told to go for lunch and to be back at one o'clock to resume the exercise.

At five minutes before the hour, J. B. and I returned to the hall and climbed into our elevated stall. I was surprised to find that none of our NCO's had yet shown up; I had thought that J. B. and I had cut it fine enough. With two minutes to go, our NCO's were still conspicuous by their absence as the other crews on the exercise settled in, got their headphones on, and made ready for business. As the last seconds ticked away, my feelings changed from uneasiness to anger.

Right on the dot, all the machinery swept back into motion. J. B. and I rushed around from one post to another like demented sentries, desperately striving to keep five crew positions going with two pairs of hands. While he was taking messages and keeping the pilot's and bombaimer's posts going, I was up and down the stairs like a Keystone Cop, racing across the hall to verify drifts, and trying madly to read and copy Morse signals from "Group HQ" at about three times the speed I was trained to take.

Every time it looked as though we were going to catch up and get back on an even keel for a few moments, J. B. would call me aloft to get some more bad news on a message flimsy, and the seething anger in my heart would boil to the surface again. Finally, at a quarter after one on the madman's clock we were using, as I was standing upstairs beside J. B. trying to scribble some essential entries into the navigator's log, the door opened and our tardy trio ambled in, first looking faintly surprised at the tornado of noise and activity all about them, then quickening their steps guiltily as they approached the elevated quarter deck from which I was trying to incinerate them with my eyes. They paused momentarily to get the good word.

"YOU BASTARDS GET ON INTERCOM," I bellowed, ready in my rage and frustration to strangle them with my bare hands.

I gave them a good two seconds to get into the room below me, and then proceeded to ream them out, jointly and severally, for three time-and-a-half minutes, with a voice and gestures highly appropriate for a winning touchdown in the dying seconds of a game, concluding with a vow to kick them all into the guardhouse for the rest of the war should they be misguided enough to treat my words lightly.

171

Breathing in less strangled fashion now that I had aired my feelings somewhat, I came down the stairway to hand the navigator's log to Sam. Expecting to see three chastened subordinates bending earnestly to the oars, I was rudely shocked to see them all helpless with laughter, Stan with tears on his cheeks.

"What in hell is going on now?" I called, mystified, my temper beginning to flare again.

Stan's attempt to answer was almost incoherent. He pointed a wavering finger at the three sets of headphones lying on the table.

"Skipper", he burbled in a weak falsetto which threatened to disappear into the dog-whistle register, "you said . . . get on intercom. The headphones were . . . practically hopping off the table . . . they could hear you back in Canada without the bloody intercom . . ." he shrieked again, holding his stomach.

I was hard put to keep from exploding into laughter myself, but managed, with a little nostril pinching, to do so. Brushing the remaining tatters of my dignity into place, I dropped the log form on the table and returned stonily to my eyrie to complete the exercise with all hands at their stations.

Late on the afternoon of May 31st, J. B. received a message notifying him that his young brother had just been killed. He had been flying Sunderlands in Coastal Command. We commiserated uselessly with J. B., but it was a deep wound. His brother was 21.

On June 4th, Penky and I travelled with our crews to Edge Hill to begin our initial flying training on the Wellingtons. Upon our arrival we could readily see how the rolling terrain surrounding the drome — the site of the first battle of the English Civil War — had given the place its appropriate name. I was at once impressed with the business-like atmosphere of the flight rooms which were bedecked with solid black models of German aircraft and with exhortative wall posters.

One of these posters, which had no application to our future circumstances as minions of the moon, showed an unsuspecting British pilot, only slightly handsomer than Clark Gable, serenely flying ahead on what was obviously a mission against the Forces of Darkness, while off to the side a German aircraft and pilot, of evil and venomous appearance respectively, made ready to launch a cowardly attack upon him from out of a tropically blazing sun. The prominent caption:

BEWARE OF THE HUN IN THE SUN,

was followed by three hand-lettered responses obviously composed by meditative aircrew *literati*, gifted linguists all:

I UND BE VATCHING ALZO, KINDER, FUR DAS GOON IN THE MOON!

II VY ZO? — ISS NEIN KRIS KRINGLE?

III BALLZ — CONZENTRATE ON DER ARTIFIZZIAL HORIZON-DEIDEN!

On June 5th we were introduced to the new pattern of collective discipline. Henceforth the captain of the aircraft, always called "Skipper" by the other crew members, was responsible for their presence when required. Roll call for flying was at 8:00 AM at the aerodrome, 15 minutes' walk from the station messes. On the roll call only the names of the Skippers were called, and a "Present" from the Skipper meant that the other members of his crew were with him, ready for whatever duty was assigned.

All the OTU's were under heavy pressure to get crews through the extensive course assignments prescribed and make them available for posting to the Main Force squadrons, or to the Heavy Conversion Units if the squadrons they were bound for were flying four-engined aircraft.[1] Because of the nightly hemorrhage in the heavily engaged line squadrons of Main Force, and the insatiable demand occasioned by the continuous expansion of the Force, there was a constant "urgent" call for more and ever more bomber crews. Flying weather and serviceable aircraft were priceless commodities in the eyes of the vigilant and harassed OTU flight commanders, and a crew could commit no greater sin than damage an aircraft unnecessarily, or waste air time when performing an assignment.

June 5th also marked the occasion of our first meeting with F/L Dwen. He was to be my flying instructor on our familiarization flights in the Wellington, or "Wimpy" as the aircrews usually called them, the name deriving from that of Popeye's pal, the redoubtable hamburger addict, J. Wellington Wimpy. Dwen struck us as a quiet, reserved type, but in his manner there were thinly veiled hints of tenseness that bespoke a capacity for hair-trigger anger best left untested. He told us that if the ground crew got certain necessary repairs finished, we should have an aeroplane for a flip that afternoon. Meanwhile, he suggested, it would be well worth my while to take my crew and my pilot's handbook on the Wellington and trek over to a distant dispersal where the erks were completing some tailwheel repairs on another plane. I should prowl through the kite for an hour or so on a familiarization tour, he said, getting used to the cockpit layout, and most importantly, memorizing the height of the aircraft from the pilot's seat as it sat in a normal position on the ground, something a pilot had to do on each new aircraft, particularly when moving from a relatively low one, like an Oxford, to a Wellington, which was over 17 feet high. We promptly departed for our inspection.

---

1. Although some 600 Wellingtons had participated in Bomber Command's first 1000-plane raid on Cologne a year earlier, Main Force bombers were now almost exclusively four-engined. By October of 1943 the Wellingtons would be completely phased out of Main Force. The quality of the Wellingtons going to the OTU's naturally improved accordingly.

The Wellington III, a Vickers-Armstrong product, was, by every measure and by broad margins, more aeroplane than we had ever handled before. Up close she looked far larger than our distant glimpses had led us to expect. Although she was a fabric-covered ship, she had the reputation of being the ruggedest aircraft, pound for pound, in the Command. She had fantastically strong metal "geodetic" body construction, in effect a spiral lattice-work fuselage, designed by the great Barnes Wallis, whose most recent piece of homework had shattered two of the great Ruhr dams only three weeks before.

The Wimpy, I repeat, was a big machine by the standards we had then developed. Fully loaded she weighed just over 30,000 pounds, a figure which represented a 400 percent increase over the Oxfords we had just mastered. With a shade over 86 feet of wingspan, the Wimpy pulled that 30,000 pounds into the sky with two 1,500 horsepower Bristol Hercules XI engines; so we now had 3,000 horsepower at the end of our throttle linkage instead of the 740 we had grown accustomed to at AFU. The Bristol Hercules, a magnificently reliable power plant when reasonably worked and properly maintained, was a sleeve-valve engine, with all the altered operating characteristics imported by that radical change. Sleeve-valve engines were a breed most of us had never even heard of before; thus we had had to absorb a substantial amount of new technical information, not to speak of a few new points on engine handling designed to ward off problems (such as oiling-up) that could literally embarrass a crew to death on takeoff. At the dispersal I looked at these well-worn radial monsters with respect, knowing from my reading that they had been excellent engines in their day (despite the limitations which their hoary old age now imposed upon them at OTU).

The Wimpy, according to our handbook, could haul 4,500 pounds of bombs to a target located within a round-trip distance of over 1,500 miles. In her tail she carried a power operated turret mounting four .303 Brownings, and in the nose a two-gun turret which the bombaimer could use to fend off frontal attacks.

A much more complex hydraulic system than we had yet had to work with, powered by two engine-driven pumps running off the port engine, provided the power required to operate the undercarriage, flaps, bomb doors, windscreen wipers and carburettor air-intake shutters. The diagram of her six tank, 730 gallon petrol system looked more complicated initially than one would have thought necessary. I recalled Freddie Taylor making specific reference to this as I pored painstakingly over the drawing showing pressure balance cocks, isolating cocks, engine master cocks, overload tank cocks, engine pumps, hand pump and priming pump. The nacelle tank cocks remained a mystery. On inspection we found that they were operated by short lengths of light chain cable, which I remembered Freddie commenting on, because the handbook, while it helpfully explained that the nacelle tank cocks were controlled by these cables, did not specify whether one drew the cable in or let it out to turn the tank on. Freddie had discovered by experience that in approximately half the aircraft the first method was correct, and in the remainder the other method gave the desired result. This meant, if you put the wrong setting on the chains initially, that you would not have any gas when an emergency arose and you went to tap the 58-gallon reserve in each nacelle. According to Freddie, the best the instructors could suggest was that each pilot have an earnest chat with one of the ground crew fitters before taking up a Wimpy he had not flown before, if there was any likelihood of requiring the nacelle tanks. Even so, Freddie had told me with a grin, we could look forward, on the rare occasions on which we would be driven to using the nacelle tanks, to enduring a few happy minutes of gut-knotting anxiety wondering whether the reserve gas was actually there, or whether we had already used it and were going to see the engines suddenly run dry and windmill uselessly. I made very sure I understood how the nacelle cables of this particular aircraft were supposed to be set before we left her.

Two minutes after the afternoon roll call we were on our way in the crew bus to Wellington Z Zebra for our first flight. I had no trouble with the takeoff, noticing simply the difference in length of run entailed by the great increase in weight; but I can still remember the feeling of incredulity that came over me just after I turned onto my final approach and Dwen told me to dump full flap.

"You'll find you have to put a bit more forward pressure on the control column as the flap takes hold", he drawled laconically. This turned out to be a bit of an understatement. As a military historian, Dwen would undoubtedly have said that Sherman's march to the sea was a bit of a nuisance to the Georgians living within the smoking swath cut by the Army of the Tennessee.

As the flap came down and I felt the stick beginning to thrust back toward me, I began pushing forward harder and harder . . . and harder . . . and harder, and harder still, until there just weren't any more harders left in the locker. If she had required another five pounds of effort, I'd have had to call for help from the second dickey seat where Dwen sat, tense, shuttling his gaze back and forth between the approaching runway and me. At 300 feet he spoke again:

"Don't ever try to do an overshoot in these aircraft once you're down this low."

He let that sink in for a moment and then gladdened my heart some more:

"In fact, the best advice I can give you is just don't do overshoots here, period. Once you've got the undercart and full flap down, your rate of climb with these old de-rated engines is about a foot and a half every 100 miles; so make your mind up early if you're thinking of going 'round again, and you'll stay alive longer. . . . All right . . . watch it . . . that's the ticket; . . . check, hold her . . . not bad; now keep her straight, we've got quite a crosswind."

Our aircraft went unserviceable after 45 minutes, but Dwen was able to get R Roger for another 45 minutes. Next day, Sunday, we couldn't get an aeroplane for love nor money; but on Monday we got another hour and a half in Z Zebra, and on Tuesday, June 8th, after another 45 minutes dual, Dwen climbed out and let me take my crew in V Victor by myself. I had had three hours and 45 minutes instruction on Wellingtons.

Another pilot on our course, C. A. Atkinson, went solo the same day, and that night he and his crew cycled the three miles over to the pub at Shenington to have a small bash in honour of the occasion. I learned from Atkinson next morning that when their host called time, the boys helped each other onto their bicycles and struck off gaily for home, led by their wireless operator, Jock Wilson. The road ran straight the last mile, leading down to the aerodrome on a moderate grade over that whole distance. As it approached the dense hedge which bounded the drome on the south side, it swept abruptly to the left in a 90 degree descending turn and skirted the field. Jock, who had felt that getting the Skipper solo on Wellingtons demanded more than a mere token libation, had worked up such a speed by the time he came to the end of the long downhill grade that if he had raised his arms at that point he could probably have flown.

In fact that was pretty well what he did. Realizing belatedly that he hadn't an earthly chance of making the turn, he hit the ditch straight on at about 35 miles an hour, left his bike over the handlebars as though the seat had been greased, and in the tradition of the great Zacchinis, the human cannonballs, soared on by himself, head first, through six or eight feet of thorn-studded hedge.

Freddie Taylor and I were standing together chatting next morning, waiting to go on parade, when Jock came up to join us, his uniform looking as though several parts of it had been caught in the chain drive of some large machine. If someone had asked me to speculate on the cause of his unusual appearance, I should have guessed that he'd been peering down the muzzle of a double-barrelled shotgun when it went off. There wasn't a butcher shop in Warwickshire with as much raw meat in the window as Jock Wilson was showing on his face that morning, but he wouldn't hear of getting the MO to take him off flying while his face healed.

Sharp at 8:00 AM, after we had all taken turns counting the

raspberries on Jock's face, and laughing uproariously to make him feel better, the flight commander came up to call the roll, and again I cursed my wireless op in lurid terms. Stanley was not on parade. Eddie Jarvis and Sam Mather said he had gone into Banbury the night before, and expressed their certainty that he would be back on the morning bus. That bus was scheduled to make a stop at the boundary of the drome at five minutes to eight each morning, so that theoretically, if one dismounted there, fought his way through the hedge that Jock had flown through so speedily the night before, and ran like Jesse Owens for half a mile, he could make parade on time. In practice, however, the bus was almost invariably ten or 15 minutes late, and no one in his senses would count on it getting him to the drome in time for morning parade. Stanley was apparently counting on it.

I braced myself as the roll call started and answered "Present" when my name was called, fuming inwardly at being put on the spot again by my scapegrace wireless operator. When the roll call was over I began fuming a lot more industriously for my name was called again, this time with orders to take my crew to S Sugar immediately for a check circuit with F/L Dwen.

S Sugar happened to be sitting in view in the nearest dispersal. I dawdled as long as I dared before getting the crew to assemble their gear and start walking toward the aircraft. Still no sign of Stanley. Dwen was not at the aircraft when we got there, but my instructions were to start up the minute the instructor appeared, so we climbed into our positions, fastened our Sutton harness, and kept a four-man vigil for the errant radio basher. In a few minutes Dwen dropped off the crew bus, walked briskly to the ladder in the nose, and climbed up to the second dickey's seat.

"Is everybody aboard, Peden?" he said as he got settled.

"Everybody but the wireless op," I said, "he's still over at the signals section getting his gen."

Dwen knew that the wireless operators had to get a bag of codes, colours of the period, and other signals items from the Signals Leader immediately before a flight; but he also knew that in the normal routine the job should take only a few moments. It was clear that he was not entirely at ease:

"Very well, if you're expecting him momentarily, go ahead and start up."

I didn't bother mentioning that I'd been expecting him momentarily for the last quarter of an hour, and went through the start-up procedure as slowly as I could; but with Dwen scrutinizing every move, I could not protract it much. In a few minutes both engines were ticking over. In another couple of minutes I was nudging them up around 1500 rpm, and shortly thereafter running the pitch controls

bombing" had the advantage that it could be worked into all our other exercises without difficulty, whereas the bombing range was usually fairly crowded, and a visit there had to be laid on in advance, and carried out in a strict cloverleaf pattern in close radio contact with the ground staff in the sighting quadrants.

One of our favourite targets for sim bombing was Banbury Cross. It stood towards the centre of the busy old market town, and offered a nice run-up, either straight along the highway or at a 45-degree angle across the prominent railway yards lying about six or seven hundred yards distant on the outskirts. The old monument was a nice target for a bomb sight and camera; but at first I could never start tracking toward it without experiencing a sharp sense of disbelief at the contrast between my ride-a-cock-horse stage of 15 years before and my present substitute for that carefree amusement, guiding a 15-ton bomber to Banbury Cross to practise blasting things off the face of the earth with high explosives.

Historical accuracy demands a minor modification of my earlier reference to the dropping of practice bombs on the Shotteswell bombing range. To be more precise, I should have said that in the earliest stages of bombing training our crews dropped bombs on or near the bombing range. Let me elaborate.

The range was situated some three and a half miles southeast of the aerodrome. By the luck of the draw — and for Shotteswell it was ill luck indeed — it lay much closer to that tiny village. Here, prior to the opening of No. 12 OTU and its continuously patronized bombing range, the hamlet's inhabitants had kept the noiseless tenour of their way far from the madding crowd's ignoble strife. But war had come, and its flail had scourged the land far and wide. Now Shotteswell's chastened citizens prayed only to be left in peace again and spared from molestation by bombers — not German bombers, for *their* crews had never cast so much as an empty gum wrapper on them, but "friendly" bombers from Edge Hill whose bombaimers all too frequently sent errant bombs hurtling through a greenhouse, in amongst nesting hens, or down a Shotteswell chimney to stir up the fire.

Conceding that a ten and a half pound practice bomb had to land pretty close to kill a person, it was also undeniable that it produced a nerve-rending flash and bang when it exploded, and shot out a billow of snowy white smoke to mark its point of impact. All in all, its unheralded arrival within half a block of any man with the normal ration of brains would cause him to spring clear out of his underwear three times out of four. And ever the menacing drone of circling bombers was present, each carrying a clutch of bombs and an overtaxed novice bombaimer. Verily, if the inhabitants of Malta merited their en bloc award of the George Cross for the months of intermittent bombing they endured in their subterranean caves, the sturdy ratepayers of Shotteswell, who moved about nimbly under the flitting shadows of bombers for a good three years, should each have been given the same medal, plus free liquor and psychiatric care for as long as the terrorists flew from Edge Hill.

Actually we found high level bombing to be a mixture of art and science that called for the utmost in co-operation and rapport between the pilot and bombaimer for success. Once a bomb was released, it continued forward at the same speed and in the same path relative to the ground as that of the aircraft. As it fell to earth, each different type of bomb developed a different terminal velocity because of variations in size, contour, and density, thus altering the time of fall from a given altitude which the bombaimer had to take into account in setting up his bomb sight. Since it took a bomb 20 to 30 seconds to fall, even from the relatively moderate heights we were practising at, it meant that the bombaimer had to release it while he was still a mile or more away from his target. If the target was a 50-foot square on the ground, his judgement had to be backed by considerable practice to hit it, because the aircraft was travelling at least 220 feet every second, and the delay of even a quarter of a second, reflex time, would cause him to miss the target completely. To be spot on, he had to learn to anticipate the target's touching the cross tip by the exact length of his reaction time, and this took practice, and more practice, and still more practice.

But no matter what degree of skill the bombaimer achieved, his performance with the sight we were then using (the Mark IX Course Setting Bomb Sight) was contingent upon matching accuracy from his pilot. All the bombaimer's settings, and his tracking of the target along the guide wires, presupposed that the aircraft — and bomb sight — would be kept dead level, and that the pilot would maintain his airspeed and height precisely on the figures set up on the sight.

It was not too difficult to keep the wings almost perfectly level, and the fuselage almost perfectly level fore and aft, and the air speed indicator almost dead on the predetermined figure, and the rate of climb indicator almost perfectly centered, and the altimeter almost exactly on the footage prescribed; but the margins between all those almosts and perfection seemed to interact in geometric progression to invalidate the bombaimer's settings and produce discouragingly large errors in the point of impact. To exploit the complicated mathematics so accurately taken into account in the sight's compensatory features, and thereby get direct hits, required nothing less than perfection; and perfection carried the customary price tag: tedious practice and intense effort and concentration.

The pilot and bombaimer had to blend their skills as delicately as two violinists in a duet. During the last 30 seconds of the bomb run, with the pilot sweating over his task of keeping half a dozen readings constant despite the basic change in "feel" and performance of the aircraft resulting from the opening of the bomb doors, the scale of the minute variations in course called for by the bombaimer had to be sensed as much from his nuances of expression as from the words themselves. A lead-footed or insensitive pilot could ruin an otherwise perfect run and skid a bomb 100 yards off the mark with a rough rudder correction where the bombaimer had sought only a gentle caress on the pedal.

My teamwork with J. B. improved, but it was not a rapid progress despite J. B.'s conscientiousness. After an exercise, we would go and get the figures supplied from the sighting quadrants, or pick up the photographs when we had been sim bombing, and J. B. would calculate our average bombing error. At first the results were such that we doubted that we would ever get less than a 100-yard error and pull our average for eight bombs down to the prescribed limit; but gradually we whittled the errors down and went on to get wholly satisfactory scores.

We encountered a ten-day period during which we were unable to get in any flying at all. This came about for a variety of reasons, including shortage of aircraft, bad weather, and the fact that the course Freddie Taylor was on was being given priority. Time was running short for them, since they were due to go back to Chipping Warden and start the final half of their course around June 18th.

This last portion of the OTU training put heavy emphasis on long night cross-countries, one of which always incorporated special exercises with our own searchlight and night fighter defences. The latter were known as "Bullseyes". In addition, the last weeks of OTU training saw the crews flying "war load" trips, i.e. flights in aircraft which had been loaded to the maximum permissible all-up weight; and, of course, more practice bombing was prescribed, plus the graduation exercise of an actual operation over enemy-occupied territory.

Freddie and I had one more thoroughly enjoyable evening together just before he took his crew back to Chipping Warden. He had racked up an above-average record at Edge Hill, particularly in the high level bombing exercises, and was eager to finish the course and get onto operations with a squadron. We sat in my hut until the small hours sharing the contents of a food parcel I had just received from the good ladies of Mrs. Plate's church in Iowa. I calculated, having regard to the exercises my own crew had completed, that it would be about two weeks before we were ready to go back to Chipping Warden ourselves. Over a few choice morsels we discussed in light-hearted vein various stratagems — all hopelessly impracticable — for ensuring that we would be sent to the same squadron.

On June 21st, three days after Freddie had gone, we began flying again. I remember the 21st clearly as the day on which Stanley nearly blotted his copybook for the last time, and with my assistance.

After a routine dual check with Squadron Leader Simpson, I was cleared to take my crew in Y Yoke and drop eight high level bombs at the Shotteswell range. We took off, dropped our bombs with painstaking care, and were back in the landing pattern at Edge Hill an hour and 15 minutes later. The control officer gave me "Turn one to pancake," and in a few minutes I was letting down and turning onto my final approach.

I dumped full flap, and became engrossed in the customary death grapple with the control column. After a full minute of this, with the runway looming ever closer, Stanley suddenly came on intercom, his accents flustered and breathless. At that precise moment, with the runway only 250 yards in front of us, I had just gained the upper hand in the pushing contest with the control column, and was simultaneously contending with rough air and a gusty cross-wind that was forcing me to crab eight or ten degrees off the runway heading; hence I was not in a position to weigh and analyze his startling communication. As unwelcome messages go, however, it was a model of its kind, brief, to the point, and crystal clear despite the over-use of one versatile word and a derivative thereof as noun, adjective, and verb:

"Don't land just yet Skipper for . . . . . sake; me . . . . . trailing aerial's still out! . . . . . me!"

I freely confess that in light of Dwen's earlier gloomy pronouncements, I jammed the throttles open and embarked upon the requested overshoot with all the enthusiasm and poise of a non-swimmer having a go at Niagara Falls on a surfboard; but Stan had sounded desperately anxious, and although I wasn't sure what the magnitude of the problem was, the rapid approach of the runway made it impolitic to ask for a restatement and analysis of the emergency.

Calling "Undercart up" to J. B., I wound the elevator trim smartly, and struggled to get the ancient leviathan rising instead of falling. In ten seconds I realized that Dwen had surely known whereof he spoke in recommending against overshoots regardless of the circumstances. The old aeroplane, engines roaring, waffled sluggishly ahead, barely staying over her stalling speed, and straining every shuddering fibre to hang in the air.

Slowly we staggered around a wide, flat circuit. I bled the flap off in infinitesimal amounts and we gradually clawed our way a few feet higher, after which I could afford to let the airspeed grow a shade healthier. Only then would I have bet with any confidence that we were going to complete the circuit as planned.

Ten harrowing minutes later we landed, J. B. and I, since we had had the best look at the man with the scythe, chalk-faced. My pulse, I noticed, was going like a flamenco dancer's heels. When we climbed out, and I had uttered a silent prayer of thanks, I turned to our good wireless operator for some clarification of this sudden trailing aerial emergency that had brought us all within hailing distance of the Pearly Gates.

It seemed that he had reeled out 50 or 100 feet of aerial while the rest of us were practising our bombing. This enabled him to do some wireless practice which he could not otherwise have done, and was perfectly proper. However, he had not been checking on the intercom to see what was going on, and when we headed for home had been unaware of the need to reel his aerial back in. It was only when he heard me throttle back on our final approach that he had realized his predicament and had blurted his pulse-stirring emergency message on the intercom.

I still had the feeling at this point in his exposition that there must be a large significant piece somewhere that I had missed. I probed.

"So what the hell would have happened if we had gone ahead and landed and torn the damn aerial off in the hedge?"

"Well, the Signals Leader would have fined me ten bob, Skipper," he said in a satisfied tone, ready to drop the subject now and head to the NAAFI for tea and a wad.

I had been braced to learn of some bizarre justification for our recent interesting circuit, something far beyond the stock emergencies dealt with in the pages of the pilot's handbook, but not for one second had I expected a bland admission that he had called for an overshoot to avoid the financial blight of a ten-shilling fine. I was momentarily speechless, but immediately recovered and launched into a high decibel policy statement designed to make abundantly clear to anyone within 100 yards of us that, in future, nonchalant calls for overshoots would result in certain death, if not in the ensuing aeroplane crash, then by manual strangulation upon landing.

We were sent back up an hour later to do a camera gun exercise in C Charlie. It took an hour and a half to complete; but when we landed again — this time without any exhortations from the wireless operator on final approach — we learned that we were still not finished. We were booked for initial night dual with F/O Attwood.

Somewhat to my surprise the night flying went very well indeed. I suddenly seemed at home in the Wimpy's cockpit, and despite her weight and her marked idiosyncracies on the final approach, I experienced no trouble whatever in landing her at night. Nevertheless, despite the uneventful progress of the exercise and my growing confidence in my night flying ability, I did not relax. We had already had one fatal accident at OTU, and the sight of a burned out Wimpy holding the ashy residue of five aircrew was not calculated to induce carelessness. I did two solid hours of night circuits with Attwood, and felt that I had earned my pay when I finally hung my helmet in the locker.

Next day we found that ours was one of four crews getting a 36-hour pass, and a quick enquiry revealed that Penkuri's was another. This set the stage for a venture I'd had in mind ever since we first came to Chipping Warden.

During the leave preceding OTU, I had visited my brother-in-law and some other friends serving with the Straths (Lord Strathcona's Horse) in 2nd Canadian Armoured Div., then stationed just outside Brighton at Maresfield. One of my friends, Con Olafson, had formerly spent some time in the Edge Hill area, and had come to know a pretty nurse living there, a pretty nurse, moreover, who had a pretty sister. In a gesture of inter-service co-operation, Con had given me the phone number (Cropredy 23) and an enthusiastic endorsement of the charms of both girls.

I had made a telephone call — all I could find time for at that stage of the course — shortly after our arrival at Chipping Warden, and had followed up with other calls, advancing my cause by degrees, until I had secured the tentative promise of an invitation to the house for two of us at some mutually convenient time. I had promised to call the moment an opportunity arose.

I cleared with Penkuri, embellishing the known facts somewhat to overcome an irrational suspicion he manifested that he might somehow draw a short straw in a venture of this type arranged by me. After a few minutes of my best salesmanship, he caught fire and became enthusiastic.

I got on the telephone immediately and broke the news of our 36-hour passes to Ruth (earlier vouched for by Con as slightly the better of the two). She responded magnificently, with an invitation for both of us to come to the house that afternoon about two-thirty, and to stay with the family until the following day. I hastily accepted and promised that we would start cycling the eight miles from Edge Hill to arrive at her place on time.

A cloud no bigger than a man's hand appeared on the horizon when I ran over the flight plan with Penkuri. One of his NCO's had just been promoted from Sergeant to Flight Sergeant, and Penky had promised to stop in at the party the boys were having in Banbury and hoist a celebratory pint with them while they wet the new crown. However, this solemn function was scheduled to start at one-thirty sharp, and since Penky's obligation as Skipper could reasonably be limited, under the circumstances, to the consumption of one token pint, he fully expected to start pedalling the five miles from Banbury to Cropredy before two o'clock. This, he calculated, should see him fetch up at the family estate within a few minutes of the appointed hour. To preclude any mistakes I double-checked, reciting once again both the route and the description of the house, then left Penkuri and embarked upon extensive slicking-up preparations myself.

Three hours later, almost exactly on time, and with my face as shiny as my brass buttons, I came up to the house, a pleasant looking country home sporting a low hedge and an attractive flower-fringed patio. But if the house had looked appealing, I could hardly credit my good fortune when I met Ruth and Sally. Con Olafson had definitely not overstated the case; they were the two best looking girls I had seen at close range since Northampton. I introduced myself, and the girls in turn introduced me to their mother, a plump, pleasant woman who quickly revealed herself as hospitality personified.

Father was a different cup of tea. One look through the viewfinder and I pegged him, despite the disguise of baggy trousers and a Harris tweed jacket, as a former Sandhurst or Guards regiment RSM, the type who liked even members of his immediate family to stand at attention, or at least sit bolt upright with all buttons fastened when chatting with him. The Uriah Heep boot-licking approach appeared to be definitely the medicine for him, and I got to work on him right away, in view of the stakes. I managed to slip half a dozen obsequious "sirs" into the early feeling-out process, asked for his opinion on the capabilities of English retrievers for pheasant hunting, simulating an intense interest in his view, and then questioned him on the lengendary durability of the locks on Purdey twelve bore doubles. A few more sycophantic straight lines, and the oblique hint that I might be able to wangle a couple of boxes of 12 gauge shotgun shells from the gunnery section, and the old boy began melting like butter under a blowtorch. In ten more minutes I had passed inspection, and he was consigning me to the custody of the girls for a survey of the property while he returned to his den, probably to gloat over old defaulters lists. Before leaving him I explained that Penkuri would be along just as soon as he completed the special air test the flight commander had given him to do at the last minute.

After a leisurely tour of the greenhouse and garden, we settled down in deep wicker chairs on the patio to enjoy the sun. The girls were not only good looking, I realized, but well endowed mentally and possessed of highly engaging personalities into the bargain. I relaxed and enjoyed their conversation. The more we chatted the better I liked them, and the more promising the whole set-up appeared. I thought fondly of good old Con as I visualized getting passes from Chipping Warden in the weeks ahead and spending numerous 48's in the company of the two charmers sitting opposite.

Time flew by pleasantly, and when Mum and Dad unexpectedly appeared on the patio carrying trays of food and dishes for tea, having apparently concluded that they could delay no longer for Penkuri, I was startled to find that it was after four o'clock. I suffered a momentary qualm, then realized that although Penky had obviously crossed me up and decided to give it a miss, the social tide was running so strongly in my favour at this point that only a lapse of disastrous proportions could prejudice the rosy future shaping up for me in Cropredy. We all tucked in and enjoyed a delicious tea. After I had gorged myself for half an hour on sandwiches, warm crumpets, and home-made strawberry preserves, not to mention friendly and animated conversation, the future looked as radiant as the summer sun.

As I was washing down the last crumpet crumbs, I glanced idly across the hedge. Down the road a distant figure was approaching. I watched for a moment. The figure appeared to be mounted on a bicycle. I watched a few moments longer luxuriating in the lassitude which succeeds gluttony. Whoever it was was using a lot of highway, as though he were pedalling shakily through a horizontal slalom course visible only to himself. I conjectured casually that this inept performer must be some novice out for his first solo on a bicycle . . . or . . . OR . . . a horrible possibility flashed upon that inward eye that Wordsworth found so useful for replays, and the image sent chills down my spine.

My lassitude left me during the ensuing sixtieth of a second as the monstrous thought began burgeoning. At 300 yards I made positive identification; it was Penkuri.

On the wobbly wayfarer came, like the highwayman, I thought, riding, riding, riding, up to the old house door, where father would no doubt look to his priming and assume the role of the redcoats. At 200 yards one readily guessed the rider had a problem. At 100 yards it was identifiable as a big problem; and when Penkuri was weathering a big problem all the muscles in his face tended to let go like leaves before the autumn gale leaving his visage hanging loose like an oversize Hallowe'en mask.

I began to pray that he would not see me or recognize the house — a distinct possibility in the shape he was in — but I could scarcely look away to heighten this possibility, for the other members of the group now had their gazes rivetted upon this spastic apparition. Tom Payne was right: these were the times that tried men's souls. I stared past him, not letting on that I recognized him, for if he kept riding his identity would ever remain a secret. Certainly I would not give him away.

But my uniform and pilot's wings had caught his eye. He kept turning further and further to the side as he came abreast of us, keeping me in view until he was looking 90 degrees to his left, his wheel working a scalloped edge on the road as he travelled. His eyes grew less vacant and he spoke:

"Hi, M . . u . . r . . r . . a . . y," he drawled, and promptly made an auspicious start by pitching onto his face as the handlebars reversed on him. There was a clanging of metal mixed up with meaty sounds.

Since he had deprived me of any alternative, I suddenly recognized him:

"Why, for heaven's sake, it's Penky," I said, as the group stood in silent fascination waiting to see what would materialize from the heap beyond the hedge.

"Hail to thee, blithe spirit" I called, striving to dissolve the gathering clouds with the light touch as I ran to help him disentangle himself from the confining embrace of his cross bar, bicycle chain, and haversack strap, all of which were cutting into various parts of his body.

I protracted the extrication process somewhat while I hissed a few Red Alert instructions into his ear, then led him over for the ordeal of introductions. He made a noticeable effort to regroup the pendulous planes of his face, and to reduce the pronounced lag in his eye movements. Unhappily, his mighty willpower could not stop him from smelling like a brewery, or stumbling over "How do you do" as though articulating a newly learned phrase from a Berlitz guide on Pushtu. Before Father he summoned up all his reserves and said: "How you do do . . . sir." In short, in about 60 seconds he proceeded to make a shambles of what had been the social success of the season, an occasion of virtually unlimited promise for both of us.

The girls did their best; they were sympathetic and understanding. I lowered the shaky warrior into a patio chair, trying under Father's gaze to make the herculean effort look like a casual steering gesture — and was almost pulled into the chair on top of him — and jammed a crumpet into his nerveless hand; from that point on, the girls did their best to pretend that he wasn't there. Penkuri made it hard to maintain the pretence. Strange rumbling and sluicing sounds emanated periodically from his interior piping, and after 20 minutes of semi-comatose immobility he had to be shown, and helped, to the toilet. Thereafter he lurched off conspicuously on the same mission at intervals of approximately ten minutes.

A pall began settling inexorably over the festivities. Upon meeting my partner, Father had figuratively donned his jackboots and Sam Browne again, and now it was apparent that despite the earlier mileage I had made with him, I was to be judged by the company I kept. It was all too clear that Father classified that company as a common, garden variety drunk. He had excused himself gruffly after sitting downwind of Penky for only two minutes, but the atmosphere continued to deteriorate steadily despite the girls' best efforts. By dinner time we were all about as gay and vivacious as a team of surgeons discussing the autopsy report on their last mistake. Penkuri himself was beginning to sober up a bit at long last, but as his inebriation wore off, his general health fell off in even greater measure, and he began to look whiter and whiter.

Dinner was a painful experience, far and away the worst social ordeal I had ever endured. By his frosty, distant manner, Father made it clear that in spirit he was wearing his bearskin, full dress and decorations. The others tried their gracious best to let on that everything was perfectly normal, but with Penkuri present and growing visibly whiter the effort was foredoomed to failure; it was like trying to pretend that everything was perfectly normal with a mute Polar bear in a blue uniform sitting at the table. He was so ill now that he scarcely dared look at the food, let alone eat it. As course after course was carried away from his place untouched, the strain mounted.

Moments after we rose from dinner the girls mercifully cut the hamstrings on the tottering evening by announcing that they were both on duty early in the morning and would therefore have to retire for the night, forthwith. They guided us to our room, and in a short time a deep silence reigned throughout the house.

Penkuri was now clearly in the grip of some terminal illness. From the position of his hands my first guess was stomach cancer, although his breath and staring eyes — particularly his breath — still offered hope that the malady might prove to be only advanced cirrhosis of the liver and alcoholic poisoning. Such was his condition that I did not have the heart to reproach him for the awesome debacle he had wrought from the moment he first collapsed amongst his bicycle in front of the house. Instead, I lay beside him quietly, turning over in my mind possible remedial measures, wondering for a start if we could retrieve the situation and undo those things we ought not to have done simply by showing up bright and early in the morning, properly contrite, looking like the airmen on the recruiting posters or the Brylcreem ads.

About midnight Penkuri put the game out of reach. He rolled over and seized me suddenly with a fevered grip, saying that he thought he was going to be sick. It was the best guess he ever made. I stood outside the toilet after helping him rapidly to the portal, wishing

I could pull another chain and ride down the pipe to some haven miles away from him. Penkuri remained in the cubicle for half an hour, alternating his performance between roaring like a moose and giving off loud straining sounds as though he were lifting a piano by himself. Residents on the outskirts of Banbury could easily have heard some of his better efforts. When he gave up, we slunk back to our room, mortified beyond description.

Half an hour later he got another mandatory summons and was back bellowing in the stall. There was no possibility of anyone sleeping through it unless he had taken lashings of drugs. Thereafter Penkuri gave two more concerts, the last one at three-thirty. I decided then and there that I could not face the prospect of two or three more such performances and then an early breakfast with Father. I began pulling my uniform on and told Penkuri to follow suit. We crept quietly downstairs, mounted our bicycles, and left, hoping that the girls would forgive us and that they would get at least a few hours' sleep following our Arabian departure.

Penky was sober now, in fact more than sober, sepulchral. As we laboured on through the darkness, I sadistically described in glowing terms the potential of the set-up he had torpedoed with his untimely orgy, and kept dribbling fuel onto the fires of his abject remorse. Twice in the course of our journey he had to dismount hastily and heave again, and it was well after five when we rode wearily up to our palatial tin shacks at Edge Hill.

Thus ended, ignominiously, the great Cropredy 23 operation, initially blessed with such good fortune. It was a sore point with me for a few days, and the fact was not lost on me during that period that Penkuri was ever at pains to steer the conversation away from any subject that appeared likely to lead to a discussion of what we might do on our next pass.

On June 26th we got C Charlie again for another camera gun exercise. On these, fighter aircraft flying from a nearby station would do simulated attacks on us using the tactics currently favoured by the German night fighters. During these attacks our gunners "defended" us with their camera guns, being particularly interested in seeing what they could do in the midst of our corkscrew evasive action. The fighters used their cameras, too, and an assessment of all the films gave a good indication of the relative efficiency of the fighter attacks, the bomber pilot's evasive action, and the marksmanship from the bomber's turrets.

Eddie Jarvis, our rear gunner, felt that he had been very successful that afternoon, and confidently predicted that he was going to be able to show us a lot of footage of the fighter. Eddie was always a modest and conservative soul when it came to making predictions on such matters, so I was satisfied that the crew would get good marks on the exercise. I gave Eddie a verbal pat on the back for making us look good, and we separated briefly for dinner. We were all scheduled to meet again three or four hours later — we emphasized the time for Stan's benefit — for another session of night flying.

Eddie Jarvis never flew with us again. After dinner, as he was sitting in the mess, minding his own business reading the paper, one of those would-be funny men, who should have been kept on a chain somewhere, came walking up to him.

"Hiya Eddie, how'sa boy?" he said, cupping his hands slightly and clapping Eddie over both ears simultaneously as his little joke.

He ruptured one of Eddie's eardrums, thereby knocking a first class gunner out of aircrew. After a day or two Eddie was gone, and I never saw him again. We flew the night of June 26th with a spare gunner.

After an hour's dual, which gave me a total of three hours night dual counting the two I'd had with Attwood, F/O Gordon cleared me to take my crew in O Oboe for an hour and a half of solo night circuits. Again things went very well, my solo landings were smooth as silk, and I landed in the early hours of June 27th well pleased with my night flying prowess in the Wimpy.

At the same moment that I was climbing out of my aircraft, enjoying my minor triumph in a Wellington, Freddie Taylor was dying in his. I learned about it a few hours later. The facts had the simplicity of classic tragedy.

On the night of June 26th, Freddie had taken off from Chipping Warden in Wellington BJ965 to do a Bullseye cross-country with his crew. Over Yorkshire, with three-quarters of the exercise completed, they ran into trouble when their port engine failed. With our old aircraft, an engine failure, particularly at night, was serious trouble. Freddie decided that there would be less risk of injury to his crew if he steered for the drome at nearby Skipton and made an emergency landing there. The alternative was to order the crew to bail out; but at night, over unfamiliar terrain, and perhaps with some uncertainty as to the exact position, the risk of serious injury to his crew was very real. Freddie rejected that option, and few aircraft captains would have disagreed with him.

He never made it to Skipton. Whether his one remaining engine also began to fail under the additional strain placed on it I was never able to find out, but I guessed that that had happened.

In any case a disaster impended, for Freddie apparently ordered his crew to take up crash positions, and at 1:15 AM attempted a wheels-up landing just outside Skipton on a stretch of ground known as Deer Gallows Plain. Complying with Freddie's order to brace themselves in the appropriate crash positions, the other crew members all survived. Freddie himself, unable to move, stayed at the controls and died against his instrument panel making the best landing he could under hopelessly adverse conditions.

Penkuri and I got permission to leave the station for a few hours to go to Chipping Warden the day of the funeral. In the bus on the way over I sat at a window, unseeing, thinking almost unconsciously of how much the loss of Freddie Taylor meant to me. The suddenness of his death had shaken me. From the time we had first gone to Dauphin he had been the natural leader of the little group we travelled with, the group which had come to include Penky, Jimmy Watson, Barrie Dean, and Watt Wilton. Freddie and I had always had a strong affinity for one another, augmented on his side by the faint suggestion of an older brother protective attitude toward me. I had been looking forward to rejoining him at Chipping Warden in just a few days; now, like Francis Plate, he had been snatched away from us.

The sight of his classmates carrying Freddie's body to the grave in a light-coloured coffin of spartan plainness stirred me deeply. Something about the pathetic cheapness of the coffin heightened the shock at first, then, as Penkuri and I followed along with the small procession, the total lack of ostentation began to seem more appropriate, the stark simplicity of the scene according with the singleness and strength of purpose Freddie had shown from the day he enlisted.

I stood at the salute as the echoes of the firing party died away and said my last goodbye to Freddie, thinking as I did so of the waves of remorse that must inevitably add their sting to his father's grief when he recalled — as he would so often — his unyielding hardness. I wished I could be with the old gentleman to help ease his pain, sharing the pride I had had in his son, and letting him know what a stalwart and cherished friend he had been to me.

The following day, back at Edge Hill, our crew flew one standard beam approach exercise and found that it completed our list of assignments for the first half of the course. On July 1st I got the times in my log book certified by the flight commander. I had done 21 different flying assignments at Edge Hill, in addition to Link time, for a total of 27 hours on Wellington III's. About seven of those hours had been dual, while for 20 hours I had flown as captain of the aircraft. On July 2nd we travelled back to Chipping Warden, and on the 3rd we began flying from that base.

CHAPTER 9

OPERATIONAL TRAINING UNIT
(SECOND PHASE)

This way the noise was, if mine ear be true,
My best guide now;

Milton, Comus

We were assigned to "B" Flight, under the command of Squadron Leader Fadden whom we met briefly. Two days after we had begun flying in his section, we met him again. We had returned late in the afternoon from a three-hour cross-country in G George to be told, before we had taxied back to our dispersal, to marshal our aircraft behind four others which were already lined up on another runway and sitting about 200 yards clear of the runway in use. When we had marshalled and climbed out of our kite, we were informed that our crew, along with the crews of the other four aircraft, would be going on a night cross-country right after dinner, weather permitting.

The weather did not co-operate. Poor when we landed, it got steadily worse. However, the demand on the OTU's to grind out assignments if at all possible, and to keep more and more crews flowing to the squadrons, was so insistent that all five crews were kept hanging about until 11 o'clock on the remote chance the weather might improve. At long last the harassed met section ruled out any hope of improvement, and the exercise was cancelled. Orders came to taxi the marshalled aircraft back to their proper dispersals and report for duty at the usual hour in the morning. I told the rest of the crew they could push off to bed, but took Stan with me to keep a lookout on the starboard side as I taxied back.

It was black as pitch and spitting rain from low scud when Stan and I got G George started. When the other four aircraft had moved off, I taxied ours down to the perimeter track, turned right, and crawled along watching for one of G George's ground crew to wave us in when we reached the dispersal. I had only a hazy idea of its location, having accumulated the grand total of two landings at Chipping Warden. Such uncertainty we considered par for the course until one had taxied around the perimeter track in daylight a few times and learned from observation which aircraft went where, and normally it was of no moment anyway, for the ground crew were generally Johnny-on-the-spot to wave their charge in.

However, G George's erks had not been called as soon as they should have, with the result that I taxied right past the dispersal unknowingly. I did see one or two glimmers of light ahead of us through the rain, but when I trundled hopefully up to them they turned out to be ground crews waving in other aeroplanes which had reached their homes before us. I taxied slowly halfway round the drome, vainly searching for the corridor and circular concrete bed which belonged to G George. The perimeter track was narrow and twisty; the blue lights tracing its boundary were widely spaced, and I got frequent warnings from Stan that I would drop a wheel in the mud if I came an inch further to the right.

Out of nowhere a shadowy figure on a motorcycle pulled past us, his machine inaudible over the sound of our own engines, and signalled me with his flashlight to stop. I complied; Stan opened the front hatch and put the ladder down, and in a moment I was looking into the face of S/L Fadden.

"You chaps at sea? Righto, follow me and I'll show you G George's dispersal."

He was down the ladder and gone before I could articulate my appreciation. I was bone tired as it was, and didn't need any more night taxiing practice. Fadden mounted his motorcycle again and led off at just the right speed, waving his flashlight behind him periodically to mark the centre of the peri track. In a few minutes we reached our dispersal. By now the erks were alert and I quickly positioned the aircraft and switched off. Our motorcycle escort was still waiting, I noted, and wondered in pleasant anticipation what other service he planned to render at this point — about all he could do, I figured, was tell us that he had already ordered the crew bus and that it was on its way.

It turned out that that was not all he could do at all. Once again he ascended the ladder briskly and spoke:

"Leave the aircraft just the way you would like to find it; be sure to put the control locks on. When you have done that, I want you two to memorize the location of every dispersal on this aerodrome, draw a diagram of the layout, and leave it on my desk before parade time in the morning."

With that, he went down the ladder, leaving me speechless and gazing unbelievingly at the hole through which he and his flashlight had disappeared. There was no point in postponing our chore until morning; getting back down to the aerodrome by seven instead of eight would cost us just as much sleep. We would have to go up to the flight room now, or over to Fadden's office, wherever we could find an aerodrome map, and prepare the diagram. I looked at my watch as Stan and I huddled under the wing out of the rain: 20 minutes before midnight.

Ten minutes earlier I had thought S/L Fadden an absolute brick. On my mental scoreboard I now rectified the obvious typographical error.

We found an aerodrome layout, and I hastily sketched the roughest approximation of it I thought I could get away with. Then we spent five minutes on memory work. This naturally entailed forehead-tapping, mumbling, and much gazing off into the distance, the performance being accompanied by a repetitive one-word refrain from Stan, who apparently felt strongly moved to liken Fadden's actions to poultry droppings.

When we felt we could stagger through the dispersal sequence with about 50 percent accuracy, a proportion we felt to be much higher than our flight commander deserved, I left the diagram on his desk and we went back outside to tackle the doubtful task of scrounging a lift back to the mess.

It began raining harder, and I wished I had come dressed for swimming instead of flying; I pulled the cover off the mental scoreboard once more and added a few more modifiers to the classification.

It was only a few days later that two Wimpy crashes took place around Chipping Warden within 48 hours, one right on the aerodrome, the other a mile or two away. The first one was noteworthy in that it yielded a few humorous overtones.

A Wimpy flying from another drome developed an assortment of difficulties just at dusk, and landed hastily at Chipping Warden, finishing up on its belly alongside the main runway, smoking ominously. The crew boiled out of it almost before it had come to a stop and went pelting down the runway. Despite the burden of their flying clothes and big fleece-lined boots, the boys gave the appearance of footing it at a shade over 50 miles an hour — exactly as I should have done in their position, next to several very large tanks of high octane gasoline, two burning hot engines, and the unmistakable indication of a sizeable fire somewhere aboard.

The officer in charge of night flying, alerted by flying control, came tearing along the main runway, heading for the aircraft on his motorcycle. He was far ahead of the crash tender, whose crew had apparently tarried to finish their hand of pontoon before setting course. As he roared down the runway on his big Enfield he met the track team from the Wimpy, and slowed down to shout some questions at them. None so much as glanced sideways at him so intent were they on their mission of widening the distance between them and the smouldering flying machine.

The officer on the motorcycle increased his speed again, still making for the smoking aeroplane. I noticed that he sat very erect on his machine, plainly intent upon setting the proper example to these craven runners, displaying Leadership and Command qualities of a high order.

Just as he drew alongside the stranded hulk and dismounted, a flaring gush of open flame banished the fabric along a goodly portion of the port side and, as we shortly learned, he caught a glimpse of something else motivating the foot racers — several 500-pound bombs baking away merrily in the open flames.

From our vantage point, 400 yards away, it then appeared that he remounted his motorcycle in one 12-foot bound that would have been the envy of any leopard, and soared away changing gears three times in as many seconds. Straining forward over the handlebars as though urging on the Derby winner, he thundered back up the runway and shot past the still energetic aircrew as though they were standing still. One thing you couldn't take away from this chap: he could extend himself when the occasion demanded.

In a few more moments the fleeing aircrew veered off the runway, and, slowing their pace, headed towards B Baker's dispersal, where we were standing enjoying the show and shouting derisive remarks at the motorcyclist now that we believed everyone to be reasonably safe. After the other crew had stood coughing and panting for a while, bent over, hands on knees, they set us laughing again by telling us that their aircraft had been carrying six sand-filled 500-pounders to make up a "war load" — the first we had known of any bombs being aboard.

There was nothing even remotely humorous about the other crash. One of our own Wimpies, up on a night exercise, crashed and burned only a mile or two from the station, killing the whole crew. We marched over to the area next morning to assist in the investigation, and were deployed in a long line, at intervals of about 25 yards, astride the path on which the aircraft had come down. Under the guidance of an officer who had been given some information on the exact site of the crash, we began walking towards the point of impact. The Air Force told us next to nothing of what was already known, but my recollection is that we were searching for some piece or pieces of the aircraft that were presumed to have fallen off only a minute or two before it hit the ground.

I walked for the best part of an hour and a half. The ground was quite unlike what I had expected, being bumpy, rough, and liberally sprinkled with brush and stunted trees. After a time the men on either side of me drew further away, and eventually they were hidden from view, although I could tell from the sounds still coming to me when I paused that they were within hailing distance.

Although our line extended over several hundred yards, I began to get a premonition that I was going to be the one who found the aircraft. I did not want to. From the sketchy information we had been given I was under the impression that the bodies had not been removed, and I was not anxious to see them. As I came up to a slight rise in the ground my premonition grew stronger, and in a few moments was justified. A hundred yards further on the earth was ripped where the plane had struck. I followed on, unwillingly, and all at once the aircraft lay before me.

It was a terrible sight. The basket-weave stringers of the fuselage, now stripped naked, had been burned over-all to an ash-grey colour and warped in some places into crazy contours that were a ridiculous travesty of the science of aerodynamics. The rear turret sat open, bereft of perspex, thrusting out four blackened and twisted pokers for machine guns. I breathed easier as I noted that there were no bodies in the wreck; someone had obviously been to the scene already and removed whatever had been left of the five aircrew. But there were unwholesome signs telling where they had been when they met their end. Over the whole scene there now floated an incongruously peaceful atmosphere; the mute wreckage lay sprawled on its scorched terminal somehow looking as though it had been there for years. The tranquil record of tragedy cast its own spell, and it was a moment before I could bring myself to lift the whistle on my collar and bring the rest of the group to the scene.

We encountered trouble ourselves on the five-hour-and15-minute cross-country we flew the night of July 12th. We were carrying a war load, and on takeoff D Dog reacted accordingly, struggling away from the earth with noticeable lethargy. But it was not our heavy load that got us into difficulty.

Sam had been having trouble with his navigation on earlier trips, and I was secretly very concerned about his ability. Like the rest of us, Sam was inexperienced; but whereas I had now accumulated over 400 hours, almost 300 of them solo, Sam had had only a fraction of that time in the air. But he was under equal pressure to elevate his craft quickly to operational standards. And there was no denying that the navigational problems on these long night exercises were demanding, particularly when Gee, one of our most helpful aids, went on the blink.

This night Sam's problems were arriving in bunches. Gee packed up about halfway through the trip, and Stan was having great difficulty getting anything on his radio. In short order Sam was reduced to the navigational equivalent of trying to start a fire by rubbing two sticks together. Another hour dragged by, with Sam's increasing doubts about the validity of his DR position becoming more and more evident from the hesitancy in his directions for course changes and in his responses to my queries about turning point ETA's. Good navigation under primitive conditions requires the odd injection of luck to make it a success. Sam's luck thus far had been uniformly bad, and it was about to get a lot worse.

We were flying in cloud, having descended to a lower altitude for the final leg of our 700-mile cross-country, when the tense silence was broken by a faint sound in the headphones that made my scalp prickle. Up and down it went, like a low, whistling air raid siren, an eerie sound that I had heard often enough in ground school demonstrations to recognize immediately. It emanated from the little transmitters of the balloon barrages, and imparted the ominous warning that there were balloons on our track. We were conditioned to fear and shun the sound. Flying through a hanging curtain of balloon cables at night promised a lethal end to the exercise.

There were no balloons on our scheduled route, and this audible warning confirmed what we had been suspecting, namely, that we were well off our intended track. The balloons were our first and most urgent problem. I clicked on my microphone:

"Balloons on our track, navigator, I'm altering course 90 degrees starboard, now."

This was the prescribed drill, to dog-leg at right angles for five or ten minutes, then resume course. I had to notify Sam of my action immediately so that he could record the radical alteration of course in his log and plot it on his mercator.

We had flown the new course approximately five minutes when, to my consternation, I heard the ghostly trace of the balloon siren in my headphones again. Once more I altered course starboard, taking us in the opposite direction to the course we had been flying five minutes earlier. Neither Sam nor I said much, but the strain he was under increased perceptibly. After back-tracking for several minutes I resumed our original heading, but tacked on 15 degrees to carry us wide of the balloons, and listened for them intently for some time. Sam was so flustered now, with the added doubts introduced by the hasty and unplanned zig-zagging and course reversal, and my last ball-park guesstimate, that the situation was beginning to slip out of his grasp. I could see the trip shaping up into a disaster and resolved to try the

Chipping Warden beam, hoping earnestly that we were close enough to pick it up.

I tuned the receiver carefully to the frequency shown on our topographic. Nothing came through but crackling static and an over-riding sound like air escaping through a leaky valve. I had to fight back the first twinges of panic as I remembered that we were rapidly getting low on juice. Then I thought I heard a faint "A," and strained to hear the tone again, but it faded, and after a few moments I feared we had lost it irretrievably. However, on another rising gush of sound the signal came through briefly again. I squeezed the right headphone tightly against my ear and struggled to retain the elusive note; I was desperately afraid that if we lost it here on the outermost fringes of the range we would never pick it up again.

It faded tantalizingly in and out like the slow wash of the sea on a shore, and after four sweating minutes I still couldn't decide whether we were getting closer to the source or not, although I had managed to pick up a faint call sign and identify it to my own satisfaction as our beam. This sort of reception was a far cry indeed from the Link, or even the radio range at the BAT course, where one could always hear the beam clearly and usually say positively in 60 seconds whether he was approaching or leaving the signal source. I had to keep on for another five minutes before I could be sure that it was not just wishful thinking and that we were in fact flying towards the station. Only then did I turn onto a course that would give me a good intercept, telling Sam at the same time that he could relax, the pilot had taken over the navigation, hence all would surely be well. Despite this display of airy confidence for the crew's benefit, I did not relax myself, being all too cognizant of our dwindling fuel supply and the fact that I had no way of estimating accurately how long it was going to take us to complete our homing.

But now the tide flowed in our favour. The signal began to come in clearly and we made a text book intercept. With our quadrant and beam leg confirmed, I began homing on the station and letting down to 2,000 feet. We had to come a shade below 2,000 to get clear of the overcast. As I broke cloud, with the on-course continuous beam signal droning soothingly through the headphones, the aerodrome flashed into view four miles dead ahead.

The glittering white circle of the outer Drem lights, the graceful curve of the funnel, the clear amber beam of the glide path indicator, and the warm glow of the parallel chain of main runway lights all combined to produce the atmosphere of a radiant fairyland wherein trouble was unknown. I had seldom been so pleased to see anything, and called Sam to come up alongside me. When he appeared, I pointed ahead, with as much nonchalance as I could simulate while feeling that

I should be down on my knees, and suggested breezily that if he had any further trouble with his navigation in future, he need only call on his pilot to take over his chores and watch the operation completed as scheduled. Sam was too grateful at witnessing the resolution of a problem that had begun to assume the aspect of a navigator's nightmare to respond to the rib in kind. Ten minutes later we were safely on the ground and heading for D Dog's dispersal.

That trip marked the watershed of Sam's career as a navigator. He reviewed his log thoroughly with the Navigation Leader, analyzed the errors and weak points, and profited from them. Thereafter he improved steadily and gained confidence in equal measure as he went along. Like the rest of us, he continued to make the odd mistake, and to learn from it; but after that trip he had a grip on the job that he hadn't had before, and our confidence in him gradually returned — and was fully justified.

We did another night cross-country of just under five hours' duration the following night, July 13th, dropping two sticks of high level bombs at the Shotteswell range upon our return. That trip went off relatively smoothly, as did the five-hour and 45-minute cross-country we flew the night of July 15th.

The latter trip marked our first experience with the use of infra-red beams for night sim-bombing, and we found it interesting. Our target was a structure in Conway, Wales, on which was mounted a device that projected an infra-red beam toward the heavens at the appropriate angle and along the predetermined line of the bombing run. In this form of bombing practice, if your bombaimer had you tracking correctly on his run, and had the target centered in his sight when he pressed the button and activated his camera, the invisible infra-red beam would leave a trace on the exposed film. When the film was developed back in the photographic section at the base, the good news, or the absence thereof, was plain to be seen.

On the night of July 16th we flew our Bullseye exercise over a route stretching about 800 miles. It took us five hours and 50 minutes, during which, as planned, we were engaged several times by the searchlight defences along the course. We were also supposed to be "attacked" by our own night fighters, who were to blink their navigation lights at us if they could get into a position from which they considered they could open fire effectively; but there was no sign of fighters anywhere along the route, much to the rear gunner's disgust.

Following our Bullseye, we did another lengthy bombing exercise, and then two and a half hours of formation practice, this on July 22nd. Friday, July 23rd, we had a day off. Before any of us was quite ready to bite the bullet, it was thrust between our teeth. On July 24th, when we showed up expecting to be sent on a high level bombing exercise, we were told instead that we would be flying C Charlie that night on a "Nickel", the code name for a leaflet raid. We thereupon gave C Charlie the most rigorous air test we had given any aircraft up to that point, test-firing the guns with scrupulous care as a final step.

Briefing was at four-thirty, prior to which time we learned that three other crews were flying the operation with us. Two of the other Skippers I knew: C. A. Atkinson and Wing Commander Bray; the other crew were all strangers.

Inside the guarded briefing room we sat for a few minutes, then rose as the Station Commander entered, accompanied by the flight commander, the Intelligence Officer, and all the section leaders. For the first time I experienced the fearful excitement of sitting before the covered wall map, watching breathlessly as the curtains parted to reveal the red route tapes, and listening to the Intelligence Officer as he beckoned with his pointer and began his unchanging but ever dramatic "Gentlemen, the Target for tonight is . . ." It struck me that, for our first warlike venture, the tapes blazed their angular red trail a long way into enemy held territory.

Our crew's target was Montargis, a town lying some 60 miles south of Paris. The other crews had objectives in the same general area. Our common route took us across the French coast just clear of Le Havre, then swung sharply southeast to the target area. Alluding to the route in the course of his briefing, the Intelligence Officer was at pains to explain how carefully it had been chosen so as to keep us clear of major flak installations and notoriously active night fighter areas.

Since it was almost inevitable that we would encounter heavy flak somewhere, he recited some highly suspect statistics purporting to show that our chances of being hit were extremely remote. Despite this laudable effort to bolster confidence, I began to experience tension of a new magnitude, a strain that left stomach muscles tighter than strings on a tennis racquet. As the briefing went on I looked in fascination at the tape and pins that traced our route, particularly the red trail leading from the sea into hostile territory, and wondered how frightening it would be to be fired upon and have shells explode near me in the darkness. Next my thoughts flitted to night fighters, wondering what our chances would be if a Ju 88 got close to us, and knowing that the answer was not very encouraging. The Intelligence Officer saved some genuine good news for the end. The trip would take just over five hours all told, and with the light load we were taking to France, we would be able to carry almost two hours of reserve gas.

When the briefing was over we had a couple of hours to wait before we went to the mess for our first operational flying meal. This treat — and it really fell in that category — consisted of a fried-egg-and-toast supper; and it was a real fried egg, the traditional bonus air crew received when they flew on ops. We knew via the grapevine that squadron aircrews got milk to drink every day, plus a fried egg snack before and after each operation. Being thus admitted to the ops fraternity did not do our morale any harm that night.

Because of the lateness of July sunsets, our takeoff was delayed correspondingly, and we waited what seemed an endless period on the grass outside the crew room. Finally, after we had smoked a lot of cigarettes, the open-backed crew bus came clattering toward us, and all four crews piled in. There was no conversation as we rolled out to the planes.

With a comfortable few minutes in hand, we climbed into C Charlie, got our gear stowed, strapped ourselves in, and started the engines. When the cylinder head temperatures were right, we ran the engines up to full boost to check the magnetos. Precisely at this point we learned that Burns was right about the frequent derailment of the best laid schemes of mice and men. Both mags on our starboard engine, which had functioned perfectly on the afternoon air test, dropped about 300 revs causing the engine to bang and splutter furiously. I coaxed it for a few moments in an attempt to clear it, but it simply wasn't having any. The next few seconds witnessed a frenzied flurry of activity as we grabbed parachutes, navigation instruments, maps and charts, code books and Very cartridges, tumbled down the ladder, and ran as hard as we could go to X X-ray, the spare aircraft. It sat 300 yards away, and we panted up to it in great disarray and confusion, lungs bursting. So much for our careful, methodical preparations, and the conscientious air check we had given C Charlie. Now we were going to venture over enemy territory for the first time in an aircraft we had never flown before, hoping that the ground crew had fueled and loaded it properly, and checked the 50 other items we'd have liked to check ourselves.

As we clambered in, pell mell, and hastily began the startup procedure again, the other three aircraft moved off, one at a time, and began rolling toward the long runway, leaving me with the sinking feeling that comes with seeing your friends leave you behind. Several people on motorcycles materialized out of the gathering gloom and strode about gesticulating and shouting inaudible instructions. The message was clear all the same: GO! GO! GO! We went, testing the engines on the run as we taxied up to the takeoff point. They were not too good on the test, but they were not too bad either. We were going to France.

The first leg, to a point on the south coast just east of Selsey Bill, took us three-quarters of an hour. There was no cloud to speak of over England that night, so that even in the inky darkness that had now closed in upon us we could make out the faint dividing line between

Fighter aircraft the author always longed to fly. Above a Spitfire VIII of 417 Squadron, and below a Mk. IX of 421 "Red Indian" Squadron.

Freddie Taylor: a natural leader. Killed in a flying accident at Operational Training Unit. (RCAF)

Above: Wellington IC Z-BU of 214 Sqn. (So identified by the code letters BU) gets airborne for a mission against Germany.

(IWM)

Below: 'X-Xray'. Another 214 Sqn. Wellington (L7843) passes overhead.

Above: This photo was taken by J. B. Waters during a simulated bombing run on Bar██
Cross

Below: One of the first Stirling bombers. The light grey undersurfaces were soon t█
repainted matt black.   (█

the two masses, land and sea. Since setting course my mind had been too fully occupied to dwell on what might lie ahead. But now the press of the routine associated with the early stages of a flight was about to ease. As soon as we were out over the sea we double-checked our navigation lights off and test-fired the guns in both turrets. I was no longer intent on making fine adjustments to trim tabs and synchronizing throttles; we had reached our height and were cruising straight and level. The cylinder head temperatures had stopped just inside the green band; oil temperatures and pressures were normal; we were on oxygen and it was now coming through properly in all positions after some early balkiness. Now, immersed in blackness, I had little to concentrate on, and between glances at the console of somnolent luminous dials my mind wandered and toyed with anticipatory thoughts. The next coastline lay 100 miles in front of us, and the people watching for aircraft along that coast meant business; they were anxious to kill us. My breathing grew shallower and under my oxygen mask I could feel the beads of sweat on my skin. We droned on with scarcely a word for 35 minutes, then Sam spoke, the prefatory click of his microphone making me start:

"Enemy coast four minutes ahead Skipper."

The tension mounted further. I braced myself against the possibility of a sudden flash and explosion close to me in the darkness. Some miles ahead there came a faint flash and then what looked like jagged visual echoes of it flashing around the horizon. We carried on, heading directly for that spot. My throat was dry now, and my heartbeat a shade faster. If I had known that one of the three Wimpies just ahead of us had already been shot down — Wing Commander Bray's — I would have been a good deal shakier.

Another coastline, barely discernible, crept into view far below. The profound significance of the event was not lost on us, although apart from Sam's navigational observation at the precise moment of crossing no one said a word. For the first time we were over an enemy-defended coast, and steadily penetrating deeper and deeper into his domain. I held my breath as I started my turn to port, and waited for bursting flak. Nothing. Then, well off to starboard, a few vivid flashes appeared. Apparently we had been fired at for the first time, and were still unscathed. I expected more, but nothing came. We were inside the coastal defences now, with 155 miles to go to reach the target, an hour's flight.

That 60-minute period dragged by with the painful slowness so frequently a by-product of strained nerves. The intercom stayed dead, except for my periodic reminder to the rear gunner to keep on his toes. Things seemed to be going suspiciously easy. Occasionally a searchlight beam wandered balefully across the sky, but never close to us, always far off on the horizon. Once we saw a group of half a dozen beams going through their restless sweeps, the beams briefly forming and re-forming a giant teepee in the heavens. At long last J. B. left the seat beside me and went forward to make his preparations for sowing our cargo of leaflets. A sense of excitement supervened as the climax of the first half of the operation approached.

As soon as we had manoeuvred into the appropriate position up-wind of the target area, we opened the bomb doors and J. B. methodically flooded Montargis and the adjacent countryside with our leaflets. In a few minutes we had completed our task. We turned away quickly and winged for home.

If time had seemed to pass slowly on the leg in from the French coast to the target, it virtually ceased to move on the reverse leg, as we waited to get back clear of the enemy coast. Straining to keep the sharpest lookout I could in the darkness that engulfed us, mentally braced for a sudden fighter attack or burst of flak, I would fly for a period that I would have estimated under oath to be half an hour, then check my watch and find that only ten minutes had gone by. But after what seemed an interminable period, we reached the coast of France again and swung north across the sea for England. There was no let-up in our continuing lookout for night fighters, the most deadly enemy we faced, but now we could at least forget about enemy flak. Ten minutes out from the French coast I checked the switch on our IFF (Identification, Friend or Foe) to satisfy myself that we would be producing the necessary protective signal as we came up to the flak batteries on our own coast. Time began to move normally again.

We came back in over the English coast uneventfully, although this time we could not see any trace of it in the murk, and began to let down slowly so that we would hit 2500 feet just before we came up to Chipping Warden. We had been flying for over five hours at this point, and the strain was reflected in the weariness that began to set in as we made our gradual descent. Offsetting this to a certain extent was the satisfaction of knowing that we would soon be on the ground at Chipping Warden with our first operation safely under our belts. Or so we thought. Little did we realize that the final hour and a half of our operation, over England, was going to furnish a far stiffer test than anything we had yet encountered.

The first hint of trouble came when we were about 15 minutes away from base. J. B. commented on the fact that he couldn't see a thing on the ground; it seemed to be covered in fog. Sam had been having no difficulty with his navigation; Gee was working and he was ready to guarantee that we were within 500 yards of where he had us plotted. But getting over the station at 2500 feet and getting safely on the ground thereafter were two vastly different things, as I had cause to know after the BAT course. I made ready to call control the moment I could see the station.

We arrived over Chipping Warden to find the outer Drem lighting practically indistinguishable, glowing feebly as though swathed in layer upon layer of dark cheesecloth. I called the tower for landing instructions and got the news that we were to be diverted. The control officer instructed me to circle the field while he got final instructions regarding the diversion. After what seemed a lengthy wait, he came back and directed us to a drome about 20 minutes flying time off to the northeast, over Cambridge way. We gathered from his tone of voice and cautious selection of pessimistic words that we should waste no time getting over there, as there weren't exactly an over-abundance of aerodromes still in business.

Off we went as fast as we could go, and in 20 minutes arrived at our diversion drome. As soon as I saw it, I felt distinctly uneasy; it looked worse than Chipping Warden. I identified our aircraft and again asked for landing instructions. The second controller had more bad news: we could no longer attempt a landing there. He did not have to say why. After we had impatiently flown two or three orbits of the field, he came on the air again and directed us to another aerodrome, this time north and west of our present position, undertaking to telephone so that they would have the flare path in readiness. His voice was not reassuring, and I suddenly began to get worried. We had now exceeded by a considerable margin the estimated time for our trip, and were correspondingly deep into our reserve gas. We set course hurriedly for the third aerodrome and laboured wearily onward, wishing more and more anxiously that we could get safely on the ground somewhere . . . anywhere.

Again it took us 20 minutes or thereabouts to reach the promised haven. If we had made it ten minutes earlier chances were we would have got in; but even as we came up to the field I could see that it was already half-blanketed with morning mist, and before our eyes it continued to roll remorselessly over the remainder of the drome. It was bitterly frustrating. On one side the Drem lights sparkled in the blackness with all their customary brilliance, bright as jewels. On the other side they could scarcely be seen, just diffuse, indefinite pools of weakly wavering light. We were prepared for unwelcome news even before I called, but hardly for the news that came after the controller told me I must not attempt a landing. Instead of coming up with an alternative field he responded to my pointed query with:

"Benchhook X-ray, I have no alternative aerodrome open. Suggest you fly inland. Good luck . . ."

This unabashed manifestation of the Pontius Pilate syndrome — rarely put on the record in such blatant form — brought the gravity of our situation home with unmistakable clarity. We had now been flying for six hours and 20 minutes. Checking back hastily on my record of the revs and boost we had used on each leg of the trip, I calculated that our maximum endurance would be another 40 minutes, just about the seven-hour total predicted at briefing. But how accurate were my observations, and how close to average consumption had X X-ray's old engines been over the past six hours and 20 minutes? I had to allow for at least a small error to make sure that the crew had a chance to bail out while we still had power, control, and some height.

With these thoughts uppermost in mind, I swung westward — the stuff had been rolling in from the east — and we all began peering ahead into the darkness to see if we could spot a Drem system, or even a pundit. Now that we were rapidly running out of juice the time did not pass at all slowly. Five minutes . . . ten . . . a quarter of an hour slipped by, and there was no sign of life anywhere below us. Although the ground was still black and almost indistinguishable, there was a suggestion of paleness beginning to lighten the eastern horizon behind us. I decided that I must now give the order "Prepare to abandon the aircraft" so that everyone would get his chest pack hooked on and ready to go.

At that moment I caught something out the corner of my eye, a dark grey line, barely noticeable against its background.

"J. B.! there's a runway!" I shouted.

But the aerodrome that had shown up so providentially, almost directly on our unplanned track, had no lights on it or around it, and it was visible only from a certain angle in the darkness that still blanketed the ground. I knew I could easily kill us all trying to land on it under these conditions, even if I could manage to find it on an approach. I did a steep turn and searched; off in the distance we finally spotted the feeble glow of a pundit. Taking a careful bearing on it, and calling to J. B. and Sam to verify its relationship to the darkened runway, I steered over, calling Stan forward with the Very pistol to fire the colours of the period, repeatedly, so as to help attract the attention of the man on duty at the pundit.

While Stan fired Very lights as fast as he could load the pistol and get it into the roof mount behind my seat, filling the air around the pundit with a great fireworks display of cascading double-coloured Very lights, I flicked the navigation and recognition lights on and off while I transmitted on the emergency frequency our plea for help:

"Hello Darky, Hello Darky, Hello Darky; this is Benchhook X X-ray, will you assist us. Hello Darky, Hello Darky . . ."

According to the book this litany and the accompanying perform-ance should have produced, almost instantly, the illumination of a giant arrow beside the pundit, (which would point directly at the aerodrome) and a phone call on a direct line from the pundit basher to flying control telling them to turn on the Drem system immediately for an aircraft in distress.

Nothing. With Stan pumping off his king-sized shotgun shells a couple of feet from my right ear, I tried to determine our best course of action. I dared not waste another second over the pundit. Should I try a landing in the dark? The alternative was to climb for a minute or two and tell the crew to bail out, which would leave me with another decision: whether to try to make a forced landing myself in the dark, or simply to bail out and turn the Wimpy loose to crash where it would. I had swung back toward where I thought the runway lay as I ran over the two basic alternatives, eking out another three or four hundred feet of altitude as I did so. I spotted the runway again. It seemed a little easier to distinguish now. I made up my mind.

"Okay, we're going to land here without the lights. Everybody to crash stations. J. B., you stay here beside me; we're going to need both pairs of eyes."

I immediately turned parallel with the runway, straining to keep it in view, at the same time throttling right back and dumping the undercarriage and some flap. I knew I would have to let the runway go out of my sight on the "downwind" leg, otherwise I was bound to overshoot, and that might well be a lot worse for everybody than bailing out.

I checked the gyro carefully so that I could come on the exact reciprocal when I turned, and began counting seconds aloud, mentally preserving the picture of how far we had been to the right of the runway when it slid from view. The big trick was going to be to use up exactly the same amount of sideways distance in my 180 degree turn, so that I would be heading right for the runway as I made my final descent into the murk. At what I judged, prayerfully, to be the appropriate second, I pulled the Wimpy into a fairly tight turn to reverse our course, and dumped the rest of the flap.

J. B. and I began to peer urgently ahead, trying in the faint light now available to spot the off-shade of the vanished runway. I was fully reconciled to making a hairpin turn, forbidden by every rule of airmanship, to reach it if necessary. There weren't going to be any second chances; we were now dropping below 300 feet.

Suddenly and miraculously the faint greyness of the strip was visible almost directly in front of us. I chopped the throttles, slid the Wimpy slightly to port to centre up, and fought to estimate how high we were over that elusive greyness. After two or three tense seconds X X-ray kissed the runway gently, and we were rolling smoothly as silk. In 30 seconds I was turning off the far end of the runway and taxiing slowly to the right around the perimeter track. I closed my eyes momentarily and breathed a heartfelt prayer of thanks. We had been airborne for six hours and 40 minutes.

After another minute, a red Aldis lamp flashed at us from the far side of the field, the signal for us to hold our position. Someone had finally spotted our moving navigation lights. I ignored the red and kept on taxiing, feeling that the personnel of the aerodrome were the last people who could afford to get sticky about a failure to acknowledge or act on signals. I had to get to the control tower sooner or later, and I had already done enough waiting. A truck came hurrying around the perimeter and pulled up in an empty dispersal just in front of us, so I asked J. B. to climb down and tell them it had been an emergency landing and that I wanted to speak to the control officer.

We followed the truck after that, without difficulty, for it was now light enough to make out clearly the distinctive outline of the control tower itself. As we taxied on toward it, the crew, who were very chipper now that they hadn't been killed at their crash stations, came on the intercom to make comment and suggestion. The general consensus was that in future I should order the control officer to turn out the Drem system as soon as I was on final approach, since I landed a hell of a lot better in the dark than with the benefit of runway lights.

We got out of the aircraft at the control tower and hastily pulled from the opened bomb bay a number of copies of our leaflet which had stuck in various corners and crannies. Opposite an Air Force roundel the leaflet bore the banner "Le Courier de L'Air". It consisted of four pages of the latest military news, written with an emphasis which even my poor French could identify as designed to boost French morale and subvert that of the Germans. Each of us concealed a copy or two about his person, then J. B. and I went upstairs to report to the duty pilot.

After we found out where we were (a place called Brunting-thorpe, situated, ironically, only 25 miles north of Chipping Warden), I told the duty pilot that we had just completed an operational flight over France and would have to make a report immediately to an officer from their Intelligence section. I then proceeded to mention, with some heat, the failure of their pundit man to respond to our emergency calls and assist us in getting the aerodrome lit. Without further ado the duty pilot rang up the culprit — he turned out to be sound asleep — and tore an imperial strip off him in our presence, concluding with the remark:

"There is an operational crew here, no thanks to you, whose lives you jeopardized. Report to me here when the lorry comes to get you." He slammed down the phone.

My sense of retributive justice had been fully satisfied by the high calibre profanity with which he had opened the telephone conversation; at the words "operational crew" my chest swelled out so far I practically had to loosen the tapes on my Mae West, and I freely pardoned the pundit delinquent for all his sins. We reversed our field in a burst of magnanimity, put a good word in for the wretch, and left to go to interrogation.

Their Intelligence bloke questioned us for a few minutes on the salient features of the trip, then, as a concluding check, inquired whether there had been any hang-ups in the bomb bay, obviously ready to confiscate our souvenirs in the name of official security. I assured him that personal inspection had established that everything had dropped out clean as a whistle, which seemed to conclude the interview, and we headed to the mess for our flying breakfast.

Other people began streaming into the mess while we were eating, giving us the novel pleasure of seeing the WAAF's covertly pointing out the fried egg gourmets as pukka operational types just back from a trip over enemy territory. We felt duty bound to remain invincibly secretive, and made no mention of the fact that all we had dropped was paper.

Back at X X-ray, the erks who had just finished refilling our tanks told us with appropriate gravity that we'd had 15 minutes' juice left when we landed. Being operational, we took the news impassively, thanked them for their help in getting us ready so promptly, and took off for Chipping Warden. The morning mist, which had put Brunting-thorpe out of service about ten minutes after our landing, had dissipated in the early sun as quickly as it had bloomed, and we flew home uneventfully. At Chipping Warden we had to submit forthwith to another interrogation. As soon as it was over, we asked how the other three crews had made out. We got another shock.

None of them had got safely home. Our crew was the only one able to fly its aircraft back to base. Of the three aircraft that had set off just ahead of us, one was at the bottom of the sea, one was a complete wreck, a total write-off, and the third was badly damaged.

Wing Commander Bray's aircraft had been shot down, but a message from Group indicated that the crew had been rescued at sea.

The Skipper whom I had not known had got caught in the fog on his return, and in atrocious visibility had landed by mistake on a "Q site" (a dummy "aerodrome" unfit to land on, constructed to baffle the Germans) and demolished his aircraft. By the greatest good luck the crew had not been killed.

Atkinson had had vile luck. Like us, he had been cast adrift by flying control, and like us, had finally stumbled onto an aerodrome somewhere deep among the untrodden ways. His aerodrome was even illuminated. As ill fortune would have it, however, the Home Guard had stumbled onto it 24 hours before he had. Of all the aerodromes in England, Atkinson found the only one on which the Home Guard had been allowed to erect lethal obstacles on the runways — in a brief rehearsal of their duties should the Germans invade and threaten the capture of the field. Through a rather glaring oversight on someone's part, an excellent sand-bagged obstacle had been left blocking the runway toward which the Wellington was settling.

Atkinson and the boys steamed into her in the gloom at eighty-odd miles an hour, instantly transforming a beautifully executed, undercart-down landing into a leaping belly-flop as they sheared off the undercarriage and left other assorted parts of the Wimpy wedged into the barrier. Although the crew suffered a considerable surprise, they somehow escaped without being badly hurt. Once they had crawled clear of the wreckage and gotten over a rather lively shaking spell, they recovered their poise and later rode home ignominiously in a truck, absolutely bursting with admiration for the realism of the exercises carried out by the dear old Home Guard.

Next day Wing Commander Bray and his crew returned. About 12 hours of bobbing around in the sea had left all their faces as weathered as though they had been wandering bareheaded in the desert sun. The story I got from Bray in the mess a few hours later provided some food for thought.

Just as he had crossed the French coast (a few minutes ahead of us), a flak battery had fired on him. The Germans had obviously not bothered to read the Intelligence Officer's statistics, because their very first salvo scored a direct hit on Bray's aircraft, causing considerable damage to the fuselage and knocking out the starboard engine. In a few hectic minutes it became obvious to Bray that they were not going to be able to stay in the air. Showing courage of a high order, he decided to attempt a ditching rather than parachute into the hands of the Germans. Losing height rapidly, he turned back towards the French coast and cranked out a spate of radio messages regarding his plight as he descended. Their aircraft came down into the sea opposite Le Havre and only a few miles offshore.

The sea was relatively calm, and Bray had exercised good judgement in getting his aircraft down in just the right position, so that when the nose went in everyone survived the body-breaking deceleration. Bray grinned over his pint as he told me that the only casualty in the crash had been his rear gunner; the impact had been so violent that his false teeth had flown out and were now lying just outside French territorial waters with the Wimpy. (I had seen the gunner shortly before, and now understood why he looked like an 80-year-old Bedouin).

Dawn found Bray and his crew tossing lightly in their dinghy in clear view of the French coast — hardly what they had envisaged when they took off. As soon as it was light, the Germans sent a couple of E-boats out to collect them; but just as they were getting dangerously close a flight of Typhoons came knifing along, barely above the wave tops, and drove the E-boats off. It was right out of a Hollywood scenario, but it was a very temporary respite; the Germans had radios too. Minutes later a clutch of Focke-Wulf 190's raced to the scene, and for half an hour the Typhoons had all they could handle in a great aerial donnybrook that saw both sides feeding in reinforcements.

At the very height of the furore, while Bray and his crew still bobbed helplessly on the waves, wondering which side was going to get them, the Seventh Cavalry galloped onto the scene for the finale in the form of an Air-Sea Rescue Hudson that came sailing majestically over the dinghy with an airborne lifeboat, something none of us had ever heard of before. They dropped it by parachute a couple of hundred yards away, and Bray and the boys showed an excellent turn of speed flailing their way over to it. They were so anxious to forego the pleasure of an E-boat ride that when they got the motor started, about ten seconds after they dragged themselves aboard, they steered for merry old England at top speed, and they kept right on going at top speed. As a result they ran out of fuel well before they got to England; but by then the issue was no longer in doubt. The navy arrived on the scene shortly afterward and brought them home.

Air-Sea Rescue told Bray that he and his crew had received the first airborne lifeboat of the war.

For 24 hours Peden's crew rejoiced in a new and unfamiliar role as the apple of our flight commander's eye. After all, of the four aircraft he had assembled for the Nickel only X X-ray was back on her dispersal and still 100 percent serviceable. It was understandable, then, that he manifested an untypical warmth and geniality toward the crew that had kept his record for that particular operation from reading 0 for 4.

We were still obliged to do two more high level bombing exercises to complete the syllabus and qualify for our clearance from OTU, one a daylight exercise, the other a final night visit to Shotteswell. We got the daylight exercise in during the afternoon of July 26th. When we landed the flight commander sent for me.

Radiating charm and friendliness from every pore, he congratulated me again on the crew's performance on the Nickel, then hinted broadly that he was looking for only one thing from me on this final night exercise — speed. The weather promised to be good for flying, and he was very short of aircraft, for obvious reasons.

"As far as bombing is concerned," he said, "your crew has absolutely nothing to worry about, you've already passed. You still have to do the exercise, of course, but if you do it quickly you can be back here in 40 minutes. So tell your bombaimer not to waste time doing dummy runs and worrying about a high score; get over there, drop your bombs, and get back. I'm giving you J Jig again tonight; but when you come back don't take it to the dispersal and switch off. Park in front of the crew room, and Penkuri will trade places with your crew. Remember now, I want to get at least three exercises out of that aircraft tonight, so don't dawdle."

I duly passed the word to J. B. and the rest of the boys that we were out for a purely recreational stooge that night, and that the magic phrase was not "direct hit", just "bombs gone."

We took off just after dusk and made a bee line for Shotteswell. In 15 minutes over the range we had dropped our eight bombs. I was steering due west out of the cloverleaf when J. B. let the last one go, and promptly asked Sam for the course to base. He came back casually with what sounded like a wet-finger-in-the-wind guess, and just as casually I swung onto that heading. In a few minutes we came sailing up to the Drem system.

"What's our pundit flashing, Sam?" I said, as I looked at the red light blinking just below us. One perfect circle of lights on the ground, as you might expect, is indistinguishable from the next at night, and with aerodromes sprinkled all over this part of the country at intervals of about five miles, I didn't want any slipup.

"Oh hell, Skipper, sorry, I forgot to bring the pundit list," Sam said after a minute's silence. He sounded embarrassed, as well he should have.

"Well, this one's flashing 'D-R', does that ring a bell?"

"It must be our drome;" Sam came back, "hell, we only had to come about seven miles from the far end of that last run, and we're right over the Drem system."

"I'll call up for landing instructions," I said, still not 100 percent satisfied. Usually this provided a fairly reliable check because at low altitude we got very spotty radio reception if we were any distance from base. Suiting the action to the word, I pressed the transmitting button.

"Hello Azure, this is Benchhook J Jig. What is my turn to pancake?"

The familiar voice of our favourite control tower WAAF came back to us loud and clear, removing all uncertainty:

"Benchhook J Jig, this is Azure; you are Turn One — Pancake. I say again: Turn One J Jig, Pancake. Over."

"Roger, Azure; J Jig Pancaking."

Recalling our flight commander's burning desire for speed, I peeled smartly over to the funnel, dumping undercarriage and half flap on the way, and in a matter of moments I was heading for the runway on final approach. I had noticed while coming cross-wind that we had a fairly strong wind blowing, otherwise everything was perfectly normal. We touched down fairly short, so I let the aircraft run on without using any brake. While we were still 300 yards from the end of the runway we ran through a shallow dip which I did not remember being there before, and I was still idly ruminating on the frailty of human memory when I came to the end, swung clear, and called the tower again:

"Hello Azure; Benchhook J Jig, clear of the flarepath. Out."

I was not expecting any reply, but my incredulous ears were now assaulted by a totally unfamiliar voice and call sign:

"Benchhook J Jig, this is Nordic Two . . . Are you in trouble?"

The proper answer, I suppose, was that if she considered the captain of the Titanic to have been in trouble, or Custer at the midpoint of the Little Bighorn, or Lincoln at Ford's Theatre when John Wilkes Booth dismounted for a visit, then yes, I surely was in trouble; but I was so taken aback and then angry at this totally unnecessary boob that I could scarcely speak at all for a few moments.

Sam picked this highly unpropitious interlude to bring himself closer to death than he had ever been before by muttering into his open microphone:

"I knew that wasn't our drome . . . the C pulse was nowhere near being right."

He was fortunate that the grip of the Sutton harness stifled my instantaneous impulse, which was to rush back and wind his intercom cord around his throat until his own pulse packed up. After all, I thought bitterly, he was only the navigator, only the person whose job it was to avoid mistakes like this by bringing along the current pundit list, only the person whose Gee box told him it was the wrong drome before we landed. I counted ten and called the tower again:

"Nordic Two, this is Benchhook J Jig. I am taxiing to the tower and will report to the duty pilot. Out"

On the way I did some fast mental arithmetic: five minutes to taxi to the tower; ten minutes with the duty pilot explaining our ancestry and why we had dropped in uninvited at this odd hour; 15 minutes to get a trolley-acc, start up again, and taxi around to the takeoff point on the long runway; 15 minutes to take off, fly home, land, and taxi to the crew room — all told 45 extra minutes wasted. Meanwhile our flight commander was doubtless glaring at his watch already and pacing his office wondering what the blue blazes we were up to. I concluded that no matter how quickly we moved from this point on he was going to be displeased, displeased and scathing.

The session with the duty pilot was embarrassing. We had landed at Gaydon, whose outer Drem system was about two and a half minutes flying time from ours. Under the circumstances, therefore, it was easy enough to explain an initial approach to the wrong drome. What was harder was explaining how a crew, now rated as fit for operational flying, had taken to the air without a pundit list, and had neglected to check its position on Gee if there were any doubt. The duty pilot laughed at my chagrin then lessened my embarrassment by saying that this happened all too frequently between Gaydon and Chipping Warden. I left feeling better, but the relief was momentary; I had a feeling that Smiling Jack at the other end would not be so understanding.

As we flew back, I ran over in my mind the complete repertoire of possible excuses I might tender to save my pride, but none would hold water under any knowledgeable questioning, and if there was one thing Fadden wasn't, it was dumb. I landed, preoccupied, not looking forward to the *tête à tête* I was expecting shortly.

But my luck was in. Just before our return an aircraft had gone off the runway into a soft spot and had to be carefully towed back to the concrete to avoid the risk of putting undue strain on the undercarriage. This had to be seen to by the flight commander. Meanwhile, to occupy him further, the met wizards had drastically modified their earlier rosy forecast, and there was a flap on to get messages to several aircraft on cross-countries, for they would be in serious difficulty if they did not get back or land somewhere else before the weather clamped. Squadron Leader Fadden, therefore, had more important things on his mind than our rather tardy return. He had scrounged another aircraft for Penkuri, I gathered, for we were told to put J Jig back in her dispersal. This latter message was not accompanied by the expected direction to report to the flight commander's office, so I gratefully melted into the darkness and disappeared while the melting and disappearing were good.

I did see Fadden the following day, however, and got another surprise. He delivered a mild barb about our carelessness — which I certainly merited — and let it go at that, turning to the business at hand, which happened to be verifying the hours I had logged at Edge Hill and Chipping Warden. When I left my thoughts harked back to my earlier disparaging assessment of Fadden and I decided that perhaps it needed a bit of revision.

I tried to imagine myself in his place, under constant pressure to turn out crews, working long and irregular hours, fighting a constant battle to keep worn aircraft serviceable, and bucking bad weather's constant erosion of flying schedules. Then I asked myself if I could do what he did, namely, tell someone (who probably seemed to him to be suffering from finger trouble) to go and memorize the aerodrome layout, bearing in mind also that this took place at what must have been the end of another frustrating night for Fadden. I had to admit that I could easily have done a lot worse. Next I recalled the verbal pats on the back he had given us a couple of times, particularly after the Nickel, and remembered too that on several occasions when we had landed at three or four o'clock in the morning I had seen Fadden leaving the mess just about the time we got there. Could it have been, I wondered belatedly, that he was assuring himself that a decent hot meal was waiting for us? Many flight comanders in his place would have been content to phone the mess and simply say that so-and-so's crew was back, see that they're fed, or perhaps just push off to bed themselves and hope the mess attendants would do their jobs. I decided that my original hasty assessment had been both inaccurate and unfair —Fadden was OK.

On August 2nd I got my times certified by the Chief Instructor. I had received a total of 26 hours and ten minutes dual on the Wellington III, and had flown as captain an additional 57 hours and 40 minutes, making a total of 83 hours and 50 minutes. In total I now had 449 flying hours, and 61 hours and 20 minutes Link time.

When I picked up my log book I got the news on our next posting. We were ordered to report August 5th to No. 1657 Conversion Unit at Stradishall for four-engined training on Stirlings. The choice of aircraft represented the Air Force's final ironic joke on the would-be single-engined fighter pilot: of the three types of four-engined bombers then in service with the RAF (Stirlings, Lancasters, and Halifaxes), the Stirling had the dubious distinction of being the biggest and heaviest.

Later that afternoon, over a cup of tea in the railway station, Stan and I relaxed while we waited for our trains, and reminded each other of a couple of the lighter moments on the course. Stan's favourite recollection was of the night flight on which he had scared the rest of us green by inadvertently pulling his intercom plug and rendering himself incommunicado while he stood by the flare chute with the fire axe, ready (on my orders) to chop the flare free if it stuck in the chute when J. B. pressed the release button.

These flares were fearsome parachute-suspended contraptions filled with magnesium. They were timed to go off a few seconds after release, and flashed explosively to generate an illumination of some astronomical number of candlepower, thus enabling the bombaimer to get high altitude pictures of the target area at night, pictures from which the point of impact of his bombs could be plotted. Several OTU Wellingtons had mysteriously exploded in the air while on exercises which included flare-dropping, and suspicion quickly centered on the flares. The theory was that the ropes of their parachutes might be catching in the older type flare chutes after the fuses of the flares had been activated, causing the flares to explode inside the aircraft.

We had been advised of this theory, hence, on the occasion in question, I had instructed Stan to leave the wireless compartment, plug in at the intercom point beside the flare chute, and listen for J. B.'s advice that he had launched the flare. As soon as he heard the fateful words, Stan was to peer into the flare chute and make sure that the flare had actually fallen clear. If, heaven forbid, it had not, his orders were to ply the axe manfully in the few seconds of life we had left to us and separate us from the magnesium monster before it exploded.

As the critical moment of flare-launching approached, the atmosphere in the aircraft, always businesslike, became deadly serious. Stan made his way back to the flare chute, the great axe in his grasp, looking like some helmeted reincarnation of the headsman from the Bloody Tower. When he was plugged in, I double checked to make sure that Stan and J. B. could hear each other clearly and that each understood the ordained sequence of events and what was expected of him.

We began our bombing run, and for a minute or so all that was heard on the intercom was J. B.'s voice calling the course corrections. Then, as he dropped our last bomb, he simultaneously pressed the button to release the flare and announced that fact clearly and emphatically.

I spoke to Stan immediately, confirming what I had said before: "Okay look in the chute and see if the flare went out properly."

Stan's voice came back in an instant, strained: "It's hung up Skipper, I . . ."

There was an abrupt cessation of sound as his intercom went dead. I sat there, suddenly fearful, counting seconds slowly to myself and half expecting a vivid flash to launch me through the air on my last trip. Everyone but Stan in fact was braced to do a flaming ride of the Valkyrie. After what seemed like a full five minutes, during which we all died a thousand deaths, Stan came back on intercom to report breathlessly that he had cleared the chute. As he had moved into a better position to jab into it, he had pulled his intercom plug out of the socket. He knew that his microphone had gone dead, but quite rightly concluded that the proper order of priorities was to keep us all alive by dislodging the flare, then report. This necessarily left the rest of us suffering from raging cases of that nervous disability described in RAF slang as high-frequency ring-twitter.

The story generated abundant laughter later, when we were safe on the ground, particularly with Stan's allegation that he could distinctly hear my breathing even after the intercom went off; but while it was taking place the scene played to the soberest, quietest audience I ever sat with.

Over our tea Stan and I went on to chuckle about another recent flight during which we had made no less than five daylight runs across the Shotteswell range in an attempt to enable Stan to fire a single smoke puff from the Very pistol. This should have been a ridiculously easy formality; but on each occasion the pistol had misfired, and each time it happened the ground staff in the sighting quadrants got more uncomplimentary about our dummy runs. Simultaneously Stan was getting generous doses of impatient advice from me about how to fire a Very pistol from the roof mount — a feat I had never performed. Stan finally decided that the pistol was not repairable, so we cleared from the range and headed home, in a distinctly chip-on-the-shoulder frame of mind.

Halfway there he came back on intercom to announce that he had finally diagnosed the trouble with certainty and suggested that we turn back to the range and knock off the exercise. We had to do it sooner or later, so with some reluctance, for we had flown a long cross-country before going to the range, I acquiesced and steered back towards Shotteswell. We could almost hear the range officer groan when I called up again. His staff had to co-operate in this stunt, making (so they led us to believe) esoteric wind calculations based not only on the observed characteristics of the smoke dissipation, but also on the information we gave them immediately prior to firing.

The radio dialogue revealed a noticeably stiff-upper-lip atmosphere below us as we lumbered into position for yet another run. The climax of the drama approached a minute or two later as I chanted out the vital statistics they wanted regarding our altitude, course and airspeed, and warned Stan to prepare. Then, in a voice that would have been appropriate had I been ordering a broadside from the Home Fleet, I gave the command: "FIRE".

In a crushing anti-climax the Very pistol misfired again, yielding the puniest possible click. This time our normally strict intercom discipline was rent in tatters as everyone followed my lead and gave Stan unreasonably harsh suggestions regarding the Very pistol and the smoke puff. I called the range officer once more before we droned off the range in disgust. The non-accidental open-mike silence that briefly trailed his curt acknowledgement of my message irritated us further — if hissing radio silence can be rebuking, scornful, and negative, his was. We smarted.

While we rang the changes on these epics of fright and frustration, Stan's train pulled in and we parted, to meet again on August 5th at Stradishall.

CHAPTER 10

HEAVY CONVERSION UNIT – STRADISHALL

Then with expanded wings he steers his flight
Aloft, incumbent on the dusky Air
That felt unusual weight.

Milton, Paradise Lost

The Stirling was such an enormous aircraft that it made the Wellington look like a half-size prototype by comparison. Even my cocksure heart quailed when I saw one at close quarters, and I secretly wondered whether people of ordinary capabilities could land such monsters at night without killing themselves. The critical feature of a plane, so far as a pilot preparing to get checked out on it is concerned, is: how high does it have the pilot sitting over the runway when it touches down? The higher he sits the more difficult it is for him to judge his position and level off at just the right height when landing. The cockpit canopy of the Stirling sat 22 feet 9 inches over the runway, the highest I had ever seen, and, except for the wingspan, which was only 99 feet where about 110 seemed called for, everything else was to scale. The wheels were as high as a man's head. The wing root itself was so thick that a man could almost stand erect inside it.

The aircraft was a mid-wing design with pronounced incidence, one result of which was the longest undercarriage and highest, most imposing posture I have ever seen, before or since. The big wheel panels which rode down with the oleo legs gave the undercarriage the appearance of having been fashioned by a designer of heavy bridge girders, although, ironically, the undercarriage was one of the aircraft's weakest features. It could withstand heavy shocks provided they

222

Stirling 'E-Easy' of 1657 Heavy Conversion Unit as seen from the cockpit of another Stirling over England in 1943.

A Stirling aloft. (IWM)

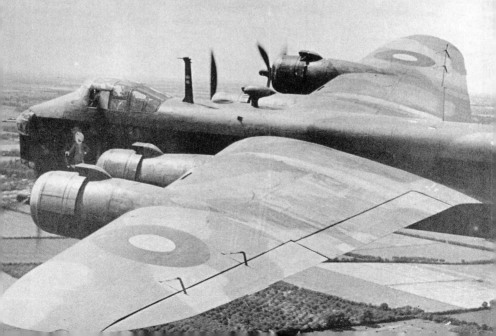

Above: The impressive stature of the Stirling is evident in this shot of 'T-Tommy' being serviced in the dispersal. Note the hard working 'erk' on top of the Matador petrol bowser, passing the hose up to fill the starboard wing tanks.   (RAF)

Below: "Former Naval Person" comes to inspect his first four engined bombers, the Stirlings.   (IWM)

This photograph, reproduced from the Sept. 1942 issue of "Flying and Popular Aviation", a Ziff-Davis publication, clearly demonstrates the massive proportions of the Stirlings' main undercarriage.

Stirling 'D-Dog' of No. 7 Squadron, RAF Oakington, about to be "bombed up".

Below: A number of 7 Sqn. Stirlings being refuelled and made ready for an attack. (IWM)

were imposed strictly in the vertical plane, but it could not, because of its abnormal height, endure very much in the way of shearing action — there was far too much leverage generated through the long undercarriage members — and even experienced pilots had to exercise great care in cross-wind conditions. Although I saw only one aircraft do it myself, there was no shortage of undercarriage wipeouts.

Nevertheless, I will gladly testify that the Stirling was one of the finest aircraft ever built. Her inability to haul a full bomb load much above twelve or thirteen thousand feet was an unnecessary limitation resulting directly from Air Ministry obtuseness in refusing to let her designer and builders increase the wingspan over 99 feet. This 99-foot requirement was imposed, well before the outbreak of war, because the then existing hangars had doors only 100 feet wide. The appalling prospect of having to enlarge a few hangars, or to build some new ones, was one the Air Ministry simply could not face, particularly when the easier solution was available of simply ruining the altitude performance of the RAF's first four-engined bomber. This insistence on the 99-foot wingspan was criminal shortsightedness, for the Stirling, apart from the weakness stemming from this stifling Air Ministry specification, flew like an exultant bird. Once aloft, with her big undercarriage stowed away, she handled like a fighter, unbelievably manoeuverable for her great size. Of all the might-have-beens in the field of strategic bombing, the potential the Air Ministry forfeited by refusing to build a Stirling as Short Brothers wanted to build her must rank as one of the most pathetic. They crippled a queen.

I immediately fancied the Stirling, from my first sight of her, to be the Platonic Idea or Form of bomber[1]. With her wheel housing panels flaring out just above the huge tires, she perched on the dispersal like some giant eagle with heavy feather-spurred talons, silent, brooding, menacing.

We plunged straightway into Stradishall's intensive two-week ground school on our new aircraft. There was much to learn. The Stirling was equipped with three power-driven turrets: a four-gun turret in the tail, and a two-gun turret in the mid-upper and nose positions. These were hydraulically operated turrets, and it was obviously essential that we start by learning which engines drove the various hydraulic pumps that maintained the pressure, which engines drove generators, which the air compressor, and so on.

There was a new and complex electrical system to learn, for the Stirling had many electrically-driven services, including the large Gouge flaps and the ponderous undercarriage. The throttle, mixture,

---

1. With fighters I could never bring myself to make a final choice, vacillating helplessly in my admiration of the Spitfire, the P-47 Thunderbolt, the P-51 Mustang and the Hurricane.

and pitch controls were "Exactor" hydraulic controls, a type completely foreign to me. Up to this point in my career — and I was not alone in this — I had never encountered anything but straight mechanical linkage.

The Exactors, we found, required careful and frequent priming, otherwise startling problems arose. We heard stories of pilots on takeoff opening the throttle levers completely, from idle to full bore, without drawing any change in engine response whatsoever. Conversely, we learned that you could cut your throttles on landing and have the engines — or any combination of them — continue to roar at full power. This phenomenon was guaranteed either to kill you or to come very close to doing so. We became very Exactor-priming conscious.

We learned that each of the deep wings carried seven fuel tanks, all but No. 7 itself being self-sealing — which made it very easy to decide which tank to use first once you were airborne. The capacity of the main tanks was 2,254 imperial gallons, and the contents of Nos. 2 and 4 on each side were jettisonable.

The Mark III Stirling had Hercules VI or XVI engines, which developed approximately 1,600 horsepower each. Her maximum all-up weight, according to the handbook, was 70,000 pounds. According to the engineers it was a shade over 71,000 pounds when she carried her designed load of twenty-four 500-pound bombs.

One other thing we learned was that our instructors at Stradishall took a touch of instability for granted. I was in "B" Flight office one chilly morning when a Flight Lieutenant instructor from another office came in and wended his way through the crowd towards the stove, where he made a brief show of innocently warming his hands. This in itself should have aroused suspicion because there was very little fire left in the stove. I noticed that everyone watched him rather closely for a few moments; and they should have watched him for a few more moments. When he had allayed their suspicions with idle chit-chat, he lit a cigarette, opened the lid of the stove, and tossed in the blackened match. To my surprise, he then threw open the nearest window, sprang up on the sill, and leapt clear with a roar of laughter. Immediately there was a mad rush to follow suit through the other windows and through the door just behind me. People were hopping out of the place like energetic kangaroos on all sides.

While I was making ready to depart myself, still wondering what had caused them all to take leave of their senses, there was a startling hiss and a hellish red glare suddenly flared and filled the little iron stove, like an instantaneous sunrise, succeeded in turn by vivid green and yellow flashes. Jets of this coloured flame and acrid smoke under intense pressure shot out from the stove's numerous fissures. It was a good thing my lack of seniority had kept me well away from it.

In half a second I was on the window ledge and then rolling on the green turf outside, close to the spot where the prankster was standing giggling at the undignified exodus he had precipitated. A minute or two later, when the choking smoke had dissipated, everyone began moving back in, satisfied that the show was over. I learned in transit, before I knew what had happened, that this had been a retaliatory visit for a similar prank pulled by "B" Flight a day or two earlier — except that they had achieved even more startling results by using a ladder and making their deposit down the stovepipe from outside.

What our visiting fireman had done was, firstly, open, in private, a couple of red and green Very cartridges and remove the powder, which was packed inside them in readily portable wafers. Next, in the course of his little social call, he had concealed three or four of these almost explosively inflammable wafers in his free hand as he lit his cigarette, and finally dropped them into the stove behind the match stub. I reiterate and confirm that the results were spectacular. His visit ensured that on subsequent calls distinguished guests from the rival flight never lacked for unblinking attention and a courtesy which extended to someone else hastily lighting their cigarettes for them.

Stradishall had been one of the permanent stations of the RAF in the piping times of peace, and still showed it in the relatively luxurious quarters and tastefully appointed mess. In the morning a WAAF batwoman came in to wake us, fetching a hot cup of tea. I was not yet all that struck on tea before breakfast, but I always thought it a pleasant attempt to make a good start on a new day.

Before we were well settled in at Stradishall, about the time we learned to call it Strad, Penkuri arrived with his crew. Needless to say I was delighted, and immediately took it upon myself to show him the principal places of interest around his new abode.

As I was showing him the attractive little ante-room just beyond the glass-panelled doors of the main lounge of the officers' mess, I pointed out the record player and radio in the corner, and mentioned that, *mirabile dictu,* the rather limited collection of records stowed below included two classics standing at the top of the Penkuri all-time hit parade: Bob Crosby's "Big Noise from Winnetka", and Clyde McCoy's "Sugar Blues". We had no opportunity to play them just then because someone else was hovering over the machine; but Penky riffled through the pile on the spot to verify that what I told him was, as he inevitably dubbed it, the real McCoy.

Directly after ground school that afternoon, he made tracks for the mess, where an uncharacteristically repulsive austerity tea was being served in surroundings worthy of edible fare. We put a notable dent into a pile of dried out bloater-paste sandwiches just the same, then Penky headed for the record player, which had not yet been commandeered.

He played Big Noise from Winnetka ten times hand running, that program of the Bobcats taking just under 30 minutes, during which there were only brief (re-starting) intervals when the talents of Ray Bauduc and Bob Haggart were not distinctly audible even unto the furthest reaches of the main lounge itself, for Penky was not selfish with good things. Temporarily sated with the throbbing of the string bass and the contrasting sibilance of the thin whistle that shared the spotlight on that selection, he turned to Sugar Blues and began a repetitive performance of Clyde McCoy's saucy theme song, hiking the volume still further so that no one would be deprived of an opportunity to check and re-check that beguiling and masterful manipulation of the mute.

My recollection is that Clyde went to bat eight times successfully before a very large officer, wearing a very large Air Commodore's stripe on his sleeves, stood up abruptly and displayed his appalling lack of taste by taking the first name of the Lord in vain an equal number of times (in a voice so loud that I wondered momentarily whether the old boy was hallucinating and thought he saw Him on the far side of the aerodrome), simultaneously stalking over to the record player, wrenching the tone arm clear in mid-phrase, and smashing the record into a thousand fragments against the radiator with a savage tennis-type overhand. He then wheeled, glared at Penky and me as though someone had just banged his bunions with a ball-peen hammer, and tramped out-of-doors. Penky waited until his receding footfalls marked him well out of earshot, then, for the benefit of our cowering compatriots of negligible rank, stood up, turned to me, hands on his hips, and in a scornful voice audible all over the ante-room declaimed:

"Fearless, I told ya we were wasting our time with that tin-eared son of a bitch — can't learn him nothin'!".

Despite the show of bravado, Penky was upset at this unusually extreme manifestation of disapproval, and after dinner he and I walked together to a pub a short distance down the road from the mess, intent upon soothing our nerves with a couple of quiet pints. Although we actually drank very little, we soldiered the evening out pleasantly so that it was past ten-thirty when we wandered back. I remembered when I got to my room that I had intended to post a letter, so Penky and I and J. B. — who had joined us — strolled back through the corridors of the mess heading for the mailbox which sat on the table just outside the main lounge. As we came up to this room, there was a sound of revelry by night that penetrated the heavy glass-panelled doors as though they were cheesecloth. Clearly the merry-makers were at full throttle. I dropped my letter in the box, and moved over to the big doors, curious to see for myself what Penkuri was staring at so incredulously.

What he was staring at so incredulously were approximately 40 officers of His Majesty's Royal Air Force singing "Roll Me Over" at the top of their lungs. What rendered their appearance a trifle out of the ordinary was the fact that they were all stark naked, except for the totally incongruous black tie that each wore around his bare neck. They were prancing about the carpet waving their pints aloft and treading exuberantly on piles of clothes that were clearly going to be un-sortable, when one of them chanced to look our way. Immediately he roared "Get them!" and the whole mob, sloshing beer about wildly, came springing across the room at us, a mind-boggling aggregation of nude flesh and waving black ties.

In one split second the three of us unanimously decided, without a formal vote, that we wanted no part of this bacchanalian binge, and took off down the hall like a trio of rabbits, followed a moment later by a screaming horde of nude madmen. We raced outside again to give them the slip, knowing that their innate modesty, and the fear of appearing before the Air Commodore on charge, would deter them from outdoors pursuit, then, minutes later, when the hubbub had flowed back into the main lounge, we slipped quietly into our rooms and locked the doors. One more quiet day of intensive training at Stradishall was over.

At this point in the course we acquired two new crew members, and a replacement rear gunner. Shortly after we had lost Eddie Jarvis with the ruptured eardrum at OTU we had been given a new gunner, a Canadian by the name of Pat Healey; but he too had had to leave us due to some medical problem shortly after we arrived at Stradishall. We found that there were two or three spare gunners around the Conversion Unit who were looking for crews. One of them was an Australian NCO named Jack Phillips who got to know the NCO's of our crew, and very shortly let it be known that he was keenly interested in joining us. I discussed it with the others, particularly Stan. They were so high on Phillips that it seemed worth my while to have a look at him for myself. I thereupon spoke to him, liked what I heard and saw, and by mutual agreement got him appointed as our new rear gunner.

We also acquired a flight engineer and a mid-upper gunner, bringing our crew up to seven members, the standard complement for the RAF's four-engined bombers.

Bill Bailey, the flight engineer, was a Londoner, close to my own age. He was more than just well grounded in his trade; he was a natural mechanic with a feel and an ear for engines, a man who knew his job inside out. Bert Lester, the mid-upper, was the youngest member of the crew, a husky English lad of 18 from Fordham. He was alert, competent, cheerful and conscientious, a crewman we were all pleased to have join us.

At the end of two weeks, having crammed into our heads as much as we possibly could about the Exactors, DR compasses, new petrol, pneumatic, electrical and hydraulic systems, not to speak of new emergency drills and equipment, we started our actual flying training, on August 22nd. My instructor was Squadron Leader Crebbin, a mature, calm and friendly flyer who wasted no time in demonstrating the idiosyncracy that clearly took highest priority on his syllabus: the Stirling's pronounced tendency to swing sharply to starboard on takeoff. Our handbook had breezily referred to the aircraft's having a "slight tendency" to swing on takeoff, so we knew it would be a bearcat.

It was. In fact, if one opened the throttles evenly, the swing would put the aircraft off the runway in a few seconds, long before it achieved enough speed to give rudder control. The answer to the problem was to stagger the throttles, opening both starboard throttles substantially in advance of the port side pair. Some pilots even took the extreme step of opening the starboard throttles fully, then catching up on the port side pair to prevent an over-corrected swing in that direction. After a few suspense-laden takeoffs under my "control" that saw us snaking frighteningly from one side of the runway to the other, I began to get a better idea of the starboard throttle lead required to keep the lofty monster straight for the critical 20 seconds until the air flow over the rudder yielded an easier means of keeping her in the centre of the runway.

So pronounced was this starboard swing that a special written acknowledgement was taken from every student pilot and pasted into his log book before he was allowed to go solo in a Stirling. The suggestive certificate, signed by me and by Squadron Leader Crebbin, appeared in mine after our flying session on August 22nd, 1943. It read:

> CERTIFIED that I have received instruction in, and am
> fully conversant with, measures necessary to correct and
> prevent swinging of STIRLING aircraft.

The implications of the endorsement ritual dampened my enthusiasm momentarily, being clearly the Air Force's oblique way of letting all pilots know that if they did something silly, like killing themselves, the Air Force would be off the hook.

The Stirling had another noteworthy characteristic, one common to most heavy bombers in some measure, but more pronounced in the Stirling than any other heavy I ever flew. When you did your flare-out and check on landing, she dropped onto the runway like a 30-ton boulder; there was no float to speak of at all. If you checked six inches above the runway the result was a beautiful landing. If you checked a foot and a half above the runway you arrived very firmly and definitely; and if you were two feet above the runway when you cut the throttles it felt as though the undercarriage were being driven through the wings. The potential violence of the consequences made for more than normal concentration on the final approach.

May I revert to the Stirling's swing and record parenthetically that a few weeks later, when we were on the squadron, I heard about one pilot on the roster who, notwithstanding the unequivocal endorsement gummed into his log book, had not mastered the requisite technique. His name was Tutt, but he was never referred to in that abbreviated form; rather, he was known to all and sundry as Tutt the King of Swing, because of his chronic inability to keep the Stirling straight on a loaded takeoff. The King of Swing was all right with an empty aircraft; he had conquered that problem. But when the Stirling was carrying a war load, all-up weight 71,000 pounds, she was much more recalcitrant, and poor old Tutt apparently found her a nightmare to handle. He had, so I was told, already wiped the undercarriage off two aircraft when they swung out of control on takeoff. My immediate reaction upon hearing the story was that Tutt and his whole crew deserved to be decorated for their persistence and their refusal to admit defeat. Every war load takeoff must have been preceded by hours of apprehension for all of them.

The grand finale came on takeoff one night when the King of Swing's aircraft got away from him again and sped off the runway in full career, carrying a heavy cargo of incendiaries wildly across the aerodrome and finishing up by hurtling along on its belly smack into the middle of the bomb dump. There it broke into flames. For several long minutes a lot of very frightened people fully expected to see the whole station soar into space in one cataclysmic explosion; but the firefighters managed to get the flames under control before the hundreds of tons of high explosives in the bomb dump started going up. The crew were uninjured physically.

Tutt was transferred to a Hurricane flight where, I was told, he was killed in an accident after only a few weeks. I often thought of the King of Swing; but although I laughed at the aptness of the title, my thoughts were not patronizing; they were admiring. Tutt may have lacked something, but it surely wasn't guts.

After two sessions with Crebbin totalling four hours and 30 minutes, I logged my first four-engine solo on August 23rd, in a Mark I Stirling. In the next two days I got in almost four hours practice on daylight circuits and bumps, following which, on August 25th, Crebbin gave me three hours and five minutes night dual and cleared me off solo for another hour and ten minutes.

Next night he sent me over to a neighbouring drome to practise circuits and bumps while the Stirlings from that station were away on ops. My first landing there is worthy of mention as the worst landing, the hardest landing, the most unsafe and terrifying landing I ever made in training. After an extremely hard "arrival" on the runway, the aircraft strained to weathercock and run off to the right; we teetered along the extreme edge of the runway for several hair-raising seconds at 100 miles an hour. If we had been at our own aerodrome, I would have taxied back to the flights after I brought the plane safely to a stop and asked Crebbin to give me another check circuit. As it was, my only alternatives were to phone Strad for an instructor and confess that I was afraid to fly the machine again — as I certainly was — or to line up on the runway and try again. I taxied around for another takeoff in a very grim silence. I think every other member of the crew was more frightened than I was — which was understandable, for they were helpless captives. At least I had some control over my fate.

But the next landing, after the tensest approach imaginable, was safe and passable — not good, but acceptable. From then on the landings got better and better. I kept going for four hours and five minutes, and after the first two hours it seemed, to me at any rate, that my landings were just as good as Crebbin's, which was really saying something. We all breathed much easier.

We were turned loose the following afternoon after our session at the flights, and evening found me sitting on the grass outside the neighbouring pub beside an attractive WAAF named Mary Stringer. While we sipped our drinks in the setting sun, a lone Stirling kept passing before us on final approach, disappearing from view just a few hundred yards away. I knew it was Penkuri getting in his circuits and bumps, so I maintained more than a passing interest in the position and attitude of his aircraft as it settled heavily across the pink-tinged sky every ten or 15 minutes.

Between his appearances I was putting my best foot forward with my companion. Her not inconsiderable physical charms, I must confess, were of less significance to me than the fact that she worked in Stores. Getting a Stores clerk to issue any item in inventory was normally only a trifle less difficult and time-consuming than making the article yourself from scratch. Bearing in mind the old maxim that love conquers all, it seemed logical that even a lukewarm affection on her part might ease our path through Stores on future clothing parades. In my own defence let me say that this grossly materialistic approach was not quite as selfish and culpable as it sounds because, so far as I was personally concerned, except for the odd article of flying clothing, there was little that sweet Mary could do for me. Officers were required to buy their own uniforms except for one initial issue of battle dress. It was my NCO's I was thinking of, little knowing that Stanley was already in on the ground floor.

NCO's were supposed to be kept presentable at His Majesty's expense. As a matter of practice, however, if they wanted a new pair of battle dress trousers, or shoes, they first had to present the worn article for inspection and have it condemned by the tailor in Stores. This functionary was not from Savile Row. Unless he could see large patches of daylight through the knees or rear-end of battle dress trousers, for example, he would not pronounce the desired verdict but return them for further service. If the assessments of the various tailors had been accepted without challenge, the RAF, by 1943, would have gone on parade with bare feet and in tatters and looked worse than Lee's Army of Northern Virginia in the days between Five Forks and Appomattox.

People with any pride in their appearance — and most aircrew had an abundance — regularly circumvented the pathetic parsimony of Stores bashers, who routinely interpreted a reasonable and sensible rule with an unreasonable and senseless extremity. As I had good reason to know, the aircrew's predictable response ran along these lines: "You want big holes in the battle dress before you condemn it chum? Right! Let's get cracking and put some holes in this stuff."

A few nights earlier I had called in at my NCO's quarters to find Stan, the dude of the crew, patiently working away at the knee of his second uniform with a piece of coke. In two or three hours, he assured me, he could add two years' fair wear and tear to any article on his clothing card, and produce worn-out knees and elbows that would defy detection by the most suspicious tailor in camp. He proved his point a day or two later.

To get back to Mary Stringer: as I fetched another round of drinks, Penkuri's Stirling droned past once more and sank steadily out of sight in the direction of the main runway. All at once came the angry roar of engines at full throttle, and we could hear the Stirling straining across the aerodrome away from us. My heart was suddenly in my throat for it was obvious that something had gone radically wrong to cause an overshoot right off the deck, and there had been something foreign about the sound of the engines just as Penky should have been touching down.

In a moment or two the Stirling appeared, safely climbing away from the drome, and after watching it for a few minutes I relaxed. Penky seemed to be all right.

Later that evening, with shamefully preferential treatment on the next clothing parade virtually guaranteed, I visited Penkuri's room to find out what had happened. He was writing a letter. When I put the question to him, he became unusually animated:

"I was just getting set to land. I was a bit short on the approach and I had a fair bit of power on coming up to the end of the runway; as I checked and cut the throttles, the port outer went practically wide open. First thing I knew, the port wing went up in the air and I was bouncing along 100 miles per on one wheel and practically scraping the other wingtip on the grass — couldn't get the damned port outer to shut off. I rammed 'em all open and we finally got levelled up and staggered around again. I'm still shaking."

Although his bombaimer, Deans, had been attending to the Exactors, Penky suspected that both he and Deans might have allowed them to go too long between primings. He concluded by cursing Exactors, their conception, construction, and continued use, and vowed that, should their paths ever cross, he would visit horrible punishment upon their inventor, whom he likened to Rube Goldberg with brain damage. His experience strengthened the resolution I had already made myself to prime these controls at very frequent intervals, for although Penky shortly treated the whole episode as a big joke, claiming he had simply wanted to test the aerobatic capabilities of the Stirling at low level, I gathered from other eye witnesses that it had been a near thing.

Twenty-four hours later, over a pint in the mess, Penkuri had another story to tell me, and again his bombaimer, Deans, was involved. On Stirling circuits, the bombaimer normally called the airspeed to the pilot at four-second intervals once the pilot had made his final turn into wind. This left the pilot free to concentrate on his approach without having to shift his gaze back and forth between the airspeed indicator and the runway or the glide-path indicator. Normally the bombaimer kept his chant going until the aircraft flared out over the end of the runway. Then he ceased, for at that point his voice would become an unnecessary and unwelcome distraction. Penkuri had been making a night approach in gusty conditions. He continued his recital to me in an irritated tone:

"Deans is sitting there saying '125 . . . 125 . . . 125 . . . 120 . . . 120 . . . 120 . . . 120 . . . 120 . . .;' then just as I'm coming up to the end of the runway he says: 'Okay, you've got her.' "

Here Penkuri took a drag at his cigarette that almost caused it to burst into flame, and continued, in a higher key:

"I don't know why it hit me so strong, but when he said 'you've got her' I nearly roared out and asked him who the hell he thought had had her for the last ten minutes. I was madder than hell. But I didn't say anything; I was too damn busy getting her down. Then to top it all off, it was a helluva landing; we flopped in so hard I thought I'd get a nosebleed. That made me twice as mad. I waited 'til we slowed down, then I shouted 'Damn you Deans!' Then he nearly ate his way through his oxygen mask sputtering, didn't know what he'd done wrong. I damn well told him what he'd done wrong. And I told him in future when he finished calling the airspeed to just sit there and squeeze his gums together."

Although my own reaction would probably have been similar, I couldn't pass up this opportunity to needle Penky, taking the line that I was astounded at his unjustly blaming Deans for his own lousy airmanship. Penky fell into the spirit of the thing at once, and we began embellishing the theme when we walked into the mess.

I brought him a pint of bitter, explaining that the mild he had ordered was unavailable until the boys carried in some new kegs (which they were in the process of doing).

"Damn you Deans", he said.

As we walked back to our rooms he paused at the mail rack to see whether any mail had come in that afternoon. His slot was empty. He turned to me and snarled again: "Damn you Deans."

My own crew were most appreciative of the story next morning, and we shortly began applying the new principle. There were any number of situations to which it could be extended.

As we were making an approach, after having been cleared to land on the long runway, the man on duty in the ACP hut just beside the near end of the runway fired a red Very light across our path, indicating a last-minute change of runway and forcing us to do an overshoot. I opened the throttles and called for the undercart, then as we began climbing away, looked sideways into J. B.'s eyes and delivered the benediction: "Damn you Deans".

The more inequitable the criticism, the better we appreciated it. If we walked into the mess and found our meal unpalatable, we damned Deans. If one carelessly knocked over a glass of water or a salt shaker, the drill was to glare at one's companion and say loudly, "Damn you Deans". Any disappointing cancellation of plans, or the issuance of orders to go flying at an inconvenient time, was ample grounds for pronouncement of the malediction upon a companion, provided the situation was totally beyond his control.

From our crew, and Penky's, the vaguely satisfying practice of damning Deans for anything and everything that went wrong spread rapidly to all the other aircrew going through Stradishall; in fact I should not have been surprised to learn that Deans was shortly thereafter being damned in the elevated society of Group or even Bomber Command Headquarters.

Now that we had demonstrated that we were capable of flying the biggest machines the RAF had, we felt entitled to stitch our conversation together with more and more RAF slang, an idiom which I always felt was particularly colourful and descriptive.

We no longer made bad landings — such miscues were now "ropey" landings. People who spoke unnecessarily on the intercom were told to quit "nattering". A new boy at anything was not a beginner or novice, he was a "sprog", and if any sprog pilot ventured an unsought or challenging opinion in the company of seasoned flyers, he risked being told patronizingly to "get some in", the reference being to flying time or ops as the occasion required. Alternatively, the sprog might be quashed by the gratuitous information that the operational type had more flying time than the sprog had sack time.

A dangerous or hair-raising flight was a "shaky do", and might easily terminate, not in a crash, but a "prang". Cities were pranged too, if a heavy raid were carried out on them. Crews did not get shot down, they "went for a Burton" or "got the Chop" on Essen, Berlin, Frankfurt, or whatever the target was. The standard adjuration to calm down or be patient was: "don't panic".

The information we required on any subject was called the "gen", pronounced "jen". A person recognized as possessing excellent qualifications and really knowing his stuff was given the ultimate accolade — he was a "gen man". If someone gave you faulty information, (usually this was some hapless wretch in the Met section going out on a limb with his predicted winds), you accused him of having given you "duff gen" instead of what you really wanted which was "pukka gen", the real McCoy. Any culprit who consistently gave misinformation was a "duff gen merchant". People who got a bad scare and responded accordingly "got the wind up" or simply were "windy". But if it was a chronic condition, and people acted unheroically as a result, they were "panic merchants".

The most overworked word in the lexicon was "wizard". It had virtually limitless nuances of meaning. A successful bombing attack was frequently described as a "wizard prang", or a "wizard show", or a "wizard do". All things approaching ineffability — and even many a comfortable way off — were absolutely wizard. The best girls were wizard; planes were wizard; carefully hatched schemes were wizard; interesting stories were wizard. I think that by September 2nd, when our crew graduated from the Stirling conversion course with 32 and a half hours of four-engine time, the word "wizard" represented a good 20 percent of our working vocabulary.

We hopefully expected to be posted to a squadron immediately after completing the course, but our expectations were not realized. Instead, I was called in to see "B" Flight commander, Squadron Leader Crebbin, who told me straightforwardly that we had done very well on our course, and then went on to explain, in guarded language evoking an air of mystery, that as a result we would be staying at Stradishall for another two and a half weeks for some special training. All he would venture in answer to my surprised query was that it would be special navigation training in a section headed by one Flight Lieutenant Omerod.

We reported for the new training immediately, but before any veils were drawn, we were told bluntly that what we were about to learn was highly secret information, not to be discussed under any circumstances, even with other aircrew, outside the inconspicuous classroom where Flight Lieutenant Omerod held sway. We discovered immediately thereafter why the security about this special course was so strict that we hadn't even known of its existence until we were chosen by Squadron Leader Crebbin and Wing Commander Cox to take it. We were going to be trained in the use of H2S, a highly secret radar navigation aid, something far more sophisticated than Gee.

It is difficult to remember today, when radar aids are old hat, how remarkable they seemed 30 years ago. In September, 1943, the capabilities of H2S sounded to us — and we had already been initiated into some of the other wonders of radar — like something from a science fiction story, a Buck Rogers device. What H2S did was nothing less than etch on a circular screen a fleeting but repetitive map-like reproduction of the terrain passing beneath its rotating scanner. The great contrast between the radar echoes generated by land and those reflected from water made the apparatus extremely effective in the vicinity of coastlines, rivers, or lakes. Unlike Gee it generated its own signal impulses and was therefore not susceptible, as Gee unfortunately was, to the jamming of German ground stations.

We began the flying exercises on September 9th, and despite what we had been told about the set's capabilities, I still recall clearly the amazement I experienced when Flight Lieutenant Oulton called me to the curtained navigation compartment where he was demonstrating the H2S's capabilities to Sam. On the screen before us each sweep of the antenna was tracing a perfect outline of the unmistakable rectangular bight of the Wash. I felt a witness to some eerie miracle, for we were over cloud at that moment, and the coastline below us was completely hidden from view; yet here before us in glowing green lines was a clear reproduction of the coast, one from which we could get a perfectly reliable "visual" fix. There was only one way to describe it fittingly: it was absolutely wizard.

We flew navigational exercises of two, three, or four hours virtually every day, during which Sam mastered the routines involved in setting up and tuning the equipment and changing scale on it at the appropriate moment. More important, he familiarized himself with the appearance of cities and towns and various types of natural topography on the business end of the cathode ray tube. Since H2S picked up strong responses from large built-up areas, it could be used as a rough blind-bombing sight. The drill was to fly within four or five miles of the mass of echoes reflected from a city, then do a short timed run from that point to the sector of the city chosen as the target area. We practised this technique repeatedly.

While these assignments were crammed with new training and experience for Sam, the duties involved were usually routine for the rest of us. But there were exceptions. On one of the early flights I suddenly found myself very busy and far from bored. We had an engine failure, and I had 20 minutes as I headed back to Stradishall to contemplate the prospect of my first three-engined landing. However, this minor crisis was resolved smoothly enough in due course, and the end result was simply to boost our confidence.

A three hour and 25 minute night flight on September 19th marked the completion of our special navigation course. We had flown an additional 35 and a half hours, bringing our total on four-engined aircraft to 68 hours, and the grand total for all types in my own log book to 517 hours.

On September 21st Squadron Leader Crebbin sent for me, and I knew that the moment I had been waiting for ever since I had walked into the recruiting office in Winnipeg was at hand: we were going to be posted to a squadron; at long last we were going to begin a tour of operations against the Germans. I had already scanned the assessment sheet that Crebbin had endorsed in my log book, and noted that he had given me "above-average" as my rating on four-engined heavies, so I went to see him with a glad and immodest heart. (At OTU I had only received the "average" assessment, a wound to my pride after having cracked the barrier for the first time at Advanced Flying Unit). Crebbin told me that my crew was being posted forthwith to 214 Squadron, RAF, a squadron in No. 3 Group stationed only seven miles away at Chedburgh. The Squadron's full title, as he recited it from the posting notice, was 214 (FMS) Squadron, the initials standing for Federated Malay States, who had at some earlier stage underwritten the cost of the Squadron's aircraft. 214 Squadron was not a Johnny-come-lately in the field of aerial bombardment; it had seen service as a heavy bomber squadron in World War I, being outfitted in 1918 with the great Handley Page 0/100. After the outbreak of hostilities in 1939 it had been re-activated, and after a stint as a training formation had been restored to its rightful place in front line service. It seemed to have some special claim to favour at Bomber Command HQ for it was already equipped with H2S, one of the first squadrons in Main Force apart from the Pathfinders to have that equipment — indeed, some of the Pathfinder Force squadrons had not yet received the device.

I left Crebbin's office floating on a wave of excitement and anticipation and went to give the glad tidings to the crew. Clearly we had been picked for 214 (which entailed the special H2S course) at the end of our standard conversion training, a fact that we were all willing to attribute to sheer excellence on the part of the crew as a whole. For the balance of the afternoon we hustled about packing our gear and getting cleared from the station in readiness for the transport which was laid on to take us to Chedburgh the following afternoon. Eating dinner that evening in the relaxed atmosphere of the Stradishall officers mess, surrounded by the snowy white tablecloths and gleaming silverware, it was hard to visualize that seven miles away the Stirlings were not being used for training flights, that men were arming them, loading them down with trolley loads of bombs, and flying them to Germany. I wondered with a mixture of excitement and dread what a real target would be like.

CHAPTER 11

OPERATIONAL FLYING — APPRENTICESHIP

For I dipt into the Future, far as human eye could see,
Saw the Vision of the world, and all the wonder that would be;

       •   •   •

Heard the heavens fill with shouting, and there rain'd a ghastly dew
From the nations' airy navies grappling in the central blue;

                              Tennyson. Locksley Hall

     We arrived at Chedburgh in the back of a truck at 3:00 PM. I reported to the Adjutant, a bluff, hearty Flight Lieutenant named George Wright, expecting to spend the remaining half-day chasing about getting quarters and going through the rest of the prosaic routine involved in getting squared away at a new station. I was wrong; the pace was a little different on 214. George put me straight in a few clipped phrases.

     "You're flying second dickey tonight, Peden — Wingco's orders. Briefing at 4:00 o'clock, so you've no time to settle in. Leave your trunk and the rest of your kit here; I'll see it gets down to the mess — pick it up there when you get back. Keep the bag with your flying clothing with you. Get your NCO's to report to the Station Warrant Officer; he'll get them fixed up for quarters. Your bombaimer can step over to the Admin Officer."

     When J. B. and the rest of the boys left, I came back, and George took me in to meet Wing Commander McGlinn, the Commanding Officer of 214 Squadron. During our two-minute meeting the only impression I was able to form was a vague one of rather distant severity — a cool businesslike gentleman.

242

Then the Adjutant took me over to meet the pilot with whom I was to fly that night. I was naturally more interested in appraising him than the Wing Commander. One of the more senior pilots on the station, he struck me as a pretty decent chap; but when he introduced me to his crew I was disappointed. For a team who were supposed to be experienced they came across as a noticeably windy lot. In adolescent style they were playing guessing games as to what the target was going to be — a practice which I decided I did not favour — and I was not at all reassured by the feverish flavour of their conversation. After a short time we joined the steady trickle of aircrew walking over to the briefing room.

Inside, the now familiar tension was easily sensed, razor sharp, despite the casual air assumed by most of the aircrew. Whatever the target was, a maximum effort had been called for; 214 Squadron and its offspring[1], 620 Squadron, had about 20 Stirlings bombed up and ready to go. All crews carefully emptied their pockets and drew escape kits, which each man then slid into the blouse of his battledress. The Wingco entered and we all stood while he and his entourage went to the stage. The time-honoured announcement came crisply as the drapes over the large wall map were drawn back:

"Gentlemen, the target for tonight is Hanover."

I felt a tremour. Hanover struck me as a pretty deep penetration for my maiden effort into the Fatherland. The red tapes ran north and east of our base to a point around Terschelling in the West Frisians, then slanted down across the mainland for most of the remaining 200 miles on a line which pointed at Berlin and carried the attacking force mid-way between Bremen and Hanover. In the eyes of the assessing German night fighter controller this line of advance would threaten both those important cities, and Berlin as well. Close to Hanover the tape turned abruptly and went directly to the target.

The attack was to open predominantly as a fire raid, in an attempt to duplicate the devastation visited upon Hamburg a few weeks earlier. The Pathfinders' TI's (Target Indicators) at a later stage were to move from the old residential quarter of the city into the heart of the industrial sector. No. 3 Group aircraft were to open the attack with several hundred tons of incendiaries. The Groups following a few minutes behind were to shift the focus of the attack, dropping a much heavier tonnage of high explosive in a pattern designed to spread the fire into the industrial area, then to blast, burn and flatten as large a

---

1. Some months earlier 214 Squadron had been enlarged from the standard two Flights to three; but on June 17th, 1943, as part of the expansion program going on in Bomber Command, "C" Flight was taken away from 214 Squadron and became the nucleus of the new 620 Squadron.

sector there as possible. Seven hundred and eleven four-engined aircraft were scheduled to attack the city.

Takeoff was at sunset. I sat up front with the skipper as the line of hulking Stirlings taxied implacably, ponderously, toward the takeoff point. On the way the perimeter track ran within a hundred yards of Chedburgh's pub, before which the locals, knowledgeable in these matters, had assembled for their nightly show. It did not lack interest.

Before our turn came, we watched four others line up, strain briefly against the brakes, then slip the invisible bond and lumber forward. Each plane would accelerate sluggishly until the tail was up, then roar heavily, faster and faster, toward the far end of the runway. The wind was between runways, and gave little help. None of the first four parted company with the concrete until it seemed certain to run off the end and pile in; but just short of catastrophe each one inched reluctantly skyward. When the green Aldis winked at us I could easily have been persuaded to switch places with the casual spectators who had given us a thumbs up with their free hands as we rolled by.

Duplicating the earlier performances, our aircraft staggered off a hundred yards from the end of the runway, and we began our slow climb. As we made a gentle turn to port I noticed that one of the four aircraft ahead of us was smoking. Like the others, he had been circling base to gain height, and I watched, sick and helpless, as the smoke streaming out from the underside of the wing root grew more and more dense, and the plane froze in a gentle dive for the earth. I kept urging the crew silently to jump, but no chutes appeared. It was like watching an impending execution.

In a flash it was over. No one spoke. My thoughts jumped to my crew on the ground; they would undoubtedly have been watching, and for hours they would not know which of the many aircraft circling the field like slow bees had crashed.

Shortly after we had set course, I spotted another Stirling softly silhouetted just ahead of us, slightly above and slightly to the right, climbing on our course. It was getting darker by the minute, so I kept a wary eye on it. Although we could make him out in the lighter sky just above us, he could easily miss us. In a few moments I noticed that he must have altered course slightly; we were now converging. I glanced at the skipper expectantly, waiting for him to dip our nose a trifle and ensure a safe crossing, for we were getting perilously close. Although he seemed aware of the other aircraft, looking directly towards it, he made no move to get out of the way. I squirmed in my seat. It was not my place as second dickey to tell the first pilot his job. Suddenly the other aircraft dropped his port wing slightly and began to slide rapidly into our path. There was no time to talk. I grabbed the controls and shoved, realizing belatedly that the skipper had not even seen the other plane. It drifted across just above us, missing colliding with us by no more than three or four feet. My skipper was clearly startled at the sudden diving of our aircraft, but the sight of that hulking shadow drifting just over our heads with an almost inaudible hum was all the explanation he required. He resumed control without a word and we carried on.

With that inauspicious start the trip proceeded to deteriorate. On the run in from the Frisians, the navigator computed a new wind and then made the incredible mistake (we later discovered) of "correcting" the drift on the wrong side. When our ETA Hanover arrived there was no sign of the Pathfinders' TI's. The skipper held his course for another ten minutes, getting more and more frustrated, before the rear gunner thought to mention that some city 30 miles behind us had been burning fiercely for most of that period. At that the skipper cursed, reversed our course, and steered for the flaming city, and the navigator, who had already been checking his suspect plotting, simultaneously discovered the glaring error.

By the time we were halfway back to Hanover the raid was over. From ten miles out the city glowed below us like some enormous fireplace full of flickering embers, reflecting the effects of over 2500 tons of high explosive and incendiaries.

As we approached, Hanover's flak batteries opened up, and since they could now concentrate on a solitary target, got in some very good shooting. Flashes all around us gave vivid testimony of their competence. Suddenly a panicky voice shouted on the intercom: "BALLOONS!". Whoever it was took ten years off my life. I wondered fearfully how the Germans could get balloons and balloon cables up to 13,000 feet.

Nothing communicates itself faster between the various scattered positions in a bomber than uncontrolled panic in someone's voice. That shout set everyone's heart racing. In a second or two the flash of more bursting shells lit the sky around us, repeatedly and rapidly, and in the momentary illumination they provided I saw that what had caused the shout was simply the billowing black smoke puffs from earlier shells. The skipper commented on it at the same time. I began breathing again, relieved, but angry with the unkown clot who had scared me so thoroughly and so unnecessarily. I knew my own crew would not have reacted with such a lack of discipline, and began to feel that there was really very little I wanted to learn from this aggregation who, between them, had violated half a dozen fundamental precepts in this one operation.

The rest of the trip was a long drawn out ordeal for me. This crew was truly windy. Fright crackled in virtually all their intercom exchanges — and there were far too many of these. Putting one's life in the hands of a group of aircrew whose nerves are shot is a harrowing experience. I longed for the moment when we would reach the English coast and relative safety — at least I thought it meant relative safety.

Eventually it came to pass, we did attain that great divide, and a short time later approached our base and called for landing instructions. I thought I detected a warmer than usual note in the response of the WAAF radio operator, and assumed that our tardiness had already occasioned concern — and some tentative mental arithmetic regarding available aircraft for the next operation.

Ten minutes later we switched off Z Zebra's engines. We had been flying for five hours and 25 minutes, and I had never experienced a sensation of relief quite as intoxicatingly satisfying as what I felt as I climbed out the rear door and stepped onto the lovely, wonderful, marvellous, fabulous, solid old concrete of that good old dispersal. I said my twentieth brief prayer of thanks under my breath as I walked forward to where some of the other members of the crew were lighting their cigarettes.

I was about to follow suit, but deferred the act momentarily while I watched the navigation lights of another aircraft, even later than our own, rounding slowly into the funnel of the Drem system and lining up to land. We were in the first dispersal clear of the runway in use, and as this aircraft prepared to land at the far end, it was heading almost directly at us. What caught and held my attention was the sight of yet another pair of navigation lights rapidly approaching those of the aircraft about to land. They were too close, vaguely disturbing; I did not quite know what to make of it. The landing aircraft was only 20 feet in the air, almost over the end of the runway, when the puzzle was speedily unravelled.

There was a stuttering thunder of cannon as the second aircraft opened fire at point blank range on the unsuspecting Stirling. In two seconds the Junkers 88 had overtaken and passed its main target and came roaring on in our general direction, hosing streams of tracers before it like flaming strings of incredibly fast baseballs. At the first bark of the guns the adrenalin had gushed again, and I launched into a workmanlike swan dive onto the concrete. Unmindful of the shock, I lay quaking in my boots and watched the intruder sweep toward us at full throttle. It seemed to me, compressing myself industriously against the tarmac, that every round of the tracer slicing out of the darkness was going to hit me between the eyes. As though not satisfied that he had terrified me sufficiently, the Ju 88 pilot dropped a shower of butterfly bombs as he whistled across the field, and a dozen of those unpredictable and vicious little canisters, each one closer than the last, exploded with jarring blasts in the course of that fiery, roaring sweep.

In 20 seconds the whole thing was over. The noise of the Ju 88 faded as he dashed at tree-top level for the sea, and the Stirling which had been his primary target wobbled to a stop clear of the runway. (The Stirling pilot, Jake Walters — of whom more anon — and the rest of the crew, had escaped physical injury by some miracle, although their aircraft was battered almost beyond repair thanks to the close range working-over from three 20 mm cannon and three machine guns.)

I climbed slowly, and very warily, to my feet, ready to plummet to the horizontal position again at the first hint of another intruder, and found that I still had a death grip on the handle of my chest pack. My heart was still racing in overdrive, and the only possible reason I could imagine for my hands not trembling as I lit my cigarette was that the multitude of shakes, quakes and tremors I was experiencing were cancelling each other out. For some hours I harboured a terrifying after-image of cannon spitting fire in my face to the accompaniment of an ear-shattering crescendo of Junkers Jumo engine noise and tooth-rattling blasts from butterfly bombs.

I went in for interrogation, took a cup of coffee liberally laced with Lamb's rum, (which tasted terrible but worked therapeutic miracles) and went down to the officers mess to find my trunk. There was a note tied to the handle, and some kind soul who noticed the vacant stare in my eye guided me through the seas of mud adorning the neighbourhood to the correct Nissen hut and an empty bed. Sleep was a long time coming.

When I woke up, after three or four hours' fitful sleep, my first thought was to contact the crew. It transpired that the previous evening all my NCO's had been on their bicycles on a road skirting the field when the unmistakable sounds of an operational takeoff had come to them and bombers had begun climbing into view from aerodromes all around the area. They had paused to watch the Chedburgh takeoff, having a proprietary interest in some unkown aircraft amongst the procession, had seen the Stirling catch fire in the air[1], and had witnessed its implacable descent and the mounting pall of smoke that marked its end. As I had realized, they had no way of knowing whether they had just seen their Skipper die and no way of finding out for some hours. They concluded, so they told me with straight faces, that if I had been in that Stirling, I was dead and there was nothing they could do for me except hold a wake. But if I had not been in the burning Stirling, the wake would either be premature, depending upon what happened on

---

1. That stricken Stirling actually appears to have been one from 90 Squadron which staggered into our circuit from the Wratting Common area while I had my attention focused on raising the undercarriage and bleeding off the flap. We lost two of our Stirlings from Chedburgh over enemy territory on the Hanover raid.

the raid itself, or completely superflous if I should be lucky enough to return — hence in either case the proceedings would not be in good taste. Consequently they had re-mounted their bicycles and carried on to the Sergeants Mess dance at Stradishall, whither they had been bound originally. Resplendent in his new serge uniform, (compliments of Mary Stringer and a tailor who could not detect his professional touch with the coke), Stan inserted the needle a little further by assuring me that he personally had had a particularly joyous evening.

I responded in kind, saying I was touched by their concern for my well-being, and with more such banter we headed for the crew room to attend a special parade the Wing Commander had called for all aircrew.

Apparently one or two of the aircraft had been late taking off the previous night, and the Wingco was determined that this would not happen again. He reviewed the situation in undiplomatic language and issued an edict that henceforth every crew was to be at its aircraft one full hour before takeoff. Someone pointed out, not nastily but with proper respect, that often the flying meals were not ready at the airmen's mess in time for the crews to meet that sort of deadline.

"I don't give a damn if you starve to death," McGlinn said icily, "you are going to be at your aircraft one hour before takeoff."

This was hardly the recommended Dale Carnegie approach for winning friends and influencing people. On the other hand, the Wingco made his point with the desired forcefulness and of course had his way, differences of opinion being so easy to resolve under the stripe system; but he left a residue of resentment in his crews. Since this was the first opportunity I had had to draw a long breath since arriving on the station, I made a few inquiries as to the Wingco's background.

He had come to Chedburgh to take command of 214 only a short time before we came over ourselves. He had had no previous operational experience, and hence was still regarded sceptically by most of the squadron's senior skippers as a handbook pilot, particularly when he was reviewing points of engine handling or tactics during briefing. The period of mutual assessment was continuing.

Every morning about ten o'clock the Wingco received a call from Group HQ. He in turn called his two flight commanders and told them accordingly that "There is a war on tonight — maximum effort", or that "the squadron is standing down." Four times out of five it would be the first message, and pilots would hurry to airtest every serviceable aircraft so that the armourers could get on with bombing-up. Even when this message came through, however, the weather conditions were frequently so threatening, either over base or over the continent, that operations were subject to cancellation right up to the last minute. The heaviest gamble, of course, involved the meteorologists' predictions of what landing conditions would be when the huge bomber force arrived back over its bases — with rapidly emptying tanks.

This morning of September 23rd, 1943, the message had already gone round: there was a war on. Further, I had been alerted to fly another second dickey trip. Meantime I was ordered to take my own crew, airtest W Willie, and then do a compass swing on it. We got at it right after lunch.

Already the station was a beehive of activity. Big petrol bowsers were making their rounds, pumping thousands upon thousands of gallons into empty tanks. Trucks laden with oxygen cylinders methodically called at each dispersal. Tractors towing long rows of bomb trolleys trundled around the perimeter track. Gunners polished the perspex of their turrets, and stripped and cleaned the guns, while armourers carefully draped long symmetrical belts of ammunition that here and there reflected the oil-dulled gleam of brass and cupro-nickel. Hundreds of men concentrated on allotted tasks; there were no idlers in sight. Before I was quite ready, it was time to go to briefing again.

This trip I was to fly with a crew skippered by an NCO, a slight chap of medium height named Flight Sergeant Sellar. I knew five minutes after I met him that I was in better hands than I had been in the night before. Sellar had an air of quiet, unflappable confidence that I liked. We sat together waiting for the curtains to be drawn.

"Gentlemen, the target for tonight is Mannheim."

Mannheim, twin city of Ludwigshafen, lay at the junction of the Rhine and the Neckar, I noticed, almost as far east as Hanover but 200 miles further south. Via the aircrew grapevine I had already learned that trips to southern Germany, because of the much longer overland routing involved, gave the night fighters a better chance to get organized against us, and that opposition in this area was usually strong. Mannheim was on Bomber Command's priority target list primarily because of its iron and steel plants, tool and die plants, and substantial petroleum storage facilities.

We went out to J Jig an hour before takeoff, in compliance with the new ordinance. The Wingco had obviously taken whatever steps were necessary to reach the staff of the airmen's mess, because we had our fried egg flying meal in lots of time — and were thus deprived of the opportunity of feeling sorry for ourselves as martyrs who had to fly on ops without being fed.

The first hour of the trip passed uneventfully, at least as uneventfully as operational flights could, seemingly. For half an hour on the climb one engine threatened to overheat, which would have left Sellar with a number of critical decisions to make, decisions which he had to anticipate before the contingency actually occurred. But the needle of the cylinder head gauge finally became stationary only a few degrees above the recommended upper limit, and Sellar settled for a minor reduction in power which he was later able to make up when we levelled out and made our general reduction to cruising boost and revs.

This trip promised to be hotter than Hanover, nevertheless I felt a growing confidence as I witnessed the performance of Sellar and his crew. They could have been demonstrating, for some Air Force film, the way an operational crew ought to carry out its duties. No one wasted a word on the intercom and, when someone did pass a message, it was in the calm, matter-of-fact voice that one would use in a classroom exercise. The contrast between this crew and my flying companions of the previous night was as wine to water.

Several times, from different sectors of the black void ahead, flashing particles of fire lashed out, looking like white sparks streaming from a high speed grinding wheel. Sometimes the first stream would be answered by a puny returning stream. But all too frequently the opening stream went unanswered, and on occasion this unsettling fireworks display was climaxed by a terrible fire blooming in the darkness, or by an explosion on the ground, as a bomber perished under the guns of a night fighter. I had seen only one or two of these, at a distance, on the Hanover attack. They were noticeably more frequent now, but the laconic sighting reports betrayed no trace of the feelings we were all experiencing.

The attack opened on schedule while we were five minutes away from the target, for we were not in the first wave. Brilliant green TI's cascaded onto the aiming point and glowed fiercely as the waves of bombers soared overhead and began unloading a heavy discharge of bombs all around and through them. Before we began our run-up, German "cat's eye" fighters — day fighters not equipped with Airborne Interception radar — arrived on the scene and dropped row upon row of chandelier flares high above us. With this illumination they had no difficulty spotting the bomber stream and many combats broke out in and around the target area, a vast arena now flooded with a pitiless light.

Sellar responded to the bombaimer's instructions with a quiet "Bomb doors open" as we began our run. As he concentrated on the run and the bombaimer's corrections, my eye caught a movement ahead of us to port. In a moment a Ju 88 flew into plain view heading in the opposite direction. For a brief moment I was able to take in every detail in the harsh light bathing the scene. The Ju 88 was on fire; flames and smoke streamed from its port engine. On the thin tubular body the identifying black cross was clearly visible in its white frame. The pilot huddled over the controls; from his attitude one sensed that he was trying desperately, before his aircraft exploded, to guide it beyond the lethal area of illumination — to get clear of the guns and the fires below and bail out. He had no eyes for us as he concentrated solely on staying alive.

I felt no sympathy for him, only relief that he was in no position to attack us. They were killers in our book, killers who had every advantage over us, the prey they stalked.

Sellar had not so much as turned his head to look at the enemy aircraft, ignoring the flak and focusing all his attention on fine course corrections as the bombaimer directed him with precision toward a fresh set of TI's just positioned by the Pathfinder "backers-up" slightly to the left of the original markers. To a neophyte like me at least the attack appeared to be heavy and concentrated. In an area of perhaps 150 acres around the TI's it looked to me as though every factory, every house, every building of every description was on fire. Over much of this expanse the colour of the fire had changed during the five or six minutes since the attack had opened, turning from the diamond white incandescence of the hundreds of thousands of incendiaries themselves to the deeper reddish flames which testified that the fires had taken hold in the buildings. As we left there were still hundreds of heavies behind us on their way in to blast and burn more of the target sector[1]. I glanced back for another glimpse of Mannheim as we were moving out of the area of illumination. The nethermost pit of hell itself could scarcely have appeared more frightful. The over-all spectacle was virtually indescribable, the product of bursting shells, a vast enclave billowing fire and smoke below, searchlights groping in slow frenzy, their beams rendered anaemic by the glare of hundreds of flares slowly descending on their parachutes — with additional rows of fresh ones being seeded far above.

Leaving the target we still had 300 miles before us to make the enemy coast. There was no let-up in vigilance. German night fighters would still be ranging in force, striving to render our attack as costly as possible. Confirmation was provided by three more combats that broke out in close proximity on the way back, a strong indication that there were many more taking place, for the bomber stream was strung out for many miles both in front and behind us. But we were not molested. Eventually we crossed the enemy coast outbound, and although no one relaxed his efforts, we knew our chances of getting home were now beginning to increase substantially. After a further suspenseful wait we approached our own base.

The weather had clamped down at Chedburgh, apparently just

---

1. Of the 622 aircraft despatched, 571 bombed, dropping 1,974 tons. Thirty-two aircraft and crews were shot down, as compared with 26 on Hanover.

before our arrival, resulting in a diversion to Waterbeach. Arriving there, we found ourselves running a bit low on juice, with nine aircraft ahead of us in the landing pattern. I grew tense as the minutes ticked by. Traffic was heavy around the drome, many other non-Waterbeach aircraft having been diverted there like us; and with 20-odd tired crews circling the field with us in the blackness we got two bad scares, one from a pilot who changed altitude without any clearance and practically landed on us, the other from a pilot who failed to turn on his navigation lights and apparently did not see ours. Through it all, Sellar remained imperturbable. After ten or 15 minutes, when we had been in the air for five minutes short of seven hours, we were given Turn One and pancaked.

Again the relief of being safely down flowed over us like a healing drug. We luxuriated in the sensation as we lit our cigarettes and waited for the crew bus. There was little conversation; everyone was too tired.

At interrogation, since I was not directly involved in the questioning, I had an opportunity to study the aircrew in the room with me. There was scant similarity between the figures around me and the keen Brylcreem-ad airmen on the recruiting posters which had equated joining the Air Force with "Adventure in the Skies". Seven hours of sweating concentration in a snug flying helmet had left everyone's hair plastered to his head like wet fur. Bleary eyes, and faces etched with the imprint of oxygen masks and the weariness spawned of acute tension and lack of sleep, complemented the sagging posture and occasional sighing exhalation of cigarette smoke to present a picture of men wrung out like dish rags — men who had had enough adventure to do them for a bit.

Waterbeach had been unprepared for this inundation of surplus aircrew, and had only a handful of spare beds. I spent three weary and uncomfortable hours vainly trying to sleep in an armchair in the officers mess, then gave up and went out to see if I could rustle up a cup of coffee from one of the cooks while I waited for breakfast.

Back at Chedburgh three hours later, I learned that our crew had not been placed on the battle order for that night, although we were down to do an air test on E Easy right after lunch. I tried to sleep for a couple of hours, then rose for lunch and made my way up to the flights for the air test.

After we had landed, the NCO's told me there was to be a dance that night at the Sergeants Mess, and invited me to come. I had a much more attractive prospect in mind — about ten hours uninterrupted sleep — so I begged off. As I learned the following morning, I should have gone, not so much for the entertainment as for the high drama.

La Belle Stringer had shown up, clearly expecting a warm welcome from Stan, who had been extremely attentive to her at Stradishall. But circumstances had altered since their last meeting. For one thing, Stan was feeling no pain when she made her entrance. Furthermore, he had no immediate need of uniforms or other articles from Stores; and of course, even if he had, Miss Stringer was no longer in a position to confer such favours. The unfortunate result was that Stan was much less attentive than he might have been. Worst of all — and this was really the *causa causans* of the climax — he was attentive to someone else, someone even more attractive than Miss Stringer, and he cruelly wounded fair Mary's pride by inviting other members of the crew to dance with Mary while he bugled after the new quarry. Nursing her wrath to keep it warm, Mary did a slow burn, a high temperature slow burn which Stan unthinkingly fanned by repeated acts of nonchalant negligence as the festive evening wore on.

The climax approached; but Mary was not yet ready to toss in the towel. Being a woman, she had no need to read Clausewitz or to study Jomini's dissertation on the Little Corporal's campaigns, to recognize that the first principle of war is the maintenance of the object, and her object was to win the undivided attention of Flight Sergeant Stanley.

She asked Stan to hold her purse while she went to powder her nose, probably thinking to immobilize him long enough for someone else to team up with his new dancing partner and take her out of the play while Mary cleared the decks for a little serious infighting.

The plan misfired. When Mary returned not only was Stan back in business with the new contender, oiling his way around the dance floor in his spanking new Stringer uniform; he had playfully twisted Mary's tail by taking a few shillings from her purse to buy the competition a drink. This was the most unkindest cut of all.

One moment after Mary confronted him and got this teasing communiqué, she provided a reasonably convincing demonstration of the truth of the old adage which avers that hell hath no fury like a woman scorned. After recovering her property in one snatch, Mary tore through the crowd on the dance floor like a Kansas twister, pausing at the portal only long enough to give Stan an exclusive piece of her mind and then to damn all his associates with the concluding shriek:

"I hope you and your whole crew go for the Chop on your first bloody op!"

I was told — and I could readily believe, for I blanched myself — that this produced an effect upon the assembled multitude much like the Count of Monterone's curse on Rigoletto. It was particularly shocking to the intended beneficiaries, the superstitious NCO's of my crew, who were now due to fly their first op with 214. They, and I, in a state of unease, considered the remark unforgivable. Ever afterward we remembered Mary, not for her beauty, but for that sweet, sweet disposition.

Half an hour after I heard the story, on the morning of September 25th, Squadron Leader Jeffries, flight commander of "A" Flight, told me that my crew was to do a fighter affiliation exercise in E Easy. He also told me that I was to take her "Gardening" that night for my first Stirling operation with my own crew.

"Gardening" was the code name for mining operations. The RAF did an enormous amount of this work, laying mines in coastal waters and harbours all the way from Norway to the Gironde estuary. By so doing they not only kept a large number of German minesweepers working constantly in an attempt to keep shipping channels open, particularly in the "inside" waterways from Norway and Denmark down behind the Frisians, but they sank a large and strategically significant tonnage of shipping and dislocated and delayed the movement of a vast number of other important cargoes.

Mining trips were usually much less risky than main force operations. But if, when the aircraft was going in at 600 feet to drop its mines, it happened to stray within range of one of the many German flak ships which were rotated at random to guard the most likely places, it stood an excellent chance of being blown to Kingdom Come before its crew knew what had happened.

Jake Walters — he who had been landing after the Hanover raid when the Ju 88 overtook him — was one of the few who lived to tell the tale after encountering a flak ship at close quarters. Jake told the story splendidly after a few pints: how he and his crew had navigated unerringly to the prescribed spot in the channel adjoining the Frisians, descended to 600 feet after going through the required procedure of checking their position again on Gee, had made their run with the bomb doors open — and flown directly over a flak ship that had heard their Stirling coming and was cocked and primed waiting for them. The first thunderous salvo had been right on target — the flak ship could hardly miss at that range — and Jake and the boys had been blown completely upside down only 600 feet over the North Sea.

At this point in the recital Jake always paused for effect, took a long draught from his pint, then looked everyone in the eye and said, straight-faced: "I wasn't afraid to die, — BUT I THOUGHT I'D FIGHT FOR THE BOYS!" — this last clause accompanied by violent foot and arm motions demonstrating a desperate winding on of aileron and a stabbing application of top rudder.

By great good fortune the throttles had been inadvertently thrust forward unevenly when Jake went for maximum power, so that full power was applied on only one side. This unintended gesture kept the aircraft rolling in the same direction and enabled it to right itself just in time to avoid plunging into the North Sea. Jake maintained, momentarily poker-faced, that the uneven application of power — and on the right side — had been no fortuitous blunder but rather consummate airmanship flowing from a most careful and unperturbed analysis of the situation performed by him whilst hanging upside down in his straps. It was a sparkling yarn, one of several in Jake's operational repertoire; but he knew, and we knew, that his miraculous escape in the riddled Stirling constituted the exception that proved the rule.

At briefing we found that our Gardening was to be done in the Frisians too, but with me, as I joshed Jake later, it proved to be a case of *Veni; Vidi; Vici;* and no problems. We took E Easy into the designated channel northeast of Texel and were back home safe and sound in three hours and thirty-five minutes. I wrote it into my log book next day with a circled "4" after it.

Next night there was no war on, so the Wingco laid on some training flying for the junior crews, and we wound up doing a Bullseye of just under five hours. On September 28th when we reported to the flights we were sent over to Stradishall to ferry a new kite back to Chedburgh, and I asked Stan, provoking an unprintable answer, whether he would like ten minutes to pop round and say hello to Mary Stringer while we were within a hundred yards of her lair.

About noon the weather clamped in and it began to drizzle sporadically. Word came through simultaneously that there was a stand-down for the squadron. I immediately thought of a few hours sleep, followed by a foray into Bury St. Edmunds. Wing Commander McGlinn had other ideas. He was clearly a charter member of that school who believed that if aircrew were allowed to lie about they would immediately get slack, and morale would decline precipitously overnight. To keep our morale sky high, he laid on a route march for the afternoon, all the way around the Drem system. I hastily guessed the diameter of the system to verge on three miles, which meant a circumferential stroll of about nine miles — three hours totally wasted. My morale collapsed.

On subsequent occasions when the squadron was stood-down the Wingco came up with other happy thoughts to keep morale soaring. We collected teapot-sized boulders, whitewashed them, and arranged them in neat borders outside various buildings to set off the inspiring period architecture, i.e. Nissen huts and other austerity monstrosities. The double row circling the flagpole compound, the very epitome of originality in design, represented our ultimate triumph in this challenging field. This day, as I slogged my way around the field resignedly, suffering from intensely low morale, the Wingco, who had not shirked the march himself, fell in alongside me.

He asked me how our Gardening in the Frisians had gone. I said "Piece of cake, sir," this being the accepted response for a pukka operational pilot. If one had just returned from Berlin with two engines out and pieces falling off the aeroplane all the way back, it would still be proper form to tell anyone inquiring that the show had been a piece of cake. The other alternative, one not employed when responding to a Wing Commander, was to magnify the exploit outrageously, in which case one's statement would likely be written into the "Line-shoot" book which most squadrons kept in the officers mess.

It quickly became apparent that what McGlinn really wanted to talk about was the second dickey trip I had done on Hanover. Having checked the navigator's log, spoken to the pilot, and, I suspect, looked at the target photos, the Wingco was not at all satisfied that the performance had served its purpose as an instructive exercise for me. He finally came out and said that he was quite prepared to lay on another second dickey trip for me before I took my crew on a main target. I wanted no more second dickey trips, and hastened to assure him that I was confident I could handle a target with my own crew. McGlinn seemed satisfied and vaguely pleased with this response, and let the matter drop.

That night I decided to forego the trip to Bury St. Edmunds. Three hours of morale building, a good bit of it across muddy terrain, had taken the edge off my appetite for pleasure. I repaired instead to the mess, with my leg tendons feeling every bit as resilient as chewed string, and settled in for a quiet and sedentary evening. When I went into the lounge after dinner, I gathered that the previous night's party, which had been moving along with considerable momentum at the time of my relatively early departure, had ultimately measured up to the usual robust limits.

I became aware of that fact as my eyes drifted casually over the top of my newspaper and fixed on a set of jet black footprints on the opposite wall, footprints which I noticed with a shock marched vertically up the wall, continued across the ceiling in unbroken train, and then came back down the near wall close to where I was sitting. I moved to investigate this intriguing spoor more closely.

The prints had been put on by someone who had taken off his shoes and socks and applied shoe polish liberally and frequently to the underside of his feet. I marvelled at the trouble he and his inebriated accomplices had gone to, visualizing the difficulty they had had in balancing and supporting him upside down, presumably while they braced themselves on top of the big mess table. No one had broken his neck, or we should all have heard about it from Doc Vyse, our MO, but I shook my head as I guessed at how many collapses, preceded by incoherent shouts of warning, and succeeded by gales of uncontrollable laughter, had punctuated this great aerial excursion.

George Wright came along at that moment and challenged me to a couple of games of shove ha'penny. I lost both ignominiously but considered it a fair exchange for the enjoyment of George's company and conversation. He had been a planter in Malaya before the war, and had a great fund of stories about life on a rubber plantation. After one anecdote, a process of word and thought association carried his conversation to aircrew, and he laughingly damned them all for rascals.

"Look here, Murray," he said, taking me over to the notice board, "I laid that picture on the bar for ten seconds last night while I was talking to Doc Vyse, and while my back was turned one of those young buggers whipped it. I didn't see it again until lunch time today. Now look at that would you."

The photograph, which showed George in tropical garb seated alongside a furry primate of some type, obviously a pet baboon, or ape, or gorilla — I wasn't sure what it was — was now thumbtacked to the notice board over a piece of paper bearing the inscription: "George and another planter in Malaya — George on the left."

"That's the sort of respect the Adjutant gets from the aircrew on this squadron," George boomed, "and then they come pestering me for passes before they are due". His appearance throughout this account was such that it wasn't hard to tell who was getting the biggest kick out of the impertinent caption.

We went back and sat down to chat over another pint. While we were thus pleasantly engaged, one of the WAAF officers strolled in. She happened to be quite good looking, so that I asked George her name as a reflex action.

"Oh, that's Bedworth, Section Officer Bedworth," he said, "I always call her Bedworthy — makes her mad as hell — what do you think?"

Trailing Bedworth by 60 seconds came two other WAAF officers: a short, plumpish brunette whose accent immediately stamped her as a Scot, and a tall, attractive English blonde named Rhoda who worked in the Intelligence Section. They struck me as friendly types; certainly they were popular with the men in the mess.

A short time later I heard the Scotch lass playfully pleading with a couple of the aircrew to teach her and Rhoda how to play a game with the unlikely name of "Are you there Moriarty?" At first the men protested that this was no game for ladies, but they bent under pressure and soon undertook to demonstrate the basic moves. Intrigued by the name, I followed the brief preparations.

"Are you there Moriarty?" was not at all demanding in terms of equipment required for team play. Rolling two good sized clumps of newspapers together, the men fashioned a pair of clubs the size of baseball bats, tied at strategic points with string. Next the two ladies were blindfolded and persuaded to lie on the floor face down. They lay head to head, separated by the length of their outstretched left arms and gripping their left hands together. In her right hand each girl held a solidly rolled newspaper club. From that point on the game proceeded with Neanderthal simplicity.

One contestant, who might aptly be termed the batter, called out: "Are you there Moriarty?" The other player, the battee or target, was bound to answer in a clearly audible voice, whereupon the batter, estimating position by sound and feel, swung her club in an attempt to hit the target on the head. Each crack on the head counted one point, and after each swing the roles were reversed.

The girls exchanged three or four very feminine half-hearted swings, scoring only partial hits or near misses and provoking much advice from the growing body of aircrew spectators, many of whom found their concentration on the finer ballistic problems of the game challenged by Rhoda, whose skirt was climbing higher with each clout. As I moved to a better vantage point it was Rhoda's turn to call again.

"Are you there Moriarty?" she giggled.

"Where?" laughed the Scotch lass, who then made the serious tactical error of rolling over on her back in an effort to vary her position quickly and substantially.

Rhoda, who was just hitting her stride and entering freely into the spirit of the game, swung her club with a new burst of speed and brought it whistling down unerringly onto her friend's upturned face, producing a shattering surprise, mild concussion, and a gushing nosebleed all in one fell swoop. The little brunette promptly burst into tears, and both girls scrambled to their feet, pulled off their blindfolds and fell into each other's arms with high pitched sobs of pain and remorse respectively. I suspected that the gladiators were all through with aircrew games for the evening, perhaps even for the duration, so I went back to the hut.

On Saturday, October 2nd, we were briefed for Gardening again, but this time it was to be no short flip to the Frisians. The target area for these mines was a shipping channel around Anholt Island off the coast of Sweden, far up in the Kattegat. Our route would take us in over Denmark, which we were told was another sensitive area so far as night fighters were concerned, and in terms of distance the red tapes traced out a round trip which looked to be somewhere between 1300 and 1400 miles.

The weather was reasonably good over England when we took off, except that it was a particularly black night; but as we approached

Denmark the visibility deteriorated steadily, with a high overcast shutting out every vestige of starlight. We flew along silently, hour after hour, in and out of unseen clouds whose presence was betrayed only after the fact by their inner turbulence. When Sam did have occasion to exchange a word or two with me — and this only occurred at widely spaced intervals — the sudden sound of his voice in my headphones made me jump. After three and a half hours we were nearing the point at which we were to start our descent preparatory to laying the mines.

Without warning the blackness surrounding us was suddenly filled with slashing white tracer coming from the starboard quarter; simultaneously Bert gave the urgent order "Corkscrew starboard!" and the aircraft vibrated to the chatter of our own guns.

I was already wrenching the Stirling into a steep starboard dive, and out of the corner of my eye watched in wild fright the hosing streams of tracer following us. Again I had the terrifying impression that the streaking cannon shells were passing within inches of my head. The firing stopped as abruptly as it had started. I kept up the corkscrew until Bert came on from the mid-upper turret a few seconds later to report that the Messerschmitt 210 had broken off.

Three minutes after we had levelled up — and well before our hearts had subsided to their normal rhythm — the Me 210 came bursting in on us a second time, from a hundred yards away on the port quarter. Again the first intimation we had of his presence was a withering hail of cannon fire, and again we dived fiercely into our corkscrew, causing parachute packs, navigation instruments, and all the other loose gear to fly wildly about the aircraft. Once more we somehow managed to stay just clear of the pursuing stream of fire. It was apparent throughout that the fighter was doing his utmost to tighten his turn and correct his deflection, but his own surplus speed and the sharpness of our turns towards him were too much; he could not obtain sufficient lead to strike home. As in the first attack, he kept up his fire as long as he could, a good four-second burst, but although his flashing tracers crept close to us, our own gunners' fire forced him to break off a second time.

My heart was beating like a frightened bird's. There are few things quite so startling as having an unseen fighter stalk you to point blank range then open up with cannons in pitch darkness. After he had broken off the second attack we kept up a mild evasive action for several minutes, but there was no further sign of the deadly twin-engined hunter.

Sam came on the intercom to point out that it was now time to commence our descent to 600 feet. At this point Stan volunteered to go up front to relieve J. B. who had been riding in the front turret. J. B.'s six-foot-four frame was about one foot longer than the turret had been designed to accommodate, with the result that spending extended periods cramped in its drafty embrace almost paralyzed him. At OTU and Conversion Unit this potential difficulty had been recognized; in fact we had feared for a time at Stradishall that J. B. was going to be taken out of our crew because of his height. We had successfully pleaded our case for keeping him with us by pointing out that our wireless operator was not just an ordinary wireless op, but a trained air gunner as well, and that he could therefore relieve J. B. as occasion required. Stanley, who was a much smaller man, now went forward to do a stint in the nose turret and let J. B. out of its torturous confines.

About ten minutes after Stan had settled himself behind the forward guns, I levelled out with the altimeter showing 600 feet. The period of unbroken silence stretched to a quarter of an hour, and my heart had just about reached its normal cadence again when Stan set it racing with a sudden urgent call:

"Climb Skipper — FOR CHRIST SAKE!"

There was no mistaking the urgency in his voice, and I shot up 400 feet before wasting any time checking on what the problem was.

When I did inquire, Stan had some difficulty emulating the calm tones of a BBC announcer while he described what he had seen. I had even more trouble keeping my poise when he revealed that we had just passed slightly *below* the mast-tops of what appeared to be some small fishing vessels. Visibility in the scud was next to nil; only by the grace of God had we missed descending another 30 feet and burying ourselves in a watery grave.

I realized immediately what had happened, and it had been my fault, and to a lesser extent Sam's, that the whole crew had nearly been killed. We had been warned at briefing that we would probably encounter a low pressure area in the vicinity of our target, and would therefore have to set a new QFE on the altimeter. The situation, cited in every textbook, was one of the classic weather hazards associated with aneroid barometer altimeters. The sudden upset of our fight to stay alive under the two fighter attacks had temporarily driven this vital detail from my mind as I started our descent, and for the same reason Sam had overlooked his written log note to remind me of the QFE setting recommended by our met officer.

I hastily made the correction, which we could now certify as reasonably accurate, having practically flicked our props through the water at the old setting, and we proceeded to sow our crop of 1,500 pound mines after Sam had verified his position.

We then altered course and started the long trail home. I looked forward hopefully to an uneventful journey, feeling that we had earned a rest, what with abysmal weather on the way in, two heart-stopping fighter attacks, and then some unintentional night wave-hopping amongst a Swedish fishing fleet. But a quiet uneventful trip home was not to be our lot.

I climbed to 12,000 feet for the return journey; however, my hopes of finding clear air went unrealized. We were still condemned to flying in and out of invisible cloud in pitch black conditions of near zero visibility. We turned onto a long, straight leg of our route, and half an hour went by without a word on the intercom. Our earlier experience with the night fighter had removed any need for me to remind the gunners to maintain the sharpest possible vigil.

Some movement below the level of my gaze caused me to glance at the yoke of the control column. I could see nothing out of the ordinary. Moments later the sensation occurred again, and once more my quick glance downward caught nothing. The third time it happened, I kept my glance lowered for a few seconds.

A spark seemed to flit between my thumbs. I moved them, and again what looked like arcing electricity flowed from the bolt head in the centre to either side of the control yoke. As I watched in apprehensive fascination, the tempo of the discharge gradually increased, and in a few minutes it became continuous. Something prompted me to glance back over my left shoulder and my heart froze in fright once again. C Charlie was sheathed in a bright phosphorescent radiance. Around the tips of the port propellers two great circles of eerie fire, pulsing like the aurora borealis, glowed in the darkness, making a giant concentric design with the ever-present dull glow of the hot engine cowlings. I was momentarily petrified by the display, ignorant of its origin and portent, and even after several minutes had passed without anything untoward happening, I remained acutely uneasy. This shimmering corona playing across the plane's wings was not the sort of furbelow I wanted around my gas tanks. I descended several thousand feet, but the frightening aura clung to us.

I had never heard of St. Elmo's fire, let alone seen it, and what we were then flying through was St. Elmo's fire at its fearsome worst. If I had known then what I know now about the unhappy possibilities inherent in critically high charges of static electricity around aircraft, I should have been even more frightened than I was — difficult as that feat would have been. Gradually the flow diminished, faded, and disappeared, to my great relief. We had been airborne about six hours.

We landed precisely eight hours after takeoff and were soon slouching wearily in the crew bus as we headed for the parachute section. Later, when we had finished our stint with the interrogating officer, Wing Commander McGlinn came up to me while I was choking down some rum-laden coffee — I hated the stuff, but the rum unravelled the mental and physical kinks at a great rate — and began chatting in a less distant fashion than he had hitherto employed. After getting me to repeat the little I could tell him about the fighter's tactics, he said: "Well, that should give you a lot more confidence. Now you know your corkscrew can fox a fighter even at close range. This one had all the advantage, and yet you kept him from scoring a single hit on your aircraft."

I hadn't really been thinking of it that way, but in retrospect I could see that there was considerable validity in what McGlinn said. The German fighter pilot had been good; of that there was no doubt whatever. To be able to find and attack us, twice, in that black cloudy void, even with the assistance of AI radar, was no mean feat, for the attacks themselves had to be delivered visually in the final stages, and to follow us as closely as he had through our violent corkscrew bespoke a highly determined antagonist who knew his business.

Thinking it over as I went to catch up to the rest of the crew, I did feel better, and at least a little more confident. I hadn't bothered telling the Wingco about forgetting to set the new QFE on the altimeter — figured I shouldn't worry him.

As we walked down to the airmen's mess for our fried egg and spam, we even found something to laugh about — (the rum was doing its job). Bill Bailey had stepped up into the astrodome for a casual look round approximately 15 seconds before the Messerschmitt's first attack. I commented, recalling the blur of motion I had caught out the corner of my eye, that he had moved back out of the astrodome at about twice the speed of the first cannon shell.

Bill grinned: "Just remembered it was time to check the oil pressure on No. 4 again" he said, then showed us some physical evidence of just how rapidly he had moved when the Messerschmitt fired. His left hand had been resting on a light screw at the base of the astrodome. His departure in the face of those fiery cannon shells had been so abrupt that he had torn right through all three gloves on that hand, including the heavy outer leather gauntlet.

Stan weighed in with a new thought. "Well boys, there's a few bods up in the Kattegat that'll be laundering their underwear tonight I'll wager. Can you imagine bobbing around quietly on a fishing boat out in the middle of nowhere, and then having a bloody great Stirling come thundering out of the night at nought feet and just about take your toque off?" We all rejoiced mightily in the probability of someone else having gotten a bigger scare than we had.

CHAPTER 12

MAIN FORCE JOURNEYMEN

Fierce fiery warriors fought upon the clouds,
In ranks and squadrons and right form of war,
Which drizzled blood upon the Capitol;
The noise of battle hurtled in the air,

Shakespeare. Julius Caesar

Seven hours after our return from the Kattegat we were summoned back to the Flights to learn that there was a war on, maximum effort, and that we were on the battle order, taking C Charlie again. The armourers had already begun bombing her up, so we could not do an air test; but she had been performing beautifully when we brought her back, so we were not overly concerned.

We attended briefing with apprehensive interest to see where our first venture as a Main Force crew would take us. The curtains slid back as the Intelligence Officer raised his pointer:

"Gentlemen, the target for tonight is Kassel."

Kassel, I noted, was in central Germany, a little over a hundred miles straight east of the heart of the Ruhr. This meant about a six-hour trip, one of the first factors to enter our thoughts after we considered the defences of the target itself. The city lay on the Fulda River, about ten or 15 miles southwest of its junction with the Weser — of Pied Piper fame. Although not industrialized to quite the degree of the Ruhr cities, Kassel stood high on Bomber Command's target priority because of its major significance as a production centre for such diverse objects as railway rolling stock, heavy machinery, and assorted types of precision instruments.

Five hundred and forty four-engined aircraft attacked the city. Our turn came a few minutes after the attack opened. The visibility was excellent, and already the city was a scene of savage destruction and garish beauty combined. In a hundred places huge cargoes of incendiaries were just flaring into life, the brilliant glare of their magnesium and phosphorous contents radiating the breathtaking beauty of gigantic handfuls of cascading diamonds on a black velvet backdrop. As we began our bomb run toward the clustered TI's, which shimmered in rich red splendour, vicious shock waves from the high explosive raining down rippled and tore across the heart of the city creating an effect like bursting bubbles in boiling porridge, and the thousands of spreading smaller fires began merging into giant unquenchable conflagrations. But it was far from being a one-sided contest.

Flak was heavy. Bright flashes ripped the sky open all round us, leaving ugly little clouds of ragged smoke, fitfully highlighted by succeeding bursts, as reminders of their intent. It took every ounce of my willpower to hold C Charlie steady and steer straight for the red radiance in the centre of this three dimensional inferno. We were using the Mark XIV bombsight now, which made J. B.'s task considerably easier. As soon as we had bombed and taken our photographs, I called to Sam to step forward from his navigator's table just behind me and come up for a look at the target. He had mentioned to me earlier that he would appreciate being given an opportunity to see what a target looked like. I banked sharply to give him a good view.

Sam took one glance out the window at the maelstrom of bursting shells, the sky filled with angry black flak puffs, and the multicoloured torrents of fire pulsing below us, then disappeared swiftly back to his curtained *sanctum sanctorum*. He had seen enough, and never again did he ask to look at another target.

I stuck the nose down a trifle to build up our speed while we cleared the target area. In Stirlings one was always conscious of the fact that the Lancs and Halifaxes were sitting about 8,000 feet above one, busily dropping bombs around, past, and occasionally through us unfortunates below them. (Jeff Bray came back from one target with seven bomb holes through the wings of his Stirling, having received a shower of incendiaries from above. Fortunately they had gone through cleanly and kept going.)

Our routing into Kassel had been excellent, the Force threatening half a dozen other cities before turning abruptly into Kassel. The success of the planners was agreeably obvious to us as we cleared the outskirts of the city. I glanced back just in time to see the first rows of flares being dropped high over the city by the German night fighters. By the time they had arrived on the scene the attack was virtually over.

However, if they had been deprived of their best chance to get the cat's eye fighters into the bomber stream, over the target, the Germans had no intention of giving up with their AI fighters; but now it was a race against time for them.

A hundred miles southwest of Kassel, a Pathfinder route marker went down. (For obvious reasons this was a measure not frequently employed.) We passed about five miles to starboard of the guide, which was exactly where we were supposed to be — Sam's navigation was spot on. A few minutes later Jack Phillips' Australian twang came over the intercom: "Fighter, fighter, port quarter level, 800 yards, Skipper."

"Roger, keep an eye on him Jack. Can you see him Bert?"

"Got him, Skipper," Bert responded from the mid-upper.

Visibility was good in the starlight. In a few seconds Phillips identified the shadowy pursuer as a Ju 88. Our exceptionally good fortune with the Me 210 the night before did not mislead us into believing that we were likely to escape unharmed again. We braced ourselves for another twisting, turning, and frighteningly uneven exchange of fire.

But this fighter pilot was apparently of a different breed. Not for him the sudden onslaught. After five minutes, five minutes which were a long time in passing, he had altered his position only to the extent of crawling a couple of hundred yards closer. Normally we would have begun our corkscrew at 600 yards, but I was hesitant about doing so until our antagonist committed himself by increasing speed and launching his attack. At 600 yards in this visibility, he could sit in position behind us with a good chance of keeping us in view all the while we corkscrewed, then close in for the serious business when I tired, and knock down a much easier target.

We sat tight, experiencing the feeling of the condemned man awaiting the tread of the executioner in the corridor, wondering what crafty trick the German fighter had up his sleeve. We had immediately thought of a stalking horse gambit involving a second confederate moving into position on the opposite quarter while all our attention was focused on the first threat; but a frequent banking search had revealed no other fighter either on our starboard quarter or below us.

In another five minutes the night fighter had crept up to 400 yards. This was getting far too close for comfort, and any remote possibility of his not having seen us was completely ruled out. At this range all he had to do was pull quickly into a starboard turn and he could rake us from stem to stern before we could move. I told Jack and Bert to draw the best bead they could on him and to fire on the count of three.

On the count they opened up from both turrets. The Ju 88 broke away sharply to port and was seen no more. Both our gunners claimed strikes, but we knew that the Ju 88 was heavily armoured up front, and the possibility of serious damage from our puny .303's at 400 yards was remote. We carried on and landed back at Chedburgh five hours and fifty minutes after takeoff. No. 6 went into the log book.

In the newspapers next day we read that the attack had cost Bomber Command 24 aircraft, which worked out to a 4.4 percent loss. On the positive side, the attack had been highly successful. (In this and a strike of similar scale carried out a few days later some 325 acres of the 375 acres comprising the main built-up area of the city were devastated.) The Commander-in-Chief sent round a communication shortly afterwards complimenting all crews involved in the Kassel attacks.

Between bad weather and a shortage of serviceable aircraft, our crew now found itself the grateful recipient of several standdowns. We did a few ferrying jobs and air tests, but much of our time was spent with our feet on solid ground. Not that we were left lounging about — the Wingco saw to it that a variety of fascinating tasks fell our way, each a guaranteed morale booster. If all else failed, he sent us off to an unserviceable aircraft to practise dinghy drill; and although we could easily have found more entertaining things to do elsewhere, we repeated the dinghy drill sequences conscientiously time after time, recognizing our own self-interest.

Invariably, during one of the dozen or so drills, someone would mock the underlying teamwork philosophy, singing out at the appropriate stage of the exercise: "Right. Cut the rope George, *I'm* in the dinghy."

Variants of the remark cropped up in conversation between members of the same crew:

Airman A: "Say, can you let me have a couple of quid; I want to go into town with the boys tonight."

Airman B, with a straight face: "F - - - you George, I'm in the dinghy."

I came to know George Wright much better during these few days. He was far beyond us in years — I suppose he was approaching 45 or 50 — but he was younger in heart than anyone else on the station. To George the sun rose and set on 214's aircrew, his aircrew, and anything that he could do, whether completely in accord with the rule book or not, to make their lives a little easier or more enjoyable, he did. If, when leave rolled around, getting off the station a few hours earlier than the passes specified meant that someone could catch a good train and get an extra day at home, George would deal with such cases on an individual basis, treating them all as urgent claims on his own time, and usually managing to clear it with the Wingco or the flight commander involved.

When a crew went missing, it was George's task to return each crew member's personal effects to his next-of-kin. It never occurred to me, because we kept our thoughts off that subject, that this could be a much more sensitive area than a casual observer would suspect. George enlightened me one evening as we sat chatting in the mess.

"I go through every single article and piece of paper that belongs to the chap, Murray. Now, according to regulation, all his effects without exception are supposed to be returned, and I could get into hot water — I've *been* in damned hot water, I'll tell you about that in a minute — for exercising my discretion. With married men, for example, I burn all the letters they have lying around except those from their wives or family, and if I'm in doubt, I burn. Otherwise you know what can happen: a fellow has a casual fling with some girl he meets on leave and she writes him a letter about the wonderful time she had and so forth. Now if that sort of letter slips through and goes home to his widow, it's a catastrophe; that will absolutely poison her memories, and scar her worse than losing her husband. I weed out any troublesome stuff like that very carefully." He began to smile.

"I got myself into one hell of a mess a few months ago. Wait 'til I get us another pint and I'll tell you."

The story was intriguing. A homeward-bound Stirling, badly damaged in combat with a German night fighter, made it as far as the English coast before crashing in flames on a rocky beach. The bodies of the unfortunate occupants were shattered in the crash, and for the most part only assorted bits and pieces could be found in and around the burned wreckage. With great effort six positive identifications were made, leaving the seventh man unaccounted for; but the possibility of his having escaped death was considered astronomically remote.

George duly despatched the signals which would prompt the issuance of official Air Ministry telegrams advising the next-of-kin of six of the men that they had been killed in action whilst flying on operations. But he was reluctant to send off the seventh signal, which, because of the circumstances, would result first in a telegram to the Scottish mother involved advising her that her son was missing on operations, then, after a six-month wait with no further word, a second message confirming the presumption of death officially. It was George's wish, considering the unusual circumstances, to avoid this protraction of the mental anguish if he could do so. He checked with the officers and men who had recovered the bodies and was assured that in their opinion there was no earthly chance of anyone having survived the crash. Further, there was no sign of a body having been thrown into the surf and washed up somewhere else. After some anxious inner debate, George, thinking of the mother, stuck his neck well out and sent a signal indicating that the seventh body had been identified.

Under these circumstances each family was asked whether they wished the Air Force to conduct a military funeral or return the body for burial by the next-of-kin. The Scottish mother replied by telegram asking that her son's body be returned. A coffin containing a few shovelfuls of unidentifiable substance from the crash was sent to Scotland and duly buried in the family plot.

Three or four days later the dead son turned up, not exactly hale and hearty, but definitely intact and moving about under his own steam. Against all probability he had in fact been thrown clear of the wreckage, and had dragged himself away from the fire, suffering only minor physical injuries and amnesia, before anyone else arrived on the scene. Somehow, the first people to come in contact with him did not connect him with the shattered Stirling, and no inkling of his miraculous survival reached anyone involved in the investigation.

The mother was naturally overjoyed at her son's resurrection, then understandably indignant at having been put through a harrowing ordeal unnecessarily. She knew nothing of the background and could not realize that George's actions had not been the stupid bungling she took them to be, but a well motivated attempt to spare her an agony of foredoomed hope.

George got hell. Hell from Group, and hell from Bomber Command; hell from the papers, and hell from the people who read the papers. Predictably the papers had printed only the fraction of the story readily available to them without any serious investigation. This apparently struck them as a great human interest story, falling into the stereotyped pattern of a moronic blunder by some incompetent official wrapped in a cocoon of red tape. They thereby missed the opportunity to give their readers a real human interest story featuring a man who had gotten into trouble because he had rejected the easy rule book solution and genuinely tried to spare a mother unnecessary pain.

George would have had considerable justification had he decided to do everything thereafter strictly in accordance with the book and not one inch beyond; but being George he did not. He kept putting himself to a lot of additional work to ensure that bereaved people (who would never know anything about his efforts) were not hurt unnecessarily.

Basically a good samaritan, George could also play the part of the avenger when he was aroused. A corporal in the parachute section was found to have been stealing personal articles belonging to crews who had gone missing on operations. He had been in a favoured position, of course, to play his despicable game; after all, no one got the word before he did. When the facts were established he was reduced to the rank of AC2 and sentenced to 180 days in detention. Ordinarily that would have been the last we ever heard of him. George, who felt like killing the wretch with his bare hands, felt that a little poetic justice was called for. He had him posted back to our parachute section for a few months after he had served his time in the glasshouse, no longer in charge, but serving under a WAAF corporal, so that he could endure the loathing glances and general ostracism he had earned as a moral leper.

In the course of our conversations I dropped one or two strong hints that Wingco McGlinn was not exactly my idea of the commander who always thought of his men's welfare first and foremost. George cut me short on this line.

"I know him better than anyone else on the station Murray, and I'm telling you you won't find a better man than Desmond McGlinn."

I dropped the subject. It wasn't that I actually disliked McGlinn, I just found him unapproachable and rather hard to warm up to.

On October 8th, we were on the battle order again — target Bremen[1]. We did not require the Intelligence Officer to tell us why this city was a high priority target. Neither did we require his warning, once we had seen the route tape, to be particularly careful when we were leaving the target and threading our way northward past Wilhelmshaven not to err to the west. It was clear, on the other hand, that if we went too far east we would stray into the flak batteries of Bremerhaven, and for individual aircraft to wander over either set of defences was to court disaster. Both places were potential targets themselves and were strongly defended by heavy flak and searchlights.

On the Bremen operation we very nearly killed ourselves again, but this time it was not as a result of forgetting to execute some detail of our orders, but rather from conscientiously implementing a stupid one. At our second turning point, just off the West Frisians, Sam reported that we were exactly one minute early and requested that I apply the curative nostrum specified by a series of navigation instructors who had not flown in Main Force operations in recent months: one orbit to use up the 60 seconds. I complied unthinkingly, having myself heard this remedy off-handedly prescribed by navigation leaders.

When I had turned through some 90 degrees a black shape hurtled past on the original course, almost invisible in the darkness. Simultaneously I became aware of other indistinct masses flashing past at lethally close range, above, below, level. Chilling thoughts crossed my mind as I realized what I should have thought of before attempting this suicidally stupid manoeuvre: true, we were a full

1. The main attack was on Hanover; but 119 aircraft were despatched to Bremen with over 300 tons of bombs.

minute ahead of ETA at the turning point; but so were a sizeable proportion of the 118 other aircraft who were in our wave and using the same met winds, and who would be adhering tightly to our own track at this point with Gee still serviceable. In a few more seconds we were in the frightening position of flying directly toward the invisible oncoming main stream. I pulled the turn as tight as I possibly could, expecting every second to be killed in an explosive mid-air collision. Throughout the whole manoeuvre we kept hitting the turbulent wakes of aircraft which had just passed, and several times Death whispered to us insistently as virtually indiscernible black hulks shot past 50 yards away. One could not actually see them until they had passed, at which time the sensation was simply awareness of a blurring streak of motion having gone by. We finally straightened up on our original course, shaken, but infinitely wiser. Doing an orbit might be perfectly all right for making a fine timing adjustment on a practice exercise, with ten other aircraft flying five or ten minutes apart, but it was just tempting fate to try it on operations at the end of 1943 with the dense concentrations Bomber Command was then achieving. Thereafter when we had to kill a minute we did what the old hands had learned to do: we doglegged 20 degrees on either side of track, but within those limits kept moving with the stream.

The sight of the target itself was another lurid nightmare which taxed my suddenly shrunken reserve of fortitude as I compelled myself to steer slowly across the centre of the vast area of illumination and wickedly flashing flak toward the glittering TI's. J. B. finally dropped our 2000 pounders and incendiaries, and we swung left to steer north-northwest for the open sea.

Twelve minutes later we were drawing abreast of Wilhelmshaven. As we were passing its picket fence of probing searchlights, I saw a group of them draw together and cone one of our aircraft — it looked like a Stirling — which had strayed too far to port. In seconds the flak was pelting up at him. At 12,000 feet even the light flak could reach him, and copious quantities of it surely did. The tell-tale signs of fighter activity in the stream were plentiful, so I could spare him only one pitying glance of short duration, during which I saw pieces the size of kitchen chairs flying off the embattled aeroplane.

Thinking "there but for the grace of God . . ." I continued on, warily skirting Wangerooge in the East Frisians, then shaping our course west and south for England. After five hours and 40 minutes of being poised mentally like a sprinter braced for the starter's gun, we touched down at Chedburgh. Once again the blessed relief from tension washed over me, and half an hour later when Bill Jeffries, our flight commander, told the night's outstanding horror story, I was in the proper state to appreciate it. Bill and his crew had bombed and were an hour clear of Bremen when he was galvanized into action by the sudden flash of boozer. Boozer was a special receiving apparatus on our aircraft, tuned to pick up the transmissions of a night fighter's AI radar. The impulses from the German fighters' "Lichtenstein" set, when picked up on our boozer, activated a red light located on the instrument panel in front of the pilot. The intensity of boozer's warning varied in accordance with the location and range of the stalking fighter. For example, if he was off to the side and well behind the bomber, the frightening little bulb would only flicker faintly and intermittently. If the fighter was lined up dead astern of his target, however, and at close range, the strength of his radar transmissions produced a clear and unwavering light on the our instrument panel.

Without the slightest warning, Bill's boozer had come on at maximum brilliance. Immediately he had thrown the Stirling into a violent corkscrew, hoping desperately that his first turn was in the correct direction. Simultaneously he called a warning to his gunners, who rotated their turrets with frenzied speed in an attempt to spot the deadly hunter so close to them in the darkness. Several terrifying seconds elapsed without the first punishing burst breaking the nerve-wracking status quo.

Despite his most strenuous efforts Bill could not shake the fighter. Boozer never even flickered throughout the wildest gyrations he could command. While the aircraft cleaved and tore the sky in its berserk twistings, the rest of the crew could only pray that the gunners would spot the fighter and drive it off before it sent them all to a fiery death.

Inexplicably spared from an early cascade of cannon fire, Bill redoubled his efforts, straining himself and the aircraft to the limit to avoid the hidden pursuer, a pursuer who seemed mystifyingly able to follow the Stirling as though chained to the rear turret.

After five minutes of this nerve-shattering pursuit, with both gunners vainly trying to find the fighter, and with his tongue practically hanging out from unremitting exertion, Bill could do no more. He levelled up, panting, hoping that the gunners could keep them alive a little longer.

At this point in the story his voice broke:

"Boozer!" he croaked, "Boozer! The son of a bitch was still on like a stoplight when I taxied into dispersal."

The room was filled with hilarious laughter. Weakened by the combined effects of intense relief, potent rum and coffee, and the unexpected humour, I laughed with Bill until the tears ran down my face, repeatedly visualizing, and commenting hysterically on, the frenzied thrashing flight from nothing, the do-or-die efforts to escape from a non-existent German fighter that stuck to the Stirling like glue —and turned out at Chedburgh to be a short in the set.

When the uproar had subsided, conversation turned to the heavy weight of the defences around Bremen and Wilhelmshaven. "Did anyone see that poor bastard that got coned over Wilhelmshaven?" I asked, turning to address myself to another pilot sitting near me.

He laughed wryly: "I *am* that poor bastard."

I was sharply skeptical, sure that the aircraft I had seen could never have survived. But he spoke the truth. The air plot and timing in his navigator's log proved it beyond any doubt; and if further corroboration had been required, his riddled and battered aircraft would have furnished it in ample measure. My faith in the durability of the Stirling was confirmed and enhanced.

In the week following the Bremen attack we got airborne only once, for some low level bombing and formation practice. On Friday, October 15th, we got leave. George performed his customary favour and slipped us our passes early in the day. I was bound for Scotland, feeling thoroughly miserable with a newly burgeoning wisdom tooth.

In London I went to Euston Station and stood in line an hour before train time to try to assure myself of a seat on the 9:10 to Glasgow. The train was packed, but I did manage to find a seat in a first-class compartment. All night long I alternated between sitting with my throbbing jaw cupped in my hands until the heat in the smoky compartment made me dizzy, and standing outside in the drafty corridor until I began collapsing sleepily and banging myself against various hard objects. When we pulled into St. Enoch's Station I tottered off with my asymmetrical visage etched in weariness and pain. A small miracle unfolded.

The first sign my bleary eyes lit on was one proclaiming the existence ten yards away of a St. Andrews hospital room. I made my way in rather pessimistically, feeling that they were unlikely to have Scotland's best doctors scrubbed and gowned waiting for me, and convinced from the pain that seemed to radiate down to my toes that that was what was required.

An elderly woman (in her early forties) wearing the white starched garb of a nursing sister sat me down and heard my one sentence tale of woe. On my fevered face her hands felt cool and competent as she carefully probed the problem area with a tongue depressor to assess the disease's ravages a little more scientifically. After a few moments she went away and returned carrying in one hand an instrument that bore all the sinister earmarks of being a useful sort of weapon to slice gum tissue with, and in the other a half-bottle of drops that looked to my jaundiced eye as though they had been fermenting in the sun since the Crimean War. Before I could say that I was feeling ever so much better, she thumbed my mouth into the maximum yawn position and made a deft stroke or two with her slasher, after which she put a few drops on the tortured spot.

The pain subsided so rapidly as to convince me that she was either a sorceress or a ministering angel in human form. Since she had a broad Scottish accent, I impartially inclined to the latter view. Half an hour after meeting the best representative St. Andrew ever had, I was on the train for Dalrymple feeling like a new man, half convinced that she could duplicate the Lazarus incident in a pinch.

Mrs. McCormick, Aunt Min's neighbour, had a niece named Betty Kean, who was a Wren Petty Officer — a very charming one — stationed in Ayr. Mrs. McCormick kindly arranged a meeting, and from that meeting flowed an invitation to a most enjoyable birthday party with Miss Kean. Despite the potential inter-service rivalry, the Air Force really won the match in a walk. Betty Kean's brother was a bombaimer on Lancasters, (she lost him six weeks later), and an older gentleman at the party very helpfully gave me an opening to impart the information that since my last visit to Ayr I had become a pukka operational type and was no longer just an F/O with a pilot's wing stooging around in Training Command.

We were having a cocktail off to one side of the dance floor. In the middle of some amiable chit-chat, in response to a statement Miss Kean had ventured about her brother, the old boy turned toward me and said, with a pleasant seasoning of paternal pride but also a trace of challenge: "My son's a bomber pilot — was on the big Bremen raid a week ago Friday — told me it was a pretty hot target".

"Your son was not exaggerating", I said, "I was there." He appeared suitably impressed, and thereafter went out of his way, in recognition of this newly-discovered bond between us, to relay the bulletin to everyone in the room and make the celebration of my twentieth birthday a convivial occasion indeed. I hadn't had the old ego fed and watered so gratifyingly since the Duty Pilot at Bruntingthorpe after our Nickel had loosely referred to us in ringing tones as an operational crew.

Upon our return from leave, the Squadron put in several days of practice flying without being called for any operations — a complete reversal of the earlier tempo. During this period we got in some further bombing practice with the impressively effective new bomb sight, the Mark XIV, including some low level bombing practice, and a brief spell of formation flying. Since our evenings were free, we had an opportunity to indulge in several visits to Bury St. Edmunds, and to relax a few times in the mess.

A rash of motorcycle accidents, most of them serious enough to hospitalize the riders involved, brought that subject into our casual conversations as a highly current topic. George Wright informally delivered himself of a few scathing comments on the brainlessness of aircrew in general, and of aircrew who rode motorcycles in particular. It was no coincidence, therefore, that I approached the notice board in the mess the following evening to discover that someone had pinned up, alongside DRO's, an authentically laid out special issue of Bomber Command Routine Orders — which appeared to have been typed on Doc Vyse's typewriter. Under appropriate headings and spurious serial numbers the body of the "Orders" ran as follows:

Z214   PART III - TRAINING

It has come to the attention of the C-in-C that the wastage of trained aircrew, not to mention useful personnel, occasioned by improper and unsafe riding practices on the Enfield 500 service motorcycle has grown to serious proportions. Henceforth the following rules of motorcyclemanship will be strictly adhered to by all ranks, viz:

1. No member of His Majesty's forces shall act as first pilot and captain of any motorcycle until he has first completed five hours dual instruction under an instructor holding a motorcyclemanship certificate issued — outside bar hours — by the Station Adjutant.

2. No member of His Majesty's forces shall solo a motorcycle for the first time in the bomb dump.

3. Every commissioned officer executing his first motorcycle solo shall wear a steel helmet and flying boots, and shall at all times be preceded by an NCO waving a red flag.

4. No officer over the rank of Squadron Leader shall ride a motorcycle as first pilot and captain on any occasion until the Station Warrant Officer has given five minutes warning on the air raid siren.

5. No pilot shall ride a motorcycle up the steps of the officers mess until he has logged a *minimum* of 10 hours (day) as first pilot on the machine; and in any case where that exercise is attempted *in formation* and after the consumption of stimulants, each motorcycle pilot shall first obtain a waiver in Form SOS 300 from every other member of the formation, (and in the case of RC personnel shall file proof, signed by the Padre, of recent attendance at mass).

6. No aircrew motorcycle pilot shall carry any WAAF on the pillion, without written permission from the WAAF "G" officer, i.e. the QUEEN BEE (unless the operation is carried out after dark).

      High Wycombe, H.Q. Bomber Command.

      Signed for Sir A. T. Harris, (A.W.O.L.) by AC 2 Flatout.

As I was about to walk away after examining these enlightening strictures, I noticed that George had never attempted to recover his stolen picture — the one featuring himself and the ape. It now bore a new caption reading: "Note George's pride at having his picture taken with a man."

Pass we on to the night of November 6th, 1943, one well remembered by me as providing an instructive lesson in the truth of the veterans' maxim about volunteering for things unasked.

The weather over the continent was foul, and over a good portion of East Anglia it was so much fouler that Bomber Command was stood down early. At Chedburgh however, it looked to our met man, Jock Bowie, as though it would get above the minimums for an hour or so about dinner time, and then again about five hours later when it would get quite respectable for a similar interval. The Wingco huddled with Jock to satisfy himself that he would not get caught out, then laid on a five-hour Bullseye for everyone he could find an aeroplane for, just to make sure that our morale did not sag a point or two. Every junior crew on the station, and there were quite a few, was sent flying — except Peden's crew; for Peden's crew there was no aeroplane. In a fine demonstration of mental instability I sought out a new friend, a fellow Canadian and Flying Officer pilot named Puterbough — pronounced Pewterboe and called Putt — whose crew had been furnished with G George. I volunteered to fly with him as co-pilot, to spell him off and keep him company in the right hand seat throughout this lengthy practice battle with the searchlights. Putt was agreeable, and I cleared it with Bill Jeffries, who seemed somewhat surprised but fully acquiescent. At this juncture I record the fact, a fact not without significance, that Putt's navigator, another Canadian named Dickie Dixon, was recognized as a gen man.

I climbed into the aircraft and parked myself across from Putt, where the disquieting information came to me that Dickie Dixon had unexpectedly been taken ill, and that Putt and his crew were making do with a spare navigator — who just happened to be the same navigator who had taken me to, and well beyond, Hanover. At this point anyone with an IQ over 20 would have left to check the tires and not come back, or recalled a previous engagement in Bury St. Edmunds and hit for the rear door; but, although less enthusiastic, I charitably acted on the premise that everyone was bound to have the odd bit of bad luck, and cheerfully belted myself in.

The first four and a half hours of the trip passed without anything untoward happening. Putt took the empty Stirling up to 15,000 feet, and after a time I spelled him on the controls. We evaded some searchlights, got caught by others, and spotted one fighter, which closed realistically before flashing its lights and breaking off. As we prepared to turn onto the penultimate leg, a 70-mile run from Bristol to Reading, I made my way back to the toilet in the rear of the aircraft without using a portable oxygen bottle to see whether strolls at 15,000 feet affected me. By the time I came panting back up front I could testify that they did. After we left Bristol, Putt cut back slightly on the power and we began our scheduled descent to 5,000 feet. We were due to level off at that altitude shortly before our arrival over Reading, whence we were to turn smartly, for obvious reasons, from our easterly heading to a north-easterly course toward Chedburgh.

The navigator came up with a modest course correction midway along this leg to Reading, coupling it with a slight postponement of our ETA. I thought nothing further of it. I should have; in fact both Putt and I should have done a little mental arithmetic when we got the first ETA.

I was checking my watch a minute or so after our ETA Reading — no word having emanated from the navigator regarding a change of course for home — when a quiet but concerned voice — I think it was the bombaimer's — came from the front turret: "Say Skipper, we're passing over one hell of a big town . . . and we've been passing over it for about five minutes."

If he had stuck a hypodermic into us he could not have caught our undivided attention half so rapidly. There was only one city that size within 600 miles of us . . . London. A succession of thoughts flew through my head, most of them depressing: this clot has done it again . . . we are only at 5,000 feet . . . we weren't supposed to come within 25 miles of London . . . London has the heaviest flak defences west of the Ruhr Valley, maybe the heaviest in the world . . . London's gunners are trigger-happy.

Putt's mind was treading the same ground, and every bit as rapidly. He was already winding on sharp port aileron when a searchlight abruptly thrust its beam up, turning us into a resplendent silver paper target a hundred feet wide. Simultaneously we were deafened by a clap of thunder. The Stirling rang like some giant metallic bass drum as a heavy shell burst immediately below us and sent fragments slashing into the aircraft. In quick succession a dozen other shells burst and flashed around us, and other searchlight beams appeared and began sliding toward us.

Putt called to the mid-upper to fire the colours of the period, always touted by Intelligence and Signals officers as a foolproof *laissez-passer*, which he promptly did, not once but several times. The guns continued to hurl their shells at us, and we bounced roughly again and again as the missiles exploded near us. Inside the cockpit it was becoming difficult to see as searchlight beams locked onto us. Once again Putt called urgently for more colours of the period, to an accompaniment of vicious sounding explosions and flashes as the gunners below warmed to their work. As I was busy expending enormous amounts of willpower and body English on the warding off of a direct hit and the final flaming curtain, the barrage tailed off as the merry men of flak decided that the British-marked, low-flying, four-engined bomber (a type the Germans did not possess), from which the proper colours of the period were being pumped like sausages out of a machine, and which was leaving London at astonishing speed after having exhibited no warlike intentions whatever, was probably British.

I luxuriated in a couple of totally impracticable but deeply satisfying plans as we left hostile territory behind us, the first one being to throw our so-called navigator out of the aircraft without his parachute. With nothing more than a pocket compass we could at least have avoided flying over London if we had not been relying upon him. Secondly, I wished we were carrying our full load of 24 500-pounders so that we could go back and dump them all on the first flak battery. Failing that, I felt that I should demonstrate to the myopic marksmen below that a kindergarten class of five year olds could learn to identify the plan view of a Stirling in two minutes flat. When I had worked off my passion through these fantasies I turned to musing over the stirring obituary notice I had nearly engendered for the local paper, the gist of which would have been: "British pilot shot down by British gunners over the capital of Britain, during a practice flight he was not supposed to be on."

Back at Chedburgh, Putt and I ascertained that our stouthearted defenders of London had knocked three holes in G George. Feeling that this warranted being recorded, I dropped a brief letter to Penkuri — who had been posted from Stradishall to No. 196 Squadron before we finished our H2S course. In a few paragraphs awash with hyperbole I let Penky know that old Fearless had aged ten years in ten seconds of the London flak barrage, concluding, so as not to disappoint his expectations: "Damn you Deans!"

CHAPTER 13

TEMPSFORD — NEW SECRETS

Each warrior vanish'd where he stood,
In broom or bracken, heath or wood;
Sunk brand and spear and bended bow,
In osiers pale and copses low;
It seem'd as if their mother Earth
Had swallow'd up her warlike birth.
The wind's last breath had toss'd in air
Pennon, and plaid, and plumage fair;
The next but swept a lone hill-side,
Where heath and fern were waving wide;
The sun's last glance was glinted back,
From spear and glaive, from targe and
      jack;
The next, all unreflected, shone
On bracken green and cold grey stone.

The Lady of the Lake. Sir Walter Scott

There was nothing about the morning of November 9th to indicate that we would be facing anything in our flying other than the pattern to which we were becoming hardened — at least not until 11:00 AM. The Tannoy sounded at that point, ordering F/O Peden to report forthwith to the Wing Commander. My conscience was reasonably clear, so, as I repaired at speed to his office, my overriding emotion was simple curiosity.

Without preamble McGlinn told me that he had selected my crew for temporary service "for a week or two" with No. 161 Squadron at Tempsford. Responding to my mystified look, responding negatively that is, he told me stonily that I would find out all about it when I got there; although he was good enough to show me roughly where the place was: 50 miles north-northwest of London, near Bedford. He also imparted the information that we were to pack our worldly belongings, take H Hal, and shake the dust of Chedburgh from our feet in two hours. Allowing for travelling time back down to the billets, that meant we actually had about 20 minutes to pack and arrange the usual ineffectual messages for the forwarding of laundry and mail. It sounded to me suspiciously like a buildup for a brush-off onto some highly undesirable Joe-job. (As usual, I was quite wrong, and in due course came to feel highly flattered at having been chosen.)

By three o'clock we had flown to Tempsford, unloaded our gear, and transported it to the Flights. The Adjutant wasted no time on me, giving me a quick speech over his shoulder as he left his office to do something more important, the gist of which was that I would be flying second dickey that night with Flight Lieutenant Dixon, that briefing was in half an hour, and that I had better look sharp as the King and Queen were coming to inspect the aircrew immediately after briefing. Oh yes, and just leave my trunk there, he would see that it was sent to the mess and that I got fixed up with a bed after I got back from wherever it was I was going to be sent. I parted from him with the vaguely resentful feeling that there must surely be some squadron in the RAF to which one could be posted and find upon arrival that he had time to squeeze in a fast visit to the toilet before being packed into an aeroplane and sent on operations.

Once at briefing the clouds of mystery began to lift. What 161 Squadron and 138 Squadron were doing quickly became apparent, and as it did, I understood why the Wingco had been so close-mouthed about it.

Tempsford was the main centre from which Special Air Service and Special Operations Executive were supplying the French resistance movement with arms and equipment. The Resistance was variously called the FFI (French Forces of the Interior), the Maquis, or simply the Underground. The magnitude of the supply program was particularly impressive, and I began to understand why security at Tempsford was noticeably tighter than anything we had yet encountered.

The big operations board listed about 20 aircraft of assorted types, and opposite their identifying letters, the components of their cargoes. I noticed that in addition to a large number of canisters that we would carry in H Hal's bomb bay, we were also carrying, inside the aircraft, several crates of carrier pigeons and one or two other large cases which would have to be pushed out the big hatch in the Stirling's belly. I quizzed Flight Lieutenant Dixon.

"Oh, that'll likely be a printing press and a radio," he said.

I turned my eyes back to the board. In the extreme right-hand column, opposite the letters of three Halifaxes, I saw beside each the inscription "1 Joe".

"What's a Joe?" I said to Dixon.

He turned back toward me: "A spy usually. We don't often carry them, because a Stirling's not the best aircraft in the world to jump from. You won't see the Joes in here though. Wait until we go out to the aircraft and you'll see them brought out." He pointed at a lower line on the board.

"You see the Lysanders?"

I nodded.

"They go right in and land on the other side. That first one's taking a Joe in with him; and you'll notice he's picking up two more in France to bring back. Things must be getting pretty hot for them." He sat silent for a moment then spoke again: "The Lysander pilots get an automatic DFC if they pull off five trips successfully."

I sat there digesting that for a few minutes, finding it difficult to realize that I was now part of this glamorous cloak and dagger operation. Then I tried to imagine what it would be like flying a slow and vulnerable Lysander to some little hay meadow in France, landing there by moonlight, exchanging one or two inbound spies for a corresponding number of outbound agents, probably with the Germans not too far off their tails, and then bringing the overloaded and unarmed aircraft home again. I concluded that they were not cheapening the DFC by handing it out to someone who had completed five assignments of that type.

Briefing was considerably different at Tempsford, since the aircraft were all bound for different destinations, destinations which were referred to only by code name on the board. Each crew received individual briefing on its planned time of arrival and the recognition signal to be flashed by its "reception committee". While other crews were getting the particulars for their drops, Dixon kept feeding me little snippets of information about peculiarities of this new type of operation and about some of the personalities involved in the work.

The first name he mentioned was that of Group Captain P. C. Pickard, well known to most of us already as the pilot of F Freddie in the RAF documentary film "Target for Tonight". Pickard had won the second bar to his DSO as the Wing Commander of 161 Squadron, and was just beginning his career as a Mosquito pilot in one of the Mosquito Wings in No. 2 Group. (He was to lose his life only a few weeks later, February 18th, 1944, leading one of the most daring and successful operations of the war, the low level Mosquito attack on Amiens Prison, an operation mounted in an attempt to free several hundred members of the French resistance imprisoned there, many of them facing execution at the hands of the Germans. The walls of the prison were breached and well over 200 prisoners escaped and remained out of the Germans' hands; but Operation "Jericho" cost Pickard his life.)

Travelling in a comparable aura of glamour was the redoubtable French navigator Philippe Livry-Level, who had escaped from France and made his way to England to carry on the war with the RAF. By lying brazenly about his age, he had wangled his way into aircrew. Dixon pointed him out to me, a distinguished looking gentleman whom I had noticed earlier because of his older appearance. As I later learned, he was approximately 45 years of age — about double the age of most of the people he was flying with — a fact which by itself was a significant commentary on his martial spirit. The boys, said Dixon, used to ask Philippe jokingly after each trip whether he had managed to drop in on his wife, for if he was anywhere in the area after the drop, Philippe used to get his pilot to fly him to the little village just out of Caen where his wife and family still lived. The deep roar of the Halifax's four engines was the welcome message to Madame Level that Philippe was there circling the house in the moonlight, only a few hundred feet away, thinking about her and letting her know that all was well with him. On one occasion, when his plane had landed in France to drop off and pick up some Joes, he had left a parcel with the reception committee, who had casually delivered it to his wife a short time later. I liked that story and made up my mind to have a chat with Philippe at the first convenient opportunity.

The moment all the crews had been briefed, we hurried out, battledress blouses betraying by rectangular bulges the escape kits buried in the inside pockets, and lined up outside one of the hangars. The timing was faultless. We had been standing there only a few minutes — in earlier days I had often waited five times as long for a corporal — when a black Daimler rolled slowly round the far corner of the hangar and came to a stop 50 yards in front of us.

The King and Queen alighted, and after a brief chat with the Station Commander and one or two other senior officers began inspecting the crews going on the night's operations. The King wore the uniform of Marshal of the Royal Air Force, his sleeve leaving little doubt of who in the group was in the best position to pull rank. He and the Queen carried out the inspection with a touch of informality, exchanging a few words here and there as they made their rounds. The whole ceremony did not take ten minutes.

I had expected to see no more of them after the inspection, but again I was to be surprised. As their car disappeared once more behind the hangar, the Flight Commander announced that officers on ops that evening would not be following the customary practice of having their flying meal in the airmen's mess. Instead, at the King's request, they would join the King and Queen for tea in the officers' mess.

Accordingly, we found ourselves in the royal presence again a few minutes later, this time for a more extended period. One of the officers present had won the Distinguished Flying Cross a few weeks earlier, and the King had fittingly decreed that he would decorate him at a special investiture in the Tempsford mess. For some minutes the hum of conversation in the lounge was stilled. In a suddenly imposed moment of solemnity the recipient, a Wing Commander, stood before his sovereign as the citation was read aloud. The King then fastened the glittering cross on his chest, shook his hand, and exchanged a few words in a confidential tone of voice before concluding the ceremony.

For a further half hour we enjoyed the distinctly unusual pleasure of rubbing shoulders with the King and Queen at a cosy tea party. Then they had to leave — and we too had to leave. The parallel went no further. They drove back to Buckingham Palace in the Daimler; we took off on an estimated six hour and ten minute flight to visit the Maquis, waiting for us in a field about 35 miles south-southwest of Le Mans.

Much about Tempsford operations differed from Main Force ops. Firstly, no bombs; just canisters and packing cases laden with a great variety of stores: Sten guns, ammunition, explosives, detonators, timing devices, radios, printing presses, and crate after crate of carrier pigeons. Further, all operations were carried out low level, so as to avoid fighters and leave little or no record with the German radar crews of routes taken and numbers of aircraft involved. Ground observers would still see and hear us occasionally, of course; but the information thus obtained was often fleeting and generalized, and the variations which it was possible for us to make in our routes made it of limited value for their purposes.

Low level operations of this type at night meant restricting the flights to about one week as the moon was waxing to full and one more week as it waned. A fair amount of moonlight was essential, even if it came through light or scattered cloud; otherwise the low flying at night became hazardous in the extreme. As Dixon took us toward the French coast at about 300 feet — instead of the 12,000 or 13,000 I was used to — I had a distinct feeling that this business was risky enough.

We had flown out over Beachy Head and swung about 20 degrees west of south to run in west of Le Havre over the Normandy beaches, practically along the line of our first visit to France with the leaflets. Crossing just west of Courseulles, we swung back to south, skirting Caen, then coming to a course of about 170 degrees. We were navigating strictly by low level map-reading, a demanding enough science even by day. I wondered pessimistically how Dixon's navigator had any hope of tracing the one small field we had to find.

All of us kept a sharp lookout. At heights ranging from 50 to 300 feet it did not pay to wander over towns or other strong points; we presented too easy a target for light flak. Heavy guns obviously couldn't even begin to track us, and had no real chance of hitting us at this height, so we were not faced with the more common problem of trying to outguess predicted flak.

We began to pass over beautiful rolling country looking like some vast Currier and Ives panorama bathed in moonlight. Cottages and small fields, fences and stacks flitted by, seemingly almost even with our wingtips. The Stirling, flame and noise belching from its glowing exhausts, was an incongruous black intruder streaking across this peaceful, undulating terrain. Not a soul was to be seen anywhere, just rolling fields and the black smudges of thickets and copses.

All at once a small house appeared on a slight rise a few hundred yards ahead of us, looking very dark against the light texture of the surrounding stubble. The moment my eye lighted on it the door flew open, and in the bright yellowish light that streamed forth a man stood silhouetted, waving vigorously. I turned my head sharply as we passed and saw him again as he flashed into view behind the starboard wing, still waving.

"He thinks he's helping us by showing a light," Dixon explained.

I found the three-second scene touching. The Frenchman had exposed himself to serious punishment by his act, yet I was to see it repeated several times in different parts of France in the next three or four trips, and every Tempsford pilot had seen these mute and fleeting benedictions.

While the low flying carried with it, as always, the wonderful exhilaration of manifest speed, it exacted its own special brand of nervous strain as we peered ahead for power lines and other obstacles. After close to an hour of this, I learned a little trade secret of the Tempsford aerial provisioners. At night, flying low level, it was frequently difficult to see or to identify landmarks which could easily have been recognized in daylight or even from a greater altitude. Here the rivers of France were invaluable, particularly the broad silvery expanse which now slipped into view as we reached the Loire. Dixon and his navigator had intentionally overshot the area we were ultimately going to be making our drop in, and flown to the Loire to get a good solid fix only 15 or 20 miles from where the reception committee would be lying waiting. Turning upstream, the navigator soon got his fix at the junction of the Indre, and we steered a northwesterly course at 180 mph, calculated to bring us to the drop field in six minutes.

Now we climbed to 500 feet to expand our field of view, and stared intently all around, trying to spot the triangle of three flashlights that would identify our objective. When our six minutes were up, we circled briefly, trying to get our bearings on the terrain below, unable as yet to detect any sign of our Maquis friends. To me the whole experience still seemed so totally unreal that their absence came as no surprise.

After a minute's consultation with his instinct Dixon spoke: "Let's swing over past that little bush and try the field on the far side."

Over we swooped, and in sudden excitement I called "There they are!" as I saw the glow of lights just ahead of us. Dixon flashed a fast signal on our recognition light, and we all stared down at the red-paper covered lights below us to see who would respond. One light, incredibly, blinked "S . . . R", the agreed upon signal. I hardly breathed.

Now three black figures could be seen running into position on the field. In a few seconds they were in a line, shining their flashlights up at us. A man at one end flashed a double light, one in each hand, the signal that we should start our drop from the opposite direction and run down the line towards the double light. Dixon made a slow turn, carefully keeping them in view, and we crawled up to about 600 feet as we opened the bomb doors and started toward them. At that height, the chutes just had time to flare open and break the fall for a few seconds before the canisters landed.

As we ran in, the reception committee disappeared from my view, hidden by the nose of the aircraft. The bombaimer's voice came over the intercom as he dropped the canisters from the bomb bay in sequence, ordering the wireless operator to push the other cargo out the huge door at the rear end. Dixon held straight on for a second until the wireless operator confirmed that he had dumped the interior cargo; then we swung in a slow turn and came back for a good look at the field.

When we had first come on the scene the field had been empty. Then the lights had been exposed. On our first pass there had been three figures, and only three, visible. Now, as we came back, there were at least 20, some of them just emerging from ditches and thickets, running hard for the ghostly line of billowing canopies. In a matter of seconds men were detaching the tell-tale chutes and rolling them up, as others seized the heavy canisters and manhandled them rapidly towards a copse alongside a narrow road. We rocked our wings in salute, then nosed down to skim low over the fields again as we made for home.

We touched down at Tempsford after six hours and 15 minutes in the air. After interrogation, I lay in bed sleepless again despite the overpowering fatigue, as my mind tumbled thoughts like a whirling clothes dryer, jumping from McGlinn to Philippe, from the King and Queen to the Maquis racing for the incriminating parachutes and canisters, from the sight of Joes walking to adjacent aircraft — some of whom I had noticed with admiration were girls — to the recurring glimpse of a stooped Frenchman in an aureole of yellow light, waving as we hurtled past him.

The following morning's battle order listed my name again, this time flying as co-pilot with an Australian, F/L Eddy. After briefing, Phillippe was issuing flying rations to the crews flying that night, rations which included two real oranges for each man. This was an unexpected and most unusual treat; fresh oranges were a good deal scarcer than fresh eggs in England, and unless one was prepared to go searching on the black market, fresh eggs were unobtainable. I stood behind the representatives of two other crews to draw the oranges for our gang, and smiled at Philippe's humour. He started off counting for each crew: "Two . . . four . . . six . . .", and each time ended "douze . . . quatorze." To preclude our being short-changed, I reminded Philippe that I was going second dickey, and that our crew therefore numbered eight; so he looked me in the eye as he shoved the last three pairs toward me and grinned: ". . . Douze . . . quatorze . . . SIXTEEN — 'ave a good trip."

The trip was virtually a carbon copy of the preceding night's. One difference sprang from the fact that the reception committee were a little harder to find after we got to the field in which we first sought them; but after ten minutes' stooging around we found them and made a successful drop. Again our roaring arrival suddenly and briefly spawned a tiny army on an apparently deserted field. Approximately seven hours after takeoff we landed safely back at Tempsford.

There was one more instructional exercise to be completed. Before sending pilots off to drop cargoes to the Maquis, the Squadron, in addition to giving them two second dickey trips in which to accustom themselves to the different tactics and techniques involved, required them to do at least one practice drop at Henlow. This was to ensure that when we found the reception committees we would be able to spot the containers where they wanted them, and not endanger or embarrass the Maquis by dumping the load two or three hundred yards away. Dropping parachute-supported canisters low level was a little different than dropping bombs, so the practice session was not an overabundance of caution but a sound idea.

We duly flew over to Henlow the night of November 12th, and two or three of us practised drops for an hour and 15 minutes. At the outset I noticed a small group of people on the ground, standing to one side of the drop zone, and realized after a moment that they were unfortunate creatures of a lower order charged with the responsibility of running about recovering the canisters and chutes we dropped and lugging them over to the truck which prowled the drop line. While I wholeheartedly approved the division of labour, I wondered sympathetically who these poor so and so's were, doomed to gallop around doing all the bull work while we stooged lightheartedly overhead showering them with canisters.

Next day I found out who these poor untrained peasant crews were. They were aircrew like us; more specifically, the very next night it was us. In putting the finger on me and my crew for a night's retrieving, the flight commander mumbled a vague and entirely unconvincing explanation about the necessity for tight security, and not wanting any more people than was absolutely necessary to know what was going on, etc., etc., etc. I found this difficult to square with the obvious fact that anyone who wanted to wander up to the boundary of the field at Henlow could stand in the moonlight and watch the Stirlings flitting about dropping things that looked like big hot water tanks on parachutes until he got tired of shivering in the cold and left. It was even more difficult to see how bringing some of our own ground crew out on the field and letting them discover that the practice canisters were loaded with sand was going to prejudice security — particularly if they happened to be the same ground crew who spent so many of their afternoons loading Sten guns and plastic explosive into other parachute canisters. However, although I detected an insultingly feeble snow job, I was not upset; in fact I thought it would be rather fun to stand underneath the Stirlings and watch the canisters float down amongst us.

My first intimation that this pastime might not be just anybody's cup of tea came after we had driven over to Henlow in an old truck, and I was sitting in the cab with the driver awaiting the arrival of the three Stirlings. We were sitting with our backs to the direction from which they would approach so that when they began the exercise we would be heading the right way and could drive straight along the drop zone picking up the canisters in order and watching the line of flight of the Stirlings and the path along which their cargoes fell. I kept the window on my side rolled up against the wintry air, but the driver, I noticed, kept his down. Every few seconds he would raise his hand for silence and cock his ear out the open window, then resume his fidgety brand of conversation. It struck me that he was not only a bit eccentric, but also as nervous as a nun in a paper bathing suit.

A faint hum came to our ears. The driver immediately started the engine, then jumped out and peered anxiously in the direction of the sound until he spotted the first Stirling.

"They're coming," he said, in a voice fairly cracking with strain.

Wondering why he was so windy, I descended leisurely to join the other members of the party, and stood gazing in admiration at the first Stirling as it swung round and made ready for a proper run, flashing its recognition light as it did so. In a few moments it was flying straight at us at 600 feet, and before it came overhead I could see that the bomb doors were open. Two long black objects detached themselves and began plummeting toward us trailing long white plumes. After two or three seconds one white plume swelled and opened with a flap. Almost too late I realized that the second chute was not going to open at all. Fortunately someone shouted, which unstuck my feet, and my brain, and I scampered clear with the rest of the group as the canister whistled down and hit the earth with a sodden thump, much too close for comfort.

Two drops later it happened again; and before the night was out, with half a dozen such experiences, I was about twice as jumpy and three times as nimble as our driver, he whom I had been patronizing. By the time we had finished loading our quota, poised half the time like blue-suited hares, I had come to realize what a perspicacious gentleman we had been travelling with. Once again I resolved not to be so hasty in my judgements in future.

The astounding failure rate of the chutes on the Henlow practice was not indicative in any way of the reliability of the parachutes used on ops, although I was disturbed enough by it to make some inquiries when I got back. The answer was understandable and reassuring. The girls in the parachute section were not too careful when they repacked these chutes, for they knew what use they were being put to, and it was hard to get too concerned about the fate of a canister full of sand. Since they did not witness the practice drops at Henlow, I supposed it never occurred to them how very unhealthy it could be standing underneath these un-retarded missiles. There were two additional factors involved: the parachutes used on these practice canisters had seen better days, and they were not kept in the same warm and dry storage area as the operational equipment.

The arrival of our jointly owned crew automobile from Chedburgh was the next event to claim our attention. We had purchased the little 1937 Ford while we were at Chedburgh, for a total outlay of £42, a contribution of £6 from each member of the crew. Bill Bailey had done all the necessary haggling with the vendor, who had sold reluctantly, protesting that if he could get even the meagre ration of petrol allowed aircrew when they went on leave, no power on earth could induce him to part with his mint-condition beauty for a mere £42.

If the price paid for the little beauty was low, I can only say in retrospect that it matched her compression. On a level road, with a following wind, the car took about a mile and a half at full throttle to work up to her maximum speed of 50 miles per hour.

The car's interior had been designed, I discovered, to accommodate four adults — four Japanese adults, travelling in their underwear. When seven of us, wearing greatcoats, wedged ourselves inside its tiny body — which we frequently did — Suraj-ud-Dowlah's Black Hole was immediately called to mind. Whenever we travelled en masse in this fashion I stipulated that pilot's wings were the only ones that entitled anyone to drive anything, (since the driver was the only person in the vehicle able to travel in a reasonably normal position.) A start with a full load of seven victims required two of them to push a little at first, to help the straining power plant break the vehicle's stubborn inertia.

While I had been occupied with my second dickey trips, Bill had managed to slip over to Chedburgh and bring our Ford status symbol to the new abode. He reported that with only him aboard, it had at times attained straight and level cruising speeds of close to 53 miles per hour. However, not wishing to punish an eager engine unnecessarily, he had done some parts of the trip at less than full throttle. J. B. and I were delighted to learn of the car's safe arrival; we had a scheme cooking in which an automobile, even ours, would be a decided asset. We served notice on the NCO's, who had endured several additional rides in it without us, that when we received the expected telephone call from two London based Wrens, J. B. and I proposed to commandeer the limousine and meet the girls for a grand *soirée* in Bedford.

On November 15th, before this landmark social event took place, we were on the battle order and briefed for another supply drop in France. However, until the very last minute, it was problematical whether we would take off or not, for the weather looked thoroughly unpromising. The met man's gloomy assessment was that if we did get off, unless some unforeseen change took place, we stood a good chance of encountering heavy icing.

His fears were borne out. Over the sea we ran into cloud that came right down to the waves, charged with the worst icing I had ever experienced. The port outer began losing power first, soon followed in lesser measure by the others, as ice jammed the oil coolers and air intakes. Gee had been unserviceable since shortly after takeoff, and Sam's problems were further complicated about the time we estimated we were over the French coast, where the ice-laden cloud turned out to have the additional malign property of affecting the compasses. Whether the problem was caused by electric charges in the clouds I did not know, but at this point both the P4's — magnetic compasses — developed a wild oscillation that rendered them useless. For the next little while we carried on using only the directional gyro, but fully aware that resetting it by means of the astro compass, on the rare occasions on which we could catch a glimpse of the heavens, would be an imprecise and unsatisfactory method for anything more than a short run.

I tried to change our altitude, in an attempt to find a level free of ice, but with scant success. Our rate of climb was slow at the outset, and as the port outer's power dropped off further, it soon became negligible. The prospects of making a successful drop had now become remote, but we were still reluctant to turn back while there was any hope of breaking out of the stuff. However, only a few minutes later, the port inner began to fail more seriously; our practicable options decreased to one — turn round and get out while we still had enough power to remain airborne.

We were all the way back to England before the engines cleared. By the time we made our uncertain way to Tempsford, we had flown about 400 useless and dangerous miles, but, far from being out of the woods, soon had to resolve a new quandary. Bill had calculated our all up weight at just over 66,000 pounds. The pilot's handbook for the Mark III Stirling cautioned against landing at any figure in excess of 60,000 pounds. There were two ways we could lighten our load. Firstly, we could jettison about 2,500 pounds of fuel. For various technical reasons adduced by Bill he recommended against this step under the circumstances, pointing out that it would still leave us well over the 60,000 pound limit in any event. Secondly, we could fly alongside the runway and jettison our cargo of approximately 12,000 pounds so that it fell inside the aerodrome. It was this latter expedient I intended to employ.

For security reasons we wanted to avoid casting the cargo to the four winds without giving the duty pilot a chance to have a crew standing by to make a prompt pickup; so I called the tower and informed him through the control officer that I proposed dropping my load alongside the runway in use, suggesting that I would stand by until he had things organized.

I was surprised to hear the voice of the OC-Night Flying in my headphones a few moments later. I had certainly not thought it necessary to call him. I shortly sensed that he was strongly opposed to my dropping the cargo — although he was careful not to issue a flat order prohibiting me as captain of the aircraft from doing so. He began by demanding that we verify our computation of all up weight, although he could have calculated it in his head within 1,000 pounds without making reference to the engineer's log.

When I finally twigged to the fact that he did not want the cargo strewn alongside the runway, I reconciled myself to attempting an overweight landing. However, to ensure that I had not misunderstood him about this clear violation of the handbook, I put one final query:

"I understand sir that you would prefer me to land without jettisoning our cargo — is that correct?"

The OC's voice crackled back: "You will exercise your own discretion."

A gasp of surprise is sometimes an effective comment, but not under an oxygen mask. Gasp with surprise I did, however, as the realization came to me of what a pusillanimous piece of fence strad-dling had just floated over the ether. Surprise was succeeded by contempt in my mind, and contempt by anger. Earlier in the conversa-tion I might have been prepared to label the OC a nincompoop for recommending a seriously overweight landing, an inconsiderate nin-compoop at that, considering that we would be subjected to higher than normal risks simply to maintain a security which was in no serious danger of being breached and to avoid some inconvenience to the ground crew; but I would still have thought of him as a man. He did not impress me as being very manly now, putting the squeeze play on a crew in the air and leaving himself carefully clear of responsibility on the sidelines, able to intone critically "Pilot error" if we pranged.

I had no clear idea how much the extra weight would raise our stalling speed, but we were on the long runway with lots of room, so I had no intention of finding out the hard way. Normally we dumped one-third flap and turned into the funnel at 145 mph, then approached with a bit of throttle at 125, letting the speed drop back to 120 just before we flared.

When I flared on this landing I was doing a good 135. She curved in beautifully, skimmed lightly onto the concrete, and rolled along swiftly. I was not in a hurry to apply brake with all the additional momentum, and I waited until the aircraft's speed had dropped back to about 65 or 70 before making the first light and tentative application. As it turned out, even at that point I was too early in view of our 66,000 pounds. There was a momentary pull, very slight, then the brakes burned out and we were rolling free again.

I was still not greatly worried, because the huge flaps of a Stirling provided a fine braking effect in themselves, and, in due course, we began to notice their effect clearly. With a hundred yards of runway still in front of me, I thought we were going to make it; but when it came time to turn off onto the perimeter track, we were still rolling about 20 miles per hour. I decided that it was better with all that weight, to let her run straight ahead off the end of the runway than take a chance on wiping out the undercarriage by turning her with throttle. I knew this way we were in no trouble. We rolled some 50 yards off the end of the runway, coming gradually to a gentle stop on soft turf. I called on the radio for a tractor to come and hook onto the tail end and pull her back onto the concrete, then we clambered out to wait for the crew bus, well pleased with ourselves in having made a good landing, grossly overweight, without the slightest damage — and in so doing preserved the OC's precious security on cargoes, and saved everyone concerned from the task of picking up a string of canisters scattered across the aerodrome.

The next development came as somewhat of a surprise.

I was told to report to the OC. On the way to his office I wondered if perhaps he was going to make amends for having been so thoroughly unhelpful by congratulating me. He disabused me of that notion with his opening remark.

"You seemed fast on that approach, Peden;" he said challengingly, "what speed did you bring her in at?"

I decided there and then that I had had enough from this specimen, and determined to give him short shrift in his obvious preparation to tick me off.

"Normal approach speed sir, 125 until I came close to the glide path indicator, then 120." I spoke just as coldly as he did.

"I should have said you were doing well in excess of that," he continued. "I went out to the end of the runway to watch you come in."

"It's not likely my airspeed indicator went unserviceable;" I rejoined, with synthetic ingenuousness "it acted perfectly normal, and we navigated on it satisfactorily even with an astro compass."

He could see I was not going to give an inch, but he tried one more feeble stroke. "At what speed did you begin to apply your brakes?"

"I waited until we had slowed down to 50," I told him.

He threw in the sponge and dismissed me. I had earlier dismissed him.

After a few hours' sleep, far too few to my liking, we rode back to the Flights through a steady downpour that showed no sign of letting up. Nevertheless, in the hope that some unexpected change might manifest itself, the Squadrons stayed on call around the Flights all morning. Contrary to what I had first anticipated, the time was not entirely wasted.

Someone produced a deck of cards and four or five poker enthusiasts fell to around a table. I ignored them at first, since my card-playing repertoire did not include poker, and in any event, ever since Freddie Taylor's educational sessions of crown and anchor aboard the *Cavina*, any aspirations I might have had to enhance my fortune through gambling had been pruned. However, Philippe came by a little later and called out the names of a couple of navigators, both of whom happened to be in the game, and in a few moments the remaining mathematicians at the table were importuning me to fill a vacant chair.

I demurred, but my excuse, that I did not know anything about the game, they overbore with hearty but inconsistent assurances that

(a) a ten year old child could absorb sufficient of the basic principles in five minutes to become a dangerous antagonist; and (b) that there would be someone knocked out early in practically every hand who would thereupon be available to assist me in assessing and playing my cards or telling me when to fold. I capitulated and sat in, pushing the peak of my cap back to the rakish angle apparently required by the rules.

For two and a half hours I waged a canny rearguard action, fighting to keep my losses within acceptable limits. Then in the half hour just before lunch I experienced remarkable success, winning sufficient to wipe out my deficit and move to a surplus and retained earnings position (converted to Canadian currency) of 14 dollars. Determined not to cloud the issue with false modesty, I put this down to a rapid mastery of the game not at all inconsistent with the demonstrated general abilities of a man with the nerve and judgement to land an overweight Stirling in the dark and make it look like child's play. At the mess I did not dawdle over lunch, and was standing first in line when the truck came splashing through the rain to take us back to the Flights.

Now that I had fully grasped the intricacies of the game, I threw off the self-imposed restraints which, in hindsight, I could see had been hobbling my morning performance, and began utilizing more paper and less silver — to the point where my former mentors began to urge caution. I saw through that transparent subterfuge without difficulty of course, pushed my cap back further than ever, and let them see how poker should be played.

An hour later someone stuck his head in and hollered the message that everything was definitely scrubbed for the night, and that the truck was coming round to take us back to the mess. I remember that call, for I was in the process of negotiating a second loan at the time, and the deal fell through with the collapse of the game. In that action-packed hour I had lost all my winnings of the morning, plus the Sterling equivalent of another 70 dollars; although there was no gainsaying the fact I was now a more seasoned poker player.

On November 18th we were briefed again to fly a full load to the Maquis group we had been unable to reach on November 15th. This time the trip went off smoothly. At a useful bend in the Loire, which we had earlier selected as a sure-fire fix for a run to the chosen field, I got a momentary fright when another aircraft suddenly sped into view, banking over the moonlit water. In a split second I breathed easier as I saw it was another Stirling. J. B. had spotted it too: "Place is like Piccadilly Circus" he rasped.

Again the Maquis band swarmed out of hiding places in force as we made our drop. Stan had a sizeable interior cargo to boost out through the big trap door, including one case large enough to house a refrigerator, so we had to come back over the drop line for a second run to drop this big box. The run was scarcely over when an indignant Stan came spluttering onto the intercom. The burden of his breathless message was that he had lost his balance as he had given the mighty heave necessary to get the last container out at the critical moment, and had teetered over the yawning hole in the floor for three or four seconds wondering if he were going to surprise the Maquis with his hardiness by leaping among them without a parachute.

Tempsford was heavily socked in when we returned, approximately five hours after takeoff, and we were diverted to Little Snoring, some 70 miles northeast. Fortunately it was still open when we got there, although the conditions had deteriorated to the point where it was easy to maintain an acute interest in proceedings until we were safely on the ground. In the crew bus, Stan was still mopping his brow over his earlier narrow escape, cursing the Air Force roundly for the unreasonable demands they made upon him, and protesting that he would be expected to chuck out pianos next. He vowed he would never open that huge trap door again without first taking the precaution of tying a length of rope around his waist and making the other end fast to a bulkhead.

The weather at Tempsford had improved by the time we got up, so we climbed into H Hal without breakfast and hurried back to see whether we were on ops again that night. Our crew's name was on the battle order, but once more the weatherman eventually had to turn thumbs down, and operations were scrubbed.

Saturday, November 20th, dawned bright and clear, and it looked as though we might get away that night. The doubtful area now was on the continent around our dropping zone. Our planned arrival time, dictated by the time of moonrise and the circumstances of the Maquis, was quite late, and before that time arrived a slow-moving front trailing rain, cloud, and ice, was scheduled to move in. Before noon the Met man became convinced that it was hopeless and again we were stood down.

As soon as the tidings reached us, the telephone lines were cleared for incoming and outgoing calls, and hardly had this been done when a telephone message came through for J. B. and me. Our two Wrens, 36-hour passes in hand, were ready to catch a train from London and could meet us in Bedford in an hour and a half if we were available. We assured them that we were most assuredly available, and would shortly be departing for the railway station in our private limousine to meet and transport them to the Bridge Hotel, Bedford's finest, prior to squiring them on a private tour the likes of which they could never hope to match.

About half an hour later we had secured permission to leave the station until noon the following day. Then we went over to the NCO's billets, commandeered the crew car, and set off for the impressive old private home — a mansion really — that the Air Force had taken over for officers' living quarters. It was our intention to spruce up, trade our battledress for our very best serge, and just generally dazzle the hell out of the two Wrens with our splendid appearance and limousine.

The mansion was situated about a mile and a half away on the crest of a gently rising ridge, a magnificent location from a purely aesthetic point of view. We headed for it happily, our only concern being that we had not left ourselves very much time and would have to change and freshen up smartly. The last half mile of our path was on the rising grade. It was so far from being a steep grade that the thought of its presenting any difficulty never even crossed my mind until we tackled it and the engine began bucking. I was forced to change down quickly to keep from stalling. In ten seconds I had to change down again . . . and yet again. It became apparent that we were not going to make it. Impatiently I turned about and went back some distance from the base of the grade to take a good run at it. This time we got better than halfway to the top before our faltering power plant gave up the ghost. Now thoroughly frustrated, we ran back over a mile on the level road to get every last revolution out of her before starting up the incline.

On we came at maximum power and the promising top speed of 50 miles per hour. We made it half way up before I began changing, and both of us thought we had the right combination to make it all the way; but with 200 yards to go to the crest, our faithless vehicle ran out of better gear ratios and we had to concede defeat. We did not have time to park and walk the remaining way, so we made our third unhappy descent and headed straight for Bedford, uttering unflattering remarks as we rolled along on the subject of how the NCO's had let our luxury vehicle deteriorate. We also recast the itinerary of our projected Bedford-and-district tour so as to avoid taking the girls on any grades, however slight. It took us but a few moments to recover our humour at this stage of the operation.

We had driven about three miles at 50 miles per hour — the vehicle, unhindered by any suggestion of restraint attributable to engine compression, having got a fine start on the down grade — when a noticeable tremor developed somewhere around the front end. J. B. looked at me questioningly.

"Next thing we know the bloody wheels'll fly off" I said jokingly, starting into a gentle right-hand turn. Suiting the action to the word the left front wheel flew off as the phrase passed my lips, shooting out ahead of us on a true tangential line even as it went down the shallow incline beside the road, and striking off independently across a farmer's field. The left front end of the car sagged sharply as the resentful wheel departed, and a harsh metallic din rent the air as we scraped to a wobbly halt on the hub, startled but unhurt. The wheel was still spinning along incongruously in splendid isolation as J. B. and I climbed out of the remains and stood laughing incredulously at the sorry state we had come to. J. B. regarded the event as the greatest coincidence he had ever personally experienced. I myself inclined to the view that it was no coincidence at all. Pure unadulterated spite.

When we had recovered our composure I went to retrieve the errant wheel while J. B. began pushing the car clear of the road. When I returned we threw the wheel into the back seat, locked the car carefully, and left it well clear of the road by the edge of the little field. (By the way, we never set eyes on it again.) We completed our journey to the railway station bouncing in the back end of an American weapons carrier whose driver had been good enough to heed our signal and give us a lift.

Despite this cheering piece of charity, however, the gala event we had been looking forward to for so long began coming unstuck in more and more places. The girls' train was late. At the hotel we encountered as a receptionist an abrasive old harridan with a sense of humour like Madam Defarge's, obviously determined to make the most of the power she presently had to treat people rudely with impunity. In the face of her opening snarls, I restrained myself with difficulty from asking if she had started her career as one of John Bunyan's jailers, since she looked ancient and bitchy enough to qualify. Instead I choked down her petulant complaints: thoughtless people who walked in without reservations, apparently unaware that there was a war on, expecting to get two double rooms just for the asking, etc., etc., etc. Pandering to her appetite for power by allowing her to abuse us for another three or four minutes, we eventually pried one double room out of her, but one was the limit.

Later, after our walking tour, dinner and a pleasant show prevented the occasion from becoming a total disaster for the girls, but J. B. and I spent the night "sleeping" in our battledress, each on a short chesterfield, entertained for three or four hours of that time by the maddening whine of the night man's vacuum cleaner as he readied the hotel lobby for a new day. When we put the girls back on the train Sunday morning and hitched a ride back to camp, we did not feel much better than if we had gone on ops the night before, although part of my pain was induced by empathy visualizing how much worse it must have been to be six foot four on one of those chesterfields.

At 3:00 PM on Monday, November 22nd, we got a hurry-up call from 214 to rejoin the Squadron. We were wanted for ops that night. We made hurried preparations, loading all our gear into H Hal as quickly as possible, and flew back to Chedburgh. But, when we hastened from dispersal to the Flights, we learned that briefing had already been held, earlier than first planned, and, since the Wingco was flying with most of the section Leaders as his crew, there was no time for them to do a second briefing. Our names had therefore been taken off the battle order.

In the morning we learned that our guess as to the target had been correct — Berlin. The Wing Commander had made a safe return, despite having encountered serious trouble. Atkinson's crew had been less fortunate. They had ditched in the North Sea after suffering heavy battle damage. The scuttlebutt was that Group had obtained a good fix on their ditching position, the wireless operator, Jock Wilson, having made contact and screwed the key down before taking his ditching position. Air-Sea Rescue searches were already being flown, so all we could do was sit around anxiously waiting for word.

There was an understandably strong bond between the crews on a squadron. This is not to suggest that they went about clapping each other on the back in a hearty Hollywood Three Musketeers atmosphere. Within the personality confines stemming from the common denominator of their having chosen air operations for their lot, there was room for wide play in personal characteristics. Thus, one liked some skippers and their crews, was neutral about others, and viewed one or two with distaste. But even with the latter group there was an underlying kinship. They were sharing the same perils. They too could crash and disappear in a thunderclap on takeoff, be killed outright or set afire in the air by fighters or flak, collide in mid-air or fly into obstacles, drown or freeze to death in a ditching, suffer anoxia or frostbite, encounter the perils of icing, struggle home uncertainly and in fear with engines dead, and get killed landing in murderous conditions. From time to time they did. With the people you particularly liked, the bond merged with natural liking and a feeling approaching that of the closest blood relationship took root.

Atkinson was easy to like, a quiet-spoken English lad with a nice sense of humour, a good pilot, and a press-on type who would go unquestioningly wherever his orders took him. His crew and mine were friendly rivals. Jock Wilson, he who had cleaved the great hedgerow at Edge Hill face-first, was a bit of a wag, a staunch crony of Stan's, and a popular personage stationwide. While we waited for word of their fate, we shopped around for details of the Wingco's trip.

Bill Bailey got the news from Pedro, temporarily the Squadron's spare engineer. As indicated earlier, the Wingco's crew was normally made up almost entirely of the section Leaders; but the Engineering Leader had been unavailable for this trip, and the Wingco had summoned Pedro into service.

Without getting beyond this point in the story I was ready to give the Wingco credit for two moves: firstly, picking Berlin as a target, for the Wingco could choose his targets, and Berlin was not one most aircrew would be eager to select if they had a choice. The Big City's defences were as hot as anything in the Ruhr, and the trip was about twice as long. Secondly, to fly a tough target when one of his regulars would have to be replaced by a spare was another plus for McGlinn in my book.

Their Stirling's engines had misbehaved badly, so badly that McGlinn seriously doubted whether they could make it back. Things got to the stage where it looked as though they would have to bail out, and McGlinn gave the order to prepare to abandon the aircraft, at which point everyone but the Wingco got his chest pack hooked on. As Pedro moved into position to resume his duties, the D ring on his chute caught on something, and the aircraft was suddenly filled with white silk as the pilot chute leapt out and foreign drafts coming in through holes in the fuselage blew the canopy out. In seconds it was in a hopeless mess, with twisted shroud lines snarled and twined over a dozen different protuberances.

Pedro was understandably upset. Now his chances of bailing out successfully approximated those of his becoming Commander-in-Chief of Bomber Command. The Wingco uttered a few unprintable words when he saw the new complications, but won himself the undying loyalty of one flight engineer by his next grim announcement that now, come hell or high water, he was going to keep that Stirling airborne until it reached England. Somehow he did, and Pedro, who was a favourite of ours, and on that account alone would have got it anyway, took a lot of ragging, particularly when he went anywhere near the parachute section.

The news which shortly came to us regarding our other crew completely swept away our enjoyment of Pedro's story. Atkinson's crew had bombed Berlin at six minutes past eight, and had then swung for home. About 20 miles out of Hanover they had been hit by flak The shells knocked out one of the outboard engines and wounded Wilf Sweeney, their Canadian rear gunner. To compound their troubles heavy icing forced them down to 1,500 feet, where they were frequently exposed to ground fire from light weapons and to searchlights. Accurate shooting by Atkinson's gunners caused many of the searchlights to be doused, however. Over the Zuyder Zee their Stirling was attacked by a Focke Wulf 190, but Wilf Sweeney, disregarding the effects of a wound in his right leg, shot the German fighter down in flames. At 10:30, Atkinson had ordered Jock Wilson to send out a distress message, since the aircraft was rapidly running out of fuel. At ten minutes past midnight their tanks ran dry and Atkinson ditched not far off the English coast. The impact had been extremely heavy, breaking the aircraft just aft of the mid-upper turret. The nose of the aircraft submerged before the other crew members, who were braced in their crash positions, had any chance to come forward and extricate Atkinson. Weakened by loss of blood, Wilf Sweeney had managed to struggle clear, but could not find the strength to make his way through the freezing waves to where Jock Wilson and the others were readying the dinghy. Jock told us later that they could hear Wilf crying to them for help and blowing his whistle. They cast off the dinghy as quickly as possible and paddled toward the sound, but they had hardly got started when the whistle was stilled. Wilfred Sweeney had died in the North Sea's paralyzing embrace. In late November few survived it.

Later, the sight of the surviving members of the crew standing around together brought home the loss of Atkinson and Sweeney more forcibly than a Tannoy announcement.

We did not get airborne ourselves until the following day, and we did not get another operation in until November 30th. We were summoned unexpectedly that Tuesday afternoon, after all but two crews had been stood down, ours and Jake Walters'. Jake Walters, you will recall, was the pilot whose luck ran to such accidents as getting blown upside down flying low over a flak ship and getting shot to ribbons by a German night fighter ten seconds before touching down after a trip to Hanover. Jake's fortunes had remained consistently malignant, and most of us just shook our heads wondering how long he could go on.

At briefing the Intelligence Officer drew the curtains and announced to a highly curious and somewhat apprehensive pair of crews that our hurriedly laid on target was the harbour of Le Havre. We were to go in low level and each lay six 1,500-pound mines in a selected belt traversing one channel. He told us that reports had just come in, reports of uncertain reliability, indicating that two German naval vessels had entered the harbour. He cautioned us that if the vessels *had* entered the harbour, and if they were still there that evening, we should undoubtedly encounter what he euphemistically referred to as "spirited opposition." I noticed that he refrained from identifying these units, or even mentioning what size or type they might be. To the initiated that did not bode well, and now that I knew who my partner was going to be, I felt it unwise to ask. If Jake was going, I figured it was better than an even bet that the *Tirpitz* and *Prinz Eugen* had somehow just slid in for fuel. In my mind's eye I could practically see their gunlayers spinning the wheels and training every gun barrel that could be brought to bear on the route which aircraft would have to take to mine their channel.

As soon as night fell — and it came all too early for me — we were on our way. Trying to look on the bright side and forget that Jake was close to me somewhere in the darkness, I rejoiced that whoever our German naval visitors were, they had not decided to drop in while there was a full moon. Flying about the harbour at 500 feet bathed in radiant moonight was not calculated to contribute to longevity.

As we raced into the harbour, I braced myself to take a pounding. Silence. Darkness and silence. We moved quickly into position, opened our bomb doors and began dropping our mines. The moment J. B. called that they were all gone, I snapped the bomb door switch and put B Baker on her wingtip in a steep turn. At that point two searchlights flicked on and began groping for us, but we dipped lower and skimmed out of the harbour before they could find us. Some shooting broke out behind us; (Jake, half a minute ahead of us, thought we had been caught) but we were right on the deck and long gone.

Back at Chedburgh two hours and 50 minutes later, Jake beamed at me. "Say, Murray, you and I ought to fly together more often. That's the easiest trip I ever did."

"Likewise, partner, and I don't mind if I do," I grinned, "if that's your jinx, keep it around."

With the hurried mining trip just two days behind us, McGlinn sent our crew to Tempsford again. Several times in the days that followed we stood by, ready to go on operations. On some occasions we actually got past briefing and were awaiting start-up time when the weather scuttled our plans. Not until December 11th did we finally get off, in M Mike, and that night the weather over much of England and the continent was misty.

The trip got off to a very bad start. In fact, it had been fully equipped with a very special built-in handicap even before it got started. Le Havre had been our 12th operation, leaving us all under a little extra strain thinking about No. 12A, as we preferred to call its successor. In addition, M Mike, the aircraft we would use next, was not nearly as good an aircraft as B Baker. Only because the operation had that very special number did we avoid telling everyone what we really thought of M Mike, namely, that in our book it was a lemon. Its performance this night of December 11th was fully in accordance with our expectations. No sooner had I lifted her off the runway and called to J. B. to raise the undercarriage than the gremlins began their work; the undercarriage refused to budge.

Two or three facts, well known to us, made this failure a matter of burning concern: we had taken off on the northerly runway, which would carry us straight towards St. Neots, five miles away. St. Neots boasted several extremely high chimneys. A fully loaded Stirling, as long as its wheels were locked down, had an angle of climb so small as to defy accurate measurement.

After a couple of verifying jerks on the undercarriage lever, J. B. hastened to get the crank and begin the arduous task of winding the undercarriage up manually. The mechanism involved was geared down astronomically, of course, and the wheels had to be brought up one at a time, making this a lengthy chore. As J. B. worked furiously on the crank, I tried ever so cautiously to turn the aircraft. With only 135 mph on the clock, and with the Stirling virtually steeplechasing over trees and hedgerows, it was mandatory to move with the greatest gentleness, difficult as that was with the thought of chimneys so prominently in our minds. For the next two minutes it was difficult to say who was sweating and straining most, me, sitting practically motionless behind the control column, or J. B., fighting vigorously with the long crank.

Handling the control column as lightly as though the grips were held together by a single fraying thread, I contrived to coax our nose nervously some 10 or 15 degrees to port, and we struggled through the air clear of St. Neots. For some minutes thereafter J. B. kept busy at his strenuous task and eventually got the ponderous wheels wound up into their nacelles. Flustered and panting, he clambered back into the cockpit just in time to hear Sam ask me to set course, Sam having shown a proper sense of priorities by keeping quiet about such matters until he found out whether we were going to stay in the air and live or collide against a couple of chimney stacks. It goes without saying that no member of the crew found these opening few minutes of 12A boring.

J. B. leaned forward and set on the DR repeater the course Sam had called, inadvertently committing the basic sin of setting the tail of the arrow on the course instead of the point. This took us off in the wrong direction for a few minutes until I smartened up and noticed it. Finally we got squared away and made a proper start on the operation.

We were due to fly to Reading, then, having cleared London, alter course to port to steer for Beachy Head on the south coast. The leg to Reading was uneventful. Although Gee was unserviceable again, Sam had the benefit of H2S, and hence was under no strain. Right on the dot of his ETA he came on intercom matter-of-factly: "Over Reading Skipper, dead on track. Your next course is . . . "

A resounding explosion directly behind the back of my seat

caused me to leap against my harness. For a terrified moment I thought we had taken a direct hit from a heavy gun, and I instinctively started a diving alteration of course to dodge any succeeding missiles. Glancing round, I saw that my first conclusion was wrong. Sam was sitting as though stunned, facing the H2S screen, which appeared to have exploded in his face strewing wisps of wire beaded with particles of glass and other debris all over his face and helmet. Confronting him now was the ugly smoking wreckage of what an instant earlier had been a flawlessly performing piece of highly sophisticated electronic equipment. He had been momentarily dazed by the violence of this unexpected and unaccountable catastrophe; fortunately he was not injured. It needed only the one glance to tell the story. There were powerful detonators in the equipment, (to be used if the aircraft were being abandoned over enemy territory), although theoretically they could be set off only by the positive act of pulling away the masking tape that covered the two deeply inset firing buttons and pushing both buttons simultaneously. So much for theory. Shorts can draw interesting new lines on any circuit diagram.

Mopping the innards of the electronic marvel from his visage, Sam composed himself again and resumed his chores while I went through some deep breathing exercises to retard my heartbeat. Beachy Head was approximately 20 minutes away. Two minutes before it was due to appear, J. B. went into the nose and lay over the perspex bombing panel to assist Sam by attempting to get a visual fix. Right on schedule the tip of a spit of land jutting out into the water appeared momentarily as part of the misty landscape shimmering in the moonlight below. J. B. identified it as Beachy Head, and Sam recorded the pinpoint in his log and gave me an ETA for the French coast.

When the time had dragged by and the ETA was up, there was no sign of the French coast, and I so stated. Sam asked that I maintain the course, expecting the coast to show up momentarily — and if this had been any trip but 12A it undoubtedly would have. But it did not. I held the course for several minutes, by which time it became apparent that the Beachy Head pinpoint had been a look-alike mistake, and that we must have been some distance further west as we crossed the English coast. To cross another little peninsula looking exactly like Beachy Head at the precise moment at which Beachy Head was due to appear was unheard of, particularly when the nearest piece of land that would qualify was Selsey Bill, a good 40 miles west of Beachy Head. Nevertheless, the impossible had happened. The gremlins had doctored the coastline. Sam requested that I hold the present course a few minutes longer, until we actually did hit the French coast, then turn left and fly along it until he got a landfall. I accepted the suggestion, but without enthusiasm. Wandering up the enemy coast at 200 feet was an unhealthy pastime, and I earnestly hoped he would get his fix quickly.

In a minute or two we did hit the French coast and I turned sharply to port. After about one minute of this, a searchlight suddenly exposed and moved quickly onto the front end of the aircraft, blinding those of us in the cockpit with its incredible glare. I managed to give it the slip in a few seconds, before it was assisted by a hail of light flak, but it was more luck than skill. I decided then and there that we had had enough of these games.

"Sam", I said, "we're going back to the English coast; we'll get a proper fix there, and then do another run across." There was no grumbling.

We flew back in grim silence, got our pinpoint, and once more turned for France. This time we ran in smoothly, hit the coast of France very close to the readily recognizable point we were aiming for, and quickly verified our position. We were fortunate to be able to do so, since the mist over France was much thicker than that we had encountered over England.

The field where the Maquis were supposed to be hiding was closer than any we had yet been to on a Tempsford operation, so it did not take long to make our way there. But as we got within about ten miles of the place, the mist and fog on the ground grew more and more dense, and at times it became extremely difficult to see the ground at all.

We circled what we were convinced was the right field for several long minutes, trying vainly to spot a signal. We moved over to the adjoining field where a clump of trees thrust up at one corner, giving us a constant reference point through the cotton-batting landscape. Still no sign of our reception committee. I was sure we were in the right area, so back and forth we flew, time after time, doing a miniature square search from the clump of trees, and peering with mounting frustration for a sign of our friends on the ground.

It was not to be. Operation No. 12A, having set out to cheat us with gremlins in the undercarriage, a reversed compass, exploding navigation equipment, spurious duplicates of Beachy Head, enemy searchlight defences and thick spreading fog, was not going to allow us the satisfaction of seeing the signals we were searching for and delivering our load. Disappointed, thinking of the trials and tribulations the Maquis had no doubt gone through setting up this drop, we finally headed home, and landed back at Tempsford after four of the most frustrating and frightening hours we had spent together in the air. No one mentioned the number of this operation. No one had to.

Some time later a carrier pigeon message was relayed to us. We *had* been over the right field. Our friends of the Maquis had heard us circling, but had been unable to attract our attention with their flashlights through the dense mist that had rolled in on them. We derived a measure of satisfaction from the knowledge that despite the obstacles strewn in our path, particularly in Sam's, we had found our way in the dark and the mist to the appointed rendezvous.

On December 13th, we were directed to rejoin 214, which had been posted in the interval to Downham Market, a station situated 30 miles north of Chedburgh. On instructions, we left M Mike behind as a bequest to 161 Squadron, an act of true Christian charity which occasioned a great feeling of joy in us. 161 would realize in due course how 'tis more blessed to give than to receive.

I took a walk by myself the next morning to do a little reconnoitering. After I had been out for half an hour, I wandered over to see the newly-installed apparatus we had heard about called FIDO. The initials stood for "Fog Investigation and Dispersal Operation" or, in the aircrew version: "Fog Intensive for the Disposal Of". FIDO was basically a system of pipes paralleling both sides of the main runway and running about a foot or two above the ground. At closely spaced intervals it was fitted with jets through which, when the system was operating, gasoline was flared under pressure. When fog settled right on the ground and a clutch of aircraft were caught aloft, the system was pressurized and ignited, converting the runway into one vast corridor of leaping flames. Notwithstanding its fearsome appearance it was remarkably effective, the heat lifting and dissipating the fog so that a pilot making his approach through the deadly shroud suddenly broke into a scary but life-saving hallway of clear visibility framed in scores of lurid gouts of flame. Effective as the system was, it had one significant drawback: it was dreadfully prodigal, consuming precious gasoline like an armada of aircraft. Downham Market had one of the first of these elaborate and costly installations, which never came into widespread use, but which were set up at our main crash dromes, and were often genuine lifesavers. It was to be my lot to have a FIDO experience very shortly, although not exactly of the type its designers had contemplated.

On Saturday, December 18th, our crew qualified for leave again, this time for nine days instead of the usual seven. With Christmas coming up, my second away from home, I had a desire to spend it with members of the family, although the nearest thing to family I had was Aunt Min in Dalrymple. I resolved to travel up to Scotland again, and left George Wright's office early, as usual, with my pass in my hand.

This time things did not pan out. In London I paid a flying visit to 9 Waterloo Place, the office of the Bank of Montreal, and picked up enough money for a Scottish holiday. Later I made my way to Euston to catch the night train to Glasgow. That train, I suppose, could have held 250 people; there were 750 already there. I waited until the train loaded, hoping that they might put on a second section; but when they had the train packed to the doors, that was it. I came back the following day, but the situation was even worse. Reluctantly I abandoned the idea of Christmas with family or friends, and decided to spend my leave in London.

I had spent my first night at Oddenino's, just off Piccadilly Circus, but they were booked solid the following night, leaving me with the problem of finding a place to stay for a week. On a tip from the kindly Welsh woman at Oddenino's desk, I telephoned the DeVere Hotel in Kensington and got a fine double room for the remainder of my leave. Not only that, there was a friendly switchboard operator at the DeVere who sounded very interesting. She spoke fractured English with bubbling enthusiasm and a heavy Spanish accent, and seemed eager to practise and improve her performance. I made a casual reconnaissance of the switchboard area as I was going out the second afternoon and determined that she was a brunette, about 20 years old, considerably above average in both appearance and pleasantness of disposition. I also noted with approval that she was constructed in such a way as to impose formidable stress on the right areas of her sweater. As soon as I returned to my room I got on the phone and struck up an extended conversation by asking for detailed directions to reach a number of downtown theatres with whose locations I was perfectly familiar. In the course of this exchange, which was repeatedly interrupted by the discharge of her switchboard duties for other guests, I congratulated her on her excellent command of English, thus scoring a grand slam homer. She explained that she had come to England with a large contingent of civilians from Gibraltar, and was working hard to improve her English. She wondered if she might practise over the phone with me when I was unoccupied, saying that she had found it somewhat taxing to attempt to answer satisfactorily the wide range of questions which the guests put to her. I assured her that I would be delighted to assist, asking in return only that she teach me a few Spanish phrases that I was particularly desirous of learning, such as how one asked a nice girl for a kiss. She giggled and rang off.

Next morning at ten o'clock, as I lay in bed luxuriating in that blissfully lazy state where one drifts in and out of sleep, the telephone clamoured. I picked it up in a mild daze, to hear her melodious voice:

"Hokay: Axe me a kestion."

My friendship with Luz Marie Lavagna developed gratifyingly; but I quickly discovered that initially at least it was to be an office hours only relationship. When she had finished her stint at the switchboard, approximately 12 burly members of her immediate family met her at the front door and escorted her home. The sentries at Buckingham Palace didn't give the King and Queen anything like comparable protection. When I did accompany her home it was amidst the entire guard detail.

Despite this restriction, I kept up my telephone campaign, for she was so pleasant and tried so hard to please that she was a tonic. In a few days I was well enough accepted around the hotel that I could stand at the counter by her switchboard and chat with her for indefinite periods without incurring the ire of the rest of the staff.

I sallied forth from the hotel each day, of course. I saw every movie that looked even remotely like being interesting, took in a symphony concert and my first opera — Rigoletto — and after four or five days found myself running out of things to do. On December 23rd I was in Leicester Square about noon, and decided on the spur of the moment to have a bite of lunch at a small restaurant I spotted on the far side of the Square. What drew me was the sign:

THE (AMERICAN) PAM PAM RESTAURANT

which was followed by some propaganda in smaller letters, the thrust of which was that Americans would swoon in satisfaction so closely did the Pam Pam resemble the "famous" hamburger establishments at home. At that moment a hamburger with all the customary trimmings struck me as a great idea. I went in and ordered, reading my newspaper until the untidy looking waitress brought my hamburger and coffee. As she set the dishes down, I focused all my attention on the hamburger. For a variety of reasons, several of them beyond the control of the management, I doubted that it would taste like the genuine article. The first bite confirmed all my doubts and caused me to remember several other reasons militating against successful duplication of the home product. In both appearance and taste the specialty of the house bore a remarkable resemblance to a skeet target in a greasy bun. I toyed unhappily with the sad substitute, trying to submerge my disappointment by concentrating on the newspaper. After three nibbles I laid the sorry thing down and reached for the coffee to rinse away the taste. Some vestige of the instinct for survival caused me to glance from my paper to the coffee cup just as I brought it to my lips.

Bobbing obscenely in a slow turn on the surface was a soggily disintegrating cigarette butt. A wave of nausea hit me. The revolting spectacle told more about the management and staff of this culinary disaster area than a ten volume critique. With nausea and anger in an emotional dead heat I strode for the door, delivering myself to all and sundry of a very loud and profane, but reasonably accurate, assessment of the establishment.

Although the leave had otherwise gone fairly well, I went out of the DeVere about 11:00 AM Christmas Eve feeling more than a little lonely. Even my new switchboard friend was off duty for a couple of days, and as I headed downtown to transact some important financial business, I was experiencing to the full the sensation of being alone amongst dense crowds of people. I came out of the tube station and bent my steps toward 9 Waterloo Place. I had gone through all the money I had drawn upon my arrival, when I had anticipated spending my leave in Dalrymple and Ayr. Spending a leave in London, even when one was staying at a hotel like the DeVere, where the rates were eminently reasonable, was a far different financial proposition from staying with Aunt Min in Scotland. Checking my wallet I estimated the difference at about £50 worth for that week, a sum which in 1943 bought a week's high living.

Twenty yards from the bank's entrance, my heart gave a tremendous leap of joy at the sight of a familiar figure. Penky was just walking out, still tucking his wallet into his pocket. I let out a shout that put the pigeons up three blocks away in Trafalgar Square. Penky's change of expression was something to behold.

"Hey, Fearless," he beamed. He came over, pumphandled my arm and clapped me on the shoulder simultaneously, and we stood grinning like a couple of kids turned loose in a candy store. "How 'n hell did you manage to bump into me in London?" he said finally.

"How did I find you in Oxford, in the dark?" I replied. "Listen Stoneface, when Fearless Fosdick goes after his man, a town with only seven or eight million people in it is too small a place to hide."

As soon as I had drawn another pocketful of money myself, we set off to do the town in style, first picking up Penky's gear and transferring it to my double room at the DeVere.

Thus it came about that my second Christmas overseas, instead of being a time of loneliness amongst strangers, as I had feared, was transformed by Penky into the best and happiest Christmas I could possibly have had anywhere. The DeVere did itself proud, preparing us a Christmas dinner that would have won the chef compliments in peacetime. Considering the wartime limitations it was unbelievable.

We spent Boxing Day loafing around, gorging ourselves again, and swapping more yarns. Penky had converted to Lancasters and was enthusiastic about their performance. I made a point of asking how many miscues he had blamed Deans for since going onto the new aircraft. He said "All of them, naturally."

I had to leave very early on the 27th, by which time Luz Marie was back on duty. Before she could call our room, I briefed Penky and had him place a call through her for King George at Buckingham Palace. Confused by the unfamiliar and unexpected voice, and the

Three popular characters of 214 Squadron (l to r): S/L Bill Jeffries, F/L Bill Doy and F/L George Wright.

Below: Radar predicted flak was often lethal. This Stirling made it home from the Ruhr after weathering a close burst.

The author (front) and F/O Steve Nessner (one of the German speaking Special Wireless Operators) prepare to lengthen 214's motorcycling casualty list.

Below: Officers of 214 Squadron in front of their sumptuous Mess at Chedburgh. The trio in the middle are Joe Bourke, the author, and J.B. Waters.

Above: Staff of 1699 Conversion Flight. In the back row, second from the left is Alfred "Stan" Stanley, the Wireless Operator of the author's crew; third from the left is Bert Lester, Mid-Upper Gunner; and second from the right is Bill Bailey, Flight Engineer. Front row, left to right: Tommy Roberts, F/L Brown, Don Bellingham (the CO of the Flight), Don Wilkinson and Paddy Moore.

Below: Carl Puterbough, one of the many Canadians on 214 Squadron, with his crew. Carl is second from the left in the front row; his navigator, Dick Dickson, is at the extreme left. The heavy white issue sweaters worn by two of the crew were officially termed "air crew frocks". (via Carl Puterbough)

Stirling 'S-Sugar' of 7 Sqn. banks away from a fellow Stirling. **(IWM)**

Above: Stirling III 'Q-Queenie' (BF382) of 214 Sqn. sits in a grass dispersal area awaiting another mission. **(IWM)**

Below: One of the first Stirlings to be delivered to 7 Sqn. **(IWM)**

F/O Dickson, the author, Tommy Crowe, George Mackie, Tony Bayliss, and (seated on the fender) F/L Jackie Furner.

Below: Part of the Wingco's crew: (left to right) F/L Bill Doy (Signals Leader), F/L Dick Gunton (Engineering Leader), W/C McGlinn, F/L Jimmie Sharpe (Gunnery Leader) and F/L Jackie Furner (Navigation Leader . . . later Air Vice-Marshal Furner).   (Tom Cushing)

unusual request, Luz went into a tizzy and everything came back Spanish. Penky then identified himself by name, rank and serial number, and asked coldly if she had been drinking. While she was still sputtering unintelligibly I took the phone and let her in on the joke, promising to introduce her to a much handsomer pilot before I left — which I did.

On December 29th, with the Squadron stood down — Bomber Command having finally made the painful decision that the loss rate among Stirlings on German targets had grown insupportable — Wingco McGlinn opted for a full schedule of training flying, both day and night, to keep everyone up to the mark and maintain morale and discipline at roughly twice the level of the Light Brigade's. By this time, let me add, he did have morale and discipline at a high level; not, I chose to think, because of his rock painting exercises and Drem system strolls, but because it was now plain to anyone with a pair of eyes that we had a Wing Commander who was generously endowed with guts. He found time for more flying than most Wing Commanders, and there had been a 100 percent correlation between the Wingco's putting himself on the battle order and the target being rougher than average. So, on the morning of December 29th, Peden's crew were slated to do an air test on L Love, and then take her on a five-hour Bullseye with other aircraft that same night, the exercise having the complementary objective of keeping the British searchlight and night fighter defences from growing slack. I had been contemplating an evening foray into King's Lynn, but my pang upon seeing the flying schedule was only momentary, replaced by the thought that if McGlinn said fly, fly I would, and cheerfully. After all, we had been assigned a brand new Mark III.

The air test was pleasantly routine; L Love was in excellent shape and ran through her paces like a lady. We landed and gave our Chiefie the news the ground crews loved to hear: "No snags." L Love smirked to herself; a malicious psychotic smirk; she intended to kill us.

That evening I noticed as I stood under the nose of the aircraft signing the Form 700 that the night was black but clear. We clambered into the kite in good spirits, considering the cold, and inhaled the unduplicatable mélange of aeroplane smells presided over by raw gas, and contributed to by traces of oil, hydraulic fluid, and de-icing alcohol. Our ground crew finished sweeping the frost off the wings, and we started the engines. Everything went like clockwork. On the run-up all engines roared proudly, and the tachometers barely flickered as we tested the mags. I gave the thumbs-up and flicked the recognition light, and the boys pulled the chocks clear.

Takeoff was to be on the main runway, and in ten minutes we were in position, looking ahead at 2000 yards of glittering Drem lights. I opened the throttles steadily and with confidence. L Love responded like a thoroughbred, and the inexorable rush quickly built up. Faster and faster — tail up — we were boring along like a runaway locomotive now . . . the ASI needle moved up steadily . . . past 70 mph . . . 75 . . . 85 . . . 90. Just as I was about to ease back and soar above the blurring lights, L Love whirled to port, the runway disappeared in a flash, and we were bouncing madly across the rough ground like berserk rodeo riders. I snatched all the throttles back, pulled the yoke into my belly, and with nothing to get a line on tried to keep straight in the blackness. For about 20 seconds L Love gave us a thrashing that would have shaken the kidneys out of a bronco buster, finishing with the final flourish of racing pell mell through a shallow ditch and tearing out with her double tail wheels a generous sample of the hedge on the far side.

She stopped, reluctantly. I called the tower a trifle breathlessly, then switched her off. I knew by now what had happened. What I could not figure out was why. At the precise moment we were about to get airborne — and I thanked the good Lord it happened then and not five seconds later — L Love's port outer engine had quit cold.

We made our way out of the aircraft and trekked back to the perimeter track, shaken in more ways than one. The driver of the crew bus came by, dropped the crew off at the parachute section, and advised me that she had orders to take me to the Wingco's office. I marched in and saluted:

"Well, short sortie, sir," I said, the feeble humour flowing, I suppose, from my relief at not being in the hospital — or the morgue.

But the Wingco's response, for good reason, was cool, at least until he satisfied himself beyond any doubt that the incident was not traceable to finger trouble on my part. In our bull-like 90 mph romp off the runway, L Love had ripped away enough FIDO piping to stock a wholesale plumbing establishment. The station Engineering Officer was going to be upset. Once the Wingco had my story, and quizzed me on my engine handling, he warmed up, and we began speculating on what had caused the sudden and complete loss of power.

In the morning the ground crew gave us the answer, confirming what Bill had guessed. The engine had oiled up, despite the care I had taken not to let her idle too slowly. The Wingco immediately issued new orders warning everyone to keep the idling rate even higher, despite the problem this created for us with our limited air supply for the pneumatic brakes.

Later, around the Flights, I heard that the Engineering Officer had been ranting about our mishap. I gathered that we had struck

FIDO at one of its main joints, automatically doubling the damage we should have done had we been a few feet further one way or the other. Apparently from his comments one might easily have gained the impression that we had gone crashing through the system at that vulnerable point for a bit of a lark.

As though to demonstrate that I was back in favour after having been wrongfully suspected of carelessness, the Wingco — with a little prodding from George Wright, I suspect — appointed me Acting Flight Lieutenant to fill a vacancy in the establishment.

CHAPTER 14

FAREWELL TO THE STIRLING

When beggars die there are no comets seen;
The heavens themselves blaze forth the death of Princes.

Julius Caesar

New Year's Day, 1944, our crew ferried another Stirling to 161 Squadron at Tempsford. It was while we were there on this occasion that we received the relayed message from the Maquis about how close we had been to making contact with them on our ill-starred trip of December 11th. While we hung about waiting for the pilot following behind us to fly us back to Downham Market, I chatted with Bob Mackett, a Stirling pilot whom I had come to know very well during my previous sojourns at Tempsford. Bob was soon regaling me with an account of an incident that had befallen him since we had last been together. I interpose a helpful word on the Stirling's plumbing facilities before's Bob's story.

Up front, alongside the pilot, a funnel hung in a clip. Running from the funnel was a tube which led discreetly to the great outdoors. Theoretically, and theoretically only, if a pilot's need to relieve himself reached serious proportions he could use the funnel, without discomfort and without leaving his seat. In practice, when such an emergency arose, remedial action was not all that easy; in fact, obtaining relief was a humbling process. After one had disposed of the first layer by undoing a bulky flying suit, the problem of avoiding the entangling tapes of the Mae West and unfastening buried fly buttons with cold fingers remained. When the blast of cold air from the cockpit suddenly penetrated to the target area, indicating that one had been successful thus far, the major problem remained, namely, finding the object of the search, which had invariably contracted in the chilly surroundings to a size approximating that of a light switch, and somehow training it over the folds of clothing to the edge of the funnel. Even with this feat accomplished, accuracy at critically high nozzle pressures was not impressive. (I attempted the feat twice during the early stages of my tour, then concluded that dying of a burst bladder was ever so much easier and less humiliating.)

If a more serious internal disorder overtook one, there was a chemical toilet (the Elsan) located at the tail end of the aircraft, just ahead of the rear turret. Since the temperature in this region was usually well below that at which Captain Scott succumbed in his last hours in the Antarctic, the Elsan was used very infrequently. But to our tale:

Mackett had been returning from a successful drop to the Maquis when some powerful catalytic agent in the alimentary canal had begun its devil's work, bringing him rapidly to the point where he could postpone a walk to the Elsan only at his peril. Fortunately, the French coast was fast approaching. He hung on with growing desperation until that all-important boundary line flashed past below him, then turned the aircraft over to his bombaimer and made his way with mincing steps to the rear. He had just let down his flying suit, battledress trousers, and long johns, when a prolonged burst of machine gun fire from the mid-upper turret froze all his internal piping solid. Clutching the half-mast clothing inventory to his posterior, he raced for the cockpit like some strangely stunted and alien creature, almost jerking his navigator's head off as he flashed past and ran full tilt against his taut intercom cord. Hurling himself into his cold metal seat, with yards of clothing trailing behind him, he seized the controls and put the Stirling through all sorts of wonderful evolutions until a moment came when he dared pause to plug in his own intercom.

"What the hell's the matter Tag?" he shouted urgently, addressing himself to the mid-upper, "What're you shooting at?"

"Aw, it's okay, Skipper," Tag replied with carefully affected calm — he had been treacherously briefed and timed by the rear gunner, who had seen Mackett perch on the Elsan — "don't get your shirt in a knot. I was feeling sleepy; just fired a burst to keep myself awake."

As Bob and I chortled over Tag's perfidy and insubordination, K King came snarling fitfully around the perimeter track, and I had to leave to join the man at the controls, Warrant Officer Mackie, for the 35-minute ride back to Downham Market.

W/O Mackie was a small, dark-haired Scot of serious mien and fiery temper; at least I thought he had a fiery temper until members of my own crew began drawing invidious comparisons between him and me in that respect, when I began to realize that the better way of describing Mackie was to say that he maintained an iron discipline in the air. He gave commands, then all smiles stopped together.

Mackie was a first-class pilot, with more Stirling hours than any other pilot on the Squadron. He and I had hit it off from the first, I think partly because I had not been put off, as some people were, by his initial reticence, and had gone on to find the tremendous store of humour and warmth that lay in him below the surface. He was rebellious, and absolutely unsparing in his acidic criticism of folly — qualities that do not normally endear people to their companions. But he won respect and affection with his honesty, for with Mackie, when the folly was his own, the criticism was honed every bit as sharp, and he told a joke on himself more readily than on anyone else. On one of our earlier *tête-à-têtes* he had sworn that after the war his first leisure time objective was going to be to expose the Air Force's crimes and stupidities in an autobiography which he would entitle "An NCO Against the World." His next project was to be Home Rule for Scotland, a cause for which I professed great disinterest, needling Mackie about it on two counts: Firstly, I told him, the best Scots, properly called Scotchmen, had long since emigrated to Canada, leaving only the poorer, unenterprising residue behind; secondly, even those torpid and immobile Scots had been exploiting the English so successfully and unashamedly since the Act of Union that if they now tried to go it alone they would be back to lumpy porridge and thin scones before they knew it. Mackie knew I was baiting him, but he could never let these calumnies pass, and gave some fine orations in disproof of my hypocritical pronouncements.

But our conversation usually centred on less contentious topics. He was better read than I, and surprised me in an early discussion by revealing himself an avid student of the O. Henry short story. Usually, however, our discourse focused either on Scotland or on flying.

After we had landed back at Downham Market this New Year's Day, Mackie told me a story I never forgot. It was a poignant tale, at once sad and uplifting, concerning a Scottish woman I had not heard of before, Lady MacRobert.

Lady MacRobert's husband died in 1922, leaving her with three sons to raise. When they grew up all three lads were drawn to flying.

One son, Sir Alasdair MacRobert, was killed in a flying accident in 1938. When the war broke out Lady MacRobert had two sons anxious to fly on operations.

On the 22nd of May, 1941, she suffered a second blow, receiving notification that Flight Lieutenant Sir Roderic A. MacRobert had been shot down and killed while flying his Hurricane on operations in Iraq.

As Mackie told the story it was easy to imagine the strain Lady

MacRobert must have been under, with her only remaining son still flying on operations. I pictured her attempting to carry on at home — a home, incidentally, which she had thrown open to servicemen — praying fervently that he be spared to her, starting apprehensively at every ring of the telephone, at every glimpse of a telegraph boy, at the knock of any casual caller.

Her mother's prayers went unanswered. Sir Iain MacRobert was killed flying on operations less than six weeks after his brother Roderic, on June 30th, 1941.

Lady MacRobert's response to this culminating tragedy, after she had weathered its cruelest hours, came like a flashing ray of light from a magnificent spirit. She donated twenty-five thousand pounds toward the purchase of a Stirling, which, upon delivery, she presented formally to No. 15 Squadron, RAF, to carry on the battle. Proudly emblazoned on either side of the Stirling's cockpit, just below the lofty canopy, was a message to fire a warrior's heart:

"MACROBERT'S REPLY"

It was a reply indeed, a reply that echoed its own fanfare of heraldic trumpets.

Her response was epitomized in that one majestic phrase and gesture; but it went even further. With another twenty thousand pound donation Lady MacRobert helped pay for the purchase of four Hurricanes. Each of these aircraft bore the family crest, and three of them the inscription, "The MacRoberts Fighter" followed by the name of one of her three sons. The fourth bore the device "The Lady."

Lady MacRobert's sons, it is clear, came by their courage honestly. I often thought of that wonderful, indomitable woman.

On January 4th, 1944, we were briefed for a target in the Pas de Calais, a target which for some reason was shrouded in a cloak of mystery. After briefing we knew only that the emplacements we were scheduled to bomb were German weapon sites of considerable importance. (Not until six months later did we learn that Intelligence had known that they were V1 launching sites.) Each of our Stirlings took off carrying 24 500-pounders. On the way in, we flew through some extremely heavy icing; but we struggled clear after a short time and thought no more about it.

The Pathfinders marked the various targets clearly, and J. B. was highly satisfied with our run, in the course of which, as instructed, he had dropped our whole load across the selected TI's in one long stick at half-second intervals.

We flew A Able back to Downham Market and were back on the ground in three and a half hours — where we got a bit of a surprise in our own dispersal. One of the ground crew went through the normal drill with me after I had positioned the aircraft, calling up to ask me if we had had any hang-ups. I double checked with J. B., who assured me that every green light on his panel had come on, indicating proper circuits and clear drops for every bomb. I shouted down to the chappie standing beyond the nose, confirming that we had no hang-ups.

"Righto," he said "open the bomb doors."

I flicked the bomb door switch, and a moment later he walked in underneath to give the bomb bay the usual perfunctory visual check. Hardly had he disappeared than I saw him come pelting out front again hollering for help in excited tones. I pricked up my ears and learned that we still had a 500-pounder aboard, adhering to the bomb bay only by virtue of a thin film of ice.

I was not at all sure what would happen if a 500-pounder fell 15 or 20 feet onto the concrete, but I was sure there were better observation posts from which to check the results than the one I was occupying over top of it. The rest of the crew seemed to share my view when I blurted out the news; without benefit of debate or discussion we all made a hasty and undignified exit. As the crew bus came along to pick us up the ground crew were racing about like the Keystone Cops in a chase piling "biscuits" — small mattress sections — under the threatened point of impact. In an amazingly short space of time they had scrounged biscuits from every point of the compass, after which they retired a prudent distance to let nature take its course.

In the morning A Able was still there and the bomb was gone. I wrote in my log book "OPERATIONS PAS DE CALAIS — 13." About 11:00 AM J. B. came out of the Bombing Leader's office. Happening to see me in the offing, he approached with a smile on his face. He had brought back the best target photo in the Group, and as a memento we were each given a print to put in our log books.

Two days later, January 6th, 1944, we took P Peter and made our last flight in a Stirling. We did not know it would be our last Stirling trip. There had been no operations scheduled for 214 that night, so the Wingco characteristically laid on a three-hour "ERIC," the daylight equivalent of a Bullseye, to keep morale at fever pitch. It was a day or two later that the word came round that we would not be flying our Stirlings again.

Now the rumours began to fly thick and fast. We were going to convert onto Lancasters. We were going to convert onto Mosquitoes. Not so, we were going to convert onto Halifaxes. We were going to be transferred to No. 8 Group. We were on our way to No. 5 Group. We were going to stay on Stirlings, but would use them for glider towing. (Some Stirling squadrons were in fact assigned that role.) We were all going to be posted to Tempsford permanently, dropping supplies to the Maquis until we completed our tours. One clot even came up with the rumour that we were going to switch to American aircraft and fly Fortresses — not with the Americans, but at night with our own Command. The purveyor of this piece of asininity was quickly made to realize that even rumour-mongering had recognized limits, and that he had let his imagination soar well beyond the pale. The smart money in 214 stayed with a Lancaster Conversion Unit and our remaining with No. 3 Group in the heavy bombing role.

One morning about a week after our last Stirling flight, as we were sitting around debating the likelihood of each of the reasonably serious speculations as to our future, one of the other Canadians, in receipt of some mail from home, asked me if I knew Max Mair. I said I did, mentioning that Max had been a star hockey player for the Portage Terriers before joining our gang on tarmac duty at No. 7 SFTS, Macleod.

"He got the chop" said my informant, handing me a newspaper clipping.

Max, who had won his Navigator's wing at No. 3 AOS, Regina, in September, 1942, had been the navigator of a 142 Squadron Wellington carrying out a raid from a base in North Africa on Turin, Italy, on the night of November 25th, 1943. The whole crew had been killed. What I did not learn until later was that a classmate of mine from Portage Collegiate, George Perry Armstrong, son of our family doctor, had also been a member of that crew.

My own mail from Canada hit even closer home the next day with the bitter news that my good friend Rod Dunphy had been killed a week after I had gone to Downham Market. The official narrative was typically blunt:

"Flight Lieutenant Roderick James Dunphy, DFC, . . . a navigator of 426 Squadron . . . Lancaster LL630 on the night of 20-21 December, 1943 . . . detailed to carry out an attack on enemy installations at Frankfurt, Germany . . . the seven crew members presumed to have been killed during air operations on December 20."

It became increasingly difficult in the face of the news to sustain the protective belief "it can't happen to me" — a belief half-doubted at the deeper levels of consciousness, but never openly. As death overtakes one friend after another, it removes, one by one, all possible grounds for differentiation of one's own case. The experienced die with the inexperienced, the religious with the non-believers, the younger with the older. Daring or cautious, competent or inadequate, death traps them all. The protective belief that somehow, even if the fighters, flak, or searchlights did get you, some miracle would take place which would see you descending safely in your parachute, was thus repeatedly strained. But, ". . . it shall not come nigh thee."

The recent names paraded through my mind: Atkinson, Wilf

Sweeney, Max Mair; and before them Freddie Taylor; and seemingly ages before him, Morris, and Francis Plate. Two other Portage la Prairie boys well known to me had also been killed flying: Leo Murray and Bobby Cole, the latter while returning from operations over Germany in a Wellington. And now Rod Dunphy.

I found myself re-creating in my mind a series of vignettes centering on him, beginning with our first meeting. In the classroom after school I had been whistling an air from Orpheus in the Underworld — our band's test piece in the Winnipeg Music Festival that year — when Rod had come up to me and said, smiling: "I know that piece; I've got a terrific recording of it at home. Would you like to come over and hear it — we just live on Home Street?" Next a vision of his mother, and his older brother, an engineering student, sitting in the living room, with Rod smiling happily over the perfection of a Toscanini rendition of some orchestral favourite. Then the night we sat together in the Winnipeg Auditorium listening to Billy Bishop's proud peroration: "23 years ago we swept the Germans from the skies . . . and we will do it again." My last meeting with Rod, in the doorway of the Royal Bath Hotel in Bournemouth: he, still with the same shy grin, more nervous, and now, in retrospect, perceptibly across the dividing line between boyhood and manhood, the line reflected in the appearance of the eyes. Rod had gone on to win a Distinguished Flying Cross for his performance on a trip that had been so bad that the bullet-shredded curtain from his Lancaster's navigator's compartment had been sent as a memento to the Canadian War Museum. And now, no more Rod Dunphy; the warmth and friendliness gone, the eager yet shy little smile quenched; the life battered out of him.

The rumours continued and multiplied. One day, a red-headed pilot whom I had met and known at AFU came to Downham Market. He was authorized to arrange the transfer of heavy bomber pilots who were interested in becoming night fighter pilots on Mosquitoes. I thought about his proposition. The Mosquito was a beautiful aircraft, particularly the fighter version. It occurred to me that if a person once got on the rolls as a night fighter, it was logical to expect that he had a better chance to work another transfer and get onto day fighters. For a moment I was sorely tempted.

But I did not seize the opportunity. I refrained because, as quickly as I thought about how wonderful it would be to fly Mosquitoes, I thought of what it would be like to leave my crew behind and go back to square one, starting the war over again with all new flying companions. So I stayed, forsaking my wonderful dream of climbing into a fighter; not in the implementation of a noble gesture, giving up everything I wanted, but to a large extent quite selfishly, because I suddenly realized that I could not give up my crew, the crew who had helped me get 13 raids under my belt and stay alive.

They had unfailingly showed the greatest confidence in me, often a good deal more confidence than my limited experience warranted, and I had enjoyed that trust. I thought of how well we worked together as a crew. I admitted to myself that I liked the discipline they showed in the air, where the skipper's word was never questioned — not because he was an officer, but because he was the skipper. They put their lives in my hands a dozen times a day, as casually and confidently as though loaning me a fountain pen for five minutes; and although less frequently, I did the same with them. While we engaged in a lot of horseplay and ignored rank on the ground, a total transformation took place when we climbed into the aircraft. There my word was law. The skipper never had to resort to pulling rank or using the Hollywood cliché "that's an order." Everyone had too much sense and self discipline to require any such nonsense in the air. There wasn't any saluting or sirring or reverential responses, but a metamorphosis took place once we climbed into the aircraft. We were no longer young men fooling around; just men with serious business on hand, men who set about doing their various jobs with inflexible discipline so as to stay alive.

I let the crew know immediately that I was not going onto Mosquitoes. They knew that the night fighter offer had been made, and were entitled to know that they weren't going to be cut adrift looking for a new skipper.

Before our time at Downham Market ran out, which it did on January 17th, 1944, I had another session with Mackie, in the course of which we found ourselves discussing the perennial topic, aeroplanes, this time Training Command aeroplanes. Mackie had said something which implied that he had not trained on Tigers, and I, in surprise, asked him point blank if he had never flown Tigers. It was a happy question. Mackie raised a finger, and his eyebrows, to make a fine distinction, allowing as how yes, he had *flown* a Tiger one memorable day. Curious, I pressed him, and the story unfolded.

In a few brief strokes he outlined the classic elements of conflict: he, Mackie, on an earlier Stirling station, enviously eyeing the Group Captain's jealously guarded personal aircraft, a beautiful Tiger Moth, in mint condition . . . his intense longing, after a long stretch on the towering Stirlings, to fly this beautiful little butterfly despite the fact that technically he was not entitled to do so until he had been given a check circuit and had his log book appropriately endorsed . . . the Groupie's antipathy toward the lowlier ranks in general, and Scottish lowly ranks in particular . . . (I gathered that the Group Captain was a

Sassenach) . . . the unexpected chance to realize his dream when the Groupie promised a group of air cadets a plane ride and was unexpectedly left with only one aircraft with which to honour his commitment, his cherished Tiger.

Mackie went on to describe how the few available pilots on the station had, at the Group Captain's reluctant suggestion, drawn lots to determine the order in which they would fly the air cadets. Mackie's name had come out on top — he was to take the first two passengers. He hurried over to No. 1 hangar where he could see the Tiger Moth perched perkily in the corner, trim and beautiful, her perspex polished to scintillating brightness, her bright yellow fabric freshly doped and glistening in the stray beams of soft sunlight probing that corner.

With staggering confidence in his own ability as a pilot, it never occurred to Mackie for one second to prejudice his opportunity of flying the little jewel by mentioning to anyone that he had never been checked out on a Tiger Moth. Bah! What problem could this toy present to the intrepid birdman who could manhandle a 36-ton fully loaded Stirling off the runway, thread Germany's heaviest flak and night fighter defences, and grease it back onto the flarepath in the darkness. Pooh! He stilled the vestigial trace of conscience by reflecting with satisfaction that there wasn't a chance in the world of being caught. The vast majority of RAF pilots received their initial training on Tiger Moths, and most of those who did not train on them initially flew them later on during one course or another. Finally, the Group Captain would never dream that any pilot on the Squadron would violate regulations and take his priceless aircraft aloft if he were not qualified to do so.

(Mackie grinned at me as he described his rapid preparations for getting airborne before someone put him on the spot by asking a direct question.)

Motioning the first lad into the front cockpit, he drew the second air cadet alongside to demonstrate the fastening of the Sutton harness, then delivered a concise statement of Mackie's Rules for Aircraft Passengers, appropriately modified for Tiger Moths: "You will sit in the front cockpit. Keep one hand up on each side of the cockpit. I want them both visible to me at all times. If you move your hands out of sight I shall hit you over the head with the fire extinguisher. Keep your feet off the rudder pedals. If something comes unstuck and I tell you to jump, go over the side and pull this D ring on your parachute. If you are fast enough you will be right behind me."

A few moments later, having found where the throttle and switches were located without arousing the suspicions of the erk who spun the prop, Mackie was airborne with his first passenger.

It was a beautiful day. The little Tiger soared upward like a rapturous skylark, the Gipsy Major purring sweetly. Floating like gossamer, enjoying the rush of fresh air and the enchanting panorama unrolling below, Mackie's spirits climbed with the altimeter. Through every pore he inhaled the grace and beauty spread before him, and momentarily forgot his passenger.

Ahead of him the River Ouse curled off to the right through the lush countryside. He indulged his long stifled aesthetic sense for a few more minutes, then bethought himself of the stringent timetable and reluctantly rolled into a slow right-hand turn, swinging back toward the aerodrome.

As the Ouse passed beneath his wing a thousand feet below, he noticed what appeared to be two females reclining on the riverbank, and his curiosity was aroused. Spiralling down for a closer look, he buzzed low over their heads and found himself being waved at enthusiastically by two very eligible looking women. Mackie's superficial dourness had by now completely evaporated, and he waved back exuberantly as he flashed past on his way home.

He landed a trifle uncertainly, for the Tiger floated longer than he had expected, quickly switched passengers, then flew like a homing pigeon for the spot on the River Ouse.

(As Mackie carried on with his story, I found myself reading between the lines and superimposing one or two complementary fragments which I felt were necessarily implied. These few addenda, which I mentally inserted at a speed far surpassing Mackie's rate of speech, related solely to his innermost thoughts and the powers of imagination he could readily have called into play at one or two critical moments of the second flight. The Lay of the Last Minstrel, thus thinly embroidered, continued.)

Again the women waved excitedly to their visitors, impressed, Mackie assumed, by this glamourous aerial flirting, and doing their utmost to show due appreciation. The taller one was particularly enthusiastic. Mackie responded, sweeping lower and lower on successive passes, and flashing his most dazzling smile for the necessary tenth of a second each time he roared by, practically at eye level.

The unaccustomed roar in the open cockpit, product of the engine note and the rushing wind's accompaniment, began to exercise a hypnotic effect on Mackie, contributing to an escape from reality to the utopian world of the imagination. In a few moments, then, the circumstances had changed. Gone was the lowly Warrant Officer flying the Group Captain's pleasure craft over the River Ouse. Gone was his whole association with the mundane surroundings of the RAF station he had just left, its mess hall odours of brussels sprouts and spam, its muddy pathways, and its snobbish WAAF officers. The Tiger's cockpit was now graced by Air Marshal Mackie, VC, DSO and Bar, DFC and two Bars; and he was piloting no training plane, but a trim fighter.

He could feel the white silk streamer which marked him as the Leader of the Squadron tugging at the top of his helmet as it tossed behind him in the slipstream. Offsetting its dazzling whiteness was the row of miniature black crosses painted in rows on the fabric outside his cockpit, 75 in all, each denoting a confirmed kill, every victim a member of Rittmeister Baron Manfred von Richtofen's own *Jagdstaffel.*

Up front his Observer was waving, directing his attention to something below. Ah yes, the women. Coming up for air momentarily, Mackie waved again with studied nonchalance and glanced at his watch. Realizing that he had only a few minutes left, he decided to do something spectacular for his audience: he would do some really low-level steep turns directly in front of the women, over the river.

As the thought crossed his mind, it was followed by a warning message reminding him that this was strictly contrary to flying regulations — and highly dangerous to boot. Unfortunately the message was addressed to Warrant Officer Mackie, and while it was in the process of being delivered, the Air Marshal resumed control and refused to accept it.

He slammed on bank and dove to within a few feet of the water, pulling the Tiger into a tight vertical turn. The aircraft transmitted warning signals herself — from her control surfaces to the stick in Mackie's hand — that all was not well. Mackie, alas, for all his vast experience on Stirlings and other aircraft was not familiar with the informative tremors of a Tiger Moth.

Round and round he roared, unconsciously tightening the turn to get a better view of the rapturous females. They were literally jumping up and down on the riverbank in front of him at this heady combination of *élan* and airmanship. He revelled in their admiration, his heart fairly bursting with joy. At this moment he felt he was soaring to the very summit of his Air Force career.

With breathtaking suddenness the Tiger went into a high speed stall due to the excessive wing loading, and in the same instant flicked over into a spin. The incipient spin Mackie killed with one desperate, stabbing application of opposite rudder; but he had no height in which to recover from the stall. Quicker than it takes to tell, the Tiger tore fiercely into the river, driving up an awe-inspiring deluge of murky water.

Before the horrified gaze of the two spectators Air Marshal cum Warrant Officer Mackie, his young passenger, and the once beautiful Tiger Moth slid quickly below the surface, leaving only the sheared lower wing bobbing in view.

But while the women's involuntary screams were still echoing between the banks, the roiled surface of the Ouse was broken again, first by Mackie's helmeted head, then by that of his passenger, whom Mackie was savagely fighting to tow with one hand.

If Mackie was a mite short of Tiger time, he was far from short of the quality now chiefly required — guts. In noisy confusion Mackie flailed his way to shore, gasping and coughing, one arm keeping the air cadet's terrorized face above water. As they struggled out and fell onto the muddy bank, their clothing plastered to their bodies and running in streams, the women waited one instant, seemingly to verify that they were both alive, then decamped on the dead run, going, Mackie assumed, for help.

Mackie lay on the bank belching up air, oil, and dirty water in approximately equal volumes, and letting installments of the catastrophic consequences now to be faced slip into his consciousness from time to time as he felt capable of considering them. After a few minutes, as he was running some fresh and frightful frames of film against the mental viewer, he became aware of strangled sobs from the air cadet.

Vaguely appreciating the stunning shock this young adventurer must have suffered, Mackie summoned up his very last emotional reserves and clapped the cadet sympathetically on the shoulder, murmuring between belches: "There . . . there . . . you're all right . . . you're okay . . . you're not hurt."

"But my uniform" the boy burbled unexpectedly, "my uniform's ruined, and the dance is tonight!"

Mackie reacted as though he had inadvertently set his hand on a red hot stove. "You young son of a bitch," he roared magnificently outraged, "is that all you have to whine about? . . . I have to go back and tell the Group Captain I've sunk his bloody aeroplane in the river and you're yapping about a lousy dance." His anger swelled, feeding on itself: "Gurgle once more, you little bastard, and I'll choke you." The air cadet's lamentations ceased abruptly.

Half an hour later an ambulance arrived, and the two somewhat estranged survivors rode back to the station. Mackie was ordered to report to Flying Control, where the Group Captain was waiting for him.

(It was not difficult, Mackie told me, to ascertain after one look at the Group Captain, that he had already been apprised of the brutal fact that his Tiger was now reposing in the mud at the bottom of the River Ouse.)

Catching a glimpse of his own reflection in the plate glass of the Flying Control Tower, Mackie was further chastened. Wearing his sodden helmet he looked like a hydrocephalous Martian. This prompted the broader realization that, taking one thing with another, Scotland's champion was not prepossessing: his boots and clinging trousers were plastered with mud, and water oozed and dripped from every quarter continuously. Above the waist, too, he looked as though someone had just turned a fire hose on him. The white silk scarf with which he had adorned himself for his rare aerial treat now hung limply around his neck like a piece of dirty sail cord.

The Group Captain's eye burned over Mackie slowly, in silence, and dropped to the puddle beginning to form at his muddy feet. He barked at the WAAF telephone operator: "Go get a bucket for him to stand in . . . Get two buckets."

She was back in a moment with two huge red fire buckets.

Mackie stepped into the containers with all the dignity he could muster, and the stony silence strained on a few moments longer, punctuated now by the tinny splash of the higher droplets striking the pails.

In response to the Group Captain's icy request, Mackie started into his recital, first breathing a silent prayer that the women had not identified themselves when they telephoned. He gave it to the Group Captain pretty well as it happened: how he'd been flying straight and level at 2500 feet above the Ouse when the engine failed and he'd prepared to make a forced landing. Knowing of the hidden barriers and traps which had been placed by government order in all fields suitable for the landing of enemy aircraft or gliders, he had deemed it to be in his young passenger's best interest to ditch the aircraft rather than take a chance of impaling it on a hidden obstacle.

The Group Captain's unbelieving sneer grew more pronounced as the story continued. He fired questions. Mackie gushed answers:

No, there had been absolutely no warning prior to the power failure. Yes, oil pressure and temperature had been normal at all times, and he had checked the petrol supply himself before the first flight. Well, sir, the only witness was his air cadet passenger. The cadet's inexperienced observations however would unfortunately add little to the accurate and detailed account just rendered. How many hours had Mackie had on Tiger Moths? . . . Why, he had never actually *flown* a Tiger Moth before, although he had seen one often enough.

At this stunning revelation of Mackie's treachery, the Group Captain's face assumed the hue of a stop light. Mackie fully realized that the only thing saving him from a kangaroo court martial was the Group Captain's knowledge that once Mackie got up and testified that he had not only been permitted but ordered to take up passengers in a strange aircraft, without even being asked if he were qualified, the Group Captain would not come out of the inquiry smelling like a rose either. At that point, choking on the gratuitous ignominy of the fire buckets, Mackie's remorse over the loss of the Tiger was superseded by a growing sense of contentment and satisfaction that the Group Captain would be unable to do anything about it.

Lady MacRobert. She gave three sons. (IWM)

Wing Commander Ogilvie, under the wing of "MacRoberts Reply", hands the crew a letter from Lady MacRobert wishing them good luck and happy landings. (IWM)

F/O Rod Dunphy (centre) and two others of his 426 Sqn. crew, F/Sgt Andrew and F/O Dodge, survey the damage inflicted upon their Lancaster by German fighters during a raid on Leipzig, October 20, 1943. The crew beat off seven fighter attacks, and despite wounds to the mid-upper gunner and damage to the aircraft pressed on to their target. (

Flight Lieutenant Roderick James Dunphy, DFC, RCAF, killed on operations over Germany, December 20th, 1943.

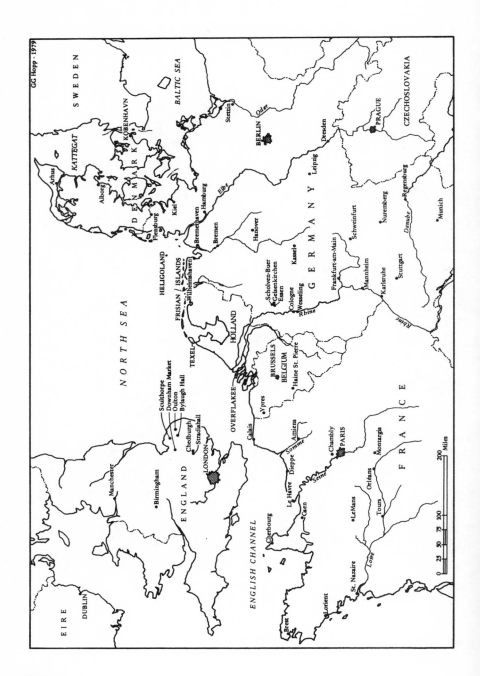

332

Left: Max Mair 'bank clerk forward' of the Portage Terriers hockey team.

Below: Max (left) with his Wellington crew. George Perry Armstrong is second from the right. Their pilot, Ouellette, is in the centre. (Joyce Ward)

Above: A Stirling standing menacingly over the bomb trolley. (IWM)

Below: Stirlings marshalled for an attack. Although grouping the aircraft this close together was in some respects risky, it was essential to an expeditious departure. (IWM)

In fact, the matter was allowed to drop, and when I was able to stop laughing at this hilarious adventure, Mackie gave me a final grin as he pointed out that, despite the fact that the Air Force had never spent one penny teaching him how to fly a Tiger Moth, he was the only pilot in the RAF to be on record as having successfully ditched a Tiger Moth in the River Ouse.

Since he was the only pilot in the world to land a Tiger Moth in the river, to the best of my knowledge, I expect his proud claim is valid, despite its being thoughtlessly ignored in every major historical work. *Sic transit gloria mundi.*

Penkuri sent me a letter two days before we left Downham Market. His news was bad. Watt Wilton, my bunk mate in Bournemouth, my fellow beer-sampler the night the Black Watch jumped us outside Burley Court, was gone. Freddie Taylor and Watt and I had been close even before we were commissioned together at Dauphin. We had delighted in the fact that our new commissioned service numbers had run in sequence: I drew J-20216; Freddie Taylor was J-20217; Watt Wilton, J-20218.

EXTRACT — OFFICIAL RECORDS
J-20218.   FLIGHT LIEUTENANT WALTER TORRANCE WILTON
F/L WILTON OF 408 SQUADRON WAS THE PILOT AND CAPTAIN OF AIRCRAFT LANCASTER DS718 WHICH TOOK OFF ON THE NIGHT OF 29-30 DECEMBER, 1943, TO CARRY OUT BOMBING OPERATIONS OVER BERLIN. F/L WILTON AND ALL MEMBERS OF THE CREW WERE KILLED ON DECEMBER 29 WHEN THE AIRCRAFT WAS SHOT DOWN NEAR LINGEN.

We left Downham Market on January 17th, bound for Sculthorpe. Until we actually prepared to drive away and leave our aircraft behind, we were not certain that we had parted with our Stirlings. Inwardly I said a fond farewell to them. The Stirling was truly a wonderful aircraft, which had rendered great service as Britain's first four-engined bomber. But for its needless maiming at birth by the short-sighted planners who conjured up the Air Ministry specifications, the Stirling might well have out-performed even the great Lancaster. She assuredly was second to none as a sturdy and dependable battler. She served us loyally, not least in providing, when she first took to the air and fought in squadron service, a morale building symbol of Britain's growing aerial offensive power. Relatively minor design changes, proposed by Short Bros., could have saved her and let her retain her rightful place in the front line. She deserved better of the Air Force than to be taken from the van — where she had carried the fight as the first real heavy, in some of the hardest hours of the battle — and relegated to glider towing. You will not find one in the war museums, or anywhere else. The Air Ministry, as though embarrassed to keep the accusatory evidence of its obvious mistake in existence, saved not even one. I am not bitter about many things connected with the war. I am bitter at that piece of rank ingratitude. The Short Stirling earned the highest honours, and never received them — except from every pilot she ever bore aloft. If nowhere else than in the mind's eye of a dwindling handful, she still cleaves the air with the proud defiance of MacRobert's Reply.

CHAPTER 15

THE AMERICANS CONQUER THE RAF

Hearts are not flint, and flints are rent;
Hearts are not steel, and steel is bent.

Rokeby.   Sir Walter Scott

The tiny village of Sculthorpe lay about a mile and a half from Fakenham, a larger center which, in turn, was only 25 miles northeast of Downham Market. Not until we reached our bleak new outpost did we make the astounding discovery that the clot who had spread the rumour about our going onto Flying Fortresses was not a clot at all; he was a gen man. 214 Squadron had been sent to take its place as an element of the recently formed 100 Group, a radar countermeasures organization commanded by Air Vice-Marshal Addison, with headquarters at Bylaugh Hall in Norfolk. We learned in due course that the new Group's activities covered a broader spectrum than we had first supposed, including complementing the vigorous bombing attacks of No. 8 Group's Mosquito equipped Light Night Striking Force with extensive night fighter intruder work by our Serrate Patrol Mosquitoes; but the Group's main role was to be carried out with the highly sophisticated weapons being conceived and developed by the electronic wizards, and 214 Squadron was to have a gratifyingly important part to play.

We were all somewhat bewildered by this sudden turn of events, and by the news that a substantial contingent of Americans, both aircrew and ground crew, would be arriving on the station almost immediately to familiarize us with the B-17. On the first count, the change of aircraft, I was more than pleased, for, much as I loved the old Stirlings, it had become painfully apparent that, unless they were modified to improve their altitude performance, the prospects of surviving a tour on them were remote. The second unexpected development, the prospect of having an American squadron come and serve on the same station with us, bothered me not at all. I had already served with enough Americans, those who had joined the RCAF, to know that, except sometimes by virtue of their accents, they were practically indistinguishable from Canadians. However, at least a third of our squadron were Englishmen and Scots, and they in particular were somewhat uncertain as to what they should expect. Many of them tended to anticipate the worst, some predicting flatly that the Americans would be lineshoot artists, pushy and garrulous, with too much money and no understanding of the problems of night operations.

In truth the Americans had no knowledge of night operations — just as we on 214 had no knowledge of daylight bombing — and they were well heeled, at least compared to the grossly underpaid British types on the station; but on every other count the fears of the pessimists proved unfounded, and somehow I knew the realization would come quickly the minute I met the Americans. For the most part they were operational types who had completed 20 or more missions, and after a very brief exposure to them we recognized their affiliation with us as veteran members of the we've-been-shot-at-brigade. They were so completely unlike the obnoxious portraits painted by the pessimistic prophets that it was laughable.

The first international mess party took place the night the Americans arrived, of course, and was a very effective icebreaker, and a good party on its own merits, despite a gaffe on my part. At an early stage I had glanced through the window and seen one of my friends approaching the mess. Running quickly to an ambush position with the well-charged soda siphon, I got off a nicely gauged high-velocity head shot as a foot came through the archway, only to see it pass just under the nose of the Station Commander, Group Captain Dickens, who entered the mess a yard ahead of my intended victim. Fortunately he was a tolerant soul and dismissed me with a rather pitying look as I hastily tried to stow the soda siphon inconspicuously into my tunic pocket — with the same measure of success I would have enjoyed in concealing a short fence post there. Nevertheless, the party went on to soaring heights 'ere the cock crew, and within a day or two, Captain Paris, the officer in charge of the American contingent, and Lieutenants Bloomer, Nickelhoff and Keating, to name only those who demonstrated heroic staying power, were as readily identifiable to us as our own blue-uniformed associates. In short order their candor and lack of pretension made them companions as comfortable as old shoes.

The greatest natural ambassador of the American aggregation, though, was a young, fair-haired lieutenant, a navigator, whose customary pleasant air of mild dissipation, coupled with crinkly eyes that always seemed to be enjoying a joke, were valid indicators of his approachability. Except when making his way into the bar for his first drink in the evening, he affected a leisurely and somewhat sloppy walk, and usually appeared with slightly tousled hair. Beyond a doubt he told us his proper name when we were first introduced, but his companion also told us his nickname, and everyone on the station thereafter hailed him as Blondie.

Blondie did better than just fit in so far as an RAF mess was concerned; he looked as though he had been there when they put the walls up. He could swap stories with anyone. If you wanted to restrict yourself to true stories, Blondie would honour the Marquis of Queensbury rules and travel under similar constraints. If you wanted to work in a bit of line shooting, Blondie was quite capable of keeping his dressing. He could hold his own in a card game, be it friendly or cutthroat, choose your weapons. He drank English beer, seeming to enjoy it, without comparing it unfavourably with Schlitz or any of the other American brews. He leered amorously at all the WAAF officers without discrimination, and was so naturally polite and courteous to them in his speech that within a few days, whenever they entered the mess, they always steered for their pet, Blondie. When they left the mess for the night, which they usually did when the decibel level threatened respectability — normally about 9:45 each and every night — Blondie joined Jake Walters (who had just received his commission) and the other aspiring operatic tenors around the piano, where, patiently waiting his turn, he showed a fine grasp of more and dirtier lyrics than even those veterans of the RAF concert repertoire. In short, Blondie was a man for all seasons, and, in my eyes at least, was the largest single contributor to the excellent rapport we established with the Americans within the first few days — and which we maintained thereafter.

Accomplishments like these were not all demonstrable within the compass of a few hours, of course, and it was not until the fifth evening, when I walked into the mess to hear Blondie and Tommy Crowe, a navigator friend of mine, engaged in a friendly conversation, that I realized Blondie's full talents as a diplomat. I gathered from the tag end of Tommy Crowe's remarks that he was helpfully proffering the inexperienced navigators of the USAAF a few pointers on the impossibly difficult art of high-level map reading at night. Blondie grinned at him appreciatively as he concluded, and then crowed over his pint in a happy voice: "Why you New Zealand bullshitter, you couldn't find your way from here to the bloody coal compound if I hung a flare over it and put a brass band at the gate" — at which point

I reckoned that Blondie clearly had another convert on the rolls.

One or two matters of professional pride that I thought might at least provoke an argument were avoided by the application of some candid common sense. One of our 214 bombaimers, ready, willing and able to launch a vigorous propaganda battle in favour of our Mark XIV bombsight over the Norden, asked an American bombardier if he, the American, seriously maintained that he could drop a bomb into a pickle barrel from 20,000 feet — this specific accomplishment being cited verbatim from the claims of a number of the more imaginative journalists inflicting their prose on the public at that time. The American was loathe to give ground unnecessarily; on the other hand he was not going to fertilize it. He grinned: "If one of you characters could figure some way for me to *see* it from 20,000 feet, I'll bet I could hit the son of a bitch." That response laid any Mark XIV vs. Norden debates to rest, permanently.

The effectiveness of daylight bombing compared with the bombing done by the RAF at night was a topic which came in for considerable discussion about that time — not in the various Air Force messes, but in the columns of assorted American journalists whose qualifications in this field were highly suspect. Most of them had obviously never taken the trouble to study the reconnaissance photographs showing the condition of various targets before and after being attacked, and the general tenor of their articles left one wondering whether they would know a bombsight from a Gee box. Largely as a result of their efforts some highly erroneous conceptions have gained wide acceptance among the uninformed. Nowadays it has become almost an article of faith for all young writers to refer, not to the Americans' daylight bombing, but, invariably, to American daylight *precision* bombing, the implication being that the RAF, (which actually did a considerable amount of daylight bombing itself, but dropped by far the greater percentage of its bombs by night) roared over at night dribbling bombs more or less aimlessly most of the way from base to the target. In fact, the results of both the RAF and American bombing were disappointingly inconsistent, particularly in the earlier stages. But the night target-marking techniques of Bomber Command improved radically from the latter part of 1943 on, with both Oboe and H2S marking being refined to the point where a night attack, under the weather conditions which obtained a good 50 percent of the time, was likely to be far more destructive than a daylight attack. The American journalists' unabashedly partisan dogma, which always accords first prize for effectiveness to daylight bombing, regardless of conditions, is not correct and should be carefully examined in the light of several factors which the journalists themselves invariably ignored.

The first of these is that the standard practice in the course of the

American daylight attacks was for the elements of the formation to toggle on the lead bombardier — that is, for the other bombaimers to ignore their bombsights and simply release their bombs the moment the lead bombardier dropped his. While there were sound tactical reasons for adopting that practice, it did not result in what an airman would normally call precision bombing, but, rather, in pattern bombing. An airman, be he Canadian, American, or British, would normally apply the term "precision bombing" to individually aimed high-level bombs falling within a circle of one or two hundred yards of the aiming point, or to a stick of bombs laid in a line running within one or two hundred yards of the intended bombing line. Under conditions of good visibility these limits could be met — and often considerably improved upon — by well trained crews in both air forces.

Most contemporary protagonists who extol the alleged superiority of daylight bombing over night area bombing — and again I remark that these are almost exclusively writers, not the airmen who flew the missions and who know the score — do not seem to understand that the accepted concept of precision bombing is simply incompatible with the concept of a large force of B-17's or B-24's spread out in a formation a mile or more wide. If the aircraft are spread out in a mile-wide formation when they drop their bombs, the individual bomb loads will be similarly spaced over the ground. Likewise if the lead bombardiers, upon whom such great responsibility rested, have their steadiness and accuracy affected prejudicially, by flak or otherwise, the errors are relayed through the whole formation.

Most of the writers seem totally unaware of the fact that on about 50 percent of our raids — both the RAF's and the USAAF's — the aiming point, and sometimes the whole target area, was partially or totally hidden by cloud. On many other occasions, the Germans guessed the target well before the arrival of the bombers, and managed to obscure the target with smoke. What the Americans usually did when balked in this manner, either by cloud, haze, or smoke, was to resort to blind bombing, utilizing a variant of the British H2S in the leading aircraft of the formations, and again having the other bombardiers toggle their loads the moment they saw the bombs appear below the bomb bays of the leaders. This was simply the timed run method that we had practised so diligently ourselves at Stradishall. If the quality of the navigation was good, the results achieved by the Americans in this manner could be extremely effective, particularly from good formation. But only a person disregarding the meaning of the word could characterize these methods as precision bombing. They were blind area bombing, pure and simple.

The effectiveness of an RAF night attack, from 1943 on, depended largely upon the accuracy of the target-marking. In the early stages, the target-marking had not been consistent, and the density of the bombing suffered accordingly, frequently being very poor. But with the development and refinement of Oboe — which could guarantee marking within two or three hundred yards in the hands of the best operators — night target-marking came into its own.

Unfortunately, the range of Oboe was limited. Beyond the Ruhr the Pathfinders, who did the marking, had to rely on various refinements of what was basically an H2S technique; at least they did until Leonard Cheshire and No. 5 Group came up with an even better method. Cheshire pioneered what appeared at first to be the suicidal method of going in over the target at ground level in a fighter — he used either a Mosquito or a Mustang — and dropping what were called spot-fires virtually dead on the aiming point. These could be seen at night, even through smoke cover or light cloud which would have prevented direct bombing in daylight, and many highly destructive attacks carried out on that basis at night proved the effectiveness of the technique beyond a doubt.

Over a target obscured by heavy cloud the RAF used different techniques, basically "sky-marking" by Pathfinder crews who dropped a special form of Target Indicator which served as an aiming point while it hung above the cloud cover. Despite the complicated mathematics that went into the placing of these sky-markers, the RAF's results, like those of the Americans, were prejudicially affected by heavy cloud cover. Since the bulk of our aircraft were fitted with H2S by the spring of 1944, the RAF could always resort to the timed run method on an individual basis.

Accompanying the refinements in Oboe and H2S techniques came the practice of using a Master Bomber, or Master of Ceremonies as we called him, over a night target. The Master of Ceremonies broadcast corrective instructions to the Main Force crews as they streamed in, and patrolled the target area during the course of the attack, calling in Pathfinder "backers-up" for additional or better marking as the attack progressed. He even used offset TI's and broadcast carefully calculated false wind settings to our bombaimers to steer the weight of the bombing in the right direction if it happened to be either going astray or becoming redundant in an area.

The net result of the various techniques was that the efficiency of night bombing in 1944 rose to the point where 200 or 300 Lancasters could do the pulverizing damage to the vital area of a target that a force of close to 1,000 had been required to do in the earlier stages of the war. At the same time, Bomber Command's first line strength continued to increase, and in the latter part of 1944 and the first part of 1945 reached a total of 1,200 or 1,300 machines, so that two or three targets could be attacked simultaneously.

Above left: Watt Wilton wearing his newly-won wings at Dauphin SFTS, October 1942.

Above right: The Americans arrive at Sculthorpe, January 1944. Capt. Preston of the US 8th Air Force meets F/L Dick Gunton, the Engineering Leader of 214 Sqn.   **(Tom Cushing)**

Below: Wing Commander J. B. 'Willie' Tait, DSO and three Bars, led Lancasters of 9 and 617 Sqns. to Tromso Fjord on November 12, 1944, and sank the Tirpitz.   **(IWM)**

Above: Lancaster LM418 PG-S. The Lancaster was far and away the best weight lifter of Bomber Command. (IWM)

Below: Grand Slam bomb in the specially modified bomb bay of a Lancaster. This monster bomb weighed 22,000 lbs.

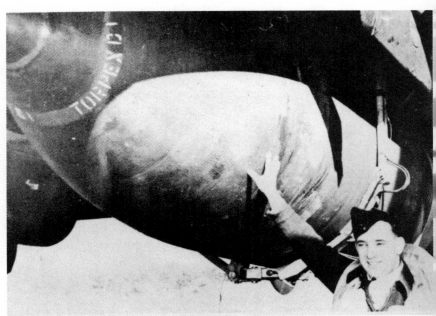

Right: This very contrasty photo shows the *Tirpitz* in Tromso Fjord before being bombed.

Below: Two seamen inspect the capsized and buckled hull of the *Tirpitz* after it was hit by 12,000 lb. Tallboys during the attacks led by W/C J. B. Tait.

Above: Canadian Pathfinders of 405 Sqn. pose with a couple of thousand pounders under the open bomb bay doors of 'Ruhr Express', the first Canadian-built Lancaster (from the Victory Aircraft Factory at Malton, Ontario). On the right is the author's friend, F/O Jack Astbury. **(RCAF)**

Flying Officer Douglas Newlands Cameron, RCAF, killed on operations over Germany, June 17, 1944.

Jack Astbury, an artist — and a pathfinder. Killed on operations, January 15, 1944.

Comparing the techniques employed in both daylight and night bombing, and the results, I think that an impartial assessment would be that under good conditions of visibility, the American approach was more effective, pound for pound, because a good tight bombing pattern with an even dispersion could be maintained so long as the formation was not badly dispersed by the flak and fighter defences. But under the conditions of light cloud or haze which so often hampered attacks, I believe the appraisal would be that the No. 5 Group type of night marking, using red spot fires, frequently produced a better concentrated attack than could be executed under comparable conditions in daylight.

During very bad weather, which was a recurring plague to both the Air Forces, the Americans, as I have pointed out, had to resort to blind bombing on H2S — just as we did — or go to a lower priority target if one happened to be within range and clear. But neither blind bombing on H2S nor pattern bombing from giant formations can accurately be called precision bombing.

Another important factor, studiously overlooked by the scribes here under indictment, is that against the American advantage of being able to throw a considerably tighter and more uniform bombing pattern in conditions of good visibility, our Bomber Command had the constant offsetting advantage that each of our aircraft carried a much heavier bomb load than the American Fortresses. This in turn was due to a number of factors. Firstly, the Lancasters and Halifaxes were equipped with more powerful engines than the Fortress and could therefore lift a larger load. Secondly, the American aircraft used proportionately more fuel on a trip because of the time required to assemble the large formations, and because formation flying itself uses a great deal more fuel than the type of flying we did. Consequently, the smaller American bomb loads were even further reduced on that account. Thirdly, they had to whittle down their payload even further because of the necessity of carrying a heavier load of machine gun ammunition than the British aircraft.

A twin-engined aircraft used by the Light Night Striking Force, the British Mosquito, routinely carried the same bomb load to Berlin as a four-engined Fortress, i.e. 4,000 pounds. The British Lancaster was the only aircraft in the European theatre capable of lifting the 22,000 pound "Grand Slam" into the air, and although there were only a few modified to carry it, they could deliver it to the Ruhr. Any Lancaster could haul a 12,000 pound bomb load to the centre of the Ruhr, and could carry 8,000 pounds to Berlin, the latter load representing double that of a Fortress. Thus, until a late stage in the war, Bomber Command maintained a conspicuous advantage in the total bomb load carried on any given operation. That weight advantage was gradually reduced, and finally eliminated, by the more rapid expansion of the American Air Force in the late stages of the war. Nevertheless, for a substantial period it was an important factor in the assessment of the relative destructive power of the two Forces.

Actually, there were only a few examples during the war of what could properly be termed precision bombing, and almost all of them were carried out by 617 Squadron, RAF, the Dam Busters. In addition to the prowess they demonstrated in breaching the Moehne and Eder Dams, 617 Squadron closed the Saumur tunnel with a "Tallboy" bomb, brought down the Bielefeld viaduct with a Grand Slam, and, under Wing Commander "Willie" Tait, first broke the back of the *Tirpitz* then on a separate raid, smashed and capsized her in Tromso Fiord[1].

Another canard that deserves a decent burial revolves around the fact that in the spring of 1941, more than a year before the Americans carried out their first Fortress attack on French targets, the British began experimenting with the old Fortress I, carrying out a lengthy series of daylight raids on German targets. These attacks, carried out by No. 90 Squadron, were almost uniformly unsuccessful. The chief weakness of the Fortress I was found to be its inability to defend itself from fighters. The results of the attacks, which were usually carried out with very small formations — and often with only a single aircraft — were so discouraging that the British concluded that daylight bombing of Germany in Fortresses, relying solely upon the defensive firepower of the bomber itself, was not feasible. To their credit, it must be pointed out that they tried some very heavily defended targets, including Kiel, Emden, Bremen and Wilhelmshaven. It is also worthy of mention that the Fortress II and the Fortress III, subsequently used by the Americans in Europe, were considerably different aircraft, in terms of defensive firepower, to the old Fortress I.

But some writers, whose chauvinism exceeds their common sense, have been inclined to dismiss the British decision to abandon the daylight bombing approach as being attributable either to a lack of intestinal fortitude on the part of the senior commanders involved, or to a failure on the part of the incompetent British pilots to understand and exploit the features of an aircraft far too sophisticated for their limited capabilities.

The fact of the matter was that the British assessment had been basically correct on the factors then under study. Without the flood of long range fighters like the Mustang, which were an essential factor in making the American daylight attacks on German targets feasible

---

1. "Willie" Tait was subsequently attached to No. 100 Group, and we had the pleasure of seeing him in our mess on one or two occasions at Oulton.

from the spring of 1944 on, the losses on deep penetrations by an unescorted bomber force relying solely upon its own defensive firepower were demonstrably prohibitive, and General Eaker was not slow to appreciate that fact. On the October 14th, 1943, attack on Schweinfurt, an epic demonstration of courage and determination on the part of the American aircrews involved, 60 Fortresses were lost out of the 291 despatched, a loss rate of 20 percent. A few weeks earlier, on August 17th, Generals Eaker and Anderson had sent the 8th Air Force heavies in a joint attack against Schweinfurt and Regensburg, and suffered the loss of 60 aircraft out of 377 despatched[1]. No bomber force can absorb casualties of that order and maintain offensive operations on any effective scale. General Eaker was forced to restrict the scale of operations severely after both these attacks; and, for many weeks, a high percentage of the 8th Air Force's efforts had to be limited to much shallower penetrations on which adequate fighter escort could be provided. The ultimate solution, daylight bombing in formations covered by heavy fighter escort all the way to the target and back, was a concept which neither the Americans nor the British had originally considered practicable, since the means with which to implement it had not been in existence.

To their eternal credit, the Americans refused to give in, marking time with a majority of shallow penetrations only until the development of the Mustang — with its original Allison engine replaced by the British designed Merlin — gave them the long range fighter cover necessary for continuous daylight bombing of German targets.

I make these points at the risk of sounding like one not overly impressed with the American contribution. Nothing could be further from the truth. I got to know many of the American aircrew. I flew with some. I saw tremendous numbers of them, in the air, on the great sorties they made against occupied Europe and Germany. It is possible that in some measure I owe my own life to the American aircrews, for they played the most prominent part in battering the life out of the German fighter force and strewing it in wreckage across the Fatherland, a dearly bought victory which had its effects upon the morale and efficiency of the German night fighter force as well. Thus, not for one moment would I hear anyone detract in any way from the truly great contribution made by the American flyers. They had every right to be proud of it. For my money, as aircrew, they were as good as the best that ever buckled on a chute. But they were well aware that their reputation and achievements did not have to rely on the ability of journalists to belittle the efforts of RAF Bomber Command. In fact the

---

1. Roger A. Freeman, *The Mighty Eighth* pp 67-69, p 78, Macdonald and Company (Publishers) Ltd., London.

operational aircrews themselves, both American and British, never knocked their allied "competition". Each knew that the men in the other uniforms were shedding blood as heavily as they were, had special problems of their own to face and conquer, and were smashing German targets in their turn. As was the case in other fields, it was the writers, safe on the deck, who fell prey to the Russian weakness of claiming the lion's share of the credit for "their" side. And the Americans weren't the only ones to indulge in that stupid pastime.

We started flying six days after our arrival at Sculthorpe, having spent a great many hours in the meantime poring over the Fortress handbook, getting used to the idea of setting engines at 28 or 38 inches of manifold pressure instead of the equivalent in pounds of boost, and assimilating a hundred and one other differences, of varying degrees of importance, between the Stirling and the Fortress. Lieutenant Keating and I were scheduled to go flying together that rather rainy morning of January 23rd. After waiting around the flight room in our harness for an hour, due to some mix-up in communications, he introduced me, upon his line chief's arrival, to that fine old American expression: SNAFU. When I asked him to render it *in extenso* for my edification, he did so with such heartfelt earnestness that the whole crew began to laugh; it rubbed off on Keating, and the session soon got off to a good-natured start. (He did not, needless to say, render the ultimate phrase as *"fouled* up".) I appreciated this new expansion of our vocabulary so much that when we packed up, after eight or nine practice landings, I dropped a line to Penky, now at Waterbeach with 514 Squadron, suggesting that he incorporate it into his continuing eulogy of Deans. I also gave Penky a glowing description of the Fortress, liberally exaggerating its performance, and commiserating with those pilots of lesser skills, doomed, in the interests of their own safety, to remain on Lancasters. In due course he responded with some unflattering statistics, more highly doctored than my own, on the comparative bomb loads and speeds of the two aircraft.

In truth, our very first impression of the Fortress, gained as we sat in dispersal starting her engines under Lieutenant Keating's supervision, was not flattering. The Wright Cyclone engines — which turned up only 1,200 horsepower each, as opposed to the 1,650 of the Hercules XVI — sounded rather hollow and tinny when they first coughed, and Keating advised us that they needed very little encouragement to develop a manifold fire on start-up. He proved his point when we started the second engine, but quickly blew it out with a burst of throttle before the fire extinguisher had to be employed. When we left the dispersal I found the squeak and jerk of the toe brakes, under my unaccustomed feet, a little distracting; but they proved easy to adapt to, and I soon preferred them to those of the Stirling. The Fortress, except for the four feet of additional wingspan, was over-all a much smaller aeroplane than the Stirling. The sensation was akin to having climbed out from behind the wheel of a Mack truck and taken over the driver's position in a Volkswagen.

My love affair with the Fortress started with the first takeoff. (The difference in weight was most noticeable — an empty Mark I Stirling weighed 13,000 pounds more than an empty Fortress.) There was no tendency to swing on takeoff, none whatever. The Fortress soared into the air like a carefree gull, and kept on climbing effortlessly. To an old Stirling pilot, her rate of climb was enough to gladden the heart. Furthermore, she was as stable as a basic trainer in the air, and at the end of the approach, when I flared out to land, I found that she floated as lightly as an Anson. In short, she was a beautiful aeroplane to fly: graceful, responsive, stable, forgiving, and as reliable as the sunrise. After the Stirling, a most demanding aircraft on takeoff and landing, the Fortress was a pilot's dream.

Next day, Keating came with me while I took her up for 40 minutes to practise stalls, feathering, and three-engined flying, then asked me to dump him off and go away with my crew and practise by myself. This we did, without trepidation, for the Fortress was obviously that rarity, an aircraft with no vices.

We found that at low level her big aileron surfaces made her a little stiff on turns; but when she climbed up beyond 20,000 feet, where she was meant to perform, she came close to matching the Stirling in her smooth and ready aileron response. In one respect, apart from her superior altitude performance, she far outshone the Stirling: because of her Stromberg injection carburettors, negative G would not cause the engines to cut; consequently, in evasive action, a much sharper start to the corkscrew was possible — so sharp, indeed, that Sam and J. B. cursed me heartily as I caused them to float weightless in the nose compartment, then brought them crashing down on top of one another as I pulled the control column back vigorously at the transitional point of the manoeuvre.

We quite enjoyed ourselves for the next little while, getting used to the Fortress in all the varying circumstances we might expect to encounter. From time to time pleasant little ferrying jobs came our way, and these we seized upon eagerly. For example, on February 2nd, we took Lieutenant Bloomer and Lieutenant Nickelhoff as passengers and ambassadors and visited Honington and Little Staughton, both American bases, to pick up more parts and equipment. The great attraction of these trips was that if we hurried, we could work in a flying visit to the PX, where they had, wonder of wonders, stacks of frosty Cokes. I hadn't had one since leaving Halifax, and they tasted so delicious on my arid palate that I invariably drank about four — then walked around like a newly charged aerosol can, burping and hissing on the slightest provocation.

On February 7th, we were sent out to night-fly the Fortress. It turned out that we would have to do this without instructors, for the Americans would have no part of checking us out at night. I couldn't say that I blamed them. They had had no occasion to do night landings for a very long time, and were no doubt pretty rusty. We decided that we would go out and start practising circuits at dusk, and simply keep going after darkness fell. To my considerable surprise, a number of the Americans wanted to come with us and refresh their memories on what night landings were like. Two of them climbed up into the cockpit and stood behind me and Bill Bailey; (in the Fort our flight engineer sat in the right-hand cockpit seat, and the bombaimer worked up in the nose compartment with the navigator.) Their surveillance put me very much on my mettle. If the Americans reposed such confidence in the RAF's night expertise, it would never do to boob and come pouncing in with a kangaroo landing, thus inviting an ambiguous interpretation by the Americans of the motto on the 214 Squadron crest: Ultor in Umbris — Avenging in the Shadows.

Fortunately, the Fortress was so easy to land at night that even the radical reduction in cockpit height between it and the Stirling — on which we were still having to concentrate — did not throw us off, and we kept greasing her on in most gratifying fashion. Our passengers were duly impressed, and after three hours without the slightest problem, we were satisfied that the Fort, as she was in so many other ways, was a first-class aeroplane to fly at night.

Bob Murray, a friend of mine who was a fitter with 427 (RCAF) Squadron at Leeming, wrote to me on February 12th to tell me that another mutual friend of ours from Portage Collegiate had been killed on ops. Jack Astbury had been a bombaimer. Our families had been friends, and indeed Charlie Astbury, his father, had been a particularly good friend to the whole Peden clan. Jack had been their only child.

EXTRACT — OFFICIAL ARCHIVES
J-21524. FLYING OFFICER JOHN WILLIAM ASTBURY
. . . AIR BOMBER OF A LANCASTER AIRCRAFT OF 405 SQUAD-RON . . . TARGET BRUNSWICK, GERMANY, . . . KILLED ON JANUARY 15th, 1944.

As though this were not sufficient bad news, I learned, almost at the same time, that Joe Bourke, one of our Stirling pilots at Chedburgh, and Earl Clare, his bombaimer, had gone missing a couple of weeks earlier. Joe had been flying with 620 Squadron at Chedburgh, slept in the same hut with me there, and had been a pal of mine since our days at Dauphin SFTS. His first second dickey target had been Munchen-Gladbach in the Ruhr. So impressed had Joe been by the terrible spectacle of the burning city that, upon his return, he had roused me out of a sound sleep at 4:00 AM to whisper an awe-struck description of what he had seen. They had just been reported missing, not killed, so we kept our fingers crossed.

Through a mix-up in communications, Bill Jeffries' ball turret gunner gave us all a noisy demonstration, a day or two later, of how not to position the ball turret for landing. Not realizing that Bill had rejoined the circuit with the intention of landing, he left the ball turret in the vertical position, so that when Bill flared out to settle lightly on the runway, a terrible rasping noise, which caught our attention a quarter of a mile away, suddenly began to flow along with him, as two .50 calibre machine gun barrels were bent into the shape of pruning hooks.

Speaking of .50 calibre machine guns: we had tried them out in air-sea firing practices over the Wash, and had been very favourably impressed, reckoning that not only did they have far more hitting power than the puny .303, but that at night the impressive size of their flaming tracers would have a far greater deterrent effect upon any pursuing fighter, even if the gunners did not manage to hit him.

On the 13th of February, just after we had completed a fighter affiliation exercise, Wing Commander McGlinn summoned me to his office where he gave me a rather searching quiz to assure himself that I had done my homework faithfully on the pilot's handbook. When he was satisfied, he told me that my crew would be leaving in a day or two to take a Fortress to the Bomber Development Unit at Newmarket. There the aircraft would be studied and subjected to various tests, which my crew would carry out under direction. Since we were due for leave in approximately ten days, he promised that Jeff Bray and I could take turns at the BDU duty.

On February 15th, therefore, we flew to Newmarket, where I found that the aerodrome was simply a grass field on the world-famous race-track. For a week we never got off the ground, as the backroom boys studied the aircraft and pondered some of the problems associated with converting it for night flying operations with Main Force. On February 23rd we returned to Sculthorpe, spelled off by Jeff Bray, and the following day we went to London for a week's leave.

I had written to Penkuri earlier to see whether we could team up on our leaves again, but he was unable to get away this time. Since the middle of November, Main Force had been engaged, whenever the weather would permit, in the Battle of Berlin. After Penky's Christmas leave things had hotted up further. Not that the German capital was the only target being attacked; the weather was never obliging enough to permit that sort of concentrated effort; but it was being given highest priority throughout this period, and Main Force was heavily committed. But for the fact that we were in the process of changing aircraft, we would have been in it with them[1].

Once in London, J. B. and I started our little interlude in quiet fashion, walking from Oddenino's, where we spent the first night or two, to Trafalgar Square. There we had our picture taken, for home consumption, in the traditional wholesome pose of feeding the pigeons. After a light lunch, not taken at the Pam Pam, J. B. mentioned that he had heard good reports of a club known as the Crackers Club. From his description it sounded like a cosy home away from home for servicemen at a loose end in London. Its exact location I do not remember, save that, judging from the brevity of our walk getting to it, a good baseball pitcher could have thrown a ball to it from the centre of Piccadilly Circus.

The Crackers Club was below street level, well below, and the first homey feature my eye lit on was a commodious, well stocked bar. Presumably one also did any necessary letter writing, chess or checker playing, etc. on its surface, since it took up most of the open space in the room. An attractive girl, whom I assumed to be the Club's social director, speedily involved me in the institution's primary if not exclusive activity, namely, drinking, and I mean drinking at prices which would clearly restrict the Club's clientele to the higher class type of patron — who had just drawn his pay.

J. B. and I engaged in the club sport for an hour and a half: he, slowly and sedately; I, much more in command of the situation, fast and furious, demonstrating that since my unaccountable lapse at the Dauphin Wings Party I had learned the ropes and taken the measure of John Barleycorn. I was drinking ale, and I ordered at brief intervals. J. B., lacking my control and sophistication, kept pouring his fresh shots of scotch into a separate glass.

By the time I had drunk five ales, he had stored the best part of a glassful of neat scotch in the spare glass in front of him. Under the gaze of the attractive witness, I felt impelled to demonstrate that we pilots were a pretty hard rock crowd. I leaned over impatiently and said, in the deepest voice I could muster, "Awright, come on J. B., quit stalling. Let's get you caught up."

So saying, I reached across, took the six ounces or thereabouts of neat scotch, and put it away like John Wayne emptying his canteen after a full day in the saddle.

---

1. Between the middle of November, 1943, and the third week in March, 1944, the RAF carried out 16 heavy attacks on Berlin. In the course of those operations Bomber Command lost approximately 500 aircraft and their crews. See: Hilary St. G. Saunders, *Royal Air Force*, Vol. III: *The Fight Is Won*, pp 21, 22; H.M.S.O.

Above: J. B. and his pilot (the author) pose for the customary "Feeding Pigeons in Trafalgar Square" picture.

Below: Halifax MZ620 begins its take-off roll.

(PAC)

A rare photo of a 214 Sqn. Flying Fortress, BU-W, in flight over England. (Tom Butler

Below: A 214 Sqn. Flying Fortress at Sculthorpe. (Rolly Harrison)

Above: Halifax LK640 of 431 Squadron undergoes regular maintenance between sorties.

(PAC)

Below: Halifaxes of 426 Squadron in dispersal.

(PAC)

214 Squadron crest. The Latin motto translates into 'Avenging in the Shadows'.

King George VI in his uniform of a Marshal of the Royal Air Force accompanied by W/C
Guy Gibson, V.C. (right).

Above: A Mosquito of 487 Sqn., RNZAF. This squadron did much night bombing and under G/C P. C. Pickard participated in the daylight raid of February 18, 1944, to free Resistance fighters from the Gestapo prison at Amiens. (IWM)

Below: A few seconds worth of 20mm ammunition is loaded into a Beaufighter of the 'Serrate' patrol. (IWM)

Tommy Penkuri's course upon graduation from No. 2 EFTS, Fort William (now Thunder Bay). Tommy is seated at the right end of the front row. (Fryer's Studio)

Below left: Tommy Penkuri; an enlargement from the above photograph. (Fryer's Studio)

Below right: Tommy Penkuri just four days before he was killed during a raid on March 16, 1944. (JD MacKenzie)

Air Vice-Marshal E. B. Addison, Commander of 100 Group from the end of 1943
Addison had been a prominent figure in radar counter-measures work from 1940.

Twenty minutes later, the unsophisticated J. B., like a seeing-eye dog, was helping me make my rubber-legged, stumbling way back to the hotel. In broad daylight, he practically carried old John Wayne become Mickey Rooney right through Piccadilly Circus to Oddenino's, pausing occasionally and dissociating himself from me by window shopping as I turned into every alcove that offered any concealment and heaved.

Although I did get back to the Crackers Club a day or two later, and managed to wangle a date with the girl I had been intent on impressing, I conducted myself much more respectably for the balance of my leave. I spent several afternoons simply walking around in Green Park where I derived much enjoyment from sitting near the water and admiring the ducks which were flying overhead, landing, and taking off almost continuously. I whiled away the time during these periods by mentally laying off what I estimated to be the correct deflection as the ducks flew around me. The last day, after I had fired about four boxes of silent shells and collected a record bag of greenheads, I was on my way out of the park when I noticed a sign tacked to a tree. Since it featured a picture of a brass band, and since I was far and away the keenest brass band fan in existence, I went for a closer look. In a moment I wished I hadn't. The poster advertised a concert by Foden's Motor Works Band, to be given the following day, either in the park or nearby, about four hours after I was due back on the station. From the 1930's on, Foden's Motor Works Band was probably the best known brass band in the world, certainly in the British Isles. Under the baton of Fred Mortimer, with his son Harry playing solo cornet, it had won more championships than I could keep track of. I was sorely tempted to stay and fulfill a lifelong ambition, but I returned to the station on time, contenting myself by acquiring a couple more Foden's records and a Black Dyke Mills.

Over the next two weeks we systematically increased our familiarity with the Fortress, doing high-level cross-countries, both day and night, more ferrying trips — and Coke flights — and another air firing exercise.

On March 16th, I found a letter from Penky in my box, bringing the cheering word that Joe Bourke and Earl Clare had not been killed, but were alive and well in a POW camp. What I did not know as I reacted happily to the good news in Penky's letter was that Penky was dead, killed a few hours before I got the letter, in an attack on Stuttgart.

The official records communicate none of the pain that a reading of their terrible litany brings to me even now: "J-21087. FLYING OFFICER KAIHO THOMAS PENKURI . . . 514 SQUADRON . . .

THE PILOT AND CAPTAIN OF A LANCASTER WHICH FAILED TO RETURN TO ITS BASE AFTER HAVING TAKEN OFF TO CARRY OUT A BOMBING ATTACK OVER STUTTGART ON THE NIGHT OF MARCH 15-16, 1944. THE BODIES OF THE . . . CREW . . . WERE LATER RECOVERED NEAR VILLARS LE PAUTEL, FRANCE."

I remained unaware of Penky's death for a fortnight. But on the night of March 30-31, a night of bright moonlight and extremely high winds that scattered Main Force, Bomber Command attacked Nuremberg, despatching a force of almost 800 aircraft. Ninety-four failed to return, most of them the prey of the murderously efficient German night fighters. Ninety-four crews; 94 four-engined bombers. It was Bomber Command's worst loss of the war. The BBC reported the sickening total next morning.

I was filled with a sudden apprehension. I left the mess without breakfast, returned to the billets, and sat down and scratched a quick note to Penky. I was afraid to telephone and ask directly. My note was returned almost immediately, unopened, bearing a large stamp across the envelope bluntly advising: "This officer missing on operations." I knew before the confirmatory word arrived shortly afterwards that Penky was dead.

I loved him like a brother.

CHAPTER 16

RETURN TO WAR – WITH NEW WEAPONS

"There!" said the Deacon, "naow she'll dew!"

Do! I tell you, I rather guess

She was a wonder, and nothing less."

Oliver Wendell Holmes, The One-Hoss Shay

From April 4th to April 12th, 1944, our crew flew a second series of exercises and tests at the Bomber Development Unit at Newmarket, then left to rejoin the Squadron once more at Sculthorpe. In trials with an AI equipped Beaufighter, we learned that visibility from the Fortress's ball turret at night was so limited that the turret was virtually useless; so it was removed from 214's aircraft[1]. Numerous other modifications were made. We found it advantageous, for example, to revert to our own high pressure oxygen system, and to modify the intercom system so that we could use our own microphones, which we preferred to the American throat microphones. Special traps were designed and fitted to the underside of the turbo superchargers to hide the tongues of blue flame that would otherwise be a dead giveaway at night. Later on we found that painting over the bottom half of the side windows of the cockpit with black paint enabled us, if we were caught in searchlights, to duck our heads below the blinding glare for at least part of the ordeal, and with luck, see what was happening on our instrument panel. This expedient actually helped quite a bit if only one or two lights were involved.

But the big changes were not so much in the aircraft as in the new equipment we were to carry — and this we learned about only in stages as we were called upon to put it to use. Everything about our operations was in the highly secret category, and we were not encouraged to ask unnecessary questions.

---

1. On one night exercise the problem was reversed. The Beaufighter's AI packed up, then he could not find us, even after we returned to the aerodrome and circled with our navigation lights on, calling to him to tell him where we were. I pointed out that it was seldom we had to do this for the German night fighters.

Our crew was now increased from seven to ten members. One of the additional bods was to be a combination window-dropper and gunner. He was stationed where he could operate one of the waist guns in a pinch, and was responsible for helping to drop the large quantities of window we began to carry. On each trip we were also assigned a special wireless operator, who had the intriguing qualification of being able to speak German. Initially we did not have enough of these German-speaking wireless operators to go round, so that, unlike the rest of us, they did not fly as a member of the same crew each time, but were rotated. We were told about their duties only in very general terms at first, and were specifically warned against trying to elicit further details from them subsequently in the mess. Apparently it was considered that if we were captured, the less we could tell the Germans about the details of 100 Group's activities the better. Even the special wireless ops themselves were not told the full story of the activities planned for them. That was to come later.

There was one other change relative to the Squadron that I have thus far been remiss in failing to mention. Because of our new role, 214 Squadron was now officially referred to as No. 214 (BS) Squadron. I had to explain to Blondie repeatedly that in 100 Group BS stood for Bomber Support. For some weeks he was determinedly forgetful when delivering the loud formal greeting he took to giving 214 (BS) Squadron members who had arrived at the mess before him.

Even before we had finished the final tests at BDU, the first 214 Squadron operation in Fortresses was launched from Sculthorpe. Naturally the first name on the battle order that April night was Wing Commander D. J. McGlinn's.

Our crew flew back to Sculthorpe from Newmarket on April 12th, and on April 24th, after having been off operations for 15 weeks, we were back on the battle order with Main Force. The target was Karlsruhe in southern Germany, some 40 miles northwest of Stuttgart. The aircraft we had drawn for the operation was F Fox, newly arrived from Scottish Aviation's hangar at Prestwick, where our Fortresses were being modified. Our ground crew had taken over where Scottish Aviation had left off, and we found on our afternoon air test that F Fox was in beautiful shape. When we landed and taxied back to the dispersal our Chiefie met me with his usual concerned look and the perennial ground crew query: "Any snags, Skipper?" I told him that his boys had F Fox humming like a top, and he relaxed and gave his expectant crew, who were standing off to one side, a railway highball. Moments later they were cycling away furiously, heading for tea at the airmen's mess.

We took off shortly after dark. Our primary role while accompanying the bombers was to blot out, as frequently as possible, the essential VHF communications between the German night fighter controllers and the fighter pilots themselves. Every minute's delay thus occasioned saw the bombers a few miles further on, and reduced the chance of an interception. With a number of our 214 aircraft spaced out in the stream, it was hoped that the traffic around the main fighter beacons could be greatly impeded. The special wireless operators were to achieve that objective by the use of a three-stage jammer code-named ABC (Airborne Cigar.).

First, the operator tuned his own receiver over the bands most frequently used by the German controllers. The moment he picked up a controller broadcasting instructions, he set ABC to the same frequency and flipped the switch, jamming the conversation into unintelligibility. Going back to his receiver, the special wireless operator then began tuning again to see what frequency the German controller had moved to in an effort to re-establish contact. As soon as he found his next frequency on went the jammer again, driving the controller to yet another frequency. And so it went, until the controllers were virtually apoplectic in their frustration.

100 Group had much more in its bag of tricks, but the time had not yet come to reveal all its wares. Once the invasion of Europe was fairly under way— and everyone felt it to be imminent — Air Vice-Marshal Addison was going to be in a position to make the German night fighters' life a great deal more difficult.

In addition to our Airborne Cigar work, we were given extensive window-dropping chores to perform in the course of our trip to Karlsruhe, and on each subsequent operation. So much has been written about window that I shall limit myself to the reminder that a package of window simply contained a large number of tinfoil strips cut to a specific length. The length of the strips was directly related to the wavelength of the main German radar detecting apparatus, the Giant Wurzburg. When a package of window was dropped from an aircraft, it immediately blossomed out, and the dense cluster of tinfoil strips reflected back an echo on the Wurzburg which was virtually impossible to distinguish from the echo returned by a real aircraft. Around the target area, with hundreds of crews dropping bundles of window, the Wurzburgs could be flooded with echoes, completely disrupting the "predicted" flak and searchlight defences. After the great July, 1943, raid on Hamburg, when the RAF used window for the first time, it was employed routinely by Main Force, and with considerable success. But with this medium, too, 100 Group had some special plans for the Germans which it was not quite time to unveil; and 214 Squadron was to learn a lot more about windowing and jamming in the very near future.

The six-hour trip to Karlsruhe seemed even longer after our

lengthy layoff; but despite the fact that I was a little jumpier than usual, I experienced a new feeling of optimism flying into Germany at 22,000 feet instead of 12,000, a feeling that now we had a fighting chance and could give a much better account of ourselves if a fighter did tackle us. The target area was certainly no easier; the gunners below didn't have any trouble getting a flak barrage up to 22,000 feet — or a lot higher — and the searchlights were just as frightening when they groped their way near one. But F Fox took us and our German-speaking jamming specialist all the way to Karlsruhe and back unscathed. After six hours of the well-remembered tension, we landed and taxied thankfully back to our dispersal, where the ground crew were waiting for us, two of them revealing their position in the darkness with shielded flashlights, having been telephoned from the control tower as soon as I called for permission to join the circuit.

The great surge of relief that I usually felt after completing an operation was augmented by the happier frame of mind stemming from the performance of our new aircraft. Karlsruhe went into the log book as No. 14.

We lay about the mess for the next two evenings, Tuesday and Wednesday, taking advantage of the fact that, until 214 had amassed a larger complement of fully modified aircraft, we would not be operating as frequently as we had on Stirlings. Thursday night, April 27th, we found ourselves free men again, and on a spur of the moment impulse — an impulse which resulted in an interesting little coincidence for me an hour later — I took a jeep ride with Tommy Crowe and one of the American pilots and visited a pub a few miles off, over Aylsham way. While we were chatting there with our friendly host, I happened to notice two brass shell cases standing on the mantle. They appeared to be of World War I vintage, and looked to be somewhat smaller than the 18-pounder type. Curious, I wandered over to inspect them. Examining their bases I discovered two things: firstly, they were German shell cases; secondly, they had been manufactured at a shell factory in Karlsruhe. The landlord laughed and stood us a pint when I told him that the bombers we had accompanied two or three nights before had probably left some British souvenirs in the same factory.

When we left the pub it was dark, and there were audible indications of the fact that, while we were having a night off, other crews in Bomber Command were plying their trade.

One of the Lanc crews flying that night was captained by my chum Jimmy Watson — my companion of the Park Lane Hotel episode a year earlier, who had led me through the lounge of the hotel past the upside down beer drinker to get Brigadier-General Frank Armstrong's autograph.

EXTRACT — OFFICIAL ARCHIVES
J-20076. FLIGHT LIEUTENANT JAMES ANDREW WATSON
(MENTIONED IN DESPATCHES).
F/L WATSON OF 622 SQUADRON WAS THE PILOT AND
CAPTAIN . . . LANCASTER . . . ND781 ENGAGED ON AN
IMPORTANT MISSION OVER FRIEDRICHSHAFEN, GERMANY,
ON THE NIGHT 27-28 APRIL 1944 . . . THE AIRCRAFT CRASHED
AT BERGHEIM. F/L WATSON . . . KILLED ON APRIL 28 . . .
REMAINING CREW (6 MEMBERS) WERE TAKEN PRISONERS
OF WAR.

Our names figured in the battle order again on May 1st, with the target being the railway yards at Chambly, not far from Paris. RAF Bomber Command, in conjunction with the American heavies, had begun the implementation of the Transportation Plan as one part of the contribution it would make towards trying to ensure the success of the impending invasion. We took F Fox again, and she performed as perfectly as she had on Karlsruhe.

The night of May 8th, in the bright light of a full moon, we went on ops again. Once more the target was a large railway yard, this time further north, at Haine St. Pierre in the historic Mons area. To confirm a belief in the Germans' minds that the main thrust of the impending invasion would be directly across the channel in the Pas de Calais area, the American Air Force and our own Command systematically dropped a substantially heavier tonnage of bombs in this northerly area than we did down south where the landings were actually scheduled to take place. The deception plan had been initiated months earlier by means of spurious army radio traffic and false pieces of information dribbled to the Germans through double agents. To complement it, both Air Forces were now going to great lengths in executing a pattern of bombing that would convince the Germans that the information they had garnered earlier was reliable, by making it appear fully consistent with the unfolding, tell-tale preparatory work of the bomber forces.

Bomber Command had been demonstrating such accuracy in its night railway attacks that it had been found possible to split it into small forces and send it to several of these transportation targets in one night. But the attempts to save infantrymen's lives and ensure their success by immobilizing the German reserves was not without its cost in blood. On the Haine St. Pierre raid we took heavy losses. Visibility in the full moon was such that the German night fighters could not long be misled, even operating under the handicap of garbled and fragmentary communications. Short as the trip was — we were back in the circuit at Sculthorpe in just under three hours — I felt the strain sufficiently to appreciate the cup of coffee the padre handed me at interrogation, containing an unexpectedly generous jolt of rum.

We awoke to the rumour that 214 Squadron and the nine crews making up the American Squadron were being transferred to a new station. I bethought myself immediately of the gen man who had mined the nugget about our going onto Fortresses in the first place, and headed for his quarters on the assumption that he must have access to a good source of information. He did, and he converted the rumour into fact, advising me that in one week we were moving to a drome at Oulton. When I asked him where Oulton was, he told me that it was located 12 or 13 miles north-northwest of Norwich, which meant it was only about 15 miles east of where we were. I thanked him politely and bided my time until I could lay to alongside George Wright.

At tea time I stationed myself at George's elbow. As I washed down the featured delicacy of the day — bloater paste sandwiches again — I turned to George exuding the very nth degree of casualness and said: "When are you going to make the announcement about us going to Oulton on the 16th?"

George stopped chewing and swung his bushy eyebrows slowly in my direction; the effect was much like watching the 14-inch guns of the *Duke of York* train onto their target. "Well I'm damned," he growled. "Only got the message myself yesterday. Has that damned WAAF in my office been blabbing this all over the station?"

"I don't think anyone on the station knowns about it except my own crew" I said, poker faced; "our special wireless op picked it up last night from a German fighter controller."

George raised his cup as if to slosh me, meanwhile his booming laugh brought over Bill Day, now Flight Commander of "A" Flight. Under the circumstances, George made the first public announcement there and then; and half an hour later there was a run on the Fakenham laundry as everyone tried to recover or get priority delivery on shirts, socks and underwear.

Above: The front of Blickling Hall, the estate of the Marquis of Lothian. It is located between Oulton and Aylsham in Norfolk.

(Rod Peden)

Below: A corner of the grounds of Blickling said to be frequented by the ghost of Anne Boleyn.

(Rod Peden)

Above: Flying Fortress 'M-Mi[...]
the aircraft the author's crew t[...]
to Stuttgart the night of July [...]
1944.			(Geoff L[...]

Left: Wing Commander Desm[...]
J. McGlinn, DFC. In the auth[...]
view the best Squadron Comma[...]
er in the RAF.		(Tom Cush[...]

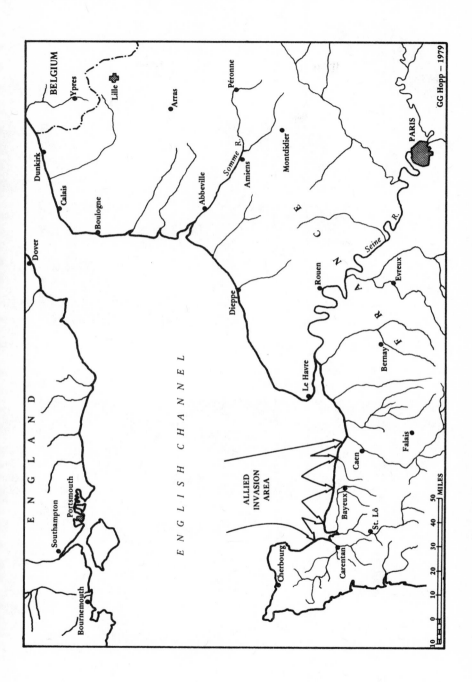

BELGIUM

Ypres

Lille

Arras

Péronne

Somme R.

Montdidier

Amiens

Abbeville

Dunkirk

Calais

Boulogne

Dover

Dieppe

Rouen

Seine R.

Evreux

F R A N C E

Bernay

PARIS

GG Hopp – 1979

Le Havre

ENGLISH CHANNEL

E N G L A N D

Southampton

Portsmouth

Bournemouth

Caen

Falais

Bayeux

St. Lô

Carentan

Cherbourg

ALLIED
INVASION
AREA

0   10   20   30   40   50

MILES

373

Above: C-47 Dakota over the Normandy beaches shortly after D-Day. (PAC)

Below: A 50-mm cannon armed Me-410 dives away from an attack on a USAAF B-17. Note the ruptures in the Fort's wing surface. (USAF)

CHAPTER 17

THE MOVE TO OULTON AND BLICKLING HALL
– THE INVASION

". . . a mass of ships lies chafing
Along the entire seaboard — bidding the trumpet
Sound for battle, . . .

Virgil, The Aeneid

On May 16th — our spy was spot on as to date and place — we crammed F Fox full of kit bags, trunks, spare parts, aircrew and ground crew, and flew to Oulton. Our elapsed time in the air, including the time taken for a farewell beat-up of Sculthorpe and a leisurely circuit at Oulton was 15 minutes. We had scarcely switched off in our new dispersal when a NAAFI wagon rolled up and we were able to have a hot drink and a cookie which, although it looked and tasted like a thin hockey puck, actually had a small bead of genuine jam on it. The wagon was operated by a very attractive young lady, whom I immediately engaged in conversation, and an old lady of about 30 who was in charge. I took the fortunate timing of the NAAFI wagon as a happy augury; and I was right.

I had not been enthusiastic about changing stations again; thus far our luck seemed to have been running bleak, bleaker, bleakest. But in a sudden reversal of fortune we had landed in a veritable Garden of Eden. The officers' living quarters were located in a beautifully wooded area of Blickling Park, a stone's throw from Blickling Hall, a magnificent seventeenth-century Jacobean mansion. This large and beautiful estate belonged to the Marquis of Lothian, but a substantial portion of it had been taken over for the duration by the RAF.

The grounds were steeped in history. Long before the great Hall had been built the property had belonged to Anne Boleyn's father, and the local legend was that the ill-fated young Queen had spent many happy hours on this spot. It went on to suggest that on particularly dark nights one might anticipate a ghostly encounter with her, walking around the lovely little lake bordering the mansion accompanied by her great mastiff — but walking in the somewhat handicapped manner suggested in the old song, i.e. "with 'er 'ead tooked oonderneath 'er arm."

Our officers mess was not in Blickling Hall itself, but in a new building which had been constructed on a little knoll 75 yards away. Nevertheless, parts of the elegant old edifice were reserved for our use. We were entitled, I discovered, to take baths in an upper storey bathroom in Blickling. I made haste to take advantage of this luxury, only to find that the water was always stimulatingly unheated, and approximately ten degrees colder than the North Sea. In a beautifully panelled room on the main floor, Jackie Furner, the new Navigation Leader, and the other classical record buffs, soon began conducting sessions of the station record club.

Oulton had other amenities to offer besides the lovely old mansion and grounds of Blickling. In a nicely treed fork in the road, a hundred yards beyond the high and stately box hedges that led to the main entrance of Blickling Hall, stood a strategically located public house, the Buckinghamshire Arms. The Buck was to see a lot of our aircrew personnel, both American and RAF, although the day after we arrived I chanced upon another pub in Aylsham, the nearby village, which thereafter became our crew's off-duty headquarters. It was called the Anchor and was run by a pleasant woman named Ena Spink. In a separate little room just at the entrance to the beer cellar she had an old phonograph and, treasure of treasures, a pile of Bing Crosby records. To top it off, as if her friendly presence and the Bing Crosby records weren't enough, Ena usually had a supply of the finest bottled beer it was my good fortune to run across the whole time I was in England: Steward & Patteson's Light Ale, brewed in Norwich by a brewmaster who must have been the unrivalled master of his trade. The first evening Stan and I were able to spend at the Anchor was a memorable nostalgia session. We screwed the tops off a fair number of Steward & Patteson's, and kept Bing performing our favourites all night: The Pessimistic Character With The Crabapple Face, Pocketful of Dreams, Ciribiribin, Yodelin' Jive, Ave Maria, Adeste Fideles, Where The Blue Of The Night, etc., etc., etc.

It will be apparent by now that everywhere we went in England we were well treated by the local inhabitants; but for some reason — I suppose because we stayed in that area longer — the people of Oulton and Aylsham made us feel more a part of the community than we had at any of our earlier operational stations. How they suffered us so uncomplainingly is beyond me. God knows they must have wearied of the ubiquitous hordes of uniformed men who established themselves in their favourite spots in the pubs, took over the cinemas, lengthened the queues at the bus stops and in the stores, and filled the tea shops and restaurants. In their place I am sure I should have been heartily sick of the invading swarms, many of them radiating the unfamiliar accents of Canadians, Americans, Australians, New Zealanders, Rhodesians and Indians, to name only the exotic dialects that flowed into the area with the arrival of 214 Squadron. But somehow the great majority of the English carried on as though we were just new families that had settled in the district. They went out of their way to strike up conversations with us in the pubs. Within a month we were on a first name basis and playing darts with half a dozen of the regulars in the Anchor, The Dirty Duck (the aircrew name for The Black Swan) the White Hart and the Buck. They invited us into their homes; and they came to our mess on the rare occasions when the war permitted us to throw a party.

We discovered the first day we were at Oulton that the aerodrome and the surrounding fields were abundantly stocked with Hungarian partridge and pheasants. A little tactical research in our Vauxhall taught us that as long as one sat in the little van with the motor running, they would not fly. We had been issued with Smith & Wesson .38's some months earlier; so I began to travel about with mine tucked in my flying boot. When I could borrow the Flight Commander's van on some pretext or other, I would prowl the perimeter track for 15 minutes stalking a covey of Hungarians. When we had collected a few, we would take them down to Ena Spink at the Anchor. A day later she would have us down and we would all share a royal feast prepared in her kitchen. All in all, we found the Oulton-Aylsham district a highly congenial one.

If I may modify the chronological order of events to a minor degree while dealing with Blickling and its surrounding area, I should mention that a little later on we were visited at Blickling by a troop of actors and actresses making the movie "The Wicked Lady." The film starred Margaret Lockwood and James Mason, and focused on the career of a wicked young lady and a dashing highwayman in that era when carriages and stagecoaches were the principal form of vehicular traffic on the English roads. I mention this for two reasons: firstly, so that if you see "The Wicked Lady" resurrected as a TV movie, which still happens from time to time, you will watch it and catch a glimpse of the surroundings of Blickling Hall and its lovely little lake — Margaret Lockwood is shown there in an early scene. Secondly, you will see a rather ornate old stagecoach which figures in the highwayman's story — and, for a few lines only, in mine.

That stage was parked for a few days just outside our officers mess, where it remained until a group of irresponsible Canadians and Americans began making use of it one night — without the benefit of a team of horses. With a little imagination we transported it 5,000 miles; with a little more it became the Wells Fargo Express, half an hour behind schedule on the run to Dodge City. Half a dozen well lubricated aircrew got hold of the tongue and the door handles and began propelling the venerable looking vehicle at a remarkable speed around the little knoll, then down towards the Buck. I was up top riding shotgun with an American navigator, and urging the horses on to greater efforts, when the producer suddenly burst from the mess and turned pale at the prospect of his rather delicately fashioned replica being battered into kindling. Before we even had a chance to run off our planned encounter with some American aircrew Indians, who were lurking at the Buck and awaiting our arrival at the more realistic pace our horses could muster on the incline, the producer testily commandeered his property and put a stop to the exercise. He had his precious stagecoach (the replacement value of which was probably beyond our wildest estimates) moved to safer storage forthwith.

Undaunted, we turned our ten gallon hats back into wedge caps and returned in high fettle to the mess, where Margaret Lockwood was holding court at the bar, and being stared at by every officer from the Group Captain on down. I rise to remark that Margaret Lockwood was worth staring at; yea and verily a real smasher. So captivating was the Wicked Lady that I cannot truthfully say whether James Mason was beside her at the bar or not. I suppose he must have been, but I do not remember seeing him, and I would wager that none of the men present, except possibly the padre, could have testified reliably the next morning on the issue of his presence. Regretably, Miss Lockwood's visit was of short duration. The only people not sorry to see her depart were our WAAF officers, who had fared poorly in the presence of big league competition.

On May 18th, with little flying in prospect, the Wingco apparently decided about noon that the whole squadron would turn Bolshy by nightfall if he didn't organize some sort of activity to keep us occupied that afternoon, something strenuous, to keep everybody in the old press-on, never-say-die frame of mind. Having momentarily forgotten his obsession with frenetic action as the great morale builder, I had already mapped out an afternoon of mouth-breathing on my cot, to be followed by an evening at the Anchor with Crosby, a few Steward & Patteson's, and some guests. But McGlinn did not consult. His new scheme was an escape exercise.

He told us that immediately after lunch we would be trucked to a spot some five or six miles from Blickling Hall and turned loose. From that point we would have to make our way back to camp across country, keeping off the roads. The Service Police would be playing the part of the Germans, patrolling the roads on motorcycles trying to catch us. If they spotted us near a road they would take us in charge and ship us back to the starting place; so it behooved us to move warily if we wanted to be back in the mess that night for dinner.

I was appalled at what this insane conception might do to my plans for the evening, since I had arranged for the two NAAFI girls to meet me and Stan in the Anchor. (I had been advised by the younger one, the one I had set my cap for, that she would venture out only on a team effort with her friend, and it had taken some strenuous salesmanship on my part before Stan had reluctantly gone above and beyond the call by agreeing to squire the older damsel.) McGlinn, with this incredible new morale-builder, could jeopardize the whole carefully arranged plan. I indulged in a little cerebration, then made a brief detour to the MT section before lunch.

At one o'clock we piled into the waiting trucks, and in short order were rattled and bumped to a point beyond Cawston, where everyone tumbled out and listened once more as the Wingco gave us our marching orders. My crew, now in possession of some intelligence to which the Wing Commander was not privy, watched McGlinn and Bill Day, our Flight Commander, strike off manfully at the head of the troops. This cost Bill Day more than the Wingco knew, for Bill had bad feet, and for him five or six miles across open country was cruel and unusual punishment that would put him in a savage frame of mind. We gradually separated ourselves from the main group and angled off to the right towards a sheltering copse, pulling up there for five minutes while the bulk of the warriors toiled up the rise ahead of us then disappeared from view. When everyone was out of sight, we hustled back to the road a couple of hundred yards from where we had first left the transport. There, to no one's surprise, we found a truck waiting for us. We climbed in and pulled the conveniently spread tarp over us, and in 15 minutes were back at our quarters. There remained only the quid pro quo: my delivery of a carton of 300 Export cigarettes, as promised, to the driver.

I had a little sleep, wrote a couple of letters, freshened up, and changed into my best serge. Then, in a contemplative fashion and a tranquil frame of mind, I strolled to the mess. I was enjoying a pint with J. B. when Bill Day came in, about 5:30, flushed and sweaty, and limping as though his feet were smoking. He looked suspiciously at me, then at J. B., noting that we were not in battledress, and that we were looking remarkably fresh.

"Where in the hell did you guys get to?" he inquired. "I didn't see you buggers anywhere on that cross-country."

"Oh, we figured all the SP's would be riding back and forth on the Cawston Road," I said, "so we struck south over to Eastgate, then came home through Marsham and Aylsham. It was nice easy walking that way." (It was also about ten miles, which Bill Day well knew.)

"The hell you went to Marsham," Bill growled. "How long you been in the mess?"

"Just got here this minute," I said, grinning.

Bill knew a cock and bull story when it was served with ice on the half-shell, but he hadn't any intention of trying to make an issue out of the incident. He merely snorted, to ensure that we knew that he knew that we were spreading the well-known substance rather liberally, and tottered off to elevate his tortured feet. Had there been some way for Bill to part company with the Wingco without arousing his suspicions, he would have been the first one organizing a ride.

As though to balance the scales of justice, our evening at the Anchor proved a disaster. The young lady I was entertaining took a leaf out of someone else's book and became very ill, to the point where, when we headed for home, we had to prop her on her bicycle and wheel her practically the whole way. Since she lived a good five miles from Aylsham, this long and dreary exercise more than made up for the one we had evaded earlier that afternoon. Next we had to see her chaperone home, and she lived a further mile or two off in the fen country. By the time we had cycled back to the aerodrome, Stan and I had decided that the NAAFI was not our best bet for female companionship at Oulton. To top it off, I discovered in the morning that my mates in our Nissen hut, "Canada House," had pinned a huge picture of Frank Sinatra over my bed while I was out. From the intense astonishment they expressed over the incident, I suspected Puterbough and Rolly Harrison.

On May 19th we flew with Main Force in an attack on the railway yards at Le Mans. In the early stages of the trip our number four engine began to act up, adding to the hundred and one regularly recurring worries that were a normal part of every operation. We nursed it along for a couple of hours at reduced power, but eventually it began to overheat even while being thus favoured, and Bill had to feather it. We had just cleared the target and were still a long, long way from Blickling Hall; but F Fox simply raised her voice, droning a little more imperiously on the remaining three engines, and, working up a bit of a sweat, carried us safely home. Five hours after leaving our dispersal we taxied gratefully back into it.

214 Squadron went on ops again the night of May 23-24, but our

crew was not on the battle order. At breakfast next morning we learned that we had lost our first Fortress. A cheerful young Australian, Pilot Officer Hockley, and his crew, had failed to return.

On June 1st the Americans launched their first radar counter-measures flight from Oulton. Captain Paris, whose temporary command of the Americans lapsed with the arrival of Colonel Scott, captained one of the crews participating. The security on the station had been so tight that I hadn't even been aware that the Americans were planning daylight operations of this type. They had scrupulously avoided talking to us about what we were doing, and we were equally careful to stay away from anything confidential when we were talking shop with them. Probably the only man on the station who knew exactly what both groups were doing was Flight Lieutenant Collins, Special Signals Leader to both Squadrons.

For the next few days we busied ourselves doing air-sea firing and two or three fighter affiliation exercises, with Mosquitoes doing the simulated attacks.

On the morning of June 5th I was in the Flight Commander's office when the expected phone call from Group came through. He passed the word along quickly: there was a war on, the Wing Commander and both Flight Commanders were on the battle order, as were my crew and the crew of Cam Lye, a New Zealand pilot. The fact that the Wing Commander had put himself at the head of the battle order was a clear indication in itself that the trip was something special. What additional significance the presence of both Flight Commanders had we could only guess. Our guess was that we were going to be in on the invasion.

At briefing, just before the curtains were parted to reveal the greatest secret of the war, the quickened pulse and respiration of everyone there, each one of them seasoned aircrew, would probably have provided a medical man with the material for an interesting paper on the effects of excitement, anticipation, and intense curiosity, combined with the normal stress associated with flying on operations.

The enormous weight of the attack to be delivered by the RAF that night surprised even us. Bomber Command, the Intelligence Officer announced dramatically, was going to pound five strategically located German heavy coastal batteries with close to 6,000 tons of high explosives. Without his saying so, we knew that the attack would be executed only a short time before the Allied infantry steamed into the area interdicted by those guns and launched their assault across the Normandy beaches. This was by far the heaviest tonnage that I had ever heard predicted for one operation.

Five Fortresses of 214 Squadron, together with a force of about three times as many Lancasters, were to establish a strong patrol line some 80 or 90 miles northeast of the beaches, protecting the left flank of the great assault from aerial interference. We would be dropping window continuously, to maintain the threat of other heavy bomber forces thrusting inland, and blanketing with a continuous and impenerable curtain of jamming every channel of communication used by the German night fighters.

As we left England in F Fox to take our station, we knew that beneath us in the darkness the tremendous drama was beginning to unfold, as thousands of ships ploughed the choppy water converging silently and inexorably on the Normandy shoreline. We steered for our appointed patrol line, situated just north and east of Dieppe, and began our run inland almost perpendicular to the coastline. We were flying well above the Lancasters, at 27,000 feet, and our orders called for us to window and carry the jamming barrier inland some 80 or 90 miles.

The outside air temperature at our altitude was 57 degrees below zero Fahrenheit, and when we had flown only a short distance along the first leg we noticed that we had begun to leave very obvious condensation trails behind us, a dead giveaway for stalking night fighters, who could ignore their window-choked AI if they got into the area and spotted the flaring white plume. Our patrol line ran roughly parallel with the line of the Somme, which lay 10 or 15 miles further off to the northeast. On the inbound legs our ground speed was extremely high because of the hundred mile an hour westerly wind at that altitude; but each time we came to the end of our beat and turned to make our way back to the starting point, the process reversed itself, and we were slowed to a crawl, stretching the outbound legs interminably.

Our orders were to patrol our lengthy beat eight times, (counting the inbound and outbound legs separately); so, for several hours we plied back and forth in the darkness, windowing and jamming for all we were worth. As we completed our fifth leg and reversed course for the French coast, Bill and I spotted, just above us, the clear vapour trail of a fighter, undoubtedly drawn by his AI radar to the maelstrom of window echoes we were sowing. My thoughts, which had strayed several times to the hazards facing the infantry approaching the beaches, snapped back to our own situation; like the fighter, we were still leaving our spoor behind in the form of the snowy white, tell-tale vapour emissions. But, unlike him, we did not possess a concentrated clutch of cannons and machine guns, or the power to add over a hundred miles an hour to our straight-and-level cruising speed any time we chose. Our gunners searched with newly-refreshed vigilance, for the fighter's revealing track was fresh and undissipated. He was close by. The strain mounted as everyone braced himself for a suddenly blurted sighting report. We flew on warily. The trail gradually diverged, ran off to starboard, and was lost.

On the last leg, we began to descend toward the coast, and immediately encountered the heaviest icing we had flown into since the night the oil coolers and air intakes of our Stirling had been jammed. In a few minutes my forward view was cut off completely as a two-inch layer of clear ice built up on the windscreen. Our rate of descent increased markedly, but F Fox never missed a beat. I kept making small, jerky movements on the controls to keep them from jamming, and in a short time we passed through the abnormal condition and the rush of drier air began eating the ice away. In about ten or fifteen minutes, while we still had lots of altitude, I could see again. Prior to this welcome improvement our only consolation had been the thought that any fighter near us would probably have encountered the same problem.

We left the French coast behind, continuing our descent, and headed back towards England. It was not yet daylight, but the darkness had begun to soften. Suddenly we saw a sight that brought a lump into my throat.

A tremendous, awesome aerial armada was passing us in extended formation a mile or two on our left side — not bombers, but C-47's: an airborne army. They were going in. We were coming out. For a long minute I watched them sailing silently onward to their date with destiny. I thought of the men squatting nervously inside and felt like a slacker. After five or six hours in the air we were on our way home, heading back to a good breakfast and a clean bed. They were only a quarter of an hour away from going in by parachute or glider — to face what? We flew in silence for some time.

After six hours and 25 minutes in the air we landed at Oulton, and shortly made our way up to the parachute section, and then interrogation. When we had finished a particularly detailed questioning on our participation, I glanced around the room to see if I could see the Wingco. I knew he was back; I had inquired and the WAAF driving the crew bus had told me that everyone was back. I asked the Intelligence Officer where the Wingco was.

"Oh, didn't you hear?" he said in surprise; "they shot down a fighter, a Messerschmitt 410. The Wingco and his crew are throwing a party in the mess."

"What do you mean?," I said, not sure that I fully understood.

"Right now, they're at it now!" he laughed. "They were so tickled at getting the fighter, they left a few minutes early and came home like a shot. Beat all the rest of you here."

Since the commoner result by far in these grossly unequal night combats was the loss of the bomber and its whole crew, we too considered that the occasion warranted a celebration, particularly since it flowed directly from the launching of our long awaited invasion. I wondered if the German night fighter had been the one whose con trails we had spotted. By the fortunes of war he had not picked the easiest target in the area. Any of the Lancasters, with their light .303 calibre armament, would have been less prickly targets than a Fortress, with its point fives and extra gun positions; and of the five Fortresses he had found the one with the squadron Gunnery Leader manning the tail turret. So be it; he had delivered his attack — and now the intended victims were throwing a party, led by their pilot.

This was the second time, and the second time only, that I had known McGlinn to unbend to this extent. Once before, in the bar, I had witnessed the phenomenon. (It was accepted protocol in our mess for a junior officer entering the bar to approach the senior officer present and ask if he could bring him something. Usually the senior officer would have a drink on the go and would decline with thanks; but it was a nice custom, which I favoured.) On the occasion in question I had gone into the bar, looked about to see who the senior officer was, and noticed Wing Commander McGlinn standing by himself. I marched over.

"Can I get you something from the bar, sir?" I said.

He glanced at his nearly empty glass. "Yes, as a matter of fact you can, Murray. I'll have a half of bitter."

I left on my errand, somewhat surprised. It was one of the few times I had known him to accept a drink, and the very first time he had ever called me by my Christian name. I brought him the drink, said "Cheers", and prepared to leave him to his reverie. Before I could turn away he spoke.

"It's a special occasion tonight, Murray," he said, with the suggestion of a smile; "it's my birthday."

"Well, good show; many happy returns, sir", I said, hoisting my pint for another perfunctory sip. I sensed he was making an effort to overcome the substantial barrier of rank and age between us, and mumbled some inane remark about anniversaries just to keep the spark of conversation alive.

"How old do you think I am," he asked unexpectedly, looking me straight in the eye.

I gave myself two or three seconds, sizing up my man carefully, then delivered a verdict based as much on demeanour and bearing as on the commoner criteria: "Forty?"

He seemed surprised with my estimate. "I'm 28," he said; and it was my turn to be surprised, for I had not been joking. His normally stiff manner made one think of him as a much older man.

Now here was McGlinn throwing a party at five o'clock in the morning. The thought crossed my mind that this boy was changing. A few weeks later I heard that he had climaxed a rather quiet affair in the mess by producing his revolver and shooting out several lights —

a finale which had emptied the mess in record time. But this departure from accepted standards I cannot personally vouch for; indeed I find it hard to credit, because it came from a source who swore solemnly that at the same time he himself had been riding his motorcycle around in tight and thundering circles directly in front of the bar. Mind you, there were some strange looking tracks on the mess floor at breakfast time next morning; there were some missing lights; there was some broken glass.

We went to London for five or six days leave the Friday after the invasion, returning on an early morning train as the first heavy concentrations of buzz bombs were falling on London. We had been told nothing about them up to this point. I remember standing uneasily on the platform in the railway station, listening to the sporadic crash of their heavy explosions against the continuous symphony of our barking guns, and watching little panes of glass in the lofty roof of the station being knocked out by bits of spent flak. Jack Phillips came marching up the platform to join us.

"Say, Skipper," he twanged in his Australian accent, his voice betraying wonderment, "you know what they're saying? These things are pilotless planes!"

"Yes Jack," I said with pitying glance and heavy sarcasm, "and if you look up there through those holes you'll see Buck Rogers and Killer Kane chasing each other in their space belts, and loosing off their bloody rocket pistols."

CHAPTER 18

GELSENKIRCHEN

Now, gallant Saxon, hold thine own!
No maiden's hand is round thee thrown!
That desperate grasp thy frame might feel
Through bars of brass and triple steel!

The Lady of the Lake.   Sir *Walter Scott*

Stan was highly indignant upon our return from leave when he found that the armourers had been instructed to remove the slabs of half-inch armour plate from behind the wireless operators' seats. The efforts I expended trying to console him — by pointing out that they were leaving it behind the seats of the pilots, men whose lives were infinitely more valuable than those of wireless operators — were not appreciated.

I lost another good friend a day or two after we got back, the night of June 16-17. Doug Cameron (F/O Douglas Newlands Cameron J-26595) had been the pilot of a Halifax of 640 Squadron which took off from Leconfield the night of June 16th to carry out a bombing attack on the oil plant at Sterkrade, a suburb of Essen. On the return journey his Halifax was shot down at Spijk, near Lobith, Holland, and the entire crew killed. Doug had been a friend and classmate of mine at Gordon Bell, and had chummed around with me and Rod Dunphy. It had been Doug who had urged me to look up his attractive former date, Joyce Wright, when I left Macleod to go to Edmonton ITS; and when, on my embarkation leave, I had gone to visit the family in Portage la Prairie, Doug Cameron had been the last man to shake my hand as I was leaving town.

On June 18th we got in our first flight since the night of the invasion. It was a very brief air test, and I record it only because I was accompanied by F/O Gilbert at the time. Johnny Gilbert was a popular pilot on the Squadron, despite the fact that he wore his blond hair considerably longer than the regulations prescribed, and at times affected an effeminate attitude. Amongst ourselves we referred to him as Section Officer Gilbert, Section Officer being the rank corresponding to his in the WAAF.

Johnny had an amusing way, when he was projecting his effeminate air, of mispronouncing his words so as to heighten the impression he was striving to create. Frequently, for example, where a "sh" sound was required, he pronounced it as a double "s" and gave it prolonged sibilance. To illustrate: once, when he and I drew the assignment of giving two novice pilots their initial dual on Fortresses, we decided that the fairest way of deciding who was to be stuck with whom was for each of us simply to pick one of the two log books reposing on the Flight Commander's desk, without first looking into them to see what experience the two student pilots had accumulated. We each chose a book, and Johnny, knowing that any unfavourable endorsements would be found at the rear, speedily flipped to the back of his, then crowed excitedly in a rising inflection as he saw the red stamp: "Not Profissient?"

Being a pretty volatile character, Johnny unwittingly made himself a natural target for practical jokes. He got married while he was at Oulton, and had scarcely returned from the nuptials when some sadist obtained access to a broken teleprinter sitting in the Met section awaiting repair, and laboriously manufactured a most authentic looking set of orders, complete with spurious code group prefixes and so forth, posting the new bridegroom to Burma forthwith. George Wright's WAAF secretary was persuaded to put it in an official envelope, plaster it with her rubber stamp a few times, and deliver it, hotfoot, to Gilbert in the Flight office. Johnny's performance left nothing to be desired, as he alternated between gasps of utter despair and bouts of energetically masculine cursing.

This day, as Johnny Gilbert and I flew together, I was reminded of an earlier joint exercise I had done, and Johnny and I laughed about it as I reminded him of the fighter affiliation practice I had done one afternoon with Jeff Bray and his gunners. My crew had performed the exercise first, with me at the controls. Then Jeff moved into the left-hand seat, and his gunners took over the turrets. The Mosquito continued to simulate attacks upon us, using the form of approach and closing speed that a night fighter would be likely to employ. Jeff Bray's crew and mine were friendly rivals, and after a particularly good rendition of the prescribed patter by one of his gunners, Jeff would turn to me and say, "Be sure your boys are getting all this, Murray." The last exercise of the day was carried out by his mid-upper gunner, who gave the spiel in flawless form as the Mosquito began to overhaul us on our right side:

"Fighter fighter . . . starboard quarter level . . . 1,000 yards . . . closing . . . 800 yards . . . closing . . . 700 yards . . . prepare to corkscrew starboard . . . Corkscrew Go!"

I had had to admit that Jeff's gunners had performed very well; indeed, their impeccably unflustered prose through the gyrations of the violent evasive action would have been the envy of any BBC announcer reading an obituary.

Jeff and his crew went to Frankfurt the next night, and I learned at breakfast the following morning, before I saw Jeff, that they had had a rough trip. Over the target they had been attacked and shot up by cat's eye fighters, and Jeff had been forced to fly home from Frankfurt with his goggles down, minus his windscreen and most of his instruments. I saw him that afternoon and approached to get the story firsthand. Jeff's face twisted into a wry grin as he responded to my query:

"The first thing I should say, Murray, is that it was not *exactly* as polished as the exercise you and I practised the other day. We were just clearing the target; everything was very quiet and tense, and all at once instead of the 'fighter . . . fighter . . . port quarter . . . down . . . 600 yards . . .' I heard a shout like: 'THERECOMESSONOFABITCH. GETTIM . . . DADADADADADADA.' "

Despite the hasty improvisation, Jeff's gunners had blown up one of the three attackers, a Focke Wulf 190, in mid-air. Johnny Gilbert and I laughed again over Jeff's description of the sudden incoherent shout drowned in two-way gunfire.

On June 21st I learned in the morning that there was to be a war on that night, and that Peden's crew were on the battle order in F Fox. We went out and did our air test immediately. It was on this occasion, as I recall, that we were standing waiting for the crew bus when it pulled up at the dispersal next to ours and we saw Johnny Corke and his crew disembarking to climb aboard their aircraft. Johnny's engineer was a chap named Barber, and he was known to the ground crew to be meticulous in his requirements. One of the erks obviously thought him too damned meticulous. As he saw Barber alight from the rear step of the crew bus, I heard him call in a low voice to one of his mates: "Oi . . . 'ere comes Ali Barber and the 40 snags."

At 4:30 that afternoon we sat in the briefing room and watched in the usual strained silence as the curtains swished noisily open to reveal route tapes running to Gelsenkirchen, in the heart of the Ruhr. Someone in the crew muttered: "Christ, Happy Valley." I responded with supreme confidence, "Piece of cake." Our target was the Nordstern oil plant in Gelsenkirchen.

I really did not feel the confidence I had expressed as I looked at the big target map in front of us. Heavy flak areas on that map were marked with red circles. The Ruhr was one solid turnip-shaped blotch of red, many inches wide, and a foot long on our map; and it had a deep belt of searchlights all round it, denoted by a continuous broad blue border framing the whole blob. Ruhr trips had one good quality: they were short. That was their only redeeming feature. Happy Valley was probably the most heavily defended industrial area in Europe. Apart from the hundreds of flak batteries and the dense concentrations of searchlights, it was well protected by swarms of night fighters, and it was extremely difficult on such a short trip to mislead them by routing as to the intended target area. When I said "piece of cake" it was just so much whistling past the graveyard; but I was to be reminded of it later.

We had skirted the fringes of the Ruhr's defences on more than one occasion, had seen that seemingly impenetrable palisade of searchlights, and knew only too well that to run through the heaviest belt of those defences — Gelsenkirchen was like another suburb of Essen — was going to be no picnic. Main Force was actually going to split as it approached our target area and attack the oil plants at nearby Wesseling and Scholven-Buer as well[1]. All these attacks, and those delivered by the RAF in the days immediately preceding, were part of the co-ordinated allied bombing campaign against German oil plants initiated some weeks earlier, with gratifying success, by the Americans. These strikes were hurting the Germans, and their fighters were reacting accordingly.

Takeoff was late these summer nights. It was just after 11:00 PM when the Aldis lamp's green flash sent F Fox roaring down the flarepath. We crossed the coast outbound near Cromer, and climbed steadily to 22,000 feet in the clear night air.

Once we hit the enemy coast, the ever-present strain mounted rapidly to the higher level that was the concomitant of being in the enemy's ball park, blindfolded by night. I always waited tensely for the first burst of flak to stab at us, hoping it would not be too close. Once that first burst came up, and I recovered from the violent start that the sudden flash in the darkness always caused, I breathed a little easier and began the game that every pilot had to play, changing altitude, course, and speed, to throw off the next burst, counting the seconds carefully and watching to see where that next burst came; then varying the course again, being careful not to "balance" the pattern

---

1. See: Sir Charles Webster and Noble Frankland, *"The Strategic Air Offensive Against Germany, 1939-45* Vol. III, page 161, Her Majesty's Stationery Office.

with a nice symmetrical correction to the other side. The German predictors were quick to average symmetrical evasions and fire a burst at the appropriate moment along the mean track.

The human system is incredibly adaptive, and what constantly surprised me, when I thought about it in safety on the ground, was how matter of factly we could play this deadly game, and even derive a certain nervous satisfaction from it, watching shells burst two or three hundred yards away, at the very spot you would have been had you not changed course as the gunners were launching their speeding projectiles on their way.

We thrust inland, threading our way through the welcoming flak, and Stan soon began reporting contacts on Monica, the radar set which he monitored in his cabin. It became apparent that Sam had positioned us well towards the middle of the bomber stream, and that the concentration of Lancasters was dense. In a way I hated these frequent radar contacts, for we always had to assume that they might be night fighters, and everyone strained unconsciously until one of the gunners came on intercom with something like: "Ah, I've got him, Skipper, it's a Lanc. He's three or four hundred yards dead astern and down just a little bit." On black nights they could not be seen at anything like that range. This night they could be spotted while they were well away from us. We had a second concern, however, even after the gunners identified the contact as a Lanc. The question uppermost in our minds then was: has he seen and identified us? The Fortress, of course, had a prominent single fin. Most of the aircraft with a single fin and rudder flying the night skies were German, and we wanted no "friendly" machine gun bullets put into us by mistake. If the friendly aircraft was slightly above you, the waiting period until you parted company was extremely tense, since it was easier for you to spot him than vice versa.

At a point about 20 minutes from the target we began to approach an outlying belt of searchlights which stood before us on either side of our intended track in two great cones. I feared and hated those baleful blinding lights more than anything else the Germans used against us. While in themselves they seldom caused death — although there were reported cases of pilots, particularly at low level, apparently becoming completely disoriented by their glaring beams and diving into the earth — they were all too often the harbinger of death. A pilot trapped in a large cone had little chance of escape. For long seconds on end the dazzling glare would render him helpless, spotlighting him as the target and making it almost impossible for him to see his instruments and maintain any sense of equilibrium. Meanwhile the searchlights' accomplices, the heavy guns, would hurl up shells in streams, and all too frequently the aircraft would explode or begin a crazy, smoking dive to the ground.

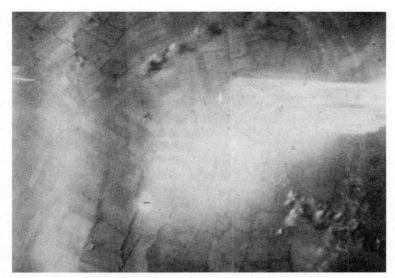

Above: This rather confusing picture is actually a very good photograph taken from the author's aircraft on the night of January 4/5, 1944. The bright traces are from flares and target markers.

Below: A high altitude photograph of the emergency aerodrome at Woodbridge (lower left). The extra wide, long runway (compare with standard size at upper right) was designed to cope with badly damaged aircraft making emergency landings. The author's arrival here was almost routine for Woodbridge. (IWM)

Above: A rare shot of a 'Jostle' transmitter (suspended from the back of the truck). On the right is F/L Collins, Special Signals Officer at Oulton. **(IWM)**

Below: The pilot of this Ju 88 landed by mistake at the RAF's emergency aerodrome at Woodbridge on July 13, 1944. This windfall provided the Allies with the secrets of the German's new SN-2 Airborne Interception (AI) radar (antenna array on fuselage nose) and its 'Flensburg' homing device (antennae on the outer wing panels). **(IWM)**

Marshal of the Royal Air Force, Sir Arthur T. Harris, B.T., G.C.B., O.B.E., A.F.C., L.L.D., Air Officer Commanding-in-Chief Bomber Command from February 1942 until the end of the war.

(IWM)

F/L Geoff Liles (front and centre) with his crew in front of their 214 Sqn. Flying Fortress 'Q-Queenie'.
(Geoff Liles)

A rare close-up shot of 'Piperack' which countered the Germans' SN-2 AI radar. The gunner in this rear turret of a 214 Sqn. Flying Fortress is Flight Sergeant Budge of F/L Liles' crew.
(Geoff Liles)

Left: F/Sgts Tom Butler (left) and Charlie Lewis, waist gunners on Flying Fortress 'E-Easy' of 214 Sqn. The chute used for dispensing 'Window' (radar jamming chaff) is visible at lower right.

(Tom Butler)

Below: Two gunners of Geoff Liles' crew pose between the aerials of 'Piperack' after cleaning the guns of their Flying Fortress. (Geoff Liles)

Above left: General Adolf Galland in front of his Bf 109 during the time when he was an operational fighter squadron commander.
(General Galland)

Above right: 'Nae man can tether time or tide; The hour approaches . . . Tom Maun Ride.'
A Lancaster crew piles out of the crew bus to begin their pre-flight checks. (RCAF)

Below: A Canadian Flight Engineer checks the oleo legs and the tires on his Lancaster.
(RCAF)

A last cigarette; then fasten parachute straps and get aboard. (RCAF)

Below: A Lancaster awaits the departure time as night falls.

Above: The strain eases after a rum-spiked coffee at interrogation. A Pathfinder crew at Gransden Lodge report. Standing at centre is F/O Jack Astbury of Portage la Prairie.

(RCAF)

Below: Following the interrogation is the usual treat of operational crews—a fried egg for breakfast, and a bottle of beer. Jack Astbury is at the head of the table. (RCAF)

As I watched these two cones warily, I noticed that they were remaining stationary for 30 seconds or so at a time, leaving a corridor between them, then abruptly moving together and establishing one giant cone right in the middle of what had been the safe passage. Twice I saw them do this, and twice when they came together in the centre they trapped a Lancaster attempting to slip by. Each time the Lancaster was destroyed. It was an unnerving spectacle to watch, particularly when your turn to run the gauntlet was fast approaching. It was Hobson's choice with a vengeance. You could not fly straight into either cone while they were standing separate; that was committing suicide; and detouring all the way around the outside would have involved a major departure from the prescribed track and thrown out the aircraft's time over target by several minutes. You had no practicable alternative but to take the black void between the two cones, knowing that the lights would swing inward and illuminate some part of the safe passage every few seconds. You headed for the open spot and prayed that you would get through. I chose a spot slightly right of centre and sweated. We were lucky.

Hardly had we cleared this hurdle than Stan came on the intercom again to report another contact, a close one. This time we were not left long in doubt. In less than a minute our rear gunner, Johnny Walker, spotted an aircraft directly astern at a range of about 300 yards. This was approximately where Stan had predicted the contact would be found, but it was another 30 seconds or more before Johnny Walker and Bert Lester confirmed that it was a Lancaster. Then, for a minute or two, we seemed to be holding the same relative positions. I was reluctant to weave away if I could avoid it, since Sam's navigation thus far had kept us dead on track, and I preferred not to mar his handiwork. However, after another minute, Johnny Walker reported that the Lanc had closed further and was now just about 200 yards astern.

"If he comes any closer, any closer at all," I said, "let me know, and I'll weave off to the side a bit."

It was at that precise moment that Fate dealt us a card off the bottom of the deck.

The Lancaster abruptly stood on its wingtip and dived away. Directly behind it, and now directly behind us and in perfect firing position, was a Messerschmitt 410 which had been stalking the Lancaster.

As Johnny Walker shouted a warning and began firing himself, the air around us was instantly filled with white flaming shells that flashed past our windows with horrifying speed, and F Fox shuddered heavily to the pounding of a hail of close range cannon fire. Through the back of my seat I felt a rapid series of staccato blows that jarred us like the strokes of a wild triphammer.

I had instinctively thrust the control column forward and twisted the ailerons to dive into a violent corkscrew; but in the second it took to initiate the manoeuvre, F Fox absorbed heavy punishment from the torrent of shells the Messerschmitt's cannons poured into us. Before I had 15 degrees of bank on, the starboard inner engine burst into great leaping flames and the intercom went dead.

As we rolled into the dive to starboard, the heavy vibration of a long burst fired from our mid-upper turret shook the instrument panel in front of me into a great blur; it was as though the instruments were mounted on the sounding strings of some giant lyre. With remarkable presence of mind, Bill ignored the tracers flying around his head, and moved to feather number three at the same time as he activated its fire extinguisher. I was dimly aware of his actions, and of the frightening flames that gushed out of the engine and were snatched back across the cowling as I rolled to begin my climb to port.

The firing ceased as suddenly as it had started — on both sides. With some difficulty I levelled up, after a fashion, and tried to take stock of the situation. F Fox was sickeningly sluggish and unresponsive; but for the next two minutes that problem paled into insignificance as I struggled to stop her swift descent, and watched Bill fight to get number three feathered so that we could get the fire under control. We had been told frequently that a fuel-fed fire, blown against the interior of the wing by the slipstream, could eat right through the main spar in as little as two minutes. If the main spar went, our chances of getting out of the aircraft as it cartwheeled earthward would be remote. Bill was unable to coax the recalcitrant propeller to feather properly, although the blades did rotate to the point where the propeller was turning over at a low speed.

Meantime J. B. had clambered back to find out what had happened in the rear of the aircraft. For all we knew, the four crew members behind the mid-upper might have abandoned the plane — or been killed.

F Fox continued to lose height, and without warning number three began to wind up. In moments it was up past its safe maximum and was overspeeding with a terrifying banshee wail. As it screamed itself into hysteria, the fire, which had been dying down, flared up in all its fury again.

Scared half out of my wits by the flames, and the knowledge that they were only inches away from enough gasoline to blow us into eternity, I tried vainly to remember what one did with an overspeeding propeller. In a moment Bill suggested throttling back the other three, and I strained to pull F Fox's nose up at the same time so that the overspeeding propeller would be carrying a substantial load.

It worked. Like a screaming circular saw suddenly deprived of power the propeller began to slow down, its terrifying note gradually subsiding like some manic thing being quieted. As it sank back below normal speed, we shifted the load onto the other three engines, staring appraisingly at number three and trying to gauge whether that fire would kill us with an explosion. Although it was not extinguished, it had subsided again with the propeller, so I turned my attention momentarily to the task of coaxing F Fox to hold height.

As though cursed with a devilish spirit of its own, number three began to overspeed again. I knew this nerve-wracking phenomenon, with its continually rising crescendo of shrieking sound was a condition which could not long endure. The propeller shaft would let go in a short time, and when that happened, in a Fortress, the propeller from number three would fly into, or perhaps through, the nose or cockpit. Despite the fact that the manoeuvre resulted in a partial stall which then lost us more precious altitude, I had no alternative but to throttle back again, haul the nose up, and try to force some load onto number three. As I did so, the flames were flaring above the cowling once more. The technique worked again, soothing the maddened outcry of the propeller and coaxing its speed back within a range the engine could tolerate. Again F Fox mushed down in a weary stall, the inevitable product of the unnaturally nose-high position coupled with the loss of power. Bill and I bent once more to the task of restoring the power very gradually, so as not to precipitate another runaway, and nursing the weary aircraft into a normal attitude.

As we levelled up, the air around us was suddenly filled with a hail of tracers again, and once again I threw F Fox into a corkscrew. But this time we could only manage a travesty of the prescribed manoeuvre, and we would have died then and there but for the good shooting of Johnny Walker. A Ju 88, drawn by the irresistible sight of fire aboard a wounded prey, had stalked us and closed to finish us off. But the German pilot had reckoned without Johnny Walker. Hollering into the dead intercom in a fruitless attempt to warn me, Johnny drew a careful bead on the German and, in the face of the fighter's overpowering weight of fire, traded lead so accurately that the German was shortly forced to break off.

F Fox had absorbed more punishment in this second combat, although nothing like what she had taken the first time. She had lost even more of her characteristic responsiveness, and her struggle to fend off the clutch of gravity was palpably less successful. Another result of the second attack, however, was that it forced us to dive again, and this in turn had immediately started number three winding up. Once more the fire flared wickedly, ugly tongues of flame visible from a great distance at night, and again we went through our scary exercise, stalling the sluggish aeroplane to get the screaming propeller back under control. The second attack, therefore, inflicted additional structural damage upon us, re-kindled the fire in number three, and cost us altitude we could not afford to give away. It did one other thing: it convinced me that it would be foolhardy to try to make our way through the main flak and searchlight defences over the target in the condition we were in. Night fighters too were clearly in the stream in force. The Ju 88 had picked us up within minutes of the first attack, and I felt it would be simply asking for it to count on escaping from a third attack in our present condition. Although we were now no more than ten minutes away from the target, I coaxed F Fox into a gentle turn and reversed our course.

Bill went forward to get me a proper course from Sam, and again I surveyed the situation with what few crumbs of equanimity I could muster. Our most worrisome problem, apart from the smouldering fire which kept threatening to flare and spread, was the generally precarious performance of the aircraft. Flying on three engines with the fourth propeller properly feathered is one thing. It is quite another doing it with an engine which is windmilling and refuses to feather, and in an aeroplane which has been torn open and battered to the point where its aerodynamic efficiency has been seriously compromised. Pulling an aeroplane through the sky with an engine windmilling is much the same as pushing a stalled car while leaving it in gear. The drag is tremendous, and the net effect is to subtract and waste a substantial amount of your remaining power. When I turned F Fox about, we were down to 15,000 feet, having lost close to 7,000 feet in the two combats and the ensuing struggle with the burning engine. We were still losing height at about 500 - 700 feet per minute, were still without intercom, and were seriously limited as to manoeuvrability.

As Bill and I were setting the remaining three engines to the most power we felt we could call upon them to deliver for a protracted period, and trying to trim the aircraft into the best attitude for its sorry condition, I felt a tap on my shoulder and looked round to see Hembrow, the German-speaking special wireless operator, standing just behind my seat. He looked dishevelled and more than slightly shaken. (In fact he had been slightly wounded, with a cannon splinter in the back of the shoulder.) His terse message registered indelibly on my brain as he raised his voice and called above the noise: "The wireless operator's been hit . . . And I've been hit . . . And we all want to go home."

This trusting message, implying that I could somehow wash out the balance of the exercise, and ordain safe delivery to Blickling Hall despite fire, battle damage, and anything else that might follow, made me feel rather fatherly. I reached back and clapped him lightly on the shoulder and told him everything was okay, that we were heading for home.

Then the first piece of good luck to come our way since takeoff manifested itself — the intercom came back on, although it remained intermittent and undependable. Actually it was not luck as it turned out, but good work by Stan, assisted by J. B. In a few minutes I had some knowledge of what had happened. Stan had been badly wounded, including at least two splinter wounds in the head which caused him to lose a lot of blood and subjected him to a great deal of pain. J. B. had promptly decided that Stan should be given an injection of morphine, and prepared to administer it; but Stan had insisted on struggling to repair the intercom before submitting to the injection. I hoped within the next few minutes to be able to make up my mind as to whether we would be likely to make it back across the North Sea or whether we should bail out and take our chances while we were over land.

It was not to be an easy decision. Time seemed almost to stand still, measured only by the intervals that elapsed between the repeated overspeedings of number three engine, which I came to loathe and fear. Time after time it went through its hellish performance, causing the flames to spring up fiercely again, and forcing us to lose precious height in each stall. I aged ten years, worrying about how long the starboard wing would stay on, and at one point ordered everyone to prepare to abandon the aircraft, so that they would at least have their chest packs on if F Fox came apart in the air. (It was at this juncture that Bill discovered that my chute had disappeared in the jinking.) However, as we neared the coast, I could not defer the decision any longer. I had to make up my mind whether we would try to make it across the North Sea or whether it would be better to have the crew abandon the aircraft, bailing out while we were over land. We had fallen from 22,000 to 6,000 feet by this time, but in the denser air F Fox was now finding her strength again, and had almost ceased losing altitude. I decided the whole crew should try to make it to England, and got Sam to work out a course for Woodbridge, on the coast in Suffolk, one of our three big crash dromes.

Over the water I told Bert to get the proper colours of the period ready for the Very pistol, thinking of our troublesome intercom and radio. Bill and I now felt justified in making a very slight reduction in power to ease the strain on the three good engines, which had laboured nobly but were showing the effort in their cylinder head temperatures. After a further tense wait the English coast appeared ahead, and in a short time we were approaching Woodbridge. Sam had brought us to it as straight as a homing pigeon, and my biggest remaining worry, or so

I thought, was that at any moment the main spar on the starboard side might let go.

I called the tower repeatedly as we approached, and although our reception of their response was extremely disjointed, I gathered that we were cleared to land. To make doubly sure, I told Bert to fire the colours of the period several times and follow with a signal indicating that we had wounded aboard. I flashed the appropriate letters on our recognition light, then began to concentrate on the all-important task of getting F Fox safely on the ground.

I kept remembering that the main spar behind number three had been subjected to the effects of what amounted to a giant blow torch playing on it intermittently for an hour and three-quarters, and as I pictured its possible condition in my mind's eye, I was at pains to avoid increasing the wing loading with any steep turns in the circuit, much as I wanted to get on the ground and far away from the 2,000 gallons of gasoline and that seemingly unquenchable fire smouldering a foot or two in front of it. I offered up a silent prayer that the under-carriage would come down when I pressed the selector. F Fox had absorbed a lot of cannon shells — I had felt them striking home — and there was a distinct possibility that the electric motors or cables which activated the undercarriage mechanism had been damaged. I had not dared try it earlier, seeking to avoid both the additional drag and the vibration it produced swinging into place.

Now was the time to find out. Bert fired another signal from the Very pistol, and after ordering the rest of the crew, with the exception of Bill, to take Stan and get into their crash positions, I turned gently toward the flarepath and flipped the undercarriage selector switch. Immediately I could hear the whine and then feel the reassuring drag effect indicating that the wheels were dropping out of their nacelles; the undercarriage motors seemed to be okay. In a few moments the green light on the instrument panel glowed: undercarriage down and locked. I stole a glance away from the flare path and peered into the gloom below the inboard engine nacelle on my side. The port wheel looked all right. Bill was having a more difficult time on his side. The smoke and intermittent showers of sparks made it difficult to see anything in the darkness. But in a few moments he straightened up in his seat and gave me a thumbs-up. I prepared to make the best landing I could.

We touched down very lightly, and for a few brief seconds I began to relax. But our troubles were not over. One of the German fighters had shot our right tire into useless pulp. F Fox vibrated roughly and began sinking lower and lower on her wounded side. I had a terrible vision of the starboard wingtip catching and the aircraft cartwheeling into one final detonation. In a second or two we were down to the hub on the right wheel, and beginning to veer to that side as the hub dragged more and more heavily. I tried to correct the swing with a touch of brake, only to discover that we had no brakes — our hydraulics had been shot out. Immediately I applied a burst of throttle from the starboard outer to see if I could straighten our course that way, but F Fox was beyond responding; she hurtled on, continuing to veer to the right. I sat clutching the control column with both hands and practically bending the rudder bar with my foot as I tried vainly to check the swing with maximum left rudder.

Out of the darkness 50 yards in front of us, the silhouette of a Lancaster suddenly loomed up directly in our path. As I threw my left arm over my face we collided with the other aircraft at 75 miles an hour, severing it completely a few feet to the rear of its mid-upper turret with our right wing. F Fox spun around violently for two or three seconds and shuddered to a halt a short distance further on. Bill and I both snatched at the master switch to cut everything off, then snapped our belts free and turned speedily to open the side windows to escape.

My window jammed. I gripped it fiercely and tugged twice more. It stuck fast. Bill had wrenched his window open and was disappearing through it, so I flung myself to the right side of the cockpit to follow him out. His foot slipped as he thrashed clear, and his heavy flying boot came back into my face like the kick of a Clydesdale. I never even felt it, but twisted through the window like a limbo dancer and sprang rearward from the battered starboard wing like an Olympic athlete.

Fast as Bill and I were, the others had had a few seconds head start and had been covering ground. They had boosted Stan out the rear door and were many yards ahead of us, running for all they were worth. When Bill and I had sprinted 60 or 70 yards I turned for a moment to look at F Fox, and remember thinking that the person who had warned us about the vulnerability of main spars had clearly had no idea of how rugged the Fortress's was. True, the outer 25 feet of F Fox's wing had been splayed open in the violent collision with the Lancaster; but the centre section was still in place and still intact.

I turned to join the other members of the crew, who were now 30 or 40 yards further on. As I panted up to them, I called out to J.B.: "Where's Stan?"

He motioned behind him to a dark bundle lying on the ground. I hurried over and took a look. Stan seemed to me to be unconscious although his eyes were half open. Even in the semi-darkness I could see that his face was as white as parchment and his hair ominously matted.

"Oh the poor bastard . . . he's had it," I said.

This was not an example of my best bedside manner, of course;

had I not been labouring under a considerable strain myself I should not have been so tactless. My sympathy and concern were genuine. (Although rather heavily drugged, Stan was still aware of what was going on, and heard my pessimistic prognosis. It made him mad, he told me later; but not as mad as he got a short time afterwards in the station hospital, when a chap wandered in beside him by mistake, saw Stan, and immediately began to throw up.)

Off to the side another Lancaster, apparently in dire straits, was emulating our performance, firing Very lights as it swung toward the funnel. After our own experience, we kept a wary eye on the Lanc — which also proceeded to swing out of control on landing and head in the general direction of F Fox and the Lancaster we had clobbered.

As the ambulance came hunting for us, the last card of the hand was turned over: the Tannoy gave vent to a strident announcement warning all ground crew to keep clear of the Lancaster we had just cut in half, advising in stentorian tones that it had a 12,000 pound high explosive bomb aboard.

I peered across to where the truncated Lancaster squatted, now pointing skyward at an unnaturally sharp angle, and guessed thankfully that we must have missed the bomb by about two feet as we slashed through the aircraft. The third aircraft had meanwhile piled in a short distance from ours. Shaken, I climbed into the second van and we were speedily borne to sick quarters to see the MO.

If you were involved in a crash, even if you walked — or ran — away from it, the rule was that you had to be given a medical inspection by the MO. In fact, the inspection varied considerably in scope and thoroughness, depending on what had happened and how busy the doctor was. We had to wait some time while they began looking after Stan. When it was my turn, the doctor called me in, looked at me, and said: "Were you hurt?"

"No, not a scratch," I said.

"You may not have a scratch, but you look as though you could use this," he rejoined, pouring what looked like about four ounces of service rum into a graduated beaker. "Toss that off," he said.

I took the medication as directed, and was unable to get any breath for approximately two minutes. But he was a better doctor than this rough-and-ready sounding treatment suggested. In half an hour my incipient case of the shakes — which he had doubtless spotted — was gone.

After everyone had been thus inspected, we went over to the mess hall for our customary reward of bacon and eggs. As I walked toward the steam table, a pilot standing with a small group ahead of us detached himself and came rather uncertainly toward me.

"You the pilot of that Fortress?" he asked.

"Yes I am," I said, "who are you?"

"I'm the pilot of the Lancaster you chopped in half," he said with a little laugh, sticking out his hand. "We were standing underneath the kite when you swung and came heading for us. We had a 12,000 pounder sitting in the bomb bay over our heads. I'll bet we raced out of there faster than you flew in."

While we waited to pick up our food, he told me that they had been attacked by a fighter just before they reached the target. In the course of the combat the fighter had shot out the Lanc's hydraulics, effectively preventing him from opening his bomb doors and getting rid of his load. His crew had been on the ground only a few minutes when they saw our Very lights and watched F Fox come in to land. Like us, they had thought everything was all right when we touched down safely; but in a moment they had realized the peril they were in. I could imagine the thoughts that went through their minds as they saw the lights of F Fox curving through the night towards their huge bomb. I suppose that for ten seconds they were more intensely frightened than I was — difficult as that is to visualize[1].

After we had eaten, we were directed to an empty Nissen hut not too far away. For an hour I lay on a cot vainly trying to relax and get some sleep; but my mind was too full of the night's events. I kept re-living the fire, the fighter attacks, and the crash. Eventually I decided to get up and go for a walk. I rose quietly, taking care not to disturb the others, and tiptoed out the door. Outside, I could see that we were only a few hundred yards from the field, and all at once I felt the urge to go back and see F Fox. I had walked no more than 50 yards when I heard a slight sound and turned to see the rest of the crew strung out behind me in Indian file.

We found F Fox without any trouble. Now she sat peacefully in the grey dawn light, the tumult of her final hours — for one glance told us she would never fly again — all too easy to recapture from her dreadful appearance. Under her wing I sank onto my knees and thanked God for bringing us home alive. No one offered any comment on the Skipper's unusual reverence.

The centre section of the fuselage was riddled with bullet holes, convincing testimony of the German pilots' marksmanship. Twenty or 30 feet of the trailing edge of the starboard wing had been ripped open and the metal pleated into accordion folds. The black rectangles of the self-sealing tanks were visible; indeed the starboard Tokyo tank lay

1. The pilot was PO "Butch" Passant, the Aussie Skipper of Lancaster JB351 of No. 61 Squadron. The whole crew, with one exception, were killed a fortnight later on another target. Dennis Copson, the rear gunner, was wounded in the attack on Gelsenkirchen and was convalescing when his crew went on their last op. The author tracked down both Dennis Copson and Mr. W. G. Francis in 1977, the latter the NCO in charge of the Crash Crew at the scene when F Fox cut Lancaster JB351 in half.

incongruously out on the ground. The cowling of number three engine was blackened and burned, and the engine itself thoroughly charred. One propeller blade, standing vertical, had a sizeable and almost perfectly circular hole punched cleanly through it just above the level of the cowling. The sight of that clean hole through thick steel gave me a new idea of the power of the fighters' cannon shells. An almost ludicrous touch was part of the sorry spectacle: the long, cylindrical master unit of the Lancaster's DR compass hung crazily on our starboard outer propeller, snatched from its mount as our propeller had flailed through the Lancaster's fuselage. After 15 sobering minutes we wended our way back to the Nissen hut.

In response to a message that had gone from Woodbridge control to Oulton Johnny Gilbert arrived later in the morning to fly us home. En route he told us that Johnny Cassan and his crew had gone missing on the Gelsenkirchen raid, and there had been some confusion at Oulton as to which crew had made it back to Woodbridge and which had failed to return. Answering Gilbert's questions, I ran over the highlights of what had happened to us, starting with the trap the first Lancaster had unwittingly sprung on us, and ending with the demolition derby at Woodbridge.

That latter part of our trip is described from a slightly different point of view in Volume III of the official history of the Royal Air Force[1]. At page 264, the author, leading up to the subject with a reference to our three main emergency landing grounds, says:

> The lighted runway in each was some 3,000 yards long and 250 yards wide, and the latest navigational aids and systems of flying control were installed. By June, 1945, 4,120 aircraft had made landings on Woodbridge alone, 1,200 of them by the use of 'FIDO'. A picture of the difficulties and conditions met with is provided by the operational records of this airfield. The date is 22nd June, 1944; the time 0220 hours.
>
> A Lancaster of No. 61 Squadron, with 11,000 lb. of bombs aboard, having been diverted with unserviceable hydraulics after an encounter with night fighters, landed direct on the 'green' flarepath, swung and then came to rest on the south side of the north flarepath. The north and central flarepath lights were extinguished and maintenance personnel rushed to tow the aircraft from the runway. At that moment an RAF Fortress called for permission to land, but did not acknowledge

---

1. Hilary St. G. Saunders, *Royal Air Force* 1939-45, Vol. III, *The Fight Is Won*, published by Her Majesty's Stationery Office.

instructions. Flashing on her identity lights the Fortress touched down on the 'green' flarepath but a burst starboard tyre caused her to swing. The crew of the Lancaster and the maintenance personnel promptly scattered but the swinging Fortress cut the Lancaster in two with its starboard wing. The 'green' flarepath was still clear and the second crash marked with 'Reds'. Immediately afterwards a third aircraft flew low up the flarepath, fired a series of Verey lights, then touched down on the 'green' flarepath when the undercarriage collapsed causing the aircraft to swing to the centre of the runway, finishing 200 yards from the halved Lancaster. This latest and third arrival was also a Lancaster with 11,000 lb. of bombs on board. As this aircraft landed a fourth arrived, again a Lancaster — from No. 57 Squadron — requesting emergency landing, as part of the undercarrige was thought to be unserviceable and the port wing was badly flak-holed. Told to stand-by the pilot replied that his endurance was 15 minutes only. Thereupon the two 10-inch control searchlights, fire tenders and ambulance splotlights were switched on and the incoming pilot was instructed to 'touch down' immediately after passing over the illuminated 'casualties', which instructions were correctly carried out for safe landing. In these four crashes, which occurred in the space of 13 minutes, no one was injured.

I would make only two comments to complement this accurate and well written account. Firstly, the "RAF Fortress" did not acknowledge instructions simply because our damaged equipment rendered them almost unintelligible. Secondly, the pilot and the bombaimer of the Lancaster we cut in half told me specifically that they were carrying a single 12,000-pounder, and, although nothing turns on it, I have adhered to their version in compliance with what in legal circles is referred to as the best evidence rule.

Johnny Gilbert got us home to Oulton in 30 minutes, where we all reported in detail to the Intelligence officer and to the Wingco. McGlinn passed a few kind words on our performance and sent us off for an early lunch and some sleep. Before I left the field, however, I climbed into the crew bus and rode by myself to F Fox's dispersal to see our ground crew. With a heavy heart I told them what had happened to F Fox and explained that she had made her last flight. I thanked them for the care they had taken of their aircraft — for she was theirs as much as ours — and told them, what I firmly believed, that if F Fox had not been on the top line when they handed her over to us the night before, we would never have made it back to England. The boys were pleased that I had come to see them, and while they naturally passed on their congratulations on our successful return, I could see that the loss of the aeroplane they had looked after so conscientiously affected them deeply. According to the Chiefie, it was the first aircraft of theirs that had ever gone missing — a record that only one or two crews on the Squadron could match.

I returned to the Flights and caught a ride down to Blickling for lunch. Stepping into the dining room, I stopped abruptly as I saw the look that came over the face of the WAAF waitress standing at the counter. She gasped, and her features contorted; then she began sobbing, and, hiding her face in her apron, hurried through the door out of sight. I was taken aback, and stood there in confusion for a moment until I guessed what had happened. I turned to the WAAF Corporal standing a little further on and said: "Is she Johnny Cassan's girl?"

She nodded.

I now understood the scene. Up until the moment I stepped through the door she had believed that Peden's crew had gone missing, and that Johnny Cassan had crash landed at Woodbridge. When she had seen me, she had suddenly realized that the facts were the reverse of the first report and that her boy friend was dead.

A couple of days later Bill scrounged some gasoline for his motorcycle, and, with me on the pillion, rode over to Ely. Stan had been taken from Woodbridge to Ipswich Hospital, then over to the big RAF hospital at Ely, where they had operated to remove the splinters from his head.

While we were milling around in the reception area trying to find out which ward Stan was in, I saw a familiar figure stumping his way along the corridor on a crutch, one leg in a cast. I hollered, and Jock Wilson, Atkinson's wireless operator, swung round and hobbled our way, beaming as he recognized us.

Thinking of his solo Ride of the Valkyrie through the great hedge at OTU, and his ditching in the North Sea the night Atkinson was killed, I shook my head at him: "Jock, what the hell have you been up to now?"

"Had to bail out the other night," he laughed, "broke my leg."

Jock was his usual cheery self, in fact he was bubbling over. A few questions overcame his modesty, and we found out that he had been awarded an immediate DFM and had just received the customary telegrams from the King and from Sir Arthur Harris so advising him. We rejoiced in his good fortune, then, promising to look him up on our next visit, obtained Stan's number and went up to see him.

My first glimpse of Stan, even with his head swathed in bandages, made me feel a lot better, for it was obvious that he had plenty of spirit. He had enough, in fact, that we felt justified in needling him after we saw his nurse, telling him that we now thought we could make far better use of the package of aircrew chocolate bars and candy we had brought than giving it to him.

Stan was not able to fly with us again until July 28th. After he regained his strength, he was transferred from Ely to the hospital at Littleport, then given leave. In the meantime, we kept flying and did three more operations using a spare wireless operator. When he was sent home on convalescent leave, Stan promptly proceeded to get married. Apparently he had overcome the imagined aesthetic handicap that had prompted his bitterest complaint in the hospital: the medics had shaved one side of his head in preparation for surgery, leaving him looking like a rooster with half a comb.

Stan too had been awarded an immediate DFM after the raid, a decoration which we all felt was well deserved — although naturally we never told him that, asking him instead what kind of line-shoot he had persuaded the doctor to send off to Butch Harris.

Some three weeks after the Gelsenkirchen trip I got a call from George Wright and was told to present myself, together with J. B. Waters and Johnny Walker, in the Wing Commander's office.

We attended promptly. When we were lined up in front of his desk, Wing Commander McGlinn somewhat formally announced that, in connection with the Gelsenkirchen trip, he had just received something he was pleased to present to us for insertion in our log books. He thereupon handed each of us a commendation embodied in Bomber Command Routine Orders for July 15th, 1944, and as he shook hands, was kind enough to say that he had put us up for decorations. Outside his office, we accepted George Wright's hearty congratulations, then for the first time paused to scan the paper we had been handed:

Headquarters, Bomber Command,   Serial No. .... A 118
ROYAL AIR FORCE.   Page No. 1
                                 Date .... 15.7.44.

COMMAND ROUTINE ORDERS
BY
AIR CHIEF MARSHAL SIR A. T. HARRIS, K.C.B., O.B.E., A.F.C.

PART 1 - ADMINISTRATIVE

A. 118

    The Commander-in-Chief wishes to bring to the notice of all ranks in the Command the commendable conduct of the under-mentioned members of a crew of No. 214 (B.S.) Squadron:-

    J.20216. A/F/Lt. D. M. PEDEN. - Pilot and Captain
    J.21576. F/O J. B. WATERS. - Air Bomber
    R.173927. F/Sgt. J. W. WALKER. - Air Gunner

2.   On the night of 21/22nd June, 1944, the above named officers and N.C.O. were members of a crew detailed to cover an attack on Gelsenkirchen. At a point approximately 15 minutes from the target area the aircraft was attacked by a M.E. 410 and in the ensuing combat the British aircraft was seriously damaged, the starboard inner engine was set on fire, and the inter-com system rendered u/s.

3.   Both Wireless Operators were wounded and were rendered timely aid by the Air Bomber, who also helped to restore the inter-com. A few minutes later the aircraft was attacked by a second enemy aircraft, but coolness and good shooting on the part of the Rear Gunner forced the enemy aircraft to break off the combat. Strikes were obtained on both enemy aircraft.

4.   With one engine still on fire, the Captain set course for home and displaying great ability successfully reached Woodbridge. He saved his crew from further injury despite a crash on landing due to a tyre having been shot away.

5.   The coolness and initiative displayed by the above-mentioned members of the crew is a fine example of captaincy and crew co-operation in very trying circumstances; their conduct is worthy of high praise.

                      Air Vice Marshal,
                      i/c Administration,
                      BOMBER COMMAND.

CHAPTER 19

PHANTOM FLEETS AND OTHER WEAPONS

He learned the art that none may name,
In Padua, far beyond the sea.
Men said he changed his mortal frame
By feat of magic mystery;
For when, in studious mood, he pac'd
St. Andrew's cloister'd hall,
His form no darkening shadow trac'd
Upon the sunny wall!

The Lay of the Last Minstrel.   Sir *Walter Scott*

After D Day, Main Force's night bombing tactics achieved even greater sophistication and effectiveness through the employment of various radar countermeasures, some new, some refined. These were complemented by a substantially expanded campaign of offensive fighter strikes executed by Mosquitoes of 100 Group's Serrate Patrol. The new elements began to be injected into the night campaign within a fortnight of D Day. They are worthy of more than cursory mention, for they involved some of the most daring gambles, bluffs, and double bluffs in military history. Perhaps not since the incredible daring of Lee and Jackson at Chancellorsville have the annals of military history recorded audacity to match that displayed by Sir Arthur Harris in the conduct of many of these operations.

The effectiveness of the German night fighter defences had increased in most formidable measure in the 12 or 14 months preceding D Day. The German fighter pilots were courageous and skillful, and their own radar weapons, like ours, were constantly being improved. They did not suffer from want of practice, and all too many of them had become past masters of their deadly art. Where the allied pilots and crews fought with determination and tenacity, their German counterparts matched their efforts, fighting to protect the Fatherland with a reckless intensity born of desperation. In the result, they were inflicting losses on Bomber Command which all too often threatened to become prohibitive. On our Gelsenkirchen raid of June 21st, for example, (when one of Bomber Command's new weapons was actually being given an early trial), the 127 Lancasters which wheeled to deliver their attack on the oil plant at Wesseling lost 37 of their number, the vast majority victims of the stalking German night fighters[1]. It requires no great facility in mathematics to foresee the effects on a bombing force of loss rates of 27.8 percent. It was because of the foreboding implications of earlier German successes against us that new weapons for 100 Group had been forged, and plans for still others advanced, weapons which gave promise of dissipating the strength of the German defenders and frustrating their efforts.

The two main radar cogs in the German defensive network were their long range detectors, the Freyas, with a range of over 90 miles, and the much more sensitive and accurate Giant Wurzburgs. The Giant Wurzburgs had an effective range of 25 miles, and fed accurate information on numbers of aircraft, course and altitude, to the German night fighter controllers and the flak and searchlight defences.

The 90-mile range of the early Freyas enabled the German defences to be alerted as soon as the first of our bombers began circling for height over our own bases. Thus, long before Main Force reached the enemy coast, the defenders were making their initial dispositions and preparing to strike the bomber stream with all the force they could muster. The first step in reducing the effectiveness of the defensive network, therefore, was to blindfold the Freyas.

The means of doing so were at hand, and in fact had actually been tested in practice many months before, when the degree of urgency had not been remotely comparable. The device which could do the job was a rather unsophisticated jammer code-named Mandrel. Our Fortresses and certain other 100 Group aircraft were lavishly equipped with Mandrel jammers after D Day, and we quickly began putting them to use. It became standard tactical practice, even when vile weather was going to preclude operations over the continent, to string a line of orbiting 100 Group aircraft a reasonably safe distance off the enemy coast and set up an unbroken Mandrel screen. The

---

1. See: Sir Charles Webster and Noble Frankland, *The Strategic Air Offensive Against Germany, 1939-45* Vol. III, page 161, Her Majesty's Stationery Office.

20,000 foot electronic curtain completely blocked the probing beams of the Freyas, causing their monitors to yield nothing but a deluge of "snow."

The Giant Wurzburgs presented a different technical problem, one that had to be dealt with by means of window. I made mention earlier of the potency of window against the Wurzburgs, pointing out that it flooded the apparatus with realistic looking aircraft echoes. It is worth noting in passing that the effectiveness of our window had not come about fortuitously. In February, 1942, British Commandos had carried out a daring attack on the radar site at Bruneval, a dozen miles north of Le Havre, in the course of which the specialists who accompanied them had partially dismantled the unknown device and seized portions of it which would yield the information they sought regarding its specifications and capabilities.

At this juncture, mid-summer, 1944, what was required, and what 100 Group produced, was a means of exploiting the Wurzburg operators' inability to differentiate with any degree of certainty between a group of advancing window echoes and the echoes produced by a genuine force of attacking bombers.

Through experimentation it had been discovered that a handful of aircraft "windowing" with precision and at a high rate — one bundle every two or three seconds — could simulate the approach of a bomber force of 500 aircraft. We were told that six of our Fortresses, with two men industriously windowing from the waist gun positions, could produce the same effect on the German radar screens as a force of 200 to 300 bombers. Thus the stage was being set for a new era in bomber tactics, and to capitalize on the situation some of our old weapons were being vastly improved.

By July, 1944, a new airborne jammer, of a capacity previously unheard of, 2,500 watts, was in the final stages of development. Code-named Jostle, this monster was to be installed in the bomb bays of our Fortresses, replacing Airborne Cigar. Whereas, in the operation of Airborne Cigar, our German-speaking wireless operator had been required to follow the German night fighter controllers by tuning manually from one frequency to the other, the great Jostle transmitter had such tremendous power that it eliminated the necessity for this and was designed to blank out simultaneously the whole spectrum of VHF frequencies being used by the controllers. Indeed, when we received Jostle at Oulton for final testing, Johnny Gilbert, whose crew was detailed to carry out one of the tests, had to fly halfway to Iceland to carry out the demonstration, lest Jostle also play hob with all BBC reception over a broad area of England and compromise security. Afterwards, when we began using it regularly on ops, we did our routine testing at very low level around the aerodrome for the same

415

reason. The Fortress, which served us so adequately in many other ways, was the ideal aircraft to carry Jostle, since it could readily climb well above the Main Force Lancasters, and thus achieve an even wider range for the super-powerful transmitter. (Despite its undoubted efficiency, I always had an uneasy feeling about Jostle after Stan reported to me that he had examined it when we were aloft, checking it as it lay in its shadowy stowage area in the sealed bomb bay, and discovered that it gave off vivid electric arcs when in use — in an atmosphere that always reeked of gasoline. The huge device was pressurized to reduce the arcing at operational altitude, but according to Stan it arced nevertheless, most unnervingly.)

A detailed description of the evolution of our Mandrel and window force tactics by reference to the individual operations carried out cannot be undertaken within the compass of this book. But a clear idea of the audacity of the tactics employed can readily be conveyed by a general description of the moves which came to be utilized routinely. When the target to be bombed lay in southern Germany, for example, the plot might shape up like this:

Just before dusk, a dozen or 14 Mandrel aircraft would fly out and take up their stations off the enemy coast, strung out in pairs in a great line so as to shield our bases completely from observation. At the appointed moment the operator in each aircraft would switch on Mandrel, blanketing all the Freyas' screens with snow. The central German fighter controller would thus have no early information on which to base his preliminary concentrations, and in fact would be unable to tell whether there were operations pending. After some considerable time, however, an attacking British force would suddenly come thrusting through the northern portion of the Mandrel screen and begin to be discernible on the Freyas. It would be several minutes before the size of the force, its altitude and its course, became apparent, precious minutes to the controller concerned; but it was essential for him to ascertain these facts in order to make a valid assessment of the threat. Even if no other factors had been introduced into the situation, the Mandrel screen itself would have delayed his reactions, to the point where fewer fighters could have been manoeuvred into position for injection into the bomber stream.

But, as the controller well knew, at least after the first time Bomber Command did it, an important new factor had been introduced. The powerful bomber stream reported to be heading for the Frisians, and potentially threatening such targets as Kiel, Cuxhaven, Wilhelmshaven, Bremerhaven or Bremen, while it certainly appeared to be a force capable of wreaking terrible damage on a target city, might only be a handful of Fortresses dropping window. The controller, therefore, delayed longer on that account, watching to see if anything further materialized through the Mandrel screen; then, when he could afford to delay no longer, began scrambling fighters from the more remote aerodromes and moving them north to meet the approaching threat. Three-quarters of an hour later, this northern "attack" evaporated in a settling cloud of tinfoil, while at the same time, Main Force, which had gone into France at low level over territory held by the Allied armies, suddenly appeared on the German radar screens far to the south, and began climbing for bombing height — already well on its way to the chosen target. Local fighter controllers along their route then had to contend with powerful jamming of their communications as they attempted to vector remaining fighters into the bomber stream.

The pattern described above was an early one, superseded in a short time by variations which became more and more sophisticated. Thus, to precipitate earlier action on the part of the German controller, we began to simulate breakdowns of the Mandrel screen. A windowing force would form up behind the Mandrel screen, strike off northeast, and fly to Heligoland, 50 miles off the mouth of the Elbe (an operation our crew did on August 25th). While the windowing force was still well on the friendly side of the Mandrel screen, two adjacent Mandrel aircraft would switch off their sets for a prearranged brief period, perhaps 70 seconds.

Through the gap thus created for their benefit, the Freya operators would catch a tantalizing glimpse of a powerful force of bombers heading in the general direction of Heligoland, again posing a threat to Kiel and the Baltic ports from Lubeck to Konigsberg, not to mention several intervening northern targets of great importance which they could attack if they swung south.

Initially the German controller would seize and act upon this valuable piece of information, gratuitously furnished by the malfunction of the enemy's equipment. Again the real bombers of Main Force would appear elsewhere later on, when the controller's dispositions favoured the attackers and embarrassed him.

After two or three feints based on this pattern had conditioned the German controller into being highly suspicious of gift information, provided by what he now realized were contrived breakdowns, Bomber Command would follow the same pattern when the target for Main Force actually was Bremen or Kiel. This was where audacity was put to the test.

Once again a portion of the Mandrel screen would collapse temporarily; and once again the Freya operators would catch sight briefly of an enormous concentration of aircraft bound for northeastern Germany. Reluctant to be caught again, the German controller would not react strongly, holding back fighters in the central and southern sectors, which he suspected would be the real target area, until the TI's went down and heavy bombing undeniably began, by which time it was too late.

A minor variant of this theme would be displayed occasionally without Mandrel breakdowns. A windowing force would pierce the veil and strike for a north German target, drawing a concentration of German fighters toward it before it reversed course and retreated through the phantasmagoric echoes it had sown. Next night the feint would be repeated and carried a little closer, and this time the German controller would be slower to unbalance his dispositions in response to the identical threat. The third night, Main Force would fly the identical route to attack, and the controller would be even less disposed to waste fuel and engine time chasing what he strongly suspected would turn out to be window echoes. Belatedly he would realize that this force was not going to turn back, and a heavy bombing attack would be delivered against a much weaker defensive response than could have been assembled.

On nights when he perpetrated a double bluff of this or the previous type, Sir Arthur Harris must have laboured under an incredible strain, remembering Nuremberg and the slaughter the German night fighters could execute amongst the lightly defended bombers of Main Force if they guessed the threatened attack was not a bluff. Bomber Command stood to receive a paralyzing blow if the German controller outguessed him.

The revelation of a manoeuvre as a bluff clearly made some new variation essential on succeeding operations of that pattern, and there was no shortage of modifications designed to promote confusion in the minds of the controllers. The basic window dropping feints were embellished at times by the addition of sizeable formations of aircraft gathered together from the OTU's. Well after the appearance of the windowing force, the OTU formations would pierce the Mandrel screen at a distant point and in their turn hold the Germans' attention for some time before turning out of danger and heading back. Additional "spoof" attacks were launched on important targets by small formations of Main Force, which magnified their strength on the radarscopes by dropping some window, and then dropped Target Indicators and flares over the city, running through all the preliminaries that were normally the harbingers of a Main Force attack, finishing off by dropping some bombs. All these facts were duly reported to the harassed controller, who frequently had three or four competing threats to evaluate and dispose his force to meet. Supplementing the spoofs were genuine diversionary attacks, carried out by sizeable forces on alternative targets widely separated from the main target for the night, attacks that were too heavy to be ignored, and which exerted strong pressure for dispersion of the German fighter force.

A change of pace that could be used only at prudent intervals was to send the windowing aircraft through the Mandrel screen heading toward a particular target, say Kiel. Half an hour later the windowing aircraft would turn for home, well inside the German defences, their feint now revealed as such. Counting on the German controller to redistribute his fighter strength as quickly as possible, and concentrate it elsewhere in anticipation of a genuine attack in another area, Bomber Command Main Force would later surge through the Mandrel screen on exactly the same track as the windowing aircraft and proceed to deliver its attack on a northern German target.

As an adjunct to the airborne jammings, the RAF engaged in a parallel campaign of ground jamming and spurious controller commentaries, using transmitters in Britain much more powerful than anything we could carry aloft. This campaign, code-named Corona, concentrated on confusing the German fighter pilots by advising them that instructions getting through to them, purporting to come from a German controller, were actually spurious directions emanating from an English trickster. The German-speaking wireless operators in our Fortresses had been trained in "verbal jamming" in their course at Stradishall; but in practice they never attempted issuing instructions reversing those of the controller. The possibilities for inadvertently betraying more than they concealed were too apparent to risk, so they stuck to jamming with their various electronic devices.

The Serrate Patrol, mentioned earlier, also figured prominently in the intensified campaign against the German night fighter defences. Additional Mosquito fighter squadrons had been added to 100 Group's strength and equipped with the latest in radar aids designed to help them find German night fighters in the air. Thus strengthened, the Serrate Patrol embarked upon a vigorous program, hunting the hunters, and waiting for them at their own aerodromes upon their return. In numbers of German aircraft shot down, the Serrate Patrol's campaign never approached the success of the comparable American effort in daylight. But apart from its less spectacular achievements in terms of aircraft actually destroyed, it had another and more significant result: its effect upon the German aircrews. They quickly became aware of the fact that the hazards of their profession had drastically increased; and the knowledge that at any given moment while they were airborne it was likely that they were being stalked themselves was not conducive to the single-minded concentration their art demanded.

The new countermeasures campaign brought us greater variety in the type of operations we were called upon to execute. Sometimes, as on the Gelsenkirchen trip, we accompanied Main Force to and from the target. Occasionally we would draw the relatively easy duty of flying as part of the Mandrel screen. On other occasions, while Main Force was preparing an imminent attack in another sector, we formed part of the windowing force, seeking to draw the fighters upon our small group.

Whenever we flew on one of these windowing feints, such as the one to Heligoland, there was always a build-up in tension as we approached the end of our run, for we were usually all too successful, from our point of view, in drawing large numbers of enemy fighters into our immediate area, a fact of which our German-speaking wireless operator would invariably inform us. As the air filled with prowling fighters, bent on our destruction, one was tempted to turn tail and beat a hasty retreat instead of carrying on steadily for the full specified length of the run and luring further squadrons of vengeful protectors of the Fatherland onto our trail.

When we first began these window spoofs, we expected — and so did the senior officers in our Group — that our losses would be exceptionally heavy; but in fact, at the beginning, they were actually lower than we had experienced on ordinary bomber operations. Later on, 214 Squadron ran into heavy weather, and for a while it seemed that we lost one of our aircraft practically every time the Squadron operated. We suspected, rightly as it turned out, that the Germans had recovered some of our radar equipment, examined it, and developed a means of homing onto our transmissions. Orders went out to curtail the use of certain devices, including our H2S and Monica, and the losses fell back to normal.

Over-all, there is no doubt that the new tactics were successful, and that they occasioned a significant reduction in Bomber Command's losses at a time when we urgently needed that relief. As the Allied armies occupied more and more of western Europe, the German defences were given correspondingly less warning of impending aerial attack, hence our infantry's successes combined to multiply the results of our own efforts. They were further enhanced by the continuing development of new radar devices such as Piperack, which came into use shortly after our crew had finished its tour. Piperack was a jamming transmitter designed to blind the new German SN-2 night fighter radar[1]. Piperack radiated a broad, fan-shaped beam to cover the bomber stream, within which the fighters' new AI radar, which the Germans had been able to design so as to pick up bombers even in a screen of false window echoes, was ineffective.

While our electronic countermeasures campaign undoubtedly had highly beneficial results, and must be counted a great success in the broad perspective, it was by no means successful on every attack. On some targets it was extremely difficult to mislead the German defenders,

---

1. See: Alfred Price, *Instruments of Darkness*, page 224, William Kimber, 6 Queen Anne's Gate, London. This excellent work provides a comprehensive review of radar development on both sides.

either by routing or jamming, and whenever their night fighters did manage to get into the bomber stream, they exacted their usual punishing toll. The July 28th, 1944, attack on Stuttgart, to which I shall make further reference, is a case in point.

While we made the German controllers' task infinitely more difficult, one should not lose sight of the fact that the Germans were not the harmless nincompoops wishfully portrayed in shows like "Hogan's Heroes." We never saw or encountered any remotely resembling those easy marks, nor did the Americans who flew with us. The German fighter pilots in particular were as tenacious as bulldogs, and until the final stages of the war, when allied bombing had deprived them of fuel even for essential training purposes, were antagonists of formidable skill and courage. They defended the Fatherland with the same determination displayed by the aircrews who gave their lives by the thousands attacking it. Some of them destroyed our Lancasters, Stirlings, and Halifaxes, in numbers which far exceeded the scores achieved by the great aces of the First War.

As I said, however, a comprehensive survey of the results leaves no doubt that our Mandrel jamming, our window and other spoofs, and our Jostle, Piperack, and other airborne jamming, detracted greatly from the success the German defenders would otherwise have enjoyed against us.

It is interesting to note the views of one of our former antagonists. A few years ago I thought I should like to consult someone "from the other side of the hill," and decided that the person best qualified was General Adolf Galland. At the time I was completing my tour in 1944, his position was equivalent to that of Commander of the whole German fighter force. I wrote to him, told him of my participation with 214 Squadron, and asked him if he would care to comment on 100 Group's efforts in the electronic countermeasures war.

General Galland replied, saying:

"I have been asked by Mr. D. Murray Peden to write down some of our experiences with the operations of RAF No. 100 Group.

"At the time when RAF Squadron No. 214 was attached to No. 100 Group, I was General Inspector of the German Fighter Arm, i.e. day and night fighters.

"I do remember very well the highly successful operations of No. 100 Group with its broad spectrum of tactics and techniques.

"Also in my book *The First and the Last*[1] I have paid special attention to the activities of No. 100 Group on page 237: . . ."

---

1. See: General Adolf Galland, *The First and The Last*, Holt, Rinehart and Winston, Publishers, 383 Madison Avenue, New York, N.Y. 10017, U.S.A.

(Here General Galland alluded to the problems our efforts had caused the Germans, recalling that 100 Group had provided "many a surprise for us" and commenting on our "feints, diversions, radio-blackouts, jamming and interferences".)

He concluded his letter in these words: "The combination of the Pathfinders' operations, the activities of No. 100 Group, the British advantage in radar, jamming and Window-techniques (ELECTRONIC COUNTERMEASURES) combined with intelligent attacking tactics, as well as on the other hand the discipline and bravery of the RAF crews have been remarkable. We had our severe problems . . . in trying to defend Germany in the air".

Another German officer, one who had been in an unrivalled position to assess Allied bomber tactics, made an equally significant comment. General Josef Kammhuber, the man who fashioned the Kammhuber line, was appointed Inspector of the West German Air Force in 1956. He was interviewed in 1959 by Asher Lee on behalf of the well-known periodical "RAF Flying Review". General Kammhuber fended off many questions, but when Asher Lee put to him a question as to "which of RAF Bomber Command's operations during the war he had thought most highly of, he answered immediately: 'Their changing electronics tactics which were always setting the Luftwaffe Night Fighter Command new problems to solve[1].' "

These are highly significant testimonials to 100 Group's effectiveness, having regard to the qualifications of the two assessors. While the success of the Group's efforts varied, the over-all effect was undoubtedly a marked reduction of bomber casualties each time the British succeeded in getting the upper hand for a period.

This became particularly true in the late stages of 1944, when the success of the Allied armies in western Europe enabled Air Vice-Marshal Addison to advance the Mandrel Screen further and further across France, and ultimately into Germany, thereby enabling the Command's aircraft to thrust into German airspace with no preliminary warning whatever.

It is clearly impossible to quantify the additional losses that would have occurred without 100 Group's contribution; but a comparison of the loss rates on operations where, perhaps because of exceptional visibility, the Germans quickly got large numbers of fighters into the stream, and those on which the jamming and the various spoofs and diversions kept fighter contacts to a minimum, demonstrates convincingly the great value of the radar countermeasures. It may not be overstating the case to say that, as things were going at the end of 1943 and the beginning of 1944, without the varied efforts of 100 Group,

1. "RAF Flying Review", November, 1959, page 46.

the Bomber Command offensive might well have had to be seriously curtailed, or perhaps even abandoned.

The fact that Bomber Command was able, not only to carry on, but to contribute decisively to the final victory, reflects great credit on the authors of the radar countermeasures plans, on 100 Group's energetic and innovative Commander, Air Vice-Marshal Addison, and, our own microscopic share aside, on the Bomber Support crews of that Group, who flew to every target with Main Force, and whose casualties were unfortunately as high as any in the Command. What they did not know was that their commanders had assumed at the outset that the casualties among the crews in the Bomber Support role would be even higher than those in Main Force itself. The radar war was not an easy one.

CHAPTER 20

OPERATIONS – THE SECONDARY TOLL

I would not spend another such night,
Though't were to buy a world of happy days,
So full of dismal terror was the time!

Shakespeare, Richard III

Our crew's next operation, after Gelsenkirchen, was a trip to the environs of Paris with Main Force, which we carried out, appropriately enough, the night of July 14th. After about five hours in the air, we taxied gratefully back to dispersal. When we had finished our flying meal in the airmen's mess after interrogation, J. B. and I, for some reason which I have long since forgotten, visited the officers' mess. It was situated only two or three hundred yards from our Nissen hut, "Canada House." As we were walking out of the mess, I saw a foreign object thumb-tacked to the middle of the notice board. It aroused my curiosity and I walked over to investigate.

It was a very dead bat, its wings extended at full stretch over a sheet of white paper which had a roughly inked swastika at the top. Below the expired aerialist a pseudo gunner's combat report was appended.

> At 22.45 hrs. July 14th, 1944, this Me 109 bat flew into the officer's mess at RAF Station Oulton (Latitude 52 degrees 50' N., Longitude 01 degrees 12' E.) at an altitude of 6.5 feet. It proceeded to carry out low level attacks at high speed, terrorizing WAAF members of His Majesty's Forces, who defended themselves by screaming.
>
> The enemy aircraft was promptly engaged by F/L Sharpe and F/L Doy, and despite the enemy pilot's erratic and violent evasive action, hits were observed on his port mainplane and in the vicinity of the landing gear — which was only partially retracted. He was finally downed with a three second burst from the officers' mess rug.

F/L Doy
214 Squadron Signals Leader

CONFIRMED
F/L G. Wright, Squadron Adjutant.

I had now completed 20 operations, and our crew was one of the most senior on the Squadron, roughly even with Jeff Bray's and slightly behind Jake Walters' in the number of operations logged. On July 17th, in company with a small force of other Fortresses, we carried out a windowing feint in D Dog across the Dutch island of Overflakee, some 15 miles southwest of Rotterdam, drawing a strenuous response from the vigilant German night fighters. We had one night's rest, then flew on ops again, this time another trip to Le Havre, but not low level as on our previous visit to the port with Jake Walters.

I was beginning to find that the strain of operational flying had a pronounced cumulative effect. Each time I found myself on the battle order the ordeal of waiting — an ordeal punctuated by the ritual of air test, briefing, and flying meal — seemed intensified, the muscles of the abdomen hardening until they felt like the extended ribs of a miniature umbrella. The tension would ease briefly as we finally got started and raced down the runway on takeoff, then it returned with redoubled force as we approached hostile territory, to reign supreme and worsen progressively as the trip wore on. Time moved with the glacial slowness that overtaxed nerves can occasion, making operational flying an exacting test of nerve and self control.

To a person wanting to visualize how intense the strain could become, how suppressed fear could swell and gnaw inside, I offer the following as a comparison, perhaps easier to imagine than the unfamilar surroundings of a darkened bomber cockpit framed in faintly luminous dials.

Imagine yourself in a building of enormous size, pitch black inside. You are ordered to walk very slowly from one side to the other, then back. This walk in the dark will take you perhaps five or six hours. You know that in various nooks and crannies along your route killers armed with machine guns are lurking. They will quickly become aware that you have started your journey, and will be trying to find you the whole time you are in the course of it. There is another rather important psychological factor: the continuous roar emanating from nearby machinery. It precludes the possibility of your getting any audible warning of danger's approach. You are thus aware that if the trouble you are expecting does come, it will burst upon you with the startling surprise one can experience standing in the shower and having someone abruptly jerk open the door of the steamy cubicle and shout over the noise. If the killers stalking you on your walk should happen to detect you, they will leap at you out of the darkness firing flaming tracers from their machine guns. Compared with the armament they are carrying, you are virtually defenceless. Moreover, you must carry a pail of gasoline and a shopping bag full of dynamite in one hand. If someone rushes at you and begins firing, about all you can do is fire a small calibre pistol in his direction and try to elude him in the dark. But these killers can run twice as fast as you, and if one stalks and catches you, the odds are that he will wound and then incinerate you, or blow you into eternity. You are acutely aware of these possibilities for every second of the five or six hours you walk in the darkness, braced always, consciously or subconsciously, for a murderous burst of fire, and reminded of the stakes of the game periodically by the sight of guns flashing in the dark and great volcanic eruptions of flaming gasoline. You repeat this experience many times — if you live.

The effects of a dozen operations, or a score, were discernible from time to time in various aircrew around the station. A Canadian gunner named Mickey Claxton, who slept opposite me in "Canada House," used to have nightmares in which he dreamed he was on operations and coming under fire. He would wake up in terror, often waking the rest of us up in the process, and then try to compose himself again. So frequently did he experience these nightmares that every night, as he punched his pillow and settled himself for sleep, he would sigh jokingly to the rest of us: "Well, chocks away."

One senior pilot, a Flight Lieutenant DFC type, when his name was on the battle order, used to grow so tense as the day wore on that his responses to unexpected questions were gasped out, and there was a note approaching the hysterical in remarks solicited from him. He would, quite literally, weep in frustration at the slightest obstacle until he got airborne, then he settled down.

In most of the aircrew, of course, the outward signs were not so readily apparent, but, with few exceptions, they were there nevertheless, in one form or another.

Jake Walters, whose tour had been far from easy, was feeling the strain. He could not hold a meal on his stomach most times when he was operating. After a raid, sitting with his coffee at interrogation, he would frequently get up abruptly, leave the little ops building hurriedly, and go and throw up outside in the darkness. Gradually we all became aware of Jake's condition, and feared that it would worsen and cause him to kill himself and his crew before he was taken off operations. Jake being Jake, we knew that he would never in this world ask or suggest that he be taken off. When we finally tumbled to the fact that his nerves were getting so bad that they were turning his stomach, someone passed the word along to George Wright. George, in turn, told the Wing Commander.

On July 22nd, 1944, Jake flew with Main Force in the attack on the railway yards at Chalons sur Marne, about 90 miles east of Paris. The following afternoon he told me the sequel.

After his return, while he sat sipping his coffee and answering the questions of the Intelligence officer at interrogation, he felt the unmistakable symptoms again, and hurried outdoors. As he stood heaving, one arm bent overhead against the corner of the building, he felt someone move in behind him, and an arm slipped firmly around his waist to support him until he finished straining. Then he heard McGlinn's voice in his ear: "I think you've had enough, Jake."

Thus came the end of Jake's tour, after his twenty-fifth operation. The rest of us on the station were almost as happy as Jake and his crew to see that they had made it, and the Wingco went up another notch in my estimation.

There were the indirect manifestations of pressure as well. Most aircrew were superstitious, some superstitious in the extreme. There were many who always did things in a certain set order, and with certain embellishments, while getting ready for a trip. Our mid-upper, Bert Lester, used to go through a little routine in the locker room every time he fastened on his parachute harness. As he bent and pulled the crotch straps in place, he always pulled them too tight and exclaimed in soprano tones: "Oooooo, my goodneth;" then, as he slacked off and clicked the ends home in the quick-release box, he dropped his voice an octave below normal to give a hearty bass "Ah, that's better."

When our crew went to draw parachute packs, we would not take one that had 13 in the number. Number 27013, for example, was out on that account; and so was Number 28021, because the digits there added up to 13.

While we sat warming the engines in dispersal before an operation, I would call the gunners as soon as I had completed my cockpit check and get each one to test his intercom while rotating the turret. Bert Lester simply counted from one to ten while traversing. Jack Phillips, when he was in the rear turret, invariably responded to my direction thus: "Roger. One . . Two . . Three . . Four . . Five . . Six . . Seven . . Eight . . Nine . . Ten . . Jack . . Queen . . King . . . Okay Skipper." After the tenth rendition, that routine used to set my teeth on edge; but I certainly was not going to tell him to change it. One had the feeling: well, we've done things this way before and come home safely, so let's stick with a winning combination. It wasn't that anyone would try to defend superstitions openly; but in the back of one's mind the thought persisted that . . . well . . . just in case . . . let's do it this way for insurance.

Many pilots, and I was one of them, refused to buy a new hat while they were on operations. When we were turning our Fortress onto the runway to take off, Bill Bailey used to lean over to lock the tail wheel on my call; and as he did so, he never missed checking to see that my old hat was hanging behind my seat over my parachute pack.

Good luck charms and mascots were a dime a dozen, of course.

Rabbits' feet, St. Christopher's, and rosaries, were seen as frequently as escape kits, flashlights and sextants. Jock Wilson carried a little yellow duck with "Berlin or Bust" written on it. In addition, he packed a small towel and soap "to wash my feet with in the dinghy." One of our pilots, a short chap named Jackson, used to carry a large panda and tuck it behind his seat. The WAAF drivers joked with him about it, but in an encouraging way, not teasing. (After about 20 trips, the panda's powers gave out.)

The vast majority of aircrew took the strain, and kept on taking it until they were killed or finished their tours. A few, after a varying number of trips, could not bring themselves to face it any longer. Duty, pride, self-respect, all inner resources crumbled before Fear, and they left silently, in shame, branded with the cruel stigma of the LMF (Lack of Moral Fibre) endorsation. All aircrew were volunteers; but while you could volunteer in, there was no volunteering out. You flew whatever duty was assigned, unless you were medically unfit. If you refused . . .

One crew flew three nights in a row on operations. They found themselves on the battle order the fourth day. This sort of thing rarely happened because the weather was seldom favourable that long. This time it did happen, and the crew were extremely tired. It is entirely possible that if they had gone to see Doc Vyse before they went to briefing, he would have ordered them, on medical grounds, taken off the battle order for one night. Instead, they discussed it amongst themselves, and took the indefensible but understandable position: "We'll go to briefing and find out what the target is. If it's a short trip, we'll go; if it's a long trip, to hell with it."

They went to briefing. The target was Berlin, an eight-hour trip. The pilot told the Flight Commander that they were not going. He in turn told the Wing Commander. The Wing Commander came over.

"Look," he said, not unkindly, "I'll pretend that this has not happened. You know you can't come to briefing and then decide you are not going to do the operation. Now get your gear together and be ready to go to the aircraft with the other crews."

The pilot and two other members of the crew realized immediately that they had put themselves in an untenable position by going to briefing before telling anyone that they felt incapable of flying a long operation. These three indicated at once that they would fly the duty as detailed. The other four members refused to go, claiming that four consecutive nights was too much for anyone, and insisting that all they wanted was one night's rest.

The recalcitrant crew members were immediately placed under close arrest. Squadron spares were pulled together to take their places, and the *ad hoc* crew made the trip — and returned safely in the morning. The four who had refused duty were posted to Uxbridge, where they were reduced to the ranks, given LMF endorsements on their records, and sentenced to 180 days detention.

I knew the pilot, an Australian, and saw a good deal of him in the weeks after this unhappy event. I did not know the crew members who had persisted in their refusal to fly, but I always felt that they had been their own worst enemies. It was harsh treatment to label them LMF, bearing in mind the service they had rendered and the ordeals they had already endured, but they had tied the Wing Commander's hands by the procedure they had adopted.

Another chap, a Squadron Leader pilot, a very personable and popular fellow in the mess while he was undergoing conversion training, had a very bad trip the second time he went as second dickey. They were badly shot up by fighters, and had their hands full making it back to base. He could not face the thought of taking his own crew on operations and possibly going through a similar or worse experience. He went LMF and was cashiered.

An NCO bombaimer, a lad we knew very well, did several trips, then simply could not stomach any more operational flying after enduring a very shaky trip, at the end of which he had had to bail out. He received the LMF treatment at Uxbridge as well.

But these cases, as I have indicated, were few and far between, and in most instances followed some traumatic experience that would have put all but the hardiest into a psychiatrist's care. One of our new pilots, on his first operation, a second dickey trip, found out what heavy flak could do if the gunners outguessed the pilot. A shell exploded under the nose, virtually amputating one of the bombaimer's legs. The second dickey spent the next three hours lying in a pool of blood, in a freezing gale, holding a tourniquet on the bombaimer's thigh and struggling to subdue him periodically when he went out of his head and began thrashing around. The bombaimer lived, and everyone who had been with him kept on flying on ops.

Remembering those who had carefully refrained from risking their precious hides, who had carefully refrained from bearing arms for their country, in any capacity, I always felt that LMF was a dirty label to fasten on someone who had volunteered for dangerous duty and had tried to carry out his commitment. The harsh treatment was necessary simply because the strain was so great. If there had been an easy and graceful way to abandon operational flying, many crews would have found the temptation hard to resist as their tours went on and the bloodshed continued.

On July 28th Peden's crew were on the battle order again. This time Stan was back with us, his first trip since Gelsenkirchen, five weeks earlier. He had arrived on the station only that afternoon. The

MO checked and cleared him for operations, although Stan later told me that he had been feeling decidedly shaky.

I felt pretty shaky myself when we got to briefing. The target was Stuttgart, and Main Force was attacking on a route that would keep us in the air close to eight hours. More accurately, I should say that the target was Stuttgart again. Bomber Command had already attacked the city twice in the preceding four days, on July 24th and July 25th.

According to the Intelligence officer, the routing on the first occasion had been very carefully worked out so as to avoid heavy flak and searchlights as much as possible. The second time out, July 25th, Bomber Command had run a double bluff on the Germans and used the identical route again. The double bluff had worked; the losses had been only 12 aircraft, a little over half the number lost on the first attack.

But tonight we were really going to fool them, the Intelligence officer told us proudly; we were going to use the same route for the third time in succession. The Germans would never believe that we would attack Stuttgart again, three times hand-running, using the same route. Their chief controller would interpret it as a bluff, and the closer we got to Stuttgart the more convinced he would be that we were bluffing and actually intended wheeling sharply to attack Frankfurt or one of several other targets north of our route. To confuse him even further, Main Force was going to attack to the north as well, with 321 aircraft being despatched to strike Hamburg while our force of 498 bombers attacked Stuttgart[1].

I felt sick. I did not normally second-guess the routing laid on by the high brass; but this conception, too clever by half to suit me, struck me as an invitation to disaster. The German controller already knew that three nights earlier we had bluffed him on exactly the same play, and had greatly benefited from his discomfiture; my feeling was that lots of poker players preferred to call rather than be laughed at on a bluff, lots of good poker players.

Later that night, after we took off, I climbed M Mike to operational altitude with grave misgivings. Hardly had we crossed the French coast than I realized that my fears were well founded. Combats broke out on all sides in the darkness, and soon the terrible sight of aircraft blowing up in mid-air, or burning fiercely as they spun to earth, was being repeated time and again. It took us three hours and 55 minutes to claw our way to Stuttgart, and by the time we got there I had long since lost count of the number of combats that had broken out in close proximity to us, all too many of them terminating in the usual

---

1. See: Sir Charles Webster and Noble Frankland, *The Strategic Air Offensive Against Germany, 1939-45*, Vol. III, page 175, Her Majesty's Stationery Office.

Above: This photo of a 214 Sqn. Flying Fortress shows some of the modifications made to suit the aircraft to RAF operations. The H2S radome, whip aerials and exhaust flame traps were added; the ball turret was removed.

F/L Jimmy Baird, P/O 'Dip' Norris and P/O Rowland Thorpe. (RCAF)

Members of 214 Sqn. pose in front of one of their Flying Fortresses.　　(RAF)

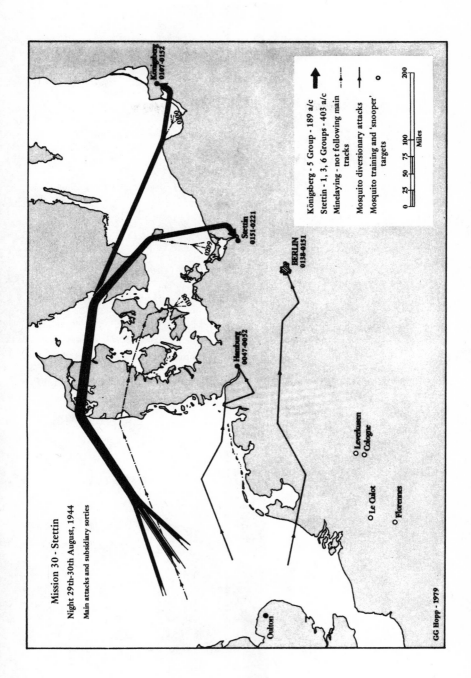

Mission 30 - Stettin
Night 29th-30th August, 1944
Main attacks and subsidiary sorties

Königsberg 0107-0157

0200
0100

Stettin 0151-0221

0200

0230

BERLIN 0139-0151

Hamburg 0047-0052

Leverkusen
Cologne

Le Culot

Florennes

Oulton

Königsberg - 5 Group - 189 a/c
Stettin -1, 3, 6 Groups - 403 a/c
Minelaying - not following main tracks
Mosquito diversionary attacks
Mosquito training and 'snooper' targets

0   25   50 75 100   200
              Miles

GG Hopp - 1979

433

Above: Wing Commander D. J. McGlinn (left), Commanding Officer of 214 Sqn., with Squadron Leader Bill Day.
Below: Marshal of the Royal Air Force Lord Trenchard with (left) General Sir Brian Horrocks.   (IW

F/L Johnny Wynne of 214 Sqn. in the cockpit window of Flying Fortress 'E-Easy'.

(Tom Butler)

Above: Irvine Bradley the day he won his wings. He was killed on night intruder operations, January 1, 1945.

Below Left: F/O Steve Nessner in front of 'Canada House'.

Below Right: F/L Jack Maguire. Killed on operations, February 21, 1945.   (Mrs J Maguire)

Above: This photo of Johnny Wynne's crew gives an excellent view of the chin radome for the H2S radar. Standing (l to r): F/O Stevens, WO Bostock, F/L Wynne, WO Godfrey and F/Sgt Richardson. Front row (l to r): F/O Moore, F/Sgt Butler, P/O Knox, F/Sgt Lewis and F/Sgt Piper.

Left: 214's gunners greatly preferred the .50 calibre machine guns of the Flying Fortress to the .303's of the British bombers. Here, F/O 'Paddy' Moore, on his third tour with 214 Sqn., has just cleaned the .5's of his rear turret.

(Tom Butler)

437

Above: Cologne cathedral standing, almost miraculously, amid the destruction wrought upon the nearby rail terminal and bridges.

Tommy Penkuri's grave, flanked by those of his crew, at Villars le Pautel.

dreadful way. It seemed that at any given moment along that route, one could look aside or ahead and see flaming debris somewhere on the ground miles below us. Time after time I called: "On your toes, gunners, there are fighters right near us," as vicious exchanges of fire tore the blackness open. Stan kept reporting contacts every few minutes, and the night air seemed alive with prowling German fighters.

The return journey was equally grim. Combats were taking place all around us, and every second I kept expecting our turn to come. It was the worst night of the war as far as I was concerned.

I sat at interrogation later feeling as though my stomach muscles would never come unknotted.

We lost 62 aircraft that night, the majority of them on the Stuttgart attack[1]. It was one of the few times that our elaborate tactics backfired — I think because the planners tried to be too clever, and the German controller was a better poker player than the people at Command who suggested trying the route for the third time. It was a particularly rough trip on Stan, coming, as it did for him, right after being shot up on Gelsenkirchen.

We did not get to bed until 7:00 AM, and went back up to the Flights at noon to find that we were on the battle order again for that night. It turned out to be another window spoof in across Overflakee. By comparison with Stuttgart it felt like a rest cure, even with our special wireless operator warning us that we had drawn large numbers of German fighters around ourselves.

Early in August, McGlinn finished his tour of duty as Squadron Commander, and was replaced by Wing Commander D. D. Rogers. I was truly sorry to see McGlinn step down. He had taken command of 214 in July, 1943, a couple of months before our crew's arrival, and, as related, had initially stirred up a strong tide of resentment. That initial reaction had long since washed away, replaced first by a measure of grudging respect, as McGlinn demonstrated that he had no intention of being a chairborne CO, then by a less inhibited feeling of friendship as his performance on the Berlin trip with Pedro boosted his stock further. By the time McGlinn had finished his period of command, having accumulated a list of targets in his log book that sounded like a calculated insult to Goering, he couldn't put a foot wrong as far as we were concerned. The extra touch of humanity he had displayed in stretching a hand to help Jake Walters put him at the head of the parade in my eyes. Jake had a backbone like a bridge

---

1. See: Sir Charles Webster and Noble Frankland, *The Strategic Air Offensive Against Germany, 1939-45*, Vol. III, page 175, Her Majesty's Stationery Office.

girder, and every pilot on the station knew that he had done more than his share by the time the Wingco ruled his tour finished. We now belatedly recognized that McGlinn's putting himself on the battle order when the target was one in the centre of that vast artillery park that constituted the Ruhr — just so that he could have it in his log book — was a typical gesture for him.

McGlinn was awarded the DFC on completion of his tour, and no one begrudged him the ribbon. He had won our respect by a peerless performance as an iron-willed bomber pilot. He had made himself a leader of an operational squadron by demanding a high standard of performance from every flyer on the station, and then imposing an even higher standard on himself — and satisfying it.

He left us without any fuss or fanfare; and once he had gone from Oulton I never saw him again[1]. I often wished I had had the opportunity to tell him that I considered it a privilege to have known him and served under him. 214 Squadron was lucky to have had D. J. McGlinn.

The Royal Air Force was lucky to have had him.

On August 7th we were on the battle order again, and after the trip flew back home about 2:00 AM to find that it had turned cold and dank and that Oulton was socked in. We were diverted to an aerodrome fittingly named Middle Wallop, situated 12 miles east-southeast of Stonehenge. In retrospect I am satisfied that a strong case could be made for the argument that both facilities were constructed under the same management. No one bothered telling us that Middle Wallop was a grass aerodrome, being used by fighters — Mosquitoes as I recall. We touched down gently in the darkness, and began rolling swiftly over the springy turf; it was only then that we realized what sort of surface we were on. In a few seconds the normal effects of friction and flap had slowed us to approximately 75 miles per hour. In a state of relative serenity now that I was safe on the ground, I was just preparing to touch the brakes when we ran up what felt like a burial mound in the middle of the flarepath. It launched poor old D Dog back into the air at an altitude of about four feet, but with insufficient speed to cushion our return journey. Thus D Dog returned to earth on the trajectory typical of a sugar bowl going off the edge of a table, and with a crash that scared me silly and provoked indignant queries on the intercom (after the brief interval required to conquer the terror which this second arrival had caused).

We taxied in with ruffled feathers, half expecting the under-carriage to collapse en route, and shortly made our way to interroga-

---

1. After these lines were written the author did locate McGlinn, and has maintained contact ever since.

tion. That exercise over, we were invited to accompany the Station Warrant Officer, who took us a few doors away to draw blankets. Back outside, in an atmosphere as black as ink, he pointed along a narrow road and told us that if we walked three or four hundred yards, we would come to some square huts that had just been built.

"Go into any of those," he said, "they've got cots with biscuits on 'em. You can have a sleep there, then come up to the mess for breakfast."

We thanked him and trudged off into the night. Sure enough, after a 20-minute walk — the SWO had been typically conservative in his estimate of distance — we realized that there were huts off to the left of us, in fact, when we turned in, we saw that we had already blundered past two or three in the darkness and mist.

In we went. Inside it was black as the pit. Sam and Bill struck a couple of matches, briefly revealing a row of empty cots — but only cots, no biscuits, just wire strung across the top. We grumbled, rolled a blanket around us, and slumped onto the wire to sleep. After about ten minutes I was sure I would look like a waffle for days afterwards; I could feel the sharp wire stamping me into neat rectangular squares from my shoulder to my heel. One other thing I noticed before I finally fell victim to the tot of rum I'd had — the inside of this hut was colder than any refrigerator.

I woke up with my teeth chattering about three hours later, and became vaguely aware that there were traces of mist in the room, and, as I rolled onto my back, that I seemed to be staring at an interesting low cloud formation. I sat up suddenly and began to shout, waking the others. In the darkness we had walked into an unfinished hut — around us were four walls and a carefully fitted door, but absolutely nothing in the way of a roof overhead. We might as well have put our cots out on the parade square.

We laughed all through breakfast over that one, and I, who had been leading the parade the night before, got full credit for the choice of accommodation. As we had noted upon emerging from our frosty cubicle, all the other huts ahead of it had been roofed in.

We returned to D Dog to find that the starter in number three engine was unserviceable. I called the tower on the radio, but after checking around, they came back saying they had no parts that would fit the Fortress. They did undertake to arrange to have one flown down to us, but explained that it might arrive that day or the following day.

Bill promptly produced a couple of tools he always carried with him, and a penny, and opened up the cowling on number three, disappearing inside it until only his legs were visible from the cockpit. In a short time he had found the trouble, and, more important, a means of fixing it. But it required his remaining halfway inside the cowling and holding something in place — perhaps a starter solenoid — while I started the engine. I was a little chary about this proposal, having gory visions of Bill sliced thin cluttering up the landscape; but he assured me that he had everything under control, and outlined a system of signals with one foot which would indicate how long he wanted me to hold the starting switch on before flipping to "mesh." I gathered this would leave him two or three seconds to disengage most of his fleshy parts from assorted rocker arms, gears, and other bits of machinery. Whatever he did, buried in the entrails of number three, it worked, and for the next five minutes he was fastening the cowling on again with the slipstream plastering his trousers to his legs. We left Middle Wallop without regret, carefully skirting the grass covered "launching ramp" halfway down the field as we took off.

On August 13th we flew another windowing feint across Over-flakee.

A day or two later the Americans were all posted away from Oulton and sent to Cheddington to carry on their work with their own 8th Air Force. I obtained all my information from the customary source — he was right as usual — and he advised me that by September the Americans would be replaced at Oulton by a new RAF Squadron, No. 223. This Squadron had had no previous operational experience in our theatre, but was to convert onto Liberators, learn to use our equipment, and share our duties.

We had spent seven happy and fruitful months with the Americans at Sculthorpe and Oulton. They had been a particularly good gang to work and train with, and we liked to think that it had been a mutually beneficial experience. The Americans had provided us with aeroplanes and had checked us out on them. We had provided them with all the latest radar and jamming equipment the RAF had been able to develop, and, through our Special Signals Section, taught them to use it. Applying to our teamwork the overworked description: "a fine example of Allied co-operation," sounds far too formal and generalized, but it happened to be quite true. The Americans were first-class aircrew, and modest ones. We all liked them, and felt a keen sense of loss when they departed to tackle their new job as the 36th Bombardment Squadron. We couldn't tell them about our feelings while we were all sober of course, but at the final party the atmosphere became gratifyingly maudlin on both sides. I made a point of telling Blondie, seven or eight times, from across the room, that we would always remember the good old 36th BS.

We flew on operations again on August 16th and 17th. The first trip was with Main Force to Kiel, and I learned at briefing that for the second time on my tour I was carrying a second dickey with me, a tall, youthful officer named Savage. The flak approaching and over Kiel lived up to its reputation and gave us an excellent workout for a while; but Bomber Command's tactics on this occasion, utilizing to the utmost the potential of our Mandrel screen and complementary window spoofs, left the German fighter defences in considerable disarray. As a result, our losses were correspondingly light. We attacked Kiel with 348 heavy bombers, nine Mosquitoes doing the marking. Only five of our heavies went missing, for a loss rate of 1.4 percent[1].

From Savage's point of view it was a good second dickey trip. He got a clear idea of what the German searchlights and flak defences could be like on a heavily defended target — and we came home from Germany without a scratch in only four hours and fifteen minutes.

On August 17th, we got a break and had an easy stooge as part of the Mandrel screen.

The following week we were summoned to the Flights on short notice one morning to be inspected by an unnamed VIP. We could not guess who it was until the door opened and the Wing Commander came in with Marshal of the Royal Air Force Lord Trenchard. If he had brought in King George I could not have been more surprised.

"Boom" Trenchard was a legendary figure in the RAF, and deservedly so, for without him the Air Force would probably never have come into existence as a separate service. Despite his advancing years he was a big, impressive-looking man, complete with walrus moustache, bushy eyebrows and piercing eyes, and a rumbling voice that still betrayed the origin of his nickname. After giving us a cursory inspection, Trenchard perched informally on the edge of a table, and beckoned us to gather close round so that he could chat. He opened this new phase of the visit by turning to an English navigator near me with this query:

"What is your service number, son?"

The navigator recited some lengthy number, in the millions, let us say 3,179,015.

"Mine is 1," said Trenchard with a boyish smile, and he meant it. That scrap of information went over very well with his audience — talk about service status symbols.

He turned out to be a fascinating gentleman, keeping us hanging on his words while he flitted from one subject to another: his conversations with Goering shortly before war became imminent; the sort of treatment we could expect to receive from the Germans if they captured us — and why[2]; the part he had played in the establishment of the

---

1. See: Sir Charles Webster and Noble Frankland, *The Strategic Air Offensive Against Germany, 1939-45*, Vol. III, page 177, Her Majesty's Stationery Office.

1. Trenchard told us that, as long as Goering retained his influence, any of us who were captured would be treated as well as the Germans could afford to treat prisoners — provided we got safely past the citizenry and Dulag Luft — because Goering was most desirous that any Luftwaffe prisoners in our hands be well treated, and would provide decent treatment on his side as the quid pro quo as far as he was able.

Royal Air Force College at Cranwell — and the basic directive he had issued to the first flying cadets:

"You Work Hard.
You Play Hard.
Hugh Trenchard."

In the course of his little chat, Trenchard mentioned a possible operation, a mass daylight raid on Berlin, to be carried out jointly by the RAF and the American 8th Army Air Force. We were left with the impression that this scheme had been touted for some time at Bomber Command Headquarters and that it might yet be carried out. After an hour or so of talking to us as though we were his own grandchildren, Trenchard left. Studying him at close range for that hour, I found it a lot easier to understand how the Royal Air Force had come into being as a separate service despite the most strenuous opposition of Admirals and Generals who would have much preferred to embody it within their own expanded empires. Trenchard displayed a highly effective combination of qualities: he was forceful; he was straightforward and totally candid; and he certainly knew whereof he spoke. On top of that, the "Father of the Royal Air Force" was very much a man's man.

For the next few days we did nothing but night flying tests. The pressure had been building up on us, for I now had 28 operations in my log book, and we all knew that our crew was due to be taken off any time. With each new summons to the briefing room there was an unadmitted and undiscussed desire to get to the target and back at all costs, to win the reprieve that went with being "screened" and made an instructor at the end of one's tour.

On August 25th, the Flight Commander had us on the battle order again. With an even keener interest than usual we went to briefing to see where we were being sent.

It was another windowing spoof. This time our Fortresses were to try to split the defences and draw fighters to the north by running in on Heligoland as though we were heading for Kiel, half an hour's flying time further along our track. When the threat posed by our force was at its height, as we were coming up on Heligoland, more than 600 Main Force aircraft would forge into Germany 300 miles south of us to bomb Russelsheim and Darmstadt, each of which lay about 20 miles from Frankfurt.

From our point of view the feint turned out to be highly successful. Well before we got to Heligoland, our German-speaking wireless operator let us know that the hive was buzzing, and as we drew nearer, the air around us was liberally populated with questing German night fighters from bases in Schleswig-Holstein and Lower Saxony. As we hit the end of our run, Sam literally did a count-down for the last few seconds, and we turned sharply to wend our way warily back across the North Sea.

On August 29th we were tapped for duty again. We headed for briefing wondering what trip No. 30 would look like. The curtains parted to reveal two targets, both of them further into Germany than anything we had flown before. Main Force was splitting its effort again. One hundred and eighty-nine aircraft were attacking Konigsberg, in East Prussia, only a short distance from the western border of Lithuania. A heavier force, 403 aircraft, were attacking the distant Baltic port of Stettin. The Konigsberg trip looked like a ten-hour operation, the Stettin attack, nine hours. Peden's crew was detailed to accompany Main Force to Stettin; Johnny Gilbert was one of those going to Konigsberg[1]. The thought of being strapped in my seat for a nine-hour session, most of it over enemy territory, and much of it over areas where the night fighters were notoriously active, was not appealing. No. 30 was going to be a long, tough grind. I consoled myself with the thought that Johnny Gilbert's trip would be an hour longer. Briefing wound up with the Intelligence officer pointing out that these attacks were of considerable strategic importance, since the attacking Russian armies were drawing close to Konigsberg, and the Germans were making great use of the port facilities of Konigsberg and Stettin to supply their beleaguered forces.

We took off at 10:00 PM in the customary climate of strain and suppressed apprehension. The operation did not start under happy auspices. As we climbed away in the deepening gloom, Bill and I could see other aircraft climbing on track below and ahead of us. Half a mile ahead I saw two Lancasters labouring for height, flying on slightly converging courses. They drew very close, and as I watched in helpless fascination, collided and locked together. The shock waves of a silent explosion blurred the picture, then they were dropping together, as though on a plunging elevator, down . . . down . . . down, into the Wash. There were no parachutes. For 14 men the operation was already over.

Our first leg ran northeast for 400 miles across the North Sea to a point on the west coast of Denmark near Lim Fjord. When we had been flying in silence for an hour, I became aware of the fact that aircraft around us were switching on their navigation lights. The bulk of them were half a mile on our port side, so that what we saw were their starboard navigation lights, pale green points like a skyful of stars floating along inaudibly with us. I do not know what prompted the

---

1. The actual routes flown by the two elements of Main Force and by the supporting Forces carrying out diversionary attacks and mining operations, are shown on Map No. 4 in *The Strategic Air Offensive Against Germany, 1939-45* supra., and the composition of the Forces and their loss rates is also shown in Vol. III of that work at page 177.

gesture — I never saw it on any other target — but it seemed as though every aircraft on the operation had been lit up. I flicked my lights on briefly, then doused them again. We had crossed Denmark and flown into the Kattegat before, and we well knew that the fighters in that area needed no assistance from us.

After a long time we came to our turning point on the Danish coast and swung east and slightly south to head across Denmark for our next turning point on the west coast of Sweden. In half an hour we were over the Kattegat and heading slightly south of east for our next turning point, 15 miles northwest of Angelholm. It took us only a few minutes longer to cross the Kattegat to Sweden than it had to cross Denmark. We steered southeast across Sweden, now making for the north corner of the island of Bornholm.

Since the Swedes were neutral, I was looking for no trouble from the ground. I thought they might fire a few rounds, a thousand feet below us, as a token demonstration against our violation of their air space. What the Swedes actually did was subject us to some very heavy and accurate flak of a particularly scary kind. This was the "flaming onion" type, a glowing red ball which seemed to move toward the aircraft at a leisurely pace for several seconds and then suddenly whistled past like the mill tails of hell. Inwardly I cursed the Swedes with every piece of profanity I could lay my tongue to. They knew damned well that they were not going to be molested, and a few token rounds a thousand feet below us, together with a protest through diplomatic channels, would have been quite adequate for face-saving purposes, instead of trying to kill us. I would have been delighted to act as Master of Ceremonies if Bomber Command's next raid had been 3,000 tons on Stockholm.

From Bornholm we ran almost straight south, crossing the German coast and running south about 35 miles on the east side of Stettin to mislead the controller.

Well to the east of the city the 400 heavies of Main Force suddenly turned southwest and began the ten-minute run that would take them across Stettin. As we neared the city I began to get extremely edgy. There was no sign of a target city in front of us. I knew we were supposed to be in the first wave; but usually the defences of a target city were showing signs of life even before the first bombs fell. In front of us there was nothing but velvety blackness. I asked Sam to check his ETA, and the slight note of doubt in my voice placed an additional and unwarranted strain on him. Just at this point some activity broke out well behind us, and was reported by Johnny Walker. Before I could ask Sam to double check, he came on the intercom to say that what Johnny Walker was seeing was probably diversionary activity over Peenemunde, a good 50 miles away. He asked me to maintain our course for another two minutes and see what happened.

Almost to the second the Target Indicators went down in front of us, and the searchlights and flak defences of Stettin flared into action with a vengeance. It had been a beautiful piece of navigation on Sam's part. In a few moments we were over the city, and the Main Force aircraft were subjecting it to heavy attack. We carried on, seemingly at a snail's pace, southwest across the city, and were within two minutes of being out of the area of illumination when a searchlight moved inexorably toward us. In a moment I was blinded by its glare. I pulled my head down behind the black paint on C Charlie's window, and tried to escape in a steep diving turn; but at 22,000 feet the beam seemed a mile wide and the blinding glare twitched and stuck with us. Providentially I caught a glimpse of a patch of cloud off on our starboard side. It wasn't much, but it was all we had. Other beams would be moving to join the first and cone us, and if that happened we were in more trouble than I cared to think about. I dived sharply toward the cloud, and in a few seconds we shot into it. It only shielded us for ten or 15 seconds, and for the first five or ten of those the light played on the base of the cloud, waiting for us. Just before we emerged, the light gave up and leaned away seeking another victim. I swung back onto course, thankfully.

The route home took us back over Sweden, and again the Swedes did their utmost to knock us down. Again we cursed their unnecessary zeal. After a while, however, we had worse things to worry about. As we swung west to thread our way across the Kattegat again, the flitting fire of air to air combats stabbed the darkness repeatedly. Once more time stood still. We had been flying for close to six hours, and had another three hours, and several hundred miles, still to go. Flak and searchlights had already made their contribution toward nervous fatigue, and we had what we knew from past experience was a particularly dangerous part of the route still before us.

The fact that I was now quite tired did not keep me from doing a strenuous banking search every two or three minutes to give the gunners a clear view below. I caught myself checking my watch repeatedly. At long last we cleared Denmark again, and steered southwest across the North Sea for home. By the time we reached Cromer, a few minutes from base, my shoulders were aching as though I had been holding a heavy weight at arms' length for nine hours.

The Minneapolis-Honeywell automatic pilot with which the Fortress was equipped was a most sensitive and efficient instrument, and I always trimmed the aircraft carefully and set up the autopilot so that Bill could snap it in if anything happened to me. But on operations I never engaged it and sat back to take a rest, because if a gunner suddenly shouted: "Corkscrew," it would take a second to lean forward and bat the bar to one side to disengage it, and that extra second in a close range night attack could mean all our lives.

When we taxied into dispersal, after eight hours and fifty minutes in the air, I switched off and then just slumped back in my seat for a few minutes, too weary to move. From the time Bill and I had started our cockpit check I had been strapped into that seat for nine hours and 15 minutes. If it had been nine hours and 15 minutes of entertainment it would have been tiring enough. The same period of intense concentration and tension, not to mention occasional spells of hard work and long moments of fear, multiplied the effect tremendously. After a bit I stirred myself and dropped through the nose to wait in the greying light for the crew bus. Johnny Gilbert came taxiing in a short time later.

On his target 15 of our bombers had been shot down. On Stettin with more than double the Konigsberg force, our group had lost 23; 38 planes and 266 aircrew for the night.

We had arrived back at Oulton around dawn on Wednesday morning. Thursday, we never stirred off the ground, and Friday we were at George Wright's office with assorted hard luck stories to get our passes and travel warrants early for the seven days' leave due us.

I went to Edinburgh and had a wonderful leave. My father's friend, Eddie McEwan, took time off to show me all round the city; from the little office where Walter Scott had worked, all along the Royal Mile to Holyrood Palace, and finally back to the Castle to the spot that Eddie liked best, the Memorial Shrine, a sanctuary whose solemn beauty commanded instinctive reverence.

I arrived back at Oulton on September 7th, and on the 8th, as I walked out of the dining room after breakfast, Wing Commander Rogers came up to me and clapped me across the sholders:

"Say, Murray," he said seriously, "would you bring your log book over to the office when you get up to the Flights?"

"Yes sir," I said, allowing my expression to betray my curiosity.

"Yes, do that," the Wingco said, now beginning to smile, "I want to write in your First Tour endorsement. You and your crew are finished."

I stammered thanks as he offered his congratulations, then left joyously for the Flights to let the rest of the crew know. There were no unhappy faces that morning. Our chances of living to see the end of the war had increased tremendously, and we reacted accordingly. At this point, unlike Tennyson's Ulysses, I was quite content to rust unburnished and not to shine in use for a bit. I thought back to the last trip, on Stettin, and was glad that we had not been told at briefing that it was our final trip.

Rogers generously gave me an "Above the Average" endorsement as a heavy bomber pilot on my Form 414(A), back-dating it to September 3rd, and telling me as he handed my book back that my crew and I would all be made instructors in 1699 Conversion Unit, a new Fortress CU that had just been established at Oulton. Our two weeks "end of tour leave" would be given us early in October, he said: meantime I was to begin my new employment as an instructor forthwith.

CHAPTER 21

CLOSING GLIMPSES, MAINLY PLEASANT

I started my career as a Fortress instructor on September 9th. Straightway I began learning how amazingly different everything looked and felt from the right-hand seat, and, more painfully, what it was like suffering through uncertain approaches and landings without putting a hand on the controls.

But a detailed recital here of my experiences as an instructor would import an unwarrantable element of circularity, for many of the same experiences and sensations I had undergone as a pupil at OTU and Conversion Unit overtook me again, but in mirror-image form, so to speak. I content myself, therefore, (until I generate sufficient ambition to write a separate book on that period alone) with the briefest possible outline of the events of the following months, interspersed with glimpses and scenes deeply etched in my memory. Against this strobe-lit account, the background of day and night flying exercises should be visualized: circuits and bumps, high level cross-countries, air to sea firing exercises, and fighter affiliation workouts — with friendly Mosquitoes simulating the heart-stopping attacks of Ju 88's and Me 410's.

1699 Conversion Unit was still in the process of being organized when I joined it. It was placed under the command of Squadron Leader D. J. Bellingham, DFC, AFC, one of the finest pilots I ever flew with[1]. We were equipped with Fortresses and Liberators, and our responsibility was to keep a continuing flow of replacement crews moving to

---

1. In 1945, when the war was over, Don transferred to BOAC and eventually became one of the line's senior pilots. He was picked to fly Prince Philip to President Kennedy's funeral.

214 Squadron and, later, to 223, the latter Squadron being equipped with the B-24's. We were not generously endowed with aircraft or instructors, so we were kept busy trying to satisfy the two Squadrons' needs.

* * *

I walked into the Castle Hotel in Norwich late one afternoon with the idea of slaking the dust of travel with a couple of light ales. As I relaxed, waiting for my first drink and gazing absently at the friendly-looking American pilot sitting facing me a few yards away, I became aware vaguely that I was looking at someone I had seen many times before. With a pleasant shock I realized that I was looking at Jimmy Stewart. At that time he was flying heavies with the 8th US Army Air Force from one of the several American dromes clustered round Norwich — probably Horsham St. Faith. To ensure that I had not missed the event, the waiter commented proudly on the presence of the distinguished guest as he brought me my drink. I tried not to stare too obviously.

* * *

On a fine evening in September, after the mail had brought a large batch of food parcels from Canada, we were winding up a great communal feast in Canada House. Vern Corbett, a resident bombaimer, having stoked his boiler to the tune of about 4,000 calories on a dozen different treats, sat propped up with pillows on his bed, his waistband open to ease the strain, even his slippers half off for maximum comfort, and prepared to enjoy the ultimate luxury as he bit the end off a cigar supplied by Steve Nessner. The match flared, the end of the cigar glowed to the rhythm of his puffs. Finally he expelled a generous billow of smoke and sighed contentedly: "Ahhhh. Ya'know, Sherman was right . . . War is Hell."

* * *

Corbett and I moved 20 yards from Canada House into a two-man Nissen hut. I found him there one afternoon, just ten or 12 yards beyond our open window, busily spreading feed on the ground for hungry pheasants and partridges. I gazed in wonderment as I dismounted from my bicycle. Here was a new and completely unsuspected side of the man, verily a breath of the good Francis of Assisi.

I entered the hut without a word. On the table, which had been moved closer to the open window, lay Corbett's service revolver, loaded, and a little pile of books which were obviously designed to steady his aim.

I made the acquaintance of a new WAAF, an MT driver of surpassing charm and beauty named Margaret Kelly. She was a Devon girl, with the peaches and cream complexion for which Devon is justly famous, and she bore a distinct resemblance to Joan Fontaine. I had been smitten at my first sight of her, which came as I was walking around the perimeter track with another chap, heading for 1699's office. This vision of all that womanhood can aspire to was reading a book as she sat behind the wheel of a crew bus which was parked just off the perimeter track behind the tower. She was on duty, awaiting calls from Flying Control. She glanced up briefly at the sound of our approach, then lowered her eyes primly to her book. I stared at her admiringly until I was abreast of the crew bus, but she gave no sign of being aware of my interest, although I suspected that her peripheral vision was being cautiously utilized. As we passed the crew bus, with no hint of any response, I resolved to find out if she was watching. I turned about smartly, then kept on my way, walking backwards to keep her in full view. Her head never moved, but the trace of a smile appeared, and I went on my way encouraged. Thereafter I found a multitude of excuses for summoning the crew bus whenever she was on duty, and after a little coaxing she agreed to come on a picnic with me on her afternoon off.

This beautiful afternoon was the afternoon for the picnic, and I was walking towards the Buck to see if I could persuade the kind lady who ran it to sell me a bit of bread and margarine and some soft drinks, something to add to the odds and ends I had assembled for the picnic from picked-over parcels at Canada House. I was feeling on top of the world generally, but not too optimistic about this specific mission. Additional food in wartime England was hard to come by; in fact Parson Malthus, had he been alive, would have been I-told-you-so-ing with gloomy satisfaction.

As I walked down the curving incline that led to the entrance of the Buck, I was happily whistling "Take a Pair of Sparkling Eyes" from the Gondoliers. I was in my very best form, unconsciously realizing all the lyrical romanticism with which Sir Arthur had endowed it. Only a lark could have rivalled my — temporary — purity of tone.

I broke off as I came up to the door and found the good lady of the Buck dabbing at her eyes with her apron.

"Is there something wrong, Ma'am?" I said.

"No, no," she said pleasantly, but sniffing, "nothing at all. I heard you coming. It made me cry to hear you whistling. My husband was whistling that tune the first time he came courting."

She gave me more food and drinks than I could stuff in my

haversack, and would not hear of my paying for it. "No, no, you've made my day," she said; the good old soul.

*   *   *

In a fine demonstration of One-Upmanship, J. B. casually mentioned, without preamble, that he and George Wright were going to London to attend the wedding of Pamela Guinness. Pamela Guinness if you please. My raised eyebrows and query brought the airy assurance that yes, this was *the* Pamela Guinness, member of the great Guinness brewery empire. And whence the invitations? George Wright, it transpired, was Lady Patience Guinness' brother, (and J. B. had been supplying George with Canadian cigarettes).

The wedding was to take place on Saturday, October 7th, 1944, at The Church of the Holy Trinity in Brompton. On Friday, the gold dust twins left for London, doing their best to leave the rest of us green-eyed, and succeeding. George, whose uniform hat looked even worse than most operational types', rented a splendid new specimen from Moss Bros. until the reception was over.

But when they returned to Oulton, it was clear that the incident which had made the greatest impact on J. B. during his absence had not been anything connected with Pamela's and Michael's nuptials, but something much easier for we of Scottish ancestry to appreciate.

With all duties at the wedding and reception faithfully discharged, George and J. B. had collected three other poker players and retired to tough things out in their posh suite at the Savoy Hotel. At a late hour, the poker players phoned room service and asked that some food be sent up. Fifteen minutes later, a magnificent liveried servitor appeared, with a rather sparse plateful of spam sandwiches — and a magnificent bill: £5, plus tip.

With each pound sterling worth about five uninflated dollars at the time, J. B. estimated that his Savoy spam sandwiches cost a dollar a bite.

Concealing our Scottish horror at the size of the bill, we coyly observed that for a couple of high rollers who ran around with Pamela Guinness, five pounds was peanuts.

*   *   *

I found myself alone, waiting for transport one afternoon, standing in front of Blickling Hall. Presently George Wright joined me. A crew bus approached, coming from the direction of the Flights; but instead of swinging round in front of us in the customary way, in preparation for the return journey, it simply carried on, without slackening speed, down the road that led to Aylsham and Norwich. As it passed, I caught sight of two WAAF's sitting beside each other in the back of the otherwise empty bus. I speculated aloud that they were probably off on some sort of joy ride somewhere. George looked at me rather questioningly, then spoke in his usual bluff way.

"Don't you know what they're doing?"

"No, what?" I replied.

"They're going into Norwich, to the hospital, for tests to find out whether they're pregnant. We lay on a run every Thursday — if we have any customers that is."

He paused for a moment to let me digest that bit of information, then spoke abruptly again: "Know what I call it? The blunderbus."

*　　*　　*

It is beginning to get light, just before dawn. The driver of the crew bus has instructions to call at two aircraft dispersals to pick up returning crews.

One crew piles in, dumping chutes, signals bags, and other equipment heavily on the floor as they flop on the seats, their weariness allowing the WAAF driver to swing them exaggeratedly off balance as she starts up again. They roll a couple of hundred yards and pull up where the second waiting crew is clustered near the entrance to the dispersal. Through the windows they see numerous fresh scars of battle on the second aircraft, savage aberrations in the symmetry that testify how fiercely the claws of the prowling night fighter raked. Instinctively they count . . . yes, all seven members of the second crew are standing there, unhurt.

The boarding performance is repeated. There is no talking for the moment, weariness again. The pilot of the wounded bomber, a pilot with Canada patches on his shoulders, slumps beside his friend, the pilot of the first crew, then speaks, aloud, but in a tone that suggests he is imparting something rather confidential: "Ya wanta know somethin'? Those bastards are using real bullets."

*　　*　　*

Jake Walters, with a couple of pints under his belt and bubbling over with fun as usual, is holding forth in front of the bar, repeating his story about the sad confusion of the uniformed bus driver stationed just outside the railway depot, charged with the responsibility of calling every few seconds for passengers staying at the Hotel Astor. The train is late and the night has been cold, Jake explains, and the driver has taken on a good cargo of anti-freeze — and continues to pull at the bottle between anouncements. Jake's accomplice at the bar is primed to chant: "What'd ya say?" after each line. Jake thickens his speech and with appropriate pauses, and growing confusion, calls for his customers:

> Free bus to the Hotel Astor;
> Free ass at the Hotel Buster;
> Bust yer ass to the Hotel Freezer;
> Freeze yer ass at the Hotel Buster.

(At this point Jake seats himself behind an imaginary steering wheel, squints glassy-eyed for prospective passengers, then goes through the motions of putting the bus in gear and leaving as he shouts: "T'hell with ya; do ya good to walk.")

*   *   *

Jeff Bray and his crew returned from operations one night and at interrogation reported firing on an Me 410 which had been manoeuvring into position on them. The gunners claimed hits on the German aircraft.

Three days later, when they went down to the mess, Jeff found a letter waiting for him. He opened it to discover that it contained a card, a card which had stamped on it the three standard silhouette views of a Mosquito. Accompanying this card, which was of the type commonly used for aircraft recognition practice, was a note indicating that it was sent with the compliments of the Wing Commander of the Mosquito Squadron at Little Snoring.

When one of his Mosquito crews had returned saying that they had been fired on by a four-engined aircraft, the Wing Commander had checked all the combat reports filed with the Group Gunnery Leader. He quickly identified Jeff's crew by the time and position of the combat they had reported.

Despite the fact that we would all have expected our gunners to do the same thing, we made great sport of this for a few days with Jeff, diving on the ground or jumping behind a building every time a Mosquito came near, and shouting: "Get down Jeff, it's a 410."

*   *   *

We received word unexpectedly one morning that a party of Federated Malay States dignitaries would be arriving that afternoon to inspect "their" Squadron and its aircraft. This caused a great flurry of activity calculated to make everything look better than it really was, and prompted the purposeful painting of "F.M.S." on a large number of articles and buildings that would be highly visible on the guided tour to be given the VIP's. Within half an hour of the telephone call the Chiefies at each dispersal had men stencilling appropriate names on the noses of the aircraft. Thus our black Fortresses soon stood arrayed in names like JOHORE BAHRU, (this on B Baker), PAHANG, (P Peter), ALOR STAR, (S Sugar), SRI GUROH (G George), and so forth.

George Wright had naturally been chosen as one of the officers to accompany our visitors. With the knowledge he had acquired as a Malayan planter, he managed to convey the impression that all the officers on 214 were intimately acquainted with the geography, politics and aspirations of the Federated Malay States. He saw to it, as well, that the visiting firemen were driven round the aerodrome with stops of sufficient length at each dispersal to enable them to read the bravely stencilled Malayan names. This appeared to go over very well.

Few of the new names lasted for 24 hours. Next morning most of the pilots, spurred by superstition, had their Chiefies paint out the exotic appellations and replace them with the battle-tested devices the Fortresses had already worn on their various operations. It was not disrespect, disdain or ingratitude, just the instinct for survival.

*   *   *

On December 11th, 1944, I was posted to Ingham, near the air base at Scampton, to take the Bomber Command Tactics Course. This was a brief but very useful series of lectures, lasting five or six days, designed to bring one up-to-date on the latest developments in aerial tactics, both our own and the Germans'. The lectures, I was soon to discover, dealt in considerable detail not only with general tactics — the Corona program, our Jostle jamming, the Serrate Patrol, the Mandrel screen, and the Main Force and Window Force variants associated with it — but also with recommended tactics for individual aircraft, including flak evasion patterns, the banking search, the specifics of the best corkscrew, etc. The course material also dealt in some detail with the capabilities of the German radar equipment. The day before I was due to be there, I persuaded Don Bellingham to lay on a training flight to nearby Scampton for one of the pupils so that I could avoid the tedious train journey to Lincolnshire. Thus it was that I arrived there in a Liberator just in time for tea.

Scampton was one of the permanent peacetime establishments, like Stradishall, so I had no trouble finding my way to the officers mess.

I had hardly entered the lounge when I met a pretty WAAF officer who had been with us on 214 briefly at Downham Market. Margaret was regaling another WAAF with a story about Peter Piper, an Intelligence officer with a reputation as a bit of a wag. I listened.

Arriving on a new station where no one knew him, Peter decided to have some fun. He had acquired somewhere a de-activated German butterfly bomb, an anti-personnel weapon that looked like a baking powder tin with round flaps or wings sticking out on either side. These wings were designed to spin it and ease its descent from an aircraft, so that it would not detonate but simply become armed when it made contact with the ground. Thereafter, the slightest touch would set it off; even a footfall near one was often sufficient. Pound for pound, these butterfly bombs were about the fiercest weapon used by either side, with a blast that would rock you to your boottops a hundred yards away.

Peter concealed this one under his coat until he got to the officers mess — which was full — then walked in holding it casually in front of him between his fingertips.

"I say," he called, "does anyone know what this contraption is? I found it caught on the eavestrough . . ."

His concluding words were lost in the wild stampede for the opposite door.

*　　*　　*

I came back from the tactics course at Ingham half frozen. Our lecture room and billets had been so cold that we sat with our greatcoats on throughout the lectures, and slept with them spread over our blankets. But I felt better equipped to take my turn giving the tactics lecture to our student crews on 1699.

Almost immediately I received official news that gave me pleasure: I had been awarded the DFC. In the same issue of Green Sheets Puterbough's name appeared, so our 214 group had two gongs to celebrate.

*　　*　　*

Our four Flying Control officers rotated the duty. Three of them were steady, calm, unflappable types who ran the show with quiet efficiency. Providing the starkest contrast, however, was the fourth Flying Control officer, a man we never referred to by name, but simply as the Panic Merchant. Whereas the other controllers usually moved quietly and efficiently to forestall impending trouble, the measures initiated by the Panic Merchant all too frequently transformed situations that were well in hand into budding disasters. Driven by some restless demon, he was the type that could never leave well enough alone.

No matter that the wind was hardly strong enough to turn the anemometer — if it sighed once at an angle exceeding thirty degrees off the runway in use, he would pick up the phone and tell the ACP[1] to move his van and change the runway — this even if someone was on final approach, ten seconds from landing. What follows is one sample of his handiwork.

An American Mustang pilot, just back from operations, with his tanks almost dry and in desperate need of an aerodrome, found himself over Oulton at 4:15 one afternoon. Dropping his undercart smartly he wheeled into an approach on the long runway. The ACP made a routine telephone call to Control to say that the Mustang, which had not had time to make radio contact and get a clearance before entering the circuit, was making an approach on the runway in use. (I happened to be on the opposite side of the aerodrome, near the Sally Ann and the hospital, and stood admiring the glinting beauty of the Mustang.) Upon receipt of this message from the ACP, the Panic Merchant soared into action.

"Give him a red," he called, "I'm changing the runway." The wind at that moment was not strong enough to bend 30-inch grass, but the ACP had no choice but to fire a red Very light across the path of the inbound Mustang.

Despite the urgency of his predicament, the American reacted instinctively as pilots are conditioned to react to such a stimulus; he opened the throttle and climbed away. But in seconds, when he had reached about 400 feet, the lifesaving snarl suddenly spluttered into silence. He turned steeply through 120 degrees and dived to land downwind on the nearest short runway. By now I was watching with anxious intensity, for the faint warning whisper of swift death was becoming audible. The American pilot sideslipped steeply to each side alternately, trying to slough off enough height to get the Mustang down. But his speed had unavoidably risen sharply in the rapid descent. The sleek fighter whistled along five feet above the runway, patently far from ready to sit down.

In the intervening seconds, the flow of circumstances had raised the stakes twentyfold. Along the boundary road, which was fringed by a tall hedge, a crew bus loaded with people going to the mess for tea rolled into view, its speed agonizingly timed to bring it directly across the Mustang's path at the critical second. From his elevated vantage

---

1. The Aerodrome Control Position, where a man kept his vigil with a Very pistol and an Aldis lamp in the little caravan parked near the head end of the runway in use.

point the pilot saw the bus, flipped up his undercart, and lifted his lifeless plane three feet higher as he came up to the road. The Mustang hurtled silently over the crew bus, which carried merrily on, neither its driver nor passengers aware that death in the form of a three-ton silver missile had flitted inches over their heads.

The Mustang dropped from view a couple of hundred yards away from me in a small stubble field on the far side of the road. As I was running in its direction I heard the two station ambulances come clanging out of the hospital grounds.

A few seconds later, as I burst onto the stubble field, I passed the ambulances. Both of them were mired to the axles in mud at the entrance to the field. The pilot's canopy on the Mustang was open, and when I came panting up he was half erect, rubbing his head vigorously where it appeared to have been banged against the instrument panel. As it transpired, he was otherwise unhurt, and we were enjoying his company in the mess three-quarters of an hour later, when Doc Vyse had finished with him.

But the beautiful Mustang, although not a complete write-off, was a mess. It sat forlornly at the end of the ugly black furrow it had ploughed, tilted slightly on one wing, showing the airscoop on the underside choked with dirt and battered out of shape, and two blades of the prop thrust violently back at right angles to their normal axis.

The American very charitably — and incorrectly — blamed himself for the event. "I should have just gone ahead and landed anyway — just ignored the Very light," he said, "but it caught me by surprise and I opened the throttle again automatically. Ten more seconds and I ran out of fumes."

To give the Panic Merchant his due, he had no way of knowing that the Mustang was in such desperate straits. But the wind, after all, had been negligible; the aircraft had been only seconds away from a safe landing; and his overzealousness had smashed one brand new aeroplane and come within a hair's breadth of slaughtering 20 or 30 people.

He carried on, excitedly, to the end of the war.

* * *

EXTRACT — OFFICIAL ARCHIVES
J-93970 — PILOT OFFICER IRVINE CLIFFORD BRADLEY

P.O. BRADLEY, OF 464 SQUADRON, WAS THE PILOT OF MOSQUITO NT231 WHICH TOOK OFF ON JANUARY 1st, 1945, TO CARRY OUT A NIGHT INTRUDER OPERATION OVER NORTH LUXEMBOURG. THE AIRCRAFT FAILED TO RETURN.

P.O. BRADLEY AND HIS R.A.F. NAVIGATOR WERE PRESUMED
KILLED DURING AIR OPERATIONS. THE TWO BODIES AND
THE PLANE WERE FOUND LATER NEAR "SIX PLANES"
NORTH LUXEMBOURG.

The last time I had seen Irvine Bradley had been at High River
EFTS. He had been walking six inches off the ground because he had
come second in his class, and because he and Bud Clarke were on their
way together to SFTS and their wings.

*　　*　　*

I went into the mess for breakfast one morning to learn that Vern
Scantleton and his crew had failed to return from operations the night
before. Vern was an Australian pilot, in the same Flight I had been in,
and we had been on the very best of terms. We had frequently alternated in the role of Acting Flight Commander when Bill Day was away
on leave. Everyone felt Vern's loss very keenly, for he had been a real
gentleman and a pleasure to have around.

About three weeks later I was in the Anchor in Aylsham, having
two or three Steward & Patteson's and playing the Crosby collection
again. I stepped out of our little sanctum sanctorum to speak to Ena
about something and came face to face with Scantleton, standing by
the main bar smiling at me. Wonderful as the surprise was, it was a
distinct shock, because by this time, not having heard a word, we were
all thinking of Vern as dead. In fact he had evaded capture and been
helped back by the Maquis. It turned into a particularly boisterous
night.

*　　*　　*

I was Officer-in-Charge of night flying one bleak January evening,
responsible for consulting the Met officer and authorizing the various
student skippers to take off on their exercises, weather permitting.
Later I would be required to be on call in Flying Control until they
were all back and heading for their flying meals. Thus far, the weather
had kept everything grounded. I had spent the late afternoon and
evening in intermittent conferences with Jock Bowie, our Met man,
unwilling to scrub the program while any chance remained of getting a
few precious hours of flying time into the book.

But a series of fronts and occlusions paraded through the area
like trained circus horses all evening, and finally, about 10:00 p.m.,
with no prospect of improvement in sight for the next three or four

hours, I telephoned the mess where the crews were waiting and told them that I had scrubbed the program for the night. As I rode back to our hut the weather was confirming to the full the pessimistic implications of the serrated lines and whorls on Bowie's chart: low scud drifted by at a few hundred feet, and a steady rain kept the windshield wipers busy. I was convinced that even the night hawks were grounded.

Upon my arrival at the site the noise told me that everyone was in Canada House, so I splashed through the puddles and entered. As soon as I had taken my coat off I was subjected to an unsympathetic and raucous barrage of sarcastic criticism for scrubbing 1699's night program. Various mentors predicted that all our pupils would go LMF after their first op with this sort of mollycoddling. My offer to clear one aircraft for circuits and bumps if anyone present would take it and bring back a first-hand weather report showing flying to be feasible finally put a stopper on that line of conversation.

As I had come in, I had noticed a string hanging over the edge of the hot water tank located beyond the vestibule. I commented pointedly on this, so someone went and pulled a tin of mushroom soup out of the hot water tank — our standard method of heating it — and shortly I was sipping some out of a cup and kibitzing on the poker game .

All at once the sound of a fast approaching aircraft came to our ears. It seemed to be low, and as the noise swelled over the next few seconds it sounded as though it were going to go right over our heads. Everyone looked at me. I listened for a moment, unbelievingly.

"Who in hell is flying on a night like this?" I said defensively. Amid a chorus of jeers I headed for the door on the run, followed by two or three curious critics.

We stood outside for only a second or two, then the aircraft roared by, 200 yards away and not very high, a glow pulsing from its tail.

It was a buzz bomb.

*   *   *

It was February, 1945. Steve Nessner, the German-speaking wireless operator who slept in the cot next to mine in Canada House, came down with tonsillitis. Doc Vyse put him in the hospital and after a few days proceeded to remove the offending tissue. Steve remained hospitalized for a while.

The day he was released and put on an out-patient basis, Steve came wandering down to the hut late in the afternoon. We chatted for a while, and he learned from me that Warrant Officer Bennett's crew, the one he had flown all of his 17 operations with, were on the battle order that night. Immediately Steve decided that he should go to briefing, relieve the other special wireless operator, and fly the operation with his regular crew. I told him that he was being stupid; but he persisted in the view that it was his duty to report to the Flight Commander and see if he could be allowed to go. Finally I asked him what would happen if he got halfway to the target and his throat began hemorrhaging at high altitude — the aircraft would have to turn round and come back low level to keep him from bleeding to death. If that happened, I pointed out, he would be responsible for prejudicing the Jostle and Piperack protection on the operation. Steve finally, albeit reluctantly, accepted the fact that he would be asking for serious trouble, and subsided.

It got dark very early. 214's aircraft departed, did the operation, and were arriving back before midnight. Meantime, I had been up at the aerodrome all night as Officer-in-Charge of night flying, had seen all my charges safely down, and was cycling back to the hut as our returning operational Fortresses began droning into the circuit. As I was propping my bike against the side of the hut, I heard the noise of an unfamiliar engine. We were so used to the sound of our own Wright Cyclones, and the Merlins and Hercs of the ubiquitous Mosquitoes, Lancasters, and Halifaxes, that anything outside that category attracted attention. This one was definitely out of place. I looked up but could not see any navigation lights in the area from which the sound appeared to be coming.

For a few moments I stood uneasily looking over in the direction of the aerodrome, then saw a pair of navigation lights heading steadily toward the funnel. A few seconds later I heard, and saw, a long burst of fire streak towards the aircraft in the funnel. It was not machine gun fire but the slower, heavy pounding of cannon fire. The target aircraft burst into flames, but maintained for several seconds its steady descent toward the runway; then, as the flames spread and leapt in the clear night air the dying aircraft slumped into a gentle curving dive and crashed a few hundred yards away from the hospital. Every member of the crew died.

It turned out to be Bennett's crew, the boys Steve Nessner had been so determined to fly with.

Bennett's parents lived a short distance out of London. Steve took the body of his former Skipper and friend home for the funeral.

*   *   *

On February 21st, 1945, Flight Lieutenant J. G. Maguire was shot down and killed in an attack on Worms. His Lancaster crashed at Dirmstein, not far from the target. One member of the crew survived to become a prisoner of war. Jack had been the president of our Lit (Literary Society) at Portage Collegiate.

Almost at the same time as I heard about Jack Maguire, I learned belatedly of the deaths of three other classmates on active service, all with the Air Force. Ted Tindall, who had been with us at No. 7 SFTS at Macleod on tarmac duty, had won his wings as a pilot, been promoted to Flying Officer, and gone missing on active service on March 22nd, 1944. Flying Officer Lorne Cruse, a friend of Rod Dunphy's and mine from Gordon Bell, had been commissioned as an Observer, and had been killed on active service on March 31st, 1944. Lorne had left Winnipeg with Strecker and me on November 6th, 1941, on the draft that went to Edmonton Manning Depot. Jack Lobb, a Warrant Officer and another classmate from Gordon Bell, had been killed on active service much earlier, away back on January 20th, 1943, eight months before I had been posted to an operational squadron. Somehow the news of his death had not reached me for over two years despite the fact that our families had a number of mutual friends.

*   *   *

An American Liberator crew returned one afternoon from operations over Germany and landed at Oulton in the face of generally deteriorating weather. It was like old times in the mess that night having a scattering of olive pinks around the bar. In an hour or so the stories were flying thick and fast, and getting louder and louder on both sides, with the line-shooting rising to epic levels. In the latter competition the RAF eventually won the match hands down, after the Americans were so unwise as to tell the truth and concede that they had flown only a few missions up to that point. The weather had kept on deteriorating, and an operation earlier planned for 214 had been scrubbed; so, with a full mess and some warmly responsive guests, the party soared to memorable heights of hilarity.

Next morning, bright and early, the Americans were in the mess for breakfast, champing at the bit to get back down to the Flights and return to base. They rode up with us in the crew bus and left us, with a volley of friendly insults, in front of Flying Control.

Twenty minutes later they were all dead.

They had taken off under a low ceiling and disappeared briefly into the cloud. Whether the pilot had then decided to make a circuit and try to get back into Oulton no one will ever know. The Liberator suddenly reappeared, diving out of the cloud in a turn, and crashed just beyond one of the maintenance hangars. Ironically, Jock Bowie told me that the poor weather was strictly local — ten miles away it was clear as a bell.

*   *   *

We had one officer with us at Oulton whose company I tried to avoid. He was doing some job on the administrative side, but what galled the aircrew was that he wore a pilot's wing and was content, among strangers, to pass himself off as one of us.

We never felt, or exhibited, any superiority complex in relation to the ground crew officers we worked with. A sprinkling were veterans of the First War. Most of them could not have passed an aircrew medical if they had wanted to; and a great majority of them were specialists whose labours in their own field were much more valuable to the war effort than anything they could have done in the air. We knew it; they knew it; and our relationship with them was excellent, based as it was on mutual respect.

But this particular gentleman got under our hides. He had obviously trained as a pilot just before the war, then thought better of it when the fighting started. He appeared to be medically fit, for he used to cadge the Groupie's Tiger Moth on occasion — or any other light aircraft that happened to be around — take it up for a circuit or two, then talk about his flying experiences at the bar as though he had just done an op on Happy Valley.

One lovely sunny spring day he somehow wangled a ride — and got in a few minutes' dual — in an old relic of an Oxford that Don Bellingham had just managed to procure for 1699 Conversion Unit. Don had been battling to get one for some time so that he could give some of the younger trainees some additional instrument flying before starting them on night flying in Fortresses.

That night in the mess, when he judged his audience to be of adequate size, this Duke-of-Plaza-Toro pilot set his pint on the bar and, very much in the Colonel Blimp style, said in loud and highly critical tones to Don Bellingham:

"Flew that Oxbox of yours today, Bellingham, . . . must say, you've got that aircraft in shocking condition, absolutely shocking."

Don did not appreciate this public lecture from an officer who happened to be junior to him in every respect. It was quite true that the Oxford was a mess; he didn't need the chairborne wizard to tell him that. It was in fact slated for extensive overhaul. But it had been on the station only two or three days, and during that period Don had had to allocate all our limited maintenance resources to the patching of our venerable Forts and Liberators.

In one of those rare moments of poetic justice, Don and I happened to be coming along the perimeter track a couple of days later, just in time to see the Groupie's Tiger Moth come taxiing out, apparently going to take off on the grass a hundred yards clear of the Control Tower. We brought our little Hillman van to a stop momentarily to give the pilot ample clearance as he taxied across the perimeter track in front of us. (The ironclad rule on our station was that if an aircraft was involved in a taxiing accident with any other type of vehicle, the driver of the latter was responsible.) As the pretty little aeroplane went by, I saw that the person at the controls was our esteemed friend, the non-operational pilot.

After a brief pause on the grass, he opened up to take off, and in only a few moments we could see that he was in trouble. The tail of the little Tiger came up too high, and Don and I both speculated aloud that he had trimmed it nose heavy — or forgotten to adjust the trim at all.

The Tiger tore across the field in this unhealthy attitude, steering straight for trouble: just ahead of it was an area of much deeper grass. I sat there using all sorts of body English trying to get the little plane airborne. All of a sudden the nose dug in and it flipped forward, end over end, and landed heavily upside down, one half of the propeller shattering and flying off. We drove over as fast as we could and ran to assist the pilot out of the wreckage. Apart from being shaken up he appeared unhurt. He had hardly pulled his helmet off before the fire truck and the ambulance came roaring over, and he was carried off to sick bay.

Don and I stood surveying the ruin of what had been a beautiful little aeroplane: its propeller splintered into kindling, its rudder crumpled and mangled, the bright yellow fabric torn and grass stained, the upside-down wheels, one wearing a patch of turf, still turning over.

Don turned to me with a grin:

"Well, I didn't do it; but I want to tell you I had to bite my tongue to keep from doing it. I wanted in the worst way to turn to him and remark: 'I must say, you've got that aircraft in shocking condition, absolutely shocking!' "

*   *   *

Place: The Control Tower, RAF Station Oulton.

The time was early in March, 1945, very late at night. I was finishing a stint in the Control Tower as Officer-in-Charge of night flying when the first movements in an episode of high drama began to take place. They took place against a background of predictions by Allied Intelligence that the Germans would likely make at least one all-out night intruder foray, delivering their attacks over British aerodromes when our returning bombers would be clustered in the circuit, in the hope that their tired crews would be less vigilant than usual.

It began to look as though this night might be the chosen one. Widespread reports of intruder activity came in, and it appeared that the hunting had been good for the German night fighters. In Flying Control my attention had been drawn to a large map of the area on which several low level "Hostiles" had been plotted on the basis of Observer Corps reports.

The telephone rang and our Controller, the receiver against his ear, called out a position and an estimated course for "Hostile 32." Someone took a grease pencil and marked an arrow in the appropriate position on the overlay, and I noted that Hostile 32 was only about ten or 12 miles away, and heading directly for Oulton if he maintained the reported course. It began to look interesting. Two or three of us decided to go out on the narrow balcony and see if we could spot him or hear him when he passed. As we left, the Controller was alerting the RAF Regiment gun post on the north side of the field.

Outside, we presently heard a few faint sounds borne on the wind from the direction of the gun post, presumably as the crew mounted a clip and got the Bofors ready. Then silence. We strained our ears and peered in the direction from which we expected the intruder to approach.

After we had been leaning on the balcony rail for about two minutes I thought I heard something; then I told myself I was imagining things; but in a few more seconds the sound came to us clearly, the sound of alien engines, swelling to a roar. Abruptly, directly in front of us and flying at right angles to our line of vision, an aircraft streaked from left to right 50 feet above the short runway. All told I saw him for only three or four seconds. It was a Ju 88, speeding for the sea at full throttle. The Bofors crew couldn't even get off a shot.

Hardly had the German engines faded to a faint hum when a new and familiar note became audible, then swelled upon us in a deep throated crescendo as a Mosquito, its Merlins snarling, swept across the field directly along the path taken by the Ju 88 and no more than 30 seconds behind it.

The hunter had become the hunted, with a vengeance. The cobra had aroused a mongoose — a mongoose with a 90-mile per hour edge in speed and four 20 mm. cannons. To the naked eye it appeared that the Mosquito's Controller had given him a perfect vector. Both aircraft seemed to have roared directly along the path of the short runway. I wondered if the German had a device like our Boozer or Monica aboard. If he did, the equipment was about to impart an ominous message as the Mosquito closed the gap between them.

We moved back inside the tower, wondering what would happen next; wondering also if we would ever know how the chase went. For three minutes there was nothing but silence. The big speaker on the wall maintained its almost inaudible hum. Then all at once it came to life as a new sibilance was born, a hissing sound like that which comes from a phonograph speaker when a needle is first set on a record. Then, from a distance, but with perfect clarity, a high-pitched Oxford accent came through, unruffled and matter-of-fact:

"Hostile 32 destroyed. Another vector please."

The German night fighter crew had had less than five minutes to live when we saw their Ju 88 speeding desperately for safety.

*   *   *

On May 1st a Mosquito from Massingham came over to do a fighter affiliation exercise with one of our 1699 crews. The Mossie navigator came into the flight office to see me, inquiring whether he could go for a ride in the Fortress while the exercise was taking place. I said "no trouble," put his name in the book, decided that turnabout was fair play, and went for a flip with the Mossie pilot.

It was a new sensation being in the fighter and attacking the bomber. The pitiful disparity between the power of the attacker and that of the defender was glaringly evident. I had realized it before, of course, but the way to have the point driven home with unmistakeable emphasis was to trade places, as I was doing. It gave me pause to think that the Me 410's and the Ju 88's that we had encountered had actually been able to slide in on us at our weakest point and bring us under their guns as easily as we in the Mosquito were now engaging the Fortress — whenever we chose, from whatever angle we preferred. The violent gyrations of the Fortress's corkscrew made it difficult to get in a good "burst" from the Mossie's cine camera gun, but it was obvious that the law of averages loaded the odds fearfully in favour of the fighter.

Even so, I felt that the Mosquito pilot did not press his attacks with anything like the determination of the German pilots who had attacked us; but I put that down to a perhaps understandable reluctance to take too many chances in what was, after all, only a routine practice exercise. If I had known then what I learned about the Mossie pilot half an hour later, I should not have been inwardly urging him to press on in another 50 yards before rolling upside down and breaking off his attacks.

When the exercise was over, we separated from the Fortress, and the Mossie pilot asked me if I would like to fly her for a bit. He slid his seat back and let me lean in front of him to take the stick. She was a magnificent aeroplane to fly; the aileron control particularly was a joy to the touch, so sensitive and effortless. For ten minutes I wheeled and turned like a child with a stupendous new toy. The Mossie pilot lost his bearings for a moment and asked me to head her back to our aerodrome, descending on the way.

As I ran across the field at 500 feet, I saw the crew bus pulling up at the dispersal of the Fortress we had been practising with. Knowing that my latest flame was driving the crew bus, I asked the Mossie pilot if I could do a beat-up right across that dispersal. He looked a little doubtful, but nodded:

"Okay," he said "but don't try cutting the grass."

I pulled her up another 1,500 feet, and then from a point a mile away from the aerodrome dove for the deck. The Mossie pilot was enjoying himself too, and pushed the throttle right forward as I dived. We whistled across the drome at about 30 feet, the airspeed indicator nudging 400 miles per hour, pulling up just over the bus and soaring up like a swallow. Reluctantly I moved out of the way and handed the controls back to the Skipper.

"God, that's a wonderful aeroplane," I said, bursting with exhilaration.

"They sure are," he replied; "but they're a little tricky to land. They're nothing but two big Merlins with a bit of plywood around them, you know, and they'll ground loop if you look sideways at them."

I mulled this over for a second or two. It was not like a seasoned pilot to be speaking in this fashion, as though he still had trouble landing the kite.

"How many hours you got on Mossie's now?" I said, looking for the assurance of his telling me that he had done a whole tour on them.

"Three," he said, "we just got to Massingham last Friday."

I was tempted to say that he only had two more hours on Mossies than I did, but thought better of it, feeling that he didn't need anyone reducing his self confidence at this point.

His landing was a bit dicey, and I could feel that the Mosquito was quite capable of ground looping if you weren't nice to her. I breathed easier as we slowed down and it became apparent that he was going to stay on the concrete.

Back at the Flights, he said, as I prepared to climb out:

"Watch your step when you jump out. I don't want to shut down the engines."

I lowered myself gingerly to the ground, extremely conscious of the silver blur which seemed about six inches from the end of my nose. As I dropped to the ground I was concentrating on not stumbling forward.

* * *

While in London on leave, I saw an ad stating that the following day a certain establishment in Leicester Square would be selling ice cream. Apparently some restrictions on the use of milk or sugar for such purposes had been eased. Not having tasted ice cream since my arrival in England, even the ersatz product suggested by the ad, I wandered over to Leicester Square on schedule and encountered a great line-up waiting to be served, almost all of them servicemen and a good 60 percent Americans and Canadians.

I found myself standing beside an American infantryman, and we quickly struck up a conversation to pass the time, since it appeared that we were going to be waiting 15 or 20 minutes to get our treat. Ever the tactful ally, I passed a complimentary remark, quite sincerely, on the results of the previous week's attack by American infantry supported by the Ninth American Tactical Air Force. The American looked at me:

"The Ninth bloody American Luftwaffe you mean," he said sourly; "those bastards have bombed us more than they've bombed the Germans."

I felt compelled to defend the Ninth, which for weeks had been going absolutely flat out and had won my professional admiration. I pointed out that in an advance such as the one we were talking about, with a highly fluid line, marking the bombing line properly for the airmen was the tricky bit. It was not a case of their airmen being either inaccurate or not careful enough. Almost invariably, I told him, it was a case of the advancing infantry changing the situation in the 15 or 20 hours that usually elapsed between the original request and joint planning for the attack and the actual bombing. Sometimes the word on last minute changes would not filter down to all formations, and the proper signals, be they red or yellow smoke or whatever, would not be displayed. I told him our Bomber Command had done the same thing at Caen the summer before, and for the same reason.

The American was a good listener, and spoke himself with a sense of humour. As we picked up our ice creams — two each — I asked him if he had anything planned for the afternoon, telling him that I was going to step over to the New Prince of Wales Theatre and take in the matinée of Sid Field in the stage show "Strike It Again." I was at a loose end until that evening, and felt I would appreciate some company.

The American was very skeptical about being my guest at this particular function; he had decided views about English comedians.

"Listen," I said, "I used to feel that way myself. Someone finally pestered me into going to see Sid Field in his earlier show, 'Strike a New Note' and since then I've never missed seeing him whenever I'm in London. I saw 'Strike a New Note' 11 times; I've seen this one six times already. I'll probably go again tomorrow. I know every line of dialogue in the show; but this guy is wonderful, believe me; he's the best."

The American allowed himself to be persuaded, but only to please me. I could sense that inwardly he was still from Missouri.

The first time Sid Field came on, with that unbeatable straight man Jerry Desmonde, I watched the American out the corner of my eye. Sid's first few sallies provoked only a mild response, but within two or three minutes the irresistible personality of the comedian Bob Hope once called the best in the business completely vanquished the American's dwindling skepticism. His chuckles became more frequent, progressed to belly laughs and finally to paroxysms of mirth.

Later in the show, when Sid did a quick-change skit in which he played a convict recently escaped from Dartmoor, the pursuing Inspector from Scotland Yard (in a kilt and on his Raleigh "Thrrrree Speed"), and the villain about to effect foreclosure on the heroine's father, the American laughed until the tears ran down his face. When Sid made his last entrance as the sour-gutted mortgagee, tripped on the tiger-skin rug and wheeled to bat the tiger two on the head with his riding crop, the American had to look away from the stage. He was whimpering in a woman's falsetto, holding his stomach helplessly, out of control. I was satisfied that he was getting my money's worth.

At the final curtain, when Sid came out with the full cast and finished up singing The King, the American turned to me excitedly:

"Do you suppose I could get his autograph if I went backstage?" he said. "Or maybe I could see him if I waited at the stage door."

"I don't think they'll let anyone backstage," I said, "but you could probably catch him at the stage door."

The American left me at the front of the theatre, determined to have a word with Sid Field no matter how long he had to wait. I had seen this wonderful personality time after time go before a brand new audience, win them over in five minutes, and thereafter have them eating out of his hand, ready to roar at every gesture and quip, so I fully understood the feelings of the new convert. I wished him luck, shook hands and left. What with the ice cream and the American's successful exposure to Sid Field, it had been one of the better days of the war.

* * *

Peden's crew made one more attack on Gelsenkirchen; but you will find no mention of this one in the Official History, for it was carried out on May 30th, 1945, a sunny day almost a year after our first disastrous visit, and three weeks after the German forces had surrendered to General Eisenhower and the Allied armies. The trip is recorded in 214 Squadron's Duty Book, but there it appears only as a tour of the Ruhr Valley with our ground crew for the purpose of

Coming home. These seven DFC aircrew from Winnipeg were grouped aboard the troop-ship Stratheden by an RCAF photographer. Front (l to r): F/O C. N. Matheson, F/L C. E. Dingle, F/L D. W. Rathwell. Rear (l to r): F/O S. W. Posner, S/L N. Thorp, F/L H. N. Scott, the author. (RCAF)

Above: There is a lot of history in this group of airmen at the airshow at Portage la Prairie during the 1976 Aircrew Reunion. At the upper left corner is Sir Denis Smallwood, then Commander-in-Chief RAF Strike Command; to the right of him is General Adolf Galland; in front of General Galland and slightly to the right, Sir Douglas Bader puffs on his pipe while he chats with Francis Gabreski, the great 'Double Ace' of World War II and Korea. To Gabreski's left, the gentleman leaning forward to peer at his program is James H. Doolittle. Next to him is Group Captain 'Tiny' White, New Zealand's representative in Ottawa for the British Commonwealth Air Training Plan during World War II. On the extreme left side of the same row, wearing dark glasses and holding a cool drink, is Johnnie Johnson, and slightly to the right sits Johnny Fauquier, Canada's most decorated airman.   (DM Peden)

Below left: General Galland, at the request of the Winnipeg Wartime Pilots' and Observers' Association, lays a wreath on behalf of the German Fighter Pilots' Association (Aircrew Reunion, Winnipeg, 1976).   (Rod Peden)

Below right: A recent photo of the author about to be flown home after delivering an address to student pilots at Portage la Prairie. At left is the Base Commander, Col. G. Brennand, at right, the pilot Capt. Jim Hunter. Note the helicopter's serial number!

Above: Two wartime passengers of the *S.S. Cavina* get together after 37 years: Dame Anna Neagle poses with the author at the RAF Club in London, October 9th, 1979.

(J. Johnstone)

Below: Sir Arthur Harris at home in October 1979.

(Author)

Left: A.V.M. Addison outside his home in Weybridge, October 1979. (Author)

Below: "Willie" Tait with Gort Strecker in the garden of Tait's home in Acton, October 7, '79. (Author)

letting them see the appalling destruction wrought, with their assistance, by the Allied aircrews.

We selected our own route, and flew to Ypres and Vimy Ridge first, to satisfy my desire to see the places where my father and my uncles had fought in the first World War. Moving further east we flew along the great line of concrete "dragon's teeth" of the Siegfried Line. We journeyed to Cologne, and at 400 feet, in a steep turn, we repeatedly circled the blackened spires of Cologne Cathedral, seemingly the only building unscathed in a desert of devastation that stretched across the entire Ruhr. The magnificent old edifice stood amidst the ruins, preserved by Providence, projecting its mute and melancholy rebuke to man's wickedness and folly. Several hundred yards behind it, forming part of the spectral backdrop, the great bridge over the Rhine sprawled drunkenly, covered for the greater part of its length by the swollen waters.

But the high point of the trip we saved until the end, when we swung north-northeast across Essen and the rubble of the Krupps works to visit Gelsenkirchen, three minutes flying time further on. As we drew near that fateful spot, Stan told us to be sure to let him know when we were approaching the sector that contained the Nordstern oil plant. At that point he moved aft to the large openings of the waist gun positions, and, while I facilitated his attack by pulling the aircraft into another steeply banked turn, he relieved himself over the industrial complex that had nearly put all our names on the casualty list.

Upon our return Stan assured us that the poetic justice of that symbolic punishment had had an immeasurable therapeutic effect upon him. While it conflicted with Portia's sentiments, it strikingly paralleled her opening remarks about the quality of mercy.

* * *

On June 27th, 1945, I left 214 Squadron and 1699, posted to the RCAF Station at Linton-on-Ouse on the first stage of my journey home. The night before I left the crew had one final session at the Anchor, and we parted company with long handshakes, misty eyes, and my truthful statement that if I had to start over again, and was given the whole roster of Bomber Command aircrew to choose from, I wouldn't trade one man in my crew.

Linton-on-Ouse was my home for all of six days, after which I was posted a dozen miles away to Dishforth, a repatriation centre for Canadian aircrew. After I had been there for about ten days, momentarily expecting a draft, the Adjutant called me to his office one morning and told me that a special investiture, largely for Canadians returning home, was being held at Buckingham Palace in two days, and that my name was on the list. He assured me that there was no draft in sight for us for at least three days, so I headed happily for London with passes to the Palace for two guests.

At the appointed hour, after a short briefing on what we were to do — one thing we were not to do was give the King bone-crushing handshakes — I stood in line with some two or three hundred other Canadians, 90 percent of them Army officers back from service in Holland, as King George presented the glittering decorations. Although he limited himself to a handshake and a few words with each man as he slipped the decoration on his chest, it took a very long time to work down to the point where it was my turn to mount the little plush-covered runway, march before the King, and bow.

During this lengthy but fascinating interlude, an orchestra in the background played Boccherini's Minuet. By my count they played it 37 times from start to finish. To this day, the moment I hear the piece I am transported back to Buckingham Palace, shaking hands with the King, then marching proudly off to show the shining silver cross to Margaret Kelly and Tom Cherry, my two guests.

I caught the first train back to Dishforth after the investiture, anxious lest something had come through in my absence — then waited for another interminable week without even the rumour of a draft. Finally the good news came. On short notice we caught the train for Liverpool, from whence, on July 22nd, we embarked for Canada aboard HMT *Stratheden.*

On July 31st the *Stratheden* dropped anchor in Wolfe's Cove, Quebec City, the first troopship to dock there since World War I. It was late afternoon when we arrived, and we were kept aboard ship until the following morning, when we boarded a transcontinental train and headed west. Early on the morning of August 3rd, another beautiful sunny morning, I climbed off the train and walked into the rotunda of the Winnipeg CNR station, the point from which I had left to start my Air Force career four years earlier. The station was jammed with people waiting to welcome their men home. I walked along with a haversack slung on one shoulder — a haversack in which I was carrying a very carefully packed record featuring Harry Mortimer and Foden's Motor Works Band — looking for a familiar face in the crush. Above the din I heard "Murray . . . Murray," and suddenly my father had me by the hand.

EPILOGUE

When I remember all
The friends so linked together
I've seen around me fall
Like leaves in wintry weather,
I feel like one
Who treads alone
Some banquet-hall deserted,
Whose lights are fled
Whose garlands dead,
And all but he departed!

Thomas Moore, *Oft In The Stilly Night*

The vivid and poignant recollections of war began to dim with one's return to civilian life. Memory's most deeply etched traces — the record of harrowing moments, or moments of blessed relief such as those when a safe return brought the knowledge that one would be alive for at least one more day — were gradually softened. The grist of a multitude of new, smaller scale experiences, like wind-driven sand, partially filled in the coarser impressions, and, over the years, obliterated completely the fainter trail of routine events.

But from time to time current happenings would reawaken fading memories, causing them to glow briefly with their old lustre. On May 6th, 1947, as one act in a program of naming previously unnamed geographical features after men who had given their lives for their country, the government assigned the name Dunphy Lakes to the extensive waters lying in Manitoba at Latitude 56 degrees 41' N., Longitude 101 degrees 34' W. If one opens the official Manitoba road map and glances at the upper left hand corner, the lake named in honour of Roderick J. Dunphy, DFC, is easy to find, some 30 miles southwest of the town of Lynn Lake.

In September, 1956, the idol of my youthful years, Billy Bishop, died. His passing stirred a flood of old memories, and the newspaper description of the lone fighter plane droning overhead as his body was carried to the graveside was an apt reminder of the legendary feats the great Canadian ace had wrought in those First War days when aerial combat had imported some of the glamour and chivalry of a bygone era.

Memories were rekindled by positive acts, too, not only by the passive reception of powerful stimuli as they chanced to occur. Some years ago, on a holiday drive from Vicksburg to Shiloh and Chickamauga, I found that my route took me into Memphis. That name echoed from the past, and I knew that I could not simply drive through the city without a short stopover. With mounting anticipation I followed the directions given us by a helpful passerby and drove to the National Guard armoury, where Memphis Belle still sits waiting for her crew.

I wonder how many thousand aircrew have stood with a lump in their throats and gazed affectionately at the old Fortress as she sits there, seemingly ready to start her takeoff roll, wishing longingly, as I did, that they could open the hatch in the nose, or the back door, and slip into the old positions again. At such times the memories are not clouded, but newly painted, fresh, and vibrant; the Chiefie is at your shoulder, ready to get you to sign.

I experienced similar moments vacationing in England, returning with Stan and Bill to all the old aerodromes, Chedburgh, Tempsford, and Oulton, and gazing unbelievingly at the quiet pastoral scenes presented by deserted and crumbling aerodromes — aerodromes that I could only remember as throbbing always with activity, alive with noise and movement, with engines being tested, bomb trolleys or oxygen trucks trundling around the perimeter track, and crew buses on sentry-go continuously between the Flights and the dispersals.

At Sandy, where the road from Sandy to the Tempsford aerodrome had been changed, leaving us momentarily baffled, we asked a local resident, a middle-aged woman carrying a bag of groceries, if she could tell us how to get onto the road that led to the old aerodrome (located a mile away).

"Aerodrome?" she said, "there's no aerodrome anywhere around here."

A few minutes later, despite that unintentional slap in the face, we stood together on the old drome, and our talk was all of Stirlings, jammed undercarriages and high chimneys, and overweight landings, as though these events had happened the previous week.

Sometimes reminders came unexpectedly and fortuitously. In the spring of 1970 I attended a conference in Washington, D.C., and on the way home was unable to get the usual direct flight to Minneapolis. Instead, I found myself on a milk run which seemed to be up and down every 20 minutes. At one point the stewardess announced that we had just landed at Des Moines, Iowa. It was the mention of Iowa that triggered the reaction. I remembered that 150 miles or so east of Des Moines was Bennett. On an impulse I left the plane and looked for a telephone. It had been 28 years . . . but maybe she would still be there.

In a few moments I was talking to Mrs. Plate. Once again the years fell away as we reminisced and brought each other up-to-date. As the plane was called and I had to leave, she told me that Wilmer, her other son, was just retiring from the United States Air Force, having made his career in the service. I had known from the letters she sent to my mother during the war that Wilmer had completed his tour with the USAAF, and that he had been awarded the American DFC and a Purple Heart.

Other little reminders come frequently. My children comment if they see a car licence with a "BU" prefix, BU being 214's squadron letters. Anything with the number 214 on it gets special mention, and a 214 with an F beside it would prompt immediate mention of F Fox.

The fall of 1970 brought a very special event. On Thursday, September 24th, I was in San Diego. I rose at 5:00 AM and caught a cab a short time later to the airport, having 2,500 miles to travel to participate in important business. On the stopover in Vancouver, I tried to telephone J. B. — as I had on the way down to San Diego — but without success. About 8:00 PM, back in Winnipeg, I changed into some fresh clothes and drove to the Winnipeg Inn.

In honour of Manitoba's Centennial, our Wartime Pilots and Observers Association had organized a great aircrew reunion and had broadcast invitations to all members of aircrew who had trained under the British Commonwealth Air Training Plan. The committee making the arrangements had looked into its crystal ball at length, gone out on a limb, and guaranteed the hotel something like 600 guests. Shortly before the event they had been sweating, for reservations made well in advance were pretty thin.

When I arrived at the Winnipeg Inn, there were close to 1,300 guests on the convention floor. Former aircrew had flown in from all over Canada, and American ex-members of the RCAF and RAF had come up in goodly numbers from south of the line. One enthusiast had flown in from Hawaii, and we had guests of honour attending from Britain and Europe.

One area had been marked off into Commands, to help people narrow their search for friends. As soon as I arrived, I got a drink in my hand and began making my way toward the sign "Bomber Command." Before I quite reached it I saw a friend from Canada House smiling at my halting progress through the crowd: Puterbough. He had come up that day from his home north of Toronto. That high note set the tone for the four-day convention.

A few minutes later, almost before Putt and I had had a chance to test London's flak defences, low level, in a Stirling again, someone took me inside the Bomber Command alcove to introduce me to one of our guests of honour, Air Commodore Johnny Fauquier, Canada's best known bomber pilot, the man who had been the Deputy Master Bomber and played such a prominent part in Bomber Command's heavy attack on the German V1 and rocket research facilities at Peenemunde, and who later commanded 617 Squadron, the Dam Busters.

Other guests of honour were: Air Vice-Marshal Johnnie Johnson, whose 38 victories made him Britain's top fighter ace in World War II; Group Captain Douglas Bader, the legless ace whose stirring display of inner fortitude in fashioning a new Air Force career after his accident has become so well known; and *General Leutenant* Adolf Galland, the best known German fighter ace, with a score of 105 aircraft destroyed. With that sort of stimulus, fanned by the company of hundreds of aircrew in a convivial mood, the lighter moments of the war were recalled in clusters, and enjoyed to the full.

I began thinking seriously about writing this book a few months after the aircrew reunion, having toyed with the idea earlier. Fortunately, my father had saved every letter I sent home during the war, scores and scores of them. Once I made the decision to write, they assumed a value to me far above anything they had ever had before. So far as the details of flights were concerned, my log book fixed all the dates and provided most of the additional details required; but there were half a dozen dates of other events that my letters had not tied down closely enough, some of which I finally had to estimate when I was unable to fix them even with the assistance of outside sources. However, 99 percent of the dates I wanted to refer to were easily ascertainable from the material I had available.

In 1972 I learned by chance that Jim Baird, our former SFTS Flight Commander, was living in Calgary. I telephoned him immediately to confirm one or two details of the SFTS chapter, and we had a delightful chat. Jim followed up our conversation with two or three letters, one of which set out the painful details of the sequel to the death of Francis Plate. I found Jim Baird's explanation gratifying, because, through all the intervening years I had never been satisfied that we really understood what had caused Plate's accident.

Our Course, No. 59, had left Dauphin in October, 1942. After our departure, Jim Baird had been taken from "E" Flight and sent to the control tower as Testing Officer for No. 2 Squadron. In that capacity he was called upon to test four or five students — and instructors — each day.

On Monday afternoon, January 11th, 1943, Baird was due to take up two students, Dewar and Dunlop, for their Instrument Wings Tests. At the very last moment, the Squadron Commander was called away. He in turn summoned Baird to take over his duties, so Baird had called on another instructor, Rowland Thorpe, and asked him to administer the tests. Thorpe readily agreed, and presently took off with Dewar and Dunlop.

At ten minutes past five, the aeroplane crashed approximately five miles north of the nearby village of Ashville. All three airmen were killed. Compounding the tragedy, from Jim Baird's point of view, was the fact that Rollie Thorpe was a close personal friend, and had himself been a student of Baird's in earlier times.

But from this tragedy, in conjunction with Plate's death five months earlier, Training Command HQ recognized that there might well be a defect in the Crane I. More intensive investigation indicated the possibility of a weakness in the leading edge of the wing as then designed. All Crane I's were immediately modified by the insertion of several extra nose ribs to strengthen the leading edge.

There were no further unexplained accidents. The mystery of my friend's sudden death was a mystery no longer as far as I was concerned.

When I became wrapped up in the writing of the book, it occurred to me that it would be pleasant to look up Brigadier General Frank A. Armstrong, or write to him, and discuss the Park Lane Hotel incident, to see if he could enhance it with further details from his own recollection. I wrote to the Headquarters of the United States Air Force to see whether they could give me the General's present address. The reply was brief:

"... I am sorry to inform you that General Armstrong died 20 August 1969."

At about the same time, I learned from Bill Bailey that George Wright had died. J. B. also mentioned his passing in a letter, putting the sadness of the loss to one side and recalling instead the good times George had given us. He went on to remind me of the first evening he and I had gone together into the officers mess bar at Chedburgh. It was on my third night on the station, the first two having been fully occupied with operations on Hanover and Mannheim. George Wright was there, saw the two new Canadians enter the bar for the first time, and, reversing protocol, came over to ask us with typically bluff hospitality what we would like to drink. J. B. and I were still highly receptive to Training Command dogma regarding the insidious dangers of strong drink to flying personnel. I therefore requested lemon squash; J. B. opted for ginger ale. Patently shocked, George backed away, looking at us as though we had openly confessed to homosexual inclinations or some other equally detestable aberration. We gathered that, in 214's mess, George did not expect soft drinks to be big sellers. We mended our ways and began nursing more robust beverages, much to George's relief. If there is a bar in the next world there is no one I would rather have welcome me to it than George Wright.

In September, 1973, I flew to Britain on a charter flight organized by the Wartime Pilots and Observers Association. Our nostalgic pleasure was at its height during the great Battle of Britain air show at Biggin Hill, and at the party in the RAF Club presided over by Johnnie Johnson and Douglas Bader.

I had advised Stan that I was coming, but had cautioned him not to say anything to Bill Bailey or J. B. Waters. J. B., I had learned, was going to be flying to London from Vancouver at almost the same time. At my instigation, Stan arranged for Bill Bailey and J. B. to join him in London for a dinner at Isow's. I kept out of sight until the three of them were on their second drink, then walked in as casually as though we met like that once a week. The results were profane and highly gratifying.

Nor were the pleasures of the trip yet exhausted. For old time's sake, I walked to the Park Lane Hotel one evening, sat in the lounge and sipped two scotches while seated where I could view the area occupied so many years before by General Armstrong and his British friend. Over my drinks I re-lived in my imagination the scene of the ultra-casual beer drinker, the General and his austere friend, and the entrance of the two Canadian pilots. In a completely atypical burst of generosity I grossly overtipped the elderly waiter and returned to my own hotel in the pleasantest possible frame of mind.

As I walked towards its entrance, a poster in a neighbouring window caught my eye, a poster advertising a show then running at the Drury Lane Theatre: "No, No, Nanette". What seemed so delightfully appropriate was the name of the star the show was featuring: Dame Anna Neagle.

On the same trip another loose end was tied off. Although I did not get the opportunity to hear a concert by Foden's Motor Works Band, I did have three highly enjoyable meetings with the dean of the world's brass band fraternity, the man who had played solo cornet for Foden's in the period of its most glittering successes, the man my old bandmaster had always avowed was the greatest cornet player in the world, Harry Mortimer. It was a thrill to discover that the musical talents of this truly great musician were matched by his kindness, courtesy and hospitality. I gratefully testify that my old bandmaster's assessment of Harry Mortimer was accurate in a much broader sense than he realized.

Still the process of erosion of our old mental images, arrested and momentarily reversed by such events, goes on. So far as the wartime experiences are concerned, it is in many ways a healthy process, helping to replace the old fires of indignation and animosity with a more charitable outlook, and a readier recognition that there were brave men on the other side, men who also underwent the strain of operations and suffered the loss of friends and relatives.

Thus, perhaps a fitting incident on which to close is one that occurred at the great aircrew reunion in Winnipeg. Douglas Bader was making some introductory remarks at the first luncheon, in the course of which he acknowledged the presence at the head table of General Galland (who has no difficulty speaking English). Sensitive to our guest's position, Bader spoke for all of us saying that we were delighted and proud to have him with us. Then Bader said:

"Put yourself in his position. How would you feel being the only British pilot at a meeting of twelve or thirteen hundred German aircrew?"

General Galland thereupon received a standing round of applause, greatly prolonged, which visibly moved him, and Bader went on to put the icing on the cake. He confessed candidly that when preparations for the reunion had been put under way, someone on the committee had telephoned him long-distance from Winnipeg, and in the course of the conversation had told Bader that it was the committee's intention to invite General Galland.

"I said," Bader continued, " 'Look, it's the most *extraordinary* thing for a Commonwealth Air Training Scheme reunion to ask a German fighter ace.' There was a sort of stunned silence at the other end of the line, and the splendid remark came back:

'Well . . . if it hadn't been for chaps like him . . . we wouldn't have had a bloody Commonwealth Air Training Scheme.' "

General Galland's laugh was swept away in the gale of laughter of his 1,300 former enemies.

THE END

APPENDIX

From:

Marshal of The Royal Air Force,
Sir Arthur T. Harris, BT., GCB., OBE., AFC., LLD.

The Ferry House,
Goring on Thames,
RG8 9DX   29.11.79

Dear Peden,

I have just finished reading your book — in fact I found it hard to put it down.

I consider it is not only the best and most true to life "War" book I've read about this war, but the best about all the wars of my lifetime — from the "Boer" war onwards.

I have only two criticisms to make 1/ That at times it made me so sad that I found it hard to retain the moisture within my eyes:-

2/ The one ref you make to Bomber Cmd bombing our own troops is not quite correct. You say the troops had moved on by the time the order to bomb in front of them was activated.

In the interests of accuracy you should know that what happened on that sad occasion was the fault entirely of both troops and the bombers.

In spite of previous agreement with the Army that the troops would *not use any* coloured smoke to indicate their position they not only used it but, unfortunately, quite by a coincidence, they used the actual colour the Pathfinders 'were' to use to indicate the target!! Thus literally bringing the wrath down on their own heads!!

But that didn't excuse the incorrect bombing, because, to doubly insure against such "accidents", Bomber Cmd's order laid down that *no bomb* was to be dropped *before the expiry of a given timed run from the coastline* — which would, if obeyed, have made it impossible to hit our own troops. Both orders were disobeyed by the troops and bomber crews concerned. But, as both troops and bombers concerned happened to be your countrymen on that occasion, I knocked their heads together and told them to sort it out between themselves. However these things, and a lot else, mishappen in war.

Warmest regards and congrats re book.

Yrs

(signed)   Arthur T. Harris, MRAF

From:

Marshal of The Royal Air Force
Sir Arthur T. Harris, BT., GCB., OBE., AFC., LLD.
The Ferry House,
Goring on Thames,
RG8 9DX
20th May, 1980

My dear Mr. Johnson,

Thank you for your letter of the 1st of May.

I have no objection to you carrying out the steps you propose, but I would like it to be made quite clear that I intend no disparagement of the magnificent Canadian crews who rendered such wonderful service in Bomber Command.

I really don't blame the bombaimers, who in the stress of action aimed at what they understood, understandably, to be the Pathfinder smoke indicators. It seems to me that the real blame for the incident, although it was of a type that is bound to occasionally occur in the stresses of war, is really to be blamed on some Staff or other Officers amongst the Ground Forces, who obviously failed to instruct the troops concerned that no smoke signals at all were to be used. It was a tragic co-incidence that that instruction was either disobeyed, or never reached the troops, and an almost incredible co-incidence is that they used pathfinder colour smoke colours designed for the occasion in question.

Yours faithfully,
Arthur T. Harris, MRAF

Mr. Eric A. Johnson,
Canada's Wings,
P.O. Box 393,
Stittsville,
Ontario K0A 3G0
Canada

INDEX

488

489

23, 24, 25, 26, 28, 463
Stringer, Mary, 234, 235, 248, 252, 253
Stuttgart, Germany, 363, 364, 421, 430, 439
Sweeney, Wilf, 297, 298, 322
Sywell, UK, 131, 133, 134, 136, 137, 139, 140, 142

T

Tait, Wing Commander "Willie", 348
"Tallboy", 348
"Target for Tonight", 280
Taylor, Freddie, 63, 78, 85, 94, 95, 96, 103, 104, 105, 106, 111, 113, 114, 115, 116, 125, 126, 127, 130, 131, 163, 168, 169, 174, 182, 183, 191, 192, 291, 322, 335
Tempsford, UK, 278, 280, 282, 283, 285, 293, 302, 316, 320, 478
Thorpe, Rowland, 481
Thrower, Pilot Officer, 153
Tindall, Ted, 463
Tirpitz, 299, 348
Tracy, Flight Sergeant, 3, 4
Trafalgar Square, 354
Trenchard, Marshal of the Royal Air Force, Lord, ix, 443, 444
Trenton, Ont., 17, 39, 43
Tromso, Fiord, 348
Tutt, "King of Swing", 233, 234

U

University of Alberta, 15
Uxbridge, UK, 429

V

Von Stroheim, Erich, 29
Vyse, 'Doc', 256, 257, 274, 428, 461

W

Waddington, Flight Lieutenant, 148, 149, 153, 154, 164
Walker, Johnny, W., 399, 401, 446
Walters, Jake, 247, 254, 255, 298, 339, 425, 426, 427, 439, 454, 455
Wangerooge, 270
Wartime Pilots and Observers Association, 479, 482
Waterbeach, UK, 252, 350
Waters, J. B., 170, 171, 182, 183, 184, 208, 210, 211, 212, 216, 220, 230, 237, 242, 259, 260, 264, 270, 288, 292, 293, 294, 295, 299, 300, 319, 320, 354, 379, 400, 403, 424, 453, 479, 481, 482
Watson, F/L James Andrew "Jim", 131, 149, 150, 151, 152, 368, 369
Wayne, John, 354, 355
Wellingborough, UK, 134, 140
Wesseling, Germany, 414
Whipple, Mr., 9, 10
Wilhelmshaven, Germany, 270, 272, 348
Wilson, Jock, 176, 177, 296, 298, 410, 428

Wilton, F/L Walter Torrance "Watt", 126, 127, 169
Winnipeg, Man., 10, 11, 28, 57, 67, 68, 90, 322, 483
Winnipeg Inn, Man., 473
Woodbridge, UK, 403, 408, 410, 412
Worthing, UK. 127
Wratting Common, UK, 247
Wrexham, UK, xiii
Wright, Flight Lieutenant George, 242, 257, 266, 267, 268, 269, 274, 275, 303, 315, 370, 387, 411, 424, 426, 448, 453, 456, 481, 483
Wright Joyce, 21, 22, 52, 386
Wright, Sergeant, 145

Y

Yokum, Pappy, 27
No. 1 "Y" Depot, Halifax, 88, 90, 92
2nd Canadian Armoured Div., 185
No. 2 Group, 280
No. 3 AOS, Regina, 321
No. 3 Group, 240, 243, 321
No. 3 Manning Depot, Edmonton, 2, 3
No. 3 Personnel Receiving Depot, 109, 111
No. 4 Initial Training School, Edmonton, 14, 15
No. 5 Elementary Flying Training School, 28
No. 5 Group, 320, 342
No. 6 EFTS, 131
No 7 Service Flying Training School, Macleod, 7, 321
8th Air Force (USAAF), 349
No. 8 Group, 320, 337
No. 10 SFTS, Dauphin, 57
No. 12 Operational Training Unit, 164, 168, 180
14th Canadian Tank Regt., 127, 130
15 Squadron, 319
No. 20 (Pilot) Advanced Flying Unit, 146
36th Bombardment Sqn., 442
57 Squadron, 409
61 Squadron, 407, 408
90 Squadron, 348
100 Group, 337, 348, 367, 414, 419, 421, 422, 423
138 Squadron, 279
142 Squadron, 321
161 Squadron, 278, 280, 316
196 Squadron, 277
214 (FMS) Sqn. RAF, 240, 242, 243, 303, 321, 337, 338, 340, 352, 365, 367, 368, 370, 377, 380, 381, 420, 451, 457, 462, 463, 470, 475, 479
223 Squadron, 442, 451
408 Squadron, 335
427 (RCAF) Squadron, 352
514 Squadron, xii, 363
617 Squadron, 348, 474
620 Squadron, 243, 352
640 Squadron, 386
1699 Conversion Unit, 449, 450, 461, 464, 475

Library of Congress Cataloging-in-Publication Data

Peden, Murray, 1923-
A thousand shall fall / by Murray Peden.
p. cm. — (Wings of war)
Originally published: Stittsville, Ont. : Canada's Wings, 1979.
Includes index.
ISBN 0-8094-9641-0
1. Peden, Murray, 1923-
2. World War, 1939-1945—Aerial operations, British.
3. World War, 1939-1945—Personal narratives, Canadian.
4. Great Britain. Royal Air Force. Squadron, 214.
5. Air pilots, Military—Canada—Biography.
6. Air pilots, Military—Great Britain—Biography.
I. Title. II. Series.
D786.P38 1993   940.54'4941—dc20   92-29448 CIP

Published by arrangement with Murray Peden
and Stoddart Publishing Company.

Cover photograph © Carl Purcell
Endpapers photograph © Rene Sheret/After Image